ARMS RACES

The International Peace Research Institute, Oslo (PRIO) has long been a forerunner in the field of peace research. Founded in 1959, it is today a thriving interdisciplinary, international institute of peace and conflict studies. All research done at PRIO is based on open sources.

PRIO's current research centres around three main programmes:
- Conflict theory and the study of ethnic conflicts
- Security and disarmament studies
- Military activities and the human environment

PRIO's publications include the *Journal of Peace Research* (1964–) and the *Bulletin of Peace Proposals* (1969–) and a programme of books; recent titles include:

Ola Tunander, *Cold Water Politics: the Maritime Strategy and Geopolitics of the Northern Front*

Nils Petter Gleditsch & Olav Njølstad, eds, *Arms Races: Technological and Political Dynamics*

Arthur H. Westing, ed., *Comprehensive Security for the Baltic: an Environmental Approach*

ARMS RACES
Technological and Political Dynamics

Edited by
NILS PETTER GLEDITSCH
and OLAV NJØLSTAD

PRIO
International Peace Research Institute, Oslo

SAGE Publications
London · Newbury Park · New Delhi

Chapters 1–15 and 17–20 © International Peace Research
Institute, Oslo, 1990
First published 1990
Matthew A. Evangelista, 'Why the Soviets Buy the Weapons
They Do'. *World Politics* 36, no. 4 (July 1984).
Copyright © 1984 by Princeton University Press.
Reprinted by permission of Princeton University Press.

All rights reserved. No part of this publication may be
reproduced, stored in a retrieval system, transmitted or
utilized in any form or by any means, electronic, mechanical,
photocopying, recording or otherwise, without permission in
writing from the Publishers.

SAGE Publications Ltd
28 Banner Street
London EC1Y 8QE

SAGE Publications Inc
2111 West Hillcrest Drive
Newbury Park, California 91320

SAGE Publications India Pvt Ltd
32, M-Block Market
Greater Kailash – I
New Delhi 110 048

British Library Cataloguing in Publication data

Arms races: technological and political dynamics. –
  (PRIO monographs)
  1. Military equipment: Weapons. Proliferation
  I. Stockholm International Peace Research Institute
  II. Gleditsch, Nils Petter   III. Series
  355.8'2

ISBN 0-8039-8220-8
ISBN 0-8039-8221-6 Pbk

Library of Congress catalog card number 89-062694

Typeset by Photoprint, Torquay, Devon
Printed in Great Britain by Billing and Sons Ltd, Worcester

Contents

Sverre Lodgaard: Preface   vii
Acknowledgements   viii

Part I: The State of the Art   1
  1 Nils Petter Gleditsch: Research on Arms Races   1
  2 Dieter Senghaas: Arms Race Dynamics and Arms Control   15
  3 Håkan Wiberg: Arms Races, Formal Models, and Quantitative Tests   31
  4 Michael D. Intriligator & Dagobert L. Brito: Arms Race Modeling: A Reconsideration   58
  5 Paul Smoker: Artificial Intelligence Models of Arms Races   78

Part II: Technological Dynamics   87
  6 Ulrich Albrecht: The Role of Military R&D in Arms Build-Ups   87
  7 Marek Thee: Science-Based Military Technology as a Driving Force behind the Arms Race   105
  8 Donald MacKenzie: Towards an Historical Sociology of Nuclear Weapons Technologies   121
  9 Olav Wicken: Modernization through Military Industry: The Creation of a 'Military-Industrial System' in Norway 1960–75   140
  10 Wilhelm Agrell: The Bomb That Never Was: The Rise and Fall of the Swedish Nuclear Weapons Programme   154
  11 Hans Günter Brauch: Weapons Innovation and US Strategic Weapons Systems: Learning from Case Studies?   175
  12 Olav Njølstad: Learning from History? Case Studies and the Limits to Theory-Building   220

Part III: Political Dynamics   247
  13 Michael E. Geyer: Militarism and Capitalism in the 20th Century   247
  14 Lars Mjøset: The Geyer Archives   276
  15 Carl Gustav Jacobsen: Arms Build-Ups under Socialism: The USSR and China   285
  16 Matthew A. Evangelista: Why the Soviets Buy the Weapons They Do   295
  17 Raimo Väyrynen: Economy, Power, and the Arms Race   314

Part IV: The Research Agenda 346
   18 Dieter Senghaas: Systemic Confrontation, Armament Competition, and Armament Dynamics 346
   19 Håkan Wiberg: Arms Races – Why Worry? 352
   20 Michael D. Intriligator & Dagobert L. Brito: A Possible Future for the Arms Race 376

Bibliography 384
Subject Index 415
Name Index 421

Preface

The 1980s have seen another wave of interest in military issues. In the beginning of the decade, arms build-ups and tense international relations triggered extensive presentations, comparisons and discussions of military forces; of the technical characteristics of weapons systems; of their destructive capabilities; of the political significance of arms acquisitions; and of proposals to limit the growth of armaments. Most of these studies were descriptive, and generally lacking any thorough examination of the causes of arms build-up – as if the urgency of the matter did not permit that kind of luxury.

Towards the end of the decade, co-operation has substituted for tension between the major powers. Fear and feelings of urgency have changed into opportunities for the better. Today, governments and public opinion do not expect the academic community to respond to the issues of the day the way it did some years ago. Neither would this be a sensible research priority. Rather, attempts should be made to organize the existing wealth of fragmented knowledge in more coherent ways, and to arrive at a better understanding of the forces that generate new armaments.

This book, from PRIO's security and disarmament programme, has come about with that objective in mind. It sets out to summarize and elaborate on what we do and do not know about the causes of arms build-up, in effect providing a state-of-the-art report on this complex matter. In so doing, it reviews contributions from Lewis Richardson (1960) to the present – a period roughly corresponding to the time-span of modern conflict and peace research.

Much attention is devoted to recent studies of the technological and political dynamics of armaments, under conditions of socialism as well as capitalism. We hope that these can prove useful for students and teachers as well as for researchers in the field. The final section, on the research agenda, is addressed primarily to the latter. For the foreseeable future, the causes of armaments will remain a central theme of conflict and peace research. So will the political relevance of such studies. Obviously, strategies for real, sustained disarmament should be designed with due regard to the factors that generate armaments.

Editors of the volume are Nils Petter Gleditsch and Olav Njølstad. Nils Petter Gleditsch is a senior member of the PRIO research staff and the editor of the *Journal of Peace Research*. Olav Njølstad is a historian at the beginning of his scholarly career. Among the authors are a number of outstanding contributors to the field of conflict and peace research.

Sverre Lodgaard, Director,
International Peace Research Institute, Oslo (PRIO)

Acknowledgements

This book grew out of an informal gathering of members of the Editorial Committee and the International Advisory Board of the *Journal of Peace Research* at the Eleventh General Conference of the International Peace Research Association in Brighton, Sussex, in April 1986. In part, it was a result of the creative confusion typical of such large and varied gatherings. Confusion, because of the impossibility of staying on any one topic for more than a very short time. Creative, because of the many ideas buzzing in the air and the opportunity to get together with a wide variety of people to discuss them. The IPRA meeting prompted this book in a positive sense by making possible the first planning session; in a negative sense because we wanted to organize a very different sort of conference.

On the long way from that first meeting to this book, we have incurred many debts: To those members of the Editorial Committee and International Advisory Board of the *JPR* who were present in Brighton, and to those who have provided suggestions later. To the Berghof Foundation in Munich and the Norwegian Research Council for Science and the Humanities (NAVF) in Oslo for providing the funds for the symposium which eventually led to the book. NAVF also provided a grant for the preparation of the final manuscript. To those non-author participants in the Oslo meeting who through their comments and critiques have helped shape the final product: Bernd W. Kubbig, Sverre Lodgaard, and Ola Tunander. To the Sara Hotel at Voksenåsen in Oslo for providing a pleasant framework for our three-day deliberations. To Eivind Lande of PRIO for helping with word processing and numerous other practical tasks, as well as translating Chapter 18 from German into English. And finally to PRIO's language editor, Susan Høivik, to the copyeditor, Miles Litvinoff, and to David Hill and Susan Haberis at Sage Publications in London.

The number of non-author participants was originally much larger. However, five of the discussants' contributions grew into separate chapters, most of them now distinguishable from the original papers mainly by virtue of being slightly shorter. All the chapters have been thoroughly revised after the symposium. In addition, three new chapters have been added, two 'classics' in the field and one specially written for this volume. Of the twenty chapters, only three have been published before.

Raimo Väyrynen and Dieter Senghaas served with us on the organizing committee for the symposium, and provided most of the ideas for topics and authors. In the end, however, it proved most practical to leave the editing to the two of us at PRIO. While this volume is in large measure a collective effort, we must assume overall responsibility for any deficiencies in the final product.

Although the project started out as a special issue of the *Journal of Peace Research*, it quickly outgrew the confines of a journal issue. The new combined publication agreement between the International Peace Research Institute, Oslo (PRIO), and Sage Publications in London has made the transition from journal issue to book a relatively painless one.

N.P.G.   O.N.

PART I: THE STATE OF THE ART

Chapter 1
Research on Arms Races*

NILS PETTER GLEDITSCH
International Peace Research Institute, Oslo

1 Internal and External Factors

This book, although loaded with 'facts' about the arms race, has been inspired mainly by theoretical issues in the debate on the dynamics of arms acquisition.

The question of the driving forces in the arms race was among the first problems to be dealt with in peace research. One important source of inspiration was the work of the British meteorologist and pacifist Lewis F. Richardson, summed up in his posthumous book *Arms and Insecurity* (1960a).[1] Richardson's starting-point was a simple, two-actor model where arms increases were positively related to the threat – the opponents' arms level – and negatively related to the defense burden – one's own arms level. This model fits well into the prevailing peace-research view of the East–West conflict in the early 1960s: a two-party conflict with actors behaving in a rather symmetric fashion – and about equally worthy of moral condemnation. At the time, this was a radical stand: a reaction against the traditional interpretation of the East–West conflict as a struggle between 'us' and 'them' – 'they' being generally malevolent and full of initiative, 'we' merely reacting to their challenges.

By the end of the 1960s this symmetric view was challenged in several ways. In colonial wars and wars of liberation the asymmetric elements seemed stronger, calling for a different sort of model. The colonizer could not be equated with the colonized, theoretically or normatively. In the East–West conflict, more emphasis was placed on various 'inner factors': bureaucratic inertia, pressure groups, the military-industrial complex, etc. German political scientists such as Senghaas (1969, 1972a, 1972b), Gantzel (1973), and Krell (1976) played a prominent role in formulating this critique, which went so far as to characterize arming as a form of 'autistic' behavior, indicating complete insensitivity to external signals (Senghaas,

---

* This chapter is a much expanded version of a paper circulated before the symposium in order to put some main issues to the contributors. I am grateful to Matthew Evangelista, Olav Njølstad, and Håkan Wiberg for comments on an earlier draft.

1974b). The action-reaction model was seen as a form of establishment thinking.[2] The impact on the state of the discipline was considerable. As a 'classic' representative of this literature we have reprinted Senghaas (1979), with slight modifications, as Chapter 2 in this volume.

A decade before this critique of the action-reaction mode of thinking, President Eisenhower had warned against the undue influence of the military-industrial complex. Thus he founded a subfield of the internal factors approach, which has generated a research tradition of its own (Rosen, 1973; Koistinen, 1980). Some of this literature emphasizes the bureaucratic and intellectual elements of the complex more than the original formulation. Galtung, for instance, refers to the complex as 'military-bureaucratic-corporate-intelligentsia' (MBCI).[3] Other studies underline the link between arms racing and capitalism as a system – cf. Geyer (Chapter 13 in this volume) and Mjøset (Chapter 14). Olav Wicken in his examination of Norwegian military industry in Chapter 9 discerns a 'military-industrial system' with elements from government, industry, and R&D, but located mostly in the public sector and thus lacking the private profit motive usually considered part of the military-industrial complex. Most empirical studies of arms-producing industries deal with the USA, but some span a number of countries (e.g. Ball & Leitenberg, 1983). Studies of the Soviet arms-building complex have not kept pace with those of the West, but are nevertheless quite numerous, and some explicitly discuss it in terms of a military-industrial complex.[4]

The 'bureaucratic politics' paradigm, which became very popular in US decision-making studies in the 1970s, was another school of thought that emphasized internal factors. But bureaucratic politics was not directed against external factors, but rather against a 'rational actor' approach which saw governments as essentially monolithic.[5] The bureaucratic politics school was aimed at foreign policy decision-making in general, and not specifically at arms dynamics.

At the same time as the action-reaction model came under attack, 'revisionist' historians and political scientists cast doubt on the symmetric view of the East-West conflict, arguing that the USA had generally held the initiative in the conflict while Soviet policy had been more reactive and cautious (Kolko & Kolko, 1972).

Asymmetric arms races could easily be worked into the Richardsonian framework by varying the coefficients indicating the sensitivity to the threat and to the burden, as well as the 'grievance' term which is not dependent on previous arms levels on either side. Theoretical integration was, however, impeded by increasing skepticism regarding formal modeling. While formal methods and quantitative data had been seen as radical innovations in the late 1950s and early 1960s, large elements of the '1968 generation' saw them as a strait-jacket and even as a conservative force.

The different schools went their separate ways and the debate petered out. The descriptive literature about the East-West arms build-up has increased enormously, but has not been matched by theoretical innovation. Even in the field of Soviet studies – where lack of openness has impeded data collection – Meyer (1985, p. 45) argues that the main deficiency is not lack of data, but failure to 'exploit such data beyond simple descriptive analysis'.

Within the 'arms racing' school, many new variants of the Richardsonian models have been published, particularly in the *Journal of Conflict Resolution* and the various publications of the Peace Science Society (previously the Peace Research Society). This literature conveys an impression of a high degree of specialization and a concentration on minor refinements. In this volume, the basics of the Richardson model and its extensions can be found in the articles by Håkan Wiberg (Chapter 3), Michael D. Intriligator & Dagobert L. Brito (Chapter 4), and Paul Smoker (Chapter 5). While Intriligator & Brito compare the Richardson model to other descriptive and normative models, Wibert surveys a large number of empirical tests, and Smoker argues for a new school of thought, an 'artificial intelligence' approach where models interact with the data and may change as a result.

The voluminous *empirical* literature on the arms build-up has concentrated first and foremost on the hardware element, secondly on doctrinal factors. Many such studies assume a 'rational actor' perspective, where doctrinal considerations dictate the number or kinds of weapons developed and deployed. Naturally, decision-makers themselves are apt to see their own arms acquisitions as rational. The policy-oriented literature here can easily degenerate into apology.

Out of the hardware-oriented literature another school of thought has emerged which instead of actor orientation emphasizes the decisive role of military technology for arms build-ups. According to this school of thought, the 'qualitative arms race' is more important than the quantitative one, and arms control should primarily be directed toward the control of military research and development and the prevention of qualitative improvements in arms. A clear proponent of this kind of thinking is Marek Thee (1978, 1986a, 1987, and Chapter 7 in this volume). The crucial role attributed to military R&D in this literature borders on technological determinism, i.e. the belief that what is technically possible will also be done. Other students of arms procurement (e.g. Stein, 1984) explicitly deny the primacy of technological developments, claiming that political decisions control the development and particularly the implementation of new military technology. In his examination of guidance technologies, an underestimated aspect of nuclear weapons technology, Donald MacKenzie (Chapter 8) leans more toward a thesis which places 'politics in command'. Ulrich Albrecht (Chapter 6) also emphasizes the limitations of a technological perspective, pointing out how weapons systems which are feasible are sometimes not developed or deployed. A prime example is offered by the Swedish decision *not* to go nuclear, examined in detail by Wilhelm Agrell in Chapter 10. The Swedish R&D program certainly got to the point where a Swedish bomb was technically possible; then the project ground to a halt through a mixture of political and military factors.

Several thorough decision-making studies have been published concerning the development of particular weapons systems or military technologies, e.g. by Armacost (1969) on the first generation of intermediate-range nuclear missiles, Greenwood (1975) on the MIRV, Ball (1980) on the missile programs of the Kennedy Administration, and Huisken (1981) on the strategic cruise missile. Such studies have sought explanations in external as well as internal factors, although they do not always refer to the earlier theoretical debate on this subject. Most of these studies are limited to single cases. Work by Hans Günter Brauch (Chapter 11 in this volume) and Matthew Evangelista (1988 and Chapter 16 in this volume) has attempted to use systematic comparisons of several cases to derive lessons from this literature for the theoretical debate. Brauch surveys ten case studies of strategic weapons innovation and procurement in the USA. He concludes by formulating a research program of structured, focused comparisons, as suggested by George (1979). Evangelista applies a similar approach to decisions to deploy regional nuclear weapons in Europe. Similarly Senghaas (Chapter 18) argues for the initiation of new case studies, as well as 'contextuating' old ones, reinterpretating them within a framework of systemic confrontation, arms competition, and arms dynamics. Olav Njølstad (Chapter 12), however, questions whether such 'structured focused comparisons' can contribute to a theoretical breakthrough. Rather he advocates a more modest program whereby historical comparisons can root out factual errors, identify possible variables in general theories, and eliminate certain theories not supported by *any* case studies. To some social scientists this would seem to leave only quantitative studies for tests of general theories – an implication not explicitly drawn by Njølstad, however.

As mentioned already, the empirical study of 'socialist' arms dynamics has developed somewhat in parallel fashion with studies of capitalist economies, although at a slower pace. Opinion is divided, however, on the application or the applicability of models developed primarily in the context of studies of the West. Evangelista (Chapter 16) discusses Soviet policy in terms of bureaucratic politics, the military-industrial complex, and other 'Western' models. Jacobsen (Chapter 15) agrees that the Soviet Union and China have 'military-industrial-research complexes', but argues that their military cultures have developed so differently from the Anglo-Saxon tradition dominant in the West that 'theorems that appear to apply in one context cannot be transposed indiscriminately to another'.

2 A Plethora of Explanations

Some of the case studies literature contains a rich theoretical discussion. Huisken, for instance, in his book on the cruise missile decision (1981) discusses no less than seven explanatory factors:

1 US strategic doctrine.

2 Technological determinism.
3 Pressure from the military services.
4 Economic incentives – (a) for military industry, (b) for employees in the industry.
5 Action-reaction in relation to the Soviet Union.
6 The bargaining card (in the SALT II negotiations).
7 US psychological self-assertion.

Huisken discards most of these explanations and ends up endorsing the seventh, which he characterizes as 'admittedly speculative' (p. 189). Interestingly, the factor selected by Huisken cannot be classified clearly as an 'internal' or an 'external' factor.

Evangelista, in a study of four decisions to procure new nuclear weapons for NATO (Evangelista, 1986a; see also 1986b, 1986c, 1988), concentrates on three competing explanations, without claiming that they span the entire spectrum of theories of the arms race:

1 Action-reaction.
2 The 'military fix'.
3 Technological entrepreneurship.

The second factor on this list is new, relative to Huisken's seven. The third is a new combination of factors. With the expression 'technological entrepreneurship' Evangelista 'emphasizes internal determinants for most of the decision process' and 'incorporates external factors at the later stages of the process, suggesting that they provide a "window" through which the new weapon can be promoted' (Evangelista, 1986a, pp. 198–199). Evangelista concludes that this factor best explains the four decisions.

Risse-Kappen (1986), in a comment on Evangelista's article, adds two factors to this list:

4 Bargaining chips.
5 Bureaucratic politics.

And he concludes that no single factor can account for the 'successful' as well as the 'unsuccessful' cases of NATO nuclear weapons deployment decisions.

Meyer (1984), in his study of Soviet national-security decision-making, lists six factors:

1 Action-reaction.
2 Technological dynamic.
3 Military superiority.
4 Interest groups.
5 National leadership.
6 Military mission.

Of these, 5 and 6 – and, to some extent, 3 – are factors which are not directly equivalent to any on Huisken's list.

Buzan (1987, chs. 6–8) examines three basic models:

1 The action-reaction model.
2 The domestic structure model.
3 The technological imperative model.

Thus, by examining four major studies (none of which, incidentally, refers to the three others) and a comment on one of them, we have come up with eleven more or less independent factors. Add to this the numerous variations of the action-reaction paradigm, and the variety of institutional interests which have been posited to lead to arms acquisitions, and we begin to face a true jungle of hypotheses.

Kurth (1971) distinguished four 'modes of change' – quantitative, innovative, renovative, and redistributive – and related these to different 'modes of causation' (bureaucratic politics, bureaucratic process, bureaucratic-corporate alliances, and the economic system). Evangelista (Chapter 16 in this volume) uses this taxonomy for studying Soviet weapons decisions. Although this helps to structure the theories and impose some order, it does not in itself eliminate any of the numerous suggested explanations from the field as a whole.

3 The Problem of Overdetermination

No wonder then that several writers have argued that arms acquisition has been 'overdetermined'. Evangelista (1986a, p. 197) argues, somewhat facetiously, that there seem to be more 'theories' than weapons decisions, and thus no clear way to choose between them. This is a well-known and real problem in studying modern war: with a cut-off at 1000 battle-deaths Small & Singer (1982) have identified 118 intra-systemic wars after 1815, i.e. wars between two or more countries each satisfying their criteria for independence, and 51 extra-systemic wars.[6] This 'limited' number – statistically speaking, not in terms of human suffering – sets clear restrictions on the amount of theoretical sophistication which can be applied to these data sets, particularly when theorists assume that their explanations may vary freely by region and time period.

However, this problem should be much less serious with regard to weapons decisions, because the number of such decisions exceeds the number of wars by many orders of magnitude. Indeed, the only practical limit to our data base here is the amount of effort we can put into identifying the cases and ordering the relevant information.

Kurth (1971, pp. 377–378) uses 'overdetermination' (or strictly speaking '*a posteriori* overdetermination') in a somewhat different sense: 'For nearly any interesting military policy . . . we can discover or invent, *a posteriori*, several alternative explanations.' While this will always be true for any particular weapons decision, it is much less likely that different theoretical explanations can account equally well for a large number of weapons decision.

Senghaas (1972a and Chapter 2 in this volume), on the other hand, has argued that arms acquisitions are overdetermined in a very different sense: they are *redundantly caused*. Thus, if action-reaction is not present to cause an arms acquisition, some internal factor will be. These redundant causes must be assumed to be non-additive, i.e. if two are present they do not lead to twice the level of arms acquisition, and they are certainly not interactive so as to cause arms levels to rise even further. If I have understood this notion correctly, we may use an analogy to some other dichotomous outcome – like choosing to drive to work rather than using public transport. One may have various good reasons for doing this, such as: (1) comfort, (2) economy, (3) time-saving. Each one of these factors may be a sufficient cause for the same outcome. When they are all present, it is impossible to tell which one is decisive. The factors are non-additive – one does not drive three cars to work or drive three times the distance, even if all three factors are present.

This notion of overdetermination somehow assumes that the factors are unidirectional in causation – that the absence of one factor does not cause the opposite outcome. But what if we can identify other people whose choice of transportation cannot be based on all three factors, but only on one or two, because the others are absent? Systematic comparison of a large number of commuters should then yield some answers with regard to the weight of the different factors. Since we do have an almost endless number of arms decisions to choose from, such comparisons should be possible – almost regardless of the imagination of the theorists.[7]

4 A Path in the Jungle?

With this optimistic program in mind I have tried to assemble in a systematic manner a very large number of hypotheses which have been (or might have been) proposed to explain arms acquisitions. I do not mean that the list is complete – no such claim would be meaningful. As Wiberg notes (Chapter 3, p. 47) there is hardly any limit to the number of variables that can be theoretically suggested as having *some* influence on military efforts.

Table 1.1 *Four levels of explanations for arms acquisition*

Level	Factor characterizing
Internal	Subunits of the actor
Actor	The actor itself
Relational	Relations between two or more actors
System	The social system or the physical context

The most basic distinction is between factors on four different *levels*: from those internal to the actor, to those pertaining to the entire social system or its physical environment. The four levels are set out in Table 1.1.

The next four tables 1.2–1.5 outline the specific factors at each of the levels.

Table 1.2 *Internal factors driving arms levels up*

- *Interest group*
  - Economic interest group
    - Ruling class
    - Industry
      - The follow-on theorem[8]
    - Workers
    - Local (e.g. community with military base or industry)[9]
  - Bureacratic interest group
  - Research interest group (e.g. weapons laboratory)
  - Military interest group
    - Inter-service rivalry
  - Political interest group
    - Arms acquisitions for internal repression
  - Combined sectional interest
    - Military-industrial complex
    - Military-bureaucratic-corporate-intelligentsia complex

Table 1.3 *Actor characteristics driving arms levels up*

- *Military mission*[10]
- *National pride*[11]
- *Expansionist ideology*[12]
- *National economic opportunity*[13]
- *Being an alliance leader*[14]
- *Internal conflict*[15]
- *Authoritarian rule*[16]

In addition to the hypotheses listed here, there are those which combine the various levels – Evangelista's notion of 'technological entrepreneurship' has already been mentioned. Another reasonable hypothesis which combines the actor level and the relational is that the USA drives the technological arms race through an inability to halt the technological momentum, whereas the Soviet Union is essentially engaged in a race to try to catch up. Väyrynen also emphasizes how the systemic factors he discusses can explain arms races 'only in combination with national and subnational factors' (Chapter 17, p. 315).

Given this wide range of hypotheses, there should be no lack of tasks for the research community. From this perspective, the empirical studies undertaken so far have only touched on a small number of the theoretical possibilities. But can we really distinguish between the different hypotheses?

Table 1.4 *Relational characteristics driving arms levels up*

- *Relations to opponents*
  - Action-reaction
    Qualitative type of reaction
    - Counter measure[17]
    - Imitation[18]
    - Imperialist competition

    Quantitative type of reaction
    - Follow-on[19]
    - Catch-up[20]
    - Stay ahead[21]

    Timing of reaction
    - Reactive (reacting to past increment on the other side)
    - Pre-emptive (reacting to present or future arms)
    - Preventive (reacting to spurious or hypothetical arms)
  - Bargaining chip[22]
- *Relations to allies*
  - 'Military fix'
  - Alliance doctrine
  - Burden-sharing[23]
  - Arms exports
  - Economic aid

Table 1.5 *System characteristics driving arms levels up*

- Upswings in long economic waves[24]
- Turning-points in international power distribution
- Technological imperative[25]

5 The Problem of Identification

An obstacle greater than overdetermination is the problem of identification, i.e. to separate the influences of various theoretical factors. This problem has two components. One is that several factors, although formulated in quite different language, are in fact the same, or logically related. The other is empirical: several factors, although different, will under certain circumstances produce identical-looking phenomena. I will deal with some *theoretical* interlinkages first.

First, on the relation between action-reaction and actor-level models: Action-reaction models may incorporate 'internal factors'. For instance, we may have a one-sided action-reaction situation, which means that the arms behavior one of the countries is influenced by factors at the actor level (or at the sub-actor level). In fact, as already pointed out, spokespersons for the superpowers tend to portray their own arming as reactive, and due to the arming of the other side. The other side's arming, in turn, is exogenous, caused by internal forces, a desire to annex its neighbors, etc. If both parties were right with regard to their own behavior, we would have an interactive arms race, but one which should never have got underway. If both were right with regard to the other party's behavior, the arms race would be caused entirely by internal forces. If one of them was right, we would have a model which bridged the gap between external and internal factors: one party was moved by external factors, the other by internal.

The technological imperative has been portrayed here as a system factor. However, if a particular country is characterized by a technological culture where the imperative is at work, it is an actor-level characteristic. The institutionalization of military R&D can also be seen as part of the action-reaction model: rivalry justifies the *enterprise* of military R&D. To be in the game requires an R&D establishment. But once you have it, it becomes a pressure group (Buzan, 1987, p. 97). A similar argument can be made for a number of other domestic factors. Specialized arms production implies that one cannot improvise arms production during a crisis through conversion of civilian industry – there is a need for a *standing capacity*.

Finally, the upswing in the long economic waves discussed by Väyrynen (Chapter 17) as a systemic factor provides an opportunity for increased arms spending by increasing the overall prosperity of national economies. Thus, it is directly related to the 'economic opportunity' factor listed under factors at the actor level.

In addition to the theoretical linkages there is also an *empirical* identification problem. Domestic factors can easily be assumed to produce national growth in armaments which resembles growth under the Richardson model. If last year's appropriation is increased by a fixed percentage, the budget will grow exponentially.[26] This is a form of 'social inertia'. A Richardson process where the two parties react only to each other can produce exactly the same growth, with the right coefficients. To give a simple example: assume that both countries start with arms levels 100. If these increase for purely internal reasons by 3% annually, they will have arms levels 103, 106.09, etc. in successive years. On the other hand, if they react to the other side only, and the 'reactivity' is 3%, the same result will ensue. If one country starts at 100, the other at 50, a 'social inertia' model with 3% increase annually will produce arms levels 103 and 51.5 in the second year. The same result could have been accomplished by an interactive process, with higher reactivity in the country with the higher arms level (6% as compared to 1.5%).

To separate internal from external 'driving forces' in such a case cannot be accomplished merely with data on aggregate arms levels. We need a wider theory which can be tested at several points. For instance, if arms levels increase in years in which there is no economic growth, while civilian budgets do not, this would point to external factors being more important than domestic inertia. If oil-exporting countries with plenty of cash increase their military spending with no visible external threat, then an actor-level explanation is called for.

6 Is There an Arms Race?

Expressions like 'run-away', 'mad momentum', 'out of control', 'irreversible', etc. are commonly associated with arms races, particularly with the present nuclear arms race. For instance, the losing candidate in the 1984 US presidential election argued: 'Ronald Reagan is determined to put killer weapons in space. The Soviets will have to match us. And the arms race will rage out of control.'[27]

Various critics of the arms race concept have pointed out that, on a number of important indicators, the nuclear arms race does not provide evidence for accelerating growth or even for monotonic growth.[28] US and Soviet military expenditures have risen in the postwar period, but not inexorably, year by year. The US nuclear stockpile has declined in megatonnage since about 1960 and in number of warheads since about 1970 (Fairbanks, 1985, pp. 81–82), and will even decline in hard-target kill capability if a START agreement is concluded.

Countering such objections, proponents of the notion of a run-away arms race tend to argue that a flattening-out of arms expenditures is only temporary and short-lived, that reductions apply only to militarily less useful weapons, and that qualitative improvements continue unabated.

Changes in military expenditure in themselves prove very little. The peaks of military expenditures in the postwar period have occurred because of the need to finance wars (Korea, Vietnam, Afghanistan) rather than running the East–West arms race. Improving the strategic forces does not necessarily require increases in military spending.

Holst (1973, p. 68) and Gray (1976, pp. 3–4) define an arms race as an adversary relationship where the two (or more) parties increase or improve their armaments at a *rapid* rate. This definition is more restrictive that the one applied by most of the authors in this book. In fact, as Fairbanks (1985, p. 8) points out, the everyday notion of a 'race' does not require fast or accelerating movement. In track races athletes do not run faster and faster. In some sports, notably bicycle track racing, the athletes for long periods may not even move very fast at all. The object of the race is victory over the opponent, and the speed in any particular part of the race is irrelevant. This seems to me a useful analogy with the arms race. The decisive aspect is the competition, the interaction between hostile actors. Thus, Intriligator and Brito define the concept of an arms race as a 'dynamic process of interaction between countries in their acquisition of weapons' (Chapter 4, p. 59).

Given the right combination of coefficients, a Richardson arms race model is quite compatible with a decelerating arms race, or even with a disarmament race. Intriligator & Brito (Chapter 20) argue that the superpower arms race (along with arms control) has contributed to a mutual deterrence regime, which is stable and promotes peace, while new arms races between lesser powers are more likely to be destabilizing. Others have a more skeptical view of the long-term stability of the superpower arms race, based in part on historical experience with arms races (Chapter 19).

While most of the chapters in this volume seem to take the interactive element in arms races for granted, the authors differ in the relative importance they assign to it. The debate concerning external and internal factors is not dead. Dieter Senghaas (Chapter 2, p. 15) feels that 'the action-reaction scheme is at least highly dubious, if not completely false'. He does not rule out external factors entirely, but argues that the main armaments decisions have been 'mainly inner-directed'. Other authors have characterized the internal–external debate as 'unproductive' (Evangelista, 1986a, p. 199) or 'outdated' (Risse-Kappen, 1986, p. 207). Certainly, at this juncture, there are not as many strong feelings attached as when the theme was first introduced in the early 1970s.

7 Arms Levels and Arms Types

So far we have skirted the issue whether arms decisions affect the overall level of armament. Some obviously do not – they only affect the type of arms adopted within a given level of strength. Is it reasonable to expect the same models to apply? The Richardson model clearly refers to levels: arming means going to a higher level of strength, although usually operationalized by military spending. Most of the case studies examined by Brauch in Chapter 11 also seem likely to affect the national level, because they concern major strategic weapons systems. Nevertheless, the relationship between acquisition of a particular weapons system and national strength is problematic. When the USA chose to develop and deploy the Polaris and the Trident ballistic missiles and submarines, this contributed to its retaliatory nuclear capacity, in the latter case also to its counterforce capacity. At the same time, the high priority given to submarine systems probably had a limiting effect on the development of land-based systems, an effect not usually examined by authors of case studies. As a result of several such decisions, and similar (actually dissimilar) decisions in the Soviet Union, the two superpowers developed nuclear forces which were structured quite differently and whose overall strength was all the more difficult to compare.

As Brauch's examination of the various case studies shows, considerations of the opponent's actions were certainly not absent. Yet several of the authors of case studies place more emphasis on explanations within the bureaucratic politics paradigm. This seems quite reasonable in view of the limited scope of their studies and does not invalidate a view of the overall arms race as essentially interactive.

8 An End to the Arms Race?

In the early 1980s, when US arms spending rose rapidly after several years of stagnation, public concern about the arms race also increased rapidly. The question of the deployment of Pershing II and Ground-Launched Cruise Missiles stood at the center of the controversy. Public statements from US officials about the possibility of limited nuclear war – inherent in any nuclear policy, but rarely discussed so openly – further increased public concern. The probability that a run-away arms race would lead to nuclear war was seen as quite high. At the end of the 1980s, the INF agreement and the rapprochement between the superpowers have led many to the opposite extreme of declaring the arms race dead. This is premature, for two reasons: the East-West conflict has seen periods of lower tension and less intense arming – but the arms race re-emerged eventually; and as Intriligator and Brito argue (Chapter 20), we are likely to see many *new* arms races, involving the smaller nuclear powers, the potential proliferators, Third World countries with unresolved border issues, etc. Many of these arms races may lead to wars or extremely wasteful arms acquisitions. Hopefully, some of the lessons learned from the study of arms races in the East–West setting can be put to use in preventing the new arms races from getting out of hand.

Notes

1. Ideas about arms races are much older than this, however. Triska & Finley (1965, p. 7) have traced ideas about the balancing of opposing peacetime forces back to 1848, to a treatise on general sociology by Eugène Duprés of Brussels University.
2. Ironically, at the same time as radical opinion in the social sciences turned against external factors in the search for causes of arms racing, the opposite happened in debates about development policy. There, explanations on the basis of internal factors (modernization) were rejected in favor of external factors (dependency, imperialism).
3. Cf. Galtung (1980, pp. 198–199, and 1988, pp. 98–99).
4. See, for example, Agursky & Adomeit (1979), Aspaturian (1973), Holloway (1982), Jahn (1975), Meyer (1984). A good guide to sources is Leitenberg (1979).
5. Important works here are Allison (1971), Allison & Halperin (1972), Halperin (1974, 1975), Halperin & Kanter (1973a). For a critique, see Art (1973).
6. Overdetermination is less probable if the threshold for including an armed conflict is lowered, as in the studies by Kende (1971, 1978), Gantzel & Meyer-Stamer (1986), and the compilations of ongoing armed conflicts in the most recent editions of the *SIPRI Yearbook*.
7. Another possible interpretation of the Senghaas notion of overdetermination is that there really is some other fundamental cause (or function) and that the other factors are merely justifications for a policy already chosen. Thus, if the real reason for driving is that the car is a status symbol, then time, comfort, or economy (whichever is present) may be cited as the reason.
8. The 'follow-on theorem' expresses the need for a continuous development of firms dependent on the military sector. Cf. Kaldor (1986), Kurth (1971).
9. Local economic interest in arms increases (or, more frequently, resistance to arms reductions) has been demonstrated in a number of studies. Cf. Gleditsch (1987 – Norway), Leitenberg (1978 – USA), Wallensteen (1978 – Sweden).
10. Meyer (1984, p. 21) defines 'the military mission model' as one in which 'decisions regarding Soviet weapons acquisition and force structuring logically follow from the designation of specific military missions devised by the Soviet military'. These missions originate in military doctrine, strategy, or acquired habit.
11. The US presidential campaigns of 1960 and 1980 share the characteristic that the winning candidate raised alarm about alleged military weakness and mobilized national pride. Cf. Buzan (1987, p. 101).
12. Totalitarian regimes are frequently seen by their opponents as having an expansionist ideology. Cf. the discussion in Jacobsen, Chapter 15.

13. For instance, the acquisition of sudden or great wealth, followed by an inability to spend all the wealth on productive investment.

14. The argument is that because defense is a public good the alliance leader will to some extent procure it for everybody. Thus, smaller alliance members can obtain a 'free ride'. Cf. Olson & Zeckhauser (1966), Russett (1970).

15. Coser (1956, pp. 87ff.), basing his argument on Simmel (1955), proposes that external conflict increases social cohesion. Thus, such a conflict may be provoked or stimulated in order to alleviate internal conflict. Since the aggravation of the external conflict is likely to lead to arms increases, the internal conflict may be posited as the underlying cause of the arms increase. Rosh (1987) has argued that ethnic cleavage leads to increased military spending, but for a different reason, i.e. the need to exercise internal control.

16. The theoretical argument here is that in democratic states domestic pressure groups have more power and the military will get access to fewer resources – thus the rate of arming will be lower. For a negative view of this hypothesis, see Jacobsen, Chapter 15.

17. By 'counter-measure' I mean the acquisition of weapons counteracting the weapons held by the opponent. A strong belief in this arms race factor has been expressed by President Reagan: 'There has never been a weapon invented in the history of man that has not led to a defensive, a counter weapon' (Reagan speaking in 1984, quoted in Fairbanks, 1985, p. 5).

18. By 'imitation' I mean that one side buys weapons equal or equivalent to those of the other side. Kissinger would have appeared to endorse this view when he argued as follows: 'Yet, in the nature of things, if one side expands its strategic arsenal, the other side will inevitably match it' (Kissinger, 1976, quoted in Fairbanks, 1985, p. 4).

19. By 'follow-on' I mean an attempt to prevent the opponent from gaining an overwhelming superiority, particularly a disarming first strike capability. Thus, one races, but not to get ahead of the opponent, merely to prevent him from getting too far ahead.

20. By 'catch-up' I mean behavior intended to match the opponent's forces. A desire to maintain the 'balance of power' is often translated into a necessity to balance military forces.

21. By 'stay ahead' I mean a form of arms racing where one always attempts to have more military force than the opponent. The justification for this may be the belief, frequently expressed by either side in the East–West arms race, that it is not going to be the aggressor. Hence, there is no cause for the other side to worry about superiority.

22. A bargaining chip is a weapons acquisition undertaken for the purpose of negotiating the removal of weapons on both sides. A prime example is NATO's double-track decision in December 1979.

23. Burden-sharing is the argument used by the alliance leader to put pressure on other alliance members to increase their arms expenditures. This is an attempt to reverse the alliance leader factor mentioned in Table 1.3.

24. This factor and the next are discussed by Väyrynen (Chapter 17).

25. Wiesner (1960, p. 679) has expressed the belief in the technological imperative as follows: 'the logic of the arms race seems to require that any possible weapon be built'.

26. A more sophisticated model can be found, for instance, in Davis et al. (1966), who assume that a US agency always requests a certain percentage increase, and that the Congress cuts the increase by a fixed percentage. Although Davis et al. do not apply their model to military spending, the same thinking is expressed by Gray (1976, p. 38: 'the best guide to the level of next year's [military] budget is the level of this year's budget').

27. Walter Mondale, as quoted by Fairbanks (1985, p. 7).

28. Fairbanks (1985), Wohlstetter (1974a, 1974b, 1984); cf. also Albrecht (Chapter 6 in this volume).

NILS PETTER GLEDITSCH, b. 1942, mag. art. in Sociology (University of Oslo, 1968); Senior Research Fellow, PRIO (1968–); Editor, *Journal of Peace Research* (1976–77, 1984–). Most recent books: *Loran-C and Omega. A Study of the Military Importance of Radio Navigation Aids* (with Owen Wilkes; Norwegian University Press/Oxford University Press, 1987); *Norge i verdenssamfunnet: En statistisk håndbok* (Pax, 1988).

Chapter 2
Arms Race Dynamics and Arms Control*

DIETER SENGHAAS
Department of Social Science, University of Bremen

1 The Nature of the Contemporary Arms Race

1.1 Détente and Armaments

The political elites in East and West so far have pursued their strategy of détente only in conjunction with a policy of unceasing armamentism. Whatever may be said on the political stage, the hard facts of a continuing growth of armament activities in the past years have proved that the intensity of the arms race between East and West has not diminished.

What circumstances today essentially determine the dynamics of armament developments, i.e. the growth of armaments and the trend of the international arms race?

1.2 External and Internal Impulses to Armaments

When the Cold War was still in full swing, it was comparatively simple to legitimize armament policies and the international arms race. The traditional explanation of the arms race dynamics has been based on the simple assertion that armament policies can be interpreted only as reactions to actions of the opponent. This action-reaction theorem conceives armament policies as being dictated from the opponent, or as *other-directed*. It is asserted that particular armament measures of one side are directly geared to the armament measures of the opponent. Since both antagonists behave (at least according to the self-image they propagate) equally other-directedly, it may be assumed that a *reciprocal escalation spiral* necessarily emerges, in the process of which weapon systems are invented and numerical plateaus fixed, and in which the supersession of old systems by qualitatively higher ones is determined.

As much research on the biography of weapon systems has shown, the action-reaction scheme is at least highly dubious, if not completely false.

---

* This is a slightly revised version of an article which appeared in *Bulletin of Peace Proposals* (Senghaas, 1979). Longer versions in English of my position can be found in Senghaas (1972c, 1973, 1974b). The original German contributions are Senghaas (1969, 1972a, 1972b, 1974a). A more recent statement of my views is found in Chapter 18 of this volume.

The main trends of the international arms race between East and West have developed quite differently from what has been asserted in the action-reaction theorem.

In the last thirty years the main antagonists – the big powers and their allies – have been, on the average, more autonomous in the self-determination of their specific armament policies than most commentators usually assume. Their main decisions have been far more geared to the needs of various segments of their societies, to be specified later on. They have been mainly *inner-directed* and less dictated by external forces. The *self-centered imperatives of national armament* policies have been far stronger than those which have resulted from the reciprocal interaction with the so-called *potential* enemy.

This alternative theorem can be empirically verified. Our observations refer particularly to the nuclear-strategic area of the present arms race. The reason for this emphasis is not that the nuclear arms race and nuclear weapons have been and still are the most dangerous and potentially most destructive war potentials; our emphasis on the nuclear-strategic arms race is of *paradigmatic value* since certain key aspects of contemporary types of arms races can be particularly well analyzed in that area. But at the same time we have to emphasize the very characteristics of the strategic arms race which cannot be transferred to an analysis of other types of arms races and weapon systems.

1.3 The Race in Technology

The most outstanding characteristic of the present arms race between East and West consists in the fact *that this arms race has been, more than any one before, a continuously qualitative one*. Most of the arms races before 1945 were primarily *quantitative* races. Although there have been many qualitative innovations in weapon technology during the last two centuries, the life cycles of weapon systems were considerably longer than the case after 1945.

The basic characteristic of the present arms race shows up in a permanent stream of technological innovations which, besides other causes, set the pace for contemporary armament policies. The reverse of this continuous innovation consists in the tremendous propensity to obsolescence of weapon systems, once produced. The many abortive weapon systems of the last decades are another sign of the same trend. In contradistinction to the armament policy of previous decades, the present arms race extends not only to *one* type of weapon system or to a few, but rather to the *entire spectrum of destruction potentials* in the possession of the political and military apparata today. The range of this spectrum begins with the subversive activities of intelligence agencies; it comprises types of counter-insurgency warfare, conventional war potentials, tactical-nuclear and strategic-nuclear weapon systems, as well as instruments of political propaganda and psychological warfare. The spectrum reaches out into a variety of new horrendous weapon programs related to types of war theaters so far unknown in warfare, like laser weapon systems.

All these programs are subject to what can be particularly observed on the nuclear strategic level: the continuous *modernization* of existing systems and the forced *innovation* of new ones. Both measures, the modernization of old systems and the elaboration of new ones, aim at the improvement of the *quality* of weapon systems: the improvement of their precision, their reliability, their invulnerability.

The *lead-time* requirements of contemporary weapon systems planning – the time from research and development to the implementation of new systems – turn the future into history: as in very few segments of highly industrialized societies, the range of options for decisive political action in the future is continuously narrowed down by decisions in the present.

2 Doctrines, Interests and Technologies

2.1 Deterrence and Worst-Case Scenarios

The intensity of technological innovations has been speeded up by the prevailing security doctrine of *mutual deterrence*. This doctrine is based on the paradoxical, yet traditional, premise that the outbreak of violence and wars in international politics can be prevented with the help of deterrence policies by the continuous improvement of the means of war. *Under present conditions, the attempt to prevent war by deterrence policies, however, leads not only potentially or with high probability but rather with necessity to its very extensive preparation, simply to guarantee mutual retaliation.*

In this connection, the so-called *worst-case doctrine* – a fundamental strategic orientation motivating the variegated contingency planning of the political and military apparata – has functioned as a speeding-up mechanism for national armament policies. This doctrine is oriented toward future potential 'catastrophic gaps' in the weapon arsenals and is based on the combined assertion of the worst possible intention of the enemy *and* its best ability to develop new military strategies and weapon technologies. The unprecedented differentiations in political and military contingency planning, a result of a deterrence policy pursued for thirty years, are no random product but the combined result of this doctrine *and* the social forces fixated to it. The same can be said about the propensity to *overperception, overreaction,* and *overdesign* in contemporary military strategy. As long as deterrence policies are pursued, military contingency planning will be geared to the expectation of the worst possible. As a consequence the image of the enemy becomes a functional value in this policy, although the degree of fixation to the enemy is quite variable.

2.2 Socio-Political Interests

It has been asserted that the intensity of technological innovations has been speeded up, though probably not exclusively caused, by the specific security policy doctrine of mutual deterrence. Other factors have been equally responsible for the maintenance of this policy and the perpetuation of the arms race.

One important factor seems to be the *proliferation of armament-oriented interests*, with respect both to numbers and to segments of the societies affected by contemporary armament policy. The political and social interests on which deterrence policies are based are as much differentiated as the existing weapon systems and the contingency planning related to prevailing escalation doctrines. Specific military missions of the armed forces are institutionally coordinated with administrative segments of the civil and military administration, with research and development laboratories, and with the production plants for weapon systems. There is presently much talk about a *military-industrial complex*, the existence of which can hardly be denied in highly industrialized capitalist and socialist societies, particularly in the USA and the USSR. However, the infrastructure of this complex is rather composed of a series of important partial alliances, sometimes mutually exclusive, and sometimes highly interlocked. Therefore it makes more sense to talk about the existence of *administrative-military-industrial-scientific complexes*.

This interest-structure of contemporary armament policy has led to a *militarization of international politics*, since the vested interests of those social groups and political institutions which participate in the planning and production of software and hardware devices for the military have generally been far better organized and stronger than the activities of other groups with a stake in foreign policy. The only really relevant exception to this, at least in capitalist countries, is represented by the socio-economic groups involved in foreign economic policy.

In order to understand the impetus of the contemporary international arms race, we have, in the first instance, to recognize this particular kind of interest-basis of armament policies. To put emphasis on the manifold interests, including psychological interest fixations, is vitally important in the evaluation of this decisive factor on which arms races are built up and which contributes to the speeding-up of the international arms race. But we must equally emphasize the tremendous hierarchization of decision-making processes related to armament policies, which justifies speaking of the existence of a *security policy oligarchy* or an *armament policy power elite*, respectively. Despite this uncontestable hierarchization of the political deliberation and decision processes in the area of security policies, we must understand the *incrementalist basis of the political deliberation process* by which certain aspects of the momentum built into military apparata can be explained. The latter aspect particularly holds for Western countries in which well-known rivalries between administrative organizations, military services, scientific laboratories, and the production plants of weapon systems have been quite openly fought through. But such conflicts do not end up in an inroad into the various activities of the military apparata: rather, they contribute to their inflation. It is far easier for interest groups and interest coalitions intrinsically involved in national armament policies to agree on the *largest common denominator* than on the smallest. In the representation of their collective interests (for example, with respect to an increase of the share of military expenditures from public budgets) all these groups tend to agree, despite their rivalries, about the modalities of how to implement basic policy postures. The interpenetration of those interest groups and their tight coordination justify our calling these a security policy power elite.

2.3 Technological Momentum

The second essential factor which helps explain the innovation intensity of the contemporary qualitative arms race could be termed the impulse resulting from technology (*technology-impulse*) and those *organizational imperatives* which emerge from it. The direction and the speed of technological innovation processes do not represent autonomous data which could be adequately analyzed apart from the concrete interest-configuration from which innovation processes emerge.

The direction of technological research and the intensity in which innovations have developed are essentially dependent upon particular political premises, which are given for a natural science and weapon technology research *within the context of predetermined political and budgetary priorities*. Within such a context, innovation processes might assume a life of their own which, in the last instance, leads to the strange fact (so congenial to all weapons designers) that the so-called threat to the nation tends to be measured by the development stage and at the technological levels of one's own armaments or by the potential technological progress of one's *own* weapon technology, and far less by armaments and technologies of the *opponent*.

In military-technological research and innovation programs, the action-reaction theorem is particularly inadequate as an explanatory device. Let us here refer to a report of the UN Secretary-General from October 1971:

> On the surface it would seem that the effort to improve the quality of armaments, or to defend against them, follows a logical series of steps in which a new weapon or weapon-system is devised, then a counter-weapon to neutralize the new weapon, and then a counter-counter weapon. But these steps neither usually nor necessarily occur in a rational time sequence. *The people who design improvements in weapons are themselves the ones who as a rule envisage the further steps they feel should be taken. They do not wait for a potential enemy to react before they react against their own creations.* (United Nations, 1971, p. 13, italics added).

2.4 Organizational Imperatives

Organizational imperatives are particularly developed by those apparata which on the basis of an exclusive specialization (as in the case of the aerospace industry) have been active at the most advanced front in the development of improved armament technologies. As has been proved by empirical analyses, the research, development, experimenting, production, and implementation phases of major weapon systems follow a rigid sequential scheme within given research and production plants, not affected by vicissitudes in the development of international politics. The theorem of the so-called *follow-on imperative* attempts to circumscribe this fact; it explicitly states what has been taken for granted in the context of the prevailing security policy and what has led to a forced arming of the participants, respectively: namely, that defense administrations and those social forces involved in the security and defense business put much effort into keeping established research and production plants going, since any interruption of the work in these institutions is considered intolerable by the political and military elites, due to the long lead-time requirements of modern weapon technology.

The interdependence of interest alliances *and* technological innovation impulses, which are largely predetermined by those interests, has to be interpreted as *the most decisive link* in the configuration of social forces, political institutions, and publicly relevant ideologies – which all together considerably determine armament dynamics today. The order of magnitude of armament policies in highly industrialized societies has led in many instances to an *auto-dynamic growth of the security apparata* to a degree which frequently does not even make any more sense within the conventional security policy rationales. The problem of overspending and underaccomplishing is, apart from the general cost explosion, intrinsic to the military apparata of given size: this does not lead so much to a problem in civilian-military relationships but rather to the impossibility of any effective control of organizations whose size is, in budgetary terms, often larger than the GNP of many countries. This can also be clearly seen in an analysis of contemporary defense planning. The latter tends today to be fairly reactive to developments which result from the interconnections between interest alliances and technological progress; it has hardly any operative function in such rational discussions of security policy options in which the substance of the discussion would deliberately not remain fixated to the premises of the conventional doctrines of mutual deterrence and threatened retaliation. As long as segments of the military apparata are not going to be completely eliminated under an increasing cost pressure, and manifold missions of the armed services will be perpetuated also in middle-sized states, defense planning necessarily leads to a policy of 'muddling through'. Also in Europe such a costly muddling through can be increasingly observed in the existing apparata. It will be intrinsic to them as long as there is no incisive reorientation both in missions and in the organization of the military buildup from the Cold War.

2.5 Psychostrategies

In the past thirty years the inflationary growth of the military apparata has been legitimized by general doctrines supposed to represent a common denominator of many specific strategic programs. Essential parts of these programs have been motivated, apart from the already-mentioned doctrine of deterrence, by so-called *balance of power doctrines* and the *doctrine of stability*, and in the West particularly by the doctrines of *superiority* and most recently of *parity* and *sufficiency*. To a large extent, these doctrines are not new; they existed as common frames of legitimization of national military policies before 1945. The partially operative function they had before World War II has, however, been lost in the face of tremendously increasing *overkill capabilities*. So the attempt to reach some level of superiority has become irrational, even in terms of contemporary military strategy. Nonetheless, the continuous arming and rearming has been legitimized by simple rationalizations; for instance, a once achieved position of strength and superiority should not be given up; and numerical inferiority cannot be tolerated (which is absurd on the given level of overkill capabilities).

We must note that the doctrines of military balance and military stability have, at various points in the last decades and under most different contexts, justified completely different, concrete security policy measures. This can easily be understood if we consider these doctrines as *psycho-strategies* and not so much as strategies related to precise *hardware* calculations. *Strategic doctrines are best understood as political weapons.* So nuclear-strategic superiority has in the West been assumed as the basic criterion for stability and balance, which has then turned the United States into an oversophisticated pacemaker of the international arms race for nearly thirty years; otherwise the many laments of representatives from Western defense administrations in the face of massive Soviet nuclear-strategic and navy deployment programs after 1967 cannot be understood. The achievement of a kind of numerical-quantitative nuclear-strategic balance between East and West in the late 1960s and early 1970s has been thus in the West quite consistently criticized as a serious undermining of 'stability' and 'balance'. Other examples could be added. They all show that those doctrines do not have, in any strict sense of the term, an *operative* meaning; they rather represent *ex post facto rationalizations* of those situations which favor, either numerically or politically, the very side which happens to propagate these doctrines. They thus represent instruments of propaganda and means of legitimization, not guidelines for a rational argumentation about security problems.

2.6 Application to East and West

We tend to assume that these phenomena can today be equally observed both in capitalist and in socialist countries. These factors are quite clearly not system-independent in their origin, but their practical consequences and implications, in the frame of an ongoing political, ideological, and socio-economic antagonism between East and West, can be labeled as system-neutral. As long as there is a heated qualitative arms race, their effects are independent of different socio-economic orders; concretely speaking, they are independent of certain basic premises of capitalist and socialist social orders, as can quite clearly be empirically observed.

There are certain important *specific* impulses of armament dynamics which cannot be compared across the borders of different social orders and which constitute additional, perhaps basic, momenta of inertiae in the growth patterns of armament policies. For example, there has been much discussion on the socio-economic functions of armaments in capitalist states, and such functions have been well documented; there has been also some discussion on the rule-preserving and disciplining functions of military apparata in capitalist states. Rule-preserving and intrasocietal and international disciplining functions of military apparata in socialist countries have been observed in many instances, as well as the particular interests of the party personnel in power to use the military apparata for their own aims. An empirical approach to further analyses of such societal (manifest and latent) functions of military apparata could start with a functional analysis of armament expenditures and with a discussion of the actual use as well as the threatened use of the military under certain conditions. Postwar history offers rich intrasocietal and international materials for such analyses.

A detailed analysis of these functions of armaments is not the object of our present study, since we are more interested in the analytical elaboration of congruent and less in the analysis of specific impulses of armament dynamics. This limited orientation can be particularly justified by the fact that the defense apparata in all major societies have become impervious to the undeniable political changes in the East–West conflict. We know well that such a substantive restriction in our arguments is very problematic; but we would like to emphasize that it is not at all arbitrary. Inasmuch as conflict potentials with warlike implications have also developed among socialist states, this type of analysis merits also special attention in studies with a Marxist approach.

3 Essential Features of Armament Dynamics

3.1 Internal and International Interaction

Let us summarize our observations so far: *Firstly, the international arms race is much less induced by external reasons than commonly assumed. Essentially the international arms race has been inner-directed*: fueled more by *internal* than by external forces. Thus, the arms race is not so much one between interacting antagonistic powers with a reciprocal escalation, as it is a competition of the various states within their own boundaries. The competitors within the scope of national armament policies are civilian, military, industrial, administrative, and scientific groupings. The 'action-reaction' scheme in armament policies is far more evident *within* nations or alliances than with respect to their interaction.

Action-reaction processes, which have been the core of so many arms race models, do exist, but not in the context in which they have usually been assumed so far. The action-reaction scheme rather characterizes the development of certain types of weapon systems (like bombers vs. missiles) or the development of individual armament technologies within certain weapon systems. The action-reaction scheme also characterizes the manifold political, military, strategic, administrative, and industrial processes which can be observed *within* military alliances. To summarize, this scheme characterizes such types of *internal* interaction patterns far more than the *transnational* or *international* interaction patterns *between* the antagonists.

3.2 Redundant Causation and Configurative Causality

The *second* observation which can be formulated about the present international arms race concerns its *redundant causation*. The emphasis on such redundant causation is of great importance, since redundantly caused phenomena cannot be altered by working on one or only a few of their constitutive causal impulses. Transformation strategies which aim at overcoming the present arms race have therefore to be more broadly conceptualized than conventional arms race control measures. Inasmuch as the loosening-up of enemy fixations does not appear to be providing an inroad into the growth patterns of the defense apparata, conventional arms control measures are not apt to restrict the *qualitative* growth of these apparata.

Aside from this type of redundant causation, a further notion has to be mentioned: the *configurative causality of the growth patterns of defense apparata* (and thus, by implication, of arms race dynamics). Conventional causal schemes have conceptualized causality in terms of the sequential interaction of independent, intervening, and dependent variables. *Configurative* causality is quite different from that type of one-dimensional causality, inasmuch as synchronous and diachronous analyses of total phenomena, like the contemporary defense apparata, show that all possible causal interactions and causal sequences can be observed simultaneously with no clear-cut, one-dimensional rigid sequential patterns prevailing. (For example, this applies between the three decisive variables of armament policies like armament interests, armament technologies, and armament ideologies.) Naturally, in the biography of individual weapon systems, a clear weighting of these factors in terms of conventional bi- or multivariate causal models can nevertheless be determined. So it can be clearly shown in the biography of some weapon systems that industrial interests were decisive in initiating a new weapon program and that the technological innovation has been the result of such lobbying pressures from the side of those groups interested in such a development; whereas in the development of other weapon systems often just the contrary can be observed, namely that a once-achieved technological innovation will be occupied by specific armament interests which then formulate certain contingency plans, with the result that such a program looks indispensable to fill certain 'gaps' in the existing weapon arsenals. The fact that all of these types of interactions do take place at one and the same time and over time between the political and military administrations, the armed services, the armament industries, technology, and scientific laboratories represents a real challenge for any conventional causal explanation of armament dynamics. We try to come to grips with these phenomena by the notion of *configurative* causality, the understanding of which is decisive for an adequate analysis of the growth patterns of armament policies, as well as for the understanding of the inertiae and momenta built into these apparata taken as a whole.

4 Consequences for Arms Control

4.1 Technological Impulses and Diplomacy

These conclusions are of immediate practical value for the evaluation of a strategy of *arms control*. If it is true that armament dynamics is redundantly caused and if major reasons for armament policies are rooted in societal configurations (within societies and within alliances) rather than in rational reactions to actions of the so-called potential enemy, then we are confronted with specific consequences: a strategy of arms control has to be based on a *multiplicity of measures* if armament dynamics is to be limited and curtailed effectively.

The question with regard to the true intervention function of arms control agreements in and their inroad into the autonomous probability of armament development trends is decisive. Past arms control agreements have been almost completely ineffective in restraining the development of armament technology.

The enormous discrepancy between the massive inner-societal impulses for further growth of armaments and for rearmament and the ritual of diplomatic negotiations is characteristic of arms control negotiations. This ritual begins with diplomatic soundings as to whether such negotiations are desired by all sides; it is continued by determining the participants, the place where the negotiations will take place, the preliminary negotiations, the long discussion on the agenda, and then, finally, perhaps the beginning of the negotiations – which may last for several years. While all this is being done in a rather spectacular way, entering the headlines of daily newspapers, the national or alliance-pledged armament policy is quietly but in a far more momentous way taking a new step toward the future. Political options in matters of arms control and disarmament are then restricted by actual armament developments.

While diplomatic delegations discuss a subject for many years in laborious sessions, this subject is often already outdated from a military-technological viewpoint at the beginning of the negotiations, and/or it is superseded by new armament-technological developments in the course of the protracted negotiations.

Arms control policies could constitute one of several *direct* strategies for the solution of imminent armament and security problems, if they could really achieve a dynamics of their own within a policy of peace promotion deliberately aspired to. *Under present conditions this would be possible only with the help of massive interferences into the research and development programs by which so far the arms race has been continuously pushed ahead.* One could talk about successful arms control measures only if these *qualitative* dimensions of the contemporary arms race could be really controlled, with the final result being a containment and cut-down of national armament policies. That is to say, arms control measures have to be evaluated not on the basis of their symbolic value, but by the degree to which they really represent an effective inroad into those factors analyzed in the previous paragraphs, particularly into manpower *and* investment (procurement) as well as research and development.

Even in that instance, arms control policies will cross decisive thresholds only if such a strategy is part of a comprehensive peace policy composed of many components, including, so to speak, roundabout strategies. By these the armament sector will not be affected directly; they rather aim to build up peace-promoting structures without which a distargeting of the defense apparata cannot come about. In this respect we are thinking particularly about peace-promoting measures in the area of socialization processes and about reorientations in the allocation of social resources geared to newly defined societal priorities.

4.2 Force Reduction in Europe

The major criterion of an effective arms control policy in Europe is the simultaneity of the reduction of all essential dimensions of the military machinery: of both the force levels (personnel) and the investment activities. The latter can be divided into two components – procurement as well as research and development programs.

If the size of military personnel is to be curtailed by an arms control agreement, then the danger exists that the other dimensions of the military machinery will be comparatively strengthened in order to achieve a compensation of the cut dimension – although it is at the moment unlikely that a cut in personnel would release any appreciable funds. Restructuring the military machineries of Europe from personnel-intensive to technology-intensive institutions requires a gradual transition from mass armies to professional armies – the latter notoriously far more costly than the first. It is therefore rather to be feared that a combination of increased wage expenditures and the reorientation of the military machineries toward personnel with a particularly high technological competence will fully absorb any sums to be released in a first step by personnel reduction. Besides, a military machinery restructured in this manner might require higher investment expenditures, thus even tending to cause an increase in military expenditures. If we assume the hypothetical case that a reduction of personnel size would cause an effective economizing of funds, then, in view of current high prices for research, the reorientation of these funds toward investment expenditures becomes almost unavoidable.

Such a development could be halted only under the condition that the growth rate of all essential dimensions of the military machinery be cut simultaneously, i.e. that all parts of the military budgets be frozen. But even the latter measure might help stimulate the intensity of armaments and military technological research – which once more shows the importance of restricting research and development funds for military technological programs, if an armaments policy is to be effective.

Summing up: only an agreement which includes all components of the military machinery and effectively excludes all possibilities for compensation or substitution, can – in view of the experiences of the past years – be considered an arms control agreement which interferes with armament dynamics to the extent of slowing it down and cutting it back effectively. This criterion may be considered the fundamental requirement of a peace-promoting arms control policy.

How important such a criterion is becomes also apparent in another connection, to be mentioned here only briefly. As soon as one engages in a discussion about politically, strategically, or purely geographically defined arms control zones, the danger of compensation and substitution appears here as well. It cannot be excluded that the limitation of potentials in a certain zone will not simply lead to an intensification of military activities in other places outside the defined zone. This example, which played a major role in arms control negotiations of the 1920s, proves that the traditional arms control paradigm requires a fundamentally new definition if it is to have any political value at all for a peace policy.

4.3 A Peace-Promoting Strategy

Our discussion until now has shown that, in the analyses of the international arms race and of the further growth of the national armament policies, the action-reaction model is a favorite justification. We have argued that in reality the national armament policies and the international arms race are more likely to be influenced by prevailing internal factors, rather than from outside. No matter how false the action perspectives derived from the paradigm of official politics, a paradigm conceived solely from the viewpoint of practice – which in a short-circuit action would take into account only our own analytical findings – would be equally false. It will have to be shown in which way a *mixture* of the action-reaction paradigm and of internal measures could be the best basis for a transformation strategy for an effective peace-promoting arms control policy. Let us first briefly explain the program which current arms control policy is essentially following.

The starting point is a certain unilateralism which seems to be acting in the wrong direction. Today this unilateralism essentially manifests itself in the fact that, in anticipating arms control negotiations, both sides are not only claiming but effectively continuing to build up their own military machinery in a full analogy with earlier experience. There are two reasons for this, officially emphasized over and over again: (1) the argument of the power policy, with the underlying notion that such a measure could enhance the possibility of forcing the current potential enemy to make certain concessions (a historically questionable and untenable assumption); and (2) the argument that such a build-up of one's own military machinery would simply enhance one's political bargaining position. When both contracting parties or partners set out from the same premises, then this policy of reinforcing the military machinery in order to obtain better initial positions in diplomatic negotiations proves a definitely doubtful and counterproductive undertaking.

In the second step, according to this official arms control program, it is then the task of classical diplomacy (supplemented by military strategic and technological expert advice) to counteract the political and technological armament processes which are always being massively pushed ahead on a national scale directly before the opening of diplomatic discussions and during the negotiations. When, after tedious negotiations, an internationally negotiated agreement on arms control is finally reached, then it can be enforced only under the invariably restrictive conditions of national and alliance-conditioned security and armament policies.

4.4 Unilateral Initiatives

What would an alternative political program look like – a program which, once applied in practice, could hold a reasonable promise of success and could have far-reaching consequences for an effective arms control policy?

This paradigm, too, begins with a certain unilateralism. However, the unilateral measures are not aimed at achieving an escalation of national or alliance-conditioned armament policies in order to gain a better initial position in the arms control negotiations: rather, the unilateral measures aim at carrying out or pushing through – should there be considerable internal social opposition to such a policy – the first effective curtailment in the existing national framework on the basis of autonomous political decisions. Such a measure could consist in reducing the share of the military expenditures in the GNP or in the national budget; it would also have to apply to a balanced symmetric curtailment of investment activities (research and development, procurement).

Then, on the basis of such a self-imposed curtailment which would lead to an effective arms control policy (if possible bindingly outlined in a plan for several years on a national scale), and after beginning the autonomous application of the curtailment (not only of a symbolical nature) of one's own armament activities, one should try to reach an international arms control agreement by means of international negotiations. This then in turn would represent a guarantee of the arms control measures already undertaken on a national scale by an internationally negotiated agreement.

Such international negotiations could also become a sort of rear cover for those national governments which might encounter considerable internal resistance against implementing the first step of such a policy on a national scale.

After the success of the negotiations, such an arms control agreement could then contribute to stabilization of the level of arms control measures nationally implemented and on a national scale effectively attained. After such a first step, this process should then be continued in an analogous way on a higher level of intensity of armament curtailment.

4.5 Practical Considerations

Which are the practical considerations for such a program?

First, unless the driving impulses for national armament and alliance-conditioned armament policy are contained, any internationally negotiated arms control agreement can only foresee those measures which are also in the interest of the then ruling factions of the national armament machinery – as clearly demonstrated by the SALT agreements. The basic consideration can be that on a national scale the maneuvering space for international arms control diplomacy must first be argued and pushed through, before it can be possible on a diplomatic level to reach any agreement of more than symbolic significance.

Second, this new arms control program is based on the realization that any form of coercive strategy ('power policy') in the contemporary East–West conflict is from its very beginning equally counterproductive, as it contributes on the other hand to the further development of the military machineries. In contrast, the program outlined here is based on the fact that those nations and those groups of states which pursue such a true peace-promoting arms control strategy would gain far greater freedom of diplomatic action, greater ability for political action, and greater ability for political maneuvering than possible with the traditional action models. It has to be taken into account that the party which takes the initiative for a nationally implemented arms control policy probably puts its own allies and particularly its opponents under psychological pressure – a situation which diplomacy, with the correct kind of staging, could well exploit for political purposes.

While at present all governments state in their official declarations that unilateral advance reductions or concessions would endanger their national security and increase the possible pressure of the current allies and particularly of the opponents on their national autonomy, in reality exactly the opposite should be the case. Additionally, we must stress once more that a policy staged this way, even if based on traditional criteria of security policies, contains no risks, since the destructive power of the military machineries has long been oversaturated anyhow. Besides, despite all assurances to the contrary, there are no military strategies for Central Europe which in the case of a military conflict would leave the substance (the population, the production facilities, the environment) of this political and geographical zone untouched.

4.6 Peace Policy Dynamics

The realism of the program presented here, with its typical sequence of specific measures on the national and international level, lies in the strategy of tackling the problem of curtailing armament dynamics from several dimensions simultaneously – although, at least in the beginning, in the form of a time sequence. Such a strategy, which is a differentiated combination of internal measures of self-limitation and of international negotiations designed to offer additional safeguards to the national measures, makes it possible to get started a peace policy dynamics which can counteract on all levels the prevailing trend of armament dynamics.

The strongest argument for such a strategy lies in its being based on feedback with the population of national communities. If we compare the contemporary arms control strategy with the strategy which we have presented as desirable and realistic, then an essential difference is that the first one is essentially oriented toward the government and the state, while in the arms control strategy introduced here state and governmental measures are of importance, but become effective only when coupled with internal interest groups.

This difference can be clearly demonstrated by an example. The current arms control strategy considers control, inspection, and verification to be the business of specialists commissioned on a national level or in an international team by state administrations; in the arms control strategy described here, however, control is essentially also a matter of *self-control*. Of course, on a national level such self-control can be effective only if the policy of self-imposed arms control curtailment is supported by interest groups. The latter will be much simpler (1) if the social-political alternative of the traditional security and armament policy and of a peace policy no more based on armaments and military machinery can penetrate the public consciousness, and (2) if the enormous social expenditures of the former and the possible social utility of the latter become concrete orientation-points in defining the interests of concrete social groups and their representatives. Such a widening of the base for a peace-promoting arms control policy is the best foundation for gradually overcoming the armament restructuring and rearmament policies which lack any rational criteria. A new movement would appear in international diplomacy, a movement which could arise only out of new political dynamics in the respective national contexts – a movement in the face of which the current arms control and disarmament diplomatic activities would reveal themselves as what they always have been: a part of armament dynamics itself.

5 Concluding Remarks

It is my personal contention that this analysis is essentially corroborated by facts, and that these practical reflections about a peace-promoting arms control policy can at least claim to be more reasonable than currently official conceptions. Certainly I cannot satisfy those who claim that the undeniably existing social and political antagonism of the systems of East and West a priori precludes such a policy. Such an argument can only be countered by saying that it is high time to start distinguishing between fundamental and non-fundamental contradictions in the East–West conflict. I am convinced that fundamental contradictions do exist and that the East–West conflict has not been created on the basis of mistaken interpretations and mistaken perceptions of elites acting in history, but that this conflict is based on antagonistic interests. Yet I cannot share the conviction that this antagonism of interests must necessarily be carried out by military means. I think that it is historically rather by chance (whose individual steps, however, can be explained) that this confrontation ever became militarized. A plea for a peace-promoting arms control policy is also a plea for more public debates on socially useful alternatives to armament activities – which means more debates about demilitarization.

DIETER SENGHAAS, b. 1940, Ph.D. in Political Science (University of Frankfurt, FRG); at present Professor of Peace, Conflict, and Development Research, University of Bremen. Most recent books: *The European Experience* (Berg, 1985); *Die Zukunft Europas* (Suhrkamp, 1986); *Konfliktformationen im internationalen System* (Suhrkamp, 1988).

Chapter 3
Arms Races, Formal Models, and Quantitative Tests

HÅKAN WIBERG

Lund University Peace Research Institute, and Centre of Peace and Conflict Research at Copenhagen University

1 Introduction

When the Massachusetts Peace Society was founded back in 1815, one of the first things it set out to do was a study of the total military expenditures in the world – and of what might have been achieved by means of these resources, if they had been put to more constructive use (van den Dungen, 1977, p. 240, citing Curti, 1929, pp. 26–27). As I argue in Chapter 19, there are several ways in which armament dynamics can be defined as a *social* problem; and they tend to affect the ways in which *scientific* problems are stated. Whether you look for determinants of armaments of individual nations or whole regions, for long-term or short-term determinants, for internal or external determinants, for determinants of input (military expenditures) or output (military capability) – it all depends on how you formulate your initial questions. These often derive from normative concerns, but may also be dictated by 'purely theoretical' considerations. For example, how to disaggregate military expenditure (milex) in a more detailed study depends on whether you are primarily interested in alternative uses of resources, or in the risks for war that may derive from different patterns of armament.

The present chapter starts with discussing various ways of formulating problems concerning armament dynamics. It then goes through some aspects of the pioneering work of Lewis Fry Richardson, looking at his epistemological points of departure and his choice of variables, parameters, methods of derivation, and attempts at empirical tests. Next, it surveys some of the revisions and improvements that have been suggested in these and other respects. After reviewing empirical results achieved from testing mathematical models of arms races by means of quantitative methodology, I finally attempt to evaluate where we stand today.

The limitations should be made clear from the beginning. This chapter is by no means an attempt at summarizing all empirical research on armament dynamics, of which the testing of formal models is only one specific kind (Leidy & Staiger, 1985). Nor does it aim to give a general, blanket overview of mathematical models of armament dynamics in addition to those that already exist (e.g. Busch, 1970; Rattinger, 1975a; Moll & Luebbert, 1980; Isard & Anderton, 1985) – it largely limits itself to models that have actually been empirically tested. Even with a generous understanding of 'testing', these constitute a rather small minority.

2 The Art of Asking

In addition to normative concerns and/or theoretical puzzles, the questions that are asked about armament dynamics depend on the underlying epistemology and cosmology of the author. We may define two pure cases of imagery by counterposing 'cataclysmic' or 'sociological' or 'causal' models with 'strategic' or 'rational' or 'actor-oriented' ones (Rapoport, 1966).

In the *first* type of models, the dependent variable is thought of as being determined by causal forces residing in the character of the international system and/or of some subsystem in it and/or of some individual state and/or of the internal dynamics of that state: we find quite a number of substantive theories using one or more of these sets of variables as independent ones. We also find different forms of causality assumed: linear, looped, etc. Furthermore, there is a broad range of formalization of the models, from purely verbal ones to sets of equations of the type

$$Y(t) = F(a_1, \ldots, a_i, \ldots, a_n; x_1, \ldots, x_j, \ldots, x_m)$$

where Y is the value at time t of some variable measuring the level of armament (or its first- or second-order derivative) of a given state, the set (a_i) consists of the *parameters* in F, and the set (x_j) consists of other variables (possibly including Y itself and its values at earlier time points). From a formal point of view, we also find quite a variety of such equation systems, both when it comes to F (e.g. linear or non-linear), a_i (estimated independently or from the solution of the equations), and x_j (variable or derivative, dependent or independent, etc.).

It should also be noted that such models are suggested by, but do not commit their authors to, epistemological determinism, as witnessed by Richardson's 'This is what will happen, unless people stop to think'. The model itself – in the more abstract sense – is deterministic, as is any more specific model of its type. *Research*, then, consists of two kinds of activities: the mathematical work of deriving consequences, and the statistical work of comparing such consequences with data by finding sets of parameter values that provide optimal fit between them and estimating how good that fit is and how statistically significant it is.

In *strategic* models, by contrast, it is taken for granted that military expenditures are not entirely determined by 'blind forces', but are decided by rational actors who – under given constraints and on the basis of the assumptions they make about reality – are trying to maximize, optimize, or satisfy some objective function defined by their sets of preferences. Here, too, we find wide variety along several dimensions. The actor under study may, or may not, be assumed to make decisions in an environment of other rational actors whose considerations have to be taken into account. We find different kinds of rationality imputed to the actors: maximizing the objective function, maximizing expected utility, seeking a minimax point, etc. In many versions of strategic analysis, the actor coincides with the state, thought of as unitary; but we also find higher actors, like alliances, and lower actors, whose interplay decides what the state does. And we find a considerable variety of substantive theories as to what *are* the objective functions of the actors. Research on a model consists in pretty much the same as in the first case, with the addition that the mathematical derivations from the specific model are sometimes offered as policy advice. (We leave it aside whether this does more harm than good.)

The ideal types thus being outlined, two things have to be pointed out. First, the polarity between them does not coincide with any of the other dimensions. Either kind of thinking can be expressed in anything between simple verbal propositions and complex mathematical models. Metaphysical preferences may affect the type of model chosen, but neither *commits* its author in that way: a strategic model author may just as well present it with the caveat: 'this is what would happen, if decision-makers were pure *homini economici*'. Purely causal models range between external determination only (action-reaction) and internal determination only (*Eigendynamik*) – but this is also largely true for strategic models, and even if I have not seen any that is purely internalist, this possibility is not logically excluded.

Second, on closer inspection, the relationship between the two types of models is a more complex one: causal and strategic analysis are not necessarily antithetical to one another. For example, Richardsonian models may be derived from strategic ones as the consequences of specific assumptions about objective functions (see Chapter 4 in this volume). One may, for that matter, dig deeper into strategic models by trying to find variables that determine the objective functions of the actors, or by showing that the objective functions of two actors in a given situation engender a process over which neither actor has control, and whose direction neither actor wants. A number of mixed-motive games illustrate this 'contrafinality'. Finally, between the extremes defined by the two ideal types we find a wide 'fuzzy' area of models with some components deriving from causal imagery and others from strategic imagery.

It is therefore relatively fruitless to try to decide which imagery is the 'correct' one. In order for us to get any good answers, the questions have to be more substantive than that. Let us therefore move one rung down on the ladder of abstraction to a question that has been much debated: what are the relative roles of internal and external forces in arms dynamics?

A first query must then be, what does the question ask? If it is understood in a causal framework, it is to be understood as a question about the interplay of *causal forces*, and a simple way of translating it would be: when some indicator of armament (of a given state) is the dependent variable, is the explanatory power of those variables that characterize the given state stronger or weaker than that of the variables characterizing its environment, and especially other states? That translation, however, already takes a number of things for granted. *If* variables can be neatly divided into internal and external ones, and *if* the relationships between them is – at least intrinsically – linear, and, especially, *if* there is no interaction between internal and external variables: then established statistical methods can provide us with neat answers, provided that the causal model tested actually contains all variables that significantly affect the level of armament.

Now we often have good grounds to question each of these 'ifs'. Should we characterize dyadic or systemic variables as internal, external, or neither? Are there good grounds to expect relationships to be linear, at least intrinsically (log-linear, etc.)? How should we categorize cases where the value of one independent variable determines whether the dependent variable essentially depends on external or internal variables?

The point of raising such questions already here is to make it clear that even the external/internal issue may not be one where it is fruitful to ask for simple and clear answers. In fact, we may have to move even further down the ladder of abstraction to get good questions.

This can also be argued, if we interpret the question inside a strategic framework. Whereas in strong versions of causal thinking the beliefs and aims of decision-makers are assumed to be irrelevant, epiphenomenal, or at least causally explainable within the model, these become crucial in strategic analysis, where the very point of departure is that decision-makers are trying to satisfy some aims, given the existing (real and/or perceived) restrictions. Are these decision-makers motivated primarily by concerns related to the position of their state in its environment (offensive and defensive capability, avenues of influence, international prestige, etc.) or by concerns related to the state itself, like employment, technological development, smooth operation of the administration, preservation of political consensus, etc? A more careful discussion of these questions will also reveal that in many cases the distinction between 'external' and 'internal' motives can be made only by fiat, and that complex relations among them may preclude any clear ascription one way or the other of 'motive force'. Furthermore – and this is also true about causal reasoning – we may well encounter a situation where the answer depends much on the level of aggregation on which we ask the question, on what decision-makers we count with, as well as on whether we study an individual system, an entire service, or military expenditures as a whole.

But enough of caveats for the moment: let us now look at some of the proposed answers and their subsequent fate, as the 'abstract model-building' of the 1960s gave way to the 'excessive empiricism' of the 1970s.

3 An Early Answer – and Its Problems

As a point of departure for our discussion we take the contributions of Lewis Fry Richardson (1960a). In his simplest model, he assumes that three things affect the 'increase of defences' of a state involved in a bilateral arms race. The surrounding menaces, represented by the defences of the other state, are assumed to affect this increase positively. Already existing military costs of the state itself are assumed to affect it negatively. 'Grievances and ambitions', like France's ambition to recover Alsace-Lorraine from Germany, are assumed to be constant and to contribute positively to increase of defences. Richardson's model (1960a, p. 16) then becomes

$$dx/dt = ky - \alpha x + g$$
$$dy/dt = lx - \beta y + h$$

where the time derivatives dx/dt and dy/dt (which we will write x' and y') represent the rate of increase in military expenditures, x and y the expenditures themselves. All the other terms are assumed to be constant parameters. Out of these, k and l represent how sensitive each state is to the military expenditures of the other state. How sensitive states are to the budgetary pressure of their own military expenditures is represented by α and β (which we will henceforth write a and b). All these sensitivity parameters are assumed to have positive values, but may differ from one state to the other. The 'ambitions and grievances', finally, are represented by g and h, which thus summarize relations between the two states. If relations are predominantly hostile, g and h are positive; if they are predominantly amicable, they are negative.

Richardson then investigated the mathematical properties of this model, and went on to compare it with the 1908–14 military expenditures of the two blocs: the Entente and the Central Powers. He concluded (1960a, pp. 32–33) that the fit was very good and that the model was therefore supported.

The essential point made by Richardson is the following: $dx/dt = 0$ means that nation X neither rearms, nor disarms, and $dy/dt = 0$ means the same thing for Y. Setting the derivatives equal to zero gives us

$$ky - ax + g = 0$$
$$lx - by + h = 0.$$

Those conditions can be represented by two straight lines. If $ab = kl$, they are parallel, otherwise they intersect at precisely one point, which therefore represents the equilibrium where neither party will rearm or disarm. The two lines divide the XY space into four quadrants, representing the four possible combinations – X rearming/disarming and Y rearming/disarming.

The crucial issue is now whether the equilibrium is *stable* or *unstable*.

Richardson shows that this does not depend on *g* and *h* (they only determine *where* the two lines will intersect), but only on the four other parameters. If *ab* is greater than *kl*, then both parties will disarm in the quadrant I, northeast of the intersection point, thus moving towards that point; and in quadrant III, southwest of the point, they will both rearm, again moving towards it. In other words, in that case, the equilibrium is stable. If the initial arms expenditures of X and Y are represented by a point in quadrant III, we will get an arms race, but a decelerating one that will eventually stop at the intersection point.

In Figure 3.1 we have taken one point in each of the two quadrants, so as to show what the equations mean in terms of tendencies. The horizontal arrows show the direction and the strength of the tendency of X to move, the vertical arrows those of Y, and the arrows in between indicate the resulting direction and strength of the tendency of the system to move immediately from the point.

Figure 3.1 *System with stable equilibrium*

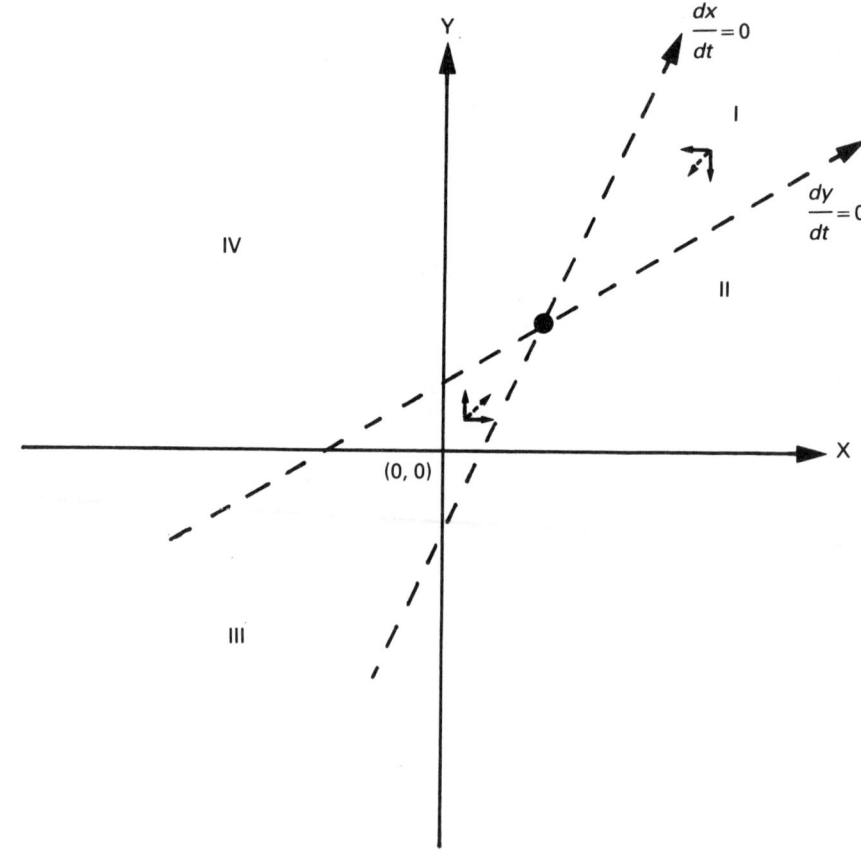

On the other hand, if ab is less than kl, then quadrant I will be the quadrant of mutual rearmament and quadrant III will be that of mutual disarmament. If the parties start in (x_1, y_1) in Figure 3.2, then they enter a 'disarmament race', which in principle is endless, but in practice must end in $(0, 0)$, where both are completely disarmed. (The same goes for any other point in that quadrant.) If they start in (x_2, y_2) (or in any other point in that quadrant), they will move northeast in an endless arms race. In both cases, the system will move *away from* the equilibrium point, no matter how close to it the parties started, and the equilibrium is thus unstable. Such 'run-away arms races', Richardson assumes, will eventually end in war, whereas this is not necessarily the case for arms races in situations with a stable equilibrium point. He also notes that unstable arms races seem to be a modern phenomenon, appearing only from the late 1870s.

Figure 3.2 *An unstable equilibrium*

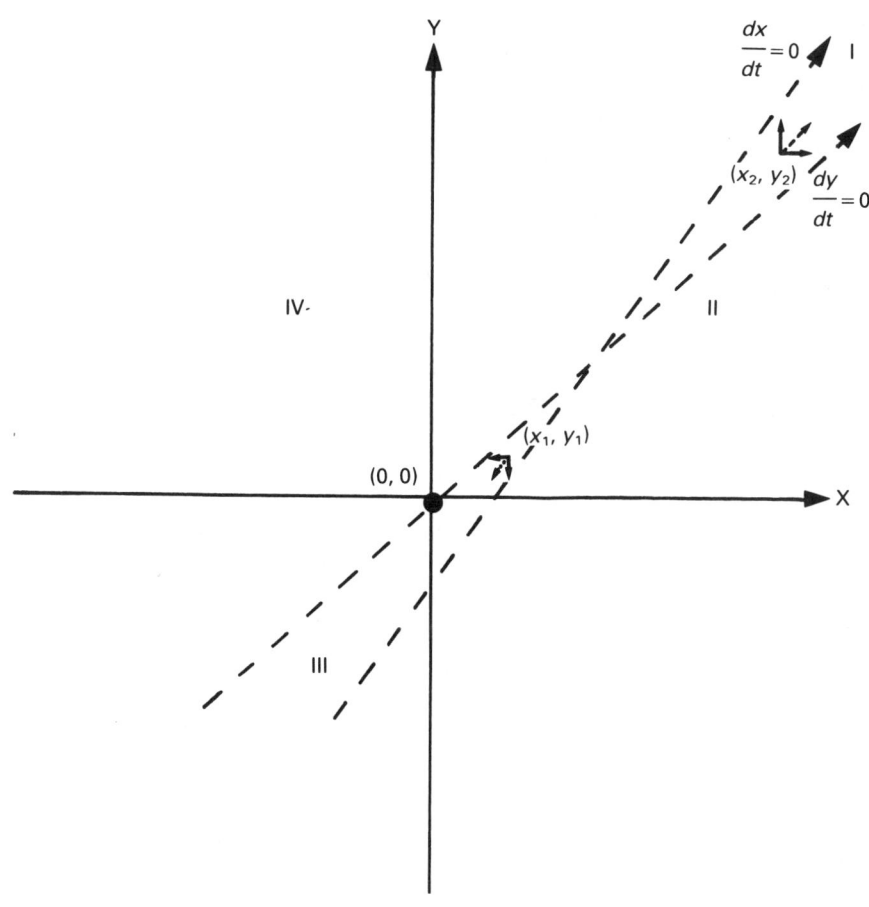

Richardson's effort was indeed a pioneering one. It is another matter that his choice of model, his mathematical analysis of it, his way of operationalizing it, his way of testing it, and his conclusions from it have all been subjected to considerable criticism – some of this by Richardson himself.

3.1 Variables

Variables x and y are to indicate 'armament'. This raises issues of conceptualization and issues of operationalization. What level of aggregation is justified: alliance, nation, or specific components of the armed forces of a nation? Should we conceptualize 'armament' in input terms – how much is spent on it – or in output terms: what is had for it? Should we think of armament as a stock variable or a flow variable?

If one were to go only to what Richardson does in his analysis of the 1908–14 arms race, his answers are: alliance, input, and flow. What he does measure is annual military expenditure of individual nations, summed up by alliance. Richardson, himself however, questions all this. In his analysis of the interwar arms dynamics, he uses the nation as unit. In his verbal reasoning, he indicates that stock would be more relevant, and also that military expenditure is to be regarded as a proxy for military capability. *If* we regard national military expenditure as the variable to be measured, then we have no validity problem – but at the expense of theoretical strength. When the theoretical justification for the terms lx and ky in the equations is that a nation is assumed to adapt its expenditure level to what the other side has or gets, then it stands to reason that what is being adapted to is what the other side gets for its money, rather than how much money it spends. Only if we assume either that the spending itself is regarded as primarily important, or that the spending level is the only information that the first state has about the level of military preparedness of the other one, can we theoretically justify identifying x and y with aggregated input, i.e. the milex figure.

If, however, we regard (assessed) military capability as the crucial latent variable, it becomes highly problematic for a number of reasons to use milex figures as the manifest one. These problems include inflation (and finding a specific military deflator), conversion of currencies (and the additional problem that e.g. the US/USSR force ratio may vary depending on whether it is measured in roubles or dollars), depreciation (which may vary among nations and services). Only under highly idealized assumptions can milex be regarded as a valid indicator of output (Wiberg, 1983).

Nevertheless, milex – or some statistical manipulation of milex – has remained the measured variable in most empirical tests of arms dynamics models. There are, however, some exceptions. In several cases, the nuclear component of arms dynamics has been measured directly by such output variables as number of missiles or warheads, or megatonnage, or yield. Authors like Rattinger (1975a, 1976a) and Lambelet (1974, 1975a,

1976) have also worked with variables like numbers of tanks, ships, fighters, or dreadnoughts, weighted by quality indices intended to measure the fighting capability of the units.

Another development in the literature has consisted in going from looking at milex to looking at what happens with the stock. The simplest way of doing this is to posit that the stock is a sum of terms

$$\sum_i p y_{t-i} q^i,$$

where p is the portion of milex that goes into the stock, y_{t-i} the milex i years before t, and q a depreciation factor.

In terms of variables, the development headed by Lambelet and Rattinger also has another aspect: away from taking the armed forces of a state as a unit to looking at more disaggregated 'races': naval, tank, missile, etc.

Working with stock, on the other hand, in principle lies closer to Richardson's original formulations (mathematical and verbal): it can be argued that we get a better (more valid) measure of what states are trying to do, and of what characteristics of other states they are sensitive to, if we use s', the first-order derivative of the stock, rather than milex, to operationalize the x and y in the model. There is a price for this, however: in Richardson's formulations, the same variable is to indicate both action (x' and y'), output (of the other actor) and burden (the negative terms $-by$ and $-ax$). Burden, however, is clearly an input variable that milex (to the extent that it is valid as such, and reliable) serves well to measure. Hence, the parsimony of the model can be saved only by assuming that some manipulation of milex figures *is* a valid measure of output, or by theorizing that it is really the milex of Alter that Ego is sensitive to, or that the theoretical role of the negative terms ($-ax, -by$) is to indicate not burden or fatigue, but satisfaction or saturation.

3.2 Parameters

Richardson's equations for the 1908–14 arms race contained six parameters in addition to his two variables and their first-order derivatives. Out of these, the grievance parameters h and g were measured independently (by means of trade figures: Richardson believed that trade was a force of amity), whereas the determination of the sensitivity parameters a, b, l, and k was left to the procedure of finding the optimal fit between the equations and the empirical data. He thus posited that the sensitivities involved were not necessarily constant over space (otherwise we would have $a = b$ and $l = k$), but that they were constant over time, at least over a few years, for each actor.

Later research with his models, as well as with modifications of them, has borne him out on the first point: parameter values often differ greatly from actor to actor. The record on the second point is mixed, however. In some cases, it has not made a great difference for parameter values whether a longer process has been broken down by time; whereas in other cases, like the analysis of 1870–1914 by Choucri & North (1975) or Rattinger's (1976a), analysis of the Middle East in 1956–73, the same parameter for the same actor has varied greatly over time.

The estimation of parameters has remained a sore point in arms dynamics modelling. One fundamental reason is that parameters usually have not been theorized and therefore not possible to measure independently, but left to statistical estimation. For Richardson, h and g constitute the exceptions (how good his underlying theory is, is beyond the point here), and some of the later research, mainly with 'rational' models, has attempted to estimate parameter values by means of calculations of military strategy (Lanchester equations and later developments). The fact remains, however, that in most cases where models have been put to empirical tests, all or nearly all of the parameter values have been left to statistical estimation. Even if it could be safely assumed that the 'true' parameter values for individual actors were constant over time, this would define some serious problems and dilemmas.

The ideal situation would consist of a long process (tens of measurement points) and very few free parameters, which there were solid grounds for expecting to remain constant. Now the longer the time-span, the more dubious is the latter assumption – but if we have several times more observations than free parameters, the assumption can at least be tested and suitably revised, e.g by breaking the process down into phases.

As the number of free parameters approaches the number of observations, however, the a priori likelihood for good fits (e.g. R^2 close to 1) increases. Or, to use Anatol Rapoport's formulation: 'Give me four parameters, and I'll give you an elephant; give me five, and I'll make it wag its tail.' At the same time, and for this reason, even good fits lose in statistical significance. Even if techniques can be found for estimating parameters in such systems of equations (as long as no single equation has more free parameters than variables), estimating the statistical significance of the parameter values becomes insuperable.

Thus a balance must be struck between theoretical simplicity combined with good testability on the one hand, and on the other hand having a model with high expected adequacy, which means several independent variables but therefore also several free parameters and bad testability. Adding theoretically unspecified dummy variables only adds to this dilemma.

3.3 Tests

Richardson seems to have been the first to combine two things: developing a (formal) model for arms dynamics *and* testing it. His claim that the test strongly confirmed the model in the 1908–14 case was not seriously challenged for a long time, and had the implication that arms races (this one, at least) were action-reaction processes, where domestic forces only served as brakes (the $-by$ and $-ax$ terms).

As it has later turned out, Richardson's claim was unfounded. In order to test the model, he transformed it into having $(x + y)$ as his variable. Later, however, Wagner and others (1975) have demonstrated that his data are also compatible with seeing the milex of the two blocs as two independent exponential processes, where thus only internal forces operate; and Rattinger (1975a, pp. 112f.) has shown that if instead one transforms the model into having $(x - y)$ as variable, the model is plainly disconfirmed by his data.

The adequacy of tests has remained a bone of contention in research about arms dynamics. Where one author has argued that his model has fared well in testing, others have often found the tests inadequate and the fit artificial.

4 Equations: Later Developments

Richardson's equations have been challenged on the grounds that the underlying theoretical ideas were inadequate, or that the equations did not adequately express them, or both. Let us therefore look at the explicit or implicit underlying theoretical ideas behind the equations and the ways in which they have been operationalized and tested by Richardson.

4.1 A Continuous Process

By using differential equations, Richardson implies that the studied process is a continuous one: changes in one variable will have immediate effects on the other variable (and on the variable itself). The clear trend in later research, however, is towards using difference equations rather than differential ones, at least in models that have been submitted to tests. The justification for this on empirical grounds – access to data – is obviously that the milex data that are easily available have years as units. There is also the theoretical justification that we have to do with discrete processes, since budgetary decisions are also annual, against which it may be held that the underlying process behind them is nevertheless a continuous one (Luterbacher 1975, p. 213).

4.2 Decision-Maker and Decision

It is implicit in the equations that each side of the race can be represented by one single decision-maker making – at each time point – one single decision. This may be theoretically challenged, on several grounds.

One of them concerns the level of the postulated decision-maker. The choice in Richardson's original analysis is a rather rare one: a whole alliance. The overwhelming majority of later research has worked with individual nations, even if one can find analyses where several nations are aggregated.

It is not difficult to argue theoretically why a single state should take the capability of two or more states into account when deciding on its own milex. Furthermore, two or more states in a firm alliance with a common definition of probable adversaries might also react in a parallel way to what happens in these other states, justifying an aggregated lx. What is less easy to see, however, is how to justify a common $-by$, unless we also assume that burden and fatigue effects are similar within the different states in the alliance. Furthermore, the ascription of common decision-making to alliances can also be questioned; nor is it easy to see how movements in one direction in one of the states should be expected to affect the other states in the alliance, when we consider both political pressures and free-rider effects (Olson, 1965; Olson & Zeckhauser, 1966).

One may also question the majority approach of using states as units, but in the other direction: that it is too aggregated. The theoretical argument might then be that we have not one, but several decision-makers, whose objectives do not coincide. To my knowledge, the only author who has tried to represent this in a formal model *and* systematically test it is Ostrom (1978). In his Reactive-Linkage models, the services, the President, and Congress are treated separately. Majeski (1983a) has developed the model further.

We have already mentioned another direction of disaggregation, dividing the armament variables into indicators of nuclear, conventional, air, naval, tank, etc. capability. There are some obvious theoretical arguments for this – and some support is given by the empirical tests – but it also creates new theoretical problems, especially concerning the fatigue factor.

4.3 The Reaction Component

In Richardson's equations, the milex of the other side appears only once – as x and y, respectively – and the parameter values k and l are assumed to be positive. This implies two things, provided that everything else remains equal: an increase in the milex of one side will be followed by an increase on the other side, and a decrease by a decrease. It is not theoretically evident why this must be so; and in addition, a number of counter-examples can be given. If A is greatly superior to B, then if A increases its milex, B may see the race as hopeless and decrease its own. Richardson (1960a, pp. 56f.), in his analysis of pre-World War II arms dynamics, tries to account for this possibility by introducing what he calls a factor of submissiveness, $x - y$, which is assumed to affect y besides x. Depending on the sign of the parameter before it, this can be interpreted as 'submissiveness' as well as 'rivalry'. The problem with this revision, however, is that it does not become *testable* in this form, unless we can find an independent measure of the new parameter. (See Taagepera, 1979–80, p. 73; Rattinger, 1975a, p. 69f.)

Another criticism is that we may well have an asymmetry, or a ratchet effect: rearmament, it can be argued, is more likely to be followed by rearmament than disarmament by disarmament – disarmament of Alter being politically easier to discount as being 'insignificant', 'faked', or 'a trick'. Several different revisions have been suggested in order to take this into account. This criticism would seem to have been theoretically formulated, but not empirically tested. To do this, one would either have to operationalize x and y as changes in stock rather than milex, or change the form of the equation, as long as one stays with differential equations. Finally, the equation is linear, implying that a change in x has a proportionate effect on the rate of change of y. This, of course, is dictated by mathematical simplicity, there being no obvious argument why the power of x in the reaction component should be precisely 1, rather than, say, ½ or 2 or anything else.

4.4 Burden Component

In Richardson's (original) equations, the rate of change in the milex of a country is assumed to depend on the magnitude of that very milex, as the terms $-by$ and $-ax$ indicate. In his theory, this effect will always be negative, expressing a 'burden' or 'fatigue' effect: the more that is spent on arms, the stronger becomes the force in the opposite direction.

This part of the equation has been criticized on several accounts. One type of criticism is that this way of expressing cost restraints is far too simplistic, unless several questionable assumptions are made. For example, it does not take into account that the cost restraint may change as the whole economy grows, or that it may depend on the structure of the economy. Some authors, like Caspary (1967) assume a ceiling for military expenditures and make the brake component a function of the distance to that ceiling. Liossatos (1980a), following arguments by Galbraith (1972, p. 231f.), suggests a curvilinear relation: if there is a slack in the economy, then increasing milex (starting from 0) may mean a stimulus up to a critical value M, and after that an increasing drain on the economy. He therefore suggests substituting for $-by$ the simplest function that has these properties, $ry(1 - y/M)$.

Whereas Richardson's equations assume that the term containing y always acts as a brake on y', Liossatos thus leaves both possibilities open. We thereby move towards a whole set of theoreticians who have focused on domestic stimulation of arms dynamics, whether in terms of a military-industrial-etc. complex, bureaucratic incrementalism, or other factors of Eigendynamik. A few examples are Senghaas (1972b), Gantzel (1973), Kaldor (1982a), Thee (1986a). (In this vast literature, however, only a minority move from verbal argument or historical analysis to expression in formal models.) The simplest way of expressing the effect of forces towards increasing milex seems to be my, where m is a parameter. The argument is that y can be assumed to be a crude measure of the size of the interest groups with something to gain from further armament, as well as giving a baseline in bureaucratic processes. Absolute size, that is: for relative size, y should obviously be divided by something, whether GNP, mobilizable part of GNP, state budget, etc.

The simplest version of this revision of Richardson's equations, thus, just amounts to adding a *my* (*m* positive) to the $-by$, in which case this part of the equation would retain the same form $(m - b)y$, but this time with a parameter that can take both positive and negative values. In other versions, this component becomes a more complicated function of y.

4.5 What Is Not in the Equations

Richardson's equations are essentially characterized by simultaneity and endogeneity. *Time* is only a variable with respect to which the variables are differentiated, the medium in which the process runs, but it does not itself play any role: neither the past nor the future enters the equations. The variables x and y (and their derivatives) are all endogenous, and their parameters left to estimation when comparing the model with data. The only exogenous components of the equations are the two assumedly constant parameters h and g.

Both aspects of Richardson's model have been theoretically criticized from different points of view, and various attempts have been made to remedy these shortcomings by introducing exogenous independent variables.

4.6 Introducing Time

There are several ways in which time can be more or less essentially introduced by revising the model.

The simplest and least essential one consists in transforming the equations to a set of difference equations. This means that the term y' becomes

$$\frac{\Delta y}{\Delta t} \quad \frac{y(t) - y(t-1)}{t - (t-1)}$$

so that the new form becomes

$$y(t) - y(t-1) = lx(t-1) - by(t-1) + h.$$

By simple transformations, the translated Richardson equations then become

$$x(t) = a_1 y(t) + a_2 x(t-1) + a_3$$
$$y(t) = b_1 x(t) + b_2 y(t-1) + b_3.$$

By substitution in both equations, they can then be written in a form where the present values of the variables are functions of past values:

$$x(t) = rx(t-1) + sy(t-1) + u$$
$$y(t) = vx(t-1) + wy(t-1) + z$$

where r, s, u, v, w, and z are the new parameters that can take any values. (I have here omitted some reservations that would have to be made in a more strict mathematical presentation.)

What has happened to the equations is only what automatically happens when such a translation is made from differential equations to difference equations: what happens 'now' is no longer a function of the situation 'now', but of the situation 'immediately before now'. (For practical purposes, that usually means 'one fiscal year ago'.) Time, or processes in time, still does not enter in any essential way.

This form obviously also keeps the property of the differential equations that, if the x and y values are now known and the six parameter values are also known, then you can calculate the x and y values for any time point in the future and the past.

Time can be somewhat more essentially introduced in another way. If we assume, for the reaction component of the equations, that I am looking at your stock, rather than at your present milex, and that I estimate your stock by looking at your milex record and introducing a depreciation factor q, then in the equation for $x(t)$ we have to substitute for $y(t-1)$ the expression

$$qy(t-1) + q^2y(t-2) + q^3y(t-3) + \ldots$$

We have no need to go into the more complicated estimates of stock that can be ascribed to the parties. The essential point is that after this revision, the equations make $x(t)$ and $y(t)$ functions of the x and y values of two or more previous time points: very few, if depreciation is assumed to be fast; several, if it is assumed to be slow.

Here, we still really have not introduced time essentially: the past record is assumed to be of interest to participants only as a source of information about the present state: they are not assumed to learn anything beyond that.

Let us now make the assumption that each participant is sensitive not only to the state of the other, but also to the trend in the milex of the other, e.g. because that trend is used as a basis for extrapolation into the future or because it is somehow read as a signal. In that case, with the other assumptions remaining the simplest ones, we have to add in the expression for $x(t)$ a term $p(y(t-1) - y(t-2))$, where p is a new parameter. In that case, we eventually get $x(t)$ as a function of $x(t-1)$, $y(t-1)$, and $y(t-2)$. If we assume this kind of learning to be based on more than one period, it becomes a function of $y(t-3)$ . . . as well.

In our theoretical reasoning, we have here moved more and more from a 'non-rational' towards a 'rational' model, e.g. by increasingly assuming the participants to look at the future in their actions. So far, it has only been assumed that past values of x and y play a role in this. In more general versions, expectations about the future can be brought in either by direct measurement (looking at what the participants say about such expectations) or by being assumed to depend on other exogenous independent variables. Before we go further into that, however, one problem should be pointed out. When we successively transformed the differential equations above, first into difference equations with the same parameters, and then by linear transformations into the equations $x(t) = rx(t-1) + sy(t-1) + u$, etc., the new parameters became increasingly more complex expressions of the old ones with their simple interpretations. For example, the new parameter s, when expressed in Richardson's parameters, becomes

$$\frac{l(1+b)(1+a)}{(1+b)^2(1+a)^2 - kl}$$

which defies any simple intuitive interpretation. In doing this, however, we did not change the number of free parameters. If we can estimate the new parameters by means of our data, we can then in principle move back to the original parameters by solving a set of equations. (However, I have not investigated exactly what reservations have to be made to 'in principle'.)

Once we go beyond this, the situation changes. For example, assume that we want to extend the model by taking into account both accumulation of stock and sensitivity to trends. If we do this in the very simplest fashion, the former means that we have to add to the equation for $x(t)$ the term $+q^2 y(t-2)$ and the latter than we have to add $-py(t-2)$, so that the equation now makes $x(t)$ a function of $x(t-1)$, $y(t-1)$, and $y(t-2)$, the last term being $+(q^2 - p) y(t-2)$. We may, of course, write this as $+ dy(t-2)$, with d as a new parameter, in which case we have added one new variable and one new free parameter, without having disturbed the balance between them. If our only aim with the model is prediction (under a number of assumptions), this is just fine: we are likely to have improved the accuracy of the prediction. If, however, our aim is to understand better what is going on, then getting back to the p and the q is essential, but our possibilities of doing so have decreased: if we are studying a relatively short process, we may be able to estimate d, but not p and q.

4.7 Bringing in the Environment

A Richardsonian arms race is largely a closed system. The only entities, apart from armament itself, assumed to affect arms dynamics are constant parameters, out of which only two are independently measurable. The theoretical argument against this limitation in the model is that there are several other things that can be assumed to affect the military efforts of a state (Busch, 1970). Apart from safeguarding against a main rival, military capability is also used for fighting wars with third parties, for colonial expansion, and for other directly instrumental uses. States may also attempt to further other aims by having a military capability and increasing it: preventing neutral states from joining the rival or lure them into alliance; securing a leadership position within an alliance; achieving influence by means of military aid; deterring or subduing domestic opposition; and so forth (Blechman & Kaplan, 1978; Kaplan, 1981). For that matter, it may also be that 'substantive military purpose seems to be of little importance', as Bobrow & Hill (1985, p. 15) conclude about Japan. In addition, it may be argued that the bigger a state is, in terms of inhabitants, GNP, etc., the more there is to defend and the higher military expenditures we may expect; and to the extent that military systems serve as status symbols, the more of national grandeur there will be to symbolize.

As for cost restraints, we have already hinted at some arguments for bringing exogenous variables in as divisors of y. One may also argue that military expenditures may be regulated by such variables as budgetary balance, trade balance, balance of payments, foreign debt, etc. (Harris, 1986).

There is hardly any limit to the number of variables that can be theoretically suggested as having *some* influence on military efforts one way or the other; and some revisions or extensions of Richardson's model – as well as some models that cannot reasonably be characterized as either – do include several exogenous variables with parameters.

We have already referred to the dilemmas this implies. They can be summarized by saying that the more 'realistic' we make the model of arms dynamics, the less testable it becomes, whether the increased realism was had by including more variables or by more complex mathematical formulations. It seems premature to state where the proper balance can be struck, but perhaps it is easier to list models that are either too simplistic or too complex to be imaginable candidates.

There are therefore good reasons for limiting the discussion to models that have been tested or where tests have been credibly proposed. They can be broadly characterized as follows. *Dependent variables* are mostly (operationalized by) absolute or relative milex figures (mostly actual milex, but sometimes decided or requested milex), sometimes by disaggregated indices of output: in terms of capability of specific military systems, whether nuclear or e.g. tanks. Some models look at only a single state or decision-maker, treating all others as environment; several model bilateral arms races; a few can be seen as bi-multilateral in the sense that only some of all the theoretically possible interactions in a set of actors are considered; and very few are truly multilateral. When more than two states are assumed to be in interaction, the maximum considered is five or six.

Independent variables: many models have no other variables than milex (or capability) variables. In these cases, the time point $t - 2$ is sometimes included, but very rarely $t - 3$ or more. As assumed accelerator variables appear size variables (GNP, population, their product, etc.); activity variables such as indicators of territorial expansion, war engagement, or battle deaths (e.g. Choucri & North, 1975; Ostrom, 1978); and indicators of domestic conflict or ethnic cleavage (e.g. Rosh, 1987). In addition, we may use 'environmental variables' as a blanket term to cover such variables as 'regional geographical instability', 'rank disequilibrium', and a number of dummy variables aimed at picturing external disturbances (like the Sino-Indian War in the Indo-Pakistani arms race, or external events in the Arab–Israeli case).

In equations for $y(t)$, we almost always find $y(t-1)$ and, when a case of bilateral arms dynamics is modelled, $x(t-1)$. In addition to these, we normally find one or two exogenous variables, sometimes three or even four, rarely more.

Form of equation: mostly both additive and linear. In a few cases of additive relationships, one of the variables appears squared or even cubed. Occasionally the form is log-linear, implying that the effect on the dependent variables is a product rather than a sum of their individual effects.

5 Action-Reaction or Autism?

Let us now return to the question crudely outlined in section 2: are arms dynamics primarily determined by action-reaction between states, or by forces inside the states? One way of clarifying more precisely the meaning of this question is by discussing what is to be counted as evidence and what would constitute clear proof for a proposition about the relative weight of internal and external forces (including the distributions 0–1 or 1–0).

This, in itself, is far from clear. What has been presented as evidence one way or the other consists of a wide array of materials. We find historical studies through analyses of various elites and of military industry; monographs about the development of specific weapons systems; general analyses of decision-making in security matters in different countries; and rigorous tests of carefully defined formal models. The results of different studies may agree, entirely or partly; they may be largely irrelevant to each other; or they may plainly contradict each other. Let us just take one example: the rapid increase in US milex in the first half of the 1950s. The simplest 'reaction' argument is that this was motivated by the Korean War; and the simplest rebuttal to this that this vast increase was already called for in NSC-68 before the outbreak of the war. At first glance, the former argument would need support from evidence that such an increase *would* have taken place even in the absence of previous planning for it, and the latter would need support by evidence that NSC-68 *would* have been realized, war or no war. Even if this latter evidence could be produced, there would be further questions, since these proposals for rapid rearmament presented themselves in 'reaction' terms of the need to be prepared for the allegedly increasing Soviet threat – to which the counter-argument may be that that threat was seen more in political terms than in terms of Soviet military build-up. And so on, and so forth: what is relatively easy to produce is evidence that, at that time, there *were* domestic forces (industrial, military, and others) that pressed for rearmament, and that US decision-makers *were* impressed by 'reaction' arguments for rearmament. It therefore seems that we can discard the two extreme positions: 'reaction only' and 'domestic forces only', but that it is much more difficult to see what would constitute definite evidence for any proposition about their precise relative weights.

This is fairly trite, for what does it contradict? There is hardly any serious analysis of domestic forces that maintains that what happens in the environment, and in particular in potential adversaries, has *no* influence on milex. As for the opposite extreme, the original Richardson equations implied that domestic forces were only (net) decelerating (the b in $-by$ assumed to be positive and hence the whole expression negative), but such an implication can be (and soon was) removed by leaving the sign of b open.

No attempt will be made here to establish a general methodology for how to weight widely different types of evidence together into an assessment of the relative weight between external and internal forces. (Such an attempt would probably show that the question was put the wrong way and would have to be reformulated and disaggregated radically to allow for even a partial answer.) I will only look at a very specific way of attempting it: the empirical testing of mathematized causal models (whether derived from 'causal' or 'actor' considerations or both). This in no way implies that I accept the claims sometimes made that this is the highest or definite form of testing hypotheses: it is *one* way among several, with its advantages and disadvantages, and in many cases other evidence would weigh heavier than even a rigorously confirmed model.

5.1 Models and Evidence

One way of rendering questions more precise and presumably answerable is to express the hypotheses to be tested in a set of equations, then operationalize and measure the variables and perform statistical tests. The two fundamental questions become: how well do the theoretically predicted values and the empirically observed values agree with each other, and how unlikely is it that a sample would show at least such a good fit with the predictions, if drawn from universe where these variables were statistically unrelated to each other? Under several ideal conditions about the data (perfectly valid and error-free), the sampling (perfectly random), and the universe (in terms of the distribution of values of individual variables), both questions can be accurately answered by means of some correlation coefficients and tests of significance – and conclusion can be drawn about the theory underlying the hypotheses. Arms dynamics are problematic from all these points of view.

Unless we trivialize by defining away the problem of validity, it will normally loom large. The observations that are made are definitely not error-free, nor can the errors be safely assumed to be randomly distributed. (Furthermore, they are often compounded, since the relative margin of error of a difference is greater, or far greater, than that of the two variable values.) The selection of cases is far from random: most empirical studies of arms dynamics have been made on sets of nations in periods where they were already generally thought to be in an arms race (at least in a loose sense) with each other. As mentioned earlier, most or all parameter values are also normally left to estimation, and the number of observation values often only slightly exceeds the number of free parameters, which can be expected to lead to good fits but questionable significance, and hence weak – if any – testing of substantive hypotheses.

Even if all these problems were solved, we still would not have reached the end of our quest. If we had had one single dependent variable and two sets of independent variables in a synchronic study, then normal regression methods would be able to provide relatively good information on the relative causal weight of the two sets in the model tested (of course, other sets might yield other results). But in arms dynamics models we normally have to do with two or more dependent variables and their interaction over time, which makes interpretation far more difficult.

To illustrate this, let us go back to Richardson again. His (as we now know, unsubstantiated) claim that his model was confirmed by pre-WWI data was taken by himself and many followers to demonstrate that an arms race was essentially an interaction process. It has later been shown (Taagepera, 1979–80, p. 72) that both this case and some other ones can be fitted to equations of the form

$$x = A + Be^{mt}$$

so that the milex of each state depends on three constants (A, B, and m, specific to each nation) and time (t). The naive reading of this would be as a confirmation of autism: milex is simply an exponential process, whose point of departure and pace depend solely on characteristics of the arming nation itself.

That would be too simple, however: 'can be fitted' is not the same thing as 'can only be fitted'. By taking these equations for two actors and solving for time, we can instead get these:

$$x' = A(y - B)^C$$
$$y' = D(x - E)^{1/C}$$

where the new parameters can be calculated from the original ones, the naive reading of this being a pure interaction process. (But how much 'process' is left, when we eliminate time?)

Thus comparing a simple Richardson model with data just cannot answer the question: the solution to the equations can be written in two ways that are logically equivalent but seem to have opposite interpretations. This is an obvious caveat against quick reading of empirical results. In this case, of course, we have a specific complicating feature: there are no exogenous variables in the equations. Let us therefore have a look at the results of other authors who have studied the same time period – and later ones – by various models.

5.2 The Proud Tower Revisited

The most encompassing study using formal models to analyse arms dynamics before World War I is Choucri & North (1975). They cover a much longer period (1870–1914); they look at each European great power separately; and they have a more elaborate model, where among their variables we can identify milex in the previous year as 'internal', together with population multiplied by income and (perhaps) colonial area, whereas military expenditures of non-allies, as well as the intensity of colonial conflicts with other great powers, seem clearly 'external'.

They achieve very good fits: but this seems true of virtually any model that includes $x(t-1)$ as determinant of $x(t)$ for almost any case. This is less true when we look at determinants of $x'(t)$. It turns out, however, that both time and space matter greatly. Thus, in Britain, previous military expenditures and population times income together account for most of the variance in 1871–90, whereas in 1891–1914 that goes for the combination of previous military expenditures and those of non-allies. Britain has thus turned more externally determined in the period. Germany and Italy, on the other hand, appear more internally determined throughout, the very greatest part of the variance being accounted for by population times income and previous milex, respectively.

As Moll & Luebbert (1980) put it, the significance of this work is that it explains milex in terms of growth processes for some of the same cases that Richardson and others have explained in terms of competition. When Wallace & Wilson (1978) looked at the same period, comparing five different models, they found that three models, the simplest one being a refined Richardsonian one, fitted Britain equally well for the 1870–1914 period. There is another important difference: Richardson implicitly models the behaviour of decision-makers, whereas Choucri & North are more interested in entire societies than in their political leaderships as such.

It then becomes interesting to see what happens when we move 'to the other side' of Richardson. Lambelet (1974, 1975a, 1976), in a series of papers on the Anglo-German naval race before World War I, focused on output, moving gradually from using as his dependent variable the numbers of dreadnoughts and later the numbers weighted by quality (broadside weight and armour). He arrived at the conclusion that over the 1905–16 period Britain was highly sensitive to what Germany had, did, and decided to do, whereas Germany was fairly insensitive to Britain in these respects, and that this agrees well with what we know historically: Germany had a long-range programme, whereas the aim of Britain was to maintain a 2:1 superiority. As Britain was unable to maintain this in terms of number of ships, it shifted to trying to do it in terms of 'crude firepower' (broadside weight), whereas the German escalation was in terms of 'effective firepower' (armour taken into consideration).

Thus, in crude terms Britain was externally determined, whereas Germany was internally determined – and in equally crude terms, this parallels the conclusion on a higher level of abstraction by Choucri and North. At the same time, we here get a warning against reading too much into 'internal' and 'external'. 'Reacting' can mean 'trying to keep on top of' as well as 'trying to keep up with'. If we see German behaviour as internally determined, we could also continue to argue that precisely Britain's reactivity was internally determined. And if we interpret Britain's behaviour as 'security-oriented' (the weak British land forces necessitating the ability to match a possible coalition of the two strongest navies of other powers – as it turned out, one of them was to become an ally), we can do the same with Germany's behaviour: the official, but faked (Tuchman, 1966, ch. 5), legitimization for its naval rearmament was protection of its civilian shipping, but military arguments seem to have had more to do with deterring Britain from joining any alliance against Germany in case of war. As it turned out, the effect was exactly the opposite.

5.3 The Interwar Period

Generally speaking, the interwar period has been less attractive to arms dynamics modellers than the earlier or later periods. There are, however, some attempts.

To start with, Richardson himself also studied this period, his first conclusion being that his earlier model would not do: if one tried to use it, it was at the very least necessary to drop the assumption about parameters being constant over time. His attempt to improve the model by introducing a 'submissiveness' factor $(x - y)$, as we have already indicated, also ran into difficulties. One of the main problems consisted in Britain and France reacting so little to the first years of Hitler's military expenditures. Another explanation for this has been suggested: the German stock in 1933 was so low that it took a few years of accumulation for it to make the Western powers worried (Taagepera, 1979–80, pp. 68f.).

Lucier (1979), studying the interwar naval expenditures of Britain, Japan, and the USA, uses and confirms a seemingly much simpler model: $x(t) = qx(t - 1)$; 'seemingly', because he does not assume the parameter q to be constant over time for the same actor, but to shift with changes in Standard Operating Procedures, which in their turn may change due to military-related domestic or international events, election of new leadership, etc. Thus, whereas at first glance his model would look purely internalist, this theorization of q (which is not expressed in substituting any function of variables for q) makes it more difficult to classify.

5.4 The Postwar Period

Most studies of arms dynamics have taken their empirical material from the post-1945 period. In some cases, the aim has been to find correlates of milex in cross-sectional studies (GNP being by far the best candidate); where nations or groups have been singled out in other studies, they have, not surprisingly, been such that are usually seen as being involved in an 'arms race'. Many authors have looked at East–West and their individual major powers over different time periods: there have also been several studies of the Middle East and the Indian subcontinent; other areas are more sparsely represented.

Wagner et al. (1975) and Taagepera et al. (1975) have looked at US and USSR milex in the period 1945–72, finding the same thing as for the 1908–14 race: the milex of the parties can be fitted to a single exponential function plus a constant (same reservations as before). The exception is the USA in the first 1945–60 phase, where two exponential functions are required to describe its sequence of disarmament and rearmament:

$$y = -350e^{-0.45t} + 530_e{}^{-0.8t} + 62 \text{ (constant dollars)}.$$

Strauss (1972), studying the 1951–69 period, assumes rational actors that anticipate on the basis of extrapolation. This leads him to a slightly modified set of Richardson equations, where the milex of each superpower in constant dollars fits

$$y(t) = a + bx(t-1) + cy(t-1) - dy(t-2).$$

The empirical investigation bears the model out by getting a high percentage of variance accounted for. However, when the model is used to simulate future milex, the conclusion becomes that the figures for 1990 are lower than those for 1970, which at the very least indicates that the assumption of constant parameters over longer time periods must be wrong. This may have to do with the criticism made by Luterbacher (1975, pp. 205f.), who asks why y is supposed to be a function of itself two time points back, but only of x one time point back.

Lambelet (1973), in studying the 1950s and 1960s, uses a more complex model: he divides the forces of each superpower into strategic and conventional; tries to measure military capability rather than milex; and uses a log-linear model, where capability A of nation X at time t is assumed to be (essentially) proportional to a product of the lagged same capability of the other power, the ratio between their capabilities of the other type, and the GNP of X. He finds negative correlations for each actor between strategic and conventional capability, suggesting that they serve as substitutes for each other. Furthermore, it appears that the patterns of sensitivities of the two superpowers differ, the USA being more sensitive to USSR conventional capability and the USSR to US strategic capability, at the same time as both sides exhibit some self-stimulation, especially the USSR. Lambelet et al. (1979), using milex of the USA and the USSR in 1949–75, also conclude that the USSR is particularly high on self-stimulation. How to interpret all this is less clear, however. As in the Anglo-German naval race, it would be far too simple to identify other-stimulation with being predominantly security-oriented, and self-stimulation with having particularly much of a military-industrial complex.

Luterbacher (1976), looking at the 1960–70 ICBM dynamics between the superpowers, uses *yield* as operationalization of capability, and constructs a log-linear model that aims at merging strategic and behavioural conceptions, and where the essential idea is

increase in ICBM potential of one nation = (costs to that nation) × (some function of the total ICBM potential of the other nation) × (second strike considerations) × (influence of past behaviour of both nations).

After operationalizing these and trying out different versions of the resulting model, Luterbacher concludes that the United States slowed down and stabilized its potential as a result of a combination of having its second strike ambitions satisfied and of cost constraints, whereas the USSR moved on in what he calls a purely Richardsonian fashion, its increase being proportional to the product of US total capability and a factor expressing USSR cost restraints. He introduces the caveat that yield has been used (the more warheads you distribute the same megatonnage over, the higher yield you get), but that no attempt has been made to weigh in the increasingly important factor of accuracy. That caveat should be underlined: if accuracy had been included in the equation for capability, the US curve would definitely not have stabilized. It should also be added that the author does not make a formal estimation of the parameters: he just makes guesses and then makes a crude assessment of how well the observed curve fits with the one predicted.

Hollist (1977b) did a comparative test of eight different models, which were modifications of the Richardson equations incorporating alone and together the impacts of economic constraints, levels of technology, and technological change. As for the two superpowers, he concluded that USSR milex was best explained by a Richardsonian model sensitized to changing levels of technology, whereas US milex was best explained by the entire ensemble of variables.

Finally, let us look at the unique study by Ostrom (1978), who seems to be the only one who has aimed not only at comparing different effects, but also at making a formal model of the internal decision-making in the United States, bringing together traditional models for arms races, for organizational processes, and for bureaucratic politics. Ostrom looks separately at the services, the President and Congress, where e.g. requests from the military are assumed to be an additive function of (1) USSR milex in the previous year, (2) battle-deaths in the previous year, and (3) the rate at which congressional DoD appropriations have moved over the two past years.

Both the separate equations and the model as a whole do very well in terms of explained variance. At the same time this illustrates a dilemma we have already broached. Its superiority to the naive model of simple incrementalism (and hence exponential growth) in terms of explained variance and error is very slight (in the former case 0.98 versus 0.96), and in fact the naive prediction is better for more years than is the Reaction-Linkage model. The price to pay for this marginal improvement is having a model that is context-dependent, and with seven independent variables instead of merely one.

Before going further into this, let us look at some other cases that have been analysed by two or more studies. The Middle East, and in particular the arms dynamics between Israel and a number of Arab states, separately or jointly, offers a similar spectrum of results. It constitutes one more of the cases of Taagepera (1979–80). For the period 1949–72, if we limit ourselves to Israel and Egypt, as well as if we add Syria, Jordan, and Iraq, the milex of the two sides can either be fitted to a constant plus an exponential function of time for each side, or their milex can be related to each other in functions of type

$$x' = a(y - b)^c \text{ and } y' = d(x - e)^{1/c}.$$

Unless we add further assumptions, this does not allow us to say anything definite about self- or other-stimulation. In the study by Hollist (1977b), it was found that both Israel and Egypt belonged to the nations whose milex was best explained by using the whole set of independent variables.

Rattinger (1976a), who does not look at milex, but looks at separate indicators of tank, ship, and air strengths, and who works by difference equations, arrives at different conclusions for the period 1956–73. First, where we find significant reaction parameters depends on what system we look at; and second, it depends on what time period we look at: parameters are clearly *not* constant over time. In the 1956–67 period, we find Israel in a tank race with Jordan, a ship race with Syria, and an air race with Egypt, generally with Israel more sensitive than the other power. After 1967, we find almost pure self-stimulation everywhere, especially in the Arab states. This is interesting in itself, but again we have to ask what it means. Rattinger's interpretation goes in the direction that the asymmetry in terms of other-stimulation means that Israel is more defensive and the Arab states more offensive, since they rearm rapidly without this being a clear reaction to what Israel is doing. This interpretation seems open to doubt: the alternative one being that the Arab states, after being knocked out in 1967 and fearing another attack, got as many arms as they could get where they could get them, without bothering too much about the precise composition of the Israeli armoury.

Lambelet (1971), finally, looking at the same states for the period 1953–65, uses a more complex log-linear model, which can be seen as an extension from Richardson's equations by (a) making the relationship multiplicative rather than additive, (b) including time lags, and (c) adding GNP and dummy variables. He gets very good fits, perhaps because of adding so many dummy variables, but reveals two kinds of variation in the parameters: the international events represented by the dummy variables affect some nations but not others, and the length of the lags changes significantly from one state to the other. In addition, it turns out that the system is conditionally stable; nevertheless, three wars did occur within eight years of the end of the period.

5.5 What Is the Use of It All?

Let us terminate our review here, by just hinting that different analyses of Indo-Pakistani arms dynamics (Ferejohn, 1976; Ward & Mahajan, 1984) also yield results that are at variance with each other, at least if we try to give them any quick translation to the internal/external issue. The theses outlined below claim to be no more than impressionistic in trying to summarize the development of the state of the art.

1 We have had a model building proliferation, some of it having developed into *l'art pour l'art* for mathematicians or for economists. Only a few of all models suggested have been tested, and only a small proportion of the remainder are even testable (at least for the present).
2 There has been progress in the methodology of testing models, but still more is needed to rescue us from the situation that there must either be something wrong with the discriminating ability of the tests, or the fundamental models, or both.
3 The most important empirical results have been negative ones, demonstrating that parameters in many cases definitely cannot be constant even for the same actor. New attempts have been made to remedy this by theorizing the parameters and substituting variables – primarily domestic ones – for them.
4 The further development and testing of formal models has not greatly helped us in resolving issues about external versus domestic determination: it is particularly here that we need better discrimination, the problems of interpreting the results of empirical studies being so great; it may also be that the questions themselves will have to be reformulated to permit good answers.
5 The general development, nevertheless, has been away from simple 'reaction-and-cost-constraint' models and towards models that incorporate more of domestic components. In addition, changes in parameters seem more often related to domestic than to interactive factors.
6 The development has been away from very simple causal imagery and towards models that attempt to portray also more sophisticated decision-making in actors. Testability, however, provides rather sharp limits to how far this is feasible – and decreasing marginal intellectual utility is another limit.

7 We are hardly much closer than in Richardson's days to finding a general and non-tautological model for arms dynamics – but at least we have better orientation as to where to look and where not to look.
8 In particular, non-decision variables seem better suited to account for trends and changing directions of trends in arms dynamics, but decision variables are necessary in order to account for the timing of such changes.
9 There has been little encouragement to the idea of being able to predict the future, e.g. by means of finding the 'true' parameters and basing stability analyses on them. In fact, to the extent that tested models have been extrapolated forward in time, they have usually been far wider off the mark than the simple assumption of exponential growth.
10 It is hardly to be expected that even improved modelling and testing can contribute more than marginally to resolve issues concerning external/internal or domestic/interactive forces. The resolution of such issues will have to rely more on systematic comparative case studies than on formal modelling.

HÅKAN WIBERG, b. 1942, degrees in Mathematics and Philosophy, Ph.D. in Sociology (University of Lund, 1977); Assistant Professor and Associate Professor of Peace Research (University of Lund, 1971–80); Professor of Sociology (University of Lund, 1980–); Director, Centre of Peace and Conflict Research, University of Copenhagen (1988–); author and editor of books on peace research, images of the future, issues of national and international security, Poland, and the Horn of Africa.

Chapter 4
Arms Race Modeling: A Reconsideration*

MICHAEL D. INTRILIGATOR & DAGOBERT L. BRITO
Center for International and Strategic Affairs, University of California, Los Angeles, and Department of Economics, Rice University, Houston, Texas

1 Overview, Definitions, and Assumptions

Arms race modeling, and in particular that body of work in this field that derives directly or indirectly from the Richardson arms race model, constitutes one of the most influential bodies of formal models in all of the international relations literature. This chapter discusses the nature of the arms race, introduces the Richardson model, presents its later variants, contrasts it to other models of the arms race, and considers the gap between arms race models and some important current issues pertaining to the superpower arms race. It does not treat empirical studies of the arms race, which are Håkan Wiberg's subject in Chapter 3 in this volume. We might note, however, that most of the empirical studies concentrate on the estimation of the original Richardson model, with relatively few estimates of later variants.

Models have been used as analytic approaches to the study of arms races, in order to describe and to predict the course and consequence of an arms race. Such models can be either descriptive or normative. The original Richardson model is an example of a descriptive model, one with neither an explicit objective nor an assumption of maximizing behavior. Another example of a descriptive model of an arms race is the stock adjustment model. The normative model, with an explicit goal and the assumption of maximizing behavior, represents another type of model which is intended to explain the underlying motivation for an arms race in terms of goal-directed behavior. One such normative model is the Brito model, and another such normative model is the differential game model.

---

* We are grateful for suggestions on this chapter made by participants in the International Theory Symposium on Arms Dynamics, particularly by Nils Petter Gleditsch, Paul Smoker, Marek Thee, and Håkan Wiberg. We also would like to acknowledge the suggestions on work reported here by William Potter and Dina A. Zinnes.

These four models, two descriptive and two normative, can all be interpreted as variants or extensions of the original Richardson model. The Richardson model can therefore be given various interpretations as arising from different approaches to the arms race. Another type of model, which also has a Richardson model interpretation, integrates strategic considerations into the treatment of an arms race and thereby provides a synthesis of the various models, with implications for arms races and the outbreak of war. Yet another approach to the arms race is that using heuristic decision rules, in which defense planners use certain rules of thumb with regard to weapons procurement, based on optimizing behavior, on strategic considerations, or on institutional aspects of the defense bureaucracy.

We begin by defining our terms and assumptions. By an 'arms race' we mean the dynamic process of interaction between countries in their acquisitions of weapons. We shall initially, like Richardson, treat only two countries, labeled A and B, thus avoiding such issues as proliferation, alliance formation, multicountry stability, etc. These issues are clearly important, however, and they are discussed, along with other potential extensions, in section 9.

There is some justification for treating the bipolar case first. From a theoretical standpoint, a theory for three, four, or more countries is intrinsically more complex than that for two countries and hence should follow the development of the simpler theory. From an empirical standpoint, much of the observed interaction to date in arms races has been that between two countries or two alliances. In nuclear weapons there is the US-USSR superpower arms race interaction (or more broadly NATO vs. Warsaw Pact), with only relatively insignificant impacts to date of other nuclear powers, such as the United Kingdom, France, and China. In conventional weapons there is the Arab-Israeli interaction, the Iran-Iraq interaction, and the India-Pakistan interaction, among others, with other nations, specifically the USA, USSR, UK, France, China, and others playing roles in supplying weapons to the participants and imposing constraints on the participants, without being active participants themselves in these bipolar arms races. In fact, the roles of these external powers are, to some extent, analogous to the roles played by the basic technological and economic constraints in the superpower arms race. For the future, however, it will become important to treat the multipolar case.

We also assume, again as Richardson did, that there is a single homogeneous weapon, here called a 'missile', where country A has M_A missiles and country B has M_B missiles. (Of course, Richardson, writing in an earlier period, did not discuss 'missiles' but rather weapons or military capabilities.) The theory can and should be extended to the more complex case of several weapons types and weapons innovation; but, as before, both theoretical and empirical arguments justify this initial assumption. From a theoretical standpoint, several types of weapons would considerably complicate the basic theory, involving both portfolio selection, as in the triad of strategic weapons, and changes over time in both weapons capabilities and the capabilities of systems to destroy such weapons, as discussed in section 9. While this is important and there is a qualitative arms race in the development and deployment of weapons systems, it is important to start with the simpler analysis of a single type of weapon. From an empirical standpoint, it is possible to aggregate either nuclear weapons or conventional weapons (but not the two together) into an overall measure of military capability. In fact, several such aggregation measures are available, such as launchers, warheads, megatonnage, and equivalent megatonnage for nuclear weapons, and the theory to be developed initially can be considered applicable to one of these aggregates. Various further extensions of the basic theory, in addition to a multipolar world and various types of (new) weapons, are discussed in section 9. While many of the models are variants of the original Richardson model, the several proposed extensions of section 9 represent further challenges to future arms race modeling.

2 The Richardson Model

The Richardson model is the best known and most influential model of an arms race (Richardson, 1939, 1951, 1960a; Rapoport, 1957, 1960).[1] It is a descriptive model of the dynamic processes of interaction in an arms race. The model is summarized by two differential equations describing the rate of change over time of missile stocks in each of two countries, A and B. For country A, if $M_A(t)$ is the stock of missiles at time t, then

$$\dot{M}_A = \frac{dM_A}{dt}$$

is the rate of change of missile stocks in country A at time t. According to the Richardson model $\dot{M}_A$ can be described as the sum of three separate influences. First is the 'defense term', where $\dot{M}_A$ is influenced positively by the stock of missiles of the opponent M_B, representing the need to defend oneself against the opponent. Second is the 'fatigue term', where $\dot{M}_A$ is influenced negatively by one's own stock of missiles, representing the economic and administrative burden of conducting the arms race. Third is the 'grievance term', representing all other factors influencing the arms race, whether historical, institutional, cultural, or derived from some other source. In the Richardson model these terms are independent, additive, and linear, resulting in the two coupled linear differential equations:

(1) $\dot{M}_A = a_1 M_B - a_2 M_A + a_3$ $\quad\quad (a_1, a_2 > 0)$
(2) $\dot{M}_B = b_1 M_A - b_2 M_B + b_3$ $\quad\quad (b_1, b_2 > 0)$.

These equations show the additions to arms levels on each side as functions of the levels of arms held in both countries. In the equation for country A weapons acquisitions (1) the constants a_1, a_2, a_3 determine, along with weapons stocks in both countries, the size of the defense term, as influenced by the opponent's weapons; the fatigue term, as influenced by one's own weapons; and the grievance term, representing all other factors, respectively. According to the theory, a_1 (and b_1) are positive, since the countries are opponents and thereby threatened by the weapons of the other side. Also according to the theory, a_2 (and b_2) are positive, since the burden of maintaining existing stockpiles reduces the extent of additional weapons acquisitions. The grievance term a_3 (and b_3) can be positive or negative.

At an equilibrium point of the dynamic process, there is no change in missile stocks, so $\dot{M}_A = 0$ and $\dot{M}_B = 0$, yielding the reaction functions

(3) $M_A = a_1' M_B + a_3'$ where $a_1' = a_1/a_2$, $a_3' = a_3/a_2$
(4) $M_B = b_1' M_A + b_3'$ where $b_1' = b_1/b_2$, $b_3' = b_3/b_2$.

These reaction functions give the number of weapons each country holds as a (linear) function of the number held by the opponent, i.e. how each country reacts to weapons stockpiles of the other for an equilibrium to be attained. The new coefficients a_1' and a_3' (and, symmetrically, b_1' and b_3') are normalized coefficients, that is, coefficients normalized by deflating by the fatigue coefficient a_2 (and b_2), assumed non-zero. If the grievance terms a_3 and b_3 are positive, then an equilibrium exists, and it is stable if the following stability condition on the slopes in (3) and (4) is met:

(5) $a_1' b_1' < 1$.

Then the equilibrium stockpile of missiles for A is given by

(6) $M_A^E = \dfrac{a_1' b_3' + a_3'}{1 - a_1' b_1'}$,

and a symmetric equation exists for M_B^E, the equilibrium number of missiles for B. The equilibrium is a stable one, in that small movements away from the equilibrium would set in motion forces that, via the basic equations of the model, would restore the equilibrium. For example, if the stocks on both sides exceed the equilibrium, then the force of the fatigue terms would offset the defense (and grievance) terms to reduce stocks on both sides to the equilibrium level. Conversely, if the stocks on both sides were both below their equilibrium levels, then the defense terms would offset the others to raise stocks on both sides. In the asymmetric case where M_A is 'too large' and M_B is 'too small', relative to the equilibrium, the force of the fatigue term for A and that of the defense term for B would reduce M_A and increase M_B, restoring the equilibrium.

For the Richardson model, the process of interaction between the two countries results in movement toward a defined stable equilibrium, assuming that (a) the basic 'causes' for an arms race – defense, fatigue, and grievance – each have independent and additive effects on changes in missile stocks, as expressed in equations (1) and (2); (b) parameters of the model, including grievance terms, are positive; and (c) the stability condition (5) on the slopes a_1', b_1' holds, which requires that neither side overreact to the other (i.e. neither a_1' nor b_1', representing the normalized defense terms, can be 'too large').

3 The Stock Adjustment Model

While the Richardson model is the best known and the most influential model of an arms race, it is certainly not the only such model, nor even the only such descriptive model. Another descriptive model is the *stock adjustment model* (Boulding, 1962; Intriligator, 1964; McGuire, 1977).[2] According to this model, each country determines a desired stock of missiles M_A^* and M_B^*, and the rate of change of missile stocks is assumed to be proportional to the discrepancy between desired and actual missile stocks, as in the two differential equations

(7) $\dot{M}_A = a_4(M_A^* - M_A)$
(8) $\dot{M}_B = b_4(M_B^* - M_B)$.

According to these equations, each side acquires additional missiles in order to offset and to overcome a perceived deficiency in its stockpile of missiles, the deficiency given by the gap between the desired and actual levels of missiles, e.g. $M_A^* - M_A$.

In general, the desired stocks of missiles depend on the level of missiles in both countries. If, as one example, each country desires a certain base level of weapons and, beyond that, to match increments of the other side's levels according to a fixed ratio, then the desired stock is a linear function of the levels of missiles held by the other side; so

(9) $M_A^* = a_5 + a_6 M_B$
(10) $M_B^* = b_5 + b_6 M_A$,

where a_5 (and b_5) are the base levels and a_6 (and b_6) are the fixed ratio of increments of one's stocks relative to the increments in the opponent's stocks. Inserting these in (7) and (8) yields the equations of a Richardson model. Conversely, any Richardson model, as in (1) and (2), can be interpreted as a stock adjustment model, with desired stock a linear function of the missiles held by the opponent.

In the general stock adjustment model the reaction curves are general functions of the weapons on both sides:

(11) $M_A^* = M_A^*(M_A, M_B)$

(12) $M_B^* = M_B^* (M_A, M_B)$;

while in the Richardson model they become the linear functions in (9) and (10). More generally, the reaction curves can take various shapes, leading to a variety of possible outcomes, depending on strategic considerations and constraints. There may, for example, be multiple equilibrium points, and the outcome may depend on the starting point.

4 The Brito Model

A normative model differs from a descriptive model in that it incorporates goal-seeking phenomena in order to explain behavior. Such a model in the arms race context formulates an explicit and specific form for the arms objective of each country and then obtains conditions necessary to attain these objectives, as in the Brito model (see Brito, 1972). In this type of model, rationality is assumed in that both countries are assumed to follow the conditions necessary for optimization, given their objectives. This assumption may be justified here in terms of the substantial costs involved in not optimizing a system involving weapons with enormous potential for damage, such as nuclear weapons.

In the Brito model each country chooses rates of acquisition of new missiles and levels of consumption so as to optimize overall national self-interest (Brito, 1972; Simaan & Cruz, 1975, 1976). For country A there is an index of defense D_A, dependent on missiles in both countries:

(13) $D_A = D_A(M_A, M_B)$,

which measures its well-being at any time in terms of security. In general, D_A increases with M_A and decreases with M_B, but for both at a diminishing rate. At any instant of time the utility function for A depends on its level of consumption C_A and the index of defense:

(14) $U_A = U_A[C_A, D_A (M_A, M_B)]$,

the former providing material well-being benefits and the latter providing security benefits. The objective of A is to maximize its welfare over all time, given as the discounted present value of all future utility levels:

(15) $W_A = \int_0^\infty e^{-rt} U_A [C_A, D_A (M_A, M_B)] \, dt.$

Here W_A, the welfare of country A, is obtained by adding (integrating) the contributions of utility to welfare at each instant of time, appropriately discounted at the rate r, given as $e^{-rt} U_A (t)$, over all time from the present time $t = 0$ into the infinite future.

The welfare integral in (15) is maximized by choice of the acquisition of missiles Z_A and the level of consumption C_A, subject to two constraints:

that the net change in the level of missiles is the gross investment in missiles less the resources needed to replace missiles becoming obsolete; and that the level of net national product, assumed given (on the basis of an aggregate production function from available levels of capital and labor), is divided between consumption and investment in missiles.

With suitable (and reasonable) assumptions on the utility and defense functions $U_A(\cdot)$ and $D_A(\cdot)$ and the parameters – namely, the discount rate and the depreciation rate and comparable functions and parameters for country B – control theory, in particular, the maximum principle, implies the existence of functions F_A and F_B where

(16) $\dot{M}_A = F_A (M_A, M_B)$

(17) $\dot{M}_B = F_B (M_A, M_B)$,

which describe the evolution of the arms race between A and B. Thus the arms race dynamics are derived as a consequence of a behavioral model of maximizing behavior, with each side maximizing a welfare integral dependent on consumption and defense. The Richardson model is then the special case in which the arms race functions $F_A(\cdot)$ and $F_B(\cdot)$ are linear, in which (16) and (17) simplify to (1) and (2).

Control theory also implies the existence of equilibrium levels of missiles for this model, levels M_A^E and M_B^E, which satisfy

(18) $F_A (M_A^E, M_B^E) = 0$

(19) $F_B (M_A^E, M_B^E) = 0$

Comparable equations for the Richardson linear variant yield the reaction functions in (3) and (4). These equilibrium levels are stable if both countries act in a myopic manner, if they do not overreact to new information, or if one or both attempts to behave as a Stackelberg leader, i.e. an agent determining optimal choices of its strategic variables given that the other agent is expected to behave in a naive fashion.[3]

5 The Differential Game Model

The differential game model is a variant of the Brito model that uses control theoretic methods to solve a dynamic optimization problem. (See Gillespie et al., 1976, 1979.)[4] Thus it is also a normative model, in which behavior is derived from a maximizing hypothesis. This model uses a utility function of the form.

(20) $U_A = U_A (M_A, M_B, Z_A, Z_B)$,

in which utility depends on the level of missiles and the acquisitions of missiles in both countries. The welfare integral is

$$(21) \quad W_A = \int_0^\infty e^{-rt} U_A(M_A, M_B, Z_A, Z_B)\, dt,$$

and W_A is maximized by choice of Z_A subject to constraints on net increases in missiles being the gross acquisitions less depreciation. This model can be solved using differential game concepts. In particular, in the zero-sum case, where the welfare of B is the negative of that of A (so $U_A + U_B = 0$), if it assumed that the U_A function is quadratic, then the problem is of the quadratic-linear variety, i.e. with quadratic utility functions and linear constraints. The solution to such problems is obtained as a linear decision rule, of the form

$$(22) \quad Z_A = a_{11} M_A + a_{12} M_B + a_{13}$$
$$(23) \quad Z_B = b_{11} M_B + b_{12} M_A + b_{13},$$

where the acquisition of missiles depends linearly on the missiles in both countries. Combining these linear decision rules for the choice variables with the investment equations for missiles, that net increases be gross increases less depreciation, yields a linear system which is the same as the Richardson model in (1) and (2). In particular, the defense term coefficient is the coefficient of the opponent's missiles in the linear decision rule equation which stems from the quadratic-linear zero-sum nature of the differential game. Thus, the differential game formulation in the quadratic-linear zero-sum case yields the Richardson model. Conversely, any Richardson model can be interpreted as if it were the solution to an appropriate differential game model of arms interactions.

6 Strategic Considerations in the Arms Race

A criticism that can be lodged against all four models introduced so far is that they treat an arms race from the 'outside', in terms of a mechanistic model, rather than from the 'inside', in terms of decisions of defense planners (Intriligator, 1975; see also Wohlstetter, 1974a, 1974b; Liossatos, 1980b; Leidy & Staiger, 1985). They all ignore strategic considerations, in particular, the roles of weapons in both deterring and conducting a war. Taking such factors into account connects the acquisition of weapons to their use in both peace (via deterrence) and war (for warfighting).[5] This section describes a model that connects strategic considerations as perceived by defense planners to the dynamics of the arms race and arms control initiatives.

In both country A and country B, at any time t, the political authorities will generally require the military authorities to justify their proposed budgets, which generally call for certain increases in the level of missiles (here used generically to represent all weapons systems). They may also question the existing levels of missiles in term of their danger and/or expense. The military authorities would typically seek to justify both their budgetary request for missile acquisitions and their current inventories of missiles in terms of national security considerations by showing their potential for deterrence or warfighting. Both the deterrence and the warfighting roles of weapons can be addressed via considering a hypothetical missile war, involving either war gaming or simulation of strategic interchanges.

A simulated missile war which starts at the present time can be described by the time-paths for missiles in both countries and for casualties in both countries. These time-paths can be considered the solutions to a system of differential equations and boundary conditions at the present time for the four state variables, namely the missiles and casualties in both countries, which provide a dynamic model representation of the hypothetical or simulated missile war. (See Intriligator, 1967, 1968, 1975; Saaty, 1968; Brito & Intriligator, 1972, 1973, 1974; Intriligator & Brito, 1976a, 1984, 1986a, 1986b; Mayer, 1986; Wolfson, 1987. For a related model, see Kupperman & Smith, 1972, 1976.) In this dynamic model the stock of missiles starts at the current level and declines for two reasons. First, each country chooses to fire its own missiles, so that there is a decline in missiles due to its own firing decisions. Second, each country's missiles are destroyed due to missiles launched against them by the other side. Casualties start at zero and rise, due to countervalue missiles launched by the other side.

The evolution of the simulated war is determined by initial missiles (which is the only actual, as opposed to simulated, factor determining the outcome); strategic decisions concerning the rates of fire; strategic considerations concerning targets; the counterforce effectiveness of missiles against enemy missiles; and the countervalue effectiveness of missiles against enemy cities. It should be emphasized that this is a model of a *hypothetical* war, e.g. in a war game or a computer simulation, and not one of an actual war.

The simulated war can be used by the military authorities to justify current budgetary requests and force levels, in particular, to justify the force levels and weapons acquisitions needed to deter an actual war. Deterrence, in this context, refers to the ability to deter the opponent from initiating a war, so it is necessary to consider what happens in the hypothetical war if the enemy initiates the war at the present time. From the vantage point of country A, suppose B initiates the war at time t by attacking A. It is reasonable for A to assume that B launches its missiles at the maximum rate of fire and that it targets only A missiles, since such strategic choices have the greatest effect in reducing the retaliatory capability of A.[6] Country A cannot respond instantaneously, but rather responds after a delay, so that over this 'window' time interval for the first strike of B it cannot launch its missiles. Country A retaliates by launching its missiles at the maximum rate of fire at B cities over a window time interval for its response, since such strategic choices have the greatest effect in terms of retaliation.[7] It is then possible to calculate from the differential equation model the number of casualties A can expect to inflict on B in retaliation for B's initiating the war.

If the military authorities in A are seeking to deter B from striking by threatening to inflict upon it an unacceptable level of damage in a potential retaliatory second strike, and if the military authorities believe that the minimum acceptable damage to B, which would deter it from initiating the war in the first place, is a certain value, then they should have enough missiles to inflict this level of casualties. It is then possible to solve for the minimum level of missiles required for country A to deter country B by inflicting this level of casualties. This minimum number of A missiles needed to deter B turns out to be a linear function of the number of B missiles. It is, in fact, a linear reaction function, as in the Richardson model and of the same form as equation (3), where the slope coefficient a_1' and the intercept coefficient a_3' can be obtained as explicit functions of certain underlying strategic, technical, timing, and social/psychological factors – namely, the maximum rates of fire; the counterforce and countervalue effectiveness ratios; the window time intervals; and the minimum number of B casualties needed to deter it, as estimated by the military authorities in A. Thus the Richardson model coefficients can be interpreted as consequences of underlying strategic and related factors.

In the case of both countries A and B each acting to deter the other, a stable equilibrium for the resulting arms race exists if condition (5) is met: which, in terms of the underlying strategic and other factors, can be expressed as a certain condition that is likely to be met, assuming it takes, on average, more than one missile to destroy an enemy missile. It is then possible to solve for the equilibrium levels of missiles on each side, which depend on the maximum rates of fire; the window time intervals; the missile effectiveness ratios; and the minimum casualties believed required for deterrence.

To give a numerical example, assume in the symmetrical case that the maximum rate of fire is 10% per minute, that it takes two missiles to destroy one enemy missile, that one missile inflicts 250,000 casualties, that the first strike initiation interval is 15 minutes, that the second strike retaliation interval is 10 minutes, and the number of casualties required to deter the other side is 40 million. Then the solution for the equilibrium level of missiles held by each side is 414, that is, with 414 missiles each side has enough to deter the other side. At this level on both sides, either side can absorb the 15-minute first strike of the other and still have enough missiles left to inflict the required number of 40 million casualties on the other in the 10-minute retaliatory second strike.[8]

Geometrically, the two reaction curves are shown in Figure 4.1 as the lines marked 'A deters', given the country A objective of deterring B, and the comparable line for B, marked 'B deters'. At points to the right of the

Figure 4.1 *Reaction curves, the cone of mutual deterrence, and regions of initiation in the weapons plane*

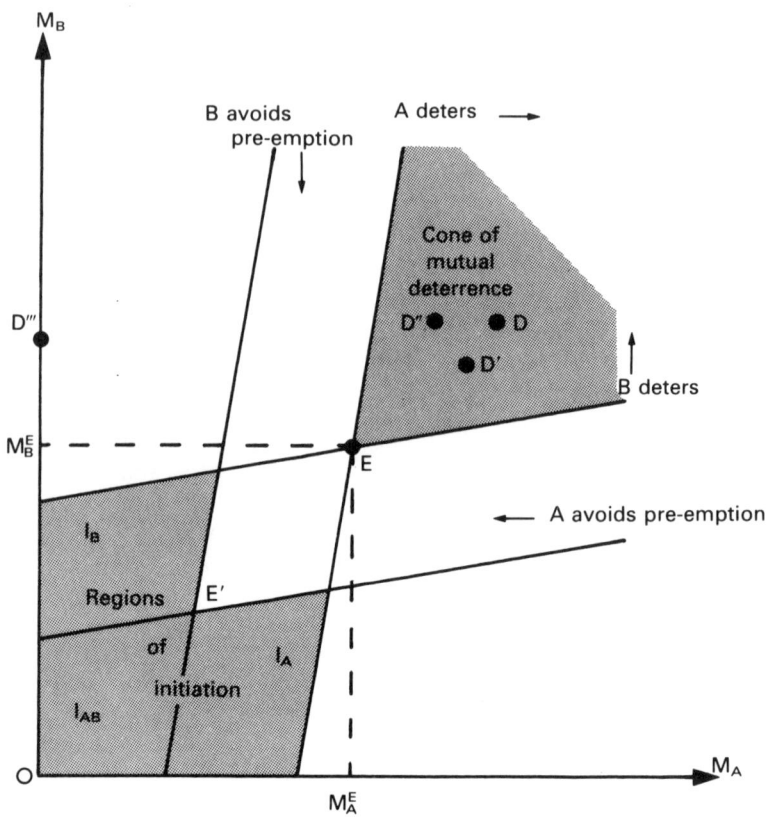

'A deters' line, country A has a sufficient number of missiles to deter B; while at points above the 'B deters' line, B has sufficient missiles to deter A. The two reaction curves intersect at E, which is the equilibrium level of missiles, e.g. 414 on both sides in the above numerical example. The shaded cone of mutual deterrence gives the region in which each side deters the other. As long as the levels of missiles remain in this cone, each side deters the other and the situation will be relatively stable against the outbreak of war. Arms control through arms limitations or reductions is feasible as long as the situation remains in the cone of mutual deterrence. Such arms control measures could include bilateral reductions, illustrated by the movement from D to D', or unilateral reductions, as in the movement from D to D'' by country A. The point of minimum mutual deterrence, E, represents a floor below which arms reductions could entail strategic instabilities.

Another goal of military authorities could be to avoid a pre-emptive strike by never having so many missiles relative to those on the other side that it may appear to the other side that an attack could be successfully carried out. If the other side believes that such an attack could be carried out, then it might be forced to make its own pre-emptive strike in order to take advantage of being the first to move, using the element of surprise. If the number of casualties inflicted on B in retaliation for its initiating the war were sufficiently large, then A would not fear an attack by B, and so B would avoid a pre-emptive strike. From the model, the maximum number of B missiles for B to avoid pre-emption is a linear function of the number of A missiles. It is again a Richardson reaction function, and it is parallel to the 'A deters' line in Figure 4.1 since it refers to the same scenario of B initiating and A retaliating. It is indicated by the 'B avoids pre-emption' line in Figure 4.1. A similar analysis for A yields the 'A avoids pre-emption' line, showing the maximum number of A missiles for which B will not stage a pre-emptive attack.

In Figure 4.1 the shaded cone of mutual deterrence is included in the area of the somewhat larger cone with vertex at E', for which both sides avoid pre-emption. The figure also shows the regions of initiation as the lower shaded sawtooth-shaped region in which one side, or both, neither avoids pre-emption nor deters the other side. For example, in region I_A country A does not avoid pre-emption since it has enough missiles to attack B with impunity, but, at the same time, neither has enough missiles to deter the other. Thus A will be forced to attack or B will be forced to pre-empt, in either case leading to war. Region I_B is the obverse case, in which either B attacks or A pre-empts. Region I_{AB} is the most dangerous region of all since each side can successfully attack the other, neither can avoid pre-emption, and neither can deter the other. Each is forced to initiate the war in order to take advantage of striking first.

Bilateral disarmament, interpreted geometrically as a movement to the origin in Figure 4.1, inevitably entails movement through the region of initiation. The movement to the disarmed state need not necessarily lead to initiation, but a movement *from* the disarmed state may be highly explosive. In such a situation, either country could acquire a small inventory of missiles which could enable it to attack the other with impunity. In fact, the danger of war may be greatest if one side detects that the other is starting to rearm, since, in such a situation, the missile levels move through regions of initiation in a crisis atmosphere.

Unilateral disarmament, interpreted geometrically as a movement by one country to a zero level of missiles, may not lead to war outbreak provided the other side has enough missiles. For example, if B has enough missiles, then A could unilaterally disarm from D to D'' or even to D'''. At this point A avoids pre-emption; A is deterred; and, while B does not avoid pre-emption, there are no missiles for A to use to pre-empt. Of course, at this point A does not deter B and thus would have to trust B's intentions. If B had a level of missiles significantly less than that of D''', however, then B would be forced to initiate.

7 Arms Races and the Outbreak of War

Figure 4.1 can also be used to study the effects of arms races on the outbreak of war, i.e. strategic stability. (See Intriligator & Brito, 1984, 1985a, 1985b, 1986a, 1986b; also Huntington, 1958; Gray, 1971, 1976; Lambelet, 1975b, 1985; Smith, 1980; Mayer, 1986; Wolfson, 1987.) Arms races are, in terms of Figure 4.1, movements in this plane, representing changes in the weapons levels of both sides. An arms race in the usual sense of increasing levels of weapons on both sides would be represented by a movement up and to the right, while a disarming race would be represented by the reverse type of movement, down and to the left. Other types of arms races can also be represented, for example, one with one side increasing and the other decreasing its levels of weapons. The shaded areas indicate the likely effect on the outbreak of war. For example, a movement from the disarmed state at the origin 0 up into the region of initiation, such as in I_{AB}, would represent an arms race likely to lead to war. It results in an explosive situation in which neither side can deter and both can pre-empt. It is precisely this potential arms race that shows the danger of a completely disarmed situation, where rearming in a crisis atmosphere without the stabilizing influence of mutual deterrence could lead to the outbreak of war.

Not all arms races, however, lead to the outbreak of war. Consider, for example, an arms race that starts in one of the regions of initiation, such as I_A. If both countries increase their levels of weapons via an arms race from a point in I_A to one in the cone of mutual deterrence, say to point D, then the arms race has the effect of *reducing* the chance of war by the stabilizing influence of mutual deterrence. In fact, this type of increase may be one interpretation of the US–USSR nuclear arms race. In the late 1950s and early 1960s, the US–USSR military balance was characterized by the instability of relatively low numbers of missiles, not sufficient to deter either side. There was, furthermore, asymmetry in the situation in that the USA, country A in the diagram, did not avoid pre-emption, while the USSR, country B in the diagram, did avoid pre-emption. Thus the situation was in region I_A, one of initiation. The fundamental instability in the situation was shown by repeated crises, culminating in the 1962 Cuban missile crisis. The mid- and late 1960s, however, saw a considerable buildup of Soviet weapons, substantially increasing M_B, and some building in US weapons, increasing M_A. The result was that by the 1970s there was a situation of mutual deterrence, a more stable situation. Thus the arms race resulted in movement from a region of initiation to the cone of mutual deterrence. Such an arms race had the effect of reducing the chance of war, as illustrated historically by the fact that since mutual deterrence was achieved there have been no crises comparable to the Cuban missile crisis or the other crises of the late 1950s and early 1960s. Both sides have become, by necessity, more restrained and less willing to 'go to the brink', due to the establishment of a mutual deterrence relationship.

Figure 4.1 can also be used to study disarming races, i.e. movements reducing weapons stocks. A disarming race that stays in the cone of mutual deterrence could be desirable in signaling peaceful intentions and building confidence, as in the movement from D to D'. However, a disarming race that went 'too far' in moving out of the cone of mutual deterrence could be dangerous and increase the chance of war, particularly if it would result in levels of weapons in one of the regions of initiation.

Another approach to the relation between arms races and the outbreak of war treats the redistribution of resources as an alternative to war (Brito & Intriligator, 1985, 1987a, 1987b). In this approach, two countries act as rational agents concerned with both consumption and the cost of a war. The countries can either consume or build arms in the first period, and they can threaten the use of force in the second period in order to reallocate resources. If both countries are fully informed, then there will be no war but rather a voluntary redistribution of resources, dependent on the arms they have accumulated. In this case there are reaction functions, showing how the arms acquired by each country depend on the arms acquired by the other side, which constitute discrete time analogs of the Richardson model reaction functions (3) and (4) in describing the dynamics of the arms race. As in the Richardson model, there exist equilibrium levels of weapons consistent with both reaction functions; but, in this case, the equilibrium depends on the allocation of economic resources between the countries. In the case of asymmetric information, however, in which one country is fully informed but the other is not, then a war can occur if the uninformed country precommits itself to a positive probability of war in order to prevent bluffing by the informed country in the latter's attempt to redistribute resources in its favor.

8 Heuristic Decision Rules and the Dynamics of the Arms Race

A realistic treatment of the arms race has to account not only for strategic considerations but also for the institutions of defense decision-making. These institutions are large, complex, and bureaucratic, and they therefore have to rely on rules of thumb or, more generally, heuristic decision rules with regard to weapons procurement. These rules may be based in part on some type of optimizing behavior or on strategic considerations; but they may also be based on history, attitudes of decision-makers, interservice rivalry, or other institutional aspects of the defense bureaucracy.

An example of a heuristic decision rule is British naval policy in the period preceding World War I, when the navy was the principal component for projecting force worldwide. British naval policy at that time was to have a navy capable of defeating the combined fleets of the two next-largest naval powers. This decision rule was based on institutions, history, and strategic factors. Another example is recent US policy on conventional force capabilities, which calls for forces sufficient to fight one and one-half wars at the same time, i.e. a major conflict plus a separate local conflict. A third example is recent US policy on strategic capabilities, which calls for force levels sufficient to enable the USA to survive a Soviet first strike and to inflict unacceptable levels of damage on the Soviet Union in a retaliatory second strike. In all three cases, decisions on weapons procurement can be described in a two-stage process involving, first, a bureaucratic-political decision to establish a certain rule or goal and, second, an economic decision on the procurement of weapons to satisfy this rule or to achieve this goal.

An important example of a heuristic decision rule is one in which the acquisition of missiles is proportional to the gap between desired and actual levels of missiles, as in the stock adjustment model (7) and (8), where the coefficients a_4 and b_4 are the adjustment coefficients (Intriligator & Brito, 1985a). If the heuristic decision rule is one in which the desired level of missiles is a linear function of those held by the opponent, as in (9) and (10), the result is a Richardson model. But suppose that the particular heuristic decision rule chosen is the deterrence one in which each side seeks only enough missiles to deter the other. The result is an arms race in which there is movement to the point of minimum mutual deterrence, point E in Figure 4.1. This point is an equilibrium of the resulting process if both sides use a deterring decision rule, and it is a stable equilibrium. In this case each country moves toward its deterrence line; for example, country A acquires missiles if it is to the left of the 'A deters' line, and it destroys missiles if it is to the right of this line.

Consider, alternatively, the case in which both sides use an attacking decision rule. In this case country A acquires missiles to the left of the 'A avoids pre-emption' line in an attempt to be able to pre-empt by attacking B with impunity. If country B also uses an attacking decision rule, then it builds its weapons up to the 'B avoids pre-emption' line. In this case the outcome depends on whether the starting point is in the region of initiation or above this region. If the process starts in the region of initiation, then the dynamics of the process drive missile levels down to the origin. If, however, the process starts above the region of initiation, then there is no equilibrium but rather an unstable arms race, moving to higher and higher levels of missiles on both sides. Thus the outcome is either a movement to the origin through the region of initiation or an unstable arms race trap: i.e. either instability against the outbreak of war, or arms race instability.

A third case is the asymmetric one, where one country seeks to deter and the other seeks to attack. The result is an unstable arms race trap but in the region of stability against war initiation. There is no equilibrium but rather a continuing arms race with a low chance of war outbreak.

These cases of heuristic decision rules in which countries seek either to deter or to attack the other side point to a fundamental difference between arms race stability and crisis stability, that is, stability against war outbreak (Intriligator & Brito, 1986a). In the case of two deterrers there can be both arms race stability and stability against the outbreak of war at the point of minimum mutual deterrence, but in the other cases treated there is either arms race stability or stability against the outbreak of war, but not both. In the case of the superpower arms race between the USA and the USSR, each side may profess to acquire weapons only to deter the other; but clearly their weapons employment policy is more salient than their declaratory policy, and each side believes that the other is, or could be, seeking weapons to attack it. The result is an unstable arms race, moving weapons levels to higher and higher levels, but one that is stable against the outbreak of war, as the situation moves higher and higher into the cone of mutual deterrence and further and further away from the region of initiation. Thus, in this case, which perhaps comes closest to describing the US–USSR arms race, there is crisis stability but arms race instability.

9 Challenges for Future Arms Race Modeling

While there exists a significant literature in arms race modeling, as described above, there remain significant gaps between the theory of arms races and several factors affecting the current superpower arms race that have not been treated in existing arms race models. These factors represent a challenge for future arms race modeling and an opportunity for arms race theorists to make their models more relevant. In the process they could contribute to a better understanding of arms interactions and arms dynamics.

A first such factor is that of *accidental or inadvertent nuclear war* (Intriligator & Brito, 1988d). The superpowers have achieved a deterrence regime via both the arms race, particularly the buildup of invulnerable strategic weapons, such as submarine-launched ballistic missiles, and arms control, particularly the 1972 ABM Treaty. In such a regime each side deters the other from initiating a war. The result is that the chance of a deliberate or intentional war is near zero. What remains, however, is the chance of an accidental or inadvertent war, due to human or technical error or possibly as a result of the actions of third parties. Such a source for the outbreak of war has not been adequately treated in the literature on arms races. This source for war can directly explain certain acquisitions, such as improvements in command and control systems. It can also indirectly explain both arms races and arms control to the extent that fear of accidental or inadvertent war leads to certain types of deployments or agreements. The concept of deterrence may, for example, be usefully modified to treat the deterring of unintentional as well as intentional war. While inadvertent or accidental war may be difficult to model or to simulate, it must be specifically treated in an analysis of arms races and arms control.

Second is *possible technical developments in weapons systems*, including possible MIRVing and deMIRVing of warheads; the development of cruise missiles; the development of stealth technology; the development of antisatellite and antiballistic missile capabilities; developments in biological, chemical, and conventional weapons; and developments in command and control systems. All of these are factors that affect the superpower arms race, but none are treated explicitly in arms race models. In fact, some technical developments such as Sputnik in 1957 played an important role in providing an impetus to the arms race, particularly the qualitative arms race. These models might usefully be extended to allow for such technical developments, perhaps by simulating the dynamics of an arms race model.

Third is *arms control initiatives*, such as the Intermediate Nuclear Forces (INF) Treaty; a potential Strategy Arms Reduction Talks (START) treaty; a potential treaty on weapons in space; potential multilateral arms control initiatives and treaties; and potential unilateral arms control initiatives. By 'arms control' we mean any initiative, whether bilateral, multilateral, or unilateral, that has the effect of reducing the chance of war, particularly nuclear war (Intriligator & Brito, 1985b, 1987a, 1988b). There should be a closer integration between arms race models and arms control initiatives, recognizing that in some cases arms races of certain types can be interpreted as a form of arms control (Intriligator & Brito, 1986a) and that, conversely, certain arms control agreements could have potentially adverse consequences, e.g. via innovations in weapons technology (Brito & Intriligator, 1981) or via instability due to reduced deterrent capability (Intriligator, 1988). Various potential arms control steps should be analyzed or simulated in the context of arms race models to determine their implications both for arms race stability and for stability against war outbreak.

Fourth is *the influence of political, bureaucratic, economic, and psychological factors on the arms race*. All of these factors play an essential role in the arms race, yet none are directly treated in arms race models. Political factors are extremely important but typically ignored, even though decisions to develop and to deploy weapons systems are influenced by domestic politics and political discourse. Bureaucratic factors also play a role in weapons decisions, which could be modeled in game-theoretic terms (Brito & Intriligator, 1980). Economic factors impose constraints on arms acquisitions (Intriligator, 1964). Psychological factors are fundamental to deterrence and other salient aspects of the arms race (Intriligator & Brito, 1988e).

Fifth is *the implications of the emerging multipolar world for arms races*. Most arms race models, such as those discussed above, treat a bipolar world, which has been a reasonable interpretation up to now for the East–West arms race. With the substantial deployments under way in the smaller nuclear powers of the United Kingdom and France and with similar possible increases for China, the world of nuclear power may very well be shifting from a bipolar one to a multipolar one. The result could be a much more dangerous world of possibly shifting alliances, threats, escalation, and inherent instability. In these respects the global arms situation may evolve into one comparable to the Middle East region, but without the global powers as moderating influences (Intriligator & Brito, 1988c). An analysis of the world of many nuclear powers will require an integration of arms race models with models of nuclear proliferation (Brito & Intriligator, 1977, 1978; Intriligator & Brito, 1981).

Sixth is *the prospects for a fundamental change in the structure of East–West relations*, such as the possible advent of a cooperation regime. There could develop over time a major change in East–West relations comparable to the post-World War II change in French–German relations or to the more recent change in Chinese–US relations. East–West relations started with Cold War confrontations and crises in the late 1940s and 1950s and evolved via an arms buildup, particularly in the 1960s, into the present deterrence regime. There could be a potential further evolution of these relations, via a verification regime into a possible future cooperation regime. Cooperation between the USA and the USSR could cover security issues, such as accidental nuclear war and nuclear non-proliferation. It could also cover global issues, such as health and environmental threats, in particular AIDS and potential radioactive damage from nuclear plants and nuclear wastes. Yet another area of potential cooperation is cooperation for the developing world, in particular Africa. US–Soviet agreement on major arms control initiatives, with verification measures, US–Soviet cooperation for Africa, and other forms of cooperation could be catalysts for changing the structure of international relations. These potential developments should be taken into account in arms race models, which should allow for certain types of phase transitions in mutual fears or suspicions, leading to potential arms reductions, whether unilateral or bilateral.

10 Conclusion

This chapter has developed the basic Richardson model and several variants of this model, including another descriptive model, the stock adjustment model, and two normative models, the Brito model and the differential game model. While these models are useful in understanding the interaction processes in an arms race and the possibility of a stable equilibrium, they tend to be mechanistic, treating the arms race from the outside and ignoring the actual or potential use of these arms.

By contrast, the model based on strategic considerations in a hypothetical war explicitly treats the use of arms in deterring the enemy and avoiding a pre-emptive strike. Reaction curves obtained using this model can be interpreted as Richardson reaction curves in which the coefficients are not given in an ad hoc way but are themselves given as explicit functions of strategic, technical, timing, and social/psychological factors. This strategic model determines the equilibrium levels of missiles as explicit functions of these same factors, and it can be used to analyze both bilateral and unilateral arms control and disarmament initiatives and the effects of arms races on the outbreak of war. Another useful approach is that involving heuristic decision rules, which implies for certain important cases, such as the US–USSR arms race, the presence of an unstable arms race that is stable against the outbreak of war.

While progress has been made in modeling the arms race, in order to make arms race models more relevant as means for analyzing and forecasting arms races and evaluating arms and arms control policy decisions, they should be extended to encompass several additional factors. Six such factors have been described: the treatment of accidental or inadvertent nuclear war; possible technical developments in weapons systems; arms control initiatives; the influence of political, bureaucratic, economic, and psychological factors; the emerging multipolar world; and the prospects for a fundamental change in the structure of East–West relations, moving from deterrence to cooperation. These six factors represent both a challenge to and an agenda for future arms race modeling.

Notes

1. Lewis Fry Richardson's seminal work became available in 1947–49 in microfilm and was published in book form in 1960, as Richardson (1960a). Rapoport (1957, 1960) provides a review and appreciation of this work. For applications of the Richardson model to arms races in the missile age, see Burns (1959), Boulding (1962), Kent (1963), Schelling (1966), Caspary (1967), Saaty (1968), Pitman (1969), Sandberg (1974), Intriligator (1975), Intriligator & Brito (1976a, 1976b, 1984, 1985a, 1988a), Lambelet, Luterbacher & Allan (1979), Majeski & Jones (1981), Majeski (1983b, 1985). See Isard & Anderton (1985) and Anderton (1985a, 1985b) for a detailed survey and bibliography. For references to other arms race models and to other differential equations models in conflict theory, see Intriligator (1982). For empirical studies of the Richardson model, see Lambelet (1971, 1974, 1976), Luterbacher (1975), Rattinger (1976b), Hollist (1977a, 1977b), McGuire (1977), Smith (1980), Cusack & Ward (1981), Ward (1984a, 1984b), and Chapter 3 of this volume.

2. A basic reference for the stock adjustment model is Harberger (1960).

3. For formal statements of existence and stability conditions and their proofs, see Brito (1972). For a discussion of the nature of a Stackelberg leader in economic models of duopolistic competition, see Intriligator (1971). The Brito model, it should be noted, treats the maximization of national self-interest, which need not necessarily entail overall maximization in terms of global welfare.

4. For a general discussion of differential games, see Intriligator (1971).

5. The distinction between the acquisition of weapons in peace and their use in war is that made by Rapoport between 'games' and 'fights', involving two different modes of thinking. See Rapoport (1960).

6. The optimality of such strategic choices for the opening phase of a missile war was shown in Intriligator (1967) and discussed in Intriligator (1968). See also Intriligator & Brito (1976a).

7. The military authorities in B, in their simulation of a missile war, would assume such strategic choices using 'worst case' analysis. Furthermore, the optimality of such strategic choices for the middle phase of a missile war was shown in Intriligator (1967) and discussed in Intriligator (1968).

8. For a discussion of the sensitivity of the equilibrium levels of missiles to changes in the strategic, technical, timing, and social/psychological parameters, see Intriligator (1975).

MICHAEL D. INTRILIGATOR, b. 1938, Ph.D. in Economics (Massachusetts Institute of Technology, 1963); Professor of Economics (1972–) and Political Science (1981–), University of California, Los Angeles; Director, Center for International and Strategic Affairs, University of California, Los Angeles (1982–); current main research and teaching interests: mathematical economic theory, econometrics, arms races, and arms control.

DAGOBERT L. BRITO, b. 1941, Ph.D. in Economics (Rice University, 1970); Peter Kin Professor of Political Economy, Rice University (1984–); current main research and teaching interests: mathematical economic theory and strategy, arms races, and arms control.

Chapter 5
Artificial Intelligence Models of Arms Races*

PAUL SMOKER
Richardson Institute for Peace Studies, Lancaster University

1 Introduction

1.1 Cataclysmic and Strategic Models

Håken Wiberg (Chapter 3) discusses arms race models in terms of two hypothetical types. The one is the 'cataclysmic', 'sociological', or 'causal' conceptualization, where macro forces are seen as dominant; the other, the 'strategic', 'rational', or 'actor'-oriented view, where rational actors provide the central focus. For mathematical model builders, Richardson models approximate the 'cataclysmic' view (Richardson, 1960a), and game theoretical conceptualizations, such as Prisoner's Dilemma, the 'strategic' paradigm (Rapoport, 1967). Clearly, as Wiberg agrees, these hypothetical types are not polar opposites, and attempts at arms race modelling include elements of both.

Two analogous schools of analysis are also present in peace research. These have been categorized the 'actor' approach, with its emphasis on individual decision-makers, and the 'structure' approach, where political, social, and economic structures are the major determinants (Smoker, 1987).

The degree to which real arms races may illustrate elements of both 'cataclysmic' and 'strategic' views is considered by Richardson when he explains that his mathematical model of an arms race simply describes what would happen 'if decision-makers did not stop to think'. Given that the 'cataclysmic' view stresses the consequences of large-scale social forces, such as socialization processes that establish the primacy of personal and national self-interest in decision-makers' minds, it is possible to speculate on what Richardson meant by 'thinking'.

In fact Richardson's equations describe what would happen if decision-makers simply pursued their own apparent national self-interest, as if

---

* I would like to thank Nils Petter Gleditsch, Michael Intriligator, and Håkan Wiberg for their comments on an earlier version of this chapter.

ARTIFICIAL INTELLIGENCE MODELS OF ARMS RACES

independent criteria of national self-interest were valid in an interactive situation, oblivious to the interactive consequences on the whole situation. In this regard there is a strong parallel between the 'cataclysmic' Richardson model and the 'strategic' Prisoner's Dilemma. In Prisoner's Dilemma the pursuit of self-interest by rational decision-makers generates a less than optimal solution precisely because mutual interest is involved but is not taken into account in defining utilities. Similarly, the Richardson equations are each developed from the viewpoint of one nation; consequently they often generate an outcome that is not optimal for the whole system, an arms race.

1.2 Interactive and Eigendynamik Models

The Richardson tradition has contributed much to our understanding of arms races, in part because of the escalatory consequences inherent in the interacting equations when the sensitivity to another nation's 'defences' is greater than the 'fatigue and expense' of armaments. Perhaps this is why the Richardson model is often referred to as an interactive or externally determined interpretation of armament dynamics, as opposed to an autistic or Eigendynamik theory such as the 'military-industrial complex'. In fact the ideas of action/reaction or externally determined, and Eigendynamik or internally determined are both present in the original Richardson equations. The defence coefficients stress externally determined forces and act to accelerate the armament process; while the fatigue and expense coefficients stress internally determined forces and act to slow the armament process.

Thus the Richardson equations

$$dx/dt = k^*y - a^*x + g \quad (1) \text{ and}$$
$$dy/dt = l^*x - b^*y + h \quad (2)$$

can be reinterpreted in terms of an external determination or action/reaction component EX and an internal dynamic or Eigendynamik component IN. This gives

$$dx/dt = EX(y) + IN(x) \quad (3)$$
$$dy/dt = EX(x) + IN(y) \quad (4)$$

where x and y are the armament levels of each side and the action/reaction function EX is defined in terms of two external influences: the first k^*y (or l^*x) reflecting the sensitivity towards the other nation's level of armament, the second g (or h) representing all other external influences, which Richardson called 'grievances'. The Eigendynamik component IN was for Richardson the negative effect, in terms of slowing the arms race, of domestic economic 'fatigue and expense' a^*x (or b^*y).

It is true that Eigendynamik approaches have tended to concentrate on internal dynamics that excite or accelerate an arms race, whereas Richardson in his original model assumed a and b to be positive and thus restraining influences. Historical circumstances may determine the degree to which external and internal determinants either accelerate or slow an arms race; a range of possibilities can be accommodated by the generalized model discussed above. The interpretation presented here is therefore not that adopted by Richardson, although the framework of his equations does in fact include both external and internal determination.

Since Richardson's original model did in fact include both action/reaction and Eigendynamik effects, classifying it as an action/reaction model is inaccurate. The fact that it has been so labelled is of some interest, reflecting perhaps the important outcomes resulting from the coupling of national behaviour encapsulated by Richardson's systems of equations.

1.3 Optimizing: the Security Dilemma

Contemporary analyses of arms races demonstrate that Richardson's interpretation of EX and IN were too simple, and as Intriligator & Brito (Chapter 4) illustrate there have been many much more sophisticated elaborations. Some of these elaborations have attempted to introduce normative concerns, such as the Brito model, where each country attempts to maximize its welfare, defined in terms of a national utility function that incorporates both consumption and an index of defence.

The problems of rationality involved in Prisoner's Dilemma and the realization that maximizing expected individual utility does not necessarily optimize either the individual or overall outcome have led to important redefinitions of appropriate optimizing behaviour in such 'strategic' situations. The 'tit for tat' Prisoner's Dilemma strategy advocated by Rapoport and others provides a 'coupled' solution for the optimization problem.

Non-optimal solutions are similarly probable in arms race models when the equivalents of utility functions are defined in terms of national self-interest. Explorations of arms race dynamics involving 'utility functions' defined in terms of coupled mutual security rather than isolated national security may provide important insights for resolving the otherwise paradoxical 'security dilemma' inherent in national self-interest in an interdependent world.

1.4 Constants and Variables

A limitation of Richardson-type models concerns the degree to which the equations describing behaviour are fixed. For example, in the Richardson equations

$$dx/dt = k^*y - a^*x + g \quad (1) \text{ and}$$
$$dy/dt = l^*x - b^*y + h \quad (2)$$

the parameters k, l, a, and b are assumed to be constant. It could be argued

ARTIFICIAL INTELLIGENCE MODELS OF ARMS RACES 81

that sensitivity towards perceived military threats by a potential adversary is likely to be influenced by both internal and external factors and that the defence coefficients k and l which reflect this sensitivity are correspondingly likely to vary. The 'constants' k and l can therefore be treated as variables whose values are determined by external determinants and by internal dynamics; this sensitivity operates upon the level of outside threat. Similar arguments can be put forward with regard to the constant mediating Eigendynamik effects, that is a and b in the case of Richardson.

This interpretation argues for four distinct sets of determinants in arms race dynamics. The first, pure interaction, results from external influences mediated through sensitivities that are externally determined. The second, mixed interaction, results from external influences that are mediated through sensitivities that are internally determined. Similarly, arms race dynamics can result from a pure Eigendynamik, or a mixed one.

Thus for a simple Richardson model the coefficients k, l, a, and b might be reconceptualized in terms of externally determined parameters ke, le, ae, and be, and internally influenced parameters ki, li, ai, and bi, to yield

$$dx/dt = ke*y + ki*y + ae*x + ai*x + g \quad (5)$$
$$dy/dt = le*x + li*x + be*y + bi*y + h \quad (6)$$

One disadvantage of this formulation is the proliferation of parameters. Much of the heuristic value of the original Richardson model comes from its relative simplicity and the consequent advantage of being able to 'test' the model empirically without the requirement that parameters k, l, a, or b should be independently measurable. But if 'constants' are not seen as necessarily constant, through the use of simulation models that interact with their data environment and self-modify as a result, then this more complex formulation could be of greater practical value.

1.5 Summing Up

As the above discussion intimates, and the chapters by Wiberg and Intriligator & Brito illustrate, it is possible to construct a very large number of mathematical arms race models of this genre. This chapter argues that such essentially 'mechanical' model building efforts should be complemented by 'artificial intelligence' models. The next section of the chapter outlines what is meant by artificial intelligence models and details significant differences between such approaches and traditional mathematical models in the social sciences.

2 Artificial Intelligence

2.1 Limitations of Traditional Models

Schrodt (1987) identifies three types of formal models that have been used to study aspects of international relations: statistical models that have mostly analysed large data sets; models of individual rationality, primarily using game theory; and two types of dynamic models, the first Richardsonian, the second using computer simulation. The second and third of Schrodt's categories resemble Wiberg's 'strategic' and 'cataclysmic' categories, although computer simulations often integrate both perspectives. Schrodt argues that

> By the early 1980s, however, it was clear that the mathematical approaches in use were not producing any magic bullets. Data collection efforts during the 1970s had produced a massive amount of data which, while imperfect, should have been sufficient to show patterns if the original hopes of the modelers – and many classical IR theorists as well – had obtained. The rational models proved useful for specific problems such as nuclear deterrence but usually either floundered or were trivialized when introduced into the low information, non-repeating, non-experimental environment of general international behavior. The Richardson arms race model proved to be not only the first, but also one of the best, of the differential equation models and any arms race models more generally were beset with statistical problems. Simulations grew and proliferated but remained largely untested and non-cumulative. (Schrodt, 1987, p. 3)

Each of these approaches can be criticized in a variety of ways, but all three manifest a common problem of behaviourism. Traditional behavioural science has for the most part proceeded as if social reality were fixed. In statistical analyses there has been a tendency to assume that relationships between variables remain constant. In mathematical modelling and computer simulation, evolving real-world situations have been represented using fixed models.

With this perspective, the future is defined in terms of the relationships that have held in the past; it includes the implicit assumption that these relationships will not change. An alternative approach does not see the future just in terms of prediction, in terms of extrapolating previous behaviour. It includes behaviour modification and alteration of relationships.

Some workers in systems dynamics have been concerned with the problem of 'Newtonian change or Darwinian evolution?' (Radzicki, 1987). Evolutionary change of social systems can be seen in terms of a mindless complex mechanical cybernetic process or in terms of an intentional systemic learning environment. Boulding has defined evolutionary change in terms of 'ecological interaction (which is selection) under conditions of constant change of parameters (which is mutation)' (Boulding, 1985, p. 25).

Social systems involve evolutionary change, but they also involve learning and intentionality; and all these components are important in considering the relationship between an arms race and models of an arms race. Mechanistic behaviourism has failed to incorporate the consequences of learning and intentionality in its model building enterprise, and the idea that models and realities can interact and co-evolve is an anathema to those who seek to establish objectivity in social science.

2.2 Sources of Artificial Intelligence

The term 'artificial intelligence' is in many ways misleading. Certainly current applications of the new model building approaches classified under this rubric have very limited, if any, 'intelligence'. But unfortunately the label has now entered into common usage both in computer science and in applications in international relations studies.

Schrodt (1987) identifies three sources from which, in his view, International Relations Artificial Intelligence models have been developed. The first source is psychological models of individual and group decision-making, particularly those models emphasizing bounded rationality rather than optimization. Here, it is argued, decision-makers do not optimize, they 'muddle through' as best they can on incomplete information. Precedent-based systems, where the model matches current and past patterns of behaviour to determine an 'appropriate' response, are an example of such an approach. The pathbreaking work of Alker & Christensen (1972) provides one of the earliest examples of such a 'trial and error' approach to 'learning'. Here the behaviour of a UN peace-keeping force is progressively modified over time as a result of the negative and positive outcomes of previous actions. Alker and his associates have continued to work at the cutting edge of AI models in international relations research.

The second source is models of knowledge representation and processing, including rule-based models, for example if 'a' then 'b'; and machine learning techniques, where the model can modify itself as a result of the data analysed. Simple rule-based systems developed in part as a result of the evolution of computer simulation of international relations, since models incorporating variations of

IF (Condition) THEN (Action)

are a natural expression of computer language. Many 'expert systems' make extensive use of such logics, and applications to international conflict include a study of the Cuban missile crisis (Thorson & Sylvan, 1982).

The third source, according to Schrodt, is 'behavioralist IR concepts of data, particularly events data, case based foreign policy studies, and increasingly textual analysis'. Alker's recent work on computational histories (Alker & Mallery, 1988) is illustrative of the use of qualitative textual material in artificial intelligence models of international conflict. His study of the 1956 Hungarian intervention by the Soviet Union uses the 'textual event data set' SherFACS, a 'computational encodable history', to generate a semantic representation. However, the technical problems involved in retrieving textual information in a usable form from such a data base are substantial (Duffy, 1988a).

2.3 Characteristics of AI Models

Artificial intelligence models in international relations, according to

Schrodt, manifest a number of features that distinguish them from earlier 'cataclysmic' or 'rational' approaches. The emphasis on qualitative information rather than quantitative data places such models closer to traditional theorists than was the case with 'cataclysmic' or 'rational' theorists. Indeed authors such as Duffy argue that artificial intelligence approaches to textual analysis can make a significant contribution to International Relations Theory (Duffy, 1988b). The storage of such qualitative information requires far more complex data structures than those used in most traditional quantitative data sets.

While this is certainly the case, it can also be argued that an essential difference between contemporary artificial intelligence models and traditional mathematical approaches concerns the nature of the interaction of the model with the data. Traditional models, such as the Richardson equations, interact with the data in the sense that patterns in the data (in the Richardson case, changes in military expenditure, however defined) are compared to predicted patterns in the model, 'defences' for example. But the model does not change as a result of interacting with the 'real world' data: it does not 'learn', 'remember', or 'forget'. It is mechanical in the sense that once the initial starting parameters are set, even in a stochastic model, the assumptions and output of the model are not influenced by the data. The model has its own 'Eigendynamik' relative to the 'real world'.

2.4 Artificial Intelligence Models: Conclusion

Artificial intelligence models are now being developed in political science and international relations (Cimbala, 1987). To some extent this can be seen, following the work of Richardson, as a development in the application of dynamic models to problems of international conflict (Luterbacher & Ward, 1985). Certainly artificial intelligence models in international relations are not static or cross-sectional: rather they present an interpretation of events over time.

Given that the original Alker/Christensen simulation of UN peacekeeping was published as long ago as 1972, and that during this period mechanistic and stochastic models have continued to be developed, it is of some interest that we do not have an equivalent to the Richardson model in the AI tradition. The increasing power of personal computers and the widespread availability of structured computer languages appropriate to artificial intelligence model building now make it possible for such models to be developed.

But the evolution of an artificial intelligence subculture within international relations research has for the most part been limited to relatively few universities in the United States. In Europe and in Asia, where substantial work is also being undertaken in fifth generation computing, artificial intelligence, and expert systems, scholars concerned with peace and war have not made significant contributions in this area, despite the availability of highly user-friendly packages such as STELLA (Richmond, 1985).

3 Future Possibilities

3.1 Heuristics for a Disarming World

Formal models can be used to represent important aspects of theories of arms dynamics and to explore their consequences. A number of paradigms from academic theories and models have become a part of public political discourse, including graduated reciprocation in tension reduction (GRIT), Prisoner's Dilemma, the idea of an arms race, and balance of power. The Richardsonian action/reaction concept of an arms race is now embedded in popular discourse.

While most artificial intelligence models have been used to describe past events, it is possible to explore evolving paths into the future. AI models can, for example, explore disarmament strategies such as drastic cuts in nuclear weapons under conditions of strategic stability. Here artificial intelligence models of the arms race would interact with a data set comprising desired world future states and events, in order to explore changes in dynamics needed to achieve the necessary drastic cuts in nuclear weapons.

One general framework for such a model might, like an AI chess program, comprise three phases, corresponding to the opening gambit, middle game, and end game. Each phase seeks to satisfy different criteria using different rule-based systems. In the opening gambit, successive moves seek to increase 'strategic stability' while reducing the number of warheads. The greater the increase in 'strategic stability', that is the capability to destroy an adversary after suffering a first strike, the better the opening gambit. As in chess there may be many possible decision paths, the best move at any time depending on previous moves and the current distribution of warheads (pieces).

During the middle game, increases in strategic stability are no longer possible, and successive moves seek to maximize the reduction in warheads, removing pieces from the board, while at the same time minimizing the loss in strategic stability. As in the opening gambit, various conditions for parity and relative 'strategic stability' would need to be satisfied by the evolving situation.

The end game begins at very low levels of nuclear warheads when strategic stability is no longer possible, and it leads to complete nuclear disarmament. A broader set of conditions, including levels of trust, verification, and interdependence, need to be satisfied by successive moves at this stage.

An important criticism of much of the work on armament dynamics is that it has focused on what has happened in the past or what might happen in the future if existing trends continue. The work so far undertaken in artificial intelligence models of international relations has also concentrated almost exclusively on the analysis of past events and short-range predictions of the future. Artificial intelligence models can provide powerful heuristics for thinking about the dynamics of disarmament; they can explore necessary and achievable behaviour modifications necessary for a disarming world.

3.2 Increased Capabilities for Artificial Intelligence Models

The model-building ideas put forward in this chapter are within the context of the capabilities of contemporary computers, although the potential for artificial intelligence models will be progressively enhanced as, when, and if the promised new technology becomes available. Such developments may make possible the exploration of alternative world futures not so limited by the constraints of yesterday's world.

The Japanese 'fifth generation' computer project (Moto-oka, 1982) has set the agenda for information technology for at least the next decade. This agenda includes dramatic advances in artificial intelligence software and expert systems. The widespread availability of personal computers with impressive capabilities will continue to open up new and challenging possibilities.

As fifth generation goals become even partially realized, computers will become less centred around numerical computations and be more able to assess the meaning of information and to understand the problem to be solved. The human–computer interface will become increasingly effective and contribute to an enhancement of human analytical and creative abilities. Artificial intelligence models are likely to replace 'strategic' and 'cataclysmic' approaches.

3.3 Futures: Conclusion

Artificial intelligence models will increasingly be used to consider armaments dynamics. On the one hand they can contribute to increasing our understanding of the complex set of interacting forces that lead to an evolving dynamic armaments process. On the other they can help us to explore the complex evolutionary dynamics that are involved in moving towards a disarmed world.

PAUL SMOKER, b. 1938, M.Sc., Ph.D. (University of Lancaster); Director, Richardson Institute for Conflict and Peace Research, University of Lancaster; co-editor of special issue of *Current Research on Peace and Violence* on accidental nuclear war (1988); current main research interests: accidental nuclear war, and artificial intelligence approaches to war and peace.

PART II: TECHNOLOGICAL DYNAMICS

Chapter 6

The Role of Military R&D in Arms Build-Ups

ULRICH ALBRECHT
Department of Political Science, Free University of Berlin

> Qui desiderat pacem, praeparet bellum.
> – Flavius V. Renatus Vegetius: *De Re Militaribus*, Lib. III, 1 AD ca. 400

> God demands peace, yet you prepare for war?
> – Erasmus Roterdamus: *Querela Pacis*, 1517

> None of all the bigoted dogmas of present politics has created more disaster than the one 'si vis pacem, para bellum'. This great truth which excels in entailing a grandiose falsehood, provides for the battle cry which calls all Europe to arms and which has constituted for such a fanaticism of mercenaries.
> – Karl Marx: 'Invasion', *Das Volk*, 30 July 1859, *MEW* 13, p. 444

1 The Issue

Peace research has long tried to come to an understanding of the arms race which could indicate ways out of it. This chapter will discuss hypotheses about one type of input fueling the arms race, military research and development (R&D). First, however, some general observations seem appropriate, also in order to put this contribution into perspective.

The by now classic line of division can be tracked back to a dichotomy introduced into social science by Riesman et al. (1950). The peace research debate distinguished between 'internal' and 'external' driving forces of the arms race. These are crude analogies to the character types of Americans that Riesman had labeled 'inner-directed' and 'other-directed'. This grand analogy suffered from a number of faults, though it dominated the peace research debate. First, the main protagonists in the arms race, according to the analogy, were treated like Riesman's individuals. This treatment defies analytical insight into the contribution of such universal factors as worldwide R&D activities. Societies do not act like individuals – to understand them, social and not person-oriented approaches are needed.

Second, the generalization from US stereotypes to all humankind, and in the next step to states as individual actors, deserves qualification – which is rarely given. The confrontation of 'internal' and 'external' direction may be helpful, also because of the fine moralistic undertone involved; but such a simplistic classification is doomed to fail to explain why nations go to war, or why the arms race continues. Rather, there seems evidence for *both* approaches, internal and external crucial factors – a not very satisfactory pluralism in such a life-and-death matter as the arms race.

The explanatory potential of other dichotomies appears considerably greater, from the accumulated writings about the arms race in the past two decades (Agrell, 1981; Gray, 1976; Krell, 1981; Lutz, 1979; Müller, 1985; Nincic, 1982; Rattinger, 1975a; Senghaas, 1972a; Thee, 1986a). Several variants draw in industrial systems as the base of weapons proliferation in the arms race. There is a host of concepts stemming from such premises – ranging from general concepts, such as the notion of the military-industrial complex (Engelhardt & Heise, 1974; Gansler, 1980; Koistinen, 1980; Lens, 1970; Nincic, 1982; Rosen, 1973; Sarkesian, 1972), to more limited generalizations, such as Kurth's follow-on theorem (Kurth, 1971). Generally, these concepts depict industrial or technological determinism vs politics in command. The regulative idea underlying this chapter also operates with this dichotomy.

This new interest in the interplay between technological determinants and politics is certainly linked to the older Riesman-type debate. Political justifications for the procurement of weapons systems tend to be articulated in terms of perceived actions by the political opponent, to cite the most important link. Technological and industrial dynamism, however, differs between the two main protagonists, the USA and the USSR, due to discrepancies in their social systems. A first hypothesis thus will be that the USA, which usually is technologically in the lead in the arms race, is largely induced to exploit its technological leadership in the field of military security as well. In the vernacular of the debate: the USA is driven by technological determinism, whilst the USSR finds itself in an uphill race to catch up. This points at a more reactive Soviet behavior, which fits in better with the notion of an 'arms race' between the two major military powers on earth.

The reader may find such basic orientations helpful in the following paragraphs. The gist of the argument should now be apparent. Furthermore, it should also be clear, in a first round, that the Riesman dichotomy about internal and external 'push' phenomena becomes too weak to delineate the issue accurately.

This contribution ends with the dictum that a static appraisal, as given by the crude circumscription of the two main protagonists above, will fail. Decades of continued arms race have sedimented into a special conduct of affairs on all sides, which will require additional reflections by the social scientist. The proposed analytical formula – industrial militarism – tries to take stock of the petrification of the two main contenders, and their disparate efforts to find a way out.

Thus, this contribution is clearly fundamentalist in orientation. The argument will start with a reflection about key terms – which are, I feel, too often taken for granted.

2 The Concept of 'Arms Race'

2.1 Nature of the Arms Race

In a strict sense, the very notion of an 'arms race' is an obfuscation: at best an oversimplified model of reality and at worst wrong. Programs for major weapons systems of the leading military powers are not launched in an action-reaction pattern or on a tit-for-tat basis (Albrecht, 1988). That is not to say that there is no race: but the sportive notion of a 'race' between personalized actors apparently has been shaped by individualist thinking. We will adhere to the term here because of its wide acceptance and political impact, but must bear in mind that it hinders analytical insight. The accumulation of weapons of mass destruction, on both sides, is something different from a 'race'.

The Palme Commission (*Common Security*, 1983, p. 9) observed that 'technology has changed the world in which we live, but understanding of its impact on international relations has not kept pace'. Analogously, it can be said that military technology has changed the nature of the arms race, but our level of insight has not risen accordingly.

The Scandinavian peace research tradition especially has portrayed the arms race as being 'out of control'. This view has been stressed in particular by Marek Thee, who asserts that 'its thrust has continued unabated' (Thee, 1986a, p. 127).

Earlier Alva Myrdal stated categorically: 'The sinister developments in the advance towards the brink to disaster all interact, worsened by the calamitous threat this book has been written to analyze: the arms race and the militarization of the world' (Myrdal, 1976, p. 3). And somewhat more recently, Inga Thorsson has submitted: 'Militarization is increasing in the Third World. An ever growing number of Third-World states have built up modern armies [. . .]. Nevertheless the arms race is pursued primarily by the two superpowers and their allies. Their arsenals, both conventional and nuclear, are constantly increasing' (Thorsson, 1984b, p. 4).

Yet this very notion provokes questions: What permits especially the arms race to develop in such a unique manner? Why are there no checks and balances? What constitutes the uniqueness of this phenomenon? And: are there indeed no limits?

Citing such alarmist writings about a seemingly endless arms race provokes a counter-hypothesis, to be discussed below. Arms races may end up in disaster, that is true, be it war or collapse of one of the protagonists. Presently, however, a third and less catastrophic limitation for the East–West arms race will be studied.

The main tendency of military technology has been to increase vulnerability. Whereas credible protection against an aggressor's weapons was once available, there is today no technology that can provide a safeguard from nuclear missile attack. The hope that an enormous research effort may produce the 'absolute' technology capable of counteracting or destroying even the most advanced offensive weapons, another highly efficient stimulus of the arms race, has so far not been vindicated.[1]

In this sense, the arms race is a qualitative one, based on a race in research and development.

2.2 Indicators

Most of the suggested specific indicators of the arms race in fact reveal nothing spectacular:

Investment in military technology has been rather constant, allowing for inflation, which would not suggest a race. A constant rate of investment or a modest increase could mean stability – at low levels.

Neither will the *numbers of weapons in inventories* show any dramatic change. In fact, because of the complexity of weapons systems and the associated costs, today the major military powers have fewer conventional weapons at their disposal than they did earlier.

Nor would *numbers of men under arms* indicate that there is an arms race. For a variety of reasons, among them economic ones on all sides, numbers of military personnel have also been reduced over time.

The observer, therefore, is left with the most intricate kind of indicators: qualitative ones. No accepted standards exist for international comparison of the quality of weapons. (And had such standards been available, the perennial problem would be to collect the required information to apply them.) So far, the measurement of the qualitative arms race has on the one hand been derived from impulse, in terms of financial and manpower resources; on the other hand, in the form of evaluations of a technical nature about relative levels of 'modernity', potential 'superiority', and the like.

The lack of convincing indicators, however, need not mean that there is no ongoing arms race. The phenomenon itself is certainly not affected by analytical problems of finding an appropriate yardstick. Refinements in methodology beyond the simplistic scheme of 'bean counting' (*Falsche Gewichte*, 1983; Bülow, 1985; Lutz, 1986) recently have used both quantitative and qualitative characteristics of modern weapons in order to find handy tools for evaluating the arms race. Throw-weight of missiles as delivery vehicles, accuracy of targeting devices, first-strike kill potential, and comparable indicators all signal that still considerable inputs into the arms race ought to be portrayed in terms of marginal returns. Economists are familiar with the argument that marginal returns in production-functions, in response to continued significant inputs, indicate sufficiency.

2.3 Meaning of R&D for the Arms Race

It would appear that R&D activities constitute a very meaningful indicator for the continuation of the arms race. Furthermore, the significance of R&D for the arms race, and for efforts to control it, is on the increase. While arms control accords of the past have mostly dealt with deployment, a recent re-orientation has led to the question: Can the arms race be controlled at its genesis, i.e. by cutting the R&D programs? (Thee, 1986a, ch. 6; United Nations, 1987).

Here a brief reference to established insights about the causality is in order. Dieter Senghaas (1971) has convincingly argued that the arms race is overdetermined, that there is redundant causality at work, and that the analyst has to look at the configuration of causes:

> As soon as one works in peace research both on the development of general theory or on specific research projects, one will quickly learn that monistic explanations [. . .] are bound to fail [. . .]. It will be apparent that we need multidimensional, multifactor and multivariate explanations [. . .]. Central methodological problems and problems of research strategy consist in the combination, linkage and interpenetration of partial analytical hypotheses into new, overarching patterns of explanation. (Senghaas, 1971, pp. 331–332.)

The arms race, although a global phenomenon, does not represent a uniform concept for all the participants, and this holds true also for the involvement of R&D in its dynamics. Magnitude of R&D spending certainly will produce differences. The three countries that each spend more than 50% of their public R&D on military purposes – the USSR, the USA, and the UK – have very different R&D establishments. Lesser countries, such as France, where roughly one-third of all public money goes into weapons research, are again different with respect to the role of this investment in general modernization strategies. The limits to generalization are rather narrow.

The following should be read in the light of these caveats. The focus on the military use of R&D here is not meant to deny the impact of other factors, but the intention certainly is to treat R&D as a prime cause in the continuation of the qualitative arms race.

In this analysis I will use personal definitions and premises on several counts. The literature, despite extensive searches, yielded few non-trivial conceptualizations. This situation may be illustrated by the problems involved in finding a useful definition of the key variable, *arms race dynamics*. A number of definitions in the literature in fact say little – if anything. Spitzer (1987, p. 250) understands by 'arms race dynamics' the 'dynamism inherent in the arms race': one of the numerous examples of vicious circles here.

The absence of useful definitions of the arms race is also reflected in the lack of agreement about the main mechanisms. Most US writings adhere to the so-called action-reaction theorem. George Rathjens summarizes this view in a critical manner:

> Although there is considerable evidence to support the claim that the action-reaction phenomenon does apply to defense decision-making, to explain all the major decisions of the superpowers in terms of an action-reaction hypothesis is an obvious oversimplification. The American MIRV deployment has been rationalized as a logical response to a possible Russian ABM-system deployment, but there were also other motivations that were important: the desire to keep our total missile force constant while increasing the number of warheads we would deploy, the long-term possibility of MIRV's giving us an effective counterforce capability, and finally the simple desire to bring to fruition an interesting and elegant technological concept. Nevertheless, the action-reaction phenomenon, with the reaction often premature and/or exaggerated, has clearly been a major stimulant of the strategic arms race. (Rathjens, 1969, p. 181)

Action-reaction phenomena may be traced in the East–West arms build-up. Reaction in most instances will be possible only after first deployment, or at least after actual testing of a weapons system. It remains difficult to assume that there are action-reaction processes covering R&D programs of modern weapons which remain highly secret at these early stages. Perhaps more plausible is that, in the absence of real knowledge, one country may start R&D work on a new line of military technology, assuming that its opponent has secretly embarked on the very same technology. This may – but only *may* – produce new weapons of a similar kind which, after becoming known, appear to indicate action-reaction phenomena. Such thought-processes appear typical for decision-makers concerned with the launch of novel R&D programs (York, 1975). The most recent innovation in military technology, Stealth, the deliberate minimizing of radar cross-sections and infrared-signatures of aircraft (Albrecht, 1988), apparently took the Soviet side by surprise, and hence does not fit into the action-reaction stereotype. Also other case studies have shown that major weapons were conceived and developed without knowledge of what the other side was doing. Again, we must conclude that the study of the arms race from the angle of R&D deserves an argument more independent from the mainstream of existing literature.

Repeated efforts have been made to encourage empirical studies by offering analytical cross-classifications (e.g. Senghaas, 1971). As usual, nobody has volunteered to fill in the various entries, so as to establish an empirical hierarchy of the theoretical models suggested. Some of these models (notably the autism formula)[2] lack support from the very beginning. There is a dearth of grand studies covering all theoretical propositions. Hence, concepts close to establishment views tend to prevail (such as the one quoted about action-reaction), because of greater persistence from these quarters. Concepts enjoying significant support from opposing quarters – such as the theorem of the military-industrial complex (MIC) – may also top the awareness of the general public. Thirdly, concepts survive which show a certain understanding of imperatives of industrial production, such as the 'follow-on' theorem.

THE ROLE OF MILITARY R&D IN ARMS BUILD-UPS 93

Again, the conclusion remains from this sketchy survey that out of a broad range of analytical approaches to the study of arms race dynamics, those dominate which, from a strictly analytical viewpoint, do not merit such assessment.[3] Peace research should therefore reflect on how suggested analytical schemes with their vague conclusions about likely prime candidate solutions might be turned into analytical hardware. The present chapter aims at contributing to this process.

3 Premises

Three premises need clarifying:

(a) *Scope of theoretical assessment.* The broadest possible approach theorizes about the relationship of state and war as a whole: a recent contribution is Krippendorff (1985). This scope is strongly connected with the philosophy that views the state as a coercive institution. Hintze (1906) originated the bourgeois line of thinking in this vein, formerly developed in the socialist tradition, notably by Friedrich Engels (the 'force theory' in his *Anti-Dühring*, 1877).

If such a broad scope is accepted, then the study of arms race dynamics becomes an assessment of secondary phenomena, and not of the prime causes of societal development.

(b) *Reach-out into history.* Some studies (recently McNeill, 1983) go back as far as to the beginnings of human civilization in order to study the impact of warfare on society. The scope mostly is not as broad as indicated under (a), because commonly one feature or at most a few selected features are traced throughout history. For the study of current arms race phenomena, the assessment should be limited to the period of the modern nation state and its emergence, i.e. the Renaissance.

(c) *Cross-sectional applicability.* Another problem of scope is related to the global importance of arms race phenomena, also for the Third World. Numerous studies have highlighted the significance of arms build-ups for these countries, culminating from 1961 onwards in the UN culture (as I would label it) of studies on the interrelationship between the arms race and underdevelopment (an evaluation is given by Volger, 1987). To simplify the analysis, Third World aspects will not be dealt with in the following, although we dismiss therewith the problems of two-thirds of humankind. But the following analytical treatment is based on the assumption that there are specificities of the arms race in industrialized societies, that there is an interconnection with industrialization, particularly with regard to the qualitative arms race.

4 Main Hypotheses

4.1 An Isolated Arms Race?

The first hypothesis relates to the debate between those who see the arms race as an isolated phenomenon, a sort of Eigendynamik, and those who link it to the East–West confrontation.

This chapter assumes that the arms race needs to be understood in the light of insight into other, possibly more basic, forms of societal dynamics (or lack of these). The intellectual Left has long considered the imperatives of capital reproduction, or the profit motive, as a prime engine of the arms race. A more pertinent view would look at the dynamism apparent in competitive capitalist settings to see if similar phenomena can be observed in the arms sector.

Such comparison will be especially fruitful in the R&D field. In a capitalist environment, as typified by US circumstances, an R&D team in a high-tech field normally will compete with another rival US team, and not so much against Soviet counterparts whose accomplishments would remain secret for some time (Mulhern, 1987; United Nations, 1987). The infighting among teams from Lockheed, Convair, Northrop, and Martin against the winning Boeing concept for the intercontinental bomber in the late 1940s opened a continuous flow of competitive efforts within the USA, up to the present 'race' for Stealth-type cruise missiles (between Lockheed and General Dynamics) or superfast reconnaissance aircraft in the Mach 5 region (Lockheed and Boeing). The competition familiar among teams of scientists is married to a commercial competition of the firms in an environment unique to the capitalist system. On top of this, Pentagon contracts are considered (and offered) as a prize to be won – there is also a competitive set-up on the demand side of the R&D budget. The dynamism of this peculiar set-up is highlighted by the US 'Independent Bid' R&D program (Adams, 1982; Reppy, 1985). On top of the huge public investment into R&D, there are, astonishingly enough, private funds going into military R&D. Such high-risk investment is seen as 'the seed money for the next generation of weapons – long before Congress or the public have heard about them' (Paine & Adams, 1980, p. 92). It is claimed that the major innovations in the US contribution to the arms race over the past two decades have stemmed from such private initiatives. Strategic cruise missiles, high-energy lasers, space-based surveillance systems, precision-guided munitions, lightweight fighter aircraft (the F-16 and F-18 concepts), and the B-1 bomber are seen by Paine & Adams as having been conceived in privately funded R&D projects. All these programs at later stages were predominantly financed by public funds, and the firms that initiated the programs were later reimbursed for their activity.

In most of the postwar period, non-military R&D has grown much faster than R&D exclusively for military purposes (Gleditsch et al., 1988). Can the private sector also be drawn upon for military purposes? Subjective estimates about present amounts are US $5 billion for the USA (according to Gordon Adams) and the equivalent of public military R&D spending for the Federal Republic of Germany and Switzerland.[4] In general, however, net private investment into military R&D, i.e. the expenditure not reimbursed by government, appears too limited to alter available statistics to any significant degree.

Occasionally, privately funded R&D projects have yielded rather dramatic innovations, as with the novel cruise missile technology (Huisken, 1981). The general public and most members of the US Congress were unaware of these weapons until the US Government unilaterally declared, in the wake of the November 1974 Vladivostok Accord, that the Agreement's ban on air-launched missiles was intended to cover free-fall ballistic missiles only. Apparently, the purely private nature of early cruise missile development helped to cheat the Soviet side. The President of the Aerospace Industries Association of America claims that the early private source of funding of lightweight fighters 'initiated a program to fill a "technology hole" – an airplane design combining supersonic speed with the superior maneuverability of subsonic aircraft', hinting at the F-16 (United Nations, 1987, p. 79). In fact, since then the trend towards ever heavier flying machines filled with electronics has been challenged by the advent of more agile, lighter aircraft, also in the Soviet inventory.

We note an even more significant example for the decisive importance of private involvement in military R&D in the case of the intercontinental ballistic missile, the principal weapon of contemporary strategies of deterrence (Beard, 1976; United Nations, 1987, p. 85). The first known contract for developing ICBMs was given in 1947 to a US firm, now part of General Dynamics. In the late 1940s, military planners apparently lost confidence in the feasibility of the concept, and placed emphasis on heavy intercontinental bombers. The firm, however, did not give up. After heavy cuts in funds, it continued the development of the first US ICBM, albeit on a reduced schedule, with its own funds. In early 1954, some six years after the military had turned their attention away from ICMBs, official interest in this technology was revived. The teams of Drs Ramo and Wooldridge, who formed a small private research company, concluded in early 1954 that the concept of combining a ballistic missile with a nuclear warhead for intercontinental deterrence was technically feasible (Nieburg, 1966, ch. xi).

Similar clashes of interest between private initiative and bureaucratic control of public funds have continued up to the present. Small research groups convinced of the potential of their findings are still searching to find private investors more willing to promote their ideas than the government. The known history of Stealth technologies, the drastic reduction of radar cross-sections for aircraft, illustrates this phenomenon.

The reasoning about the dynamics of the arms race has produced a number of strands of debate. This race is certainly not without a subject – the systemic contradiction between the modes of production and state organization of the world's two principal military powers. This role induces both powers to project power virtually everywhere on the globe where deemed necessary (seemingly more so for the USA than for the USSR). The relationship of these issues with the ongoing arms race here is seen as a rather intermediated one: the East–West conflict is at the roots of the arms race, but it does not determine this race into specifics.

Another level of debate deals with the 'rational actor' assumption. The rationality of decision-making has been challenged on a number of levels.

First, the calculation and articulation of the respective national interests at stake provoke questions about the rationale used. Second, the perception of the vital interests of the other side leaves much room for debate, again using the yardstick of rationality.

Third, the conclusions drawn on each side about appropriate steps for safeguarding own national interests provoke question. This is not to say that top politicians must be accused: the articulation of national interests itself reflects the pursuit of power, and contradicting views within domestic politics about current priorities will find their way into foreign policy. Because of the roots of foreign politics in the domestic scene, and the inherent compromises, the rationality of an international political concept might be challenged on grounds of principle.

Fourth, the perception of decision output, and what from this becomes apparent to the other side, puts a simplistic action-reaction model into question. In several cases, the Soviets simply would have been at odds to understand what a certain US move meant. They would want to react in kind, but did not know how or with what. Lack of sufficient evidence from the other side induced decision-makers to resort rather to their own principal assessment of the East–West conflict. Despite decades of mutual understandings and misunderstandings, there is still no general consensus about how the nuclear alphabet should be written. The US way of doing things is not accepted, also for reasons of pride, by the Soviet Union. Unwilling to see themselves as pupils to a US headteacher, the Soviet side feels rather that a life-and-death matter such as nuclear warfare should be read in their own vernacular. And they are afraid that the US understanding of their views lacks both competence and sophistication.

Yet another strand of assessment focuses on the relationship between economics and politics in the arms race. The enormous economic effort unfolded in this East–West context provokes the search for specific dynamic contributions in the interaction between the two spheres. The paradigm of military-industrial complexes appears to have lost in persuasive power on both sides. The Soviet literature is proud of announcing 'complexes' of all kinds, such as 'agro-industrial complexes', or 'complex programs' in the activities of Comecon (Albrecht & Nikutta, 1989). But even the most patriotic texts have not copied the US right-wing position, that the establishment of a national military-industrial complex is necessary to provide the armed services effectively with the kind of equipment they require. On the US side, the theorem has also lost reputation and tends to be superseded by the older notion of 'militarism' (see below).

In a more fundamentalist manner, Marxist concepts (or concepts claiming this label) also appear to have lost ground. After 1968, a brief passage in the writings of Friedrich Engels about the state as 'ideeller Gesamtkapitalist' (ideal macro-capitalist) stirred up considerable debate. Engels presumably would have been amused (and Marx angered) about the over-extension of a polemical remark in a serious work of analysis. Again, this is not to ridicule the substance matter involved. I do hold that the clash between the USA and the USSR is predominantly one between two political economies. But the analytical understanding of this fact still leaves much to be desired.

Both the Pentagon and its Eastern counterpart, despite checks and balances such as the Defense Advanced Research Projects Agency (DARPA), must be described mainly as huge bureaucracies, characterized by internal rivalries, indecisiveness, and offsetting of unconventional ideas by opponent forces. The slight edge which the Western organization regularly is able to secure must then be explained by the capitalistic high risk-taking, and the dim prospects of later generous refunding. Thus organizational features in the armament effort of the West may be crucial in topping the arms race between two huge machineries, which may have more in common than not, on both sides of the East–West divide.

4.2 Dimensions

Our second hypothesis concerns dimensions of the innovative effort in the arms race, or magnitude of industrial involvement. This aspect of the arms race tends also to be neglected by peace researchers, who have rarely been inside a factory. Yet, proper assessment of this aspect is crucial for understanding the dynamics of the arms race. The combination of quantum leaps in innovative technology (the 'vertical' dimension of the arms race) with the breadth of industrial effort (the 'horizontal' dimension) may be portrayed by the mathematical formula of product-moment correlation. This illustration may also help to understand the perennial Soviet drawbacks in catching up with Western technology. They are fighting a hopeless race in the horizontal dimension of the arms race, because the integration of novel technologies into the East–West arms build-up places additional strings on the national technology base of the country. Nuclear research, jet engine technology, making of missiles, building fast naval combatants, the multitude of demands posed by modern combat electronics, laser and particle beam weapons technology, topped by the requirement to experiment with, to calibrate, and to produce and test this equipment – all this illustrates these demands of 'dimension' or 'width' which certainly could push a national economy of limited sophistication, under any organizational circumstances, to the limits. The Soviet desire to opt out of the arms race for economic reasons becomes more easily understandable, if this dimension comes under consideration. It is not only the waste of public funds for military purposes which otherwise could be used as seed money for investment into economic growth. The real threat to the Soviet economy is the vision of continued uphill races in advanced technologies, with an economic base which expands at a much slower pace. The continued qualitative arms race is going to become costlier and costlier to the USSR, in terms of opportunity costs which the average citizens actually can grasp, forced as they are to look at the losses in everyday economic life.

4.3 Finite Aspects

Our third skeptical inroad into debate about the continued arms race, and the role of R&D in it, is linked to the debate about finalism in socio-technological development. Credit for raising this question should go to a small group of senior scientists at the by now defunct Max Planck Institute at Starnberg near Munich (Böhme et al., 1973). Taking up their argument and applying it to the topic is the main focus of this section.

Arms race dynamics in general reflect an image of unabated growth. Table 6.1 depicts over history the increase of lethality of man-made weapons. The figure provokes at least two questions, the main one being the validity of indices used to show that there is an arms race. I conclude, cautiously, that a mix of indices will help to overcome this problem. The second question is whether such a chain of technological inventions through history can be meaningfully portrayed in such a manner, or whether some inventions such as the atomic weapon ridicule any effort to find a common denominator for destructiveness.

Table 6.1 *A long-term view of the lethability of weapons**

Weapons/weapon system	Lethality index
Javelin (till 17th century)	18
Sword (till 17th century)	20
Bow and arrow (till 17th century)	20
Crossbow (10th–17th centuries)	32
Culverin, 12-pounder (16th century)	43
Flintlock gun (18th century)	47
Minié gun (mid-19th century)	150
Field gun, 12-pounder (17th century)	230
Breech-loader (end 19th century)	230
Repository gun (World War I)	780
Gribeauval field gun, grenades (18th century)	4,000
Machine gun (WWI)	13,000
Machine gun (WWII)	18,000
Field gun, 75 mm explosive grenade (end 19th century)	34,000
Tank, 2 MG (WWI)	68,000
Aircraft, 1 MG, 2 bombs (WWI)	230,000
Field gun, 155 mm explosive grenade (WWI)	470,000
Howitzer, 155 mm (WWII)	660,000
V-2 missile (WWII)	860,000
Tank, 1 gun, 1 MG (WWII)	2,220,000
Fighter aircraft, 8 MG, 2 bombs (WWII)	3,000,000
Hiroshima atom bomb, 20 kt TNT (1945–48)	49,000,000
Lance missile, 0.05 kt TNT warhead (1971–80)	60,000,000
Lance missile, 1 kt TNT warhead (1976–)	170,000,000
M 109 howitzer, 0.1 kt TNT warhead (1969–)	680,000,000
Pluton tactical missile, 20 kt TNT warhead (1973–)	830,000,000
F-4 fighter bomber with B-61 bomb (1968–)	6,200,000,000
M-20 IRBM (1977–)	18,000,000,000
SS-18 ICBM (1976–)	210,000,000,000

* Reprinted from Kaldor & Robinson (1978, p. 353) and slightly reduced. The source of the data used by Kaldor & Robinson is Dupuy (1964). The 'lethality index' is a purely comparative computation of characteristics of weapons with no direct meaning in reality. The methodology is given in Dupuy (1964). A revised version is found in Dupuy (1980, p. 313). Reproduced with permission from Jane's Information Group Limited.

THE ROLE OF MILITARY R&D IN ARMS BUILD-UPS 99

Regardless of the validity of this US Army index – it is certainly illuminating. It took centuries to raise the lethality of weapons by one order of magnitude. After World War II, with the nuclear arms race, quantum jumps are discernible across two orders of magnitude within a few decades.

There are also elements pointing at a finite barrier to further escalation of destructive power per weapon. With the hydrogen bomb, the decreasing marginal utility of further increases in lethality becomes evident. The main reason is not that the size of the diameter of destruction grows only at the rate of the cubic root of yield. This has always been the case, and this narrow margin never prevented the arms race from continuing. Marginality rests on the recipient end: human measures become negligible if compared to potential growth of nuclear fusion. The Soviet SS-18 missile may well represent the ultimate in destructive potential assembled within the nosecone of a single missile.

The second common denominator of arms race dynamics is economic in nature. World military expenditures are growing more rapidly than GNP per capita. Again, this portrait can be honestly challenged. 'World military expenditures' remains a highly disputable aggregate when we consider the problem of currency exchange rates. Yet the upwards trend seems to be unbroken. Time series of performance increases are mostly used to indicate the prolific contribution of R&D for the continuation of the arms race. Numbers of warheads and their carriers (Cochran et al., 1984, pp. 14–15) or more technical data about jet engine performance (Ponomarev, 1984) appear to signal all prospects for a massive continuation of present trends, given the required R&D investment.

The upward curves reflect, however, only half of the story. The potential for a straightforward continuation of these curves certainly is limited. Mary Kaldor has introduced, in a grand analogy to economic analysis, the thesis of diminishing returns to R&D investments in 'ripe' or even 'decaying' technologies (Kaldor, 1982a). The useful life of given lines of technology is finite. And *indeed*, the argument is by no means a theoretical one. Empirical studies clearly show that there are signs of saturation, e.g. in the significant case of nuclear stockpiles (Cochran et al., 1984, p. 14).

The data about nuclear stockpiling indicate several facts not in line with a simplistic hypothesis of an ever-expanding nuclear arms race. First, there is again the notion of saturation, a finite element to the quantitative expansion of the stockpile. The size of the maximum stockpile (25,000 to 30,000 nuclear warheads) as well as the time it was reached (ca. 1965; cf. Cochran et al., 1984, pp. 14–15) leave a lot of room for debate. The recent accord between the two nuclear superpowers to eliminate IRBMs indicates that the definitive answer to the question 'How much is enough?' still remains to be formulated. Second, the pace of the build-up deserves scrutiny. We now know that the first decade of the Cold War saw only a modest build-up of the US nuclear stockpile. The second half of the 1950s represents a steep increase – by a factor of ten over a five-year period

(Cochran et al., 1984). The creation of a minimum deterrent stockpile in the late 1940s led only to a few hundred bombs altogether, a modest program indeed.

Alongside quantitative saturation at levels analytically difficult to understand, there is the technological aspect of limits. The well-known charts of the development of missile accuracy over time may serve as a striking illustration (Sivard, 1976; *Bulletin of Peace Proposals*, 1988; Spitzer, 1987). Normally these charts are also read as indicating unabated progress. Seen from Kaldor's point of view, the diminishing returns in accuracy become apparent. In an even more radical perspective, the curves tend to approach the time axis in an asymptotic manner. To increase the accuracy of latest generation of ICBMs, an outrageous R&D effort would seem needed.

Defenders of the development of the US Army Pershing III missile (a four-stage vehicle with intercontinental range; Cochran et al., 1984, pp. 132–133) have argued that such high-accuracy missiles with a true pin-point hitting ability would make it feasible to concentrate on conventional rather than nuclear weapons. Hence every effort should be made to proceed in missile development towards this end. In fact, however, the most likely outcome – if we compare with today's cruise missiles – would be a military dual-use option, again an expansion of the arms race.

5 Conclusions

In past analysis, peace researchers seemed to have shown a highly instrumental understanding of the R&D element in the qualitative arms race. R&D was seen as merely the gestation stage in the life-cycle of weapons. Only recently have there been questions as to whether the R&D predicament shows some dynamics of its own, and whether the role of R&D could be crucial in fueling the overall arms race.

Furthermore, the dynamics of the qualitative arms race have commonly been seen as a rather isolated phenomenon, with little or no interconnection with other spheres of society. This view does not hold, however. Studies of couplings between arms race dynamics and dynamics in other fields will bring better analytical insight (Thee, 1986a).

My main conclusion is that there indeed exists a strong link between dynamic structures in society and the dynamics of the arms race. Such an approach is likely to prove helpful in understanding the leadership role of US military technology – that the USA normally is in the lead with military-technological innovation. More thorough efforts seek to combine insight about the relative lack of societal dynamism in the Soviet system with the well-known role of Soviet arms technology as a 'catch-up' racer (Albrecht & Nikutta, 1989). The prominent linkage in this view is, besides the regime of politics, that between militarization of R&D and the progress of industrialization. This linkage has long been debated as the relationship between militarism and industrialism (Smith, 1985; Edgerton, 1988).

The R&D paradigm may be helpful in delineating a new concept of militarism: industrial militarism. The conviction that there is a strong influence from industrialism, the serial manufacture of mechanical products on a large scale, on to militarism may be traced both in the socialist and in the parochial critique of modern societies. (The third dimension, the liberal strand of criticism, has for understandable reasons failed to develop into this direction. See Albrecht, 1987.) In order to highlight the less parochial variant: Franziskus Maria Stratmann, OP, a noted Catholic intellectual pacifist of the 1920s, denounced militarism (a) as a consequence of industrialization of state and society, (b) as a consequence of the industrialization of warfare, and (c) as a consequence of the kind of industrial contest which modern war provides (Rajewski & Riesenberger, 1987).

The recent debate – admittedly limited – about a proper analytical understanding of current militarism has also taken this direction. Volker Berghahn, in a careful evaluation of available contributions, finds a new kind of militarism 'of high-technology industrial systems orientated towards and pledged to, mass consumption' and calls for 'future work [. . .] to test the argument presented' (Berghahn, 1981, p. 123). Wilfried von Bredow (1983) appears to support similar conclusions, although less explicitly.

The old-fashioned concept of militarism, albeit in a grossly altered manner, hence appears to be increasingly useful to delineate the complicated interrelationships between civil and military bureaucracies, industry, and the general public, all interacting in the continuation of the arms race. It also appears that the notion of a 'military-industrial complex', the assertion of undue influence of elitist groupings in industrial-military affairs, is now shrinking to become a specific subvariant of the general concern about resurgent militarism.

Established concepts of militarism, with its various roots (liberal criticism of undue military influence in the civilian sphere; the socialist tradition of denouncing it as societal maldevelopment; the parochial concept seeking to combat chiefly the ideology), remain hardly applicable to the problem we face today. Among the phenomena which sustain contemporary militarism, the industrial dimension, R&D for the production of sophisticated weapons, is prominent. The question is then whether there is a special relationship between militarism and industrialism (giving a special momentum to the arms race), and how this special relationship can possibly be specified.

Berghahn mentions a post-modern kind of militarism: he feels it 'likely that one day we may be studying a militarism of a third type: that of a computerized post-industrial no-growth society' (Berghahn, 1981, p. 124). The idea has never been taken up: what does 'the industrial system', or, by now, 'the post-industrial system', actually mean for the militarism which is under scrutiny? Senghaas's call for an extended notion of militarism has likewise remained without substantial response.

Some explanations can be offered for this glaring failure of peace research. There are virtually no peace-related studies, and very few historical studies of a more traditional nature, which have analyzed in depth the three major formations where militarism and industrialism intermeshed in high intensity: Nazi militarism with its impact of modernization, paralleled by Japanese militarism, and 'Red militarism' in the Soviet Union.

The most relevant test for Europe may be research into the interrelationship between militarism and industrialism during Hitler's Third Reich. Yet what the victorious powers prohibited at Potsdam in 1945, Nazi militarism, seems non-existent for the academic history of the Third Reich: Nazi militarism (and its industrial implications) remains a grossly neglected topic (Berghahn, 1981, ch. III). Prussian militarism has led to a great debate in Germany after World War II, however. The question remains, whether Nazi militarism deserves its own analytical concept (possibly linked with the analysis of fascist ideology), or whether it should be understood more properly as a wave of modernization (as a few historical assessments suggest). It may well be that this very combination of a determined striving for industrial modernization, plus a backwards-looking, non-modernist ideology directed to the masses, can explain the two pillars of contemporary militarism/industrialism. This formula would embrace not only Nazi and Imperial Japanese militarism before 1945: potentially, it could cover more recent developments as well.

With reference to literature, the situation is somewhat better with respect to the Soviet Union. There are a number of writings about the question of a Soviet military-industrial complex (Albrecht & Nikutta, 1989; Kapitza, 1988). At least Stalin's Soviet Russia is not a counter-example to the hypothesis about the linkage between militarism and industrialism, and the pre-Gorbachev USSR may also fit into this concept. The political mobilization for war there may remain comparable, at least with a view to the effects, to what happened in Germany and Japan. The principal difference, however, will be found in the aspirations of industry, which in the case of private ownership showed a strong determination to prevail. Industrialists in a non-private, government-oriented political system apparently tend to subsume their sectoralist ambitions. The statement should be read with caution: I argue that a specific linkage, a mutual reinforcement of militarism and industrialism, may exist also in the USSR, but 'Red militarism' and the Soviet road to industrialism do not intermesh with private industrialism in the dynamic way known from Western and Japanese militarism.

One vital topic within the study of R&D and arms race dynamics has apparently failed to attract the attention of peace researchers: basic innovation of explicitly new lines of technology. The brief hint to privately funded R&D programs resulted in, among other things, the insight that the real innovations which have given the USA the decisive edge in military technology over the Soviet Union are not a product of the huge apparatus otherwise set up to turn out exactly this product. The Pentagon and its opposite number(s) in the USSR would appear to have far more in common than features which separate them. Both are enormous bureaucracies with comparable ways of seeking solutions to technological challenges. And both apparently fail to turn out really revolutionary innovations, the 'quantum jumps' which in fact both contesters are striving for.

Nor will methods applied on both sides in the past be appropriate for the future. In the USSR, the Politburo chose 'shock therapy' for design teams, asking for excessive jumps in technology in combination with excessive rewards. The political leadership itself used marathon-meetings for briefing about the particulars of new tanks or fighters (something incomprehensible for Western Cabinets). There is no future in this heavy approach, given the intricacies of various lines of laser technology in military application, or the exotics of VHSIC computer chips. On the other side, all tricks in contracting techniques accessible to the Pentagon may have been exploited in the past, yet with little prospect of finding another, superior system of incentives which might induce industry to make a 'great leap forward'. The analytical assessment of those 'quantum jumps' and their effect on the arms race seems to require a far more general approach than the one suggested and accepted in this presentation.

Peace research must also, in addition to improving analysis along the lines suggested, debate the conversion of R&D to peaceful purposes (Albrecht, 1986a). The general conversion debate has tended to overlook precisely those problems which would arise if the major contesters should ever opt to regear their high stakes in the military application of science into alternative directions. The great debate about ways out of the arms race certainly will also have to deal with the intricacies of military R&D. Otherwise, the observation made by the Red Queen to Alice will continue to be true, that participants in the arms race have no choice, because 'it takes all the running [they] can do, to stay in the same place'.[5]

Notes

1. Any 'absolute' weapon indeed would end, at least in theory, further R&D and the arms race. A number of weapons have been labeled 'absolute' in the course of history, without such a consequence. The atom bomb also presented such claims (see Brodie, 1946).
2. See the self-critical remark by Senghaas (1986, p. 11).
3. Cf. e.g. the assessment by Müller (1987), where the above-noted action-reaction concept is labeled *Legitimationsgewäsch* (gossip about legitimacy; Müller appears to mean *Legitimität* instead of 'legitimation', because he does not challenge the formally legitimate aspect of the phenomenon).
4. Personal comment by Henry Ergas of OECD. See also his 'Does Technology Policy Matter?' (Paris: OECD, mimeo, 1988).
5. Lewis Carroll [Charles L. Dodgson], *Through the Looking-Glass. What Alice Found There*. London: Macmillan, 1872.

ULRICH ALBRECHT, b. 1941, Dipl. Ing. in Aeronautical Engineering (1967), Ph.D. in

Political Science and Economics (Stuttgart University, 1970); Professor of Peace and Conflict Research at the Free University of Berlin, Department of Political Science (1972–). Author of articles and books, mainly in German, about arms trade, conversion, and international relations.

Chapter 7

Science-Based Military Technology as a Driving Force behind the Arms Race*

MAREK THEE
International Peace Research Institute, Oslo

1 Militarization of R&D: Order of Magnitude

'Military R&D' is here used to subsume mission-oriented R&D activity comprising basic and applied research, with the development, testing, and experimental production of new weapons and weapon systems. The term also covers the improvement and modernization of existing weapons and weapon systems.

No exact data on the size and dimension of global military R&D are available. Secrecy is here practised to the extreme, far more than in civilian R&D. A few Western countries do publish some figures, but their accuracy is uncertain and may not disclose the full range of involvement. Various aspects of military R&D can be concealed under diverse budgetary expenditures: in the case of the United States, for instance, nuclear-weapon R&D in the books of the Energy Department, while military space exploration goes under the budget of the National Aeronautics and Space Administration (NASA). The Soviet Union does not publish any data on its massive military R&D;[1] nor does China, another of the six major powers engaged in military R&D.

However, some useful indicators on the order of magnitude of world military R&D can be found in existing scholarly computations on global manpower and expenditure on military R&D.

Colin Norman of the Worldwatch Institute, in his 1981 study on the state of science and technology in the 1980s, produced an estimate of the 1980 world R&D budget 'based on data from national sources and international agencies'. The figures, as Norman stresses, 'are approximate and should be regarded as no more than a rough guide to relative expenditure'. Norman's estimates of the 1980 global R&D budget are reproduced in Table 7.1.

Norman concludes that the 'feeding of the world's military machine is thus the predominant occupation of the global research and development

---

* A longer version of this chapter has been published as Thee (1988). It includes a discussion of the impact of military R&D on development.

Table 7.1 The global R&D budget (%)

Military	24
Basic research	15
Space	8
Energy	8
Health	7
Information processing	5
Transportation	5
Pollution control	5
Agriculture	3
Others	20
Total	100%

Source: Norman 1981, p. 72

enterprise' (Norman, 1981, p. 72). The exact proportion of global R&D expenditures devoted to military R&D still remains a matter for further study; this relates mainly to the military share of basic research, space (satellites), energy (nuclear), information processing (computer science), transportation (avionics), and 'other' types of research. Assuming even that only a tiny percentage of the above R&D endeavours is of a military nature, this may well yield a total figure of 30–35% of the 1980 global R&D budget devoted to military R&D. Moreover, we should note the rapid recent growth of military R&D – at least one-third from 1980 to 1986, according to SIPRI (Acland-Hood, 1987, p. 153). Thus, today's share of military R&D in total R&D may be still larger.

The comprehensive 1982 UN study entitled *The Relationship between Disarmament and Development* contains a thorough discussion of the bearing of military R&D on total R&D. Central here is the question of opportunity costs lost for development, due to the concentration on military R&D. This study recalls that the UN study on *Disarmament and Development* ten years earlier estimated the share of military R&D at 40% of global R&D expenditures. Reflecting on this estimate, the new UN study takes a more conservative line, stating that 'the most recent estimates point to a share of resources used for military R&D of the order of 20 to 25% as regards both manpower and expenditure'. Still, the study adds, 'if a more accurate accounting were possible, the figure presented above would almost certainly appear conservative' (United Nations, 1982, para. 150).

The 1987 *SIPRI Yearbook* has calculated: 'World spending on military research and development (R&D) is roughly a quarter of world spending on all R&D and in 1986 was approximately $85–100 billion a year at current prices' (Acland-Hood, 1987, p. 153). Further: 'Of the world's four million R&D scientists and engineers, probably over three-quarters of a million are engaged in military R&D. If support people are included, there are probably at least one and a half million people in the world working in military R&D' (op. cit., p. 154). As to the national distribution of this manpower, the *Yearbook* adds: 'Two-thirds to three-quarters of all military R&D scientists and engineers are either in the USA or the USSR;

more are found in the USSR, where research is more labour-intensive' (ibid.).

This may be a cautious estimate. Eugene Skolnikoff of the Massachusetts Institute of Technology has a higher assessment. Referring to R&D expenditures in 1987, he concludes:

> The funds devoted to R&D worldwide have reached astonishing proportions. No accurate tabulation is available, but a rough calculation would indicate a total of some US $400–500 billion per year. Of that amount, a reasonable estimate, probably conservative, is that one-third to one-half is motivated directly or indirectly by military/security concerns. (Skolnikoff, 1987, p. 16)

Skolnikoff divides this estimate of global expenditure devoted to R&D into US $240 billion each for the USA and USSR; US $70 billion spent in Western Europe, US $40 billion in Japan, and the remainder in the rest of the world (Skolnikoff, 1987, p. 16).

Thus, according to Skolnikoff, world military R&D would currently be consuming US $133–200 billion a year, or even higher, up to US $167–250 billion. This is about twice the SIPRI estimate of the size of global expenditure for military R&D. On the other hand, the two assessments are similar as concerns the national-geographical distribution of the global R&D venture. SIPRI states that the world's six biggest spenders on R&D – the USA, the USSR, FRG, France, the UK, and Japan – account for some 80% of world expenditures on total R&D; the six biggest spenders on military R&D, with China here replacing Japan, account for some 90–95% of world expenditure, with the USA and the USSR in the mid-1980s responsible for altogether 80–84% of this expenditure (*SIPRI Yearbook*, 1987, pp. 153–154). Characteristically, the major powers have a share in military R&D far higher than in total R&D, with the USA and the USSR again occupying a distinctly predominant position in both manpower and expenditures.

Coming from different scholarly sources, the above computations may not be fully comparable. However, taken as a whole they reveal a situation in which military R&D is expanding rapidly and appropriating the lion's share of world R&D. Recent years have seen the spread of military R&D to almost all disciplines and branches of science and technology – from physics, chemistry, information technology, and space exploration to medicine and social sciences, so as to master war-fighting capability in all environments. Clearly, then, this evolution indicates a process of preemption of civilian R&D. This is done both quantitatively, by arrogating a massive part of resources earmarked for R&D; and qualitatively, by penetrating and assuming control in key segments of total R&D.

Another indication of the magnitude and impact of military R&D is the share of military expenditures devoted to military R&D on the one hand, as against the share of national resources earmarked for all R&D and diverted to military R&D on the other hand.

According to SIPRI, before World War II military R&D consumed on the average less than 1% of the military expenditures of major powers (Huisken, 1974, pp. 126–127). These were themselves, in the years 1925–38, in real value more than ten times lower than in the 1980s (Tullberg, 1986, p. 17). Today, however, if we take 1981–84 averages, we find that military R&D as a percentage of military expenditure amounted to between 11 and 13% of the military spending of the major Western powers: the USA, the UK, and France (Acland-Hood, 1986, p. 29). Military R&D has become the fastest growing military expenditure item of major powers. For the USSR, no precise data are available on these or other military expenditures. However, there can be no doubt, given the drive of the USSR to catch up and even surpass the US performance, that Soviet outlays on military R&D are at least equal to those in the West, if not larger.

2 Armaments: A Race in Modern Military Technology

This burgeoning expansion of military R&D has served as a powerful impulsion of armaments, generating a dramatic transformation in the nature and intensity of the arms race. Between 1948 and 1985, the volume of global military expenditures increased fivefold, in constant prices (Tullberg, 1986, p. 18). Though this escalation may also be attributed to various politico-military circumstances, a vital role has been played by the shift in the centre of gravity of armaments: from competition in quantities, to rivalry in science-based military technology. The emergence of newer and newer weapon systems has accelerated the process of obsolescence and replacement of military hardware. The end-result has been an unprecedented increase in the cost of arms and in the destructive power of the war machine.

Command of the most advanced military technology has become the crucial variable of military efficiency, with qualitative superiority a central objective in the arms race. This pursuit of qualitative advantages has trickled down, from the competition between the giants, to regional and local conflicts. As the arms race has turned into a global phenomenon, its horizontal quantitative expansion has become dominated by a qualitative-vertical race. In the process, highly sophisticated conventional arms – supersonic jet fighters, armed vehicles and artillery, air-to-air and air-to-surface missiles, guidance and radar systems, and assault ships – have filled the arsenals of Third World countries, finding their way on to the battlefields of Asia, Africa, and Latin America (Brzoska & Ohlson, 1987). At the same time, the proliferation of nuclear weapons and of nuclear weapon technology has acquired alarming proportions: by the 1980s not only were the nuclear stocks of the major powers saturated with stupendous quantities and a bewildering variety of nuclear explosives, but nuclear weapon technology and know-how had spread to several 'threshold countries' in politically and strategically sensitive spots of the globe –

countries that, at a moment of crisis, might indeed use such acquired capability (cf. Spector, 1984; Lomas, 1988).² Through the impulse of high military technology born in R&D laboratories, our world has become a far more dangerous place to live in. Today, the very survival of the human species is in jeopardy.

These advances in science-based military technology and their application in armaments have proceeded thanks to major scientific-technological breakthroughs followed by the conjunction of different technologies in the plants of military R&D, and through the carefully pursued modernization, improvement, and refinement of new weapons and weapon systems. This mission-impelled exertion of military R&D has generated a revolution – or rather a perpetual ongoing revolutionary process – in the development of implements of war, in the art of warfare, and in strategic thinking.

Of the basic military scientific-technological breakthroughs of the post-WWII period, three are of monumental importance:

(a) the epoch-making discovery of nuclear weapons, which increased, almost infinitely, the explosive destructive power of arms;
(b) the quantum/qualitative leap in the mobility and reach of modern weaponry, through the development of such high-speed intercontinental carriers of nuclear and conventional weapons as supersonic bombers, intercontinental ballistic missiles, submarine-launched ballistic missiles, multiple independently targetable re-entry vessels, and long-range cruise missiles;
(c) the extension of the military thrust from land, sea, and air to the near-orbit and outer-space environment, through the launching of satellites and the progressive militarization of outer space (Thee, 1986b).

These accomplishments in military technology have been accompanied and furthered by constant progress in a range of specific technologies. These include nuclear fission and fusion techniques, micro-electronics, computer sciences, solid-fuel rocketry, a variety of sensors, artificial intelligence, and what is otherwise subsumed under 'new emerging technologies'.

Military R&D has as its chief day-to-day objective to operationalize the achieved knowledge in science and technology in new weapon design and development, so as to make arms more instrumental and efficient. Thus nuclear warheads have undergone a basic transformation from unwieldly behemoths to versatile miniaturized versions, their weight-to-yield ratio constantly perfected; missiles have been made more expedient in accuracy, speed, range, manoeuvrability, non-detectability, penetration, and target acquisition; precision-guided munitions, in themselves a revolutionary leap, have been developed and improved. Updating and upgrading the quality of arms has affected almost each of the millions of small component units of modern weapons systems.

This scientific-technological exertion has had a profound effect on the quantities and qualities of the military arsenals, especially nuclear stockpiles. Up till the late 1950s, in line with the ongoing modernization of nuclear arms and the shift from the fission to the fusion bomb, the megatonnage of nuclear stockpiles grew immensely, and nuclear warheads multiplied. But from the 1960s onward, the achieved technological perfection of these weapons brought about a radical change: while operational capability was further streamlined, high redundancies were disposed of and obsolete non-functional weapons eliminated. For instance, according to official sources, the megatonnage of the US nuclear stockpile was reduced between 1960 and 1980 by a factor of four. Out of 71 different types of nuclear warheads manufactured between 1945 and 1986, 42 types have since been fully retired (Cochran et al., 1987, p. 5). Another example was the 27 October 1983 Ottawa decision of NATO defence ministers to reduce unilaterally the European nuclear build-up by 1,400 expendable theatre and battlefield nuclear weapons.

Bearing in mind these points, we might wonder if the December 1987 US–Soviet agreement on eliminating intermediate-range nuclear forces (INF) – important as it is from the viewpoint of improving the international political climate – was simply not one further step in this trend of getting rid of expendable weapons. On the one hand, intermediate-range nuclear weapons were aimed at targets already well covered by the many long-range ground-, air- and sea-based nuclear weapons. On the other hand, the INF accord – and perhaps even further partial cuts in nuclear stockpiles – would seem to reflect more than merely a trend towards redundancy-reduction. It may also reflect a rethinking of the very war-fighting utility of nuclear weapons – weapons which by their overkill capability and massive radioactive fall-out threaten the survival of assailed and assailant alike. This has been explicitly spelled out by the policy conclusions of the January 1988 *Discriminate Deterrence* report elaborated by the Commission on Integrated Long-Term Strategy set up by the Reagan Administration. Composed of thirteen high-level US strategists, including three former National Security Advisors (Henry A. Kissinger, Zbigniew Brzezinski, and William A. Clark), this Commission stated explicitly that 'we cannot rely on threats expected to provoke our own annihilation if carried out . . . we must have militarily effective responses that can limit destruction if we are not to invite destruction of what we are defending' (*Discriminate Deterrence*, 1988, p. 2). Similar sentiments have been repeatedly aired recently by Soviet spokespersons as well: 'Were nuclear war ever to become a reality, it would inevitably put an end to the existence of mankind. No one wants to join a suicide club' (Beglov, 1988, p. 35).

Today's nuclear weapons cannot possibly be used in any sound military way, nor for any sound political purpose. Moreover, in the case of INF weapons, both sides have seemed uneasy about their vulnerability to false alarms, computer failure, or human error. A matter for deep concern has been the danger of a sudden nuclear conflagration in times of crisis which could not be brought under control with still imperfect command, control, communication, and intelligence (C^3I) technologies. This is underlined in the *Discriminate Deterrence* report, which stresses that 'control of space in wartime is becoming increasingly important . . . our space capabilities – critical for communications, intelligence, and control of our forces – must be made survivable or replaceable' (*Discriminate Deterrence*, 1988, p. 2; see also Carter, 1987).

Clearly, today the index of military power and efficiency is tabulated more in technological terms than in sheer numbers of military hardware items. As for nuclear arsenals, the time seems ripe for major cuts, so as (to restate the slogan of President Reagan) 'to render them impotent and obsolete'. Yet we should also remain on guard against replacing them with technologically even more effective and ominous weapons. This may especially be the case with the SDI-impelled race to develop new generations of nuclear and exotic weapons based, as the 1972 Anti-Ballistic Missile Treaty so prophetically foresaw, on 'other physical principles'.

3 A Rush to New Frontiers of Military Technology

Assessed from the angle of effective war-fighting capabilities in the nuclear age, two generations of military R&D accomplishments have generated in the 1980s a process of future-oriented rethinking of existing military potentials, with a view to scientific-technological refinement and enhancement of weapon systems to suit true war-fighting and war-winning objectives (cf. Kissinger, 1979; Keeny & Panofsky, 1981–82; Halperin, 1987). The main concerns of the military, the strategists, and the military R&D community have centred on the vulnerabilities inherent in the devastating potential of nuclear weapons; on the absence of defence against nuclear arms; and on the constraints intrinsic in the offensive potential of nuclear weapons, to attain a true war-fighting and war-winning capability by operationally combining offence and defence (in the Clausewitzian tradition). Other concerns have related to scientific-technological exigencies for conventional weapons in the new military environment, and to the consequences of possible new breakthroughs in military R&D for the superpower balance of forces.

From these considerations, several new concepts have emerged as to the direction of the military scientific-technological endeavour. The greatest impact here has been made by the Reagan Administration's Strategic Defense Initiative (SDI). Essentially, SDI aimed to take advantage of high-level esoteric technologies to build a space-based country-wide shield against nuclear missiles. This would mean an offence-defence strategic capacity, complementing nuclear and conventional offensive capabilities with space-strike weapons: a perfect scenario for a first-strike capability. Yet this 'Star War' vision has met with strong criticism, especially pointing out that the SDI scheme still lies beyond the reach of available technology. In consequence, several derivative 'strategic defence' scenarios have evolved, calling for the establishment of a ground-based anti-missile defence system to cover missile sites, command centres, and other military installations: this is the concept of Star War II (Blackaby, 1986).

In a typical action-reaction process, also the Soviet Union has intensified its pursuit of new technologies for ballistic missile defence based on 'other physical principles'. Its professed goal has been to develop cheaper countermeasures against space-strike weapons (cf. Brokaw, 1988). In these controversies, military R&D has appeared, even within the concerned scholarly community, as a compelling hedge against the military scientific-technological race of the adversary.

Two exotic breakthrough technologies, earth- and space-based, related to 'other physical principles' have become the centrepiece of a new fierce arms race: hypervelocity Kinetic Energy Weapons (KEWs) and Directed Energy Weapons (DEWs) (Jasani, 1986). KEWs derive their destructive potential from the very speed and momentum of electromagnetically or rocket-propelled objects directed by railguns or laser beams. DEWs, on the other hand, rely on high-energy chemical or nuclear-pumped X-ray lasers, and may appear in the form of particle beams or so-called radio-frequency weapons. The actual development of KEWs seems more advanced and has become the main current in SDI exertions, earmarked for deployment by the mid-1990s (Weller & Bruce, 1987; Patel & Bloembergen, 1987).

In the meantime, the *Discriminate Deterrence* report, commissioned in 1986 by the Reagan Administration, provides a glimpse into the intended course of the general military scientific-technological push into the next century.

> Military technology will change substantially in the next 20 years. . . . If Soviet military research continues to exceed our own, it will erode the qualitative edge on which we have long relied. . . . Both our conventional and nuclear posture should be based on a mix of offensive and defensive systems. . . . We need strategic defense. . . . We need a capability for conventional counter-offensive operations deep into enemy territory. . . . We and our allies need to exploit emerging technologies of precision, control, and intelligence that can provide our conventional forces with more selective and more effective capabilities for destroying military targets. . . . We will need capabilities for discriminate nuclear strikes. . . .
>
> Carefully designed reductions in nuclear arms could lead to a safer balance of offensive and defensive forces. . . . We must maintain a mix of survivable strategic offensive arms and command and control capabilities. . . .
>
> In the Third World, no less than in developed countries, US strategy should seek to maximize our technological advantages. . . . Here too we will want to use smart missiles that can apply force in a discriminate fashion and avoid collateral damage to civilians. (*Discriminate Deterrence*, 1988, pp. 1–3, 21)

A special chapter on 'Managing technology' stresses the programmes of 'highest priority' to widen the options to future US Presidents:

> We would assign a high priority – higher than it has been getting in recent years

– to spending in the accounts for basic research and advanced development. Among the programs meeting these criteria, four seem especially urgent:

1. the integration of 'low-observable' (Stealth) systems into our force structure;
2. 'smart' weapons – precision-guided munitions that combine range and high accuracy;
3. ballistic missile defense; and
4. space capabilities needed for wartime operations. (*Discriminate Deterrence*, 1988, p. 49)

In sum, the study envisages the pursuit of futuristic technologies, including SDI ballistic missile and space technologies, to arrive at a nuclear-conventional and offensive-defensive war-fighting and war-winning capability – and this on a global scale. It envisages 'discriminate' nuclear strikes, military operations deep into the territories of the adversary, and 'discriminate' war-fighting in the Third World.

In operational terms, as a military correspondent of the *International Herald Tribune* puts it, the study postulates that 'the West should concentrate on high-technology weapons capable of delivering nuclear strikes and move away from weapons that threaten nuclear Armageddon ... [i.e.] without triggering a massive reprisal.' Moreover: 'the report presses the case for new technology by saying that missiles can be accurate enough for conventional warheads to provide the same long-range capabilities as nuclear weapons do now' (Fitchett, 1988, pp. 1, 5).

This blueprint for 'discriminate' war-fighting, charting the course of military technology into the 21st century, in fact means projecting ongoing military R&D into the future. Given the current parallel course followed by military laboratories, and the correspondence of high-tech military deployments by the USA and the USSR, the US scheme can be seen as marking the general direction of the East–West technological arms race.

The process should be perceived not in static but in highly dynamic terms of the technological race. While negotiations are proceeding for 'carefully designed reductions in nuclear arms' (as stated in the *Discriminate Deterrence* report), military R&D laboratories East and West are working full speed to achieve new technological breakthroughs, to design, develop, and produce new types of weapons and weapon systems. Again, by default of Soviet openness in this domain, US pieces of information must be taken as indicative. Thus *US News & World Report* stated in autumn 1987:

> Over the next three years, nearly 50 major weapon systems are scheduled to move from prototype to production. . . .
> Since 1981, military research and development has grown twice as fast as overall Pentagon spending. . . . According to the House Armed Services Committee, every dollar for military R&D generates about $10 in subsequent defense spending. Pentagon planners concede that early orders for 47 new weapon systems expected to come on line during the next five years will cost more than $150 billion. . . . In the next five years, more than a half-dozen aircraft are scheduled to begin production. . . . New generations of strategic missiles – including the Trident 2 D-5 and the single warhead Midgetman – are

also in the pipeline. . . . The Pentagon puts so much into R&D that nobody can back out of it. (*US News & World Report*, 1987, pp. 32–33)

These developments are seldom fully open to public view. Whenever concern about the race in military technology is voiced, arguments of national security are evoked to justify military R&D. There follow then odd additional contentions that military R&D is beneficial for arms control since it produces better tools for arms control and verification, and that it actually has contributed to reductions in nuclear megatonnage and types of weapon systems.

There may well be some truth in such argumentation. However, as with all half-truths, this tends to obscure basic reality. It should be obvious that national security is not enhanced but weakened by the spiralling arms build-up. Likewise, the massive military R&D investments and constant new inventions in intelligence – be they different kinds of spy satellites, sensor technologies, or C^3I installations – can hardly serve the arms control exercise: on the contrary, they stimulate the arms race and tend to perfect war-fighting capabilities. And concerning the reduction of nuclear arsenals, as we have seen, this has gone hand in hand with progress in their efficiency.

The race in modern military technology has a distinct destabilising effect on the military environment, as well as marring the climate of international relations. The pursuit of technological 'fixes' for arms control only clouds over the need for genuine disarmament and for political solutions to our arms race predicament.

4 Military R&D and Armaments Dynamics

From the foregoing analysis of the quantitative and qualitative aspects of the militarization of R&D, we hope to have indicated the extent and role of military R&D in fuelling armaments and sustaining the momentum of the arms race.

Contemporary armaments dynamics in the East–West context are a multi-dimensional and multi-causal phenomenon. From the perspective of the military competition between the superpowers, there is mutual stimulation between the internal and external motor forces of the arms race, as expressed in action-reaction or mirror-image paradigms. This is illustrated in Table 7.2.

However, from a broader methodological point of view, taking into account economic, socio-political, and systemic factors, we must differentiate between underlying structural determinants on the one hand, and a set of behavioural-doctrinal and functional determinants to the arms race on the other hand (see Thee, 1986a). These correspond roughly to the dialectical relationship between the material base and ideological-functional superstructure: structural determinants match the substantial material base, and the behavioural-doctrinal and functional determinants are akin

SCIENCE-BASED MILITARY TECHNOLOGY 115

Table 7.2 Action-reaction in the superpower competition

		Nuclear weapons				Conventional weapons		
US	1945	Atomic bomb	1949	USSR	US	1952	Main battle tank	1958 USSR
US	1946	Electronic computer	1951	USSR	USSR	1949	Nuclear-powered submarine	1958 USSR
US	1948	Intercontinental bomber	1955	USSR	US	1955	Large-deck aircraft carrier	1975 USSR
US	1952	Thermonuclear bomb	1953	USSR	US	1955	Wire-guided anti-tank missile	1972 USSR
USSR	1957	Intercontinental ballistic missile (ICBM)	1958	US	USSR	1959	Photo reconnaissance satellite	1962 USSR
USSR	1957	Man-made satellite	1958	US	US	1960	Supersonic bomber	1975 USSR
USSR	1958	Early-warning radar	1960	US	US	1960	Computer-guided missile	1968 USSR
US	1960	Submarine-launched ballistic missile (SLBM)	1968	USSR	US	1961	Nuclear-powered aircraft carrier	1992 USSR
US	1966	Multiple re-entry vehicle (MRV)	1968	USSR	USSR	1961	Surface-to-air missile	1963 US
USSR	1968	Anti-ballistic missile (ABM)	1972	US	US	1962	Long-range fighter bomber	1973 USSR
US	1970	Multiple independently targetable re-entry vehicle (MIRV)	1975	USSR	US	1964	Air-to-surface missile	1968 USSR
USSR	1971	Sea-launched cruise missile	1982	US	USSR	1970	High-speed attack submarine	1976 US
US	1983	Neutron bomb	199?	USSR	US	1972	Television-guided missile	1987 USSR
US	1985	New strategic bomber	1987	USSR	USSR	1972	Heavy attack helicopter	1982 US
USSR	1987	Single warhead, mobile ICBM	1992	US	US	1975	Jet-propelled combat aircraft	1983 USSR
US	199?	Stealth bomber	199?	USSR	US	1976	Large amphibious assault ship	1978 USSR
					USSR	1978	Multiple-launch rocket system	1983 US
					US	1987	Binary (chemical) weapons	199? USSR

Source: Sivard 1987, p. 14; reprinted with permission. © World Priorities, Washington DC.

to the reciprocally reactive phenomenon in the attitudinal and operational superstructure.

Two primary motor forces are at work. The first one is the management of the political economy of armaments, dominated by what has been subsumed as the military-industrial complex, i.e. the socio-political corporate constituencies most interested and involved in the procurement of arms. These include the military, the military industry, and increasingly the state-political bureaucracy with its keen interest in armaments as an instrument of policy and diplomacy (obviously true for both the East and the West). The second major force here is the uninterrupted forceful exertion of military R&D.

These two structural forces interact in a reciprocal way: the technological allure of power from the military laboratories activates the various armament constituencies in pursuit of more and better arms: and vice versa, the executives of armaments constituencies relate back to military R&D their specific requirements for the assortments of arms. The actual interplay between these two fundamental arms race determinants is essentially a problem of the egg and the hen. At technological breakthrough junctures – as in the pursuit and development of nuclear weapons – the scientific-technological community generally takes the lead; on the other hand, requirements for improvements and modernization of weapons, if not the outcome of the laboratory R&D momentum, often come from the armaments constituencies as well.

On the superstructural level, the arms race is nurtured by ideological dogma and perceptional and attitudinal asymmetries, as well as by the personal idiosyncrasies of individual leaders. A potent stimulus comes today from rigid military doctrines such as 'nuclear deterrence'. This is a speculative tenet with no hard evidence to validate or invalidate it. It may seem to possess a ring of plausibility: however, the historical record of deterrence theories like 'si vis pacem para bellum' (if you desire peace, prepare for war) is unequivocal. In the long run, this doctrine has served not to preserve peace but to sustain preparation for war, indeed not infrequently leading to war.

Between the structural base and the doctrinal-behavioural superstructure lie functional energizers of the arms race (Figure 7.1). Chief among them we find bureaucratic politics combined with institutional inertia; this is reflected in the way the arms flow is amplified in the protracted competitive process from the laboratory, through production, and up to acquisition and deployment. In a mix of clashes and compromises between the various corporate armaments constituencies, including the three branches of the armed forces, the numbers and varieties of weapons get levelled up to the highest common denominator.

As a totality, armament dynamics are highly influenced by the thrust of modern science-based military technology. Various ingredients of military technology and the impulse from military R&D permeate all aspects and levels of the base and superstructure of the armaments momentum: the

Figure 7.1 *Great-power armaments dynamics*

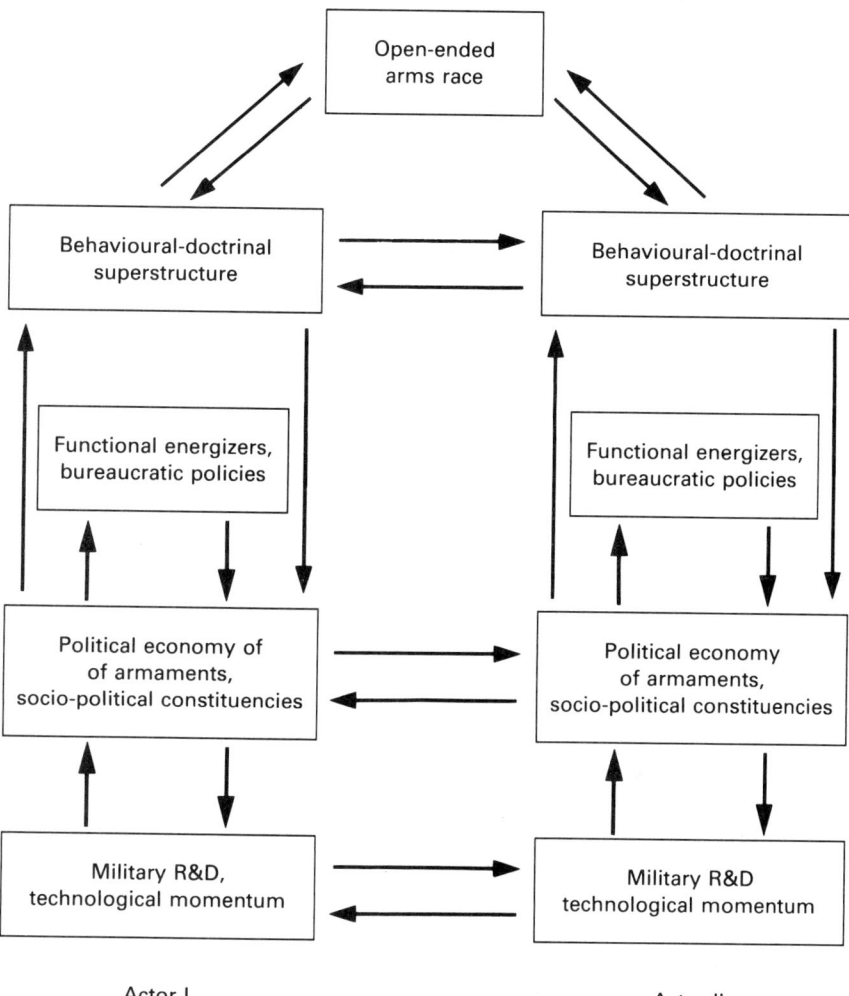

structural, behavioural-doctrinal, and functional corridors of the arms race. In particular, military R&D too often acts to pre-empt the political decision-making process. By sketching captivating technological visions of force-aggrandizement, and expounding narrow, one-directional options at moments of decision, military technologists actually leave the decision-makers with little alternative choice (see York, 1976, p. 11).[3] A good recent example of the influence exerted by hawkish sections of the military scientific-technological community on the political decision-making process can be seen in the circumstances of the launching of the Strategic

Defense Initiative. As is now widely known, the inspiration for SDI came from the military laboratories (Blackaby, 1986).

Assessed in its entirety, the impact of military R&D on the arms race emanates not only from its quantitative weight – the million or more top scientists and engineers employed by military R&D, and the hundred billion dollars or so feeding the military laboratories East and West each year – but more so from the tight institutional set-up close to the seats of power, and its mode of operation that invigorates and perpetuates the arms race. Military R&D is a prestigious establishment, the 'tail that wags the armaments dog' (DeWitt, 1984; Stein & Hippel, 1986).

We need to perceive clearly the work regularities and operational imperatives of military R&D. These are embedded:

- in the years- and decades-long *lead-times and gestation periods* of research, design, development, repeated testing, prototype production, and product improvement that infuse constancy and petrify the arms race. The moment a long-haul new weapon project is undertaken, and corporate support behind it builds up, any withdrawal becomes extremely difficult, even should the weapon prove faulty (cf. the history of the MX missile and the B1 bomber);
- in the *follow-on imperative* driven by scientific curiosity, ambitional cravings, and professional routine, requiring the pursuit of excellence and constant perfection of produced materials. This also requires alternating the development of arms of offence with arms of defence and vice versa, on the assumption that the adversary is certain to acquire similar or even better weapons; the result is to end up racing against one's own achievements. Evidently, more than in other domains of R&D, military R&D is conscious of requirements for high-tech performance, with the very R&D process becoming a continuum without any specific end to the scientific-technological exertion and with little regard for the costs involved. No new opening can be left unheeded and new venues have to be sought with utmost vigour; each new stage in the R&D endeavour becomes a starting-point for a fresh departure to yet another round in the arms spiral. Achieved capacities have to be maintained and extended. There is a self-stimulating effect in the 'follow-on-imperative': the more advanced the technological race, the greater the reliance on military R&D. Consequently, military R&D itself has a propensity to grow and intensify its prowess;
- in *worst-case projections and planning*, far beyond prudent assessment of the achievements and capabilities of the adversary. Part of this propensity stems from the general secretiveness of the armaments endeavour, further intensified by the nervousness, fear, and uncertainty that pervade technological competition. This then generates the urge towards pre-emption, towards over-design and over-reaction – a drive out of proportion with real challenges; it institutionalizes excess.

All of the above operational imperatives of military R&D meet and intertwine. The synergetic effect is to routinize and petrify the thrust of the arms race. The non-synchronized efforts of R&D in East and West, reinforced by perceptional asymmetries, amplify this momentum. Cycles of moves and countermoves, crossing each other in unexpected ways, put their imprint on the arms race. Weapons in the armouries of today are thought to be obsolete, while those on the drawing boards project the arms race further into the future.

Trying to depict the arms race drive generated by military R&D, the scientific community has coined the term 'technological imperative'. By this is meant, as formulated by Wolfgang Panofsky, that 'new technology tends to generate its own momentum' (Panofsky, 1981). Anatol Rapoport has defined the technological imperative as follows:

> The technological imperative can be seen as a massive compulsion to engage the full potential of scientific knowledge in the service of the war machine. The compulsion is inherent in the self-propelling dynamics of burgeoning technological progress. The ever-increasing complexity of weapons systems necessitates a further increase in the complexity of the supporting systems, which, in turn, creates opportunities for making weapon systems even more sophisticated. . . . When we consider that by analogy with similar processes in other fields of endeavour, the burgeoning complexity of weapon systems is conceived as 'progress', we realize how strong are the pressures for escalation (Rapoport, 1987, pp. 176–177).

Expansion is inherent in the very nature of military R&D. The uninterrupted innovative process of military R&D generates abundancies of weapons and weapon systems. In it lies the push which has produced the enormous redundancies in the nuclear arsenal (cf. McNamara & Bethe, 1986, p. 127). This innovative process is also responsible for weapon systems which have 'evolved without a well-defined conception of why they were needed, and without an assessment of their full implications', as was the case with the emergence of long-range cruise missiles and MIRVs (Betts, 1981, p. 1; see also York, 1973, p. 23).

5 Conclusion

In sum, no matter how contemporary armament dynamics are conceived in theory and however they are described in their multi-causal complexity, we must recognize the central role of the running drive of military R&D. High military technology dominates priorities in the arms race. Military R&D has become the crucial variable in armament dynamics.

Let us close by reiterating the statement made in the UN study on the relationship between disarmament and development: 'One of the most conspicuous distinguishing features of the military scene since the Second World War has been the extraordinary rapid rate of change in weapon technology. It is this feature of the post-war arms race that is primarily responsible for the unique intensity of this race' (United Nations, 1982, para. 146).

Notes

1. Soviet secrecy on armaments and military R&D expenditures should be of special concern. If the Soviet Union is serious about disarmament and development, as it persistently claims, it should be interested and helpful in making the armaments machine more transparent by revealing its dimensions and mode of operation. One should hope that Secretary-General Gorbachev's promise, in his message to the 1987 UN International Conference on the Relationship between Disarmament and Development, to reveal exact data on Soviet armaments in line with 'glasnost and openness' so as 'to come up to a realistic comparison of military budgets' will indeed be put into effect.

2. 'Threshold countries' are generally considered to be India, Pakistan, South Africa, Israel, Argentina, and Brazil. Aspiring to acquire nuclear weapons are also Iraq and Libya.

3. In this case, York is describing the circumstances surrounding the US decision to proceed from the production of the atomic bomb to the development of the hydrogen bomb.

MAREK THEE, b. 1918, M.A. in Journalism, Dr. in Political Science, and Dr.hab. in Contemporary History; Senior Research Fellow, PRIO (1968–88); Editor, *Bulletin of Peace Proposals* (1970–88); currently Senior Research Fellow Emeritus, PRIO; main research interest: the impact of science and technology on peace, war, and development.

Chapter 8
Towards an Historical Sociology of Nuclear Weapons Technologies

DONALD MACKENZIE
Department of Sociology, University of Edinburgh

1 Arms Dynamics and Technological Change

To assert the centrality of technological change to the processes of armament and disarmament is, at least since 1945, to assert a truism. Trite the point may be. Exaggerated it sometimes is: Cynthia Enloe (1983, p. 8) is right to remind us that a military force is more than 'what it launches'. True, however, it remains.

William McNeill's *The Pursuit of Power* (1983) and more recently Michael Mann's *The Sources of Social Power* (1986) remind us how intertwined our capacity to control each other and our use of material artefacts have always been; indeed, a provocative argument can be made that it is precisely our use of technology (including writing, irrigation, buildings, transport, etc., as well as weaponry) to control each other that sets us apart from other primates (Strum & Latour, 1984). Ever since systematic technical innovation in weaponry began – it is scarcely more than two centuries old – state power has come to depend more and more on technical change. Those who wish to build up the power of states, and those who wish to dismantle it, cannot help but attend to this topic.

They will find a large academic literature to help them, a literature full of insights and replete with fascinating case studies.[1] Yet it is notoriously hard to reach well-founded general conclusions on the basis of this literature; that difficulty, indeed, was one rationale for holding the symposium on armaments dynamics which led to this book.

The overall difficulty of generalizing from case studies is intensified when it comes to trying to use them to assess the role of technological change in arms dynamics. Here we find sharply contrasting theoretical positions. To the extent that we can identify an 'official' view of arms dynamics, it is of course that the process begins with rational assessment, by military and political leaders, of the threats faced. Technologies are then fostered, and weapons created, as needed to meet those threats.

A 'counter-orthodoxy' has, however, emerged to challenge the complacency of this official view. This counter-orthodoxy we might call the 'technology-out-of-control' position. Far from being in rational control of the processes of arms dynamics, military and political elites are here seen as the captives of technology or technologists. Technologies change, following either their own internal logic or the career, institutional, and financial interests of their developers. The demand to incorporate these changes into weapon systems, and then to deploy those weapon systems, becomes irresistible. A technological 'momentum', 'imperative', or 'creep', rather than rational political decision, is the fundamental causal mechanism in the arms race. A range of authors have eloquently advanced this analysis, and supported it by reference to examples such as the shift from the atomic to the hydrogen bomb, the introduction of MIRVs, and the growth of missile accuracy – all seen as developments embraced because they were 'technically sweet'. The number and influence of the authors adopting a form of technology-out-of-control position are what justifies calling it a 'counter-orthodoxy': see, for example, Barnaby (1980), Schroeer (1984, 1985), Shapley (1978), Thee (1986a), Thompson (1980), Turner (1985), York (1975), Zuckerman (1980).

A smaller number of writers, however, have concluded that the technology-out-of-control position has 'bent the stick' too far in its opposition to the official view: see Krass (1981), Roberts (1985), Stein (1984, 1985). According to their analysis, which we might call the 'politics-in-command' position, technological change is a *dependent*, not independent, factor in arms dynamics: the servant, not the master, of political power. In arguing this, these authors are not reiterating the official view. They take a bleaker view of the interests and goals of political and military elites than do the proponents of the official view or, indeed, many of the proponents of the technology-out-of-control position. Thus many of the latter see the apparent shift from 'classical deterrent' nuclear strategies (targeting cities in retaliation) to 'warfighting' nuclear strategies (targeting nuclear forces and command and control facilities with its implications of potentially attacking first) as the prime case of technical change, such as increasing missile accuracy, imposing its own logic, and dragging strategy after it. Krass (1981) and Roberts (1985), however, see matters the other way around. Warfighting arsenals have been consciously and deliberately brought into being to make warfighting strategies apparently implementable. Roberts argues that elites on both sides have actively desired the political clout that a warfighting, rather tnan simply a deterrent, nuclear arsenal might possess.

The case study literature *is* drawn on by authors debating the role of technology in arms dynamics but only to a limited extent, and anecdotally – typically it provides examples of episodes that are used to make points in favour of preferred theories. There would, however, be great difficulty in making more systematic use of the case study literature to address this theoretical issue. For the typical case study concerns a *programme* (e.g. a particular missile system), the circumstances that gave rise to it, the obstacles its proponents had to overcome (generally case studies are of 'successful' rather than 'failed' programmes), conflict surrounding it, and the outcomes of that conflict. The *technologies* used in the programme will, by and large, be treated as given – at most the opportunities offered by their development, or obstacles posed by the lack of it, will be described, perhaps together, in the best case study literature, with a discussion of selection between available technologies.

To draw a biological analogy, *studying programmes without studying the development of their component technologies is like studying organisms without studying their genes*. Without systematic study of both, we cannot properly address the relationship of programmes to technologies, a relationship which is analogous to that of organism to genetic structure, of phenotype to genotype. The technology-out-of-control and politics-in-command positions are the analogues, in the study of arms dynamics, of hereditarianism and environmentalism in biology.

Of course, the biological analogy should not be pushed too far, at least unless one is prepared to commit oneself a priori to a strong version of technological determinism. For there is evidence (see MacKenzie & Wajcman, 1985) that technologies exist in many more 'allelic forms' than do genes; that both programmes and technologies are consciously shaped (not just blindly, by selection) with adaptation to the environment in mind; and that technological evolution is Lamarckian rather than Mendelian – that the life-histories of the programmes that incorporate technologies affect the nature, as well as the distribution, of those technologies.

Nevertheless, the biological analogy does highlight the difficulty of assessing the role of technology in arms dynamics on the basis of case studies of programmes. It also shows what is problematic about at least one stimulating attempt to apply a quantitative, rather than case study, approach to the problem: Schroeer (1985). Schroeer demonstrates a close correlation between the growth through time of computer power and missile accuracy. He asserts that this correlation is evidence for the conclusion that 'computers may be a major driving force producing a technological imperative towards improved missile accuracies' (1985, p. 61). Since computer capabilities are confidently expected to continue growing exponentially for at least the next two to three decades, 'there seem no insurmountable obstacles to continuing improvement in CEP [Circular Error Probable, the conventional measure of the accuracy of a missile] at present rates for another twenty-seven years. . . . Policy-makers clearly will have to cope with almost unbelievably accurate ICBMs in the future' (1985, pp. 67–68).

The problem with this argument is familiar to anyone acquainted with the heredity/environment debate: it is the step from correlation (missile accuracy and computer capability have changed roughly in tandem) to causation (improvements in computer capability are the cause of increasing missile accuracy). If that step cannot be made – and no *direct* evidence for it is provided[2] – then both the overall technologically determinist conclusion and the predictions for the future become perilous.

I would argue, then, that one source of current theoretical difficulties in the study of arms dynamics is the almost complete lack of detailed study of the development of the key component technologies that go into weapons programmes – particularly, in the light of their substantive importance, of the technologies that go into *nuclear* weapons programmes. There are, of course extremely helpful and instructive 'technical' treatments of such technologies (for instance, for the technologies discussed by Schroeer, 1985; see Bunn & Tsipis, 1983; Hoag, 1971). But there is little that in a genuine sense analyses their *development*. My argument is that such studies – which I will characterize as *historical sociologies of nuclear weapons technologies* – are both necessary and feasible.

In what follows, I will seek to explain and justify in turn three aspects of that characterization – the study of *technologies*, its *historical* nature, and its *sociological* nature. In doing so I shall draw examples primarily from missile guidance technology. This is central, contested terrain for the 'technology-out-of-control'/'politics-in-command' divide (see not just Schroeer, 1985; but also Barnaby, 1980; Roberts, 1985; Shapley, 1978)[3]

2 Technologies

Much of the case for a focus on technologies has already been made: that without it we lack systematic insight into the 'developmental genetics' of weapons programmes. Only one supplementary point is necessary: that I take a focus on technologies to imply a *comparative* focus in two senses. *First*, there should be comparison internationally. Ideally, international comparison allows study of both the development of a technology, and of the ways it is incorporated into programmes, in a range of contexts, especially political contexts. By holding one 'variable' (the type of 'technology') constant and letting others (such as 'political context') change, some theoretically relevant insights should be gleaned.

Unfortunately, the world is not in that methodological sense ideal. The number of cases to be dealt with is limited. In the area of missile guidance, where there is rightly concern about the proliferation of this key technology (Steinberg et al., 1981; Steinberg, 1983; Karp, 1984–85; North, 1987), there are only two, or perhaps four, genuine post-1945 cases of the sustained indigenous development of sophisticated ballistic missile guidance technology. These cases are the US, the USSR, and possibly France and China. (The French case is marginal because of the importance, early in the development of French ballistic missile guidance capability, of technology acquired from the US guidance firm Kearfott; acquired technology seems likely to have been important in the Chinese programme too.)

Of course, the Soviet and US cases cannot be assumed a priori to be wholly independent. Only if there was a strong *Eigendynamik* element in arms dynamics, in which the external world was irrelevant, would that be so. Nevertheless, the direct effects of US *guidance* technology on Soviet *guidance* technology, and vice versa, seem to have been relatively weak, however strongly other aspects of weapons technology have been affected (the perception of the growing accuracy of Soviet missiles has of course been central to the debate in the USA over MX, for example). The prime supposed channel of direct influence – Soviet acquisition of Western technology – is, in the guidance case, much less important than conventionally assumed (MacKenzie, 1988a; Intelligence Community Report, 1982). The USA and the Soviet Union have developed reasonably distinct technological 'styles' in missile guidance. One fascinating example is the earlier deployment, and different design, of Soviet by comparison with US stellar-inertial guidance systems for submarine-launched ballistic missiles (MacKenzie, 1988b).

So international comparison is feasible and of some interest. A *second* dimension of comparison is also available, at least in the case of some nuclear weapons technologies – comparison between their development in nuclear weapon applications and in conventional military or civilian applications. The significance of this second form of comparison lies in its bearing upon an often implicit, but none the less important, assumption in much technology-out-of-control analysis. In the words of Schroeer, that assumption is that 'the progress of much of the science and technology of the nuclear arms race appears inevitable. The rate of progress can to some extent be modified, but probably not its ultimate direction' (1984, p. 3). So not only does the development of technology exert, in the absence of quite deliberate policy measures to prevent it doing so (which is what Schroeer is calling for), a determining influence on the weapons programmes incorporating it: but the development of technology is autonomous, self-explaining, or 'natural'.

Missile accuracy is an obvious apparent instance of a 'natural trajectory' of technology (the term is taken from Nelson & Winter, 1982, p. 258). What, after all, could be more natural than for the scientists and technologists involved in guidance to seek to improve accuracy? Not surprisingly, then, Shapley (1978) takes increasing missile accuracy as her prime instance of 'technology creep' influencing arms dynamics.

The possibility of comparison of the second kind (across 'application areas') arises here because the dominant technology for guiding strategic missiles (inertial, 'self-contained' guidance) has close analogues in the navigation of submarines, modern military aircraft, and long-range civil aircraft. The inertial navigators found in these were in the 1960s structurally quite similar to missile guidance systems, and indeed used similar components. (A major risk of the proliferation of ballistic missile guidance technology is, in fact, the possible diversion of aircraft inertial navigator technology for ballistic missile use; Israel, in particular, seems to have enjoyed good access to aircraft inertial technology.)

The 'technological trajectory' subsequently to be found in the development of aircraft inertial navigators – both civil and most military types – is, however, quite different from that found in missile guidance. In aircraft applications, ultimate accuracy has *not* been pursued. There has been general satisfaction with an 'adequate' level of accuracy – an average error of around one nautical mile after an hour's flying time – that has been obtainable in 'state-of-the-art' systems for over twenty years. Instead, the chief technological effort has gone into reducing the weight and volume of inertial systems and also reducing their 'lifetime cost of ownership' by increasing their producibility and reliability.

This should not be understood as 'low tech' by comparison with strategic missile 'high tech', nor should it be seen as simply a matter of different choices of how to apply the 'same' technology. Rather, two different forms of technological change have evolved. In the first, that characteristic of strategic missiles, 'ultimate accuracy', has been pursued, primarily by evolutionary refinement of traditional gyroscope and accelerometer designs and traditional, complex electromechanical 'stable platform' configurations. In the second, that characteristic of aircraft, these traditional approaches have, in the USA at least, progressively been abandoned. At the level of components, there has been a shift in aircraft systems first from traditional mechanical gyroscopes to sophisticated 'tuned' designs, and then away from mechanical designs altogether, to laser gyroscopes, in which the gyroscope's function of detecting rotation is performed by contra-rotating beams of coherent light. Simultaneously, complex 'stable platform' system designs are being replaced in aircraft navigation by mechanically much simpler 'strapdown' designs, where the inertial instruments are simply fixed to the body of the vehicle being navigated, and what was previously done mechanically – keeping the system in a known geometric frame of reference – is now done computationally.

This second form of technological change is the closer to that found more generally. The move from electromechanical devices to optical and digital ones, and the shift from mechanical complexity plus computational simplicity to mechanical simplicity plus computational complexity – these are obviously far from unique to inertial navigation. *But it is a form of technological change that has yet to make a decisive inroad into strategic missile guidance.* It came closest with the Small ICBM, where the *cost* of the guidance system is a major concern (since in this single-warhead system it is not 'amortized' over several separate warheads). But the laser gyroscope option was eliminated from the competition in December 1987 (*Aviation Week and Space Technology*, 1987), and the eventually victorious system is a minor modification of the MX Advanced Inertial Reference Sphere – an ultra-sophisticated 'stable platform' carrying extremely sensitive, but quite traditional, floated mechanical gyroscopes and accelerometers.

Viewed in comparative perspective, then, what looked like a 'natural' form of technological change – the pursuit of ever-greater accuracy – begins to look almost 'unnatural'. Certainly, it involves standing aside from the main direction of technical change in inertial navigation, and indeed arguably from that characteristic of 'modern technology'. What are the reasons for this distinctive form of technological change? The answer must be postponed to a later part of this chapter, but for now I would note that it has been the comparative perspective that has opened it up as a question. The assumption of a 'natural' trajectory of technological change prevents us from finding an answer, because it prevents us from formulating a question in the first place.

Of course there is need for caution in any comparative analysis. In comparison across 'application areas', an obvious difficulty lies in the extent to which differences in technology may be caused by 'physical' differences between the areas, rather than different social, political, or economic priorities. It is, for example, evidently true that guiding a ballistic missile (with its short time of guided flight, great acceleration, and harsh physical environment) is a different task from navigating an aircraft (with longer flight times, but lesser acceleration and a less extreme physical environment, and greater ease of access to 'non-inertial' navigational information). It turns out that these explain some, but not all, the differences between the two forms of technology. 'Physical' differences do not, for example, on their own explain why aircraft inertial navigators offering an order of magnitude improvement in performance over the 'mile per hour' standard have not been adopted, or at least have not been adopted widely, even though at least two such systems (the Bell 'Hipernas' and Honeywell 'SPN-GEANS') were developed a considerable time ago.

3 An Historical Approach

What then of the justification for an historical form of study? Again, part of the argument has already been made. The comparison (international, and between different application areas) referred to in the previous section was comparison between the *development* of technology in different circumstances. Static comparisons, made only at one point in time, offer little insight – it is very hard to ascertain the reasons for differences found in this way.

Another advantage of an historical approach is pragmatic – access. In the guidance area at least, participants seem positively to welcome a study framed as history of technology. It fits well their self-image either as direct technical contributors or as sponsors of technical development. So 150 interview requests met with only 3 refusals, while others volunteered help without it being directly requested of them. Unusually, interviewees seem at least in certain cases prepared to be named in print as the source of particular statements and pieces of information. This case may have peculiarities: because of its wide range of uses, inertial technology is 'less secret' than, say, nuclear weapon technology per se. So historical work done without a security clearance – no clearance was sought for the guidance work – is probably somewhat easier in this area than some others. Nevertheless, the point remains that an historical, rather than, say, political science, approach seems to offer the better chances of getting the level of participant cooperation that detailed study requires.

An historical approach also allows the identification of continuities that may be hidden by the 'slice in time' case study method: continuities of institutions, people, and issues. Studying the technical decisions involved in a range of weapons programmes makes clear the extent to which the same actors and interests operate across a wide variety of circumstances.

Let me draw three examples from the guidance field. The first is an institutional continuity. One organization, the Charles Stark Draper Laboratory Inc. of Cambridge, Mass. – formerly MIT Instrumentation Laboratory – has designed the guidance system for *every* US submarine-launched ballistic missile and for Thor, Titan II, MX, and the Small ICBM. Given the importance of guidance for missile accuracy, and given the centrality of accuracy to the nuclear strategic issues at the heart of controversy over US weapons programmes, one would have assumed that this would make the Draper Laboratory an organization of some interest in the literature.

Not so. Case studies of each individual weapon system may *mention* the Draper Laboratory (not all even do that), but none has devoted any serious analytical attention to its role. Was it a mere servant of other interests, or was it a political actor in its own right? The silence on the issue may indicate that case-study authors assume the former; and, indeed, in any *particular* case this may be justified. But when one considers the pattern as a whole – a single organization being central to strategic weapons programmes over more than three decades – one gets a disturbing sense that, again, a potentially important question is simply not being asked.

Personal continuity is as striking as institutional. For a long time the most important contributor to missile accuracy was held to be accelerometer accuracy. *One person* – Mike Sapuppo of the Draper Laboratory – has essentially been responsible for the design of the accelerometer for *every* currently deployed US strategic ballistic missile (and the yet-to-be-deployed Trident D5 and Small ICBM). Yet to the best of my knowledge, Sapuppo has never been interviewed by any of the case-study authors. It may be that if this is so it is because accelerometer design has been taken to be 'mere technicality'. But that, again, would be a dangerous assumption to make. For example, one basic choice in accelerometer design is between the PIGA (pendulous integrating gyro accelerometer) and PIPA (pulsed integrating pendulous accelerometer): not, on the face of it, an exciting issue, I must admit. However, the two devices are seen as offering contrasting advantages. The PIGA is seen, at least within the Draper Laboratory, as the ultimate in accuracy, but is a notoriously hard to produce and expensive instrument. The PIPA is seen as less accurate but more producible and cheaper. So the changing circumstances of the US submarine-launched ballistic missile can be traced, in miniature as it were, in accelerometer design for that programme. While PIPAs were used for Poseidon and Trident C4, the shift to overt prioritization of counterforce capability has been marked with the adoption of PIGAs for Trident D5.

The submarine-launched ballistic missile programme offers my third example, which is an example of continuity of issues. The technical decisions surrounding each of the MIRVed generations of US submarine-launched missiles has been marked by essentially the same twin, interlocked disputes: over accuracy specifications and warhead yield. At stake was the desirability or otherwise of counterforce capability. The same actors have clashed each time – the Strategic Systems Projects Office, the Office of the Chief of Naval Operations, the Office of the Secretary of Defense; with important roles being played by the Draper Laboratory, Kearfott Division of Singer, Lockheed, and some members of Congress. But the outcomes have dramatically shifted. In the case of Poseidon they favoured the opponents of counterforce, while with Trident D5 they have decisively favoured its proponents (Trident C4 is a complex transitional case). But the one extended case study of Trident (Dalgleish & Schweikart, 1984), bizarrely, does not even clearly formulate this difference in outcomes as an issue worthy of investigation.

The ultimate hope from an historical approach would be that it would help to *explain* differences such as this, and help to answer *causal* questions about weapons development. Here I would emphasize '*help* to answer', for it would be naively empiricist to expect historical work in this area to prove more decisive in settling causal questions than it has in others. Nevertheless, the help given may prove useful.

Take, for example, the question of whether increased computer power is really the *cause* of increased missile accuracy, and not merely *correlated* with it. As Schroeer (1985) rightly points out, a key index and driver of computer power is the number of components that can be formed on the one semiconductor chip. Originally, ballistic missile onboard computers were indeed 'state-of-the-art' on this parameter. The Minuteman II onboard computer was one of the first major users of integrated circuits. But since then a distinct 'lag' has opened between the levels of integration achievable and that actually employed in onboard computers. Though later than Minuteman II, the Poseidon onboard computer, with nine 'logic gates' per chip, was still close to state-of-the-art integration when it was being designed in the mid-1960s. But the guidance computer for Trident C4, a 1970s design, incorporates only medium-scale integration, when large-scale integration had been achievable since the beginning of the decade. Similarly, the Trident D5 onboard computer, a 1980s design due for deployment in 1989, is close to the lower end of large-scale integration ('as high as 1,500 gates per chip', private communication), not the very large-scale integration now commercially available.

In part, of course, this is to be explained by the very specific requirements of strategic system computing, notably radiation hardening.

But it also seems to reflect the judgement expressed to me in a letter by a senior figure in the guidance decisions for US submarine-launched ballistic missiles: 'About computers in ballistic missile guidance: their capabilities or limits have never caused more than trivial effects on overall accuracy compared to imperfect sensors and imperfect models of the physical world' (private communication).

This sort of judgement cannot necessarily be taken as unproblematic (see the next section), nor does it address the possible indirect effect of growing computer power on improving 'imperfect sensors and imperfect models of the physical world'. But it may be that this belief is part of the reason for the emerging lag in integration levels – that even when high accuracy is a clear-cut requirement (as it is with Trident D5 but was not with earlier generations of US submarine-launched ballistic missile), little advantage is now seen in pressing to the limit of the state-of-the-art in microfabrication technology.

So while nothing is *proven* about a causal connection, or lack thereof, between computer power and missile accuracy, this historical evidence does suggest that a computer-based 'technological imperative' explanation is simplistic.

4 A Sociological Approach

The third aspect of my characterization – an historical *sociology* of nuclear weapons technologies – requires the most explanation. The kind of sociology I believe to be most relevant is that originating in the sociology of scientific knowledge.

To describe a whole field of study briefly but adequately is impossible, so let me simply select out one central conclusion that can be drawn from this field and related historical and philosophical work. That conclusion – the heart of the oft-debated 'relativism' of the field – I would summarize as the claim of the *in-principle challengeability of all technical arguments*.

There are various ways of arguing for this radical conclusion. Perhaps the best known is that called the Duhem–Quine thesis, which led Quine to the conclusion that 'Any statement can be held true come what may, if we make drastic enough adjustments elsewhere in the system. . . . Conversely, by the same token, no statement is immune from revision' (Quine, 1964, p. 43). The attachment of the name Pierre Duhem (1861 – 1916) indicates the role of the French physicist and historian of science in first formulating the thesis in *The Aim and Structure of Physical Theory* (1954). Since Duhem and Quine, the argument has been elaborated and re-presented by several authors.[4]

This is a sophisticated body of literature, and the authors involved are far from in complete harmony. But rather than engage in lengthy discussion, I shall provide a summary exposition of what for present purposes is the basic point. Suppose we wish to test a theory T. A simple way of thinking about how to do it – a way the Duhem–Quine thesis suggests is *too* simple – is to deduce the implication *I* of the theory for a particular empirical situation. By experiment or observation we then check whether *I* is in fact the case. If *I* is not the case, we reject theory *T*. If *I* is the case, we retain *T*, at least until the next test.

The flaw in this way of thinking that the Duhem–Quine thesis focuses on is as follows. To draw an implication from a theory for a particular situation always involves the assumption of more than just the theory. Auxiliary assumptions, *A*, are involved too. Thus in testing Einstein's theory of general relativity by studying the orbit of Mercury around the Sun, auxiliary assumptions had to be made about the shape of the Sun in deducing the implications of Einstein's theory for Mercury's orbit. Auxiliary assumptions are further to be found, typically, in the method by which we gain our knowledge of the particular situation in question. If, for example, we are using some apparatus, we will be assuming that the apparatus is working correctly, and that the theories according to which it is built (geometric optics for a telescope, electromagnetic theory for a voltmeter, say) are correct.

So we are never testing the theory T *on its own, but the combination of* T *and the auxiliary assumptions* A. If *I* is found not to be the case, then the fault may lie with *T*, but it may also lie with one of the auxiliary assumptions. Without violating logic, we can choose to retain *T* and throw into question *A*. 'Any statement can be held true come what may, if we make drastic enough adjustments elsewhere in the system.'

We can of course then proceed to test the auxiliary assumptions, but this procedure could potentially be endless. Each test of an auxiliary assumption will itself involve auxiliary assumptions, and so on. One way of expressing the aspect of knowledge highlighted by the Duhem–Quine thesis is to say that knowledge forms a *network* (Hesse, 1974; Barnes, 1982). Neither facts nor theories stand on their own. Certainly, concepts bear a relation to reality. But they also bear a relation to each other. As our knowledge changes, we are not abstractly compelled to maintain either relation at the expense of the other. Even apparently quite basic, 'observational' terms can be revised (Hesse, 1974, ch. 1).

Taken by itself, the Duhem–Quine thesis might seem to imply complete contingency in the development of our knowledge – complete voluntarism, the capacity to believe and say whatever we wish. But of course in actual practice neither 'contingency' nor 'voluntarism' captures at all well the development of knowledge. Necessity and constraint there certainly are. The question is, whence do they come? What the arguments I have presented rule out, I believe, is the answer that they come *simply* from 'reality' or the abstract demands of logic.

At the most immediate level, of course, the answer is that certain links in the network of knowledge are so well entrenched that, whatever might be the case abstractly, in practice they cannot be shifted. Take the example of Millikan's oil drop experiment. A working Millikan experiment should show only integer electrical charges: fractions of the charge of an electron should not exist and should not be found. Routinely they are found, however, both by Millikan himself and in the thousands of oil drop experiments performed in schools and universities annually. Universally, the finding of a fractional electrical charge is deemed a failed experiment: to revise the atomic theory of matter on the basis of it is not a practical alternative.

What is central is *credibility*. An undergraduate physicist finding a fractional charge in an oil drop experiment just does not have open to her or him any other option than defining what she or he has done as a mistake. It is not simply a matter of low status; it is also a question of the lack of available credible ways of refashioning the links in the network of knowledge. To succeed in having the fractional charge experiment defined as competent would require possessing either a viable alternative to existing theory, or a plausible argument that existing theory did not of necessity imply only integer charges. Interestingly, in one episode these conditions were nearly met, when a high-status group of physicists, led by the respected experimenter William Fairbank, found fractional charges in a sophisticated version of Millikan's experiment, and interpreted these as the result of a type of particle known as a quark. Though the existence of quarks was widely accepted by physicists, they were not however believed to exist in isolation as 'free quarks' in the way Fairbank's interpretation necessitated. Fairbank's results did not, ultimately gain acceptance (Pickering, 1981).

The question of credibility is what turns the *in-principle* challengeability of all technical arguments into the practical unchallengeability of many. Why this is a *sociological* and not just a philosophical issue is because credibility is a social matter. It indicates at least a minimal sense in which the 'negotiation of knowledge' is social. Even if we may be individually free to believe what we wish (which I do not think is psychologically correct), the options that are open are a matter of what other people are prepared to believe. If we press for alterations in the network of knowledge that are too lacking in credibility, we run the risk of being seen as incompetent, foolish, or mad. If nothing else, avoiding this outcome means that we have to take other people's beliefs into account.

A fuller sense in which we could say that the negotiation of knowledge was social would be if we understood the social determinants of credibility and of preferences in terms of which links in the network to protect and which to revise. I do not think that the *only* determinants are social: the biological and psychological nature of human beings must play its part in what we do and do not believe; and I do not doubt that 'reality' plays its part too. But historical and sociological studies of scientific knowledge have also shown the operation of at least two sorts of social factor (Shapin, 1982). The first has to do with science itself as a social system. Scientists develop 'investments' in particular theories, particular experimental skills, and the like. These investments can then play a part in shaping scientists' preferences about which network links to protect and which to revise. The second social factor concerns the wider social significance of the knowledge produced by science. Quite often scientific knowledge has been drawn upon for purposes of legitimation – for example, to defend an institution as 'natural', or to condemn a form of deviance as 'against nature'. This too can create a vested interest in the preservation or revision of a particular link in the network of knowledge.

Note that the presence of social factors of either kind does not imply inadequacy of the knowledge in question. The physics of Boyle and Newton provides an example that has been extensively studied by historians of science. Unquestionably, this is 'good science' by all normal criteria. Yet as David Bloor (1982) has shown, drawing upon the work of historians, there is strong evidence that amongst the interests supporting the protection of key assumptions in their physics were religious and political concerns.

Such considerations may sound very abstract, and having little to do with the world of nuclear weaponry. But the processes studied by sociologists or science can be found there too; and they have, I would argue, major consequences for the analysis of the role of technology in arms dynamics. But before turning to these, let me briefly discuss one important, though largely forgotten, episode in which issues of the challengeability of technical arguments became dramatically manifest. The example is a debate that took place relatively early in the history of US ballistic missile programmes. The question was whether we know that nuclear missiles will work. 'Work' here does not have a fancy meaning. The issue at stake was whether, having carried its nuclear warhead to the rough vicinity of the target, the warhead would then explode. It was not *just* the question of whether a certain percentage of missiles might not, for one idiosyncratic reason or another, fail. At least some of the time, the issue seems to have been whether *any* would work, or certainly whether there were any grounds for assurance that any would work.

Perhaps surprisingly, those making the challenge were not outsiders, but very senior figures in the United States Air Force, and their supporters in Congress. The best single statement of the challenge came in 1961 from the Armed Services Committee of the US House of Representatives (Johnsen, 1961, p. 22):

> Who knows whether an intercontinental ballistic missile with a nuclear warhead will actually work? Each of the constituent elements has been tested, it is true. Each of them, however, has not been tested under circumstances which would be attendant upon the firing of such a missile in anger. By this the committee means an intercontinental ballistic missile will carry its nuclear warhead to great heights, subjecting it to intense cold. It will then arch down and upon re-entering the earth's atmosphere subject the nuclear warhead to intense heat. Who knows what will happen to the many delicate mechanisms involved in the nuclear warhead as it is subjected to these two extremes of temperature?

By 1961 the USA had conducted many nuclear weapons tests; it had also conducted many flight tests of ballistic missiles. But all US missile tests had been conducted on missiles without warheads, while the bombs in ordinary nuclear weapons testing had been either detonated in fixed positions or dropped from towers or aircraft.[5] The challenge mounted by the Armed Services Committee was therefore this: testing the components of nuclear missile systems separately was not adequate against the risk that some feature of the way they were combined would prevent the nuclear missile from working.

The challenge was not treated as absurd. The Joint Chiefs of Staff apparently recommended that missile tests be conducted with warheads on board (Wilson, 1964, p. 26). *Aviation Week and Space Technology* (1962a) reported that there were plans to launch an Atlas missile with a live warhead from Vandenberg Air Force Base in California. The trajectory would take the missile 'near some populated areas', but it was reported that 'Administration and Defense officials feel the need to proof-fire the warhead outweighs the risk of the Atlas exploding during launch or in flight and damaging surrounding communities'. *Aviation Week* further noted that the 'nuclear warhead itself is arranged so that it would not explode in such an event'.

We will never know whether the Kennedy Administration would in fact have authorized such a test, because a politically more palatable alternative had been found – one where any populated areas contained Pacific Islanders, not Americans. In what my source (Lockheed Missiles and Space Company, n.d., p. 20) describes as 'an almost forgotten historical event', shortly after noon on 6 May 1962 the submerged Polaris submarine USS *Ethan Allen* fired a live Polaris missile on a 1400 mile trajectory towards the nuclear testing ground at Christmas Island. Squeezed between more conventional tests on 4 May and 8 May, 'Operation Frigate Bird', as it was called, attracted little public attention. It was a 'success'. *Aviation Week* (1962b) reported that the shot 'hit "right in the pickle barrel"'. The warhead was reported as exploding with a force estimated at half a megaton.

The Duhem–Quine thesis should alert us to what happened next. The 'success' of the experiment did not end the challenge. If anything it intensified. Certainly, the stakes were raised. In 1964 Air Force Chief of Staff General Curtis LeMay went public with his concerns. 'There are some unknowns and uncertainties you should know about', he told the Defense Appropriations Subcommittee of the House of Representatives. 'One is that we have only had one test, it was not under fully operational conditions, we fired one Polaris out in the Pacific with a warhead on it. It was not truly operational. It was modified to some extent for the test' (Wilson, 1964, p. 26). The issue was taken up by Republican Presidential challenger Barry Goldwater, who charged the Democratic Administration with building a 'Maginot line' of untested – and, following the signature of the Partial Test-Ban Treaty, untestable – nuclear missiles.

What is of interest here is the fluctuation in credibility of this kind of challenge. Abstractly, matters could be said to be little different now from

1964: Frigate Bird has not been repeated (we now think we know that its success was fortuitous, and that most Polaris A1 warheads suffered from a defect that would have prevented detonation – Hussain, 1981, p. 13 – but that is not of central relevance here). Yet the credibility of the challenge has certainly declined. That nuclear missiles might fail to work in the drastic sense suggested by the early 1960s critics is not now seriously entertained, at least not as influentially as it was then.

This is perhaps too straightforward a case. The challenge was not highly technical, and a clear social interest underlay it – the critics were supporters of an alternative weapon, the bomber. And it is of course quite unusual to find the abstract possibilities for challenge actually taken up: most technical arguments pass unchallenged. Yet the general case for in-principle challengeability of all technical arguments, and for the social nature of credibility, seems to me to stand. From it, two things appear to follow.

The first is the case for a subtle shift in research agenda. A great deal of attention quite rightly goes into debating the truth or falsity of technical arguments (for example in connection with the Strategic Defense Initiative). It seems to me that there is also a case for researching the bases of the credibility of technical arguments. To the extent that this is done at all, it is typically for technical arguments deemed false. But the Duhem–Quine thesis suggests that the question of the causes of belief can be asked for all technical arguments, whether deemed true or false.

This may sound like an esoteric direction of research. But it is actually of considerable policy importance. One frequently discussed means of restraining arms dynamics is by restrictions on certain kinds of weapon tests. The effects of such restraints are entirely dependent on the credibility of certain technical arguments. What constitutes an adequate test of a weapon is a socially negotiated matter. As we saw, the credibility of the belief that at least some ballistic nuclear missiles will 'work' has not been damaged by banning the only form of test a significant sector of military opinion took to be valid. This is not to say that test restrictions are not useful – they are – but that it is worth remembering that their effects operate through the medium of belief structures. If, say, missile flight tests of a certain kind were banned, would laboratory tests plus computer simulations be *believed* to be an adequate substitute (not just *would* they be an adequate substitute, which is how the question is normally posed)?

The second thing that appears to follow from the in-principle challengeability of technical arguments is a major theoretical difficulty in the explanation of arms dynamics. This difficulty is best expounded concretely, with reference to the problem outlined in section 2 above of why a distinctive form of technological change exists in missile guidance in the USA, a form that emphasizes the evolutionary refinement of complex, traditional electromechanical systems, rather than novel mechanical designs, optical sensors, and the use of computer power to reduce mechanical complexity.

There is of course a straightforward 'politics-in-command' explanation that can be given: that decision-making elites want, and have for some time wanted, counterforce capability, and thus have selected the form of technological change that has offered and offers the greatest missile accuracy, even if it is not 'technically sweet'. I do not want to reject this explanation, which seems to me to be in broad-brush terms correct,[6] certainly more correct than the 'technology-out-of-control' alternative.

Note, however, that this explanation rests upon a technical argument – that this form of technological change offers greatest accuracy. As all technical arguments, this is challengeable; and while it is not challenged publicly, it is privately. It tends to be quietly doubted by more than one inertial specialist outside the Draper Laboratory. The objection was posed most sharply in a 1986 interview with one of the pioneers of alternative technology, the 'dry' tuned-rotor gyroscope, who quoted the opinion that the evolutionary refinement of the traditional 'floated' gyroscope at the Draper Laboratory was 'like polishing a turd'. The best dry gyro could outperform the best floated one, and the extraordinarily low drift rates quoted for Draper gyroscopes were, he said, 'bullshit', the product of an artificial test environment.

This man had his own sociology of missile guidance to offer, in terms of the separation of 'instrument' specialists (dominant, he would argue, at Draper) from 'system' specialists who understood the place of the inertial instrument in guidance as a whole, and in terms of what he called the 'political clout' of the Draper Laboratory having ensured, at least to date, the continuance of their preferred form of technological change.

Though his analysis is not unique, we should not accept it unproblematically. The principle of challengeability applies equally to *his* technical arguments, and Draper engineers certainly would dispute them vigorously. Rather, his analysis highlights the difficulty of explanation. Paradoxically, the 'politics-in-command' explanation grants too much to technical argument. 'The technical' is not a transparent world from which political or military elites can select. So the explanation for the distinctive form of technological change in missile guidance has to include a crucial extra clause: elites have selected the form of technological change that has *appeared to them* to offer the greatest missile accuracy. But that seemingly innocuous phrase 'appeared to them' is an analytical Pandora's box. For there is a whole realm of politics – almost wholly unnoticed in the case study literature – in the construction and maintenance of that appearance,[7] and also in challenges to it. 'Micro-politics' we might call it, but it has macro effects, and also on occasion necessitates forays into 'macropolitics'.

Thus one of the great skills of Charles Stark Draper (1901–87), founder of the Draper Laboratory, was his command of this 'micro-politics'. He was a superb salesperson, with a powerful personality and a considerable network of personal contacts, especially in the key senior circles in the US Navy and Air Force. At the construction and maintenance of technical reality for elites he was at the least the equal of his better-known contemporaries, Edward Teller and Hyman Rickover – indeed, his relative lack of fame is perhaps indicative of his success, for unlike them he never became nationally controversial.[8] Draper *could* be beaten, but sometimes at least beating him involved overt resource to 'macro-politics'. Thus Draper seems to have believed that stellar-inertial guidance for submarine-launched ballistic missiles was unnecessary – that sufficiently refined inertial navigation and guidance could achieve requisite accuracies. Proponents of stellar-inertial guidance from the Kearfott Division of Singer, its key pioneers in the USA, circumvented Draper – and also those within the Navy who were opposing it for different reasons, bureaucratic and strategic (MacKenzie, 1988b) – by a direct approach to the Department of Defense, with one of them indeed deciding, as he told me in an interview, that to gain acceptance for stellar-inertial he had to 'join the power structure'. He in fact did so, obtaining a senior position in the Department of Defense, where he played a significant role in setting the specifications for Trident C4, the US missile where stellar-inertial guidance was first adopted, the stellar-inertial option for Poseidon having previously been cancelled.

In emphasizing that the realm of 'the technical' can actually be seen as a realm of 'micro-politics' – indeed one that interacts with 'macro-politics' – I have no wish to support Zuckerman's analysis (1980) that it is the 'men in the laboratories' who are the driving force in the arms race. That is grossly to overestimate their power; even Draper, exceptional as he was, could not foist a goal on an unwilling elite.[9] The point, rather, is a more methodological one. Satisfactory explanation of arms dynamics cannot afford to 'black box' technical argument – even, or perhaps especially, technical argument that appears to the analyst to be correct. Ultimately, we need, not to *abandon* the politics/technology dichotomy (that would be too glib a response to these analytical issues), but to understand how, out of the in-principle 'seamless web' (Hughes, 1986), apparently separate spheres of 'technology' and 'politics' are normally constructed.

5 Conclusion

I hope I have made the case for an historical sociology of nuclear weapons technologies. To end, it is perhaps proper to be modest and to admit that this approach is no analytical panacea. As we have seen, it cannot be expected to *settle* causal questions in straightforward empiricist fashion, and it tends to lead to reformulation of issues such as 'technology-out-of-control' versus 'politics-in-command' rather than to resolving them. In the same way as there are problems of generalizability in the case study literature, so would there be problems of generalizability in the historical sociology of nuclear weapons technologies. For these technologies are many-fold, and each would require specific, detailed study. No doubt the patterns that would emerge would differ from one technology to the next.

As yet, we quite simply lack an adequate general theory of technological change which could make full sense of the results of a multiplicity of studies.

Nevertheless, such studies still seem to me to be of great interest. To take but five examples: historical sociologies of re-entry vehicle design, of strategic anti-submarine warfare, of command-and-control technologies, of anti-ballistic missile technologies, and of the technology of thermonuclear weapons would singly, but above all collectively, greatly enhance our understanding of the processes of arms dynamics in the nuclear realm.

Detailed accounts of nuclear weapon system technologies are beginning to appear. Even though not framed in precisely the analytical form advocated here, they still seem to me to bolster the argument of this chapter, in that they demonstrate the insight, both substantive and in policy terms, that can be gained from study of what at first sight might appear to be matters of 'technical detail'. Wilkes & Gleditsch (1987) show how much can be learnt about the relations between superpowers and subordinate states, and about the connections of these to nuclear strategy, by pursuit of the apparently unpromising topic of radio navigation aids. And although the precise lessons to be learnt are not spelt out, Hansen (1988) shows how close research can get to the very heart of nuclear weapon systems – the history and design of atomic and hydrogen bombs themselves.

Notes

1. See, for example, Armacost (1969), Beard (1976), Dalgleish & Schweikart (1984), Greenwood (1975), Holland & Hoover (1985), Holloway (1977, 1982), Huisken (1981), Sapolsky (1972); not all of these are 'case studies' in the sense the term is used in the text.

2. Schroeer is of course aware that in a direct technological sense missile accuracy does not depend solely on onboard computer capacity, but also on a wide range of other technologies and sciences such as inertial components, geophysics, and geodesy. He notes (1985, p. 63) that 'all these aspects involve to a great extent computers in design, construction, sensing, evaluation and control'; the problem, though, is that they also involve much else besides.

3. Where empirical claims are made in this chapter, without citation of published literature, the reference is to this study conducted by the author in 1984–87 with funding from the Nuffield Foundation. Some results of this study have already been published in MacKenzie (1986, 1987, 1988a, 1988b).

4. See e.g. Hesse (1974, ch. 1), Barnes (1982, ch. 4). In a general sense the work of both Kuhn (1970) and his apparent opponent Lakatos (1970, esp. pp. 97–103) is congruent with the Duhem–Quine thesis.

5. Some nuclear warheads had been lofted into the upper atmosphere or space for explosion there, but that obviously left out the re-entry phase. We now know that the Soviet Union had conducted some live tests of missiles before 1963, and the People's Republic of China was to do so in 1966 and 1976 (Hussain, 1981, p. 53; Fieldhouse, 1986, p. 104); but this did not seem to influence the US debate.

6. It does underplay the extent of elite divisions over counterforce in the USA, notably the resistance of a crucial section of the US Navy to counterforce, for which see Sapolsky (1972), Greenwood (1975).

7. To repeat, in using the term 'appearance' I am impartial on the correctness or otherwise

of the appearance; I do not restrict analysis to false appearances! Impartiality – in the sense of not allowing one's sociological explanations of belief to be affected by one's assessment of the truth or falsity of those beliefs – is a central methodological tenet of the sociology of scientific knowledge. See Bloor (1976, esp. p. 5).

8. One of the few substantial references to Draper in the literature of the arms race is by Herbert York (1970, pp. 54, 86, 89). Although York is sceptical of some of Draper's claims he describes Draper as knowing 'more by far about the science and technology of inertial-guidance systems than anyone else in the Western world' (p. 86). Controversy surrounding Draper has been local to Cambridge, Mass. – where it surfaced particularly in the successful attempt to force divestiture by MIT of Draper's Instrumentation Laboratory – and to the guidance community.

9. Thus in Draper (1959) he sought to persuade Navy leaders to seek to rival the accuracy of Air Force ICBMs, a tactic that they in practice avoided until the changed circumstances of the late 1970s.

DONALD MACKENZIE, b. 1950, Ph.D. in Social History of Science (University of Edinburgh, 1978); Lecturer in Sociology (1975–88), Reader in Sociology (1988–), Edinburgh University; author of *Statistics in Britain 1865–1930: The Social Construction of Scientific Knowledge* (Edinburgh University Press, 1981), and (with Judy Wajcman) *The Social Shaping of Technology* (Open University Press, 1985); current main research interests: strategic missile guidance technology, super-computers, and national defence laboratories.

Chapter 9

Modernization through Military Industry: The Creation of a 'Military-Industrial System' in Norway 1960–75

OLAV WICKEN
Institute for Defence Studies, Oslo

1 Introduction

The 'boom years' of 1960–74 saw a rapid expansion in military consumption and the defence industry in many countries in Western Europe (Ball & Leitenberg, 1983). This was a period of relatively low international tension. While the Cold War had been regarded as one of the most important incentives for military-industrial expansion in the 1950s, emphasis was now placed on internal factors. In US literature 'the military-industrial complex' became the central concept in a number of studies which looked for an explanation for the rapid growth in military consumption and production.[1]

The empirical foundation for theories about this state of affairs is to be found in the great powers, particularly in the United States. The openness about military-industrial relations in the United States and the efforts made by researchers to utilize this information have resulted in US studies forming the basis of a more general understanding of the incentives behind military industry and consumption. However, this does not mean that explanations of the US situation are necessarily true for other countries, e.g. the European states.

In order to understand the situation in Western Europe we must base our investigation on European experiences. However, we cannot assume that the reasons for the expansion in military industry in Western Europe were the same in all countries. For example, it is probable that the size of the countries and the need for national defence have led to differing interpretations of the significance of military industry, and that therefore the motives and reasons for the expansion of defence industry have differed from country to country.

This chapter discusses some background factors for why the military industry expanded in a small Western European country, Norway, in the postwar period. It emphasizes the construction of a 'military-industrial system'[2] consisting of munition companies, a military research institute, the procurement system, a long-term planning system, etc. This system was regarded by its initiators as a means of modernizing both the military system and Norwegian industry in general. Military-industrial expansion is therefore regarded as one aspect of a broader modernization policy of Norwegian governments after World War II.

The Norwegian military industry was modest until the 1970s. Most production took place in three state-owned companies: an ammunition works, a weapons works, and a naval shipyard. Only a few privately owned companies had substantial interests in production of military equipment, mostly in electronics (telecommunication, detection equipment, etc.) and explosives. The growth rate of the military industry can be illustrated by the military sales volumes of the two most important companies (Raufoss Ammunisjonsfabrikk and Kongsberg Våpenfabrikk), which increased from NOK 0.6 billion in 1960 to 2.1 billion in 1975 (fixed 1984 prices).

We argue here that the construction of the 'military-industrial system' was made possible by the state system in the early 1960s. Politicians encouraged an active interventionist state in economic matters, without establishing any central political control of all the aspects of the new public functions. This made it possible for small groups and individuals to establish a 'military-industrial system'. In Norway such a system was constructed without a central political decision having been taken and without private strong profit interests being involved. Also, most of the military establishment did not favour the expansion of a national military industry.

This chapter will first discuss the ideology of modernization in Norwegian politics, then look at the construction of some elements of the new 'military-industrial system', and lastly discuss the Norwegian state system.

2 Motivation and Ideology

What was the motivation for creating the 'military-industrial system'? We may distinguish between two types of arguments: the role of military industry for national security (primary objective) and all other kinds of motives (secondary objectives). We will claim that 'secondary objectives' were of substantial importance as arguments to strengthen military-industrial production in Norway.

2.1 *Primary Objective: Military Industry and National Security*

In the early postwar period military-industrial growth was given low priority, and Norway's armed forces relied on obtaining good contracts for buying war material abroad, first and foremost in Britain. The US Mutual Defense Assistance Program (MDAP), which had started in 1950, solved the dilemma of whether to use the country's resources for civil- or military-industrial purposes.

In general, the military establishment did not regard a national military industry as a necessary part of the country's military defence, at least not until the 1970s. In the 1950s military professionals and defence politicians were not particularly interested in encouraging national military industry, and there were often conflicts between military professionals and the existing military industry. The military felt that a national industry would limit their choice of purchases. They wished to be free to choose equipment offered on the international market instead of being tied down to national development and production programmes that could prove unsuccessful.

The arguments for military expansion presented in various White Papers to the Norwegian Parliament (*Stortingsmeldinger*) for military-industrial expansion have mainly been indirect. Having national military-industrial production would make it possible to carry out repairs on equipment and to improvise on unfamiliar equipment in wartime. Apart from readiness (ammunition production) there was one direct military reason for Norway to have a military industry: equipment produced abroad would be unlikely to suit topographical and climatic conditions peculiar to Norway. This was the military argument given for technical research and industry from as early as 1946 (Forsvarskommisjonen, 1978).

2.2 *Secondary Objectives: Economic Considerations*

Norway was one of the founding members of NATO in 1949 and had a long tradition of close contact with the Atlantic powers, particularly Great Britain. Even though the country belonged to the rich Western world, it was at the same time among the peripheral states of Europe. The Norwegian economy at the beginning of the 1950s is described as semi-industrial with a weakly developed engineering industry (Balassa, 1969). Therefore the government (Labour from 1945 to 1965) advocated the strengthening of civilian industry. The aim was to modernize Norwegian society through industrialization, rationalization, and centralization.

Norway was to be modernized by expanding capital-intensive industry and by exploiting the country's natural resources effectively. This was in accordance with the economic expertise and theories of the time: a high investment rate would yield rapid economic growth, which was the government's primary aim. This called for Norway to use a great deal of real added value for investment purposes; the country was in fact one of the world leaders where level of gross investments was concerned.

By the early 1960s there were clear indications that the economists had been mistaken. Despite large investments, growth in the Norwegian economy was lower than the average for Western Europe. The argument about growth through capital-intensive production was weakened. In its place came a new economic theory: growth was only to a limited degree dependent on the size of investments, the labour force, and natural resources; *qualitative* conditions were at least equally important (Bergh & Hanisch, 1984; Hanisch & Lange, 1986).

This realization was of course not fundamentally new; but because it gradually found acceptance among economists, it came to influence politicians in the 1960s. Earlier it had been mainly engineers who had argued that technology was vital to the modernization process – naturally enough, since technology was their profession.

As the Norwegian authorities in the first half of the 1960s gained a new understanding of how to achieve their main political objective, the USA began to signal a gradual reduction of the MDAP. This meant that the Norwegian government would have to finance technical material for its own defence in the future. This was an enormous challenge, particularly at a time when the cost of military equipment and weapons was rising rapidly and the armed forces increasingly needed modern technical equipment to replace WWII material that was becoming obsolete. Military plans indicated that the investment share of the defence budget would increase up to 30–40%.[3] With a modest national military industry this meant increased imports; and defence would become a heavier economic burden for the nation, as hard currency was still scarce. In about 1960 former UN Secretary-General Trygve Lie visited other Western countries in an attempt to attract foreign investment to Norway. In this situation increased military imports could come into conflict with the dominant political ambition of the Norwegian government: modernization through industrial growth.

The construction of a 'military-industrial system' may therefore be regarded as a way of solving the potential conflict between two political objectives: modernization of the society, and modernization of the military establishment through investment. In Norway this potential conflict was solved by linking the development of a national military industry to modernization – military research and industry were to be an instrument of modernization.

2.3 Modernization through Military Technology

Throughout the entire postwar period in Norway, economic arguments weighed heavily in the appraisals of military-industrial expansion. This applied particularly to the early postwar years when the political authorities chose to give priority to civilian economic growth by keeping military industry on a low level; lack of hard currency made participation in the 'Off-Shore Procurement Program'[4] particularly attractive; and the balance of payments was one argument for expanding industry in the 1960s.

A small group of people introduced a new type of argument for expanding military industry that was coherent with the Labour Party's ideology of modernization. Such attitudes were first expressed in the 1950s, but it was not until the 1960s that they became significant. This new movement was the first to express the possibility of using military research and development to raise the standards of both the armed forces and civilian industry.

The proponents of military industry thought that military research and development would help to modernize the armed forces themselves, which in the future would experience a similar transformation as modern industrial production characterized by efficiency measures and automation. This could take place only by using new technology. In qualitative terms, the armed forces in Norway as in other Western countries regarded technology as the major competitive means in relation to the Soviet Union. In addition there was an international tendency for military weapons and equipment to become steadily more technically complicated and advanced.[5]

Military research and industry were also regarded as a means of modernizing civilian industry. In the mid-1960s they were used in the public debate as an argument for engaging in military-industrial expansion (i.a. Leine, 1968; Rørholt, 1966; Stokke, 1968). Military industry was technology-intensive; it had to cooperate closely with research establishments and it required a high degree of technical and administrative competence in the companies concerned. There was a lack of industry of this type in Norway. Norwegian companies did not have experience in following exact contracts with delivery deadlines and work schedules, and they were not used to following exact, demanding specifications that would be subsequently inspected and tested. 'It was undoubtedly the duty of the armed forces to "train" industry in these fields in order to make it more competitive on the export market' (Wicken, 1984, p. 169). Indeed, the major means of making Norwegian industry more internationally competitive turned out to be research and development contracts, which had been used very little in Norway before the 1970s.

Such views were based on experiences from other countries, first and foremost the United States and Sweden, which were the most advanced industrial countries in the world and Europe respectively at the beginning of the 1960s. The United States had the most advanced economy in the world and there was talk of a technological gap between the USA and Europe (OECD, 1969). It was this gap that, according to the argumentation, could be reduced by using the military industry to function as a crane to lift the country's general technical level up to greater heights as had been done in Sweden: 'The secret of Swedish industry and Swedish defence is that Sweden has used industry to develop defence, and defence to develop industry' (Hurlen, 1966, p. 446).

It may be claimed that the ideology of 'modernizing through military industry' was only a varnish to make military rearmament more acceptable in Norway's Labour Party and among Norwegian politicians. It is difficult to decide whether this ideology indicates the basic views of the participants or was used as a secondary motive to promote a policy that otherwise would not have been acceptable – an empire-building strategy for individual institutions. More important in our context is, however, that the modernization argument was seen as coherent with the dominant ideology of the parliamentary political system. Military-industrial expansion was

MODERNIZATION THROUGH MILITARY INDUSTRY 145

thus more easily accepted by politicians, and created the condition for the construction of the 'military-industrial system'.

3 The Construction of a System

In the boom of 1960–74 a 'system' was created that became the foundation of Norway's military-industrial expansion. This was done by expanding the state research institute and industrial companies; by establishing the regulations for military procurement; and by adjusting the decision-making structure in the Ministry of Defence to make it possible to consider the needs of industry before purchasing. This section will look at some of the basic elements of this 'system'.

3.1 The NDRE–Kongsberg Alliance

In the course of the 1960s what we may call the 'Kongsberg model' for military-industrial expansion became evident. This was an alliance between the country's only military research institute, the management of Kongsberg Våpenfabrikk (hereafter called Kongsberg), a few technical personnel in leading positions in the armed forces, and some of the Labour Party's defence and industrial expertise. In the political and economic environment of the 1960s this alliance was able to allocate adequate resources and build up an organization for military procurement that laid the foundation for the expansion of military industry, first and foremost at Kongsberg.

This alliance originated in the 1950s between Kongsberg and the Norwegian Defence Research Establishment (NDRE). The institute was founded in 1946 and was in practice a continuation of the work of Norwegian researchers in Allied research institutes in Britain and the United States. In the beginning the NDRE was a 'foreign body' both in Norwegian research and in the Norwegian armed forces. Whereas the armed forces discovered that the NDRE did not cover their needs, civilian researchers were sceptical of military research in general and were afraid that the new institute would drain resources away from civilian research.

Nevertheless the NDRE created a platform for itself in Norwegian society that made the institute a power factor in questions of military kinds, both technical and industrial. The most important elements were the close contact the institute managed to make with the top defence politicians and its professional competence in certain areas of major military importance.

Shortly after the establishment of the institute, Norway's young and dynamic Minister of Defence Jens Christian Hauge gave it high priority. Hauge, who had led the military resistance movement in Norway during WWII, had clashed with the old military leadership shortly after the war. This disagreement was basically a conflict between old and modern concepts of defence, where Hauge represented the new elite defence concept based on modern weapons and technology. In 1947 Hauge transferred NOK 10 million from the army to the NDRE – a symbol of the transfer from the old to the new defence system – for nuclear research and missile development.

By the 1950s the NDRE had become the country's largest and probably most advanced research establishment in the basic areas of modern weapon technology: electronics, automation, and chemical explosives. From 1948 nuclear research was moved to a newly formed separate civilian institute, the Institute for Atomic Energy, which continued to cooperate closely with the NDRE. Immediate neighbours at Kjeller, just outside Oslo, the two institutes formed one of the largest technical research communities in the country.

Kongsberg was an old munitions company, founded in 1814. After WWII it needed modernizing. As Minister of Defence, Hauge saw it as his task to begin modernizing the military companies, but the work reached only the discussion stage. Even though Kongsberg was given low priority in connection with NATO, it managed to obtain a contract for production of the Bofors anti-aircraft artillery L/70 in 1953, and this order marked the beginning of the modernizing process. Hauge, who had been Minister of Defence up until 1952, was the man behind the contract and behind the reorganization of the company to enable it to carry out the new production. Hauge also had to persuade the administrative leaders of Kongsberg that the future of the company lay in advanced military-industrial production. This suggests that the expansion was a result of external pressure – from an ex-Minister of Defence and some officials in the Ministry of Defence. Through their positions as negotiators on behalf of Norway they could allot assignments to a Norwegian state-owned company – against the wishes of its directors (Wicken, 1987a).

The modernization of Kongsberg was accelerated in the early 1960s. At that time Kongsberg had a new management: Hauge himself had picked out the new managing director; the earlier director of the NDRE was chairman of the board from 1962, while Hauge was deputy chairman, a position he held right up until 1983. There was thus close cooperation between the NDRE and Kongsberg,[6] and Kongsberg became the only Norwegian company willing to enter into large-scale technically advanced production based partly on research from Norwegian institutes and partly on collaboration with foreign companies. In the course of a few years Kongsberg established itself as the country's leading technological company, and it initiated a number of new spheres of activity: production of car parts (1956), ASW Terne missiles (1957), numerical control systems (1961), missile systems Sidewinder (1962) and Bullpup (1964), gas turbines, proximity fuses, fire control systems, SSM Penguin weapons systems, and minicomputers (Wicken, 1988).

Thus by the mid-1960s both the NDRE and Kongsberg were among the leaders of Norwegian research and industry in areas of future industrial growth. This gave them influence in Norway's industrial policy, first and

MODERNIZATION THROUGH MILITARY INDUSTRY 147

foremost among politicians concerned with the role of technology in growth and reconversion.

3.2 Public Procurement as Industrial Policy

A market was required for the developing military industry. Until about 1960 Norway had lacked a national market for military equipment. In the defence sector there had been little need for a link between military procurement and Norwegian industry, since the MDAP had meant that no purchasing projects of any size existed until 1960 when Norway decided to build 48 new ships for its navy. This 'Fleet Programme' brought up the question of whether it was right to order the ships abroad and thus get the best value for money or whether consideration should be given to Norwegian industry (Wicken, 1987b).

In the knowledge that there would be other big projects financed nationally, an organization and a system for defence purchases were established. The initiative was taken partly by the armed forces, but was also forced through by the Royal Norwegian Council for Science and Technology (NTNF), which wanted to introduce public procurement as industrial policy in more general terms. It is interesting to note that representatives of military industry and of the military research institute were among the most eager to see the NTNF involved in this matter. The most influential individual was the director of the NDRE, Finn Lied, who was also a member of the board of the NTNF from 1958.

In about 1970 the foundations were laid for a procurement organization that would systematically protect the interests of industry. This was done partly as a practical way of implementing the 'Fleet Plan' of 1960, and partly by compiling regulations for military procurement.[7] Procurement policy that would benefit industry was speeded up under the non-socialist government of 1965–71, whose Minister of Defence Otto Grieg Tidemand was a champion of such policy. In the years 1967–68 a great deal of work went into developing a military procurement system which became the foundation for corresponding civilian legislation. When the Director of the NDRE, Finn Lied, became Minister of Industry (1971–72) in the new Labour cabinet, much of the initiative behind this policy was moved to the Ministry of Industry.

3.3 The Decision-Making System

The same group of officials that had strengthened Kongsberg and the NDRE and had taken the initiative in developing a military procurement policy to benefit industry were also responsible for ensuring that technical expertise in the armed forces gained a more powerful position in the leadership. In 1963 a Royal Commission was appointed to assess the kind of leadership the armed forces were to have in the future.[8]

It was proposed that the armed forces be led by a troika consisting of an administrative leader, a scientific leader, and the Chief of Defence. In our context it is the scientific leader that is of most interest. This post was to be filled by the Director of the NDRE, Finn Lied – who was also a member of the committee. His task was to take the initiative at an early stage to promote production of military material based on Norwegian research. In addition the scientific leader was to present the technical possibilities of the future to the military and political leaders.

He was also to be responsible for system analyses, for support of long-term planning in the armed forces, and for operations analyses of how the armed forces' resources could be most effectively put to use. This would give the NDRE a powerful position within the planning system of the military establishment. At an early stage the NDRE had become the only centre for applied computer research in the defence forces. A group for operations analysis had been established as early as the late 1940s, and a systems analysis group was set up in 1960 which became important in furthering the NDRE's influence in political defence planning in the decades to come. With its monopoly of computer expertise, the group could develop tactical and strategic models and also influence the decision-making process in weapons procurement.

Not all the recommendations of the Royal Commission were accepted, but the NDRE managed to attain a powerful position both in the general long-term planning of defence and in procurement. This was illustrated by the Director of the NDRE being appointed to the Defence Council (Forsvarsrådet) in 1963. We may see the strong position of the NDRE in the defence planning process during this period as part of an international pattern. Also in the United States, scientific advisers were to become particularly influential after the 'Sputnik shock' of 1957 (Killian, 1982).

4 The Role of an Active and Expansive State

The 'military-industrial system' was developed largely between 1960 and 1975. It consisted of two powerful elements, the NDRE and the state-owned munition companies, and a military system with a code of regulations that made it possible to consider the needs of industry in military procurement.

At the same time the Norwegian state was undergoing a period of rapid growth while the predominant political ideology was that the state should take an active part in solving economic and social questions. Economic growth made it possible to build public institutions at a brisk pace, but nobody was in a position to carry out any responsible political control or administration of the many initiatives taken. The 'system' we have described was the result of a number of initiatives – and few people could have realized that the end result would be a kind of 'military-industrial system'.

4.1 The Active State

The discussion about the Fleet Plan in 1960 showed widespread willingness in the Norwegian Labour Party to utilize the state's role as customer in order to promote industrial development. The debate also expressed a general will to use the state actively in order to promote the dominant political goals at any time. Priority was placed on achieving the objective, while the procedure was considered less important. In 1960 the issue was whether Norwegian companies should be given orders even when they did not have the best tenders. Some members of the Opposition thought that this would lead to lobbying in the ministries: decisions would no longer be taken on the grounds of purely economic assessments, but through general evaluations of the effects the different options would produce. This would open the way for greater arbitrariness in the choice of purchases and enable those who wanted to influence the political decision-making process to lobby in the ministry (Wicken, 1987b).

We may look on this debate as an expression of the more general attitude to the use of the state apparatus to promote definite political goals which were highly dominant in the political life of this period, both in socialist and in non-socialist governments. This opened the way for the political support of several initiatives to increase the numbers of state organs and develop systems to solve specific social problems. Such initiatives often came from groups involved in an individual social sector, and their ideas were largely accepted by politicians after the relevant expert committees had delivered their reports.

The state needed economic resources to be able to expand its area of activity and develop organs to carry out its more active tasks. The active state also implied an expanding state, and this expansion required fresh resources. State revenue increased rapidly, both as a result of the collective revenues increasing and because the state controlled a steadily increasing share of the Gross National Product. From 1960 to 1974 public expenditure, calculated in fixed prices, increased by more than 150%. As GNP increased rapidly, public expenditure as a percentage of GNP increased 'only' from 11 to 16%.

This expansion and the new activities opened up the system to entrepreneurs who wanted to exploit the state apparatus to promote the particular interests or political views of certain groups. The combination of an active and an expansive state meant that the state apparatus was not permanent and rigid, but that new 'systems' could be developed to enable the state to undertake new tasks. We may speak of an open and flexible state system.

At the same time the state was not a monolithic power structure with political organs or individuals able to control and govern this expansion in relation to superior political objectives. The growth of new 'systems' took place through initiatives from persons outside the formal parliamentary political system. This can be seen from the development of the military-industrial system we have described.

When it was possible to utilize Kongsberg for 'private' industrial policy, this was because of the position of the state company in relation to the Ministry of Industry as owners and the Storting (Norwegian Parliament) which granted funds for development projects. In practice the ministry did not inspect what the company did; and the ministry's strong man from about 1960 to the mid-1980s, Odd Gøthe, expressed it thus: 'The military company has lived its own life in splendid isolation. There was not much the Ministry of Industry could do with strong personalities like Hurlen, Jens Chr. Hauge, and Møller from NDRE' (Gøthe, 1988). Nor was there anyone in the Storting who was able, or found it appropriate, to check the details in the state company, so that proposals for investment funding were largely approved without any real check being made.

Similar views were expressed by the Ministry of Defence as early as 1960: 'It is the clear opinion of the Matériel Directorate that it has always been difficult to keep a check on the military company. One may say that the military company has had a tendency not only to keep a check on us, but even to direct us' (Wicken, 1987a, p. 68). Later many people might have made similar statements about the influence the NDRE had in making decisions about defence policy.

5 What Is a 'Military-Industrial System'?

The Norwegian 'military-industrial system' had some similarities to the US 'military-industrial complex', but it also had its peculiarities. The term military-industrial complex has its roots in the writings of C. Wright Mills (1956) and attained popularity thanks to President Eisenhower's 1961 farewell address in which he warned the American people against the extension of the influence of the military-industrial system beyond essential national security interests. In US literature the military-industrial system is most frequently defined as a coalition of powerful groups and bodies that share economic, institutional, or political interest in intensifying defence expenditure. At this general level we see clearly the similarities between the Norwegian and US systems.

The idea behind the MIC concept was to analyse how factors other than purely military ones influenced the arms race, e.g. economic motives. The strongest groups in the complex were the large military-industrial companies and the professional military establishment. Together they managed to influence the political decision-making process to increase the defence budget more than would otherwise have been the case (Galbraith, 1969, 1972). In most writings on the US military-industrial system, the profit motive of the large industrial companies is regarded as one of its main driving forces.

Looking more closely at the motivation and social structure of the Norwegian 'military-industrial system', we note how it differs from its US counterpart. The Norwegian munition companies were state-owned, as was the only national defence research institute. There was therefore no private profit motive behind the construction of a 'military-industrial system'. Also, the military establishment cannot be regarded as a main driving force in the process described, as it did not show any particular interest in a strong national military industry until the 1970s.

The lack of private profit interests and military interest involved in its construction meant that the motives must be found in the public sector:

First, there was an attempt to strengthen the military technical research community and the state-owned military company. Expansion of military-industrial production would attract resources to these establishments. Second, the motive was to contribute to the modernization and strengthening of the Norwegian military forces. Third, having a national military industry would reduce imports and hence save foreign currency. Fourth, military industry was seen as a locomotive in a broader modernization process in Norwegian industry.

In his farewell address President Eisenhower warned the American people that factors other than national security decided military-industrial expansion. In Norway only a few regarded non-military motives as a political danger. On the contrary, the dominant political attitude at the time was that non-military factors would be taken into consideration in military decision-making. In the 1960s it became more common in political decisions on all kinds of economic matters (including military) to take secondary objectives into consideration: the primary objective to improve the quality of the military forces and the secondary objective – economic growth – were to be balanced (Wicken, 1987b).

What President Eisenhower had really feared was 'technology-out-of-control' (MacKenzie, Chapter 8 in this volume): that is, out of political control. The Norwegian system was not constructed as a result of parliamentary decision-making processes; it cannot however be described as totally non-controlled. Leading personalities in the system were close to – or even part of – the formal political system. Hauge continued to keep a strong political position even after having left the government; Lied became Minister of Industry in 1971–72. The third individual who linked the construction of the 'military-industrial system' to the formal political system was Otto Grieg Tidemand, who was Minister of Defence 1965–70 in the non-socialist cabinet.

The construction of the 'military-industrial system' was not implemented after political decisions were taken by the formal parliamentary political system. It was constructed as a consequence of operations by politically influential groups working mainly through non-parliamentary decision-making channels. This did not however create political tensions or interference from the Storting or the Government. We may understand this lack of reaction as a consequence of the consensus in both defence and industrial matters in Norway in the period 1960–75 (Sejersted, 1984).

The construction of the system was part of a broader change of the modern state, from a 'corporate state' (Rokkan, 1970) to the 'segmented state' (Maktutredningen, 1982). From the 1960s a number of 'politico-economic systems' with a high degree of internal self-government were established. These 'systems' consisted of private or public economic interests in coalition with public establishments, politicians, and public administration. In accordance with this tradition we may call our system a '*military-industrial segment*'.[9]

By 1980 the military-industrial segment had been integrated in a 'defence segment' which also included the armed forces and leading military politicians (Tamnes, 1986). An important aspect of the segment at that time was to allocate the largest possible amount of resources to the military. This objective unified the segment, but at the same time we may observe a new critique of the 'military-industrial system', i.e. that it had obtained too much power in military planning and procurement processes, giving less influence to military professionals and the administration of the Ministry of Defence. In this perspective, then, Eisenhower's 1961 criticism of the US military-industrial complex was to find its counterpart in Norway some twenty years later.

Notes

1. A few of the classic discussions on MIC are Galbraith (1969, 1972), Melman (1970), Mills (1956), Pursell (1972).

2. The military-industrial system is an analogue concept to the 'technological system' used by Hughes (1983). The idea is that social, political, and economic interests are closely connected to a technology or a product. The participants in the system have certain interests in promoting this specific technology or product. Together they form a 'system' of interrelated and mutual interests groups. Such a system, first constructed, will reach a phase of 'momentum' when it is 'out of control' of other social forces.

3. *Stortingsmelding* no. 15, 1963–64. *Forsvarssjefens forslag til forsvarsprogram for perioden 1964–68.*

4. The Off-Shore Procurement (OSP) Program was part of the Mutual Defense Assistance Program whereby the USA paid for munitions production in Western Europe. The programme had a double duty: to provide recipients with added foreign exchange while at the same time providing for the production of munitions (Kaplan, 1980).

5. *Stortingsproposisjon* no. 23, 1957. *Om hovedretningslinjer for Forsvaret i årene framover.*

6. Aslak Bonde, 'Terne-rakettens venner. Om utviklingen, produksjonen og salget av det første norske våpensystemet 1953–62'. Unpublished thesis in History, University of Oslo, 1988.

7. See *Innstilling fra Utvalget for utarbeidelse av nye bestemmelser vedrørende anskaffelser til forsvaret.* Oslo: Ministry of Defence, 1970. The breakthrough years for developing a military procurement organization and regulations were during the non-socialist government of 1967–70. This procurement system was to a large extent copied by other public procurement agencies in the years to follow.

8. The chairman of the Royal Commission was Jens Chr. Hauge; the other members were the Director of the NDRE, Finn Lied; Chief of Defence from 1963, Bjarne Øen, who was one of those who took the initiative in establishing the NDRE; and the Minister of Transport and Communications from 1965, Håkon Kyllingmark. Cf. *Om den øverste ledelsen av forsvaret*, *Stortingsmelding* no. 80, 1965–66 [Haugeutvalget].

9. When the system was established it opened for activities which may be described as *technological entrepreneurship* (Evangelista, 1986a). The alliances between the elements of the system created pressure groups which were able to promote technological and industrial programmes which politicians hardly would be able to control. We should however treat the

creation of the system as a separate social phenomenon from the utilization of the system when it was constructed. This chapter deals only with the former problem.

OLAV WICKEN, b. 1950, Cand. Philol. in History (University of Oslo, 1977); visiting Research Fellow at the London School of Economics (1978–79); Research Associate at the Norwegian Institute for Defence Studies (1982–); among his publications are studies on Norway's military-industrial policy in the post-World War II era and on Norwegian industrial and technological history.

Chapter 10

The Bomb That Never Was: The Rise and Fall of the Swedish Nuclear Weapons Programme*

WILHELM AGRELL
Research Policy Institute, University of Lund

1 Introduction

In 1945 the newly established Swedish Defence Research Agency (FOA) initiated a high-priority research programme on the nature and effects of nuclear weapons and the premises for a national weapons programme. During the 1950s Sweden embarked on a massive development of the high technology of the nuclear age, including wide employment of heat- and power-producing reactors, a complete domestic fuel cycle, and a defence based on tactical nuclear weapons.

Of these giant steps into the nuclear age, almost all were to lead to a dead end. The heavy-water reactor programme failed to create a technologically and economically feasible alternative. With light-water technology taking over in the nuclear industry, the domestic fuel cycle became pointless from the perspective of energy production. And the Swedish nuclear weapons programme never crossed the threshold where it was officially sanctioned. In fact its existence was, and still is, publicly denied. The largest and most far-reaching attempt in the history of Swedish defence to develop a new weapons technology not only failed: it never was.

This officially non-existing nuclear weapons programme – with its determinants, progress, failure, and consequences – is of vital importance for an analysis of the development of Swedish defence, of the role of defence research, and of the links between civilian and military use of

---

* This chapter is based on two books in Swedish and an ongoing research project on the Swedish nuclear weapons programme and its impact on Swedish postwar policy. The first book (Agrell, 1985) dealt with the transition in the defence doctrine from a WWII-influenced concept to a doctrine influenced by the theories of nuclear deterrence and limited war. The second book (Agrell, 1989) deals with the institutionalization and development of Swedish defence research during and after the war and the links between defence research, procurement, and domestic arms production.

national efforts for high technology. This aborted weapons development programme can also be relevant in a general discussion of weapons acquisition and the role of political, strategic, and technological determinants.

First, there is a strong tendency, discussed by other authors in this volume, to focus on the process of weapons development and procurement in the United States, the interaction between the United States and the Soviet Union, and a limited number of strategic weapons systems. Virtually all analysis of the arms race is directly or indirectly based on empirical data, case studies, or theoretical approaches originating from this narrow field. It is of course true, as Hans Günter Brauch points out in Chapter 11, that this field constitutes the forward edge of the postwar arms dynamic; the USA has been the leading developer of military technology, and strategic weapons have been regarded as the political and military core of the arms race – with the most far-reaching consequences. It goes without saying that an analysis of weapons development and the arms race that failed to deal with this field would be of very limited general value.

On the other hand, a focus on strategic weapons only would disrupt an overall analysis of the social ramifications of military technology. As in all research the definition of the research object determines the kind of questions likely to be asked and answered. Ulrich Albrecht in Chapter 6 points to the lack of research on the interrelation between social structure and weapons development, between militarism and industrialism. The history of strategic weapons tends to stress the importance of planning, programme management, and the interrelation between succeeding generations of weapon systems. If the main theoretical purpose is to deal with the relationship between militarism and industrialism, a number of other research fields, from other periods and other environments, could be equally or more important.

Second, the focus on weapons development is almost exclusively on systems that have actually been selected, produced, and deployed. This focus is justified if the aim is to study the causes behind existing arsenals but is more questionable if the purpose is wider: the social factors affecting arms technology cannot be properly studied unless failures and aborted innovations and projects are studied in parallel with the successful ones.

Third, the focus on the USA as the primary engine of the development of military technology tends to overlook the complex pattern of impulses, technology transfer, and independent lines of development in other countries. The US (and Soviet) development of military technology in the postwar period is important not only because of its direct political and military consequences on superpower relations, but also because of its impact on other countries and regions.

Fourth, a theoretical framework and general conclusions based mainly on US postwar experiences will tend to overemphasize the importance of the specific factors in political life, industrial structure, and military organization in the USA. Any attempt to deal with the fundamental issues concerning the social context of the development of military technology must look beyond the US (or Soviet) perspective and determine the importance of the specific cultural and social dimension. Such a perspective is more widely acknowledged in the study of technological development and diffusion in the non-military field.

Fifth, study of the nuclear weapons programmes of the non-superpower nations is essential for the continuing discussion on proliferation and non-proliferation.[1] Much attention has been paid to why countries 'go nuclear' and opt for an overt or covert nuclear capability. Less attention has been paid to the far more general pattern: why so many threshold countries have not developed weapons programmes.[2] From the point of view of arms dynamics, the mechanisms behind the reluctance of a large number of countries to cross the threshold of nuclear weapons are as relevant as the factors behind proliferation.

The history of the Swedish nuclear weapons programme, and its military, political, and scientific dimensions, certainly does not in itself answer the array of questions raised in the five points above. The brief discussion below can, however, serve as an illustration of the potential value of broader or more specific case studies dealing with arms development outside the superpower contest over strategic weapons.

2 The Hard Lesson: Coping with the 'New Means of Warfare'

In World War II, Sweden, along with Switzerland, became an island in a continent shattered by war and Nazi German *Neuordnung*. Swedish defence, demobilized and largely neglected in the mid-war period, was still in poor shape; parliamentary decisions for improvements had been implemented only partially when the war broke out; and Sweden found itself more or less cut off from an arms world market closed down by demands for national mobilization. For Sweden the only alternative to achieve a badly needed rapid build-up of national defence was to rely on the domestic industry. Isolated from the world market, large parts of Swedish industry, mainly the paper and metal industries, were running in low gear. Manpower as well as production capacity could be diverted to the new urgent goals of national self-reliance concerning raw materials and arms production (Olsson, 1977).

But Sweden was faced with more than a problem of establishing a national basis for a rearmament programme. This programme, and the whole national defence effort, would rapidly become obsolete and thus insufficient unless Sweden could adjust to the rapid development in weapon technologies and their employment by the major powers in the war. The extraordinary situation tended, in Sweden as among these powers, to break down much of the conceptual and structural resistance to new technology within the armed forces. The intensified armament programme made this easier, since virtually everyone got more. But Sweden was not only isolated from most sources of arms imports: the country was also sealed off from information concerning new technologies, new weapons, and their tactical employment by the warring parties.[3] Swedish defence attachés and other intelligence sources tried to pick up information on the new weapons technologies but were in most cases prevented by tight security and considerable suspicion.[4] For instance, it was only towards the end of the war, when Swedish political terms of trade improved, that Sweden managed to procure some radar equipment.[5]

Sweden emerged from World War II with the overall political lesson that neutrality and national rearmament had worked and that also in a postwar world Sweden would have to rely on its own resources, on national mobilization within the concept of a 'total defence'. The armed forces had been built up and were well equipped, and a new extensive military-industrial network had been established. The division of Europe in two blocs and the emerging Cold War served to confirm these lessons and made them the cornerstone of Swedish postwar defence policy.

One of the most imminent tasks for this new and extended defence policy was to assess the lessons from the war and the impact of the new means of warfare. In the years 1945–47 the Swedish Defence High Command carried out an extensive investigation of the changes in warfare and their impact on Swedish defence (Agrell, 1985, pp. 82–94). The main conclusion, as presented to the 1945 Parliamentary Defence Commission, was the importance of the rapid development in the means for air warfare demonstrated in the (assumed) devastating effects of the Allied bomber offensive against Germany. Thus air defence had to be improved considerably, and among the key elements of the 1948 parliamentary defence decision was a very substantial reinforcement of the number of fighter squadrons.[6] Air defence was, according to the doctrine presented by the Supreme Commander and endorsed by politicians, an independent and crucial element in Swedish defence, since an aggressor (assumed to be the Soviet Union) could direct severe blows at Swedish cities, industry, and power stations.

According to the assessment of the Supreme Commander the most important single technological innovation during the war was radar – an assessment reflected in intense Swedish efforts during and after the war to develop and procure radar stations.[7] Nuclear weapons were, in the long perspective, regarded as a radical new means of warfare, but in a highly detailed analysis the Supreme Commander attempted to downgrade the immediate importance of the new weapon; nuclear stockpiles were assumed to remain strictly limited for a long time to come, and Sweden was, due to its large territory, less vulnerable to nuclear attack than densely populated areas elsewhere (*Vårt framtida försvar*, 1947). Still the general conclusion of the Supreme Commander was that the numerous technological breakthroughs during the war had created a basic uncertainty that made impossible long-term decisions concerning the structure of Swedish defence. The impact and prospects of the new technologies had to be examined closely.

3 Into the Atomic Age

One of the many organizational innovations decided during the war was the establishment of a joint Defence Research Agency, Försvarets forskningsanstalt (FOA). The agency was set up in 1945 by merging three dispersed research bodies, the Defence Chemical Agency, established before the war, the Institute for Military Physics, and the Defence Telecommunication Laboratory – the two latter ad hoc institutions set up during the war. The overriding purpose of the new agency was to coordinate and carry out the necessary research, experimentation, and testing concerning 'new means of warfare', areas where industrial development work along established lines would not be sufficient. (For a further discussion, see Agrell, 1989, ch. 4.)

FOA was, as a result of the merger, organized in three departments: for military chemistry (FOA 1), military physics (FOA 2), and military electronics (FOA 3). Each research group basically continued with the type of work it had carried out during the war. But one new high-priority task was assigned to the agency as early as 1945: the investigation of nuclear weapons technology.

The political and psychological impact of the atomic bombs dropped over Japan was not limited to the major powers. In Sweden, as in Norway, the idea of national development of this new technology was soon raised (see Forland, 1987, 1988). Sweden had one considerable advantage, already investigated by the British on behalf of the Manhattan Project towards the end of the war: very large deposits of the mineral kolm in oil shales, containing a low concentration of natural uranium.[8]

In the autumn of 1945 a major research programme was initiated at FOA covering a wide range of problems concerning nuclear energy and nuclear weapons. FOA 1 started research on the enrichment of uranium from kolm, and FOA 2 focused on the basic principles for reactor technology and general information concerning nuclear weapons and their effects. At the same time the Swedish government appointed a Parliamentary Atomic Committee to investigate the need for basic research in the nuclear field. In its reports of 1946 and 1947 the Committee suggested a general strengthening of basic research, a programme for constructing a research reactor, and an advisory board to the government (Atomkommittén, 1946, 1947). Neither the directives to the Committee nor its report mentioned the possibility of military utilization of Swedish nuclear research. The declared motive for strengthening nuclear research was instead the possibility of producing energy from a domestic raw material.

In 1947 the company AB Atomenergi was set up, with the state as the largest owner. AB Atomenergi was to develop methods for uranium production and start work on a research reactor. So far the visible side of Swedish nuclear research was entirely civilian, for civilian purposes only. In the years 1947 to 1950 the bulk of research on uranium enrichment and reactor technology initiated at FOA was transferred to AB Atomenergi along with parts of the research staff (Agrell, 1989). Behind the scenes, things looked very different, however.

Even though the assessment of the Supreme Commander in 1947 downgraded the impact of nuclear weapons, this did not mean that the Swedish defence community lacked interest in the possibility of developing nuclear weapons.[9] The assessment dealt mainly with the threat posed by nuclear weapons, but it also underlined the potential of these weapons for a defender inferior in manpower and fire support. In 1948 the Supreme Commander thus secretly instructed FOA to investigate the premises for developing nuclear weapons or other forms of nuclear warfare and nuclear propulsion in Sweden and the time needed for such a programme.[10] The investigation presented by FOA became the key document for Sweden's nuclear research and development efforts in the coming decades.

The FOA plan concluded that a national Swedish nuclear weapons programme had to proceed along the plutonium line and be based on heavy-water reactors with a core of natural uranium from the Swedish deposits. A small research reactor would be useful for gaining experience, but the key element in such a programme would be a large reactor that could produce plutonium in quantities necessary for the construction of nuclear charge. Prior to this, considerable research would have to be carried out in the fields of plutonium chemistry and the theoretical and practical problems associated with the construction of a nuclear device. The total time-span of the programme was estimated to be between eight and thirteen years. Because of the time-lag for the development of a large plutonium-producing reactor, the main task foreseen for FOA in the short perspective was general support and supervision of the development of reactors so that the military component would not get lost. Research on plutonium had to be started and was gradually to increase so that construction of the charge could proceed swiftly once the large reactor began to turn out sufficient quantities of plutonium.

In order to secure links to the reactor programme of the civilian AB Atomenergi various measures were taken. The most important was a secret agreement 1950 between FOA and AB Atomenergi stipulating a division of labour 'in order to facilitate planning and the incorporations of the resources of FOA and AB Atomenergi in a joint plan' (Larsson, 1985; *Svensk kärnvapenforskning 1945–1972*, p. 16). Thus the agreement stipulated a free flow of personnel, know-how, and raw material between the two organizations; in the event of a more tense military situation the whole of AB Atomenergi would be incorporated in FOA. The research department established at AB Atomenergi was in reality an extension of FOA, headed by a former senior researcher from FOA 2 and, in accordance with the agreement, working on the reactor development within the framework of the joint plan. But it was not until the mid-1950s that this plan was actually launched.

By then both the military and the political situation had changed considerably. With the rapid development of nuclear warfare and the nuclear doctrine of the United States in the first half of the 1950s, the earlier assessments from Sweden's Supreme Commander no longer appeared valid. In the years 1952–54 a major reorientation in the military attitude towards nuclear weapons occurred, affecting threat perceptions as well as the question of Swedish nuclear weapons. (For further discussion, see Agrell, 1985.) In the new long-term plan presented by the Supreme Commander in 1954 the development of new means of warfare was declared as the main element affecting future Swedish defence. The threat from nuclear weapons against cities and military targets was now regarded as considerable: through massive nuclear strikes at the outbreak of a war, an aggressor could wipe out a large portion of the Swedish population, paralyse essential functions, and prevent the Swedish defence forces from operating in large formations (*ÖB-54*).

To cope with this new situation, the Supreme Commander suggested several radical adjustments in Swedish defence strategy. Civil defence had to be reorganized to cope with an extensive plan for swift evacuation of the population from large and medium-size cities.[11] For the armed forces the Supreme Commander foresaw changes in organization and tactics in order to adjust them to a 'nuclear climate'. It is obvious that the ongoing re-evaluation within the US Army of the future role of ground forces in a nuclear war influenced Swedish conclusions on this point.[12] But the most important element, as presented by the Supreme Commander, was that Swedish defence itself could benefit from the new means of warfare and not only adjust to their consequences. For this reason, he requested a gradually increasing long-term allowance under the general heading 'new weapons' (*ÖB-54*, p. 342).

'New weapons' in reality meant a *nuclear* weapons programme even if this was not stated outright. The sum, divided over ten years, and presented in *ÖB-54*, was in fact based on the plan originally drafted by FOA in 1948 and revised in 1953 on the time-frames and annual costs for a nuclear weapons programme. In the 1953 revision, total programme costs were calculated to SEK 500 million (Larsson, 1985; *Svensk kärnvapen-forskning 1945–1972*, p. 17). In *ÖB-54* the total sum was just over SEK 600 million – a fair adjustment to rising costs. According to the FOA plan, the major costs of the programme would start in year 5. In *ÖB-54* the funds for new weapons started in fiscal year 1960/61, so if this was year 5 the programme must have run from fiscal year 1956/57. Thus, the years 1955–56 must have been crucial for the formal initiation of Sweden's nuclear weapons programme.

4 Big Science and the Blue-Yellow Line

Until 1955 a Swedish nuclear weapons programme had been a political non-issue. Officially no such programme existed, no preparations were carried out, and no formal proposition for a programme had been made.[13]

The turning-point was to be a decision on the development of large plutonium producing reactors, huge long-term investments in an untried technology.

In December 1955 a new parliamentary committee was appointed – Atomenergiutredningen – this time to study the possibility of a large-scale national reactor programme. The Committee worked quickly, presenting its report in March 1956. Two months later the government presented a bill to the Swedish Parliament.[14] With its 1956 decision on nuclear energy, Sweden was to embark on a large-scale national programme for heat- and power-producing heavy-water reactors fed with natural uranium enriched from the domestic deposits at Ranstad in Västergötland. The declared motive for selecting the alternative using natural uranium and heavy water was the need for improved self-reliance in energy production. By the end of the century the programme was to make Sweden more or less self-sufficient in power production and heating. It is, however, worth noticing that these arguments were presented before the Suez Crisis with the drop in oil deliveries due to the closing of the Canal; the main argument instead was the general risk of future problems in the uranium and oil markets.[15]

On the surface the so called 'blue-yellow line' for the development of nuclear energy was one of several national programmes for the development of 'big science' in Sweden from the mid-1950s and onwards. (The designation 'blue-yellow' refers to the colours of the Swedish flag.) This policy was based on widespread optimism, not least within the Social Democratic Party, about the prospects of technology for ensuring economic growth and hence social progress (Erlander, 1976; Wittrock & Lindström, 1984).

Neither the 1956 parliamentary report nor the government bill mentioned any specific linkage between the proposed nuclear energy programme and preparations for Swedish nuclear weapons. Officially the Swedish government maintained that there was no need to discuss or decide on nuclear weapons since any military application of nuclear energy could not become relevant for several years (*Svensk kärnvapenforskning 1945–1972*, p. 19). But behind the official scene things looked different: here the design of the blue-yellow line was dictated by specific demands for a programme to produce plutonium.

The secret agreement between FOA and Atomenergi was still in force, which meant that all actions were closely coordinated in a joint plan. Thus a direct link existed between FOA (and the Supreme Commander) and Atomenergi – a link which neither the Parliament nor the public was aware of when the civilian programme was debated.[16] In November 1955, just before the crucial cabinet meetings where Atomenergiutredningen was appointed, FOA in cooperation with Atomenergi and several university research groups completed a new and considerably more detailed investigation on the premises for developing nuclear weapons (*Svensk kärnvapenforskning 1945–1972*, p. 19).

This investigation included calculations on the size and construction of a 'tactical atom bomb', requirements as to the purity of the weapons-grade material, and the costs and staff needed. A reactor programme designed exclusively for plutonium production would, however, lead to competition for sparse manpower between a military and a civilian programme. The investigation could therefore not recommend an exclusive military plutonium production programme. The solution to this problem was a dual-purpose programme with low-temperature reactors producing plutonium and heat, as well as high-temperature reactors producing plutonium and electric power. These reactors would, however, require frequent fuel exchange and therefore a more complicated construction. Extra costs were to be covered by the defence budget within the overall civilian programme.

Thus Atomenergi (and in reality FOA and the Supreme Commander) could sit on two chairs and simultaneously propose the design of the civilian nuclear energy programme and the additional military specifications of the civilian programme 'which was to be initiated anyway'. Research Director Sigvard Eklund could, both as an author of the early drafts for the weapons programme and as an expert in the parliamentary commission on the nuclear energy programme, supervise the continuing coordination of effort under the joint plan. With the blue-yellow line, Sweden would within four or five years have a modest-sized plutonium production reactor operating (R 3 in Ågesta) and somewhat later a large reactor (R 4 in Marviken). A uranium enrichment plant at Ranstad was under construction, and heavy water was being procured from Norway. Thus, Swedish plutonium production would not be affected by any international restrictions imposed by the nuclear powers.

Until the 1956 parliamentary decision, the joint plan did not run into any serious difficulties. Swedish nuclear weapons, although from time to time a topic in the public debate, were not yet a policy issue. But with the decision on plutonium-producing reactors, the whole programme had to be set in motion if the time-frame of the FOA studies was to hold. And now problems began to mount.

5 A Crumbling Consensus on National Defence

In November 1955 the Swedish cabinet – at the time a coalition between the Social Democratic Party and the Agrarian Party – for the first time considered the nuclear weapons issue.[17] Several prominent Social Democratic cabinet members argued the necessity of retaining the option to equip the Swedish armed forces with nuclear weapons if an international agreement to ban these weapons could not be reached. Others, first of all Foreign Minister Östen Undén, were clearly opposed: Swedish nuclear weapons would, in Undén's opinion, in themselves make Sweden a target in a future war and therefore undermine the overall goal of Swedish non-aligned policy.[18]

Prime Minister Tage Erlander did not take a clear stand for or against.

His basic line was that there were good reasons to postpone a decision. From the perspective of party tactics it would be suicidal to display an open split in such an important issue shortly before the autumn 1956 elections. And, according to Erlander's own diary, 'we would lose nothing by waiting, since we anyway have to build our reactors first' (quoted in von Sydow, 1978, p. 62). In February 1956, the Executive Committee of the Social Democratic Party discussed the nuclear weapons issue; several members came out strongly against nuclear weapons. Erlander managed to convince both wings of the necessity of postponing a decision and refraining from public intra-party debate.

The Social Democrats were thus weakened by an internal division on the important issue of national defence, a split that could easily be exploited by the Opposition parties. This situation was complicated by the fact that all parties were engaged in intricate negotiations on a long-term decision on national defence based on the *ÖB-54* plan from the Supreme Commander. The nuclear weapons issue did not in itself create the division in the Social Democratic Party: it merely opened up an old conflict between the proponents of a strong national defence and the pacifist wing that had unsuccessfully been pressing for reallocation of defence resources in the immediate postwar years.

This internal split could, however, not be kept out of the public debate for long. In early 1957 the FOA Director stated that Sweden had resources to produce nuclear weapons and that the first bombs could be operational by 1963–64, thus triggering a major public debate in which proponents and opponents within the Social Democratic Party confronted each other (Ahlmark, 1965). Defence negotiations, complicated by the inability of the Social Democrats to formulate a line in the nuclear weapons issue, were further delayed, and it was necessary to request an updated long-term plan from the Supreme Commander.

This new long-term plan, *ÖB-57*, was a strong and consistent argument for the procurement of Swedish nuclear weapons. Swedish defence was described as impossible in the long run without access to tactical nuclear weapons. In *ÖB-57* the Supreme Commander developed the operational principles already outlined in earlier plans: faced with the threat of nuclear strikes, Swedish forces had to disperse in order not to present the aggressor with nuclear-worthy targets.[19] By possessing nuclear weapons, the Swedish defence could force the aggressor to disperse in the same manner, so the battle would be fought on equal although fundamentally changed terms. On this nuclear battlefield an 'area war' was to be fought – a kind of warfare demanding strong mobile conventional forces. Tactical nuclear weapons could therefore, in the concept of the Swedish Supreme Commander, not be employed to replace conventional forces.

In *ÖB-57* the Supreme Commander increased pressure on the government. With a clash approaching on the issue of the new comprehensive pension system (eventually leading up to a new election in the summer of 1958) the Social Democrats decided to opt for an agreement with the

Opposition concerning defence. Military expenditures were to rise sharply, but no decision was to be taken on the increasingly controversial issue of nuclear weapons. However, by the autumn of 1958 the nuclear issue was back again, this time in terms of a formal request from the Supreme Commander for funding for nuclear weapons research at FOA.

FOA planned to perform advanced research and experimental development in plutonium and in various aspects of bomb construction until the plutonium-producing reactors started to deliver weapons-grade material. FOA was already well under way in many of these fields, and funding for nuclear research was sharply increasing.[20] The FOA request was made on the direct order of the Supreme Commander. The Supreme Commander, General Nils Swedlund, however, disregarded increasingly desperate signals from the pro-nuclear wing that he should stick to the low profile. Instead, General Swedlund and the defence staff moved ahead with a vigorous campaign line pushing the Social Democratic Party towards open division on the issue of nuclear weapons (von Sydow, 1978, p. 352). Relations between the Supreme Commander and the Defence Minister Sven Andersson were to remain frosty until the former left office in 1961.

Nuclear research at FOA now became the main issue in the public debate, where new popular anti-nuclear movements like the AMSA (the action group against Swedish atomic weapons) played an increasing role.[21] Tactics to postpone the decision with reference to the reactor programme could no longer work, and the Social Democratic Party had to unite the opposing wings in one way or another. The approaching party conference in 1960 determined the time available. In November 1958 the party commissioned a special group to study the nuclear weapons issue – in reality to find a formula to unite the two wings, at least temporarily.

Erlander chaired the group himself, assigning most of the negotiating work to his young and talented assistant Olof Palme. Palme approached the problem by trying to find a formula broad enough for both wings to accept and yet satisfying their demands at least to an extent where they would refrain from open rebellion against the party line. The key element was how the purpose of the research programme should be defined. FOA experts and scientific advisers of the government both argued that there was no clear-cut dividing line between research aimed at construction and research aimed at improving protection against nuclear explosions and fallout (von Sydow, 1978; Socialdemokratiska partistyrelsen, 1960). The official line was that all research carried out so far had been motivated with the aim of protection against nuclear attack. Now the experts argued that a further expansion of the protection or S-programme was in fact needed but not possible with current instructions. The S-programme, according to the experts, consisted of a 'pure' protection part and a 'bomb' part which dealt with the principles of nuclear weapons. The knowledge gained in the 'bomb' part was necessary for the overall programme but could – in theory – be used in a future construction programme, the so-called L-programme (L for *laddning*, i.e. charge) presented in 1958 (Socialdemokratiska partistyrelsen, 1960).

Erlander noted in his diary that 'the borderline between protection and construction research grew more obscure every day' (von Sydow, 1978, p. 359). This, however, offered a formula for a compromise between the two wings: extended protection research. The line worked out by Olof Palme in the report presented in November 1959 involved continued postponement of the decision on the main issue; not until the mid-1960s, when the greatly delayed Ågesta reactor began to produce plutonium, would a decision have to be made. In the meantime, general research competence should be maintained, but only within the limits of the aim of protection against nuclear weapons.

To this conclusion the opponents had no objections, and the proponents were also pleased. They had reason to be, since this line in practical terms satisfied the demands of the Supreme Commander under the flexible concept of extended protection research. The 'freedom of action line' thus saved unity in the Social Democratic Party by giving both wings what they demanded. In reality this double bottom compromise meant very little, but its political implications were clear for the inner circle: it would never, under the given circumstances, become possible to push the opponents a single step further. Although the compromise allowed for considerable expansion of nuclear weapons research, the issue of Swedish nuclear weapons was politically dead, unless some fundamental change should occur in the international situation.

6 Inter-Service Struggle versus Programme Momentum

The idea of Swedish nuclear weapons had its earliest and most outspoken advocates within the Swedish Air Force. The reasons for this were both professional and organizational. After the war the Swedish Air Force developed close contacts with the RAF, which was regarded as a model air force. The Swedish Air Force built up its air defence system after the British model and purchased British radars and British fighters. The role of Bomber Command in the new British nuclear strategy obviously had an impact on attitudes in the Swedish Air Force, an impact amplified by the fact that atomic bombs would give the attack wings a new and crucial role in the overall defence strategy.[22]

Initially, the other services showed considerable reluctance to the idea of nuclear weapons. The Navy feared a strategy that would make its large surface battle-groups obsolete and force it back into a concept of coastal defence. The Army feared a development where new means of warfare would replace reliance on the large field Army and the conscript. Army opposition was overcome by the strategy developed in *ÖB-54 and ÖB-57*, that nuclear weapons should be employed to make the battle more even. The Navy was left aside and overruled by the Supreme Commander: *ÖB-57* clearly stated that the role of the Navy had diminished, that there was no need for major surface combatants in the Baltic in a nuclear war, and that the role of the Navy in forward defence could be taken over by the Air Force.

The Navy of course objected violently; but in fact all three services were displeased with the Supreme Commander's heavy emphasis on nuclear warfare and nuclear weapons and his, in their view, too limited interest in the problems of modernizing the existing defence organization.[23] With his nuclear line Supreme Commander Swedlund and his defence staff thus became increasingly isolated not only from the political decision-makers in the Defence Department but also from the three most powerful organizational actors, the services.[24] Officially and publicly the services supported the nuclear line decided by the Supreme Commander, but this was not active support and they did not really take part in the campaign (Agrell, 1985, ch. 10).

In 1961 Swedlund's term of office expired and a new Supreme Commander took over: former Air Force Chief Torsten Rapp. In parallel to this, the defence staff and the services were to produce a new long-term plan for a parliamentary commission to be appointed in 1962. The team working on the long-term plan, Ag ÖB-62, was headed by the new chief of the defence staff Major-General Carl-Eric Almgren. The central issue for Ag ÖB-62 was how to proceed with the campaign for nuclear weapons. Almgren's initial suggestion was to continue the line from *ÖB-57*, to push for nuclear weapons as an indispensable element in a future Swedish defence. This suggestion, however, met with immediate opposition, and the whole issue was transferred to a special secret investigation commission known as Kärnladdningsgruppen (the Nuclear Charge Group).

Discussions within Ag ÖB-62 continued, and especially the Chief of the Air Staff voiced increasingly critical comments on the value of Swedish nuclear weapons. (See Agrell, 1985, ch. 10, for a more detailed account.) One important point was that the military had committed itself to handling the nuclear weapons programme within the existing defence budgets. This would have been no problem with the initial calculations and with the 2.5% real increase for new technology decided in 1958. But by 1961 it was clear that the cost of a domestic programme was rising rapidly, since an exclusive plutonium-producing reactor again had to be considered.[25] At the same time the original 2.5% increase was reduced in 1961, and a large number of modernization programmes had to be initiated to maintain the standard of the forces.

In this situation the service chiefs put pressure on the Supreme Commander to specify what number of conventional forces they could get instead of the nuclear programme (Agrell, 1985, p. 326). The Air Force had a special reason for this reluctance to a new cost-consuming programme. In 1961 the first decisions were taken by the Supreme Commander to go ahead with the development of a new combat aircraft, the System 37 Viggen, a multi-purpose aircraft designed to replace all existing aircraft in the Air Force. (For further discussion of the history of System 37, see Dörfer, 1973.) System 37, developed by SAAB, was to be by far the largest, most advanced, and most hazardous technological undertaking by the Swedish defence and defence industry ever. The

Viggen Project was crucial for the size, capacity, and status of the future Air Force. Compared to this, nuclear weapons were a secondary issue.

This internal dispute was solved through a compromise: formally the Supreme Commander, backed by the services, continued to argue for somewhat extended research and continued freedom of action. But in reality the priorities in the plan were shifted from nuclear weapons to improvements in the conventional forces: the defence strategy outlined in the plan mentioned the role of nuclear warfare only briefly; instead the need for powerful forces to meet an invasion was stressed without the previous reference to the necessity of establishing a 'nuclear climate' (*ÖB-62*; Agrell, 1985). Further debate on nuclear weapons was regarded as harmful for political consensus on the 'big issue': the modernization of the existing defence organization.

This new military consensus on how to handle the nuclear weapons issue affected the highest levels in the military hierarchy and the organizational policy adopted towards the government and the parliamentary committees. It did not, however, have any immediate effect lower down in the hierarchy, on the levels which supervised, planned, and executed preparations for the nuclear weapons programme.

In 1960 the government issued new instructions for FOA nuclear research, instructions based on the recommendations of the Social Democratic Study Group. According to the new instructions FOA was prohibited from carrying out research aimed at the technical and economic basis for the production and testing of nuclear weapons (*Svensk kärnvapenforskning 1945–1972*, p. 40). The word 'construction' was not mentioned. The instruction therefore appeared to prohibit FOA research on Swedish nuclear weapons, while it in fact admitted all research and development efforts up to the prototype level.

Within the newly established Department for Nuclear Research, FOA 4, work was expanding rapidly. In the spring of 1961 FOA reported to the defence staff that most theoretical problems concerning the construction of a nuclear charge had been solved and that a simple prototype could be assembled if the necessary weapon-grade material could become available (Agrell, 1985, p. 313). The research programme at FOA had obviously been following the original plans fairly well; research had kept pace with the planned reactor programme, but this programme had in turn failed to produce the fissile material on schedule.

Within the wide framework of the new instructions, FOA now proceeded with the long-term build-up of the research programme, moving into the specific construction details of an implosion charge and advanced plutonium research, especially the problems of plutonium separation.[26] In requests for funding, the amount for nuclear research increased from the SEK 8.5 million in 1958 to 18.8 million in 1961, or from 34% to 55% of the total proposed research budget. The largest single research field was plutonium (Agrell, 1989). The research programme was thus proceeding towards the goal of the joint plan – but without the necessary link with the reactor programme and with decreasing support from a military leadership more concerned with approaching changes in the economic situation of Sweden's national defence.

7 Scientific Demobilization and Political Cover-Up

Towards the mid-1960s it became increasingly obvious that the 'freedom of action line' was quietly being transformed into a 'silent no' through a number of non-decisions. FOA by now possessed a large capacity to handle plutonium and had completed the development of most construction details. By 1965 the first charge of uncontrolled burnt-out fuel became available from the Ågesta reactor. The obstacles were mainly military and political. Research at FOA was continuing, but the Supreme Commander started to cut funding for nuclear research in 1964–65 (*Svensk kärnvapenforskning 1945–1972*, p. 48). In the new long-term plan *ÖB-65* nuclear weapons were hardly mentioned.

On the political scene the situation was similar: the nuclear weapons issue was in reality dead, but the way out from the freedom of action line was extremely complicated and full of domestic and international concerns. Pressure from the proponents, also among the non-socialist parties, was declining, but the Social Democratic government had to find a formula to legitimize a cancellation of the freedom of action line which was appearing more and more superfluous. International developments were to supply the main arguments here.

With new doctrines on limited war being accepted in the USA and NATO it seemed less likely that any future conflict would have to be fought with nuclear weapons. In a limited war Sweden's conventional forces were assumed to play a key role in deterring the Soviet Union from committing its forces on yet another front.[27] A 'local war', with an isolated Soviet attack on Sweden in an international crisis, had been regarded as a substantial threat in the 1950s but was now ruled out as improbable. Swedish nuclear weapons would thus not be necessary for successful deterrence in this new doctrine where Swedish defence efforts should be limited to a manageable level of warfare. In an article in the journal of the Royal Academy of War Science, Under-Secretary of Defence Karl Fritiofsson outlined this argument, concluding that Swedish nuclear weapons were no longer needed from a security political perspective (Fritiofsson, 1966).

The strategic arguments against Swedish nuclear weapons had already been clarified in the extensive strategic studies carried out by FOA and the Swedish Institute for International Affairs in the years 1963–65 (Utrikespolitiska Institutet, 1965). These studies dealt with a large number of complex issues that had not been observed in the 1950s: the large organization and costs required to maintain a standing nuclear force, the problems of deterrence and self-deterrence in a conflict with a nuclear aggressor, and the political effects in the Nordic area and beyond if Sweden were to join the nuclear club.

The arms control aspect also became increasingly important for the attempt to formulate a way out of the freedom of action line. The Partial Test Ban Treaty of 1963 seemed to indicate that an international disarmament process was making progress in the nuclear field. Negotiations for a non-proliferation treaty supplied the Swedish government with the final argument for the decision already taken – to abandon the nuclear option for Sweden.

One problem remained, however. Officially Sweden had only held the question of nuclear weapons open. No specific investments or preparations had been made for the nuclear weapons programme. Formally the 300-person research staff at FOA and Atomenergi was engaged in a programme for protection against nuclear weapons and the civilian use of nuclear energy. In reality FOA had come very far in the development of nuclear weapon systems. Although the military and political reasons for this research had vanished, it continued throughout the 1960s and was not to be dismantled until the years 1969–72. As late as 1972 FOA conducted some experiments with small-scale models of implosion charges of plutonium (Larsson, 1985).

The reasons for this slow dismantling of nuclear weapons research were both political and organizational, although there was hardly any desire to continue some kind of clandestine research programme for the sake of a future nuclear option. The research programme could not be abandoned straight away, since formally it was a programme for protection. The retreat had to be made in good order and legitimized by a downgraded nuclear threat perception. The size of staff also posed a serious, although very different, problem. FOA could not just sack them: personnel would have to be transferred to other research programmes, and this process took time. Some wanted, for personal professional reasons, to complete their projects in order to publish reports and dissertations. In 1972, when the curtain finally went down, the only thing left of Swedish nuclear weapons research was a small staff maintaining a thin competence, empty laboratories, and a huge amount of accumulated knowledge in the FOA archives.

8 The Reasons for Not Going Nuclear

Several attempts have been made to explain in retrospect the Swedish line in the nuclear weapons issue and the decision to drop the nuclear option in the 1960s (Andrén, 1971; Jervas, 1983; Prawitz, 1967; Quester, 1970). These attempts have focused mainly on the international political situation around the mid-1960s, with the increased emphasis on deterrence on various levels and Sweden's active policy in the field of international disarmament. The Swedish decision has thus been regarded as an adjustment to changing strategic premises (Jervas, 1983) or as a consequence mainly of ambitions in the field of international disarmament (Quester, 1970). The latter interpretation was based largely on the circumstances that Swedish officials in the mid-1960s, among them Alva Myrdal, ambassador at the Conference on Disarmament in Geneva, proposed using the Swedish nuclear option as a bargaining chip in negotiations with the nuclear powers.

These interpretations seem, however, to focus too much on the circumstances that affected the overt political reorientation in the mid-1960s, an approach that was inevitable in official and semi-official analysis. For observers at the time, furthermore, vital aspects of the nuclear weapons programme and its political and military prehistory were unknown. Today, in a historical perspective the reorientation appears inevitable, given the political and military deadlock in the nuclear weapons issue that had already existed for several years. The compromise in the Social Democratic Party saved the consensus around the freedom of action line. Vague definitions of research instructions permitted continued and even expanded nuclear weapons research. But the political tide had definitively turned against the nuclear weapons programme. Even the most devoted proponents in the party leadership realized that the battle was lost, and that the probability of a go-ahead decision was rapidly fading away (Agrell, 1985, p. 359). This change in the political climate was apprehended in leading military circles and was reflected in rising internal doubts about the feasibility and usefulness of the new weapon. The revival of the organizational interests of the services on the internal military arena finally made the issue stone dead: lacking an active and unified military campaign, a new weapons system without a clear supporter in one of the services did not have a chance of survival. The main organizational carrier of the programme, FOA, was rapidly losing its influence in the military bureaucracy.

Thus, there was not one single or even one major reason why Sweden did not go nuclear in the 1960s. A number of interacting factors, both external and internal, that appeared over a long period of time, determined the outcome. One important factor was the split within the Social Democratic Party and the inability of the pro-nuclear party leadership to bridge this and proceed with closed politics in the nuclear weapons issue. Behind this were both internal and external reasons, the underlying division of the Social Democratic Party on the defence issue and growing international opposition to nuclear weapons and nuclear tests.

Another obviously important factor involved developments within the Swedish defence forces and the growing and inevitable structural problems created by the policy of keeping and even expanding the number of formations in the postwar years. 'Modernizing' as the prime goal was eventually to take over from 'new means of warfare', and the policy of military technology was to shift from a revolutionary to an evolutionary concept, with the focus on the successive replacement of heavy equipment in the services.

Applied to the Swedish nuclear weapons programme many of the concepts and models developed in the US–Soviet arms race debate seem too general. The dividing line between 'internal' and 'external' factors does not seem very useful; at every stage the Swedish nuclear weapons issue was affected, directly and indirectly, by an inseparable mix of domestic and international impulses and concerns.

Neither can a clear dividing line be discerned between 'technology push' and 'demand pull'. These concepts seem to fit better the kind of process they have been designed for, continuing series of development and procurement decisions within specific fields of weapons technology, and not a single unique venture into the realm of revolutionary military technology. The Swedish defence doctrine influenced by the experiences of World War II created a climate for radical innovations in the field of military technology. The formula of 'new means of warfare' included both a technology push and a demand pull. But in the field of nuclear weapons the links between technology push and demand pull were not firmly institutionalized, as was the case with research, development, and production of combat aircraft. Here a well-established network was created, a network that made a weapons technology invulnerable to fluctuations in the political, military, and industrial environment. This pattern is hardly unique for Sweden, but the Swedish experience points to the importance of the aborted innovations and weapons programmes, of the specific circumstances under which a military-industrial network is transformed to encompass radical technological innovations.

The story of the rise and fall of the Swedish nuclear weapons programme also underlines the importance of the link between overall attitudes to technology and technological change and developments in the field of arms technology, between what Ulrich Albrecht in Chapter 6 discusses as industrialism and militarism. With the concept of 'new means of warfare' Sweden embarked on a policy whereby national resources, not only industrial but also scientific, were to be systematically employed to enhance national defence. The basis of national defence was no longer only economic resources, manpower, and industrial capacity, but increasingly also ability in terms of science and technology.

With its population of some 8 millions, Sweden is a small country, but a country that entered the postwar world with a considerable technological capacity and equally considerable political, social, and economic ambitions. The whole idea of a large-scale national nuclear energy programme designed to produce plutonium for a nuclear weapons programme appears inconsistent with the well-established international policy of the Social Democratic Party devoted to bridge-building and disarmament. (For this policy, see Misgeld, 1984.) Sweden's efforts in nuclear energy and nuclear weapons must be understood in connection with another and more overriding goal: the development of the big technologies of the future – nuclear power, computers, aircraft, and spacecraft – where Sweden with advanced know-how and a superior social system could compete with the great powers on their own terms. Things did not exactly turn out this way.

In the end the 'bomb that never was' merely stands out as one aspect of this fading dream of Sweden as a technological great power.

From this perspective, much of the general debate on arms dynamics seems to focus too narrowly on specific aspects of the weapons development process, on specific weapons categories, or on the interpretation of the decision-making process. The impact of the overall development in the postwar world – from a system dominated by the technologies of the 'Nuclear Age' and the industrial capacity of the United States to an increasing technological competition in a vast number of fields between new and old economic powers – is often overlooked in analyses which regard the specific circumstances of the 1950s and 1960s as an eternal and self-evident background for all further analysis of weapons development and arms dynamics.

Notes

1. A considerable literature on the problems of nuclear proliferation was published in the late 1960s and early 1970s. (See for instance the two SIPRI books *The Near-Nuclear Countries*, 1972, and *Nuclear Proliferation Problems*, 1974.)

2. A study dealing with the motivation of nuclear and non-nuclear states is Goldblat (1985).

3. During the war Sweden managed to procure a few small Italian prewar destroyers, a large number of Caproni light bombers (known as 'the flying coffin' in the Swedish Air Force), and a smaller number of old Junkers Ju-86 bombers, along with German and Czech artillery pieces. The deliveries from Germany were the result of trade agreements where Sweden exchanged large quantities of iron ore and ball bearings needed by the German arms industry. The equipment from Germany was delayed several times as one of the means to put pressure on Sweden, and it was less modern than the technology delivered to the German forces. See Ekman (1986), Hägglöf (1958), Olsson (1977).

4. Swedish intelligence was regarded as unreliable, especially by the British authorities, due to cooperation with the German Abwehr. See Carlgren (1985).

5. A few radar sets were delivered from Britain in 1944 in exchange for the wreck of a German V-2 missile that crashed in Sweden.

6. The relationship between fighter and bomber squadrons in the Swedish Air Force was 15:15 in 1945 and was altered to 32:12 in the 1948 decision, which also included a rapid change from propeller to jet aircraft and the procurement of radar-equipped all-weather fighters.

7. The most extensive domestic military R&D effort carried out during the war concerned radar. When Sweden managed to buy some British sets, and further surplus deliveries became possible, the domestic development of surveillance radars for the Air Force was abandoned, and research efforts were redirected to the problems of operations use and maintenance of the imported equipment (Scheiderbauer, 1981).

8. The British carried out explorations of the deposits of kolm (a kind of coal) through the leading Swedish mineral company Boliden. A draft agreement was discussed with the Swedish authorities that would guarantee British and US exclusive rights to the supplies for a period of 30 years. After the US dropped the atomic bombs, the Swedish government withdrew from the negotiations, citing political reasons, but promised to control the export of material containing uranium in the future (Gowing, 1965, p. 314).

9. During this period the term 'High Command' (*Högkvarteret*) was used for the three service chiefs and their staffs together with the Supreme Commander and his staff. This 'defence staff' had overall responsibility for coordination of planning and budgets and the responsibility for ground operations, while the chiefs of the Navy and the Air Force had independent operational responsibility.

10. The author has been able to study the documents in accordance with the Swedish system of 'conditional declassification', through which researchers get access to material on the condition of a security screening of the manuscript before publication. Thus the documents as such are not declassified. See Agrell (1989, ch. 5).

11. This extensive evacuation planning was presented by the Board for Civil Defence in 1955 under the title 'Civilförsvaret inför atomåldern' ('Civil defence facing the atomic age'). The goal was to virtually empty all cities with more than 20,000 inhabitants prior to a nuclear attack and thus disperse between one-third and half of the population in remote and sparsely populated areas.

12. The development in the US Army nuclear doctrine was frequently discussed in Swedish military journals. A book on *Atomic Weapons in Land Combat* by two US Army officers, Reinhardt & Kintner (1953), with its optimistic view of the possibilities of employing ground forces with new organization and new tactics on the nuclear battlefield, received considerable attention. The book was translated and published in Swedish by the military literature association in 1955.

13. On a few earlier occasions questions had been posed in the Swedish Parliament concerning the nuclear weapons issue, but each time the government gave assurances that no such programme was being considered and that no preparations were being carried out (*Svensk kärnvapenforskning 1945–1972*, pp. 16–22).

14. The bill *Angående riktlinjer för utvecklingsarbetet på atomenergiområdet* (Kungliga Majestät, 1956. Stockholm: Riksdagen) was, in accordance with standard Swedish procedure, largely based on the report *Atomenergien* (1956) from the parliamentary commission. In Sweden parliamentary commissions are normally appointed by the government after consultation with the Opposition parties, which also nominate their representatives in the commission.

15. The argument of self-reliance vanished from the nuclear energy programme in the years 1958–62 as cheap uranium became available on the world market and the interests of the nuclear industry began to focus on light-water technology. Instead industrial and technological arguments became central; Sweden had to proceed along the heavy-water line in order to keep up the pace in the general build-up in technology and industry.

16. In the bill one of the most debated points was a ban against other parties than Atomenergi carrying out research and development work on the construction of reactors. This received harsh criticism as a measure to protect the state interests in Atomenergi from competition from private enterprise like ASEA. But this ban was primarily a necessity for the joint plan, since ASEA and private firms were not covered by the secret agreement for cooperation.

17. This meeting was held on 23 November; at an earlier meeting on 18 November the civilian programme had been discussed. From 1951 to 1957 the Social Democrats ruled in coalition with the Agrarian Party.

18. Undén had already formulated his critical view of Swedish nuclear weapons in a memorandum of August 1955. According to Undén, nuclear weapons would not only become a threat to the Soviet Union, they would also be pointless in a conflict since the Soviet forces under all circumstances would possess more tactical nuclear warheads (von Sydow, 1978, pp. 55ff.).

19. According to the revised tactical manuals of the Swedish defence forces a minimum central distance of 2 km between companies was to be employed when deploying combat formations for defence (Arméstaben, 1963. *Arméreglemente*, del 2, pp. 1, 34).

20. In 1957 FOA asked for SEK 4 million for research under the heading 'Nuclear Weapons'. In 1958, 2.8 million was taken up under the new heading 'Construction of Nuclear Devices', but under the headings 'Effects and Protection' FOA asked for 8.5 million. Even without the controversial construction research FOA was to double its high-priority work in the nuclear field (Agrell, 1989, p. 209).

21. AMSA was regarded by the military and the security service as an element in Soviet clandestine warfare, employing formally independent 'front organizations'.

22. The first senior Swedish officer officially to raise the issue of Swedish nuclear weapons

was the commander of the Air Force, Lieutenant-General Bengt Nordensköld, in a speech in 1952 (Ahlmark, 1965, p. 21).

23. All three service chiefs wrote reservations to the main text in *ÖB-57*, some of the formulations being very harsh.

24. According to the memoirs of the commanders of the Air Force and Navy, an important role was played by Swedlund's personality, especially his lack of flexibility. The contact between the service chiefs and the Supreme Commander became strictly formal after 1958, and the former were not informed about the measures taken by the Supreme Commander in the nuclear weapons issue (Ericsson, 1968; Ljungdahl, 1972).

25. The reactors of the blue-yellow line had been continuously delayed due to construction problems. At the same time, military demands concerning the size of the planned nuclear stockpile were increasing. The study *Svenska kärnstridsmedel* – written by the defence staff in spring 1961 and used by Almgren as an initial bid in the negotiations – saw a minimum of 50–100 warheads as needed to force an opponent to disperse his units. However, for waging a tactical nuclear war it was estimated that the Swedish defence forces would need between 1,400 and 1,500 warheads (Agrell, 1985, p. 319).

26. In 1963 the FOA opened a plutonium laboratory where research was carried out until the laboratory was closed down in 1972.

27. This doctrine of 'marginal deterrence' was formulated in *ÖB-65* and in the 1965 parliamentary defence commission. Its strategic rationale was that the Nordic area as a whole, and Sweden in particular, was of limited importance to the parties in a future conflict which was assumed to be focused on operations on the front in Central Europe (for further discussion, see Agrell, 1985, ch. 6).

WILHELM AGRELL, b. 1950, PhD in History (Lund University, 1986); Researcher, Swedish Air Staff and Defence Staff (1974–78); Research Fellow, Lund University (1978–87); Assistant Professor of History, Lund University (1987–). Author of a series of books in Swedish about the arms race, Swedish military policy, and submarine incidents in Swedish waters.

Chapter 11

Weapons Innovation and US Strategic Weapons Systems: Learning from Case Studies?

HANS GÜNTER BRAUCH

Institute of Political Science, Heidelberg University, Frankfurt University, and Peace Research and European Security Studies (AFES–PRESS)

1 Introduction

Since the end of World War II we have experienced the longest and most intensive arms competition in human history, both in quantitative and in qualitative terms. During that war new weapons systems such as radars, cruise and ballistic missiles, and two atomic bombs had been incorporated and used in warfighting. In the United States, the process of military research, development, engineering, and testing for war requirements was instrumental for the creation of new institutions, procedures, and social relations between the military, the scientists and engineers, and industrial companies, as well as universities and newly created think-tanks. Many of the structural changes induced by World War II survived, as did many of the new institutional settings. This was partly due to the changed global situation of the Cold War and superpower confrontation, and partly due to domestic processes, e.g. in the United States the intensifying service competition between the Army, the Air Force, and the Navy. The war experience and perceptions of the new Cold War were conducive for the emergence of a 'National Security State' (Yergin, 1977). This new institutional, procedural, and social environment had a direct impact on the process of weapons innovation and procurement in the United States and elsewhere (Brauch, 1976).

This chapter will focus on ten case studies on the weapons innovation and procurement process for strategic weapons systems in the United States, dealing with launchers (bombers, ground-, and sea-based intercontinental ballistic missiles), multiple independently targetable re-entry vehicles (MIRVs), and ballistic missile defence (BMD) or anti-ballistic missiles (ABMs).

These case studies were selected for the following reasons:

- Strategic weapons systems have dominated the US/USSR arms race.
- In this strategic arms race, the United States has generally been considered the technological pacesetter.
- Intercontinental ballistic missiles (ICBMs) and sea-launched ballistic missiles (SLBMs) and bombers have become the central means for employing nuclear weapons in war and for deterrence; MIRV has become the major force-multiplier and ABM/BMD the major effort to counter both ICBMs and SLBMs.
- The USA was chosen as a focus, because more information has been made available on its weapons innovation and procurement process and more empirical case studies have been published than for any other country.

1.1 Ten Case Studies

In the nuclear age, *strategic weapons* are generally associated with nuclear weapons that can put at risk not only whole nations but the future of civilization as well. Four functional sectors may be distinguished in the development of military R&D for new strategic weapons systems:

(a) *New weapons systems of mass destruction* (nuclear warheads of the first, second, and third generation as well as biological and chemical weapons).
(b) *Launchers and launch platforms* for weapons of mass destruction (intercontinental bombers, intercontinental land- and sea-based ballistic and cruise missiles, surface ships and submarines).
(c) *New support systems* (military electronics, command, control, communication, and intelligence systems, satellites).
(d) *Space-based weapons systems* (ASAT and space-based ballistic missile defence).

Nuclear weapons themselves are generally classified in three categories: *strategic weapons systems, theatre nuclear weapons,* and *tactical nuclear weapons.* In the SALT negotiations, particularly in the SALT II Treaty, *central strategic systems* meant those weapons capable of reaching the heartland of one country from the home territory of the other.

In this survey we deal solely with launchers for such central strategic nuclear weapons: with bombers, ICBMs, SLBMs (and their submarine carriers), with new technology for re-entry vehicles (MIRV), and with systems and concepts of ballistic missile defence (the ABM systems of the 1960s and 1970s and the SDI concept).

With respect to strategic bombers, two case studies will be reviewed: Robert J. Art (1968) on the joint Air Force–Navy experimental fighter bomber TFX, and Robert E. Coulam (1977) on the F-111 – as it was later renamed and built in smaller numbers as a medium-range bomber of the US Air Force. Three case studies focus on ICBMs: by Michael H. Armacost (1969) on the Thor–Jupiter Controversy; by Edmund Beard

(1976) on the development of the first ICBM; and by Lauren H. Holland & Robert A. Hoover (1985) on the MX decision. SLBMs are analysed by Harvey M. Sapolsky (1972) on Polaris and by D. Douglas Dalgleish & Larry Schweikart (1984) on Trident. Concerning MIRVs we have chosen the case studies by Ronald L. Tammen (1973) and by Ted Greenwood (1975).[1] On the BMD systems, the case study by Ernest Yanarella (1977) on the years 1955–72 will be reviewed.

These ten case studies by US scholars provide a representative sample of systems that have played a major role in the USA, both in the weapons innovation and procurement process of all three military services and in the US–Soviet strategic arms competition. One system went into production with a different name and a more narrow mission: TFX, replaced by the F-111. One system (ABM with the Spartan and Sprint missiles) representing a mission (ballistic missile defence) was inactivated immediately after deployment. However, in his 'Star Wars' speech on 23 March 1983, President Ronald Reagan called for a renewed effort to develop a ground- and space-based BMD system in the context of what was later to be called SDI.[2]

While in our sample the 'success stories' prevail, there exist even more cases of 'failures' – of weapon system projects being stopped prior to the procurement or deployment stage. At present there are only few case studies and no comparative analyses as to why these projects have been cancelled.

1.2 Questions to Ask

To make valid generalizations relevant for a theory of armaments dynamics, we need to ask:

• What can we learn from these studies or weapons biographies to understand, interpret, and perhaps explain the weapons innovation and procurement process of the United States?

• What generalizations do the authors of these case studies offer about the weapons innovation and procurement process of the United States?

• What theoretical lessons may be drawn from the empirical evidence presented in these case studies and from their theoretical conclusions?

• What conceptual conclusions may be deduced for future research projects on the weapons innovation and procurement process of both sides in the strategic arms race?

• What practical conclusions may be drawn for policies of arms limitation and reductions from empirical analyses of factors that have stimulated the innovation and procurement process for strategic weapons and that have destabilized the strategic balance?

2 Theoretical Approaches to Armaments Dynamics: Revisited

We may distinguish at least three phases in literature on the determinants of national armaments policies, on the US–Soviet arms competition, and on global features of the arms race in the nuclear age.

First, the traditional school, primarily in the framework of the theoretical notions of the power politics approach and of balance of power, saw US armament policy in terms of an action-reaction phenomenon or of an action-reaction process.[3]

This rather crude model was challenged in the late 1960s and early 1970s in the United States and in Western Europe by many social scientists who focused on domestic processes: technological innovation, bureaucratic policy formulation, development of strategic doctrines, and economic interests. This *revisionist school*[4] claimed that domestic factors were the primary determinants for the US weapons innovation and procurement process. Primarily US representatives of this school focused on bureaucratic politics and on the military-industrial complex (Pursell, 1971; Sarkesian, 1972; Schiller & Phillips, 1972; Rosen, 1973) by relying on pluralist models of influence groups. European peace researchers, largely influenced by the works of Senghaas (1969, 1972a, 1972c) and Gantzel (1972, 1973), emphasized the predominance of internal determinants (Innenleitung or Eigendynamik) that comprised ideological, technological, bureaucratic, and even psychological factors. A third group here, influenced by Marxist concepts,[5] emphasized economic factors: interests or functions as a major factor of the arms race. They used the concept of the military-industrial complex in the context of theories of state monopoly capitalism.

And finally, the theoretical challenge by the narrower US and by the broader European revisionist school, as well as by Marxist scholars, stimulated case studies that focused on the specific features of the armament policies of individual countries and on specific weapons systems.[6]

None of the many German case studies dealing with non-strategic systems have been included in this sample, because of their limited comparability with the selected cases. Many of these empirical case studies have analysed the specific mix between internal (domestic) and external (e.g. threat-stimulated) determinants. Most of the authors in our sample may be referred to as representatives of this third *post-revisionist empirical school* of armaments dynamics.

Only a few reconceptualizations have been offered so far (e.g. Evangelista, 1986b, 1988) that try to overcome the polarization between the traditionalist and the revisionist schools of the 1970s by drawing inductively on the wealth of empirical research.

In the West German debate, Albrecht (1986a, 1986b) and Brauch (1986, 1989d) have shifted their analytical focus, from the dichotomy of internal and external determinants, to the interrelationship between politics, strategy, and technology, and political, military, and scientific actors, and to the different levels of analysis. Three US authors have suggested that in analysing the armaments innovation and procurement process two layers of decision-making should be distinguished: an internal secret layer and an external layer involving the active participation of the US Congress and the public at large (Holland & Hoover, 1985); and that the process of weapons innovation should be analysed for five stages (Evangelista, 1986b).

3 Common Empirical Research Focus

3.1 The Budgetary Dimension

Since 1939, the growth of military R&D expenditures and of the R&D establishment has skyrocketed. From 1920 to 1935, the US government spent annually an average of US $4 million for military R&D. By 1944–45, the military R&D expenditures of the War and Navy Departments – without the outlays for the secret Manhattan Project – had reached a level of $513 million. By 1945, the Manhattan Project alone had employed up to 125,000 persons at a time.

This war-induced collaboration between scientists, military personnel, and industrial contractors led to long-lasting structural changes: the Manhattan Project had become the prototype for big science, for project research, and for secret research funded by the military, linking together military-controlled and independent research institutes funded by the military but also university and industrial research institutes. Research projects and professional careers became increasingly dependent on military funding.

This is not to say that the US military R&D establishment is a unified factor of political influence on the weapons innovation and acquisition process. It is relatively competitive: companies, university research laboratories, and private think-tanks all compete for R&D funds, as do the individual services with respect to allocations for their own branch. The perspectives and time-range also differ – from that of the development engineer, convinced of a new technical approach, to that of the military commander who has to solve more immediate problems of manpower, training logistics, and doctrine. 'Comparable gaps exist between the military services and the Pentagon planners: the one group is interested in responses to current threats: the other is trying to produce a balanced structure for the future.' (Long & Reppy, 1980, p. 17)

In current prices the US military R&D effort has increased dramatically: from $418 million in FY 1945–46 to $35,467 billion in FY 1986. In constant 1987 prices appropriations increased from $225.1 billion in 1981 to $311.6 billion in 1987; while the respective figure for research, development, test, and evaluation rose from $20,974 to $41,969 billion. During the first six years of the Reagan Administration the overall defence budget increased by 38%, while military R&D expenditure was raised by 100% in real terms.

Writing in April 1987, Judith Reppy summarized the economic significance of US military R&D spending for the US economy:

Since World War II, military R&D has constituted a large fraction of total R&D funding in the United States, roughly 40 percent for the postwar period as a whole. It is a larger proportion of government-funding R&D, rising to over 70 percent under the Reagan administration. The military component is larger for R&D than the military-related share in other spending categories, such as total military spending as a percent of the gross national output. (Reppy, 1987, p. 2)

In FY 1984, of the $26.6 billion the US Department of Defense then spent on military research, development, test, and evaluation, about 30% each went to tactical and strategic systems, $1.4 billion to advanced technology development, and $3.1 billion to the technology base. In FY 1985, the Pentagon requested $2.8 billion and in FY 1986 $5.5 billion for advanced technology development, most of which was programmed for SDI.[7] Gansler (1980, p. 99) pointed to four negative trends in post-Vietnam defence research and development:

The development time has lengthened for each succeeding generation of weapons systems [. . .]. This results in higher program costs and the deployment of obsolete equipment.
The large expenditures on engineering of complete weapons systems [. . .] result in significantly less money going to the critical advancement of new components and materials [. . .].
There has been a clear shift of R&D funding from the small, inventor-led companies to large firms. [. . .]
The extreme R&D emphasis on equipment performance has rapidly increased the cost of military equipment [. . .] and thus greatly reduced the quantities of equipment procured.

The increasing emphasis on military R&D has often come at the expense of production: 'Since 1945, the ratio of defense R&D to production expenditure has gradually increased from around 5 percent to a peak of over 50 percent, with cyclical variations during periods of conflict' (Gansler, 1980, p. 101).

The ratio of military R&D outlays to procurement outlays had first peaked in 1950 at 20%. Then it fell to 10% following the Korean War, reaching a second peak with close to 50% in FY 1965, to fall to 25% in FY 1969, reaching an all-time high at close to 60% for FYs 1975 to 1977.

When procurement requirements dwindled after the US involvement in the Korean and Vietnam wars, military R&D expenditures tended to more than double, only to be reduced by half during the next war. It is within this budgetary framework that the US weapons innovation and procurement process has evolved since 1945.

3.2 Formal Stages of US Weapons Innovation and Procurement Policy

The formal stages of the weapons innovation and procurement process differ for the United States and the Soviet Union. For the US, Kossiakoff (1980, pp. 61ff.) has distinguished among three different aspects of weapons systems acquisition: institutional, functional, and procedural. In

WEAPONS INNOVATION AND US WEAPONS SYSTEMS 181

Figure 11.1 *Phases in the life of major defence systems*

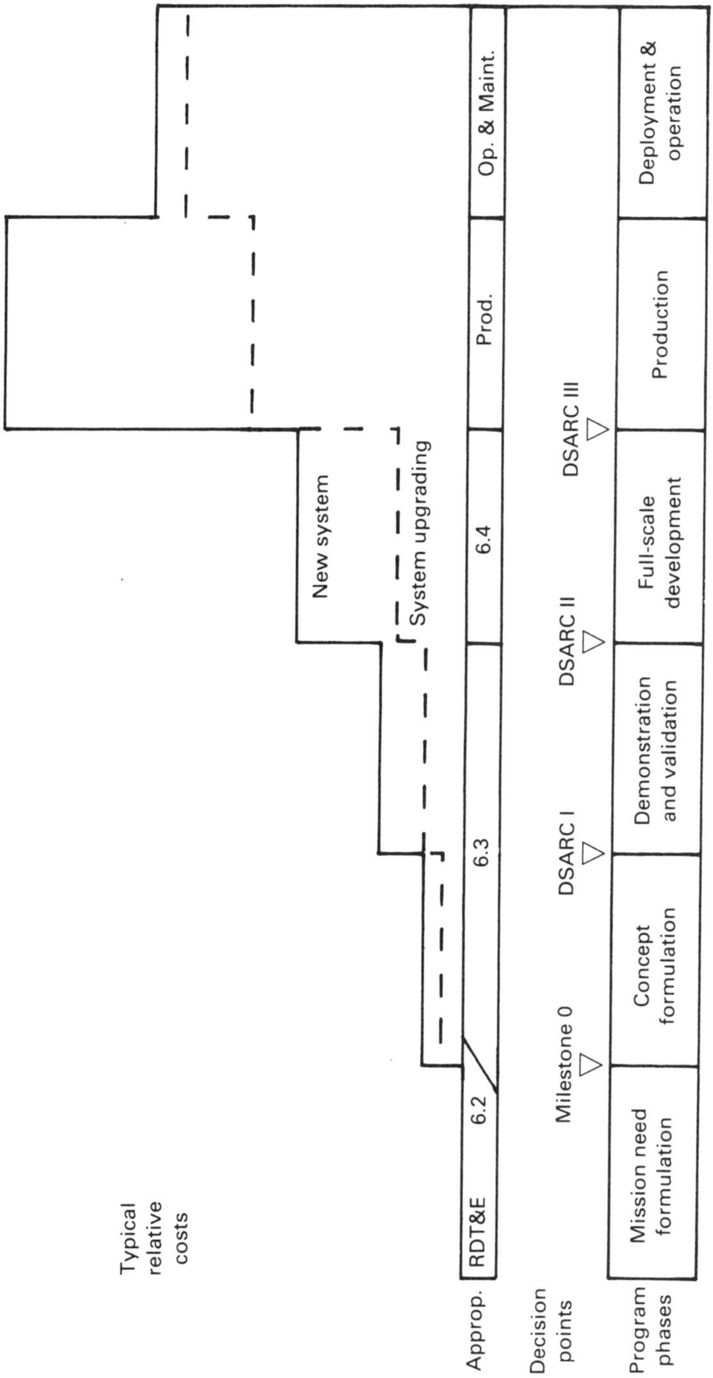

Source: Kossiakoff (1980), p. 72. Reprinted with permission.

institutional terms he refers to defence R&D centres (in-house R&D centres of the military services, government-sponsored university laboratories, and independent, non-profit organizations established to support certain defence missions) and commercial companies. In functional terms, he points to four elements in originating and implementing a military weapon system: (1) assessment of operational effectiveness and need, (2) advancement of knowledge and technology, (3) production of new or improved operational equipment, (4) definition of solutions to operational needs.

For the late 1970s, in the formal programme phases of the development and procurement of major weapons systems we may distinguish among: (1) mission need formulation, (2) concept formulation, (3) demonstration and validation, (4) full-scale development, (5) production, and (6) deployment and operation. (See Figures 11.1 and 11.2.)

Robert Perry, a Program Director for R&D and Acquisition Studies at RAND, has used the term 'R&D style' to designate the policies, procedures, and preferences that characterize R&D programmes. R&D styles have changed over time with respect to institutional and procedural elements. In Perry's view:

Figure 11.2 *Major systems acquisition cycle – mission analysis*

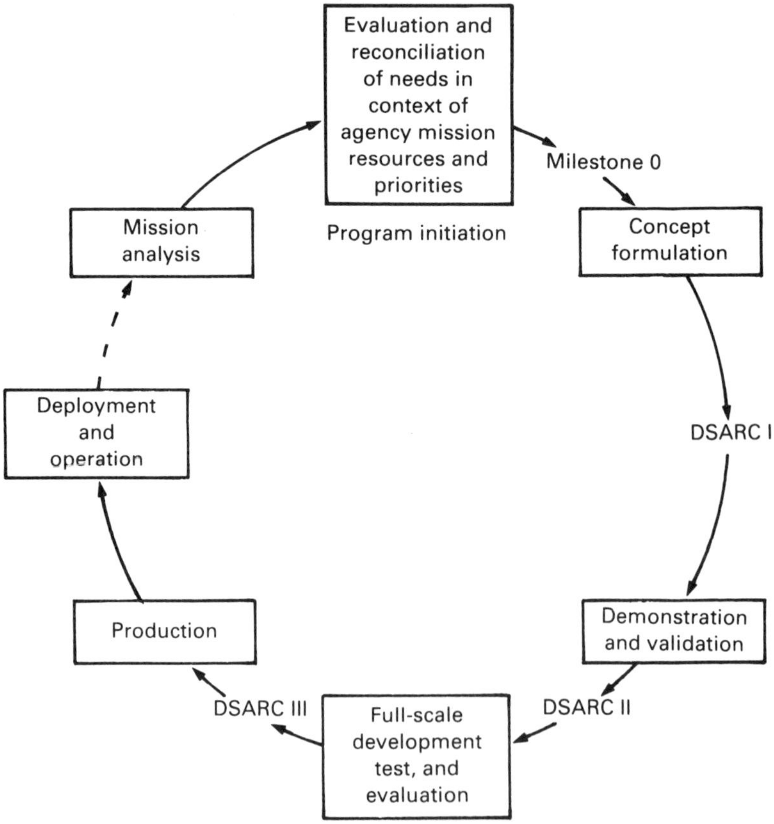

Source: Kossiakoff (1980), p. 73. Reprinted with permission.

The best of American military R&D is characterized by pragmatism, adaptiveness, flexibility of approach, and a decent respect for the occasional intractability of technology. The striking advances often made by relatively small groups led by skillful, imaginative American innovators attract much attention. But it is also true that much vital American military R&D depends on recurrent increments of performance improvement that are increasingly difficult to achieve. (Perry, 1980, p. 93)

Perry concludes his discussion with these observations:

American military R&D style is characteristically inconsistent in many aspects. It includes both derivative designs and innovative ones. [. . .] In general, the USSR prefers an R&D process that proceeds from the orderly improvement of previously developed systems, and for the last 35 years the United States has preferred starting systems from scratch and seeking bold technical advances. Of course there are exceptions to both generalizations, and in the American case, styles are changing. [. . .] the American system is astonishingly resilient, able to survive rapid starts and stops and changes of direction, scope, or goal. It accommodates effectively to technical, financial, and procedural 'instability' [. . .] Skillful managers are able to create new initiatives and to compose alternative goals, to reallocate resources, and to exploit unheralded technology. (Perry, 1980, pp. 107–108)

These formal structures of the weapons innovation process and the generalizations offered by Gansler, Kossiakoff, and Perry provide only few insights, however, into the decision-making process for new US strategic weapons systems.

3.3 The Political Decision-Making Process for Weapons Innovation and Procurement: Layers and Stages of Analysis

In their case study Holland & Hoover (1985) use two layers. Evangelista (1986b, 1988) distinguishes five stages, as does Baugh (1984) in his survey of the strategic weapons acquisition process.

Holland & Hoover challenge the conventional wisdom according to which defence decision-making, especially for procurement, is seen as more hierarchical and dominated by the executive branch. They question the implicit contention that factors important in domestic politics, such as Congress, interest groups, and public opinion, are less important and even peripheral in the defence process. They make a distinction between two layers of defence activities: an *inner* and an *outer layer*: 'The *inner layer* focuses on decisions about design, research, development, and testing of prototypes of weapons. The *outer layer* refers to decisions related to the acquisition and deployment of weapons' (Holland & Hoover, 1985, p. 2). In their view, the outer layer of the MX decision-making process differs radically from previous acquisition and deployment decisions, or at least those prior to the 1970s. To a much lesser extent, according to Holland & Hoover, this has also been true for the inner layer. For the first time in the post-World War II history of the procurement process, the ultimate power of such decisions is no longer the exclusive prerogative of the executive branch.

Ironically, the access to weapons procurement decision making for newly activated public input was an unintended and unforeseen result of recent legislation for non-defense issues, [. . .] such as the National Environmental Protection Act (NEPA) of 1969, the Federal Land Policy and Management Act (FLPMA) of 1976, and the Freedom of Information Act (FOIA) of 1965 [. . .] These new acts facilitate public input in the outer layer of the decision-making process. (Holland & Hoover, 1985, pp. 6–7)

According to Holland & Hoover, the first or inner layer of the procurement process (which comprises activities concerned with the origins of the idea, the design, and the research, development, and testing of a weapon system) is barely visible and in most cases inaccessible for outside actors; while the second layer (which focuses on the decisions preceding the actual purchase or acquisition and construction as well as deployment of the system) is more visible and accessible to those concerned with weapon procurement policy. It is on the first layer that most case studies – influenced by the bureaucratic politics approach – have focused.

The character of the procurement political process has changed, starting with the public controversy about the ABM, the issue of refining US counterforce capability in the early 1970s through improved warhead design and guidance improvement, culminating in the MX controversy, they argue. Evangelista (1986b, 1988) has offered the following generalizations for the USA:

> Impetus for innovation in weapons technology comes 'from the bottom' – from scientists in government or private laboratories and the military officials with whom they are in close contact. The new proposal is pushed up through the bureaucracy until it attracts the attention of supporters in the Congress and the Executive. In this respect, a new weapon starts with a technological idea rather than as a response to a specific threat or as a means to fulfill a longstanding mission. *Thus, internal factors are paramount for most of the process of innovation, while external ones come into play at a later stage when a justification for the new weapon is required.* (Evangelista, 1986b, pp. 9–10, emphasis added)

Comparing innovation and organization of military R&D in both the USA and the USSR, Evangelista concludes:

> According to the criteria developed by organization theory as well as economics, one would expect to find the United States far more innovative than the Soviet Union in the field of military technology. The centrally-planned, secretive Soviet system should discourage technological innovation, except when high political authority is brought to bear in order to implement specific programs. Innovation should be much more common in the United States where a decentralized market system and a relatively free flow of information encourage low-level initiatives. (Evangelista, 1986b, p. 104)

Influenced by James Kurth (1971),[8] Evangelista proposes an idealized five-stage pattern for US weapons innovations:

> The pattern described is one whereby scientists in weapons laboratories and

> military officials in close contact with them recognize technical possibilities for new weapons. They actively promote the military applications of their technological discoveries in a process of consensus-building that starts with the military-technical community and is gradually pushed up to include high-level military officials, Congress, and usually the Executive. At some point, advocates of the innovation may be assisted by an often unrelated foreign development of the appearance of a threat. In the later stages, as supporters seek advanced development and production of the new weapon, they appeal to a more specific threat, sometimes quite different from the one that provided the earlier opportunity to promote their innovation. (Evangelista, 1986b, pp. 106–107)

Evangelista argues, with Kurth (1971), that, due to vigorous activity at the base and weak control at the top, 'technocratic' forces dominate the *first* stage in the process of US weapons innovation. However, technology is no autonomous force; so, for an idea to attract political support and funding, at the *second* stage promoters try to build a consensus in its favour. During the *third* stage, scientists and their military and industrial associates in the R&D community promote the new weapon proposal within the military services, the Congress, and the Executive, until it gains influential supporters.

> An external threat is often useful for breaking through organizational and bureaucratic barriers of change. [. . .] In the US system lower-level actors try to promote their programs from the bottom, by invoking threats. Such threats arise not only from potential enemies, but perhaps more often from competing programs in rival military services. [. . .] Although *internal* threats (from rival services) appear to constitute the primary motivation for pursuing programs that meet bureaucratic resistance during this third stage, promoters of an innovation tend publicly to invoke an *external* threat. They are often thereby able to make the organizational changes necessary to carry through the innovation. (Evangelista, 1986b, pp. 122–124)

In the *fourth* stage, after a weapons system has received sufficient support from the services and from Congress to enter into advanced R&D, in order for it to go into production as a prototype, its promoters must engender a certain bureaucratic momentum and appeal to 'strategic fears', according to Kurth. At this stage, weapons systems are often justified on the basis of an external threat, or a projected threat that is still rather vague. External factors, Evangelista argues, 'should be understood as catalysts – in the sense of speeding up the process of getting a new weapon adopted but not initiating it. The weapons promoted as responses to new external threats were often unnecessary, or did not meet the particular threat for which they were supposedly intended' (1986b, p. 129).

Finally, in stage *five*, promoters of a new weapons system seek wider public and Congressional support in order to secure full funding for its large-scale production.

> Often under greater scrutiny than during earlier stages, the program typically must be justified with reference to a more specific threat or opportunity. Because, however, promoters of the new weapon have already amassed

considerable support, rationales for producing the system need not have much grounding in reality. [. . .] The 'external' factors, the military threats or requirements, generally appear only in the later stages of an American weapons innovation, and then mainly as justifications for weapons that are desired for other reasons. (Evangelista, 1986b, pp. 133–137)

A more traditional interpretation of the interrelationships among strategic doctrine, weapons acquisition, and arms control has been suggested by Baugh (1984). In his survey of the strategic weapons acquisition process, Baugh differentiates horizontally between conceptual columns of basic process, primary feedback interactions, and constraints, and vertically among a five-step sequence of

(a) intelligence-gathering, to garner information about the external environment; (b) interpretation and assessment to determine probable needs; (c) program option generation, including selection and funding of program options in light of expected needs, existing programs and capabilities, and a myriad of constraints; (d) research and development; and (e) actual production of weapons and their deployment and incorporation into the arsenal. (Baugh, 1984, pp. 87–88)

While the assessment of needs should lead to the generation of programme options designed to meet them, Baugh argues that in practice

program options are generated more or less continuously, as natural products of the ongoing research and development process and as routine outputs of every organization. Indeed, it is central to the argument [. . .] of 'technological creep' [. . .] that evolutionary increases in capability will be generated as routine R&D outputs. *It is thus difficult to determine categorically whether program options precede or follow doctrine and needs-assessment.* (Baugh, 1984, p. 90, emphasis added)

To interpret the functioning of the strategic weapons regime, Baugh organizes the arms literature into four themes. Two stress international factors – *action-reaction* and *war mobilization* – and two emphasize domestic factors: *bureaucratic politics* and *political-business cycle (military-industrial complex)*. However, Baugh does not opt for any of these four models. He concludes his sketch of an 'integrated, systemic view of the political and management processes which unite the disparate elements of arms control agreements, strategic doctrine, new weapons acquisitions, historical patterns of action, technological possibilities and forecasts, stocks of existing weapons and major domestic and foreign actors' with a sense of helplessness by pointing to the obvious: 'With so many elements, that regime is characterized by a tremendous number of interactions, and routinely exhibits unresolved conflicts and apparent contradictions' (Baugh, 1984, p. 120).

After this brief review of the formal structures we turn now to the dynamic process of weapons procurement by asking of the ten case studies in our sample:

WEAPONS INNOVATION AND US WEAPONS SYSTEMS 187

- What is the scientific working context of each author: scientific discipline, scientific school, and direction?
- Which research questions are pursued, and what research focus has been chosen: domestic or international input or output factors, internal or external layer of decision-making, and level of analysis?
- What weight is attributed to analysing questions of causation and legitimation, and what significance is given to technological, strategic, economic and political factors as well as actors?

4 Analytical Framework

4.1 Scientific Context

All ten case studies have been written by political scientists with a specialization in international relations, public administration, organization theory, management techniques, strategic affairs, and military history. Eight of the studies were published between 1968 and 1977, and the two more recent ones on the Trident and MX in 1984 and 1985. Six of them grew out of PhD dissertations.

The first two studies by Art (1968) and Armacost (1969) have been influenced by the decision-making process analysis. Their research focus is rather narrow, on aspects of the political control of the weapons innovation process (Art) and on its management (Armacost), and on how to improve management techniques. In his analysis of the TFX controversy during the McNamara era in the Pentagon, Art presents 'what the civilian and military leaders thought, how they acted, and from their own testimony, why they thought and acted as they did' (Art, 1968, p. xi). Armacost pursues the following purpose:

> to contribute to an understanding of how the content of weapons policies is influenced by the character of the political process through which those decisions are made. Specifically, this study presents an analysis of the ways in which interservice competition affected the development, production, and deployment of the novel weapon system: the intermediate-range ballistic missile. (Armacost, 1969, p. 8)

The studies by Sapolsky (1972), Tammen (1973), Greenwood (1975), Beard (1976), Coulam (1977), Yanarella (1977), and Holland & Hoover (1985) have been influenced by the bureaucratic politics approach that had been developed by Allison, Halperin, et al. in the early 1970s and that was increasingly being criticized in the later 1970s and in the 1980s.[9]

Sapolsky focused on the following research questions:

> In what way does the organization of the military affect the generation of weapon proposals? How do weapons proposals gain approval? What factors influence the development of approved projects? What type of government–contractor relations are the most effective in large-scale technical projects? What is the role of science advisers in the formation of government policy? How can large-scale projects be controlled? What organizational structures and

management policies facilitate the development of technology? Why was the Polaris development successful? (Sapolsky, 1972, p. ix)

To answer these questions, Sapolsky was permitted to read and analyse the papers of the Special Projects Office responsible for the Poseidon systems development, and he conducted about 400 interviews.

Beard deals 'with the events, decisions, and perceptions that led to the original situation of 1957' by trying to demonstrate 'the process leading through the development of an American ICBM and describe why the weapon appeared when it did. By so doing, I hope to cast new light on the interrelationship between technology, strategy, organization and politics' (Beard, 1976, p. 4).

Coulam focuses 'on the influence of bureaucratic phenomena on the F-111 development'. He attempts 'to demonstrate the value of the cybernetic paradigm for evoking, and giving logical coherence to these phenomena' (Coulam, 1977, p. 9).

The studies by Tammen, Greenwood, Yanarella, and Holland & Hoover are broader in design and have more ambitious theoretical aims. Tammen and Yanarella have been influenced by the German debate on armaments dynamics, most particularly by the writings of Dieter Senghaas. In his interpretation of defence strategy, Tammen reviews the theoretical relevance of literature on the action-reaction phenomenon and the perspectives on the balance of power, in order to interpret the MIRV case. He places special emphasis on the domestic drives of the action-reaction process, particularly on the technological imperative.

Yanarella has three objectives: first 'to provide a general historical narrative of the most important events in the evolution of the ABM between 1955 and 1972'; second 'to analyse the five most salient decisions to deploy an active defense against ICBMs'; third 'to weigh the impact of the strategic, technological, political, organizational, and economic factors' (Yanarella, 1977, pp. 2–3).

Greenwood analyses

> the process of technical innovation within its broad historical and institutional context. The development programs for the Poseidon and Minuteman III, the strategic missiles that carry the first generation MIRVs, are examined, as are the several competitive warhead systems that were one by one abandoned. The relationship of MIRV to fluctuations in strategic thinking, and to perceptions about Soviet weapons programs is analyzed. The organizational environment and the changes in domestic politics that affected the MIRV programs are explored. (Greenwood, 1975, p. xv)

As a basic hypothesis, Greenwood claims:

> It is the complex interplay of technological opportunity, bureaucratic politics, strategic and policy preferences of senior decisionmakers and great uncertainty about Soviet activities that fostered the development of MIRV. Although one or

another of these factors may have dominated at one particular time or for one particular actor, each made an important contribution to the course of the programs. (ibid)

For Holland & Hoover, the MX case 'is the clearest manifestation of the changes in the pattern of procurement decision making for major weapons systems in the post-Vietnam/Watergate era'. In their view the importance of their book 'rests on discovering and analyzing the reasons for MX's departure from the norm of procurement decision making in the 1950s and 1960s, and explaining why it is the harbinger of decision making concerning a certain type of major weapon programs' (Holland & Hoover, 1985, pp. 1–2). They offer a descriptive model of procurement decision-making derived from the bureaucratic politics literature of the 1970s, adapted to the new environment of the early 1980s.

The study by Dalgleish & Schweikart is methodologically far less ambitious. It seeks simply 'to show how the Trident affects and is affected by a vast array of military and nonmilitary factors'. The authors pursue four major themes. First, they study 'the problems facing constitutional democratic governments as they try to achieve continuity in, and financial support for, large defense programs'. This involves a re-examination of a point discussed by Gansler (1980): how capitalist competitive processes may be employed in essentially non-competitive programmes. Second, they challenge the view of most media reports of the Trident; third, they discuss 'the interrelationship of the Trident in the strategic equation in a broad sense'; and finally, they 'repeat the studies of other policy analysts by investigating the political and military considerations affecting weapons selection in a democracy' (Dalgleish & Schweikart, 1984, p. xvii).

While Art, Coulam, Armacost, Beard, Sapolsky, and Dalgleish & Schweikart offer many insights into the inner layer of the weapons innovation and acquisition process, they have not focused on identifying those factors that stimulate the strategic arms competition, or on contributing to a theory of armaments dynamics. Rather, they discuss such constraints to weapons innovation as the conservatism of the services that prevents cost-effective solutions – i.e. the intra- and inter-service competition. Only four studies of our sample discuss the interrelationship of technological, strategic, and political factors (Tammen, Greenwood, Yanarella, Holland & Hoover), with two stressing the importance of a technological impulse (Tammen, Yanarella). Only two offer propositions that permit generalizations for a theory of armaments dynamics. Holland & Hoover go beyond the traditional assumptions and propositions of the bureaucratic politics paradigm of the 1970s. However, they do not discuss the role of economic *input* factors, e.g. the interests of defence contractors in follow-on contracts and of defence-dependent regions and states in future federal defence contracts, as well as the economic *output* factors, for example the impact of specific defence contracts on industrial sectors, on the business cycle of growth and inflation.

4.2 The International and the Domestic Political Context

What of the international context when the ten weapons projects were being initiated? To what extent can they be interpreted as a direct reaction to the status of East–West relations, to war requirements, to international crises, to Soviet technological advances, and to specific intelligence information?

Four case studies focus on weapons systems initiated during the mid- and late 1950s: the Thor and Jupiter IRBMs, the ICBMs (Atlas, Titan, Minuteman), the Polaris, and the Nike Zeus ABM system. Four case studies focus on systems of the 1960s during the McNamara era in the Pentagon: the TFX and the F-111 bomber, and the MIRV, while those systems initiated during the Eisenhower Administration (Thor, Jupiter, Titan, Minuteman, Polaris) were deployed in the 1960s during the Kennedy and Johnson Administrations. The two most recent cases – Trident and MX – were initiated during détente as part of the price President Nixon had to pay for obtaining military and Congress acceptance for the SALT I Treaty. Six weapons systems were initiated during the Cold War (1946–62) period; two systems (MIRV, Sentinel) were launched during the limited détente (1963–68) period and introduced during the brief détente interlude.

The concept of land-based missiles (IRBMs, ICBMs) as well as of using nuclear-powered submarines as missile launchers had been pursued by experts since the mid- and late 1940s. Various factors had slowed down their development: the Korean War had caused cutbacks in R&D in favour of war requirements for procurement; the budget ceiling of the Eisenhower Administration did not favour new weapons systems that could challenge established missions of the Air Force bomber force or of Navy carriers and surface ships. Such domestic constraints in an era of East–West confrontation were overcome as a consequence of the Sputnik shock of October 1957. This provided the stimulus for organizational innovation within the individual departments: thus the newly established Special Projects Office of the US Navy was given planning and budgetary responsibility for developing the Polaris. In the Office of the Secretary of Defense (OSD) two new organizational units were established in 1958: the Office of the Director of Defense Research and Engineering (late DDR&E), and the Advanced Projects Agency (ARPA later DARPA); and in the White House the position of the Presidential Science Advisor was created.

During the McNamara years new management techniques were introduced to strengthen civilian control over the military and to overcome constraints which, due to inter-service competition, often favoured competitive developments among the services. After World War II a new organizational structure for US defence policy was established in two stages: between 1945 and 1947, the Atomic Energy Act, the Unification Act, and related laws provided the legal framework for the creation of the US Department of Defense, the Air Force and the Central Intelligence

Agency. In the aftermath of the Sputnik shock, advanced technology now became a major element of the East–West competition and was given its many institutional voices. In his Farewell Address, President Eisenhower warned against the negative impact of a structure that had begun to evolve since late 1957:

> [. . .] we must guard against the acquisition of unwarranted influence, whether sought or unsought, by the military-industrial complex. The potential for the disastrous rise of misplaced power exists and will persist. [. . .]
> Today, the solitary inventor, tinkering in his shop, has been overshadowed by task forces of scientists in laboratories and testing fields. In the same fashion, the free university, historically the fountainhead of free ideas and scientific discovery, has experienced a revolution in the conduct of research. Partly because of the huge costs involved, a government contract becomes virtually a substitute for intellectual curiosity. [. . .] In holding scientific research and discovery in respect, as we should, we must also be alert to the equal and opposite danger that public policy could itself become the captive of a scientific-technological elite. (Eisenhower, 1961, p. 1038)

4.3 The Research Focus: Input vs Output Factors

Two different sets of questions may be raised with respect to any weapons system. First, what reasons (causes), social forces (actors), organizational and political frameworks (processes), and internal and public justifications have been given for any new weapon system? Such questions refer to *input factors* or *determinants* or armament policy. Secondly, what have been the implications of specific weapons innovation and programme decisions for the future structure of the armed forces for the formulation of military doctrine, for the national and the international political system, and for the strategic arms competition between the two superpowers, specifically as regards strategic stability? These questions refer to *output factors* or to the manifold *impact* or *implications* of strategic weapons innovations.

All ten case studies have focused primarily on *input* factors, i.e. on the role played by technological factors (scientists, military officials, and defence contractors who have been primary promoters), strategic factors (strategic rationalizations in terms of mission requirements and the threat from the competing military service or superpower), bureaucratic factors (organizational routines, management techniques), and political factors (civilian political actors, organizations, interest groups, elections) in the weapons innovation and procurement process.

However, these case studies have neglected a detailed analysis of the *impact* of these new weapons systems on the domestic and on the international system, often serving as new inputs or legitimations for yet a new round in the arms competition. Tammen in his case study on MIRV only peripherally discusses the stability implications for the arms competition (arms race stability), during international crises (crisis stability) and for command and control systems (command stability). One fundamental shortcoming of input-oriented case studies on the weapons innovation and procurement process has been that their retrospective narrow focus has not been able to provide any prospective early warning system that could have predicted e.g. the destabilizing impact of MIRV on the ICBM vulnerability issue. Such concerns have been reflected only to the extent that they have been discussed during the weapons innovation process, either within the Executive or during debates in Congress.

4.4 Level of Analysis

Holland & Hoover correctly note that both the bureaucratic politics paradigm and most case studies on the weapons innovation and procurement process have focused only on the *internal layer* of decision-making within the Executive. This may have been appropriate and sufficient until the late 1960s as long as a bipartisan consensus existed on foreign and defence policy matters in the United States.

Only three case studies go beyond the narrow focus on the organizational subunits that promoted, developed, and administered a specific weapon system and their superiors within the Pentagon. All three cases deal with controversial weapons systems: the MIRV (Greenwood), the ABM (Yanarella), and MX (Holland & Hoover). Only the MX case study analyses at length the 'public arena', especially the role of the states and civilian groups critical of the MX in general and of a specific deployment mode. However, equal emphasis has not been given to the lobbying of the proponents – organizations representing the interests of the military and the defence contractors and their allies – in the media.

On the internal layer, weapons innovation and procurement decision-making has been analysed in at least five stages or levels: (1) concept formulation (e.g. between scientists, military officers, and defence contractors; (2) programme definition (e.g. between officers in R&D subunits and their superiors within each service); (3) programme promotion (within each service, intra-service consensus building); (4) programme salesmanship (within the Department of Defense, inter-service competition, and consensus building); (5) policy integration (inclusion of domestic and foreign policy considerations). The *internal layer* of decision-making is usually not accessible to the public. Information on this layer can be obtained for historical cases only after the documents have been released to the public, and through intensive off-the-record interviews with participants.

The *external layer* of the arms innovation and procurement process involves the budgetary process within the US Congress and Executive–Legislative relations. This sixth level is the focal point for public interest groups for and against a specific weapons programme, experts, and the media.

While US case studies influenced by the bureaucratic politics approach have dealt primarily with the early levels of the weapons procurement process, case studies on armaments dynamics of the Czempiel school[10] at

Frankfurt University have concentrated on this sixth level. The present author has tried to analyse the external factors that influence the budgetary process and Executive–Legislative relations (Brauch, 1979b, 1980, 1981).

4.5 Bottom-Up vs Top-Down

In his comparative case study on the weapons innovation process on tactical nuclear weapons for the United States and the Soviet Union, Evangelista concludes:

> The factors that come into play at various stages reflect differences in the organization of military research and development in each country. These differences in turn reflect more fundamental differences at the level of the political system. To summarize, the centralized, secretive system in the USSR imposes innovation *from the top down*, generally in response to foreign initiatives. The more open, decentralized system in the United States fosters initiative and initiation *from below*. (1986b, pp. 164–165, emphasis added)

This pattern holds true for at least eight case studies in our sample. The TFX decision by Defense Secretary McNamara was initiated from the top against the will of the Air Force and the Navy, both of which wanted to have their own fighter. In fact, in the long run they were to prevail, as the F-111 fighter bomber was built only in the Air Force version, while the Navy version, the F-111B, was cancelled.

One case, however, contradicts the dominant feature of postwar US weapons innovation process: SDI, initiated from the top (Stein, 1984; Herken, 1987; Brauch, 1989b). The history of the formulation of President Reagan's 'Star Wars' speech of 23 March 1983 shows that neither new intelligence information about a new Soviet BMD challenge, nor detailed initiatives that had come up through the bureaucracy, were the decisive factor. Crucial here were President Reagan's own political and strategic predilections. Suggestions he picked up from the members of his 'kitchen cabinet' and from unofficial defence advisers like Edward Teller and General Daniel Graham provided the conceptual input for the speech (Brauch, 1989b, pp. 366, 368).

4.6 Causation vs Legitimation

Have new US weapons programmes been stimulated by intelligence information on specific Soviet weapons programmes? Or have they subsequently been legitimated with intelligence information in the consensus-building process within each service and in competition with the rival service? Has there been an action-reaction process between US and Soviet weapons decisions, as claimed in McNamara's classic San Francisco speech?

> The Soviet Union and the United States mutually influence one another's strategic plans. Whatever be their intentions, whatever be our intentions,

actions [. . .] on either side relating to the build-up of nuclear forces, be they either offensive or defensive weapons, necessarily trigger reactions on the other side. It is precisely this action-reaction phenomenon that fuels an arms race. (McNamara, 1967, p. 387)

Senghaas (1969, 1972a, 1972b) has challenged this classic interpretation of the action-reaction process or the predominance of external threat factors; his hypotheses concerning the foreign threat have also been supported by several case studies in our sample. Evangelista has cogently summarized this point: 'The external factors, the military threats or requirements, generally appear in the later stages of an American weapons innovation, and then mainly as justifications for weapons that are desired for other reasons' (1986b, p. 136).

Gray (1976) has distinguished six patterns of interaction: (1) *Eigendynamik*, (2) random response, (3) macro response, (4) limited response, (5) differential response, (6) mechanistic response (Gray, 1976, pp. 100–125). The analytical relevance of the model selected depends on the analytical lens used, or on those aspects of the arms race the analysis focuses on: technological, strategic, bureaucratic, or political history. Each of his six models, Gray has argued, 'seems to fit some of the evidence of Soviet–American arms race behaviour' (Gray, 1976, p. 99). With the specific focus of most of the case studies on the bureaucratic policy-making process, it is not surprising that domestic input factors prevail in most of the case studies.

Gray's macro-response model may help in interpreting the military R&D input in new weapons systems immediately after the Sputnik shock. According to Gray's definition, the macro-response model

> suggests that the record of the strategic arms race shows a series of often severely time-lagged, broad-fronted, almost lurching responses. [. . .] Model 3 suggests that the significant action-reaction process is the one that pertains to the perceptions of major shifts in the political intentions of the adversary and/or major shifts in his overall strategic capability. [. . .] Model 3 is an attempt to politicize what is all too often a technical exercise – the analysis of plausible arms race action-reaction chains. [. . .] Action-reaction, in this view, is no tidy, hygienic thrust and parry exercise. The arms race activity of a state moves from one plateau of effort to another, as a consequence of a shifting of arms race controlling gears by the political leaders. [. . .] Broad responses to broad perceived challenges may have to await favourable electoral political circumstances, and will not be reflected in weapons developed and deployed for many years to come. [. . .]
>
> There is good reason to claim that the arms race had its genesis, has been sustained by and has been moved into higher or lower gear as a consequence of the perceptions of broadly understood political threat. (Gray, 1976, pp. 104–105)

This model may help explain why there have been two major periods of drastic increases in US military R&D expenditure, immediately after the Sputnik shock in 1957 and after the Soviet intervention in Afghanistan in 1979. The Sputnik shock was accompanied by the Gaither Report, an internal re-evaluation of the Soviet threat conducted in 1958. A second re-evaluation of the Soviet threat was initiated in the United States in 1973 and 1974, catalysed after 1976 by the activities of the Committee of the Present Danger. Such re-evaluation of the Soviet threat by major portions of the US security elite was to overcome the implications of the shattered post-Vietnam consensus. This new consensus remained latent during the Carter Administration, but manifested itself immediately after the Soviet invasion of Afghanistan. By changing the public mood in the United States, the Afghanistan impulse brought into power perspectives associated with the Committee on the Present Danger. This led not only to a most dramatic increase in US defence expenditure but also to a doubling of US military R&D expenditures in real terms (Acland-Hood, 1985).

4.7 Analysis of Internal/External Input/Output Factors

Art, Coulam, and Armacost focus primarily on the decision-making process within the Executive branch. They deal with the success (Art, Armacost) or failure (Coulam) of the management and budget reforms introduced by Secretary of Defense McNamara during the Kennedy and Johnson Administrations. External input factors (e.g. intelligence information on related Soviet weapons programmes) did not play a causative role in the early stages of these specific weapons innovation processes; the Soviet threat was used, however, in the effort to legitimize weapons projects within the service, in the inter-service competition, and in the budgetary process in Congress. Internal and external output factors that explain the impact on the national economy and on the international system have not been studied. Art emphasizes:

> The revolutionary manner in which McNamara made his decisions [. . .], transformed the 'expert' career bureaucrat into the 'novice' and the 'inexperienced' political appointee into the 'professional'. By demanding that decisions be made through a cost-effectiveness analysis, McNamara freed himself from the secretary's usual dependence on the experience and knowledge of the military officer and the career civil servant. (Art, 1968, pp. 160–161)

Coulam is more sceptical on post-WWII weapons acquisition reforms:

> Established organizations resisted any broad proposals for reform. [. . .] Little actual change resulted, other than the reinforcement of organizationally conservative [. . .] myths of success for concurrency and the weapon-system concept. Robert McNamara confronted a similar problem during his tenure. His major procurement reforms involved changes in planning procedures and changes in contract types. [. . .] The procedural reforms apparently weeded out the most extreme cases of unrealistic and duplicative programs, though at the cost of further rigidifying the requirements process and generally reducing the number of projects committed to hardware development. The contractual reforms were nearly a complete failure, however. (Coulam, 1977, pp. 376–378)

Armacost believes that the following political factors have constrained any rational choice: inter-service and inter-agency rivalry, and budgetary ceilings. With respect to the IRBM, he argues that allied influence 'on the design of IRBM was indirect and negative'. On the strategic and organizational reforms initiated by McNamara he is more positive:

> The pace and character of technological innovation were substantially influenced by revisions in strategic doctrine. The McNamara strategy initially encouraged an acceleration of the procurement schedules for strategic delivery systems as well as impressive efforts to improve and safeguard those systems. [. . .]
> Participation in the qualitative arms race was by no means abandoned, despite the evident interest in controlling its pace. On the contrary, since 1962, annual expenditures for research, exploratory development, and advanced development – precisely the areas of new technology formation – have been increased by more than 25 percent. [. . .]
> Interservice strife was not a prominent feature of defense politics during the period of the massive buildup and qualitative improvement of strategic forces [. . .] (Armacost, 1969, pp. 286–287)

In Armacost's assessment, McNamara's organizational reforms of defence planning and budgeting shifted

> the balance of influence in the Pentagon away from the service departments to the Office of the Secretary of Defense. [. . .] Although the traditional services were not formally assaulted, their independence and authority were significantly diminished. Some of the functions formerly performed separately by the service departments were delegated to new agencies. Thus communications, intelligence, and security responsibilities were consolidated in the Defense Intelligence Agency and the National Security Agency; procurement services in the Defense Supply Agency; common and long-line communications in the Defense Communications Agency. [. . .] The initiative and influence exerted by the Secretary of Defense and his staff [. . .] was enormous. (Armacost, 1969, pp. 288–359).

In his longitudinal study on bureaucratic politics and weapons innovation for the ICBM case, Beard refers to the close linkage between service organization and weapons innovation:

> The strategic bomber and the ICBM both illustrate that a revolutionary new weapon may be subordinated to outdated doctrine or outdated methods if it is not assigned to an agency designed to foster it. The bomber was promoted by the Air Corps during the early years, but was persistently opposed by the Army General Staff in favor of combat support and reconnaissance. The ICBM was developed by a totally new organization, the Western Development Division. [. . .] Polaris too was developed by a 'Special Projects Office'. (Beard, 1976, p. 232)

> Any new weapon system is bound to compete with already existing commitments simply because it is new and has therefore never had a budget line of its own. Similarly, *all* of the budget will already be allocated to the existing functions. [. . .] There is a built-in and inevitable resistance to new ideas that will cost money unless additional outside funding appears available. But such funding is unlikely, particularly for a seemingly revolutionary development, until after the item has proven its worth. (Beard, 1976, pp. 238–239)

Holland & Hoover, in their MX case study, extend their analytical focus, from the narrow internal layer of weapons procurement prevalent in the first four studies, to broader external domestic input factors: the debate in Congress and the influence of states and of environmental and church groups on the central deployment issue.

Dalgleish & Schweikart concentrate on internal input factors: on Trident's budgetary birth (1968–74), and its planning, programming, and budgeting (1974–82); but they also discuss external threat-induced input factors with respect to the Soviet ASW capability and Trident operational survivability. One chapter also deals with the impact of Trident on NATO reform, and the concluding chapter has a casual reference to the impact of such large government projects on the role of defence contractors in a market economy.

Tammen in his interpretation of MIRV discusses both the external and the internal drives of the action-reaction phenomenon. Among the internal drives he mentions (1) technological uncertainty, (2) technological obsolescence, (3) intelligence uncertainties, (4) unpredictability of the market due to a single consumer, (5) Congressional authorization and appropriations, (6) constraint of lead-times, costs, risks, quality, (7) inter- and intra-service rivalries, (8) inter-functional conflicts (theorists vs engineers), (9) political influences, (10) innovation, and (11) amount of concurrency desired (Tammen, 1973, p. 31).

Tammen briefly surveys the opposing assessment of the impact of the MIRV on strategic stability that have been made both during the internal debate within the Executive branch and the budgetary process in Congress, and in the limited public debate:

> MIRV has also raised doubts about the stability of BOT [the balance of terror]. Since MIRVing a force greatly multiplies the number of reentry vehicles, the fears of the 1960s about instability resulting from accidental launches, preemption, and qualitative arms races remain relevant. [. . .] A large MIRV force also creates mathematical prospects for land-based preemption and consequent blackmail. [. . .] On paper these possibilities, though remote, are definite factors contributing to instability. On the other hand, better command and control facilities may have reduced some of this uncertainty. (Tammen, 1973, pp. 132–133)

He also summarizes the arguments of a second school of thinking which has emphasized the stabilizing influence of MIRV on US defence policy: 'First, MIRV relaxes the pressure for additional deployment of new launchers which look provocative. Second, it is said that MIRV redresses the Soviet advantage in throw-weight or megatonnage. Third, MIRV reinforces the logic of deterrence by making it senseless to contemplate attack' (Tammen, 1973, p. 133).

Tammen does not opt for any of these conflicting assessments of the MIRV, nor does he offer any prospective discussion of the impact of Soviet MIRVed missiles on the vulnerability of US land-based forces, which was to dominate the US defence debate in the late 1970s and early 1980s and provided one of the rationales for a massive defence build-up by the Reagan Administration.

For Greenwood, who also focuses primarily on the domestic input factors in the development and procurement of MIRV, this programme was in part

> a reaction to the intelligence information and intelligence projections concerning Soviet ABM and offensive missile build-ups. But the word 'reaction' can only be used with great care.
> [. . .] It was the anticipation of potential Soviet actions that helped generate support for MIRV. Although the Soviets did little more than hint at the possibility of a large-scale ABM deployment, American defense planners felt obliged to hedge against that possibility. Because the Soviets were deploying missiles that, with accuracy improvements and MIRVing, could have been regarded as a potent threat to the Minuteman force, means were sought to compensate. (Greenwood, 1975, pp. 103–104)

Yanarella pursues three objectives by offering a general historical narrative of the most important events and by analysing the five most salient decisions in detail; instead of simply delineating the various factors affecting each of these decisions, he tries to weigh their impact upon the history of the ABM development. This relative importance of domestic input factors will be reviewed next.

4.8 Technological, Doctrinal, Bureaucratic, Economic, and Political Input Factors

Art emphasizes the predominance of *political* factors, or more specifically, civilian control of Secretary of Defense McNamara over the weapons procurement process implemented by new techniques of analysis and budgeting. Art argues that by centralizing the defence decision-making process within OSD, McNamara not only gained effective control but also strengthened civilian control over the military.

Coulam is more sceptical with respect to the shift of power and influence from military to civilian leadership during the McNamara years:

> The military's sustained pursuit of maximum performance through an inflexible development process has resulted in a tenfold increase in unit acquisition costs every twenty years. [. . .] If this trend continued, it would, by itself, severely disrupt acquisition organizations and operational commands. [. . .] Any changes it induces could as easily be perverse as meliorative. Yet there are few immediate alternatives one can envision that really hold out the prospect of substantial improvement in our acquisition experience. (Coulam, 1977, pp. 387–389)

Armacost, on the other hand, is much closer to the evaluation offered by Art.

Beard, in his discussion of the linkage between technological, strategic and political factors, restates the obvious:

The interrelationship of politics, strategy, and weapons choice must be recognized. The nature of the weapons possessed by a nation can strongly influence its strategic thinking and political-military actions. Current strategic doctrine should not totally constrain research and development efforts, just as current technology should not determine the full range of strategic speculation. If either or both phenomena occur, a process of reinforcement may inevitably follow whereby doctrine restrains research and research then only supports the prevalent doctrine. This is not the best solution. If war is too important to be left to the generals, so too may be the choice of weapons which may determine whether or not you get into a war and how you fare once there. (Beard, 1976, pp. 245–246)

Holland & Hoover conclude with respect to the interrelationship of various domestic inputs to the MX decision that the insights of previous procurement studies and of the bureaucratic politics approach no longer provide an adequate explanation (Holland & Hoover, 1985, p. 8). They argue that during the 1970s 'a new defense policy system has emerged in Congress, and members are scrutinizing and modifying executive initiated weapons policies in unprecedented ways' (p. 34), and that new groups – arms control specialists from think-tanks, universities, and foundations, who had a major impact on new weapon decisions like the ABM – have become important political factors through lobbying and elections. They claim:

> The MX decision-making [. . .] also differs significantly in three critical ways from the pattern suggested by the bureaucratic politics propositions. First, strategic considerations as they related to MX were important factors in the decisions made about the new missile, especially the basing mode considerations. [. . .] Senior officials in the executive branch outside the Pentagon would not normally be instrumental in [the early] phase of MX decision making. On the contrary, they were and strategic factors most often dominated their motivation. (Holland & Hoover, 1985, p. 124)

Secretaries of Defense James Schlesinger and Donald Rumsfeld had played a major role in promoting the MX early in the process; however, the origins of MX, at least in the Carter Administration, Holland & Hoover argue, 'were not the result of deliberate strategic analysis, but rather the product of organizational doctrine, technological opportunities, and changing perceptions of the threat. MX was a result of SAC, DDR&E, and design labs in industry interacting on these issues' (1985, p. 148). In the period from 1973 to 1979, in their view,

> deliberate strategic decisions as well as political expediency crucially affected the character of MX and the various basing modes considered for its home. In fact, strategy was as significant as organizational doctrine in shaping the characteristics of MX during this period. The impact of strategic considerations and political expediency were far greater than one would expect given the propositions for the inner layer of the bureaucratic politics literature. (p. 148)

During the final year of the Carter and the first year of the Reagan Administrations, 'the Congressional arena was critical in MX decision-making, and strategic, foreign policy, as well as traditional constituent, factors were salient (Holland & Hoover, 1985, pp. 151ff.). As a consequence of legislative reforms in the 1970s, Congress could force the President to modify earlier deployment decisions. In 1980 and 1981, environmental and sociopolitical issues did have 'a significant impact on MX decision-making', according to Holland & Hoover (p. 209). From 1981 to 1983, strategic, foreign policy, environmental, and socioeconomic considerations were factors important in MX procurement decision-making, in both the Executive and Congress. Furthermore, the President was a central actor in MX negotiations with Congressional and state leaders.

Holland & Hoover offer the following interpretation of the interrelationship of the individual factors:

> In sum, then the case of policy-making for MX illustrates the interplay of several factors that may never converge again:
>
> (1) a weapon system capable of massive and irreversible impacts, both nuclear and nonnuclear;
> (2) a lack of consensus on the foreign and strategic policy objectives that inform the development of a weapon system;
> (3) a system that is technically flawed or unsatisfactory;
> (4) a project so controversial that consensus-building is difficult in the executive and in congressional arenas;
> (5) congressional and public actors equipped and willing to use their power to influence the nature and direction of procurement policymaking;
> (6) a project for which a movement of opposition has mobilized and operates in several decision-making areas simultaneously;
> (7) a system so expensive that it threatens to preempt other domestic goals. (1985, p. 253)

The MX decision-making pattern shows that the process by which certain types of procurement decisions are made has changed; and that this change has been in the direction of expanding the arena of conflict. Whether this dispersion of power will create good policy is a two-edged sword. On the other hand, competition, it is said, breeds compromise that guarantees the 'best' decision will not be made (Holland & Hoover, 1985, p. 255).

Sapolsky rejects the hypothesis of a technological imperative by pointing to the long list of cancelled projects. In his view, the choice among weapons projects 'is the choice among defense strategies. Conflicting views abound. Without agreement on strategy it is impossible to agree on evaluation' (Sapolsky, 1972, p. 237).

Tammen's interpretation supports the prevailing influence of domestic factors:

> At no point in the line of technological progress were Soviet intentions or capabilities a direct influence on these specific engineering practices. This engineering solution was then seized upon by civilian think tank strategists who saw advantages resulting from the use of multiple warheads. Once the technology was present, it was initially adopted for targeting reasons. When the

Soviets began experimenting with ABMs, MIRV was coopted for a new role and justified solely on the basis of penetrations, even though penaids were available and multiple unguided warheads would be just as effective and much cheaper. MIRV *became a technological hedge against a nationwide Soviet ABM system which was expected by some but which never appeared.* [. . .]

MIRV development created self-generating requirements which justified the continuation of the program. [. . .] The threat changed, but no modification occurred in the MIRV program. It remained flexible enough to proceed without interruption. (Tammen, 1973, pp.106–107, emphasis added)

In Tammen's view, primarily technological factors have driven the MIRV development: 'The engineering origin of MIRV was only remotely related to specific Soviet intentions or capabilities' (p. 138).

For Greenwood,

The decision to deploy MIRV was not made by a single policy choice at a particular moment in time. It was an evolving process requiring a myriad of separate decisions and activities. [. . .] Strategic arguments are employed in order to advance the programs that the technical organizations need in order to remain active, to maintain their technological and organizational independence, and to expand or protect their roles and missions. But strategic preferences also form part of the belief structure of military personnel and are thereby influential in their own right. (Greenwood, 1975, p. 80)

For the Air Force, MIRV offered the advantage to advance their central mission, fighting nuclear wars by improving the capability to penetrate a Soviet ABM. 'If one adds together the ideological perspectives of the service bureaucracies, their organizational interests and procedures and the opportunities afforded by new technology, an explanation of the main features of the MIRV programs can be generated.' (Greenwood, 1975, p. 80)

Greenwood disagrees with the interpretation by Kurth (1971), who claimed that the MIRV programme could 'best be explained by bureaucratic process: bureaucratic doctrines, bureaucratic standard operating procedures, including in this case normal procedures for the research and development of technocratic interests, and bureaucratic programs for organizational preservation and growth' (Kurth, 1971, p. 385). Greenwood rejects any of these partial explanations, 'the determination of technology, the inexorable drive of bureaucratic process or the preeminent role of central decisionmakers, as *the* explanation of the MIRV programs' (Greenwood, 1975, p. 81). In his view:

All were involved and all must be included if an accurate explanation of the MIRV programs is to be given. [. . .]

The best that can be done is to suggest that at some times and at some levels in the government hierarchy one aspect was most important, and at other times and at other levels different aspects were. No single policy determinant predominated across either the span of time or the breadth of diverse organizations. Technical and organizational factors, for example, were much more compelling within the services, particularly the technical organizations, than in OSD, and within OSD they were stronger in DDR&E than in Systems Analysis or to the Secretary. Strategic objectives, on the other hand, were more compelling in their own right at the level of responsible decisionmakers. But, as discussed above, even their dominant strategic objective changed with time. To Secretary McNamara, moreover, the utility of MIRV as a means of controlling the bureaucracy was a major advantage in 1964 and 1965. By 1967 and 1968 he was trying, with less success, to use MIRV as an argument against the ABM advocates in Congress. [. . .] MIRV's role in domestic politics probably did predominate in President Johnson's mind. It was a counter to his defense critics and helped him delay an ABM deployment while trying to get the Soviets to agree to SALT. In short, technology, strategy, politics, and organizational factors were all woven together in an intricate, unique and changing fabric. Until 1968 the main strands all tended in the same direction, carrying the MIRV program forward. (Greenwood, 1975, p. 81)

For Yanarella (1977), 'the United States' strategy of technological planning and weapons innovation flowing from the technological imperative may be most aptly termed as a 'technological-breakthrough approach', comprising the following features: (a) maximization of uncertainty, (b) non-generic prototype design, (c) multipurpose design, (d) quest for technological superiority, (e) breakthroughs are constitutive of the strategy, (f) problems of stability and control, (g) a common technological impetus projected on to one's adversary, (h) the breakthrough approach is self-referential as to ends.

Yanarella claims:

The United States based its strategic planning and programming upon a presumed identity of development by the Soviet Union. Yet planners showed little concern to structure the actual Soviet strategy of weapons development and innovation into the American R&D weapons planning process. Moreover, nearly all serious analyses of Soviet behavior in developing and deploying strategic weapons systems contradict this assumption of strategic and technological symmetry. Actually, the Soviet military R&D process seemed to be directed by what has been called a strategy of 'technological incrementalism'. (Yanarella, 1977, pp. 191–192)

The Soviet approach to technological weapons development includes the following features: (a) minimization of technological uncertainty, (b) generic prototype design, (c) single-purpose design, (d) acceptance of technological inferiority, (e) reliance on numbers and/or megatonnage, (f) successive incremental changes, (g) political use of strategic power, (h) deterrence and defence strategy (Yanarella, 1977, pp. 192–194). For Yanarella, military technology played the crucial role in fuelling the arms race; bringing military R&D under effective political control would be tantamount to controlling the arms race.

5 Generalizations on the US Strategic Weapons Innovation and Procurement Process

What are the empirical conclusions of the authors of the case studies?

What generalizations have they drawn to explain the strategic weapons innovation and procurement process of the United States from 1945 till 1984? Have they formulated theoretical propositions for a theory of armaments dynamics?

Art's focus is too narrow to permit broader generalizations, nor is this his specific interest. He concludes that McNamara successfully

> asserted his independence from the bureaucracy. [. . .] In reversing the unanimous recommendation of his military officers, McNamara laid himself open to the charge of ignoring the judgement of experts. [. . .] McNamara resolved to strengthen his control over the process by which sources for the development of advanced weapon systems are selected. [. . .] He 'rigged' the decision-making procedures in order to prevent them from blocking the outcomes he wanted. (Art, 1968, pp. 161–165)

Coulam summarizes his conclusions:

> The F-111 program began in 1962 as the symbol of a new order in the Department of Defense. It ended ten years later as a measure of the failures of that order. In the intervening period, much had gone wrong, technically and politically. In all of these unfortunate problems, the underlying influence of cognitive simplifications and organization routines was decisive. (Coulam, 1977, p. 337)

Armacost draws the following general conclusions:

> The increased authority of the Office of the Secretary of Defense and the techniques of systems analysis might as easily facilitate as inhibit the pace of military-technological innovation. [. . .] During the 1960s, much of the systems analysis [. . .] has been responsive to a new doctrinal consensus on the major strategic issues. [. . .] In order to reduce expenditures on nonessential projects, there emerged a tendency to promote a vigorous developmental effort only on those projects for which an explicit military requirement could be stated. Secondly, perspectives regarding the likelihood and the desirability of strategic weapons innovation underwent a substantial metamorphosis. Many prominent defense officials expressed the conviction that a technological plateau had been attained which rendered radical scientific or technological breakthrough extremely unlikely. This conviction was perhaps reinforced by the anxiety shared by scientists and strategists alike that a perpetuation of the arms race would disclose increasing hazards while new weapons promised little additional security to the United States. Thus the conscious effort to manage and contain the arms race. The implications of such perspectives on the weapons innovation process are obvious. (Armacost, 1969, pp. 292–293)

Beard concludes that in the early stages long-range ballistic missiles

> were virtually ignored at the highest levels of the Air Force, as the minimal funding and statements of knowledgeable personnel make clear. The concept of the self-fulfilling prophecy consistently operated during this period. If the decision is made that something cannot be developed because of technological impossibility, and then that judgement is used to justify a refusal to provide development funds, the item will not be developed and the judgement will appear true. Hence the circular ICBM history. (Beard, 1976, p. 239)

In Beard's analysis, control over the budget has been vital for the choice of weapons systems:

> Whatever faction controlled the money tended to control the choice of weapons and thus to determine overall organizational doctrine. Once the missile people got their own budget, the bomber people were in trouble. [. . .]
> The whole history of the American ICBM is one of attempts by the missile's advocates to generate interest in the weapon in the existing organizations or to create alternative (and more favorably disposed) organizations. [. . .]
> The ICBM might have been developed earlier than it was had an agency free of Air Force perspective existed, had it enjoyed access to all relevant information, and had it been heeded. (pp. 240–241)

To overcome those bureaucratic hurdles, Beard suggests that a 'well funded and independent review agency with high-level support and full technological access should produce more efficient and economical choices. Not only might unusual technological or strategic concepts receive a more objective hearing, but old and potentially outmoded weapons and doctrines might also face valuable scrutiny' (pp. 244–245).

However, by the 1970s and 1980s the situation had changed, as has been stressed by Holland & Hoover. They offer the following findings:

> The idea for a new experimental missile was a response to the desire of the air force to develop a third generation of ICBMs as a logical follow-on to Minuteman. The movement of the MX and its basing mode through the design and development stages was influenced by the interplay of organizational doctrine (the Air Force and SAC), technological opportunities, and projections of the enemy threat in the late 1970s and 1980s. Thus, during this phase of procurement activity, decision making was dominated by engineering groups in DDR&E, the design labs of defense industries (especially TRW), engineering elements of think tanks (RAND), and SAC. Moreover, the decisions about research, design, development, and testing of MX were incremental rather than synoptic; the result of hundreds of separate yet interconnected actions by individuals in the above groups. Finally, SAC was the dominant force during the early stages of MX development. (Holland & Hoover, 1985, p. 250)

While internal factors have largely dominated the research and development process, foreign policy considerations, particularly due to the SALT agreement, have complicated deployment (basing mode) decisions since 1972. For strategic reasons, OSD and several Senators opposed a more accurate ICBM:

> It is in the period after 1974, and especially between 1979 and 1983, that the propositions associated with the bureaucratic politics paradigm provide insufficient insight into MX decision making.
> After 1975, the pattern of MX decision making was more synoptic than incremental. With the increasing dominance of strategic, foreign policy, and domestic political issues in the MX debate, the preeminent position of SAC declined, and the influence of senior national security officials, especially the President, increased. At the same time, actors in Congress and the public arenas had begun testing their power and forcing reconsideration of basing decisions.

Between 1976 and 1983 the MX received five fresh basing mode reviews and many less broad reexaminations by three Presidents and their senior officials.

It was Congress [. . .] that forced the Ford Administration to postpone its plan to temporarily retrofit the MX in Minuteman silos; that compelled the Carter Administration to affect changes in the MPS. (Holland & Hoover, 1985, pp. 250–252)

When the Polaris programme was conceived in the late 1950s, the USA was already committed to a rapid expansion of its ballistic missile programmes. In summarizing his findings, Sapolsky states:

> The launching of *Sputnik* strongly reinforced the perception of danger. [. . .] By the time the Polaris was ready for production, there was no question that the United States would deploy ballistic missiles in large numbers.
> The Polaris and the other ballistic missile programs were thus clearly the beneficiaries of an unusual convergence between technological opportunities and a consensus on national needs, a convergence with parallels perhaps only in the Manhattan and Apollo projects. In the mid- and late 1950's the United States had a sharply defined defense problem and a compelling desire to pursue a given technological opportunity as it appeared to offer a solution to that problem. [. . .] The breakthrough that permitted the rapid development of ballistic missiles was *political* rather than technological. When the consensus was reached on the direction of national policy, however, the technological opportunity was there to exploit. This convergence between technological opportunity and consensus on national policy was, I argue, a facilitating factor in the success of the Polaris program since, with it, came potential access to unlimited resources and a favorable political environment. (Sapolsky, 1972, pp. 240–241, emphasis added)

However, a favourable foreign and domestic political context was not sufficient for the success of the Polaris programme:

> The success of the Polaris program depended upon the ability of its proponents to promote and to protect the Polaris. Competitors had to be eliminated; reviewing agencies had to be outmaneuvered; congressmen, admirals, newspapermen, and academicians had to be co-opted. Politics is a systemic requirement. What distinguishes programs in government is not that some play politics and others do not, but rather that some are better at it than others. (Sapolsky, 1972, p. 244)

In order to promote and to protect the Polaris, its proponents used four bureaucratic strategies: differentiation, cooptation, moderation, and managerial innovation. 'Through the pursuit of these strategies the FBM [fleet ballistic missile] proponents were able first to generate a unique demand for the development of the Polaris and then to gain autonomy for the Polaris development agency, the Special Projects Office' (Sapolsky, 1972, p. 245).

In his interpretation of defence strategy, Tammen concludes:

> MIRV was developed out of a complex relationship of factors, the vast majority of which were domestic. The few inputs that were related to Soviet weapons

programs were so muted in influence as to be of little importance. MIRV is not an example of ARP; on the contrary, MIRV calls into question many of the basic assumptions of ARP.

Second, MIRV has demonstrated a great deal of flexibility along many axes: bureaucratic, cost-effectiveness, targeting, ABM, and arms control. [. . .]

Third, ARP was considered by Defense planners, but in a far different way from its commonly accepted meaning [. . .] moving toward the perfect weapon – the weapon that could not be redressed by Soviet actions.

Repeatedly one is drawn to the two facts that most characterize MIRV: that it was justifiable by a wide set of circumstances and that it was responsive to domestic pressures. [. . .]

The lesson for arms controllers may well be to concentrate on bureaucratic and domestic factors as determinants of weapon systems development, rather than on the programs of potential adversaries. (Tammen, 1973, pp. 139–140)

Greenwood's views contrast with this analysis, especially with the notion that technology was the major determinant of MIRV.

In the case of MIRV, innovation was not very difficult and no significant organizational changes were necessary. It was not an organizational or structural innovation, but a purely technical one within organizations whose purpose was the exploitation of technology. The innovation was fully consistent with existing organizational and policy objectives. [. . .] MIRV was clearly a technology whose time had come. It was firmly grounded in the technical developments of the 1950s and was primarily an extrapolation of concepts of the same period. It is therefore not surprising that MIRV was 'invented' almost simultaneously in several places within the technical community. It was rapidly accepted within both the military and civilian sides of the Defense Department, with only a brief and scattered resistance. All concerned increasingly saw MIRV as a solution to their own particular problems. The consensus in favor of proceeding solidified rapidly. By 1965 it was fully formed. (Greenwood, 1975, p. 14)

Of the five quasi-independent inventors of MIRV, four were associated with the Air Force community. For the initial stages of the weapons procurement process, Greenwood's analysis supports the conclusions of most of the other case studies:

MIRV was originally conceived by the technical and industrial community that supports the service missile organizations and was suggested to these organizations and to DDR&E by this community. Because it was not viewed as a new weapon system, but only as an improvement of one that was already authorized or being planned, it was able to advance quite far in conceptual design without receiving explicit authorization from either the services or DDR&E. (1975, p. 35)

However, Greenwood's argument continues, MIRV was not only a product of the technical community:

It was just as much a product of McNamara's policy preferences. He saw the Minuteman MIRV as a means of reducing opposition in the Air Force and the Congress to a freeze on the land-based force and a reduction in manned bomber forces. He saw both Minuteman and Poseidon MIRV as a certain hedge against the possibility of a large-scale Soviet ABM deployment and as a system that would increase the available options in the event that deterrence failed. (p. 48)

Once the decision had been made to begin engineering development of MIRV in 1964, support for the programmes solidified rapidly, and neither McNamara nor any other official had any interest in retarding the MIRV programme. MIRV seemed to offer something for everyone by contributing to the objectives of all major organizations and decision-makers in the weapons innovation process: 'In OSD target flexibility, counterforce and war-fighting capability were desirable attributes of MIRV, but its usefulness as a hedge against the possible deployment of a large Soviet ABM system became more important' (Greenwood, 1975, p. 50).

Strategic considerations became more decisive on the political level in order to manage bureaucracy below, to articulate national interests, and to follow their own belief systems. New development projects are generated directly as a result of the decision-maker's strategic perspectives, which also play a role in determining which programmes will survive and which will not. MIRV was a programme that never lacked strong support from Secretary McNamara and his staff, because for them MIRV also offered a tool to achieve several military and strategic as well as economic goals simultaneously: to keep down the size of Minuteman force, to cut back the projected force the Air Force wanted, and to increase the target list. MIRV allowed the cancellation of the bomber project without a decline in force effectiveness. When in 1966 intelligence reports of Soviet ABM were leaked to the press, MIRV offered a cost-effective countermeasure by providing a clear advantage for the offence. In November 1966, the decision to deploy Poseidon reduced the increasing pressure for a deployment decision for the Nike-X ABM system. The release of MIRV was timed for political effect, to counter pressure for BMD deployment. MIRV made the United States confident of being able to overcome Soviet ABM.

Greenwood provides the most elaborate discussion of the relevance of the MIRV case for generalizations, with several theoretical propositions for future research. With respect to the action-reaction interactive processes in armament policy he claims:

> The linkage existed, although it was far from the sole determinant of the programs. Soviet actions were sporadic and often confusing to American intelligence analysts. [. . .] One could conclude that to the extent that the United States reacted to Soviet actions it did so as much or more in anticipation of what the Soviets *might* do than in response to what they *were* in fact doing. Moreover this anticipation was based largely on the presumption that the Soviets had knowledge and technical capabilities similar to those available to American development programs. One could argue therefore that there was no reaction, but that the reaction was as much self-generated as Soviet-generated. (Greenwood, 1975, p. 104)

In Greenwood's view, MIRV was unnecessary as an ABM penetrator. It was an overreaction to Soviet ABM. Its survival was partly due to the uncertainty of intelligence information:

> Advocates [. . .] were able to point to Soviet activities as a means of justifying the MIRV programs. The service technical organizations that needed new programs for their own organizational purposes could argue that MIRV was required to nullify Soviet ABM systems. Later, Administration officials could dwell on Soviet multiple warhead tests in order to discredit those who sought to delay or stop the American MIRV tests. They could also point to Soviet technical advances and to their numerical advantage in ICBMs in order to argue that American technological superiority must be maintained. In particular, this meant MIRVs, including the accuracy improvements, reentry vehicle designs and warhead advances that are indivisible components of MIRV. MIRV's role in a variety of political and bureaucratic disputes, the very mention of which might have weakened the case, did not have to be discussed because a convenient and acceptable justification was available in the Soviet ABM system. (Greenwood, 1975, p. 105)

Discussing theories on the weapons acquisition process (bureaucratic politics, technological determinism, systematic strategic analysis, action-reaction process) Greenwood concludes with reference to the MIRV case:

> Both the partial applicability and the inadequacy of each of these separate models or explanations has been demonstrated for the MIRV case. The importance of strategic doctrine can be seen in the initial Air Force resistance to MIRV and in the process by which its acceptability gradually increased. [. . .] The role of uncertainty and the impetus of action-reaction cycles can be seen in the overwhelming concentration on the penetration problem in the early and middle 1960s. [. . .] Bureaucratic process played a key role in the early formation on the MIRV concept within the technical community [. . .]. (1975, p. 142)

Greenwood discounts the popular notion that MIRV was a reaction to Soviet ABM, domestic factors (Tammen, 1973), bureaucratic process (Kurth, 1971), and the insistence of York (1973) and Lapp (1970) that MIRV deployment was inevitable once its feasibility was recognized.

> No single-factor explanation [. . .] captures the full complexity or illuminates the interaction between and fluctuations in the many separate strands that together produced the MIRV programs. [. . .] General predictive theory is simply not possible in this field. [. . .] The problem derives not from a lack of research or a paucity of case studies to serve as a data base (the claims of some social scientists notwithstanding) but from the very nature of human personality and human society.
> What should then be the task of an analyst of an historical case study? The first is to bare the inner workings of a decision process, identifying the various strands and showing how they converged and diverged, overlapped and intermingled to produce the observed outcomes. [. . .] The second is to suggest some generalizable propositions or hypotheses about the interrelationship of these variables that may on the one hand be testable by other scholars and on the other be useful to policymakers. (p. 143)

Before we turn to a brief review of Greenwood's propositions, let us remark that Yanarella's theoretical conclusions are noteworthy because they offer a clear preference with respect to the importance of the domestic input factors that drive the arms race. Summarizing the two idealized portraits of the conflicting and asymmetrical technological planning processes of both superpowers that affected the arms race of the 1960s, he concludes: 'Not the action-reaction phenomenon, but rather the "technological imperative" – operating within the administrative agencies of OSD and guided by the technological breakthroughs approach – was the major impetus of the strategic arms race' (Yanarella, 1977, p. 194). Yanarella sees the following consequence of this assessment for the United States military policy:

> Through the interaction of this technological imperative flowing from this 'continuously reciprocating process' and the consequences of the McNamara twin revolutions in defense policymaking, then, the United States eventually found itself in the worst of all possible technological worlds – one comprised of a strategic arsenal many times more powerful than necessary, a modest ABM system strictly ancillary to its strategic offensive forces, and a dynamic arms race fueled overwhelmingly by its own R&D efforts in both offensive and defensive spheres. (pp. 194–195)

In order to contain military R&D that fuels the strategic arms race, Yanarella believes, it is not sufficient to rely on arms control alone. Rather, he suggests addressing those multifaceted elements that drive the dynamics of the strategic arms race, which have been explained in terms of 'redundant causality' by Dieter Senghaas:

> Redundantly caused phenomena generally cannot be changed by only attenuating a few of their elements. Even if within a major complex – composed of as many parts as a military-industrial complex – some elements lose in importance (e.g. if the enemy is pictured in a less hysterical manner), the growth patterns of such complexes remain almost untouched; there may even be compensations by the strengthening of other elements. (Senghaas, 1972a, pp. 361–365, and 1972b, pp. 81–86)

Greenwood summarizes his theoretical conclusions in the following eight propositions:

(1) Without adequate political support a weapons innovation cannot survive to be deployed as part of the force structure.
(2) The management 'techniques' and style of the Secretary of Defense affect the degree of control he exercises over the weapons acquisition process and his policy preferences can affect the type of weapons developed and deployed.
(3) The critical event in the life of a weapon system is the decision to enter into engineering development.
(4) The technical community plays a central role in the weapons acquisition process.
(5) Strategic preferences and intelligence projections can have important impacts on weapons choices.
(6) Mechanisms exist by which Congress can influence weapons acquisition decisions. By repetitive and reinforcing actions Congress can set general policy guidelines and identify special issues of concern.

(7) The Arms Control and Disarmament Agency and special interest groups gain influence through the sufferance of more central actors.
(8) Significant unilateral reduction in the rate of modernization of the American offensive strategic forces would be very difficult to achieve. (Greenwood, 1975, pp. 144–156)

Holland & Hoover (1985) have summarized the results of their case study in 21 propositions distilled for the inner layer from the bureaucratic politics literature, and for the outer layer added by the authors:

A. Propositions for the inner layer
(1) Ideas for new weapons or refinements of old weapons are seldom the result of deliberate strategic policy analysis. Rather they are the product of organizational doctrines, technological opportunities, perceptions of enemy threat, and/or incomplete and often vague strategic attitudes. More accurately, these ideas involve the interaction of engineering groups of the Director, Defense Research and Engineering (DDR&E), design labs in industry, engineering elements in think tanks, and the subunit of the military service with ultimate responsibility for the use of the new or refined weapon. [Confirmed]
(2) During the design, research, development, and testing stage, procurement decisions about weapon ideas continue to be determined by the interaction of engineering groups of the DDR&E, design labs in industry, engineering elements in think tanks, and the subunit of the military service with ultimate responsibility for the use of the new or refined weapon being the most significant actor. [Partially confirmed]
(3) The mission of the subunit of the military service with the ultimate responsibility in the military for the use of the new weapon along with the power of the subunit are more important factors in the success of a weapon system (e.g. the attractiveness of the weapon to draw support within the Pentagon as compared to other alternatives) than the larger strategic and force posture considerations of US national security policy. [Rejected]
(4) Senior political officials outside the Pentagon may disturb decisions at this layer of action on procurement but rarely control it. [Rejected]
(5) Political officials outside the executive branch as well as extra-governmental individuals will seldom seek to influence the inner layer procurement decisions, let alone disturb or even control them. [Rejected]
(6) The hundreds of interrelated yet individual decisions during design, research, development, and testing cause the character of procurement decisions in this layer of activities to be incremental rather than synoptic. [Partially confirmed]
(7) The likelihood that a weapon idea will reach design, research, development, and testing depends on the effectiveness of its advocates to continually promote the economic and political well-being of their project, for the longer a new weapon system survives during this inner layer of procurement activities the greater the momentum that builds for the weapon. The repeated individual choices begin to establish an irresistible bureaucratic inertia. [Confirmed]

B. Propositions for the outer layer
(8) When the decision for a weapon program reaches the point of acquisition and deployment, the number of participants with interests in a particular weapon system tends to increase significantly, especially inside the executive branch. [Confirmed]

WEAPONS INNOVATION AND US WEAPONS SYSTEMS 211

(9) During the acquisition and deployment stage, more actors from the congressional and public arena are activated. However, the congressional and public arenas remain indirect and peripheral to the decision process for weapon procurement. [Rejected]

(10) The principal factor for producing what congressional involvement there is in procurement is porkbarrel. [Rejected]

(11) The acquisition and deployment of a weapon program continues to depend on the capability of its advocates to promote the economic, strategic, and political well-being of their project. [Confirmed]

(12) Those weapon systems being considered for acquisition and deployment most likely to engender significant support (i.e. that will be least controversial) are those where

(a) the missions of the organization responsible for the new weapon converges with the capability of the weapon;

(b) technological opportunity converges with a consensus on national policy;

(c) the strategic requirements or foreign policy needs converge with the weapons system's capabilities;

(d) the cost of deploying the weapon system in domestic terms (i.e. money, land, environmental impacts, and jobs) are likely to be relatively less than other alternatives; and

(e) the advantages of deploying the weapon system in domestic terms (i.e. contracts and jobs) are likely to be relatively greater than other alternatives. [Confirmed]

(13) Weapon programs are seldom slowed or overturned once initial approval of acquisition is achieved in the executive branch, and only a presidential directive is likely to slow or overturn that decision. However, the decision to modify, while executive based, may be made in anticipation of public or congressional resistance deemed threatening enough to warrant change. [Partially confirmed]

(14) The 'rules of the game' introduced by the Secretary of Defense and the President shape how and by whom acquisition and deployment-decisions will be made within the executive branch. [Confirmed]

(15) Strategic policy considerations will be significant factors in procurement decisions in cases where the weapon system's strategic advantages are uncertain. [Confirmed]

(16) Foreign policy considerations will be significant factors in procurement decisions in cases where the weapon system's foreign policy advantages are uncertain. [Confirmed]

(17) Environmental considerations will be significant factors in procurement decisions in cases where the weapon system will be environmentally costly. [Confirmed]

(18) Socioeconomic considerations will be significant factors in procurement decisions in cases where the weapon system will consume large amounts of resources (material and financial) and be socially costly. [Confirmed]

(19) The President will be a decisive participant in cases where the strategic, foreign policy, and/or domestic considerations of the weapon system are in conflict with administrative policies. [Confirmed]

(20) Congress will be an important arena in cases where the strategic, foreign policy, and/or domestic considerations of the weapon system are in conflict with constituent and/or personal policy preferences. [Confirmed]

(21) The public arena will be an important one in cases where the costs and/or benefits of deploying the weapon system pose a clear and present threat to the interests of individuals. [Confirmed] (Holland & Hoover, 1985, pp. 246–250)[11]

6 Ten Lessons for a Theory of Armaments Dynamics

(1) The empirical conclusions and the theoretical generalizations offered by the authors of the case studies do not add up.

The ten case studies in our sample have not pursued comparable research questions. They have not used a common research design or paradigm even though many have been influenced by writings on the decision-making process and on bureaucratic politics. Their research focus on the decision-making process within the executive branch (internal layer) or on the budgetary process in the Congress and the public debate (external layer) has been too diverse.

(2) Findings concerning the weapons innovation and procurement process for strategic weapons of the United States may not be applied to the Soviet weapons innovation and acquisition process.

Due to the differences in social, political, economic, and administrative systems, research findings on the US decision-making process do not mirror the situation in the Soviet Union. Yanarella (1977) and Evangelista (1986b, 1988) offer a few suggestions for the differences in the procurement processes of both superpowers. Perry (1980) and Holloway (1980) have analysed US and Soviet styles of military R&D.

(3) Findings concerning the US weapons innovation and procurement process for strategic weapons systems may not be applied to interpret and explain the weapons innovation and procurement process in Western Europe.

Relatively little empirical research has been conducted on institutions, processes, and individual cases of weapons innovation and procurement policy for the United Kingdom, France, the Federal Republic of Germany, and other West European NATO countries. Weapons innovation and procurement policies have a different economic significance for those countries that have to some extent purchased, produced under licence, or co-produced weapons systems with other West European countries or with the United States.

(4) The functional stages for the weapons innovation and procurement process are similar for all countries.

At least seven functional stages may be distinguished: research, development, engineering, production, procurement, deployment, and employment in war. The concepts used for these stages in various countries are often different. A good illustration for this point has been the debate between the United States and the Soviet Union on the boundaries between research and development in the ABM Treaty of 1972.

(5) Only a few comparative case studies exist on US and Soviet strategic or tactical nuclear or conventional weapons systems that try to address the same or similar research questions for both countries.

Evangelista's dissertation (1986b) and subsequent book (1988) are a positive example for a research area still to be developed.

(6) The focus of the case studies in our sample has often been so narrow that even generalizations for the innovation of one group of weapons systems for the postwar period are not possible.

The studies of Art (1968) and Coulam (1977) show opposite conclusions reached by both, based on the development history of one specific weapons system (TFX or F-111) during the McNamara years. No effort has been made by most authors to draw conclusions for the weapons innovation and procurement process in the United States since 1945.

(7) Most of the case studies in our sample deal only with the input factors for the early stages (in the internal layer) of the weapons innovation and procurement process.

For most studies, domestic input factors prevailed for the early stage (causation) of new weapons systems. These have often subsequently been legitimized in terms of the specific mission of a service and the Soviet threat (external input factors).

(8) Output factors for these weapons systems on both the national and the international level have hardly been analysed, and if so only as a topic of Congressional debate.

The impact of specific weapons systems on selective industrial sectors, regions, states, counties, or towns has been discussed with only one particular focus on the deployment effects for the MX case. The economic impact of major procurement decisions on defence-dependent regions and the feedback via the political process have not been analysed at all. The intensive discussion on the military-industrial complex in the United States has had hardly any impact on the case studies in our sample.

The impact of specific weapons on the international system in general and on strategic stability in particular has only briefly been noted in Greenwood (1975), Tammen (1973), and Yanarella (1977), as topics in the Congressional debate.

(9) These studies have not had a specific input for a theory of armaments dynamics, nor have most of them aimed at this.

The studies by Greenwood, Tammen and Yanarella offer generalizations and theoretical propositions of relevance for theoretical approaches to explain dynamic competitive armament processes on the national and on the international systems level.

(10) These case studies have not had any specific practical political impact on the domestic selection process or on international arms control negotiations.

These case studies have not functioned – nor have they pretended to – as early warning systems to sensitize the public at large or the political actors about destabilizing weapons systems. Nevertheless, both the political experience of the Vietnam War and to some extent also the findings of studies influenced by authors of the bureaucratic politics paradigms have had some impact in strengthening the position of Congress.

7 Ten Propositions for a Comprehensive Research Design

(1) A methodology is needed that makes case studies comparable with respect to design and results.

George (1979) has offered very useful suggestions in his methodological writings dealing with structured focused comparison. Meyer (1984) has ably summarized the attractiveness of an analytical framework based on focused comparison case studies:

> Here fixed sets of questions are systematically applied across a number of individual case studies. In this way not only are important similarities, patterns and trends illuminated, but significant deviations from past behavior are noted as well. [. . .] Focused-comparison case studies allow you to bring together, in a systematic and synergistic way, the truly large amounts of data that are currently floating among many disjointed studies. (Meyer, 1984, p. 287)

(2) At least four different types of comparable case studies are needed: on the weapons innovation and procurement process for specific sectors (weapons biographies), longitudinal studies on policies and processes within selected countries, comparative studies dealing with similar weapons systems for the United States and the Soviet Union, and comparable studies for Western Europe.

(3) Case studies on the weapons innovation and procurement policies and processes must combine the analysis of input and output factors for the national and international level.

(4) Case studies should distinguish elements of causation and legitimation during the weapons innovation and procurement process.

(5) Case studies should also focus on the domestic output factors of the specific weapons systems to be analysed.

(6) Detailed case studies are needed that analyse the past, present, and future impact of new weapons systems on the international system, particularly on strategic stability.

(7) A set of internationally agreed criteria is needed for the evaluation of weapons systems in terms of arms race, crisis, and command stability.

(8) More transparency on the weapons innovation and procurement

process is a major precondition for any evaluation of new weapons systems in terms of their impact on strategic stability.

(9) Institutional and procedural innovations are needed on the executive and legislative level for a prior and independent assessment of new weapons systems in terms of strategic stability.

(10) An international analytical and negotiation framework is needed in order to recognize new destabilizing weapons systems and to prevent their development and deployment.

Where do these ten lessons and ten conclusions lead us with respect to our initial research interest? What can we learn from the case studies in our sample about the mechanisms of the qualitative arms race, and what theoretical lessons may we draw for reassessing the theoretical propositions on armament dynamics as formulated by the revisionist school in the early 1970s?

8 An Input-Output Model

We have distinguished between determinants (input factors) and implications or the impact (output factors) of armaments decisions on the level of the national and the international system. In the context of a simple input-output matrix, the three models on armament dynamics may be differentiated:

- The *traditional action-reaction model* has analysed the relationship between stimulus (input, e.g foreign threat or specific weapons decisions of the competitor) and response (output, e.g. the impact of a specific weapons system on the armament behaviour of the competitor).
- *Revisionist models* have shifted the focus of analysis primarily to domestic input factors (technological impulse, strategic interests and rationalizations, economic and bureaucratic interests) and, in the context of the debate on the existence of a military-industrial complex, on the linkage between domestic output (impact of weapons procurement decisions on economic growth, on specific industrial sectors, on regions, states, counties, and towns) and new political inputs via the political process.
- *Post-revisionist empirical approaches* of the late 1970s and 1980s have tried to focus on the interdependence between domestic and international determinants for specific weapons systems (e.g. for the medium-range missiles of the Soviet Union and NATO).

An *input-output model of armaments dynamics* should focus systematically on the many interrelationships, linkages, and feedbacks between input factors (determinants) and output factors (implications) for the national and the international level of analysis.

The MIRV case illustrates the lack of systematic analysis of the impact this weapons innovation would have on international stability once the competitor had introduced it as well. In the late 1970s, Soviet MIRVed heavy missiles were instrumental for an intensive debate in the United States on the emergent window of vulnerability. This argument was used both to criticize the SALT II treaty and to call for new US strategic weapons systems, most of which had already been initiated during the détente period.

The suggested input-output model of armaments dynamics combines an analysis of the specific historical global and domestic context with a systematic assessment of factors that have caused the initiation of new weapons systems and of arguments used to legitimate them during the weapons innovation and procurement process, during the budgetary process involving the legislative branch, and during the deployment stage that brings in regional concerns.

The international political context has to be analysed to show to what extent the involvement in wars, international crises, or the completion of arms control treaties has had a stimulating or a restraining influence on specific weapons decisions.

On the national level, various factors have to be taken into account: how the ruling elite perceives the competitor; the state of the economy and the government's economic policies and priorities; the organizational framework (institutions, bureaucratic routines); military employment policies; and the declared strategy. Systematic analyses of the weapons innovation and procurement process should:

• formulate a set of structured and focused research questions addressed either to several weapons projects of the same country, to both superpowers, or to third countries, e.g. West European NATO countries, so as to make research results comparable;

• develop several functional stages of the weapons innovation and procurement process applicable to both the United States and the Soviet Union and also to West European countries for the analysis of the input factors;

• state, for each functional level, the position and arguments of the proponents and opponents and the outcome, to the extent that public information is available (domestic input factors);

• discuss, for each functional level, the relevance and the political use of intelligence data in support of or opposition to new weapons systems, information permitting (international input factors);

• address, for each weapons system that has gone into production, the economic impact for the companies and for industry, for specific defence-dependent regions, states, counties, and towns, as well as its impact on the advancement of technology (spin-off), depending on the overall focus of the case study (domestic impact or output factors);

• evaluate, for all major weapons systems, especially for comparative studies on the US and the USSR, the implications of specific weapons systems for the overall defence posture of the competitor, in terms of strategic stability (international implications or international output factors).

Depending on the specific research interest and on the research design, the focus on different aspects of the broad input-output analysis of armament dynamics suggests different levels of political activities with the same aim of slowing down the process of weapons innovation and avoiding the introduction of new destabilizing weapons systems that may help to erode East–West relations if fielded also by the opponent. At least four different levels of political action are thereby addressed:

- For studies that focus on domestic input factors, questions of institutional and procedural reform of the weapons innovation and procurement process are relevant.
- For studies that focus on international input factors, the establishment of an independent intelligence service decoupled from the military service is of relevance.
- For studies that address domestic output factors (e.g. the domestic economic implications of specific weapons systems or of their cancellations), strategies for industrial diversification and conversion become specifically relevant.
- For studies that address international output factors (e.g. the implication of a specific weapon system on arms race, crisis, and command stability), an analysis of the impact on the strategic balance and on strategic stability becomes vital. Some of the problems may be addressed either by international arms control treaties or by national self-restraint.

Stability considerations should be addressed at each stage of the weapons innovation and procurement process by independent players with no specific service or industrial interests in mind. Such a prospective defence technology assessment in terms of stability could be institutionalized both in the executive and in the legislative branch in Western democratic countries, or in the political review bodies in the state socialist countries.

This highly ambitious research design may be developed for specific weapons systems of both the United States and the Soviet Union, for components of the strategic offensive (ICBM, SLBM, and strategic bombers) and for research projects on strategic defensive forces (e.g. BMD). Such case studies should comprise the following components:

- a joint research design by employing the methodological suggestions made by George (1979) for structured, focused comparative case studies;
- an analysis for the specific input factors in the USA and in the USSR (technological impulse, service interests, political and ideological interests, etc.);
- an analysis of the observable domestic economic output factors that often generate political input factors of their own (pork barrel politics);
- an assessment of the prospective impact of these weapons systems on the strategic balance and on strategic stability a decade into the future.

Such broadly designed, specifically structured, and sharply focused comparative case studies could provide new insights, and not only for more adequate theoretical propositions. They could also serve as part of an analytical early warning system to sensitize the public and the political process to destabilizing weapons developments that should be constrained by mutual agreement. The political lesson to be learned from the MIRV case – not from the case studies that have analysed the MIRV programme of the United States – is that a defence technology assessment in terms of stability criteria could contribute to such an early warning system. However – as the case of the arms control impact statement well illustrates – no institutional or procedural reform will suffice without the political will to use those tools.

Notes

1. Several former defence officials like Herbert York (1970) or diplomats like Raymond Garthoff (1985), as well as representatives of the bureaucratic politics approach like Graham T. Allison (Allison & Morris, 1976), have commented in detail on this case, for strategic (its impact on strategic stability) and methodological reasons.

2. This case has been discussed by this author elsewhere; see Brauch (1984, 1986, 1989b); see also the bibliographical references in Brauch (1987, pp. 572–587, and 1989c), Stein (1984).

3. See Waltz (1959, 1979), Gilpin (1981), Rosecrance (1982), Posen (1984); for a recent summary, see Evangelista (1986b, pp. 23–31). For classic treatments of the action-reaction phenomenon, see McNamara (1967), Rathjens (1969); and for a brief debate, see Senghaas (1972a,b, 1973c), Tammen (1973), Greenwood (1975, pp. 104–106).

4. See in the United States: Huntington (1961), Allison (1970), Allison & Halperin (1972), Halperin & Kanter (1973a,b), Halperin (1974), Allison & Morris (1976). For more recent surveys, see Holland & Hoover (1985), Evangelista (1986b).

5. See e.g. Perlo (1973), and a Soviet text, Faramazyan (1974). For Western studies influenced by Marxist notions, see Schmidt (1975), and Gerhard Bräunling, Peter Schlotter, & Manfred G. Schmidt, 'Rüstungspolitik und Rüstungsproduktion in der BRD. Vorarbeiten zur Analyse des Verhältnisses von Staatsapparat und Kapital' (unpublished manuscript).

6. The armament policy of the United States has been analysed by such West German scholars as Krell (1976), Brauch (1976), Müller (1985). For similar studies on France, see Sirjacques (1977, 1979); on the Federal Republic of Germany, Schmidt (1975), Bielfeldt (1977); on the Soviet Union, Tiedtke (1978). Important studies on specific weapons systems in the United States are Art (1968), Armacost (1969), Sapolsky (1972), Tammen (1973), Greenwood (1975), Beard (1976), Coulam (1977), Yanarella (1977), Dalgleish & Schweikart (1984), Holland & Hoover (1985), Evangelista (1986b). Case studies on West German weapons systems have been presented by Schlotter (1975), Mechtersheimer (1977).

7. See 'Table No. 544: Federal Research and Development Funding for National Defense: 1980 to 1986', p. 332 in US Bureau of the Census, *Statistical Abstract of the United States: 1986* (106th edition). Washington, DC: GPO, 1985.

8. Kurth distinguished among four modes of change in the US weapons procurement process: *quantitative, innovative, renovative,* and *redistributive*; and four modes of causation: *bureaucratic politics, bureaucratic process, bureaucratic-corporate alliances,* and *the economic system*.

9. For a critical review of this approach, see Caldwell (1977), Freedman (1976).

10. See Czempiel (1964), Krell (1976), Medick (1977), more recently Kappus (1985), Kubbig (1984, 1988), Witzel (1988). See also my review of early studies in Brauch (1979a).

11. Reprinted with permission of Westview Press, Boulder, CO, and London.

HANS GÜNTER BRAUCH, b. 1947, Dr. Phil. (Heidelberg University, 1976); Chairman of Peace Research and European Security Studies and of the Study Group on Weapons Technology and Disarmament of the International Peace Research Association; teaches International Relations at Frankfurt University; Research Fellow, Lecturer on International Relations, Heidelberg University. Most recent book: *Military Technology, Armaments Dynamics and Disarmament* (Macmillan/St. Martin's, 1989).

Chapter 12
Learning from History? Case Studies and the Limits to Theory-Building*

OLAV NJØLSTAD
International Peace Research Institute, Oslo

1 Introduction

In four well-received case studies on the US decision to build the H-bomb, four distinguished US scholars and arms race experts – Warner A. Schilling (1961), Herbert York (1976), David Rosenberg (1979), and Jonathan B. Stein (1984) – have come up with an equal number of answers to the key historical questions: How, actually, did the decision come about? Which factors, most likely, determined the outcome of the decision-making process? Taken together, their differing causal explanations seem to cover most of the main factors usually referred to as arms race dynamics: international action-reaction mechanisms (Stein); bureaucratic politics (Schilling); technological entrepreneurship (York); military strategy, inter-service rivalry, and budget policy (Rosenberg).

At a first glance, therefore, these four case studies seem better suited to illustrate the problem of overdetermination – 'the fact that there are too many plausible explanations for the same phenomenon and no clear way of choosing between them' (Evangelista, 1986a, p. 197) – than to deepening our knowledge about the H-bomb decision. As for those arms race analysts who believe that historical case studies should play a more substantial role in theory-building, the implications seem even more discouraging, since a general theory cannot be based on a series of case studies with ambiguous conclusions, and still claim to be valid. Hence, analysts must either find a reliable method for choosing between rival historical explanations, or desist from using the H-bomb example (and other ambiguous weapons surveys) for theorizing purposes – an alternative which, in turn, would fatally question the representativeness of any pool of selected empirical examples.

I will consider these case studies more thoroughly in section 3 of the chapter, using them to illustrate some of the methodological problems

---

* I am grateful to Håkan Wiberg, Nils Petter Gleditsch, Ottar Dahl (Department of History, University of Oslo), and my fellow historians at PRIO for comments on an earlier draft of this chapter.

involved in formulating general arms race theories on the basis of individual case studies. This section will also include some brief remarks on the method of 'focused, structured comparison'. Here, my general conclusion will be that it is very hard to see how historical case studies can contribute to any breakthrough in our theoretical understanding of the arms race phenomenon. Then, in the fourth section, I pass on to discuss some positive corollaries of the negative conclusions in section 3: namely, what theoretically relevant contributions we, after all, *can* obtain from armament decisions of the past.

In section 2, however, the approach will be a more abstract one, as I address two of the oldest methodological questions related to history as a distinct scientific discipline: What characterizes the kind of past that we are dealing with in an historical survey? And, second, what kind of understanding can be obtained through such scientific endeavor? Without at least a brief preliminary answer to these questions, we can hardly hope to cope with the more specific and urgent problems confronting us in the final two sections of this chapter.

2 Historical Past and Historical Understanding

In a trivial sense, all arms race theories are based on some kind of structured interpretation of past experiences: without it, they could hardly claim any empirical relevance. For example, how otherwise different they may be, both the statistical methods used by Richardson and the sociological methods used by Senghaas and other advocates of the Eigendynamik model are indeed empirical methods, using carefully selected data somehow believed to represent real-life cases of the arms race phenomenon.

Nevertheless, this way of scientific dealing with the past is certainly not what we would refer to as an historical inquiry. Nor are the methods implemented historical methods, the questions asked historical questions, or the understanding ultimately reached historical understanding.

Why not?

First of all, because social scientists' interest in the past is fundamentally different from that of historians. Generally speaking, they look to the past only insofar as it can support or disprove their hypotheses about some present and/or future phenomenon. This, in turn, implies that their primary interest in a particular past event has to do with its similarities or dissimilarities to other events which are supposed to belong to the same 'category', 'class', or 'type of phenomenon'. Because of this generalistic approach, the particularities which make the event a unique occurrence in time and space will usually be stripped off, thereby making it easier to see whether the event fits in with some broader or general pattern. Historians, on the other hand, generally agree that although there are resemblances among complex social events (e.g. decisions on nuclear weapon production), no such events are identical; and they often add that their aim is to understand an event as 'unique' rather than as typical (Mink, 1966, p. 183).

2.1 The Singularity of Historical Events

While social scientists concerned with the arms race phenomenon are dealing with the past in its present or present-future modalities, historians are concerned with the past *as past and past only* (Oakeshott, 1983, p. 101). This is not to say that historical research is conducted without influence from its surroundings, or that historians are without hopes and ambitions regarding the political relevance of their work and findings. But insofar as they are involved in historical inquiry, the available empirical data (and such data are themselves present survivals of the past) are analyzed only because of their supposed relevance to a certain historical question. And though historians – for didactic or heuristic reasons – may be interested in 'similar' or 'comparable' cases from a more distant or recent time, the explanatory gain from such cases is nil: all conclusions must be inferred from the remnants of *this particular past alone*. Ultimately, the reason for this lies in the spatio-temporal singularity of the past searched for by historians: their retrospective scope focuses on the possible unique relationships between various human actions of the past. These relationships are what we usually refer to as 'historical events': dynamic social situations where some particular actions (speech acts included) are being performed, thus changing the relationship between the actors involved and/or their relationship to the surrounding physical environment. To explain an historical event, therefore, is to reveal its unique – rather than general – characteristics, causes, and consequences.

2.2 The Indeterminacy of Historical Interpretation

Obviously, this historical past is not identical with the present remnants or survivals used by historians in their analyses. Neither is it the social, economic, political, cultural, and environmental totality of which the events under study once were a part. Instead, the historical past is to be found in the intellectual *terra incognita* between this vanished totality (which can never be revoked or fully grasped by any kind of scientific endeavor) and its still-existent but more or less randomized left-overs. More precisely, historical past is not some sort of reconstructed past reality, like an old town uncovered and rebuilt by archaeologists, but an *intellectually constructed universe of possible past events* – that is, events which might or might not have happened, and whose presence in this cognitive universe solely hinges on the quality of the inferences made by the historian from the present available remnants (Oakeshott, 1983, p. 33).

Their curiosity somehow aroused, historians start putting the surviving artifacts under close and careful investigation. Step by step, they create a cognitive universe of possible past events – historical *eventualities*, so to speak – consistent with the information obtained from the primary sources.

This is done by asking historical questions. These questions – the *whats, whens, wheres, whos, hows,* and *whys* of an historical inquiry – are the tools used to establish not only the list of characters, their social and institutional framework, the chronology of relevant actions and happenings; but also the unprecedented relationship between these characters, actions, and happenings. Such relationships – which are what history is basically about – are described with words and notions indicating why some kind of event did or did not materialize. In other words, they are 'causes' explaining some individual or collective human actions, *res gestae*, of the past.

At this point, things are complicated by the fact that, in an historical explanation, the causes and reasons referred to are *themselves* inferred relationships between empirically established actions and happenings in the past. Or, to rephrase Michael Oakeshott, in history 'the relation *between* events is always other events', which implies that 'the conception of cause is thus replaced by the exhibition of a world of events intrinsically related to one another in which no *lacuna* is tolerated' (Oakeshott, 1966, p. 209). Consequently, the causes and reasons which are said to 'explain' a particular historical event are only one of *many possible interpretations* of the linkage between it and other events equally established by empirical evidence – and equally open for rival interpretation. The inescapable conclusion is that no matter how detailed and thorough an historical inquiry may be, it certainly cannot leave us with a unique correlation between the various empirical variables which will force all observers to make identical inferences and conclusions. Instead, the available evidence allows for a number of more or less plausible interpretations.

Now, 'plausibility' is a relative concept, inseparably intertwined with our total intellectual and cultural experiences. Thus, why one among the alternative interpretations is singled out as *the* explanation of an event cannot always be adequately justified by methodological arguments alone. According to Morton G. White, the most obvious reason why historians will often single out different causes of a given event is that there are 'basic differences of interest, basic differences in concern and curiosity' among them, leading them to ask different questions. But their conflicting explanations may originate from other and even more fundamental sources as well: the lack of objective criteria for deciding which interpretation reveals the *true* cause of an event may also reflect the fact that historical documents contain 'the same possibility of variety as one finds in ordinary language' (White, 1965, pp. 125–126).

This leads us, finally, to the notion that I shall call the *indeterminacy of historical interpretation* – thereby indicating that it, in many ways, parallels the problem discussed by analytic philosophers like Willard V. Quine and Donald Davidson as 'the indeterminacy of translation'. In short, this problem arises whenever we want to communicate a certain insight – say, a physical hypothesis on the origin of black holes – to a person who either does not speak our language or speaks it without sharing our underlying theory of nature. Here, some kind of translation is needed: in the former case between two different languages; in the latter between two different paradigms or world views. At this point the question arises: how to ensure that our insights will survive such translation?

According to Davidson, there are two basic requirements which a translation should meet to avoid serious loss of information. First, the translation must secure that all the structure needed for a theory of truth is carried over from one language to the other.[1] Second, the translation should maximize agreement – that is, in translating A's hypothesis into B's language, sentences on empirical observations that A assents to should as much as possible translate into sentences that B assents to; correspondingly for dissent. The purpose of this requirement being to minimize the risk of misapprehensions.

The crucial point is that even when these requirements are met, there is always more than one possible connection between the two languages (or paradigms) that can qualify as translation. Most of these possible translations may be identical, or synonymous, in meaning. Others are not, thereby having the capability to distort slightly the information as it crosses the language border. This leaves us with a small but inescapable amount of uncertainty whenever exchange of insights with another human being requires translation: some nuances in meaning may not be carried through. More important, it implies the possibility that there do exist types of information not necessarily translatable from one language (or paradigm) to another: for instance, sentences which are neither true nor false, and on which there is nothing whatsoever to agree or disagree about (Davidson, 1975, pp. 20–21; Føllesdal, 1975, pp. 30–39; Quine, 1975b, pp. 90–91).

In history, sentences which are not truth-functional may often be considered as highly relevant evidence in the causal argumentation. Most relevant, perhaps, many speech acts fit into this category. Such utterances – also called 'performatives' since they are used to perform some kind of ritual or symbolic action – can be understood only if one is familiar with the cultural institutions and social sanction-systems involved. For example, everyone acquainted with the scholarly debate on the crisis between Church and State in medieval Europe will know the explanatory importance of how various speech acts and rituals – say, the coronation of Charlemagne, the excommunication of Henry IV and his subsequent oath at Canossa – are interpreted. With arms race phenomena in Western societies after World War II, the interpretative challenges are – for obvious reasons – less demanding. Nevertheless, even regular historical documents from our own time and our own political culture contain much of the same ambiguity. As Deborah Larson has pointed out in a recent study on content analysis in foreign-policy research, also 'minutes of intra-governmental debates and diaries contain conversational language, which is idiomatic, elliptic, imprecise, and difficult to pin down into analytical categories'. For example, even after careful reading and extensive discussion, researchers could not agree on how to codify George F. Kennan's famous 'long telegram' of 26 February 1946. Their general conclusion was that the inherent ambiguity of this type of document is the major source of unreliability in the field of diplomatic history and foreign-policy studies (Larson, 1988, pp. 250–251).

Summing up, since historians have to construct their universe of possible historical events on the basis of partial and randomized documentation; since they have to consider survivals containing sentences of which there may be no unique translation; since they have to interpret performatives and make inferences from speech acts to beliefs; and since their final criteria of plausibility will always be a function of their own cultural experiences – there can be no definite, non-ambiguous explanation of complex historical events. Instead, we are left with alternative interpretations, of varying probability.

Let us now turn to the implications that follow from these suggested essentials of historical understanding – the singularity of historical events and the indeterminacy of historical interpretation – with regard to historically based theorizing on the arms race.

3 Case Studies and Theorizing: Some Limitations

Few scholarly attempts have been made at using case studies on single weapon decisions and weapon programs to develop a comprehensive and historically based arms race theory. In view of the problems involved, this reluctance is not hard to understand: the case studies have focused on very different types of cases; using different types of sources; applying different concepts, categories, and methods; and asking different types of question. No wonder, then, that skeptics have questioned the possibility of comparing and synthesizing the findings of these studies.

So far, the most thorough and promising attempt at overcoming this problem would seem to be the 'method of structured, focused comparison'. This research design, proposed by Alexander L. George, has the explicit aim of converting the lessons of history into 'a comprehensive theory that encompasses the complexity of the phenomenon or activity in question'. While George acknowledges that this is not easily obtained, he argues that the perils of bypassing systematic study of relevant historical cases have proved so damaging for theory-building in political sciences that it, nevertheless, must be attempted (George, 1979, pp. 43, 48). He concludes that the task is manageable, provided that the following three prerequisites are fulfilled: (1) The case studies – focusing on a series of single examples of a certain socio-political phenomenon – should employ *general variables for purposes of description and explanation*. (2) Those conducting these studies should *define adequately the 'class' of phenomena* for which they are attempting to develop explanatory theory. (3) Also, the investigators should be 'selective and focused' in their treatment of each single case: that is, they should make sure that *all cases are addressed by the same set of standardized, general questions.* In this way, George suggests, the 'all-too-familiar and disappointing experience of traditional, intensive single case studies in the past' could be avoided, thereby making it possible to cumulate historical insights into a valid general theory (George, 1979, pp. 50, 54–55, 60–62).

Brauch, in Chapter 11 of this book, argues that this method or research design could profitably be applied to the arms race phenomenon as well. Also, at least one attempt at doing so has been made in the scholarly debate (Evangelista, 1986a). Two main questions have emerged from these contributions. First, whether the proposed method is really suited to produce comparable single case studies which, in turn, could be used to develop valid generalizations. Second, whether it may solve the problem of overdetermination, which has puzzled and frustrated so many arms race theorists in the past.

Now, it may be objected that both questions are rather irrelevant as long as the tacit premise that it is possible to reach unambiguous conclusions on the level of single case studies has not been firmly established. As indicated in my discussion of the indeterminacy of historical interpretation, this may not be the case, however. In this section, therefore, I will analyze this problem somewhat further; for a while leaving the method of structured, focused comparison and starting instead at the opposite end: with the problem of ambiguous case studies or, rather, independently designed case studies on the same particular weapons decision which have apparently come up with incompatible conclusions. The reasoning behind this approach is simple: unless we are certain that we can reach consistent and unambiguous conclusions at the level of individual case studies, there is hardly any use in discussing how to make non-trivial and valid generalizations about the arms race.

As mentioned, I will use four different case studies on the US hydrogen bomb to illustrate my general methodological points. Since these studies present very different conclusions as to the character and causes of President Truman's decision to initiate accelerated H-bomb research, they seem a sample well suited for our discussion.

3.1 Constructing Four Possible 'H-bomb Decision' Universes

Chronicle, as Croce once observed, is the corpse of history. From a careful reading of the four selected case studies on the H-bomb decision, the following 'skeleton' of the event emerges:

In mid-September 1949, US military and civilian experts were convinced that the USSR had tested a nuclear device some two or three weeks earlier, thereby breaking the US atomic monopoly. The sensational news was made public by President Harry S. Truman on 23 September. His announcement, very brief and matter-of-fact, was obviously aimed at reassuring the public that the government had not been caught off guard. Any need for extraordinary counter-measures was explicitly denied. At this time, however, a secret debate on what the adequate US response should be was already developing inside the Administration. Very soon the options narrowed as to whether or not US nuclear scientists should be instructed to develop, if possible, a totally new weapon – the 'super' or 'hydrogen' bomb – based on the fusion of the hydrogen nucleus and believed to be 1000 times more powerful than an ordinary Nagasaki-type fission bomb. These deliberations involved not more than approximately a hundred people, most of them belonging to three governmental agencies: the Department of Defense, the Department of State, and the Atomic Energy Commission (AEC). In addition, the Joint Chiefs of Staff (JCS), the Joint Committee on Atomic Energy of the US Congress (JCAE), and two expert groups closely associated with the AEC – the General Advisory Commission (GAC) and the Military Liaison Committee (MLC) – participated in the decision-making process. Among these, only the GAC (headed by elite atomic scientist J. Robert Oppenheimer) was unanimously opposed to the H-bomb. The five commissioners of the AEC were divided: three favoring and two opposing the proposed 'crash' program. All other agencies wanted the program initiated, differing only on its size, urgency, and future implications. Before making his final decision, Truman asked a special committee of the National Security Council – members being Secretary of Defense Louis Johnson, Secretary of State Dean Acheson, and Chairman of the AEC, David E. Lilienthal – to advise him on the matter. Although Lilienthal was very much against a crash program, the Special Committee came up with a unanimous report, asking the President to take all necessary action to accelerate the development of a thermonuclear weapon. On 31 January 1950 Truman decided accordingly. In the United States, his decision was widely acclaimed. Less than 40 days later, on 10 March, he decided to stress the urgency of the effort even more: this time instructing the AEC to prepare both *testing* and *quantitative production* of hydrogen bombs as soon as (or if) the weapon had been proved scientifically feasible.

Thus far, there is no disagreement between the four authors. But as soon as we proceed to look at how they interpret the causal relationship between the various elements of the event, the common ground between their analyses begins to shrink fast. This is somewhat surprising since, in this case, there is no doubt that international action-reaction mechanisms played a crucial role: in fact, all authors agree that the Soviet nuclear explosion triggered the US debate. But did it decide the *outcome* as well, or did other factors play a more influential role as soon as the debate got started? Here is a brief summary of the four rival answers to that question:

1 *Consensus building and bureaucratic politics.* According to Schilling, the decision to implement a moderately accelerated research program was basically a result of a major characteristic of the US governmental process: the need to avoid conflict by avoiding choice. Since there existed incompatible preferences among President Truman's advisors, and since Truman 'in this instance, saw no reason to go out of his way to stir up a

momentous struggle within his administration', both the President and his advisors settled on a so-called minimum decision: a solution which contained some political or organizational gains for each major participant and which left unsettled all controversial issues that did not require an immediate answer. (Schilling, 1961, pp. 37–40).

2 *Technological entrepreneurship.* York claims that Truman's decision to go for the H-bomb was a result of strong, coordinated political pressure from an alliance between key members of the defense establishment, the Atomic Energy Commission and the Congress. In short, technology is the key word in York's analysis: technological advances made the situation ripe for a crash program; agents within or in close connection with the nuclear research community – with the elite scientists in the GAC as a notable exception – joined forces in favor of the H-bomb; and, finally, the strong technological optimism among US policy-makers made them ready to counter the loss of the US atomic monopoly with an expensive effort towards nuclear superiority on a higher level of quality (York, 1976, pp. 58, 62, 74).

3 *Perception of an intolerable Soviet threat.* Stein, while not blind to internal factors, is very much against the notion that the state of the art in nuclear science and/or bureaucratic pressures alone forced the decision upon Truman and his closest advisors. On the contrary, 'the urgency instilled in the AEC, State Department, and Defense Department administrators could have come from only one source: their individual and organizational interpretations of growing Soviet power' (Stein, 1984, p. 42). Hence, in Stein's view, the H-bomb decision was basically a political response to a political challenge (Stein, 1984, pp. 48, 51).

4 *Strategic necessities.* In the fourth case study, Rosenberg argues that military agents played a more significant role in the secret debate on 'the Super' than recognized by historians so far. Also, their perspective on the hydrogen bomb question is found to have been very different from that of civilians: while civilian agents discussed the crash program proposal 'largely in reaction to the Soviet atomic test of August 1949', planners inside the military establishment analyzed the new weapon concept 'in the context of strategies for war with the Soviet Union, developed prior to the Soviet test' (Rosenberg, 1979, p. 63).

According to Rosenberg, this made the military participants slow starters in the quest for the H-bomb. Seen from Pentagon, there was simply no need for a crash program – for several reasons. First, it would take the Soviet Union a couple more years to acquire an offensive nuclear capability which could threaten the USA. Second, during this period US research on the thermonuclear bomb could proceed at natural speed, without interfering in the fission program in any demanding way. Third, in the meantime the US stockpile of advanced fission bombs could probably blow out almost every strategic Soviet target outside Siberia (Rosenberg, 1979, pp. 80–83). Although never against development of the H-bomb, the military chiefs were at first reluctant to support the idea of a crash program. However, their moderate stand – presented to the President in mid-January – furnished Truman with the arguments needed for a compromise between the governmental agencies involved. Only a few weeks later, the JCS took part in a renewed internal campaign which convinced Truman that his decision of 31 January was too narrow and should be followed up by a decision to test and produce the weapon as soon as scientifically and technologically feasible (Rosenberg, 1979, pp. 84–87). In both instances, therefore, strategic considerations had a crucial influence on Truman's thinking and actions.

Now, which of these historical explanations gives us the true picture of the event? How should we proceed if we were planning to embody the 'historical lesson' of the H-bomb decision in a general arms race theory?

Obviously, it would not be possible to use all the explanations suggested in the four case studies, since their conclusions do not seem to add up. Our first step, therefore, should be to check out whether the main assumptions and conclusions of the four case studies are really incompatible or, alternatively, whether a coherent and consistent synthesis could be developed. Finally, if we are able to answer those questions, we should also consider whether the conclusions reached by this approach – which we could call the method of *intensive cross-interpretation* – could possibly have been obtained through a case study based on 'structured, focused comparison'.

3.2 Analyzing Discrepancies

Discrepancies between historical explanations of the same historical event may be of two different kinds: factual or interpretative. In the former case, the discrepancy can be tracked down to an asymmetry between the empirical evidence of the inquiries in question. Although there are several examples of such factual discrepancies in the four case studies in our sample, we do not need to consider them here, since it is usually a manageable task to decide which explanation has the most solid and relevant empirical basis and, hence, to exclude interpretations not able to account for all relevant evidence in a coherent way. In the latter case, however, discrepancies cannot be accounted for by empirical asymmetries alone: instead, they should be regarded as alternative interpretations of approximately identical selections of evidence. Even though it is sometimes possible to eliminate one of the rival interpretations because it violates accepted rules of logic or methodology, more frequently we are faced with a situation where interpretation is pitted against interpretation, and no objective criteria exist which can enable us to decide which is the most valid.

In the following, I will present some results from a cross-reading of the four H-bomb studies and some of the related primary sources in regard to this type of interpretative descrepancy. The purpose is *not* to discuss the H-bomb decision per se, but to illuminate a dual methodological point: that there is a certain indeterminacy involved in historical interpretation which makes it questionable to use case studies as a basis for theorizing, and that these ambiguities are not likely to be discovered or accounted for by the method of structured, focused comparison.

Among the interpretative discrepancies identified by this analysis, four seem of particular relevance to our problem:

1 *There is disagreement on the status and vigor of the US thermonuclear program at the time of the Soviet nuclear test.* While Schilling, Rosenberg, and Stein agree that progress in thermonuclear research had been very limited at the time of the Soviet explosion and that only a handful of people had been working on the problem since the end of WWII, York presents a more mixed picture: he claims that, despite poor financial backing and numerous setbacks, important advances had nevertheless been made, particularly in computing techniques and in the calculations of different kinds of thermonuclear devices. This progress, York adds, and the fact that such understanding theorists as Teller, von Neumann, Ulam, and Carson Mark were increasingly devoting themselves to the problem, made the situation ripe for an accelerated program from the moment the US atomic monopoly broke down (York, 1976, p. 27).

A careful reading of the empirical evidence reveals that both interpretations may have their merit. On the one hand, neither side ever claimed that the effort had so far been more than marginal, nor did any of the consulted experts dare to guarantee success should a crash program be implemented. Not even Teller, the strongest advocate in the scientific community for a crash effort and the man who some eighteen months later was to work out a brilliant solution to the complex scientific problems involved, was willing to put the stakes higher than a little above 50%. AEC commissioner Lewis Strauss, definitely among the most influential H-bomb proponents, gave the same figure in a private letter to Truman. Stein, thus, seems to be on the safe side when he stresses 'the undeveloped and very uncertain status of the hydrogen bomb program' before Truman's decision (Stein, 1984, p. 44).

York, on the other hand, counters that the estimate of the superbomb proponents was shared by the leading opponents as well. For example, the GAC scientists concluded that the bomb had a better than 50-50 chance of being developed within five years, provided that a strong group of scientists were recruited to work on the problem and that all necessary resources were made available. Moreover, he argues that the many setbacks also had certain promising aspects, quoting Teller's statement: 'We still don't know if the Super can be built, but now we don't know it on much better grounds' (York, 1976, pp. 27, 50).

The crucial question is, therefore, whether the common estimate ('a little higher than 50%') should be interpreted as an *optimistic* or *pessimistic* forecast. And, next, whether it actually reflected an open-ended situation where no certainty as to the final outcome could possibly exist – which is Stein's position – or rather, as York indicates, that somehow beneath their cautious calculations the elite scientists *knew* that very soon the requested answers would be within reach.

Here, the available evidence turns out to be inconclusive, able to support both interpretations. In the last resort, our choice of interpretation would probably depend on our general philosophy of science, especially how we are inclined to explain major breakthroughs in the natural sciences. If we believe in the progressive cumulation of scientific knowledge – and also interpret Teller's much-quoted statement that scientists 'are not responsible for the laws of nature but only for finding out how these laws operate' as typical of the attitude among leading H-bomb proponents – then we may agree with York that the H-bomb decision illustrates how 'technological momentum can determine the course of the arms race' (York, 1976, p. 11). On the other hand, if we see scientific progress as a function of more fundamental economic, social, and political factors, then the modest progress in the US thermonuclear program before Truman's decision may lead us to endorse Stein's conclusion that the H-bomb decision provides an example of 'the primacy of political developments and political forces over technological pull in the postwar Soviet–American arms race' (Stein, 1984, p. 51).

2 *The threats and opportunities perceived by US policy-makers in the wake of the Soviet explosion do not appear the same in the four studies.* Richard Herrmann has argued that the key premises in any theory that 'purports to explain real phenomena of politics are the empirical assumptions about goals and, even more important, about the ways in which people characterize the choice situations that face them'. Moreover, these goals and characterizations are seen as resting not on immutable first principles but, rather, on time-and-place-dependent perceptions of *threat*, *opportunity*, *capability relationships*, and *cultural differences* (Herrmann, 1988, pp. 175, 183). In this connection, it is noteworthy that while all authors in our sample take care to introduce the reader to the strategic and foreign-policy background of the H-bomb debate, they describe this background in very different terms. This, in turn, influences how they interpret the perceived challenges and options of major US policy-makers.

Here, I will focus on only one participant, Secretary of State Dean Acheson, since the interpretative discrepancies are very clearly stated in his case. Also, he is commonly regarded as the single most influential participant in the secret H-bomb debate. This is by no means surprising, since his cooperation with Truman – described as 'one of the most successful partnerships between a chief executive and his secretary of state in the annals of American diplomacy' (Crabb and Mulchany, 1986, p. 122) – was very close during these months.

The three authors who deal specifically with Acheson's role (York, Schilling, Stein) agree that, during the fall of 1949, the Secretary of State was getting increasingly concerned about the overall trend in international politics. The 'loss' of China, together with the Soviet nuclear test, had, once and for all, convinced him that it was no longer possible to check the communist threat with economic and political initiatives alone. Kennan's approach to containment seemed progressively out of date. When the secret H-bomb debate broke out, therefore, Acheson was already eagerly looking for some new type of counter-measure that could help the USA regain its edge on the diplomatic scene. Also, although Acheson initially was somewhat concerned about international reactions to an accelerated US H-bomb program, by mid-November he had definitely come out in favor of accelerated research. In the current situation, Acheson explained to his friends and advisors, the USA simply had no other choice than to speed up research and find out whether an H-bomb was scientifically and technologically feasible.

But why were all other alternatives excluded? Which factors made Acheson feel that he had no other choice?

According to York and Schilling, Acheson had one overriding concern: the *political* consequences of a Soviet H-bomb monopoly. He accepted the argument that the Soviet Union was in all probability already at work on its own superbomb. If the USSR won the race, Acheson feared that this would provide a dangerous diplomatic opportunity to blackmail the East European neighbor states. At the same time, Schilling adds, Acheson wanted a solution which did not cut off too many future options. Accordingly, he favored a decision for a moderate speed-up of thermonuclear research while the questions of whether the bomb should also be tested and deployed could be left open for discussion at a later stage (Schilling, 1961, pp. 38–39; York, 1976, p. 66).

Stein agrees that the prospect of a Soviet monopoly in thermonuclear weapons was a major concern for Acheson. He claims, however, that what bothered Acheson was not only the possible diplomatic consequences but the worsening of the overall military balance between East and West as well. A Soviet monopoly would make a Soviet military attack on Western Europe more probable, and fatally weaken the US ability to repel such an attack. On the other hand, if US scientists proved that they could develop an H-bomb, this would add considerably to the credibility of the US deterrence strategy. Consequently, the most efficient way of minimizing the risk of Soviet military aggression seemed to be to get the H-bomb before the Soviets could get it. Moreover, Acheson had become 'a strong believer in the diplomatic utility of a powerful military' and felt that, if it added to strategic deterrence, the weapon would be an efficient tool with which to further US political and diplomatic ends (Stein, 1984, pp. 20, 46). This leads to Stein's second and most controversial point, namely that Acheson *used the H-bomb issue to gain bureaucratic support for a radical review of US national security policy.* As already mentioned, the Secretary of State had become increasingly critical of the current containment strategy. Looking around for alternatives, however, his frustrations deepened. As long as the USA was relying solely on nuclear deterrence, its foreign policy would remain impotent, since no effective intermediaries between diplomatic pressure and all-out war were at hand. Only a major build-up in conventional forces could make US foreign policy more flexible. In this light, the Soviet nuclear explosion could only deepen Acheson's concerns. Inspired by Nitze, he asked the Policy Planning Staff to conduct a major review of current US national defense policy – obviously hoping for a substantial increase in conventional capabilities. Since such a build-up was incompatible with Defense Secretary Johnson's conservative budget policy, Stein argues, Acheson now became involved in a sophisticated bargaining with the AEC and the Department of Defense. In this game, the H-bomb was *not* the bigger issue as far as Acheson was concerned. Instead, he traded the H-bomb (which he did not exactly want but felt the US could not afford to forgo) for the defense review (which he very much wanted but which others were equally eager to stop). This strategy succeeded because Lilienthal, the only H-bomb opponent in the Special Committee, shared Acheson's wish for a defense review, while Johnson, at the opposite side of the table, wanted the H-bomb more than he opposed the review (Stein, 1984, p. 30).

So, while Schilling and York stress that Acheson supported the H-bomb program because it was necessary to deter unpleasant Soviet diplomatic action, Stein claims that Acheson saw it as a tool both to deter Soviet military aggression and to obtain bureaucratic support for a substantial build-up in conventional weapons. This build-up was considered a necessary precondition for a more offensive US diplomacy in the Cold War.

Now, how can we decide the relative probability of these two rival interpretations? Would it be possible to rely on methodological principles and empirical evidence alone?

The answer is mixed.

No doubt, there are some factual misunderstandings in Schilling's argumentation – for example, he erroneously assumes that the initiative for the strategic defense review came from Lilienthal, thereby overlooking the crucial fact that, more than anything else, this was Acheson's doing. This fact may seem to support Stein's interpretation, which receives additional backing from Acheson's behavior *after* Truman's decision (he gave up his opposition against test and production as soon as he had secured presidential support for the defense review). There exists, however, no clear evidence in support of the key premise in Stein's interpretation, namely that Acheson used the H-bomb issue as a tool in a sophisticated bureaucratic horse-trading. On the other hand, such purely tactical motives were not likely to be put in print or communicated to other participants. The absence of empirical evidence, therefore, does not in itself falsify Stein's argument.

What about the discrepancy regarding the exact mixture of diplomatic and military fears? Here, the available sources seem to support both interpretations. For example, in a handwritten document on the H-bomb debate found among Acheson's papers in the Truman Library, the Secretary of State indicates that he was influenced by *both* military and diplomatic considerations; some offensive, others defensive in character.[2] The complexity of this motivation has been confirmed by other sources as well (Gaddis Smith, 1972, pp. 153–158). In the last resort, therefore, our interpretation of Acheson's perceptions and motives will strongly depend on how we determine the development and final breakthrough of NSC 68 concepts in his thinking. Most probably, the fall of 1949 was a transition period in this respect. If so, this makes room for alternative interpretations. In other words, even if we agree that Acheson held the balance of opinion, the exact character of his influence may be interpreted variously depending not only on what evidence is used but also on the larger analytical perspective.

3 *The question of how Truman's budget policies may have influenced the outcome of the debate is unsettled.* Among the most distinct features of the Truman presidency before the outbreak of the Korean War was its strong commitment to the principle of a balanced budget. Since Truman was not ready to make major cuts in his social welfare programs (the 'Fair Deal'), it became necessary to reduce military expenditures and implement low, conservative defense budget ceilings. In May 1948, Truman placed a $14.4 billion ceiling on the Fiscal Year 1950 defense budget, thereafter refusing to raise the limit despite heavy pressure from the military services and Congress. A year later, he put the ceiling even lower, at $13.5 billion. At the time of the Soviet explosion, both Truman and Secretary of Defense Johnson were forcefully defending their budget proposal, while high-ranking Air Force and Navy officers were engaged in a bitter fight on Capitol Hill, desperately trying to make the rival service take the lion's share of the curtailments. Among the agencies and institutions belonging to the national defense establishment, only the AEC was able to gain presidential support for a substantial expansion program. In early 1949, the JCS managed to convince the AEC that a major increase in the production of plutonium was necessary to bridge the gap between available nuclear warheads and the number of strategic targets in the current plans for nuclear warfare against the USSR. An ambitious production program, calling for a $300 million supplementary grant, was worked out and presented to the President, who approved it in mid-October.

So far, there is no disagreement between Stein and Rosenberg – the only two to discuss economic and budgetary aspects of the H-bomb decision in any detail. Their ways part, however, when it comes to interpreting how this budget conservatism influenced the H-bomb debate. Stein argues that, in 'the austerity-conscious Truman administration', the leading government officials would not 'ordinarily advance huge sums of money to any project whose certainty was barely 50 percent assured' (Stein, 1984, p. 42). The implication was that the budget policy per se would not incline these agents to favor an expensive crash program; on the contrary, only an important change in the balance of power between the US and the USSR made them set aside these economic considerations.

Rosenberg takes the opposite view, arguing that budget policy was among the factors that added to the pressure to go for the thermonuclear bomb. On a general level, budget policy had long increased the US dependence on nuclear weapons, since the atomic monopoly enabled the United States to reduce its conventional forces and to tolerate a Soviet superiority in such weapons in Europe. Consequently, if loss of the monopoly were to be compensated for by an adequate conventional build-up, the costs would have to be tremendous – as was later confirmed by the $30 billion program coming out of the NSC 68. So, from a fiscal point of view, an R&D program calculated to some $300 million might easily prove the cheaper way – provided that some kind of military response was deemed necessary. In addition, most expenditures to the atomic weapons program were channeled through the AEC, not through the military services. Hence, if a decision were made in favor of accelerated research on the H-bomb, it would be possible to make a military response to the Soviet explosion *without increasing the defense budget*. Considering the ongoing fight between the services on how the defense budget should be apportioned, this made accelerated H-bomb research an attractive option: with no immediate consequences for the distribution of defense resources, it was not likely to be considered a threat by any of the services. This is probably why the so-called 'Admirals' revolt' – the intense criticism of the current nuclear-based defense strategy put forward by leading naval officers during the 'carrier versus B-36 bombers' debate in Congress in the fall of 1949 – did not give rise to any naval opposition to the H-bomb. In other words, budget politics tended to make the H-bomb *a service-neutral issue*, in contrast to most other conceivable military responses to the new Soviet challenge.

Even though Rosenberg's argument may seem the more compelling, available evidence does not itself exclude either of the two interpretations. In fact, the background documents contain very little evidence of economic considerations. On the other hand, it would be an illegitimate example of *argumentum ex silentio* to infer from this fact alone that budget policy played no crucial role in the debate. The long-run economic advantages of a 'technological fix' could very well have been so obvious that this was never systematically deliberated by H-bomb proponents. If so, it is equally understandable why the opponents did not bring up the subject either: it simply would not have raised their stakes.

The ambiguity of the situation is well demonstrated by the following piece of evidence. Five days after the decision was made, Truman told his White House staff that 'there actually was no decision to make on the H-bomb' since this 'really was a question that was settled in making up the budget for the Atomic Energy Commission last fall when $300,000,000 was allotted'. Now, obviously, this may have been hindsight on Truman's part: serving, perhaps, the purpose of convincing his staff that the decision was a logical consequence of his previously established atomic energy policy. In fact, several observations make it difficult to accept Truman's assertion: the nuclear expansion program had been proposed long before the Soviet test; presidential endorsement of the program had been made several weeks before the H-bomb emerged as a major issue inside the governmental system; and, most important, none of the other participants who took part in the decision-making on *both* the expansion program and the H-bomb – Acheson, Johnson, Lilienthal – has ever indicated any direct connection between the two issues. On the other hand, we cannot completely rule out the possibility that Truman, when considering the H-bomb issue, felt that it would be against logic to endorse the first while turning down the other; even more so since he was advised by the experts that the money put into a thermonuclear program could easily be channeled back to the fission program if future research proved the H-bomb infeasible.

On this point, therefore, we cannot put forward decisive empirical support for either of the two rival interpretations. We may, of course, feel that they have unequal degrees of probability. In the end, however, our choice will reflect assumptions and evaluations that cannot be referred back to any particular piece of evidence.

4   *The authors are equally divided when it comes to the exact character of the debate preceding Truman's decision as well as the character of the decision itself.* Here, discrepancies relate to two different type of questions. First, while all authors seem to agree that the H-bomb debate was a mixture of political, military, technological, and moral arguments, and that these separate elements were combined and intertwined in many different ways, the four case studies present no congruent opinion as to which questions were topping the agenda. For example, there is no agreement on how much attention was paid to the technological and scientific aspects of the problem. Indeed, there is a long way from Stein's claim that 'in a very real sense, technology was suspended from the deliberations' to the rival conclusion of York, that 'the ideas and proposals put forth by the technologists eventually created a set of options that was so narrow in the scope of its alternatives and so strong in its thrust that the political decision makers had no real independent choice in the matter' (York, 1976, p. 11; Stein, 1984, p. 18).

This leads us directly to a second and much more important discrepancy concerning the political realness of the debate. As indicated above, there is a deterministic implication in York's position on this point which should not be overlooked: the technological momentum left the politicians with no real freedom of choice. This is tantamount to saying that, given the internal drive of the US nuclear establishment, there was in fact no realistic rival option to consider and discuss. Rosenberg, on the other hand, concludes that the decision Truman reached in mid-January and formalized on 31 January had all the characteristics of 'a real and conscious political choice' (Rosenberg, 1979, p. 86).

It seems fairly clear that any choice between these rival interpretations cannot possibly be made on a strictly empirical basis. For instance, our assumptions with regard to the philosophical problem of human free will would, at some point, start to influence us. And as soon as this happens, we are back to where we started: the indeterminacy of historical interpretation.

If we adopt a deterministic stand à la York, the debate preceding Truman's decision gets a touch of the unreal – something that just had to continue toward its foregone conclusion. It is interesting to note that this theme – the profound insignificance of the debate – has some non-deterministic variations briefly touched upon by Schilling and by Stein. In both instances, the pseudo-character of the debate is ascribed to the alleged overriding concerns of the main actor on the scene, President Harry S. Truman.

As outlined above, Schilling argues that Truman could probably have lived with other outcomes of the debate as well, *but he could not have lived with an intra-governmental split on such an important foreign policy issue.* Consequently, he initiated a bargaining process where the overriding goal was accommodation. In this sense, the secret debate was a fake, since the 'real' issue was not to find the best response to the Soviet challenge but rather to find the solution best suited to please all major participants. The decisive factor, therefore, would not necessarily be the quality of the alternative options, but the organizational strength and political skill of the various participants.

Another possibility is that the debate was mere window-dressing, primarily intended to add at least *some* democratic color to a presidential decision taken before the debate ever began. Both Stein and Rosenberg, who discuss this at some length, conclude that the evidence indicating that Truman had made up his mind as early as October 1949 is unreliable.

There are, however, some pieces of evidence, not mentioned by any of the authors in our sample, which may seem to support the assumption that Truman had decided what to do long before January 1950. For example, when he was first informed about the possibility of making a thermonuclear bomb – during a private meeting with Admiral Sidney Souers, Executive Secretary of the National Security Council, in early October – Truman's immediate response has been reported as, 'Tell Strauss to go to it and fast!' According to Souers, Truman listened carefully to all arguments from the opponent GAC scientists, but he was not influenced by what he read and heard. He did not need any advice from H-bomb proponents like Souers and Acheson either. In fact, Souers remembers, 'Neither of us could have kept him from doing it'.[3]

But if Truman really was that sure, why did he bother to consult a special committee and waste so much time on analyzing the question?

One possible answer might simply be that, in Truman's eyes, *this was the natural way to handle it*. Back in 1945, he had sought advice in another expert committee before deciding to drop the A-bomb on Japan. In January 1946 he had similarly appointed an advisory committee, headed by Acheson, to analyze the problem of international control of atomic energy. Three and half years later, he set up a special committee of the NSC to handle the JCS/AEC request for an expanded fission production program.

Thus, a tradition for this kind of procedure was already at hand. Moreover, so far Truman had every reason to be content with this set-up, since the experts' advice had never seriously contradicted his own preferences. We may suspect, therefore, that when Truman reappointed this committee to study the H-bomb question, his intention was both to follow established routines (thereby foreclosing any future criticism for having rushed into a decision without listening to competent advice) *and* to secure expert confirmation of the kind of decision he was already inclined to make.

However, even if we should hold with this interpretation, we would probably not be able to support it without some highly speculative interpolations from a more general interpretation of Truman's belief in atomic diplomacy and his normal decision-making procedures in atomic energy affairs. Its validity, therefore, is very much open to question. Consequently, not even the exact development in the Chief Executive's thinking on the issue seems possible to figure out in an unambiguous way. In the last resort, this implies that we may never be able to exclude altogether the possibility that the debate – despite the unquestionable sincerity and strong commitment of most participants – had a foregone conclusion and basically did serve as a kind of political window-dressing.

3.3 Overdetermination or Indeterminacy of Interpretation?

As indicated above, a careful reading of the four case studies in our sample clearly suggests that, while most of the major discrepancies between them should probably be regarded as a function of empirical asymmetries, others should not. Instead, they are of an interpretative character and cannot be chosen or excluded as the 'most probable explanation' of the event on the basis of empirical evidence alone. The next question to consider is, therefore, whether the four case studies on the H-bomb decision confirm Evangelista's thesis that detailed case studies of individual weapons decisions will unavoidably lead to overdetermination, and that the method of 'structured, focused comparison' represents the best solution to this problem.

According to Evangelista, a structured, focused comparison of similar types of decisions cannot *prove* one theory of the arms race indisputably better than another. On the other hand, he claims that this offers a way to eliminate weaker explanations in favor of those with greater explanatory power. Consequently, the method is supposed both to solve the problem of overdetermination and to offer 'more meaningful (albeit, still tentative) conclusions than does the approach that relies on single case studies' (Evangelista, 1986a, p. 197). In fact, the way Evangelista himself applies the method – in his comparative historical study of four decisions on nuclear weapon production for NATO – strongly indicates an ambition toward some sort of *experimentum crucis* between rival arms race theories. Analyzing the decisions (1) to produce and deploy the Thor and Jupiter missiles in 1959–69, (2) to produce and deploy the Multilateral Force during the mid-1960s, (3) to begin production of the 'neutron bomb' in 1978, and (4) to produce and deploy cruise and Pershing II missiles, he intends to test three alternative explanations – identifying the strongest explanatory factor influencing the decision as 'action-reaction', 'military fix', and 'technological entrepreneurship', respectively. From the assumption that the strongest explanatory factor should, as a necessary condition, be able to explain *all* four decisions in a consistent and convincing way, Evangelista excludes both the 'action-reaction' and 'military fix' models (both failing to explain why the neutron bomb was being produced), and thus ends up identifying 'technological entrepreneurship' as the strongest explanatory factor.

Now, if the observations made in this chapter are correct, Evangelista is attacking the wrong problem at the wrong end. Taking the latter first, it is *not* the research designs and methods used in individual case studies that create the ambiguities he classifies as 'overdetermination': instead, these ambiguities are rooted in the very character of historical knowledge. Consequently, if case studies based on the method of structured, focused comparison yield more unequivocal conclusions, it must be at the expense of something important – their historicity.

Second, the notion of 'overdetermination' is problematic. As used by Evangelista, it implies that a sample of case studies presents incompatible causal explanations of the *same* event or *same type of phenomena* without offering a reliable way to choose among them. As we have seen, this incompatibility – which appears only in connection with what I called interpretative discrepancies – is usually a function of some *preceding fundamental choices* in terms of philosophy of science, overall interpretation of a historical period or national culture, theories on human nature and human free will, etc. Now, the crucial point here is not that such incompatibility can be traced back to these underlying assumptions, but rather that the assumptions create different cognitive universes and correspondingly different historical events out of approximately the same selection of evidence. In other words, we may accept the thesis that there is no social fact incapable of being scientifically explained and yet hold without inconsistency that there are other ways of understanding the 'same' facts, simply because what will count as a fact is in part prescribed by the adoption of an explicit methodology (Mink, 1966, p. 168). It may seem, therefore, that the whole problem of overdetermination – at least as far as historical explanations are concerned – boils down to irregular or misleading use of language. For example, when Evangelista (1986a, p. 197) defines 'overdetermination' as 'the fact that there are too many plausible explanations for the same phenomena and no clear way of choosing between them', we should ask what the word 'same' is supposed to mean in this context. If we accept, at least in principle, that historical events have a singular character, we might be reluctant to accept that the strategic, bureaucratic, technological, and socio-economic background factors behind the Thor/Jupiter decision of 1959 and the neutron bomb decision almost twenty years later were so similar that it makes much sense to describe these acquisition decisions as two examples of the same phenomenon. Moreover, as pointed out by Thomas Risse-Kappen in his critical reply to Evangelista, it could even be doubted whether the decision in the early 1960s *not* to develop a neutron bomb could accurately be described as a decision on the *same* issue as the go-ahead decision in 1978 (Risse-Kappen, 1986, pp. 209–210).[4]

Also, we might wonder whether the overdetermined character of any particular weapon decision could possibly have persisted if the proponents of the rival explanations had agreed on all underlying assumptions. This question is important since, if the answer is in the negative, it may turn out that Evangelista's claim to solve the overdetermination problem through structured, focused comparison might become a mere analytic proposition. As we recall, two major prerequisites involved in this method were that the investigators should develop a common definition of the problem under study, and a common set of general, standardized questions. Now, it might be argued that this procedure is tantamount to excluding exactly those basic assumptions from the cognitive universe which would otherwise have allowed alternative interpretations to be formulated in a consistent way. If so, what is gained in unambiguity might easily be outweighed by a corresponding loss in explanatory power. The method of structured, focused comparison should then be seen not so much as a superior method for developing relevant and empirically based theories but rather as a methodological procedure which 'solves' the problem of overdetermination in a self-fulfilling way – simply by excluding those assumptions and questions most likely to produce ambiguous explanations. If so, all but one theoretical approach will be systematically eliminated from serious consideration.

A very different and to my mind far sounder approach to the problem has been offered by Quine and Davidson. They claim that an important by-product of the indeterminacy of translation theory is that it dissolves the problem of overdetermination.[5] Interestingly, this dissolution is not obtained by any kind of research design aimed at excluding all possible ambiguities but, on the contrary, by accepting that, because there exist various theories of nature and there is no unique correlation between their various propositions, various alternative causal explanations of the same phenomenon are always possible. The better the translations are, the more coherent the theories will be. Instead of excluding all rival explanations, one should always try to improve the translations involved. This does not mean that all theories are of equal quality. It only implies that, when we *do* have two or more explanations of the same phenomenon which are equally able to account for all evidence in a consistent way, then the existence of rival conclusions should be seen as a function of the indeterminacy of translation between different languages or theories of nature. A good example is the rival explanations of light (explained as photons and waves, respectively), which should be considered as equally valid, depending on whether the phenomenon is described with the theoretical vocabulary of Newton or of Einstein (Hempel, 1966, pp. 26–28; Føllesdal, 1975, pp. 28–30; Quine, 1975a, pp. 79–81).

In history, the indeterminacy of interpretation leads to a similar situation. Causally different explanations do not necessarily imply 'overdetermination': instead of being logically incompatible, they may each be the most plausible interpretation within their own cognitive universe of possible historical events. This fits with Popper's assertion that historical interpretations 'may be incompatible; but as long as we consider them merely as crystallizations of points of view, then they are not' (Popper, 1966, p. 267).

Summing up, then, the method of structured, focused comparison may be well suited if our primary aim is unambiguous conclusions. If, on the other hand, our primary aim is to analyze the arms race phenomenon in its whole complexity – from all relevant angles and backgrounds – then this method is not only unsuited but directly incompatible with our scientific ambitions.

Returning to the H-bomb decision, we might wonder how a single case study based on the method of structured, focused comparison could possibly secure the same valuable insights obtained by the fundamentally different research designs used in the four studies – designs which, obviously, reflect the very different personal and professional backgrounds of the authors. Equally important, we might doubt whether the method would be able to point out the empirical gray zones and explanatory uncertainties in a similarly efficient way as obtained by intensive cross-interpretation of the findings of the 'unstructured' and 'unfocused' case studies in our sample.

4 Understanding Arms Race Dynamics: Some Possible Contributions from Historical Case Studies

If we remain skeptical to the possibility of using historical case studies for theory-building purposes, what role could still be left for them in our search for a better understanding of the arms race? The following are some suggestions:

1 *Identifying factual errors and misunderstandings.* Case studies are not flawless. Probably not a single case study can be found which does not contain one or more factual errors. It is also astonishing to see how persistent such errors can be: how they may outlive one revised version of a particular book after the other, or be adopted by a wide range of authors working on the same problem or in the same field. In some cases, such errors may even have strong impact on the causal interpretation of the event under study. For example, the way one of the authors in our sample misconstrues the circumstances around the so-called Klaus Fuchs affair has no doubt influenced his overall interpretation of the H-bomb decision.

Fuchs, a German-born British nuclear scientist who had been deeply involved in the Manhattan Project and the early H-bomb deliberations, was questioned by British intelligence officers on 26 January 1950, who suspected that he could have been passing on atomic secrets to the USSR. Fuchs not only confirmed this but stunned his interrogators by admitting that he had been an atomic spy ever since 1942. Now, how did this scandal influence the US H-bomb debate? The answer will, for obvious reasons, depend on *when* the news of Fuchs's arrest reached Washington, on *how* it was circulated among US decision-makers, and finally on exactly *what* the first messages revealed about Fuchs's activities.

Here, Stein makes the erroneous assumption that Fuchs was *arrested* on 26 January and that the news of his spying 'added to the pressure to make an immediate decision' on the H-bomb (Stein 1984, p. 35). The truth, however, is that Fuchs – after the first questioning by MI5 – was *not* arrested. The intelligence officers had to consult the British government first. Consequently, Fuchs was still a free man when Truman's formal decision was being made: in fact, he was even asked by the BBC to comment upon the decision (Moss, 1987, p. 146). It was not until two days later, on 2 February, that he was arrested; and the primary sources contain no evidence that any information indicating that his spying could also affect the thermonuclear arms race had reached Washington prior to that date (Lilienthal, 1964, p. 634; *FRUS*, 1950, p. 524).[6] All in all, it is very unlikely that the Fuchs scandal had any real influence on the outcome or timing of the H-bomb decision.

On the other hand, when timed correctly, Fuchs's arrest and confession emerge as a key event when it comes to understanding the reasons for the renewed military pressure for a crash program in February/March 1950. According to Rosenberg, all available sources indicate that the Fuchs affair triggered a radical change in the intelligence estimates and strategic thinking in the Pentagon. For the first time, the JCS now seriously considered the possibility that the USSR might have an H-bomb under production. As late as in mid-January, the military chiefs had not argued for anything more than a moderate H-bomb program. Now, however, they asked Defense Secretary Johnson to inform President Truman that it was 'incumbent on the United States to proceed forthwith on an all out program of hydrogen bomb development if we are not to be placed in a potentially disastrous position with respect to the comparative potentialities of our most probable enemies and ourselves' (Rosenberg, 1979, p. 85; Donovan, 1982, pp. 156–157). In Rosenberg's account, the Fuchs affair becomes a major causal factor in explaining the changes in the military planners' attitude toward the H-bomb between 31 January and 10 March. Correspondingly, missing this point, Stein has great difficulty explaining why the military agencies so suddenly dismissed the compromise they had approved in late January.

The method of structured, focused comparison does not offer any guarantee against such factual errors. On the contrary, since the bulk of the questions will not be formulated on the basis of the particular kind of evidence available but rather on the basis of some preconceived assumptions of a general character, they may be even harder to detect. It is, on the other hand, difficult to conceive of a method better suited for detecting such mistakes than intensive cross-interpretation.

2 *Identifying possible theoretical variables.* Instead of trying the impossible – to make valid generalizations on the basis of a number of ambiguous weapons decisions – we should pursue the less ambitious goal of identifying those variables that should, in some way or other, be included in any arms race theory. For example, from the four inquiries into the H-bomb decision, at least eleven variables proved of critical importance for our interpretation of the decision. The way the authors interpreted the *strategic*, *political*, and *budgetary background* had great impact on their causal interpretations of the decision. Also, the exact status of the thermonuclear research program before the Soviet explosion emerged as a much-disputed issue with crucial implications for the authors' overall conclusions; consequently, the *state of the art in this particular field of weapons technology* and the *organizational and scientific push* toward various technological options should be accounted for. Then, two international events – the Soviet nuclear explosion and the arrest of Klaus Fuchs – did, in all probability, directly influence the US debate: the former initiated the decision-making process, while the latter may seem to have reopened it again only two to three weeks after Truman's 31 January decision had been made. *International triggers*, therefore, emerge as an important variable. Also, the participants' *perception of threats and opportunities* proved of considerable importance. In addition, there was at least some element of compromise-seeking in the decision-making process: hence, *decision-making routines* and *intra-governmental bargaining mechanisms* should be included as well. Finally, as was clearly demonstrated in regard to Truman's and Acheson's roles in the H-bomb decision, the interpersonal relationships between the main participants should not be neglected. In other words, the way *confidential information* and *access to top governmental officials* are distributed among the participants proved crucial factors in this particular debate.

Obviously, other variables will emerge from case studies of other weapons decisions.[7] Together they make up the universe of causal factors relevant for analyzing past or present arms race decisions.

3 *Testing of general theories.* Instead of launching a crash program of historical case studies on *different* weapons decisions – identically formed and asking the same preconceived questions – we should concentrate on the conduct of *intensive cross-interpretations*: that is, a number of case studies focusing on the same historical events, analyzing them from different angles and perspectives, using somewhat different methods and empirical sources, and, predictably, reaching somewhat different conclusions. Thereafter, a careful reading of these studies could help us locate the lacunae in our cognitive universe of possible historical events – where available evidence is too scarce to exclude contradicting interpretations –

indicating *in what areas we should look for additional evidence*. In other words, case studies may also have an important function of initiating new and better case studies.

Moreover, such comparative inquiries into a single weapons decision could be instrumental in identifying which discrepancies have a factual and which an interpretative character. The former should be analyzed in the light of all available evidence; some interpretations may thereafter be excluded because of inconsistency or poor empirical relevance. The latter should be linked more explicitly to their underlying general assumptions or theories (paradigms). This would, at least to some extent, enable us to *track down the explanatory limits of rival theories*. For example, our sample of case studies on the H-bomb revealed a number of key questions that were not answered or accounted for by the four authors in an equally satisfactory way. Whether the proponents of a certain arms race theory should regard such negative outcomes as a falsification of their theory may be open for debate. They should, however, be encouraged to *look for adjustments that could improve the theory's validity*. Correspondingly, a theory that *survives* this kind of intensive cross-interpretation would – especially if conducted on a sample of major but in many ways different decisions – increase its general credibility in a substantial way; even more, perhaps, than if confirmed through a series of similar constructed case studies on a much larger number of historical events. The reason for this is obvious: the more cases to examine, the more undue simplifications are needed to make them appear comparable, and the higher amount of uncertainty is embedded in the causal inferences. Intensive cross-interpretation, on the other hand, has the advantage of bringing both factual and interpretative discrepancies to the fore. The danger of self-confirmation is thus substantially decreased.

5 Concluding Remarks

There are two main arguments in this chapter: one pessimistic, the other optimistic, in regard to the possible theoretical contribution of historical case studies on individual arms race phenomena. First, I share much of the skepticism expressed by Evangelista and Brauch concerning the direct utility of individual case studies. My skepticism is, however, founded not on any general disapproval of the methods used by the authors of such studies, but rather on the recognition of the singularity of historical events and the indeterminacy of historical interpretation. Correspondingly, I am unable to share Brauch's and Evangelista's optimistic view that the limited usefulness of historical case studies could be dramatically expanded by new methods and research designs. To my mind, the methodological novelties presented so far 'solve' the problems only by committing a sophisticated analytical fallacy which, in the last resort, would strip the case studies of their historical character. Here, the crucial point is not that structured, focused comparison would take place at the expense of historicity – a minor problem, one could say, if the method would not otherwise suffer from any major methodological shortcomings. Unfortunately, though, this does not seem to be the case: as we have seen, the method of structured, focused comparison is highly overadvertised, since it falsely promises to eliminate the weaker causal factors behind the arms race in favor of one factor with greater explanatory power.

On the other hand, I am convinced that there exist several more limited and less ambitious ways in which historical case studies may contribute to our understanding of the arms race phenomenon. In section 4 above, I have offered some suggestions in this respect; particularly emphasizing the possible gains from an intensive cross-interpretation of carefully selected weapons decisions. Used in this way, historical case studies may also serve to highlight the main observation in this chapter: namely, that there are certain aspects of the arms race phenomenon *which we may never be able to explain in a coherent and unambiguous way*. In accordance with the principle of the indeterminacy of historical interpretation, these aspects will always remain potential objects of rival interpretation.

This does not imply that all theories are equally relevant and valid; nor does it mean that we are notoriously unable to understand what factors are feeding the arms race. It does mean, though, that we should start reconciling ourselves to the possibility that we may be unable to determine – not to mention predict – the exact way these dynamics blend and interact in each single case.

Notes

1. For example, the logical and grammatical modalities which enable the scientific community familiar with A's language to decide whether A's explanation is false or not should be translated so that a similar decision is, in principle, possible for B.

2. See undated longhand notes on the Acheson–Lilienthal Report and the H-bomb decision in *Papers of Dean Acheson*, Box 89, 'Atomic Bomb and Atomic Energy, 1953–59' folder, Harry S. Truman Library, Missouri, USA.

3. Oral history interview with Admiral Sidney Souers, 16 December 1954, in Post-Presidential Files, 'Memoirs' file, 'Sidney Souers' folder, pp. 1–7. Harry S. Truman Library, Missouri.

4. According to Risse-Kappen (1986, p. 210), 'a brief examination of what several explanatory models can contribute to account for the four cases will show that the comparative case study method does not result in putting the emphasis on only *one* decisive factor'. This is a conclusion fully shared by this author.

5. In fact, their discussion focuses on the problem of underdetermination, starting with the assumption that every theory of nature is empirically underdetermined. However, from a logical point of view, there is no substantial difference between these problems, since the empirical underdetermination of theory is *complementary* to the casual overdetermination of a particular empirical phenomenon.

6. See also 'Memo for the Office of the Secretary of Defense', 3 February 1950, in Record Group 330, Box 7, 'Security' folder, Papers of the Department of Defense, Modern Military Records, National Archives, Washington, DC.

7. Gray (1979) provides a good example. Here, he compares three weapon biographies – Sapolsky (1972), Greenwood (1975), Beard (1976) – and convincingly shows how the composition of causal background factors did change during the time period covered by the three case studies, thereby strongly indicating that there were several variables of crucial importance behind the weapons acquisition process in the United States.

OLAV NJØLSTAD, b. 1957, Cand. Philol. in History (University of Oslo, 1987); Research Assistant, PRIO (1988–89); Research Fellow in the Department of History, University of Oslo (1989–); current research interest: US–Soviet relations in the 1970s.

PART III: POLITICAL DYNAMICS

Chapter 13

Militarism and Capitalism in the 20th Century

MICHAEL E. GEYER
Department of History, University of Chicago

1 The Discourse on Militarism

'Militarism' – one word and so many meanings. Even within Marxist discussions, definitions of this concept seem quite arbitrary. Therefore theories on militarism – or on militarization – always pose problems of communication. What some have called the 'interparadigmatic dialog' is especially difficult in this field. The difficulties of communication which normally exist between different theoretical paradigms seem here particularly condensed. It is as if militarism has developed its strength primarily in discourses on militarism, which seem to ban militarism from the text by thematizing it.

I wish I had been the first to formulate this statement. At least I did think something similar, poring over this century's many definitions and redefinitions of militarism or militarization, which indeed are characterized by the 'dis/articulation of other paradigms purely on the terminological level, playing on equivocations, within one's own paradigm'. Alas, these are not my words, but Wolfgang Fritz Haug's (1987) – and he was writing not on militarism but on ideology. I suppose he might have written just the same about capitalism – which only confounds our task of writing on militarism and capitalism. If it were not for the very urgency and the very deadliness of the subject-matter, we might want to approach it in a distinctly post-modernist mood: rearrange the texts once more, make them dance, and thus turn them, quite the way Marx himself had thought of doing, into the subject of an ideological inquiry which then could be decoded by intellectuals like Haug. For the very fact of militarism vanishes behind the echoes and amplifications of texts and phrases about the subject-matter which these texts try to understand.

It is not *this* game which I want to play. Rather, I want to show that the discourse on militarism, militarization, and arms build-ups in the 20th century constitutes a single 'archive', to use a phrase from Foucault (1969). This is not the result of a continuity of thought; the genealogies of thought which exist are sometimes enlightening, but mostly trivial. Nor is it due to the continuity of a particular social formation: though, again, one could establish this continuity in the simultaneous social reorganization of capitalism and militarism from personnel-intensive to capital-intensive modes of production and destruction and their concurrent global expansion in the 100 years between 1880 and 1980. This would be less trivial: but it is not the task of this paper.

This 'archive', which itself consists of many and contradictory statements, is shaped by a profound loss, and by the century-long effort to recover this loss. This is the loss of 19th-century political and social project(s) for the formation of a civil society, to be constituted separately and autonomously on the basis of the organization of production. It is the loss of the notion of civil societies set against a clearly delineated and identifiable military sphere and the rampant violence of the absolutist international order. It also consists in a pervasive anxiety about the replacement of these projects of civil society by militarized social and institutional structures. Only a very truncated and impoverished notion of militarism would underestimate the traumatic impact of this social transformation which sets the 19th century apart from our own. It is only within this context that we can locate the debate on arms build-ups. In the archive of knowledge about militarism in the 20th century it is but one element. If it has become the predominant theme in the debate on militarism after 1945, this is not simply due to the centrality of arms races – as if 'reality' were ever perfectly mirrored in social discourse or, for that matter, in intellectual or social scientific debate. Rather, it is the one element which was chosen for debate in a process of elimination, which has subordinated or eradicated others. This 'hegemonic' debate, in turn, is closely tied to the rise of knowledge professionals – for example, in the creation of a discipline of international relations – as substitute civil society, whose claim to autonomy derives from their expertise: the analysis of the systems-world of arms build-ups which was linked to the expectation that a more perfect understanding of this world would create the tools for controlling or even reducing it.

With very few exceptions, this expertise was linked to a persistent belief in the instrumental rationality of the social sciences and the therapeutic quality of an expertly set up, rational organization of national and international security. The other side of the coin of this belief is an extraordinarily tenacious disbelief in the very existence of militarized social formations, except as deviant or dysfunctional systems structures to be analyzed as the special difference between functional and rational organizations of violence, and non-functional, 'excessive' ones. In this respect, these social scientific approaches continue an enlightened tradition which had also shaped 19th-century social movements, yet they insist on the reasoning rationality of knowledge professionals – rather than on the powers of social classes and their inherent quality to guarantee peace – and their ability to define what is utilitarian or instrumental and what is 'baroque'. Not infrequently they reveal a subtle distrust in the ability of individuals and social classes to make this choice for themselves.

These initial observations are not meant to underwrite the current vogue of debunking experts: experts have played an immensely critical and important role in the debate on armaments and arms build-ups. However, they clearly are products of the systems world of armaments in the 20th century as well. While their true breakthrough came only after World War II, they did not simply rise like a phoenix out of the ashes of 19th-century dreams and expectations. Rather, their knowledge lent meaning to an ever more amorphous and anonymous process of armaments, and, as such, they were a key constituency in our understanding of armaments.

Our 'expert' texts on arms build-ups fill the void between the hyper-reality of arms races – which can only be appreciated metaphorically in the 'purest' of all representations: in numbers and games – or in the hyper-concreteness of military hardware, its development, production, display, and use. In these capacities, they could and did serve the optimization of armaments as well as the decoding of the process of arms build-ups, which has become universally dangerous and oppressive, yet increasingly incomprehensible and anonymous. The debate of experts is located in all four quadrants of this matrix, which is the origin of the earlier-mentioned 'difficulty of communication'. The complexity of these word-games, however, allows us to overlook that they constitute merely one 'text' in a much larger archive on militarism. Despite its complexity and seeming comprehensiveness, the debate on arms build-ups remains tied to the systems world of armaments.

My efforts to uncover the full dimensions of this archive, then, are not simply a matter of antiquarian curiosity, dusting off some old ideas in order to see whether they contain some hitherto ignored nuggets of insight, or to provide authority for one or the other position on arms build-ups today. In uncovering this archive, we can rather begin to see the contours of the trauma of militarization in the 20th century and the efforts to cope with it. We can also locate the actual place of experts in this context and indicate the 'space' of public discourse which they have vacated in their pursuits. This should help us to understand the 'helpless anti-militarism' of experts – quite as important as understanding the growth of expertise on militarism.

Thus, my main argument in this chapter should not come as a surprise. I do not intend to follow the convenient road of explanation which leads from an initial rejection of militarism as capitalist formation and its definition as pre-modern force to an increasingly sophisticated understanding of the capitalist nature of arms build-ups. Rather, I want to show the nature of systemic interpretations of arms build-ups, and their limits. In the course of the 20th century, social scientific experts have developed a better understanding of the *Systemwelt* of armaments. Altogether this has been an extraordinary success, and they have amassed a most comprehensive understanding of arms build-ups. To be sure, this debate is in need of rationalization and organization. However, as useful as this exercise may be, it does not help to overcome the growing gulf between the systems world of armaments and the *Lebenswelt* of everyday experience which shows all the scars of militarization.

A recovery of the full archive of knowledge about militarism indicates that experts on arms build-ups are overwhelmingly located only on one side of the divide. Since this gulf grew with the expansion and intensification of the forces of destruction, these knowledge professionals were shut off in a 'golden cage' of expertise. At the same time, however, the two worlds were mediated in an initially poetic and aesthetic but increasingly vulgar language of violence, one which made destruction and its organization into a key metaphor for the very arena which experts had vacated and where the loss of the hopes and expectations of 19th-century civil society was most serious: the cultural and political process of social organization, the creation of identity for individuals and societies. This condition is at the heart of the habitualization of violence which characterizes our century.

More of the same expertise will not reverse this process. The recovery of the trauma of militarization, laying bare the full dimensions of the collective knowledge of militarization, is a stepping stone on the way. The re-creation of a language to make transparent the link between the system world of armaments and the everyday world of social conduct could be the next step. This can be completed only in the reconstruction of alternative projects of civil society.

2 The End of Civil Society

Concepts of militarism in the 20th century try to explain a phenomenon which would not have occurred, if 19th-century expectations had been proven out – the militarization of the world in the expansion and the intensification of the forces of destruction as manifested in the continuity of arms build-ups over the past 100 years. This process occurred against the predictions of almost all the masterthinkers of the 19th century, who linked the success of their intellectual agenda to the certain coming of an age of peace, based on the flourishing of civil society. Moreover, it happened against the desires and political goals of the predominant social and political movements of the time. And it surprised and shocked the ruling and governing classes – be they the liberal economic or a republican bourgeoisie, or military and state officials who had thought that they had contained and controlled the forces of destruction after the cataclysm of the Napoleonic Wars. The process of militarization effected a most radical and remarkable transition of political and social-cultural beliefs and outlooks. All social and political movements which had once proclaimed as their main goal peace and its prerequisite, civil society, have now learned to live with war or a permanent state of military preparations, reshaping the political and social order accordingly. The phenomenon of militarism, then, is as much a cultural-political as it is a political-economic one. It has eroded political beliefs as much as it has become a physical danger. It has reshaped social identities as much as it has reorganized interests.

We need not distrust the sincerity of individuals or of whole social movements who have fought for the creation of a peaceful, civil society, and failed: but we must question why we tend to forget such failure. Western societies seem awestruck by the process of industrialization, while they neglect the collapse of civil society in its wake; or they wonder whether, of all phenomena of the contemporary world, arms build-ups are genuinely part of our world – rather than being an aberration – and whether militarism can be interpreted as a social formation, rather than an extraneous factor. All the more important that we ask not simply what militarism *is*, but what it is *in our collective memories* which makes us forget the process of militarization and overlook the transformation of the social and political consciousness in the transition from the 19th to the 20th century.

This problem of cognition must begin with acknowledging the powers of forgetting. Practitioners of historiography draw a straight line from the ideas of early-19th-century 'peace advocates' to the late-19th-century and early-20th-century distinctions between militarism and industrialism, which, in turn, have become the bases for our own debates. They tend to acknowledge a certain hiatus in mid-century, but this brief disruption seems but a small gap. However, small elisions of this kind are first acts of forgetting. And what is forgotten here is something important. Whereas the critique of mercenary armies, arbitrary princes, and military *gloire* can be traced back to early modern times, the word 'militarism' came into usage as a neologism only in the 1860s. As such it soon became associated with many and diverse meanings, carrying along older debates. However, it was not simply a new word for an old phenomenon: it expressed strong passions, a great deal of anxiety, and a growing awareness that the forces of destruction could not be tamed and that Europe faced a process of 'rebarbarization', bringing to an end an era of civil progress.

Whether or not this was 'really' the case is yet another matter, but the hiatus between 1850 and 1880 suddenly gains meaning. If it is so that 'militarism' described a phenomenon which was not entirely alien, but unexpected, and which was not quite understood, but named, then the subsequent efforts of the social sciences to establish lineages into the past should no longer be understood as strategies of uncovering the past, but as strategies of myth-making or as 'invention of tradition'. Thus, it becomes possible to think of the distinction between militarism and industrialism as inventions against an unpleasant reality – a reality shaped by the loss of 19th-century hopes and expectations. And we may also begin to consider the association of 'militarism' with a 'feudal' past (Schumpeter, 1919) as an imaginary device, or a metaphorical strategy to explain something for which there was no immediate precedent but the aura of History. Continuities of History were established against the discontinuity of social and political practices. This act of forgetting was amplified by later historians and social scientists who, themselves eager to establish continuities, fell prey to the same act. They have a share in the repression of knowledge about a rupture in the history of bourgeois society – the dissolution of civil society – and, hence, cannot understand what militarism was: the beginning of a long struggle for the reorganization of society.

Diffuse and emotional as early statements on 'militarism' were, they described a comprehensive social syndrome or a 'calamity'. In England this agitation centered around a new sense of vulnerability occasioned, according to contemporaries, by new technologies. The communication and transportation 'revolution', coupled with the shift from wooden to iron warships, set off invasion panics and, more generally, political and social sensibilities that saw the autonomy of the island and the impenetrability of British society, its whole way of life, as threatened. Such fears were heightened by simultaneous developments in the arch-enemies France and Prussia. There, the introduction of universal conscription within the context of a professionally organized *Militäranstalt* – as opposed to the previous system of selective, property-, or merit-based conscription and part-time training in militias as extensions of bourgeois society – led to vociferous protests against the rise of an oppressive system of institutional domination. This uproar fused the opposition against militarism and Bonapartism with protests against the concentration of industrial capital and financial speculations, as well as the exploitation of the countryside, and the systematic transfer of resources from agriculture to industry, or from one region (the German South) to another (Prussia). It was a protest against the loss of control over individual and collective identities which targeted its manifest expressions – the encroachment of state and private (industrial) institutions – on the public and the private sphere.

The 'arms race' of the 1860s shows up as merely a small kink in the statistics. It is noteworthy for the expansion and intensification of the military grip on social resources (whether or not this hold was controlled by parliament) which initially concentrated on 'human capital' and after the 1880s/1890s extended increasingly into the sphere of production. But as much as these quantitative aspects mattered, their social-cultural face was at the center of contention – inseparable from the concurrent industrial transformation of society. Capitalist industrialization and institutional militarization had the same impact. At stake was the separateness of the nation, the autonomy of civil society, and the integrity of the individual – indeed, the very fundaments on which civil society had been built. The debate about these conditions, their origins and consequences, as well as possible ways of coping, permeated late-19th-century social and political thinking and practice. It is the proper site for the discussion of militarism and arms build-ups.

The initial shock of the 1860s slowly gave way to the formulation of strategies to cope with the process of militarization. These responses may seem strange in the light of subsequent developments, but they become understandable if we recall that the major challenge was not simply armaments or the expansion of the military sphere, but the recasting of social identities and the rebuilding of social order.

Most studies of militarism turn to what is most familiar to us: instrumental strategies which aim at containing, limiting, and rationalizing the military sphere and militarized sentiments. However, such strategies have already made a decisive step, which was all but self-evident and was mostly rejected at the time. They acknowledged the transformation of society under the impact of industrialization and militarization, and aimed at organizing and containing the *systems* which controlled the process. They saw militarism not primarily as a mode of organizing social existence, but as a state of affairs in which society was not sufficiently or at least not rationally organized, in which politics was normative rather than professional, science experiential rather than value-free, and the organization of violence shaped by extraneous considerations – both preindustrial or capitalist interventions were mentioned – rather than by instrumental concerns.

These rationalizers developed their own imaginary social order. The fantasy of a (rationally) 'organized' society dissolved the public sphere into a series of complementary functional divisions. Civil society thus lost its encompassing and hegemonic quality as the public space of bourgeois politics and gave way to partial systems and subsystems of social organization which together made up society. Production, destruction, and reproduction were parceled out into separate domains and linked together in the pursuit of an optimal, equilibrating social organization.

The immediate consequences of this construction should be evident. The loss of civil society as a unifying social and political space was compensated by a functional division of society in which the organization of production and of destruction were separated: but both reigned supreme as organizers of society, limited only by the imperatives of reproduction. It is this division between militarism and capitalism most subsequent theories of militarism operate with. It is a division which, contrary to historicizing myths, does not grow out of the construction of a (bourgeois) civil society, but presupposes its destruction as a unified, politically organized space.

However, it was not at all clear who and what controlled the logic of this social division of labor, beyond the growing sense that it should be done by professionals or experts. The nature of their expertise was a point of contention, and the organization of production was by no means considered self-evidently central. It was the whole point of (and the oddly neglected reason for) the quite famous intervention by Hintze (1906) to argue that territorial state-building and militarism as its constitutive principle were the organizing center. And Hintze's ideas were drowned out, not by those who pleaded for production, but by those who argued that the politics of space and population – of social reproduction – were supreme. We need not repeat these arguments and their national peculiarities; but we must recognize that this new social imagery instantly created new divisions, and shaped new political struggles over the hegemonic principles which informed the social division of labor. As such, they became the new currency of political discourse. Their fate was decided not by scientific merit, but by political conflict – and ultimately by war.

Before these divisions could become virulent, however, another and altogether more important battle had to be fought and won. The rise of a functional organization of society required an acquiescence into subordination under the imperatives of what Max Weber (1921) aptly called *Herrschaftsbetriebe* (producers of domination) and what has been ineptly translated as 'bureaucracies'. It is one thing to recognize the competition between these producers of domination as it unfolded in the competition of social theories; it is another to realize that all of these aimed at silencing the challenge against domination by externalizing and reifying the imperatives of a functional organization of society in secular and ultimately immutable processes.

The laws of territorial state building, which Hintze analyzed as the very foundation of militarism, could not be changed once set in motion. The same was true for the process of bureaucratization: it was the very condition and the essence of modernity. The nature of technologization/industrialization was less well defined, but it gained a similar status of a meta-historical force. Power was omnipresent and universal (as the systems of domination were), but the conditions of maintaining power were beyond social and political theory. Rationalizing experts objectified the ulterior causes of institutional domination and rationalized it as an inadvertent force. They 'naturalized' the ability to organize society and explored the development of tools. Theorists of militarization analyzed the logic of militarized competitions, but disembodied the actual process of organizing domination and subordination on a national and international level. It is here that we see for the first time the simultaneous tendency to create a hyper-real aura for militarism and the tendency to analyze it in terms of hyper-concrete military hardware, a tendency which was to become the predominant mode of interpretation after the 1940s.

On this basis the social and political practice of organizing civil society could be replaced by a new instrumental praxeology, which entailed two contrary options. Instrumental knowledge could be used as a means to maximize national resources in international competition (arms management) as much as it could be employed in the management and control of it (arms control). We see both tendencies emerge in the arms race before World War I.

Contrary to social science mythology, they have not shaped the debate on militarism and arms races ever since. Both arms controllers and managers of armaments have faced stiff opposition against any instrumental organization of society and the subordination which it would entail. This opposition is not immediately recognized as such, because subsequent scholarly debate has missed the crucial link: that the charge of militarism entailed conflicting strategies, not so much over arms build-ups, but over the reconstruction of bourgeois order in the 20th century. These challenges aimed at (1) the creation of an imaginary bourgeois identity, (2) populist rituals of affirmation and appropriation of militarism, or (3) the destruction of the emerging monopoly capitalist order.

The predominant bourgeois strategy consisted in transferring 'militarism' on to an imaginary 'other', a society which formed the radical opposite of what bourgeois intellectuals and politicians preferred their own society to be. Strategies of transference were used widely, because they allowed the continuation of well-established discourses about the military state and the military caste. The attribution of 'militarism' to 'feudal' elites was not only an entrenched political practice: it also allowed one to acknowledge militarism as a social and political phenomenon and to deflate it, at the same time, into a force with no foundation in the present. Militarism was seen as an unfortunate hold-over, one which surely would have to fall sooner or later and yield to a better society. This construction quickly entered national and international competition. Liberals declared German elites as 'militarist' and 'pre-modern', much as British public opinion did with Germany (dropping France in due course). German elites, in turn, wore the epithet proudly as a badge of distinction. These word games have to be understood for what they are – political attributions to establish difference and otherness without having to define oneself.

The popularity of these attributions among historians, who read back such rhetorical constructions first into 'facticity' and then into History, should not distract us here. It is more important to realize that this common strategy has systematically interpreted the world upside-down. Of course, the military sphere contained older social formations, even if they had nothing to do with 'feudalism', but militarism was rapidly shedding its old skin in the dynamic reorganization of violence. At a time when Schumpeter finally codified the otherness of militarism, there was in fact little left of the old military elites and their habitus. By World War I, militarism had become the bourgeois self, rather than being the other. Militarism was at the core of establishing bourgeois identity. On the other hand, the political opposition against militarism as an expression of absolutist rule was indeed a hold-over from the past – a memory of past battles which were either not fought or lost (in Germany) or which were fought and won, but no longer mattered in the face of militarization (in France and Great Britain). These strategies reflected the slow demise of 19th-century liberalism all over Europe; and what survived was not this liberal tradition, but the militarized organization of society and industry. Their brief and altogether unsuccessful recovery during the interwar years shaped subsequent scholarship, but did little to reverse the trend.

This is what the more profound theorists of transference came increasingly to expect. A superficial reading of Spencer (1897) and Freud (1930), to take two of the most prominent ones, yields only the result that they pushed back or transferred militarism on to a 'militant society' in the distant past or on to a primordial *Mordlust* as part of the unconscious – a state of pre-civilization. Both projected the problem of militarization into 'primitive societies' or the 'savage mind'. One was separated from present civilization by industry, the other by *Kultur*. What scientific discourse prohibited being said, Thomas Mann's poetic license made abundantly clear. These social constructions of atavistic societies were fantasies of the 'other', which sheltered the dream-like existence of their creators. Spencer envisioned a society in which the organization for war was an involuntary association and as such the opposite of bourgeois liberties: but it was also a society in which male 'warriors' dominated women/reproduction and those who worked for the maintenance of both – an underclass of workers. Freud's primordial human beings had all the trappings of skilled and ruthless competitors whose status was defined by (violent) activism and by a possessive individualism which created society in accumulating wealth, women, and power. Whatever Greece had really been, this 'Greek' society served was a metaphor for contemporary social formations, not unlike the description which socialists gave of capitalist society.

In fact, Freud's and Spencer's musings about their own times indicate rather clearly that they recognized them as projections of current dangers. Spencer conceded grudgingly that he most likely misjudged the inescapable development from involuntary association (militant society) to voluntary ones and came more and more to identify the militant type of society with current practices on the European continent. Others, like Hobson (1902), pointed to similar practices in the British colonies. Freud's skepticism about the thin veneer of 'civilization' gave way already during World War I to deep depression about the state of mankind. Both Spencer and Freud erected dream worlds against their time, which were soon to go up in flames much like Knin's library in Elias Canetti's novel *Auto-Da-Fe*.

The nature of these current dangers becomes evident if we take seriously the mass appeal of militarism which Freud and others desperately tried to project into the uncivilized past. If Spencer's 'other' were the rising *Herrschaftsbetriebe* on the Continent and if his political project was the defense of free-trade imperialism, then Freud's 'other' were social formations which gave themselves a militarized identity. We find at the turn of the century a quickly growing number of intellectuals as well as populist movements who chose to identify themselves with militarist practices, playing out 'heroic' roles. These strategies of identification, the formation of militarized identities, were potent forces indeed. They had prominent spokespersons – political theorists like Pareto (1901) and social theorists like Michels (1911) and, most of all, Sorel (1925) – but social scientists always remained on the margins. The main intellectual core formed around a distinctly modernist aesthetic (represented by the Futurist avant-garde) which long before the war used the metaphor of (war-) machines to imagine the rise of a new, dynamic, steely, and masculine race which wrecked havoc on the stale bourgeois order of the 19th century. And it formed around a core of 'therapeutic' experts (as in the eugenics and hygiene movement) who aimed at creating a potent, physically perfect, and violent master-race. These experts and aesthetes only go to show that the formation of militarized identities did not indicate syndromes of backwardness, as some historians hold, but turn-of-the-century modernism.

Strategies of militarized identity formation organized the world and society in an age of institutional domination. They acknowledged subordination, but at the same time turned the act of subordination (military service, white-collar work, civil service) under the new *Herrschaftsbetriebe* into an act of establishing 'difference'. They gave up the right of self-determination in exchange for the subordination of others. Militarism was thus indeed a mode of social organization, but a surprising and unexpected one. It established social and national difference in an age in which no longer property, but capital, defined relations of domination and subordination, and in which the autonomy and integrity of social classes and of the individual were no longer defined by their control of the public (which was usurped in the functional organization of society by *Herrschaftsbetriebe*), but in the subordination of others – women, workers, colonials, Jews.

There was a good deal of heroic theater in all of this. But there is no reason why we should consider these performative acts of militarization as somehow less genuine than instrumental ones. This heroic theater provided an answer to the dissolution of the autonomy of the individual, society, and the nation. Heroic theater was not simply *accoutrement*, as much as it was staged and quite consciously directed in propagandistic efforts. Surely, it was the game of privileged societies – or the 'excess' of decadent societies as Veblen (1915) argued. But what some intended as social theater ('social imperialism' in the narrow sense of the word) was appropriated by social groups in processes of mass mobilization and turned into a practice of organizing society. If we can speak of 'resistance through ritual' we must not forget the equally powerful 'affirmation through ritual'. Militarism as a strategy of identification became a means of organizing identities of class, gender and ethnicity, establishing in the process the hegemony of male, white/Aryan, bourgeois society after the collapse of 19th-century civil society.

Militarism was thus neither an elite phenomenon nor an objectified systems structure, but a mode of social organization. Today's historians and social scientists have great difficulties with this view. They prefer to interpret social militarism as false consciousness or *Überbauerscheinung* – the superimposition of a militarized rhetoric on to social classes and social groups which could (and should) have known better, and whose interests, in any case, pointed into a different direction. They argue that militarism occurred because the confrontation with the working class forced bourgeois groups, against their genuine interests, into an alliance with pre-modern (military) elites. Now, it is always hazardous to second-guess interests, because these second guesses reveal so clearly the intent of those who are guessing. It is thus the interest to forget the powers of a militarized construction of identities by transferring them on to a past which is sealed off. They presume that the systemic organization of violence, if done properly and rationally, is the appropriate and 'modern' way of coping with militarization. This denial – that the rationalizing, institutional organization of subordination, and the destruction of civil society which it engenders – provided the opening for militarized movements and their efforts to establish identity and arenas of domination outside their own context of subordination.

If the affirmation of militarism through ritual is to be understood as a 'genuine' social movement, we should, on the other hand, not neglect the element of theater in the rejection of militarism through ritual. Antimilitarism or pacifism was not as popular, but it was as populist and theatrical as social militarism. It had its own 'folk-devils' and its own 'folk-medicine' and was tied only loosely into high bourgeois culture. The latter of course was represented by the initially small, but growing, group of international law experts who argued in favor of a code of international behavior and a system of arbitration to enforce the code. Their key problem consisted in establishing an international civil society against the cut-throat competition of an anarchic international society. It would be disingenuous to confuse their 'moral' politics of international relations with instrumentalist ones which aimed at the management of international conflict. The difference between these two groups was not erased until after World War II.

These internationalists stood in a quite uneasy relationship with populist anti-militarists who gained some notoriety before the war. Theirs was a quest for 'purity' – or, for that matter, for motherhood, healthy living, or hygiene as much as for peace – linked to the rejection of an interventionist state. Though there were considerable national variances, they aimed, as a whole, at the moral-cultural reform of society. In England this frequently entailed a defense and revitalization of liberal commercialism, in France a defense of republicanism, and in Germany a defense of Graecophilia and *Kultur* – key elements of the respective national bourgeois identity. They recreated a vision of a bourgeois society against the militarist order of the day, but they were most popular in exorcizing the new folk-devils of armaments. Armaments as a conspiracy of corrupt elites against the welfare of the people (Angell, 1910) were their most successful rhetorical weapon; 'collective security' became their most important antidote to corrupt politics. 'Collective security' of course was to become a political strategy during the interwar years, but it had originated as counter-myth against the 'cult of violence'. This 'myth' insisted on the peaceful inclinations of 'the people' at large, and linked democratic representation to international peace.

Of course, it also tinkered with the notion that some people were, by nature or geography, more democratically inclined than others and hence should rule the world: but this only goes to show that there was no social-cultural strategy which was not geared to establishing social identity and difference. As strategies of international salvation and as populist revulsion against arms races and their instigators, they always also managed to salvage bourgeois hegemony – and the more organized the working class, the deeper ran the insistence on difference. Popular anti-militarism was distinctly class-based.

If bourgeois society faced the collapse of civil society and developed a range of substitutes for it, socialist thinkers faced another, related quandary. For one thing, Marx and Engels had in their own writings left a quite ambivalent heritage about the role of the state and the military in capitalist societies, even if there was more than enough to reject any notion of violence as an autonomous force in History – the objectification of militarism in the instrumentalist discourse – to be seen independently from capitalist social formations. But there was yet a more puzzling problem. If the organization of violence was an extra-economic means of coercion employed in class struggle, one could expect it to wither away with socialist revolution. However, if the organization of violence was an an essential and integral part of the capitalist process of accumulation, then it would not suffice to expropriate the expropriators in order to create a socialist society: this would require the reorganization and redirection of the whole system of production. Socialism could not build on capitalism – a fundamental challenge to Marxist 'modernism' and 'progressivism'.

One could very well argue that the so-called 'revisionists' were continuing Marx's agenda if they argued that militarism was not an inherent, systemic aspect of capitalism but an extraneous, extra-economic element. They quickly came to share the bourgeois sentiment that militarism was a phenomenon of an ill-adjusted capitalism; and that the rationalization of production and of class struggle would eliminate the internal *raison d'être* of militarism, much as the rationalization of international competition and arms control/disarmament would eliminate the external causes and thus allow a gradual transition toward socialism. The cooperative management of production in a corporate system of bargaining and the organization of international competition would permit dispensing with this tool. If class struggle could be managed, militarism could be avoided altogether. If militarism persisted nonetheless, then this was a matter of conspiratorial elite politics and its 'excesses' which could be checked by popular participation.

At the surface, it seems that Karl Liebknecht (1907) had a radically different, revolutionary perspective on the same matter; indeed, he did not share in the 'revolutionary attentism' of the revisionists. But his militancy should not obscure the fact that he also shied away from locating militarism within the system of accumulation. Leibknecht argued – much as Anthony Giddens (1986) was to do 80 years later – that 'coercion'/militarism was a general feature of all class systems, but that capitalism – faced with rampant competition abroad and the challenge of the proletariat from within – required militarism more than any other social formation. Militarism was an extra-economic 'articulation' of class struggle, and the more advanced the class struggle, the more intense the militarization – to a point where the 'transaction costs' of militarization would be so high that the whole system would fall under its own weight. Not only was this view extremely mechanic, but it also allowed for a separation of 'militarism' as tool or instrument and the actual system of production and accumulation. Militarism was employed by capitalism, but remained external to it. As such, it was denied social status of its own. It was a social formation only insofar as it was a function of capitalism. Liebknecht shared a corporatist vision of a socialist future, at whose core lay the rational organization of society. His revolutionary zeal notwithstanding, this vision presupposed the acquiescence into the organization of private and public life, if only the working class (or its vanguard) could be the organizing party. It is not by chance that Liebknecht figures prominently in orthodox Marxist anti-militarism.

Neither is it by chance that French socialism and British Leftism do not. Their anti-militarism always contained a strong 'syndicalist' or Left-populist element – the rejection of any form of subordination and the appeal to an autonomist socialist culture. Jaurès's defense of the militia (1911) was neither an empty formula nor a military-instrumental alternative to standing armies, but involved the expansion of working-class society into the military, and the subordination of the military organization under a socialist public. Rosa Luxemburg (1913), though coming from a different background, had similar concerns and developed them in her theories of spontaneous mass-action.

At the same time, she was less sanguine than the Left populists and pacifists, as well as her French comrades, about sidestepping organized capitalism and the process of institutional militarization. Militarism, she argued, should not be understood simply as a tool of capitalism. If militarism were to be essential to capitalism at all, it had to be situated in the very process of capital accumulation, which itself would have to be understood as a political-economic phenomenon where class struggle was an integral (rather than an externalized) part.

Luxemburg agreed with Engels on the simultaneity of the development of the forces of production and destruction, both pointing to an ever-higher degree of *Vergesellschaftung* of the means of production and coercion without equivalent participation. Militarism thus reproduced and made transparent class rule. She agreed with Liebknecht and others on the intensification of violent competition in capitalism, though she was less concerned with competition as such than with what she saw as the inherent necessity of capitalism to prey on non-capitalist societies in order to reproduce itself. However, these two elements had to be situated properly in the process of capital accumulation.

In order to make her case, Luxemburg proceeded cautiously in several steps. In a first approximation she considered military expenditure as a state-centered form of consumption. Indirect taxation allowed for a transfer of resources from the worker/consumer to the state. As long as civil servants and soldiers used this transfer in order to maintain themselves, nothing much changed in the system of reproduction, except that the laboring classes were financing the tools of their oppression. However, with the industrialization of weapons production a more significant transfer occurred – not simply from one mouth to another, but from consumer to capital goods. State expenditures thus became a 'splendid' area of capital accumulation. This, of course profited first and foremost certain groups of capitalists, and one could be inclined to interpret armaments simply as an outgrowth of intra-capitalist competition and, *ceteris paribus*, of international competition – a competition, moreover, in which the state systematically favored concentrated forms of capital or possibly even a new breed of state-centered *comprador* capitalist. This view – which, incidentally, was particularly popular among Russian Marxists (because it linked state-centered extraction with international capital formation) – was to shape much of the debate in subsequent decades and was reinvented in the conceptualization of a Military-Industrial Complex.

Luxemburg, however, went from this analysis of *Einzelkapitale* and their competition to a political-economic analysis of the system of accumulation from the perspective of the *Gesamtkapital* in advanced capitalism. Expenditures for armaments, she argued, provided a 'second' cycle of capital accumulation beyond the first cycle of exchange between capital and labor. This second cycle became increasingly important as trade unions gained power and reduced the possibility of surplus extraction in the first cycle of accumulation. Simply put, the higher the wages and the higher welfare expenditures (of enterprises), the more there is a need to recycle capital beyond the transactions between capital and labor (or behind their back) as it is achieved through taxation. Under conditions of successful class struggle, then, capital accumulation was increasingly maintained on the basis of transfers of the state which created a second and growing field of accumulation. Armaments became a systemic feature of capitalism due to the political struggles engendered by capitalist social relations. The defense of this secondary cycle of capital accumulation, in turn, became the main issue in the rejection of parliamentarization and mass politics. As a result, the strong militaristic state was not an absolutist hold-over, but a novel phenomenon which grew in consonance with the new requirements of capital accumulation.

This theory of militarism interpreted militarism as a political-economic formation which was the product of the organization of capitalism and of the 'rationalization of class struggle'. The more advanced the latter, the greater the need for arms build-ups – both from the perspective of competing *Einzelkapitale* (as transfers from consumers to capital goods) and from the perspective of the *Gesamtkapital* (as state-mediated substitute for primary accumulation). Rosa Luxemburg did not systematically explicate the link between the formation of militarized social identities (consumption) and 'secondary' accumulation, but this link could, no doubt, be established on the basis of her argument. Luxemburg rather expanded her political-economic analysis in a second direction.

As powerful as secondary accumulation was in re-creating an area of accumulation, it remained tied to capitalized social relations and as such was strictly limited by the very system of capitalized social relations. This led Luxemburg to search for other sources of state-centered extraction and pointed her back to the role of non-capitalist consumers: peasants and petty commodity producers. Why she did not consider colonies as targets for such extraction remains unclear. But in the final analysis she argues that non-capitalist segments (in capitalist societies) are the strata who are a significant source for state-centered extraction: they are forced (through taxation) to enter capitalist social relations and thus expand the sphere of capital accumulation in the first place; their living standards are repressed, since their maintenance is of no interest to capitalist producers (who must have some interest in the reproduction of labor); and their surpluses fuel the process of concentrated capital accumulation. In other words, militarism is not just a capitalist social formation: it is the social formation which as a whole feeds on non-capitalist ones. In short, this is a theory of militarization and underdevelopment.

We have thus run the course, from the nascent instrumental approaches to militarism and the imaginary attribution of militarism to pre-modern societies to its reversal which interpreted militarism as an advanced capitalist formation preying on non-capitalist social formations. Whichever way we choose to go in our own analysis, the elements for all subsequent interpretations of militarism were in place by the turn of the century. They all reflected the newness of the phenomenon, a surprise over its very existence or over its (re-)invigoration. Some of these approaches were cruder than others, and there was plenty of room for subsequent elaboration and differentiation. But the refinement of basic strategies is only one element to consider. Of equal importance is the forgetfulness of subsequent debates, the mis- and non-reading of texts and the displacement of others – a destruction of knowledge about militarism which has been part and parcel of the growth of militarization. Hence we must be concerned in our further discussion with the growth of knowledge as much as with the shrinkage of our archive.

3 *Lebenswelt* vs. *Systemwelt*

Despite contending and conflicting approaches, the prewar debates had left an unambivalent heritage. The debate on militarism served the purpose of defending a class-based bourgeois and socialist *Lebenswelt* against militarization. Socialist and bourgeois interventions differed quite profoundly in their definitions of the nature and the logic of these oppositions, but they were unified in their opposition against the

Verherrschaftlichung of daily life – so much so that they tended to reduce militarism to a manifestation of systems efforts to control society. We find instrumentalist approaches in both camps, but they played an altogether subordinate role at the time. Not only did the notion of rationalizing national and international conflict seem incongruent with the intensity of national and international conflict, but the very expectations of a rationalized organization of national and international conflict seemed a mere 'ideological' project – rationalizing militarism more than the defense against it – and as such quite as dangerous as militarism itself.

This was to change radically during the interwar years. Within twenty years the defense of the *Lebenswelt* and, with it, any notions of a massive popular insurgence against militarism were virtually abandoned. In fact, the roles became radically reversed. The *Lebenswelt* became the very 'site' of militarization, while professionally (or technocratically) organized systems structures and their mobilization of society seemed to provide the sole defense against rampant social militarization. What at the turn of the century had been seen as the main danger – the rational and functional organization of society – was now considered the only safe haven against militarism. Toward the very end of this period, we may note some voices of doubt about the wisdom of this choice. But these voices remained quiet into the 1960s and they never recovered from the loss of a base in popular social mobilization – the sure expectation that there were social groups or social classes whose rise to dominance would bring an end to militarism and arms build-ups.

It is not too difficult to explain the grand conjunctures of this development, the shifts in the hegemonic organization of the Western world, the accompanying rationalization and organization of capitalism, and the concurrent reorganization of socialism with the rise of the Soviet Union. But an analysis of these grand conjunctures describes as necessary and obvious what was in fact a major defeat of all those efforts which aimed at a reconstruction of civil society against popular militarism and against the increasingly pervasive, systemic organization of violence. This defeat was so thorough that for a long time it was almost impossible to think of a rejection of militarism as a process of popular insurgence; indeed, it is still quite difficult to think of it as an effort of constructing a civil and peaceful society rather than as unfocused protest, a diffuse social phenomenon which lacks the power of political concepts and strategies. It is this defeat which requires explanation.

We might be inclined to seek the causes for this reversal in WWI. The intensification of destruction, the expansion into intercontinental dimensions, and the comprehensive mobilization of national resources effectively cut through many cherished notions of the prewar years. Any pretensions about the incompatibility of war and capitalism had to be abandoned: industrial production fueled the war effort. Any notions that civil governments would act as firebreaks against the expansion of industrial war likewise had to be aborted: civil leaders or, in any case, civil institutions organized the war and provided the infrastructure for organizing war; war expanded the 'cage' of institutional domination. Most of all, however, WWI destroyed one of the most enduring notions about war and peace in Europe – the notion that people as such are peaceful, while princes are belligerent. This was a war of the masses who did not cease to fight for four long years. World War I rendered obsolete all strategies of transference. The source of the war was not some 'other', but industrial society itself. The initial shock of the 1860s about the potentials of militarism had become reality on an unimagined scale, wiping clear any pretenses that the development of the forces of destruction was anything but a 'modern' phenomenon. Of course, it also destroyed the heroic theater of the prewar years. Industrial societies had to face themselves as destructive societies; the taboo had been broken, but all the more imposing was the problem of how to control the sources of destruction.

If the answer was ultimately management of conflicts, arms build-ups, and militarism rather than popular insurgences, this was a surprising outcome. For war was seen as industrial-institutional Leviathan, an industrial dance of death, engineered by a giant mechanism which subordinated whole nations under the imperatives of war mobilization. It was commonly acknowledged – not only in Germany – that the feat of destructive engineering had destroyed the remnants of a bourgeois civil order of the 19th century. But it had also generated massive insurgences which aimed at eliminating war and constructing a peaceful national and international society. The Russian anti-war strike fed into the Bolshevist revolution against imperialism and militarism. Close to defeat, the German war effort was brought down by an anti-military strike at home and at the Front. Although the Western allies did not face open ruptures, war led to concerted efforts not just to contain military conflict and to manage international order, but – under the impact of the US intervention – to democratize the political order of nations as a prerequisite for organizing peace. These trajectories pointed in different directions, but it did seem that mass war had produced its own antidotes. And these antidotes were the people who had fought the war never to fight war again. And yet, only twenty years later, war was to be associated with the people, while its limitation and potential elimination were to be linked to the rational working of systems structures.

The first sign of this transformation came from the Soviet Union. Here the Soviet discussion of militarism can interest us only insofar as it had an indirect effect on socialist concepts of militarism and arms build-ups in Western capitalist countries.

This impact was profound in at least two ways. First, the Bolshevik revolution reinforced the deep prewar splits within socialist thinking about militarism and capitalism. It set the notions of militarism and arms build-ups as a product of un- or ill-adjusted capitalism against those which had argued for the identity of militarism, capitalism, and war; it also separated gradualist-progressivist approaches from revolutionary ones. The separation of the two was to reshape socialist approaches to militarism and arms build-ups. We should not be sidetracked by the fact that social democrats now began to tinker with military budgets like everyone else and mostly had no conception of how to organize capitalism or how to contain militarism and arms build-ups. There was a remarkable dearth of original thinking about militarism and capitalism in the social-democratic camp. But to the extent they did have a conception, it rested on delegating the task of containing armaments to experts. This is not to say that this strategy was flawed. In fact, what debate there was on disarmament and the prevention of war was supported by socialists and social democrats. And any efforts to develop supranational understanding were promoted by them. Likewise, any efforts to outlaw war were endorsed by them. But this very strategy demobilized popular mobilization against war and armaments. The link was severed between social mobilization and the political organization of capitalism as prerequisites for containing militarism. Those who had gone on strike for peace were turned into consumers of security, itself organized and managed by political professionals who relied on the knowledge of experts.

Second, communist thinking was not just shaped by the 'treason' of socialists, but it had to face deep disillusionment about the limited revolutionary potential of the working class. Here we cannot launch into a debate about how the search for substitutes and for alternative strategies divided the Soviet and international communist movement. But the waning of the revolution in capitalist countries raised the problem of the defense of the revolutionary autonomy of the Soviet Union. The first Four-Year Plan had many features, but among its most important ones was the belief that communism could be saved only by the systematic organization of production and destruction in the defense of autonomy, rather than insurgent proletarian or peasant mobilization in capitalist and non-capitalist countries (Trotsky's and Bukharin's strategies, respectively). To be sure, this was a revolutionary process contrary to similar state- and military efforts of reorganizing the social organization of production along autonomous lines in Latin America, in the Near East, and in China. But it was also a revolutionary process which hinged on the institutional organization of society in the defense against capitalism (whose militancy grew with the strengthening of communist autonomy). It was not the people, but the formation of a militarized revolutionary counter-state, which was to provide the antidote to militarism and capitalism.

This development, in turn, influenced Western Marxist/communist thought on militarism and capitalism. Rather than problematizing the mass appeal of militarism (and of anti-militarism), the debate on militarism, as far as it existed, centered around systems structures and the nature of inter-state competition.

This shrinkage of knowledge is most evident in the discussion of Fascism. Here the debate was less unanimous than it may appear, but it presumed throughout the need of capitalism to foment militarized social movements and the ability of capitalism to do so. The difference between this argument and the ones in prewar years is evident. No longer is the militarized sphere seen as an instrument of coercion. It has now become interpreted as a full-fledged social formation, but analyzed quite in the same way as the police and the military – as a readily available instrument of capitalism. The rise of militarism as social formation was explained by the advanced nature of *Vergesellschaftung* which found its equivalent in the *Verherrschaftlichung* of society. While the process of capitalist armaments was understood as a problem of the competition between *Einzelkapitale* (or monopoly group factions) within the capitalist world and thus the domain of national communist parties, the class struggle of the *Gesamtkapital* was internationalized in the contradiction between capitalist militarized social formations and the Soviet Union's scientific and instrumental use of violence in defense of revolutionary autonomy. This peculiar division of labor reflects a nationally fragmented capitalism and an internationally organized class struggle.

Whether or not militarized social movements like National Socialism in Germany were an instrument of capitalism has been hotly debated ever since the interwar years. The current orthodoxy is a fusion of Marxist elements devoid of any systematic political-economic analysis, and liberal assertions about the peculiar nature of German society occasionally infused with a heavy dose of a Durkheimian notion of *anomie*. Interpretations emphasize the importance of WWI and the world economic depression in the formation of militarized movements. It depends on the political predilections of authors whether they interpret these two formative factors as 'calamity' or as an outgrowth of the anarchic and imperialist quality of capitalism. Both serve, in any case, as *deus ex machina* to explain the explosive rise of a movement whose social-cultural basis is considered essentially German. In this respect, most authors pick up interwar-year liberal sentiments which had interpreted 'paramilitarism' as an outgrowth of either pre-modern or anti-modern ideologies. The latter difference simply indicates to what degree authors have been willing to give these ideologies a concrete social base. While anti-modern ideologies have been conceived of as a 'spirit' (*Geist* mentalities) capable of integrating disenchanted elements of bourgeois society, the notion of premodernity has tied paramilitarism to the continuing power and influence of pre-modern elites. Both share the conviction that paramilitarism must be seen as a 'deviant' development in the modern world, contradicting the normal functioning of a modern industrial society. It is not by chance that this orthodoxy came to be formulated in periods of relative stability of internationalism – in the mid-1920s in Germany and in the 1950s and 1960s in the United States.

It is not my intention to provide an alternative interpretation of these movements and of National Socialism in particular. Rather, I want to show that National Socialism indeed occupied the *Lebenswelt* literally and metaphorically and thus not only destroyed populist anti-militarism, but also made the *Lebenswelt* into the 'site' of militarism. This ultimately physical process of destruction added momentum to the general shift from interpretations of militarism based on social movements, to explanations based on systems worlds.

Both anti-militarism and paramilitarism rose simultaneously in the context of total mobilization during WWI. *Both* were defeated and demobilized in the stabilization of capitalism after 1923–24. As far as anti-militarism and pacifism are concerned, the extremely popular, broad-based, and insurgent quality of this movement during and after the war is worth our attention. If 'pacifism' was a liberal sectarian movement and anti-militarism an element in socialist mobilization, it became, after 1916, a mass movement against the institutional domination and organization of society: it opposed war, but in opposing war it protested against an oppressive system of domination of everyday life. Indicative for this kind of movement was that the defense of the integrity of the family, for example, always lay much closer to its heart than the expressionist anti-war literature, and that the spontaneous reaction against 'the system' was far more pronounced than any political-conceptual analysis of the system. The popularity of this movement is manifested not only in the huge anti-war demonstrations after the war, but also in the success of the plebiscite for the 'expropriation of the princes' in 1926 which gained four times as many votes as the 1929 (Rightist-radical) plebiscite against the Young Plan and reached far into the bourgeois camp. The demobilization of this movement cannot be attributed to National Socialism – which eventually destroyed its organizational remnants – but is a result of the stabilization of the Weimar Republic.

However, National Socialism, as it gathered, unified, and transformed the paramilitary movement, was its main competitor and in many ways played on the same sentiments. If paramilitary movements were defeated between 1920–23, they re-emerged as militaristic protest movements – against stabilization rather than as a reaction to the depression. Nowhere is this more evident than in the wave of war literature. Its interpretation is of concern here only insofar as this genre grew out of the stabilization period, using the war in order to develop an alternative Utopia of society directed against organized capitalism. Unlike in prewar literature, the enemy was always 'the system', and not anti-militarism. Large segments of bourgeois society could conceive of a popular order only as militarized order. Nowhere is this agenda more clearly expressed than in the writings of Ernst Jünger. This is not to say that Ernst Jünger explains National Socialism: but a careful rereading of Jünger provides us with clues about the extraordinary popularity of militarism.

Ernst Jünger's (1932) writings are manifestos of mass mobilization. Here there is nothing left of the old individualistic heroic ideals of the prewar years nor of the violent anarchism of the 'cult of violence'. His description of the *Materialschlacht* reminds us of Engels's insight into the simultaneous rise of the forces of production and destruction and the industrial organization of death. Jünger ridiculed both liberal traditions, which represented to him the ideals of a hopelessly lost age, and the romanticism of the old military and its supporters. All this is generally agreed upon, but these rudiments of an argument are only prolegomena to what really matters. The *Materialschlacht* is not simply the fusion of technology and human spirit (which is denied in capitalism). If this were the case, there were no need for militarism as a social formation. Militarism would sink back into the role of mere instrumentality, which Jünger detested. Indeed, Jünger is far more perceptive than most of his interpreters. The *Materialschlacht* is not a system of production, but one of organized and excessive consumption. It is functionally organized consumption, and in this sense quite different from the exchange- and gift-oriented excess of Bataille (1949): but it is consumption all the same. This is a most important intervention which thoroughly relocates militarism. In the prewar years, militarism was generally interpreted as the binary opposite to production or as a process complementary to production. It is understood in this way by 'totalitarian' militarists like Ludendorff and generally by the new managers of violence in the interwar years. As such, it survived in the post-WWII era and, in a remarkable act of forgetting, was to become the very conceptual fundament for the 'production of security'. But Ernst Jünger interprets militarism as an appropriation of the tools of production and destruction in the process of consumption. Thus, militarism plays very much the same role as monumental architecture – the link to Keynes on the one hand and to Speer on the other should be obvious, but also the difference to all those past and present theorists of militarism and arms build-ups who locate militarism in the realm of production, simply because weapons are industrially manufactured.

Only if we understand the nature of militarism as consumption can we understand the tensions between totalitarian managers (of industrial and military *Herrschaftsbetriebe*) and National Socialist militarized mobilization. But we also may begin to understand the specific role which Jünger allotted to militarism; for militarism is not (yet) simply another mode of (state-centered) consumption. First of all, Jünger understands consumption as a force which 'erodes' the 'security' and permanence of things, property and all its simulacra (like gold) among them, and thus undermines the very foundations and the habitus of bourgeois society. He sees militarism as the only means to save consumption against its own corrosive impact – an idea which incidentally, is also picked up by Hannah Arendt: militarism as a mode of consumption gives meaning and direction to consumption in that it makes consumption 'memorable'. Militarism thus is not false consciousness: it is, much as Baudrillard (1966) puts it, the simulacrum which does not conceal the truth, but is, instead, the truth that there is none. Militarism, then, is least of all 'weapons': it is 'language' which gives meaning and thus appropriates and controls the consuming techniques of destruction. In making consumption/destruction memorable through language, militarism subordinates systems of production and destruction and their technicians (*zügelloses Spezialistentum*). Militarism becomes the revolt of a consuming *Lebenswelt* against the *Systemwelt* and a means to re-establish permanence in the face of the consuming destructiveness of consumerism.

But this is a revolt based on consumption, and consumption's prerequisite is the power to control producers. The consumption of weapons – much as the building of monumental architecture and thus the whole process of lending permanence to excess in the creation of simulacra – requires *Herrschaft*. It demands subordination – subordination under the regime of production in order to consume. Consumption thus becomes a deadly serious undertaking. It requires subordination and it consumes death. Keynes, of course, is able to forget both, because he is concerned solely with economic transactions (expressed in his notion of savings). And Sweezy, like all American 'institutional' communists, can forget it because his Puritan Marxism can conceive of accumulation through consumption – in the employment of idle capital – but not consumption as a violent and deadly social formation. Jünger links producers and consumers in the *Gestalt* of the worker who combines subordination and memorable excess in one person. What makes this conception of militarism so serious is Jünger's insistence that consumption must have meaning and that the production of meaning be controlled – not by specialists – by the producer/consumer, the worker. His militarists are not atavistic creatures but producers/consumers who engage in deadly excess. They are situated in consumer society and aim at establishing dominance over the 'technique' of production – the latter includes both the managers of violence and their critics as well as all those who deliver the necessary raw materials and are seen as an equivalent to Nature, as exploitable as Nature itself.

Whatever Jünger's actual relations to National Socialism were, his writings were exorcised with the defeat of National Socialism, and we may think this is all for the better. His enemies, however, were not the successor-generation of the liberal-bourgeois *Friedenswindbeutel*, to use Marx's expression, which had gained considerable popularity in Great Britain and the United States during the interwar years. Before National Socialism could be defeated, these individuals and groups suffered defeat themselves. They were subordinated in the mobilization for war against National Socialism. The interwar internationalists have since become something of a laughing-stock or, at least, held up as an example of the impossibility of popular anti-militarist politics. It is not for us to judge whether their politics were irresponsible in the context of the 1920s. However, it is worth noting that on both the national and the international level, populist militarism and populist anti-militarism were antagonistic expressions of an opposition against a systemic organization of society; and both were subordinated in a mobilization for war which brought to the fore systems-managers, their intellectual pundits, and eventually their critics.

George Egerton (1983) has pointed to the similarity of militarists and anti-militarists:

Differing radically, of course in content, and steeped in mutual hostility, the competing ideologies each served similar socio-political functions. They shaped the inchoate perceptions of reality of a social group into an order of consciousness; they explained the origins and the causes of present evils while prescribing the appropriate remedial programme; they projected a utopian future; they furthered social integration of a group and legitimated the leadership of a political elite.

Egerton does, however, not fully appreciate the socio-political nature of these liberal myth-makers, if he considers them merely as another 'pressure group', albeit an extraordinarily popular one. They exerted pressure, no doubt; however, they did not push 'interests' but rather defended a way of life in the face of the experience of WWI. Their infrastructure in Great Britain consisted of the main socializing agents of the liberal bourgeoisie, churches and schools, and their program lacked 'political' practicality, because it served the socio-cultural 'practice' of reconstituting civil society against its detractors – not just militarists, arms producers, and arms merchants, but all those who had transformed Britain in the arms build-up before the war and in the total mobilization for war. How much this was a holding operation against overwhelming odds becomes evident, if we consider that they exercised a virtual ideological hegemony over the British middle class, but never held actual power; that they were able to mobilize millions of people, but never were able to shape politics; and that they gained support of individual industrialists, but were entirely unable to alter the course of industrial politics. Like their counterparts in pre-and post-war Germany, they considered themselves vanguards of a new age, fighting against the demons of the past, but in fact they were fighting rearguard actions in an age of organized politics.

The striking thing about the League of Nations Union as well as the plethora of US internationalist organizations is *not* their rosy-cheeked optimism and progressivism based on the assumption that peace would surely come if 'people' only exercised their power and if the 'essential harmony of interests' and the natural 'desire for cooperation' could be set free. These elements were certainly present. But if we think of these organizations as 'interest groups' and of their ideologies as naive 19th-century progressivism, we follow the infantilization strategies of their detractors. A closer examination of such groups rather indicates three elements.

First, the actual 'internationalist' core was extremely small. They all lived off a complex associational infrastructure, which in Great Britain was firmly middle-class and in the United States ran the entire gamut of grass-roots organizations of farmers, churches, and workers. Internationalism was deeply embedded in the social-political struggle of these groups, which was always anti-corporatist, but otherwise ranged from the defense of free-trade liberalism to the demand (in the United States) for state-centered redistribution. The popular revulsion against the 'merchants of death' was only one of the more manifest and evocative elements of a much broader, though highly disorganized, front of opposition against an economic and political system which effectively disenfranchised and marginalized large groups of the voting public. If they demanded a new social contract and if they caucused against arms dealers and arms producers, this was not just pious rhetoric but a challenge against the incorporation of society. If they pursued 'moral politics', this was not sentimental politics, but a quite interventionist social action program. In fact, many of these internationalists did not believe that 'people' were naturally peaceful, but that they had to be organized and re-educated in order to make them peaceful. This therapeutic intervention of course was not always what we expect it to be. But the link between the temperance movement and anti-militarism only goes to show the importance of their agenda for a moral reconstruction of society.

By the same token, it is not at all self-evident that these internationalists were altogether innocent and dove-ish internationalists. Again, we find a wide variety of actions and suggestions, which reached from bleeding-heart politics, to isolationism, to an extremely coercive and aggressive internationalism which demanded coercive power for international arbitration, but also the opening of underdeveloped countries – and not just the opening of the British and French Empires, but also of the nationalist, import-substituting regimes in the 'Third World'. There is, however, one thread which runs through all these various demands and propositions: internationalists rejected the corporate elite politics of the time and sought to replace it by a new international social contract. The nature of this social contract varied from being a contract among privileged nations to being a contract between privileged and subordinate people, but it was always a contract of the people against the *Herrschaftsbetriebe* – again often characterized and caricaturized in the international cartel of arms producers and arms merchants – which undermined the morality of the individual, the autonomy of society, and the integrity of the nation.

And thirdly, these internationalists were by no means 'quietist': they were not necessarily in favor of a passive international policy. In fact, this issue led to deep splits among the internationalists, though the lines of division are difficult to fathom. In any case, there was a persistent current which favored interventions and activist collective security; and the demand for interventions and sanctions rather increased during the 1930s than decreased. The nature of these demands varied again very widely, but it cannot be said that the internationalists had no sense for the reality of power.

This brief survey cannot do justice to all those groups which were labeled 'liberal internationalists', nor cannot it even begin to make sense of their dynamics. They were many things, but mostly not what they came to be seen by the late 1930s. These groups were collectively made responsible for the failure to maintain security and international order in the interwar years and to protect Europe and the United States from Fascism and militarism. The most common charge against them was the imputation that they exchanged a Utopia of moral politics for the reality of power. In fact, it now rather seems that they had no power, though at least in Great Britain they had considerable mass support. 'Liberal internationalists' can be accused of many things, but they were certainly not responsible for the crisis of the interwar years.

And yet this label has stuck to them, branding them as either high-minded or infantile moralists. The problem is obviously not whether we may find such moralists among them, but why the diverse assembly of popular anti-militarists were so successfully marginalized. The answer to this problem cannot be found in any particular politics, nor in the grand conjunctures of international affairs in the late 1930s, that is, the rising tensions in the international system and the militarization of international competition. Rather, it consists in the wholesale abandonment of the project of civil society and the turn to the professional authority of experts, a change perfectly represented in the mass conversion of liberal and Left intellectuals from Utopia to realism. Again, this is not the place to review the full breadth of this phenomenon which is epitomized in a whole genre of 'corporatist' literature in the United States or in the reception of Max Weber and the transmogrification of his ideas into structural functional theory – which, in turn, served as the foundation of the 'imperial presidency' in the United States. A few famous and orthodox texts must suffice in this context.

In one of the classic texts on interwar politics Carr (1939) juxtaposes utopianism and realism and makes a plea for practical fusion of both in a new politics. But what is read as a tract against liberal internationalists (about whom Carr says little) is in fact an act of exorcism of liberal-imperial British politics, informed by the realization that British hegemony which had underwritten liberal Utopias was gone. It is an argument which says that the utopians no longer hold power, rather than that the utopians did not know power or were unable to exercise it. But where was power situated and how is it exercised? Carr is remarkably sketchy on this issue. He points not merely at a reconfiguration of power centers – a shift from Great Britain to the United States – but predicts 'with some confidence' a growing transnational organization of power which obliterates national sovereignty – and implicitly popular sovereignty as well. Oddly enough, Carr considers this development to be an inadvertent and amoral process. The new concentration of power, however, cannot rule on the basis of coercion alone, but 'presupposes a substantial measure of consent'. Consent in turn is achieved not by popular representation, but by negotiation and arbitration between organized interests. It is this organization of interests which requires the abandonment of Utopia. On a national level, this has been achieved in a 'rationalization of class struggle': 'Employment has become more important than profit, social stability than increased consumption, equitable distribution than maximum production.' Carr foresees the same trend on an international level, *'once the issue of power is settled'*. International stability can only be achieved by establishing power-political hegemony, but this hegemony can only last in the 'frank acceptance of the subordination of economic advantage to social ends, and the recognition that was economically good is not always morally good'. This of course is the return to Utopia: but to a rather feeble Utopia after the issue of political power has been settled. It is the return to Utopia as practical and incremental politics of professional politicians – the organization of society by moral rationalizers for the benefit of the people, once the initial resistance against the reconfiguration of power has been broken. The political public as a force has entirely vanished from these considerations. Civil society has become a social formation of the past, and it is now no longer even seen as a morally upright one. For while of all groups organized interests can be convinced of 'self-sacrifice', the utopians of the past were self-centered and relentless egotists who pushed their interests in the name of universal civility.

In this assessment of what after all is the liberal-bourgeois tradition E.H. Carr is not far from Hans Morgenthau (1946), who proclaimed 'the lust for power' a universal human phenomenon. There is no way to escape this human condition, and any flight into liberal illusions would only compound the disaster because they would set free the lust of the common man. These are, according to Morgenthau, 'the illusions of international law as a standard for political action, the illusion of a naturally harmonious world, the illusion of a social science imitating a model of the natural sciences which the modern natural scientists themselves no longer accept' (p. 121) – all struggling to eliminate or to conceal what is 'beyond the ability of any political philosophy or system', and that is the very baseness of human nature and of popular social movements. The challenge is to eliminate not power politics, but 'the destructiveness of power politics'. The latter can be achieved only by the 'wisdom and the moral strength of statesmen'. This solution, a plea for a morally and philosophically tempered power politics, differs of course radically from that of E.H. Carr. But it locates power again not in the people, but in the expert as 'statesman' who is

> indeed the prototype of social man himself; for what the statesman experiences on his exalted plane is the common lot of all mankind. Suspended between the spiritual destiny which he cannot fulfill and his animal nature in which he cannot remain, he is forever condemned to experience the contrast between the longings of his mind and his actual condition as his personal, eminently human tragedy. (Morganthal, 1946, p. 221)

So much for power politics and the nature of democracy. It is the philosopher-statesman who carries the burden of this world for the people of this world.

A third variant of the same trend is reflected in Vagts (1938), who points to a wholesale reversal of the nature of militarism. He considers the militarism of the military a matter of the past, and the militarism of the masses a pre-eminent factor of the present and the future. This militarism is partly a hold over the military state, but it is most deeply embedded in the nature of mass society itself, which according to Vagts counteracts a process of atomization by a turn to 'mass movements and processions in which the equal step, the music of bands and mass chanting drown out temporarily, the dissensions of ordinary life'. One can of course argue in defense of Vagts that this description only reflects his experience of National Socialism. However, Vagts insists that it is rather a phenomenon of all modern mass societies. In fact, Vagts insinuates that militarism is the collective expression of the dispossessed, 'of millions of workers and farmers, finding no great profit or enjoyment in their new freedom'. It is a rejection of all kinds of popular mobilizations. This kind of mass militarism has become a highly comprehensive social phenomenon. 'It covers every system of thinking and valuing and every complex of feeling which ranks military institutions and ways above the ways of civilian life, carrying military mentality and modes of acting and decision into the civilian sphere.'

But what is civilian life, and how can it be saved? And what is a military, as opposed to militaristic, way? Civilian life and the military way fuse in the purposeful, functional, and instrumental organization of violence undertaken by military professionals in conjunction with civilian experts. Both define military necessity and have 'an informed and realistic conception of society's interests'. We have in Vagts's *History of Militarism* not just a case of moral panic in the face of mass mobilization, but most clearly a substitution of civil society by the rule of professionals and experts who proceed 'scientifically'. Why Vagts's theory of militarism is such common currency today, especially on the Left, is worth further consideration.

It is not difficult to associate Carr with the socialist tradition, Morgenthau with the conservative, and Vagts with the liberal. But it is more important to reflect on the extraordinary transition of all three traditions and their convergence in one point. All three agree that people and particularly mass social movements must be distrusted, and that the only appropriate site of enlightenment is the realm of professionals. All presume or argue for the organization of society in the pursuit of national and international stability as a prerequisite of anti-militarism. All reflect the triumph of the *Systemwelt* and seek, in various ways, to rationalize this world. Their political prescriptions differ widely, but they establish new cleavages between militarism as 'romantic' popular politics and civilianism as the rationalizing discourse among professionals. And contrary to Harrold Lasswell, they are all extraordinarily optimistic that the organization of society will serve to maintain peace and civility. They have abandoned both bourgeois and socialist traditions of politics in favor of the technocratic organization of everyday life in the 20th century. They forget or suppress the original agenda of anti-militarism: that is, that the organization of society entails domination and that it is exactly this process of domination which destroys civil society and gives rise to militarism. The revolt against the rise of *Herrschaftsbetriebe* which was so powerful a momentum in the first half of the 20th century is now branded as either infantile or Fascist, or both.

Ever since, theories of militarism have become prisoners in the iron cage of the logic of a system which militarism helped to create and to legitimize. And if things went wrong there was always the consolation with which Quincy Wright ends part II of his *Study of War*:

> Modernism [. . .] has envisaged society as a process by which institutions and beliefs are continuously adjusted to the most accurate forecasts which science can offer of the future. Modernism has hoped to eliminate human catastrophes and conquests by social and scientific procedures for continuously testing the present value of ideas and beliefs. It has, however, recognized that such procedures can be effective only if humanity becomes less reluctant to accept the new and to abandon the old than it has been in the past. (Wright, 1965, pp. 404–405)

It has taken a long time to discover that the logic of these rationalizing systems may be what is wrong, and not humanity. And it may take even longer until we can find ways out of this predicament. In the meantime we remain inside the cage, experts talking to experts. We have to recognize that, in their popular battles, the anti-militarists were thoroughly defeated – not by the militarists, but by rationalizing experts. As long as we forget this, we can pace out and measure the cage, we may feather it, hold monologs or engage in world games: but it is hard to imagine that we can break out from our confines.

MICHAEL E. GEYER, b. 1947, Dr. Philos. (Albert Ludwig Universität, 1976); Professor of History, University of Chicago (1986–); formerly with the Department of History, University of Michigan (1977–86). Author of *Deutsche Rüstungspolitik, 1869–1980* (Suhrkamp, 1984) and other works on militarism, fascism, and German history.

Chapter 14
The Geyer Archives*

LARS MJØSET
Institute for Social Research, Oslo

1 Three Preconditions

In his chapter, Geyer refers a number of texts concerning 20th-century militarism. These texts have been selected from an 'archive' of the whole 20th-century 'discourse on militarism, militarization, and arms build-ups'. Some of these texts are contributions by intellectuals and social scientists. But there are also references to the views of protest movements and social reformers, as well as to the iconography of society. Geyer finds that this archive 'is shaped by a profound loss and the century-long effort to recover this loss':

> This is the loss of 19th-century political and social project(s) for the formation of a civil society, to be constituted separately and autonomously on the basis of the organization of production. It is the loss of the notion of civil societies set against a clearly delineated and identifiable military sphere and the rampant violence of the absolutist international order. It also consists in a pervasive anxiety about the replacement of these projects of civil society by militarized social and institutional structures. Only a very truncated and impoverished notion of militarism would underestimate the traumatic impact of this social transformation which sets the 19th century apart from our own. It is only within this context that we can locate the debate on arms build-ups. (p. 248)[1]

From this quotation, we can extract a number of preconditions. These are substantial views, conclusions, or judgements about basic social transformations in the 19th and 20th centuries, but they are not explicitly discussed by Geyer. He has decided to deal solely with the texts in the archive. But on the other hand he also states that his aim is not just another post-modernist exercise which tries to make the texts dance. But to avoid such post-modernist relativism, I feel it necessary to include an explicit discussion of what I see as his preconditions.

The *first precondition* is Geyer's claim that one can trace a specific 19th-century project, namely the construction of a genuine 'civil society'. Geyer

---

* This chapter is a comment on Michael Geyer's contribution (Chapter 13). References to Geyer are given with page numbers only.

defines this project as 'the cultural and political process of social organization, the creation of identity for individuals and societies' (p. 250).

The *second precondition* is Geyer's view that the basic transformation of social structures from the 19th to the 20th century is fully described by the term 'militarization'. Hence, there is a spread of 'militarized social and institutional structures' in the 20th century.

The *third precondition* concerns an alleged intimate relationship between militarism and capitalism. Geyer simply asserts that capital defines the relations of domination and subordination.

These three preconditions constitute a specific philosophy of history. Indeed, there was a 19th century project, more than just a utopian vision, aiming at *peace*. As world history turned into the 20th century, this project broke down, and there was an encompassing militarization of social structures. This gives the impression of some kind of *fall of man* from a 19th-century 'peace project' to a 20th-century 'state of militarization'.

This chapter scrutinizes Geyer's three basic preconditions, and provides some final comments on his judgements about other interpretations of militarism.

2 Civil Society

The first precondition is one found in the writings of every 19th-century 'master-thinker': the 'expectation' of 'the coming of an age of peace, based on the flourishing of civil society' (p. 250).

From the few hints given, we must guess that such a Utopia had some connections to 'liberal capitalism'. At one time, Geyer seems to regret the 'slow demise of 19th-century liberalism all over Europe' (p. 255). We can also see that England is his basic reference here. Further, he makes it clear that the idea of a 'peaceful civil society' was carried by the bourgeoisie. Describing its opposite, 20th-century 'militarized social structure', Geyer links it to 'an age in which no longer property, but capital, defined relations of domination and subordination, and in which the autonomy and integrity of social classes and of the individual were no longer defined by their control of the public' (p. 257). Conversely, the 19th-century situation was one in which property defined relations of domination. It seems safe to conclude that Geyer here wants to establish the contrast between early (or liberal) and 'late' (or 'monopoly') capitalism.

The 19th-century project is described as 'the coming of an age of peace, based on the flourishing of civil society' – and its failure 'happened against the desires and political goals of the predominant social and political movements of the time' (p. 250). But it seems exaggerated to claim that the predominant social and political movements at that time all wanted a flourishing of civil society, at least if civil society is defined as an autonomous sphere, securing the political and social integrity of the individual (p. 252). Rather, many wanted to retain their privileges.

Autonomy therefore basically pertained only to privileged groups: most members of the working class were not allowed suffrage. England was in fact an extreme case, witness the failure of Chartism.

The 20th century saw the fragmentation of civil society, which lost its 'encompassing and hegemonic quality as the public space of bourgeois politics and gave way to partial systems and subsystems of social organization which together made up society' (p. 253). This was a loss 'of civil society as a unifying social and political space' (p. 253), a failure to reconstruct civil society against militarism and systematic organization of violence (p. 263).

In the 20th century, anti-militarists failed to maintain effective social movements, due to their 'wholesale abandonment of the project of civil society and the turn to the professional authority of experts, a change perfectly represented in the mass conversion of liberal and Left intellectuals from Utopia to realism' (p. 272). Referring to the 'functionalization' and militarization of society in the 20th century, Geyer criticizes the creation by intellectuals of an 'imaginary social order', a 'fantasy'. He also criticizes the 'invention of tradition', as elements of a contemporary militarization of *Lebenswelt* are projected back in history, giving rise to the theory of capitalism as the opposite to militarism, with militarism as an 'atavistic' (Schumpeter), pre-modern element. But we might well ask whether also Geyer himself is inventing tradition by constructing this 'civil society', abstracted from the concrete relations of class and power.

It is, however, possible to interpret Geyer's 'civil society' as his version of what Jürgen Habermas (1962) has called *bürgerliche Öffentlichkeit*. This was the first practical incarnation of the principles of freedom and equality, as realized in a peaceful *herrschaftsfreie Diskurs* where only reason counts. These were bourgeois ideas, and they are explained by Habermas (1973) with reference both to the extension of the commodity exchange relationship *and* to the secularization of basic ideas from the European Enlightenment. Despite their bourgeois origins, the ideas of freedom and equality could be taken up by all protest movements. Habermas shows that the working class took the ideology of freedom and equality seriously, as a 'kernel of truth' in bourgeois ideology.

In the 19th century, liberal capitalism faced severe legitimation problems; by the turn of the century, the wave of democratization and suffrage extension was roaring over Europe. This was part of the background for the transformation of capitalism into organized, welfare capitalism, what Habermas has called late capitalism and the French regulation school has dubbed 'Fordism'. It is described by Habermas as a form of capitalism which has solved the problems of 'material distress'. The real ideologies – those containing a kernel of truth – are all dead. In that sense, 'bourgeois civil society' as a project has broken down. According to Habermas (1973), the 'surrogate ideologies' of late capitalism cannot protect modern Western society from the 'crisis of meaning' which follows from its inability to solve problems of 'spiritual distress'. The French regulation school has focused more on the transformation into an 'American way of life' under postwar Western European Fordism and the fact that the specific articulation between mass production and mass consumption explains the specific type of a crisis which we have experienced in the 1970s and 1980s (Aglietta & Brender, 1984; Boyer, 1986). Certainly, there is tradition for a *Kulturkritik* against this type of 'one-dimensional society'. But in comparison to British 19th-century liberal capitalism, we must at least acknowledge the fact that late capitalism involves substantial political and material progress for the working masses. This is clearer today – after some ten years of austerity – than it was in the late 1960s, when Habermas formulated his diagnosis of a 'crisis of meaning'.

These are extensions of the analysis of the breakdown of the 19th-century civil society. But they contain nothing about militarization. Hence, for his second precondition, Geyer turns to another source of inspiration, the structuralism of Michel Foucault.

3 20th-Century Militarized *Lebenswelt*

Our 20th-century '*Lebenswelt*' of everyday experience . . . shows all the scars of militarization' (p. 250). Industrialism failed to create civil society. The archive on militarism consists of attempts to forget this failure: 'All the more important that we not simply ask what militarism *is*, but what it is *in our collective memories* which makes us forget the process of militarization and overlook the transformation of the social and political consciousness in the transition from the 19th to the 20th century' (p. 251).

Like the fall of the *civil society* project, this hiatus is not explicitly dealt with. The specificities of the historical constellation are dealt with only briefly: new technologies, communications/transport 'revolution', the shift from wooden to iron warships, the emergence of universal conscription and *Militäranstalt* in Prussia and France. All these trends created a new sense of vulnerability within the elites of the hegemonic power at that time, England. From the 1860s, militarism became a notion, reflecting this shock experience. Earlier, criticism had been directed only against mercenary armies, arbitrary princes, and military *gloire*.

The division, however, is not so firm. In a nice historical account, Geyer later (p. 263) shows that World War I was a dividing line. This war was to show that capitalism and militarism were compatible, that civil forces could organize war, and it decisively disproved the belief that only princes were belligerent while people were peaceful. World War I was the war of the masses, with industrial society as its source. But it also created the last major protest movements: the Russian Revolution and the German near-revolution, as well as important reforms also in the allied countries.

Geyer wants to make a much more specific point. With reference to the focus of late-19th-century protest movements, he shows that they fused the criticism of militarism and Bonapartism with criticism of capital concentration and financial speculation. He interprets this as an attempt to attack the 'socio-cultural face' of what we – creating a parallel to Polanyi's (1944) famous notion – may call 'the great militarist transformation'. Geyer concludes that the debate on this change 'permeated virtually every aspect of late-19th-century social and political thinking and practice' (p. 252). But examples and illustrations are lacking. The crucial point is that Geyer fails to substantiate his claim that the militarist transformation influenced social structures so thoroughly. I feel he turns dogmatic when he just asserts that militarism in the 20th century became 'a mode of organizing social existence' (p. 253).

Nowhere is the dramatic radicalism of Geyer's claim clearer than in his use of the distinction between *Systemwelt* and *Lebenswelt*. *Systemwelt* is the 'functional organization of society', the notion of an overarching *Herrschaftsbetrieb*, where bureaucratization, technologization, and industrialization work together as seemingly 'metahistorical forces' (if Geyer's reading of Weber is right). The development of this 'machine' has certainly contributed to the *'Verherrschaftlichung* of daily life' (p. 263). According to Geyer, the weakness of 20th-century theories of militarization is the claim that militarism stems only from the *Systemwelt*, 'from above'. Against these claims, Geyer insists that militarism has a mass appeal.

He finds proof of this in the writings of intellectuals like Pareto, Michels, Sorel, and in futurist art. From this he concludes that militarized identities are very modern elements, not backward ones. In the 20th century militarism has been made a strategy of identification, organized according to gender and to ethnicity: male and Aryan. 'Militarism was thus neither an elite phenomenon nor an objectified systems structure, but a mode of social organization' (p. 257). Militarism flowed from *Lebenswelt* itself.[1]

In his second main subsection, Geyer tries to confirm this idea with reference to the 20th-century history of ideas. He emphasizes events in interwar Germany, where Nazism made *Lebenswelt* a site of militarism. The intellectual consequence of this – so to say the consequence within the archive – was to speed up the transformation away from explanations based on 'social movements' to such based on *Systemwelt* (p. 267).

Through these quite radical formulas, Geyer has established a Foucault-inspired view of militarism as a discourse, reflecting 'that the organization of society entails domination and that it is exactly this process of domination which destroys civil society and gives rise to militarism' (p. 274). In this way Geyer prepares the ground for an overall criticism of the 'knowledge professions' which formulate this discourse.

Before turning to his criticism, let us return to our earlier reference to the regulation school. Their contribution may in this connection be seen as the modern version of the *Annales*-school, since they emphasize the importance of the inert structures of daily life. In the 20th-century postwar period, these structures have been marked by mass consumption. Of course, segments of the modern mass consumption culture may be violent (for instance, the teenage rocker 'car culture' of the US 1950s), but it is very hard to see that such a lifestyle can be reduced to the one characteristic of 'militarization'. Actually, the mass consumption way of life is often seen as peaceful, as conducive to political consensus, even low political participation, to detachment from nationalist hysteria, and to concentration on leisure and mass media experiences.

Geyer would obviously not agree with such an interpretation of the Fordist 'iconography'. In one respect he is right: we know that the American way of life since the late 1940s has been imbued with a feeling of Cold War emergency. Partly, this has also been formulated ideologically as the superiority of the 'American way of life'. But the extent to which the USA has succeeded in spreading such sentiments has varied according to receiving country, to connection to US alliance networks, and to historical periods. (In the 1960s, for instance, many European countries were critical of US warmongering in Vietnam.) Furthermore, the 'Cold War consensus' has largely been a creation 'from above', not a general feature of the postwar world. Attempting a more general approach, we may of course search for images of life and death competition in modern sports and in other mass media events. But an exclusive focus on peace-promoting or militarist elements here fails to address the crucial question: what is the relationship between these elements of the modern way of life typical of postwar Western capitalism? Is the relationship dependent on modern capitalism as such, or are there variations according to social groups or nation states? Further analysis of this relationship is also important if we are to be able to judge about potentials for protest against militarization.

Geyer, however, seems to choose an even higher level of abstraction. He draws on one particular file in his archive, the file containing the writings of German writer and essayist Ernst Jünger (b. 1895). Here, Geyer finds confirmation for his view that the popular 20th-century bourgeois order is a militarized one. Discussing Jünger's notion of *Materialschlacht*, Geyer finds that it is not defined only by human spirit fused with technology, but also as organization of excessive consumption. Militarism, according to Jünger, appropriates the tools of production and destruction in the process of consumption. It can be likened to Third Reich 'monumental architecture'.

Particularly inviting for Geyer is the view that consumption erodes the security and permanence of things, thereby undermining bourgeois society, property, and all its 'simulacra' (similarities). According to Baudrillard, *simulacrum* indicates the telling of the truth that there is no truth. Militarism is not weapons, but language, which constitutes meaning, 'and thus appropriates and controls the consuming techniques of destruction' (p. 268). Militarism is the revolt of a 'consuming *Lebenswelt* against the *Systemwelt*', a 'means to re-establish permanence in the face of the consuming destructiveness of consumerism' (p. 269). According to Geyer, the production of meaning is controlled by the producer/consumer.

Militarists are not 'atavistic creatures but producers/consumers who engage in deadly excess' (p. 269).

In line with such views, one could argue that, in the postwar phase of Pax Americana, militarism has become even more strongly embedded in the *Lebenswelt*. The identity of the demobilized public of the Western nations would be established by the consumption of weapons. In this way Geyer could relate his perspective on militarism to the American way of life and its iconography. But it still remains to shore up this general perspective by analysing the social history of the two interconnecting factors mentioned above: the 'Fordist' consumption patterns of the American way of life and 'Cold Warism'. Until this has been done, it is difficult to decide whether Geyer's look at militarism through post-modernist lenses is really all that fruitful.

4 Capitalism Defines Militarism?

Turning now to Geyer's third precondition, it concerns the group of 'knowledge professionals' who in the 20th century have been occupied with the presentation of theories which make us forget the 19th-century project of peace. We shall look a bit closer at Geyer's treatment of some such theories.

The important tradition of 'liberal-bourgeois' reactions to the decline of the peace project has already been mentioned: militarism is here seen as an atavism. Militarism was constructed as a negation of what the bourgeoisie would like their society to be. Militarism was a feudal remnant. Schumpeter's (1919) theory became the final codification of such an 'otherness of militarism'. Geyer shows that Spencer's and Freud's 'fantasies' about this 'otherness' were actually projections of current dangers. While 19th-century bourgeois ideology contained a kernel of truth, Geyer reads this version as no more than 'pseudo-ideology' in Habermas's sense, or a 'dominant discourse' in Foucault's sense.

Geyer fails, however, to address a revised version of Schumpeter's approach. In Arno Mayer's (1982) analysis, *fin-de-siècle* militarism is linked to the strength of aristocracy. But Mayer argues that aristocracy at this time still had its main power bases intact. Hence, they did not represent atavist elements in the social structure: their power was real, and the bourgeoisie subdued to this dominance.

As already mentioned, Geyer holds that most studies of militarization in the postwar period have disregarded the transformation of *Lebenswelt*. Instead they accepted the *Systemwelt* which emerged from 'industrialization and militarization', and made this into an 'imaginary social order', a 'fantasy' of a 'rationally organized society' (p. 253). This rationalization is the basis for postwar theorists: militarization as hyper-real and military hardware as hyper-concrete. There is a new 'instrumental praxeology': a complementarity between 'arms race managers', maximizing national resources in international competition, and 'arms controllers', who manage and control international competition. The discourse on arms build-up has become the dominant element in the debates, that is, in the archive. It is marked by its 'disbelief in the existence of militarized social formations', and it is voiced by social science 'international relations' experts. All these experts deny the militarization of daily life. Technocratic experts and the internationalist idealists converge in their distrust of social movements. This is a variation on Habermas's (1968) theme of science and technology as pseudo-ideologies.

Geyer also levels criticism against Social Democratic parties, which demobilize popular mobilization against war and armaments, fooling people into becoming 'consumers of security' (p. 265). Geyer in particular addresses a theory attributed to Karl Liebknecht and Anthony Giddens (1986). This theory holds that coercion and militarism are a general feature of all class systems, but since capitalism faces both the challenge of the proletariat from within and external competition from abroad, capitalism requires militarism more than any other social formation does. (Mayer, 1982, holds many similar views, but regards *aristocracy* as the class most fearful of proletarian mobilization, at least before World War I.) Geyer rejects this view of militarism as an extra-economic articulation of class struggle as 'extremely mechanic' (p. 260). If militarism is seen as external to, but employed by, capitalism, it is 'denied social status of its own'. Clearly, that is not in harmony with Geyer's view of a thoroughly militarized life world.

This leads to perhaps the most striking paradox of Geyer's contribution. The title is 'Militarism and Capitalism in the 20th Century', but the problem of this relationship is never discussed explicitly. Geyer's most fundamental precondition, it seems, is the advance solution of this problem. Provided he is not just dancing a post-modernist dance with Rosa Luxemburg, it seems that he agrees with her classic analysis of militarism as 'situated in the very process of capital accumulation'. In a situation where unionization and other successful strategies of class struggle prevent capital from extracting more surplus directly from the workers, the state/capital relationship (where the state orders militaristic capital goods from capital, spending the taxes payed by the masses) is a compensatory circuit for accumulation. Luxemburg regards the state as realizing the imperatives of 'total capital'. She even extends this view, as she argues that capitalism needs to exploit non-capitalist strata and areas, that is both the domestic traditional sector and foreign colonies, by hooking them on to this 'emergency' circuit. Geyer sees here a nutshell theory of underdevelopment and militarization, and he even states that this theory could be linked to his own idea of 'militarized social identities (consumption)' (p. 261f.).

But this theory seems deficient, both with respect to Luxemburg's own time at the turn of the century and with respect to the later 20th century. The argument – at least as Geyer presents it – totally disregards two important features. The first feature is technical change, and in particular labour process rationalization, which certainly is a part of the general disciplination that Geyer is well aware of. The second feature is the 'capital/capital circuit', i.e. the fact that other capitalists demand productive equipment from capitalists producing capital goods. (For such a criticism of Luxemburg, see for instance Brewer, 1979.)

Furthermore, as we have noted, the emergence of postwar 'Fordist' capitalism implies that the purchasing power of the broad masses (which now consume even durable goods produced by large-scale industries benefiting from returns to scale) becomes crucial. This – almost 'Keynesian' – circuit shows that at least through the postwar Golden Age of Western capitalism there was compatibility between increasing consumption power of the masses and a further surge of capital realization and accumulation.

This compatibility may have faded with today's long economic downturn. What we need is a study of the specificity of militarism during the different phases through which modern capitalism has passed since the 'great militarist transformation'. We need to scrutinize its national varieties. In this way we can free our arguments of implicit philosophies of history like the one which Geyer has built into his three preconditions.

Note

1. Geyer here obviously departs from Habermas's (1981) definition of the notions of *System* and *Lebenswelt*, where the latter is the site of the irreversible ideas of enlightenment. Actually, while Geyer's notion of 'the civil society project' is close to Habermas, his views here seem closer to Foucault. Given Habermas's (1985) recent criticism of Foucault, it may be doubted whether these sources of inspiration go well together.

LARS MJØSET, b. 1954, Mag. Art. in sociology (University of Oslo, 1979); Research Fellow, PRIO (1981–84); University Fellow in Sociology, University of Oslo (1985–87); Research Fellow, Institute for Social Research, Oslo (1987–). Author of 'Nordic Economic Policies in the 1970s and 1980s' (*International Organization*, 1987) and other works on economic sociology and sociological theory.

Chapter 15
Arms Build-Ups under Socialism: The USSR and China

CARL GUSTAV JACOBSEN
Department of Political Science, Carleton University, and Canadian Institute for International Peace and Security, Ottawa

1 Western Theory and 'Socialist' Reality

Arms dynamics and arms build-ups in the USSR and China expose the hazards of superficial extrapolations from Western theoretical models. The Soviet Union and China clearly have military-industrial-research 'complexes' (see below). But whereas those of the West grew apart from the State and have remained distinct from the State – notwithstanding post-1970 trends towards an increasingly incestuous relationship between the two – those of Moscow and Beijing have always been part of the State and integral to it. Russian/Soviet and modern Chinese political-military cultures (as well as some of the oldest Chinese traditions) have always allowed more military influence over non-military policy considerations as well as more non-military influence over military matters, strategy, and doctrine. The bureaucratic weight of military and related concerns may indeed be greater than that found in the West, but it is qualitatively different: in essence, in implications.

Extrapolations based on Western experience and assumptions about the impact of expansionist ideology are hazardous: in the Soviet and Chinese contexts the concept of expansionist ideology is in fact more misleading than revealing. The related theory, that lack of democratic restraint and absence of the kind of competitive environment that the West associates with the profit motive contribute to arms build-ups, is also inappropriate to Soviet and Chinese experience. In fact, the record suggests that as concerns military procurement decisions Soviet and Chinese reality imposes more restraint and more competitive pressures than does the Western norm.

2 The Impact of Military Culture

Military culture, with the ramifications of ethnocentrism, constitutes the single most crucial variable usually missing from strategic debate and consideration. It has significant impact on strategy and doctrine. And it defines the socio-political roots that sustain military endeavour.

Russian and Chinese military cultures have not escaped foreign influence – the former by Prussia, the latter by Meiji Japan. But both developed independently of and remain qualitatively different from the Anglo-Saxon tradition of the dominant Western power. There has been some functional convergence during recent years. In the United States the Anglo-Saxon model of the military as a clearly separate adjunct of the State withered under the post-World War II impact of dramatically higher rates of military funding; by about 1970 there had emerged a new demonstrably incestuous career pattern expectancy that intertwined military and military-industrial agencies with civilian executive (and to a lesser extent legislative) military procurement and oversight bodies. But, as noted by former President Dwight Eisenhower in his Farewell Address (when he warned that the then still incipient 'military-industrial complex' already exercised 'influence – economic, political and even spiritual – [. . .] in every city, every State house, every office of the federal government'), the process of functional integration has been distinctly asymmetrical (Eisenhower, 1961, p. 1038; Jacobsen, 1982, pp. 109–126). This has reflected enhanced military influence, not symbiotic integration.

In Muscovy and also in the Sun Tsuian strain of Chinese military culture that found expression in Maoist thought and Chinese 'communist' practice, the relationship of military and society was symbiotic. This qualitative essence was reinforced by the advent of Bolshevism[1] – a consequence of both theoretical predilection and force of circumstance.

Lenin's approving notes on Clausewitz confirm and develop the Marxian view (which complements that of Clausewitz) that military power is an element of, a reflection of, and an extension of State power; State power is defined by its socio-economic essence; it is a composite of inherently interrelated components, one of which is military might (David & Kohn, 1977, pp. 182–222). Strategic power is an amalgam of each and every component of State power – economic, military, cultural/ideological, and others. The exercise of State power may be expressed through the (integrated!) projection of one, several, or all component elements. By the early 1980s Moscow had emphatically disavowed the notion that nuclear war could be encompassed within the old dictum that war is a continuation of politics. Yet this reflected the divorce of nuclear power (as non-rational, non-controllable, and indiscriminately suicidal) from military power; it did not reflect any change in views on the nature of the State, or the role of military and society.[2]

The force of circumstance was to work in the same direction. The early Bolsheviks were embattled, fighting potentially superior White armies (in the Baltic, the Ukraine, and Siberia), potentially superior interventionist troops, German, British, French, Italian, American, Canadian, Japanese, and others (on the Kola Peninsula, in the Baltic, in Crimea, and in the Far

East), amid war-weariness, disillusionment, and economic calamity. To be a Bolshevik was to be a soldier: the corollary, that a Red Army man or woman was also a Bolshevik (and propagandist and agent of State power), was also a truism.

This pattern persisted through seven decades – of threat, real or potential, from a more potent enemy or enemy coalition, combined with continuing economic problems and weakness (1913 production levels were not surpassed until 1927; 1939 output was equalled only in 1949; and, more recently, there has been near-stagnation caused by systemic resistance to the need to switch from resource-intensive to technology-intensive growth). Military power was never a luxury. It was a societal imperative; so was the need to limit its cost.[3]

The military remained integrated within a larger socio-economic composite. Military officers serve on party and State bodies, at all levels. Party and State officials serve on military councils, at all levels, in peace as in war (Scott & Scott, 1984).

The defence imperative provided military industries with priority access to resources and personnel; as *quid pro quo* the military acquired responsibility also for the production of higher-technology civilian goods – from cameras and refrigerators to TVs and video machines.

The military, a universal organization (as opposed to the strictly limited membership of Party structures), became the main post-school non-media organizational actor for inculcating societal values; it became a crucial adjunct to the drive for literacy; and it became the vehicle through which minimal all-union competency in the *lingua franca* of the Empire-State could be ensured.

Military contributions to the State also extended to help in harvest gathering, laying of sewage pipes, construction of dams, railways, bridges, universities, civilian housing, and to other tasks.

The socio-economic drag of military costs and burden was also eased by the doctrinal requirements that maximum military benefit be wrought from civilian potentials. Civilian air (Aeroflot) transport was designed in part to serve military crisis requirements. The Merchant Marine was designed to complement and hence minimize the need for purely Naval supply and transport vessels. The Fishing and Oceanographic Fleets were calibrated to serve as intelligence extensions of the Navy. It is important to note that these civilian agencies should not therefore be viewed merely as military auxiliaries. They remained essentially civilian, and their primary (in peacetime) civilian tasks are themselves vital to the State. The external services of Aeroflot, and even more so the Merchant Marine, are essential sources of foreign exchange. The Fishing Fleet has become crucial in meeting the nation's protein requirements. There is no peacetime precedent for civilian Fleet construction or dock requirements being impaired as the result of Naval priority; in fact, there is some evidence that the reverse has occurred. The operating rule in times of peace is that military needs are served whenever and wherever this can be accommodated without undue damage to civilian goals; only in crisis or war do military needs become paramount. Nevertheless, access to complementary civilian resources obviously does alleviate military needs (Jacobsen, 1975).

But the demand that the military maximize its provision of services to civilian purpose, and optimize its own utilization of complementary civilian resources, does not exhaust the realities of restraint under which the military must operate. The realities of relative underdevelopment have always imposed real issues of choice, substantive choice. The preference for quantity, imposed by historical memory and geography, has been bought at the expense of quality – fewer flying hours, less training with front-line equipment, far lower at-sea schedules, and significantly lower day-to-day readiness levels, across the board, than in Western force structures (Jacobsen, 1982, 1987b).

3 Changing Doctrines and Threat Environments

The above description, though focused on the Soviet case, may be said to convey the essence of both Soviet and 'Communist' Chinese tradition as concerns the role of the military in society: the military permeates society, but does not dominate it; there can be no question of military opposition to the State, for it *is* of the State; military factions do exist, but they are not functional separatists – on policy issues their weight reflects the weight of the composite political-economic-military-social factions of which they are integral, component parts.

Changing military-political doctrines and changing threat perceptions in recent years have not affected the essence of this integrative military culture,[4] but as they have affected its ramifications for policy, they therefore warrant comment and consideration.

Soviet policy priorities have been dramatically affected by new military doctrinal, political, and socio-economic dynamics. As concerns the former – and with the a priori caveat that real evolution is a matter of zigzags and the impact of ongoing debates – we must start by noting that, in the nuclear arena, Soviet doctrine developed quite differently from that of the United States.[5] US nuclear doctrine evolved from Eisenhower's posture of Massive Retaliation, which saw nuclear weapons not as military tools but as the Damoclean sword of ultimate deterrent, through the various phases of Flexible Response, which envisioned the use of nuclear arms for ongoing military purposes, through Secretary of Defense Schlesinger's 'Selective Targeting' and former President Carter's PD 59, which envisioned even earlier use of nuclear dissuasion, to the quite explicit doctrines of nuclear war-fighting and SDI that dominated the early Reagan Administration. In the USSR, however, the progression was reversed. Secretary-General Khrushchev's dramatic demobilizations of armed forces personnel during the late 1950s was accompanied by a guarantee of more fire power: Soviet forces were nuclearized; nuclear war-fighting became accepted doctrine. But the military utility of nuclear weapons was subjected to increasing question, and Soviet doctrine gradually modified and changed, through SALT and its concomitant acceptance of Mutual Assured Destruction (MAD), to Secretary Brezhnev's Tula speech and the appointment of Marshal Ogarkov as Chief of the General Staff in 1977. The 'New Revolution in Military Affairs' relegated nuclear arms to the role of admittedly suicidal final deterrent (Massive Retaliation), and focused instead on developing new conventional and exotic weaponry that might acquire nuclear-type efficacy without the nuclear weapon's attendant albatross of loss of control and purpose (Fitzgerald, 1985).

The differing developmental trends intersected about 1972, when SALT I was signed. The acceptance of MAD, and its apparent imperviousness to foreseeable technological change, persuaded Moscow that all-out strategic war between the superpowers was inconceivable, at least as a matter of conscious policy; that if war should nevertheless break out, even nuclear war, both would be compelled to grant the other homeland immunity; that the foreseeable threat therefore was not mortal, so attention could switch to the longer-term task of ensuring strategic health and power for the year 2025. Nuclear modernization programmes went ahead. But the CIA testifies to the fact that the share of the Soviet defence budget allocated to strategic nuclear systems decreased after 1972. By the early and mid-1980s it was clear that changing doctrine had indeed altered procurement patterns. In the Soviet Navy, for example, all-nuclear armaments and single-shot, no-reload norms were replaced by new designs that accommodated conventional and other options, and reload.

But the larger US polity was not yet ready to embrace the de facto concession of parity (and acceptance of or resignation to MAD) that constituted the core of SALT I and the Basic Principles Agreement (and the *leitmotif* for SALT II) – with its notions of 'sufficiency' and concomitant rejection of 'superiority'. Détente began to break down in 1973, when Washington vetoed a Soviet role in Mid-East peace negotiations; the breakdown accelerated with the Jackson–Vanik US Senate amendment of 1974, which gutted the Nixon–Brezhnev accords. Previous developmental trends reasserted themselves – culminating in the Reagan Administration's pursuit of unilateral advantage and the wherewithal to 'prevail' in nuclear war. The announcement of SDI in 1983, and the President's confidence that the USA could secure immunity from Soviet strike or retaliation, threw Soviet strategic policy councils into turmoil. This negated the postulate that defence against the plethora of superpower penetration options was an illusion: Moscow's long-standing Ballistic Missile Defence efforts were directed at third-party prospects – China and France; the task of defending against US potentials had been acknowledged as insurmountable since 1967. Moscow could not discount US technological prowess and ingenuity. Soviet calculations appeared wrong; Soviet complacency misplaced. There was a clear and present danger.

By 1984–85, however, Moscow became more sanguine. President

Reagan did not renounce his vision. But Soviet (and US) studies soon suggested that even esoteric SDI components might be vulnerable to relatively cheap counter-measures; the scientific, technological, and computer software requirements of Reagan's SDI appeared as far in advance of current realities as the 747 or Concorde were from the Wright brothers' plane; Pentagon SDI funding in fact focused increasingly on more limited ambitions (in effect, SDI II or III, or 'Son of SDI') that would not negate MAD – and that were not totally dissimilar from the ambitions of Moscow (Committee of Soviet Scientists for Peace, Against the Nuclear Threat, 1985, 1987; Jacobsen, 1982). The Pentagon also ameliorated the impact of other deployment decisions that might precipitate nuclear engagement: few Pershing IIs were put on alert; most Pershing warheads were stored off and at demonstrable distance from the warheads. US Army doctrine diverged from nuclear preoccupation, to increased emphasis on non-nuclear, conventional, and exotic options. December 1987 brought the INF Treaty removing theatre-range nuclear weapons from Europe. Soviet attention reverted to the long-term prospectus of 'the Ogarkov agenda'; the US military appeared similarly inclined.

This restored the congruence between Soviet military-doctrinal and politico-economic dynamics. The latter coalesced under former Secretary-General Yuri Andropov. Deeply perturbed by economic stagnation and by the corruption, cynicism, and apathy that had prevailed during the late Brezhnev years, the Andropov coalition embraced the banners of discipline, moral regeneration, and re-industrialization – recognizing that the only way to achieve this would be through a change from resource-intensive to technology- and capital-intensive growth patterns, a change that could be brought about only through increased population participation and commitment, and that would at best be costly, dislocating, and time-consuming.

The Gorbachev embodiment of this programme (as also its initial thrust under Andropov, prior to SDI and the exacerbation of superpower tensions) has clear support from military reformers. The year 1987 brought acceptance of the efficacy of 'defensive defence'. With military requirements again focused on the uncertainties of a more distant future, the 'fundamental' underlying theme of Soviet military thought – that military prowess must rest on socio-economic well-being – came to the fore. The military were as perturbed by socio-economic problems as Andropov/Gorbachev. The military's long-term high-tech priorities complemented those of their civilian counterparts. The military accepted that the technological base must be diversified; military-technological dynamism demanded the creation and emergence also of a more dynamic interactive civil industry (Cooper, 1987, pp. 388–404; Jacobsen, 1987b, pp. 8–9).

Quality control procedures developed within military industries were now introduced into the civilian economy. Prominent military industrial managers were transferred, to lead the scientific-industrial and technological conglomerates now established as 'the leading edge' of the

'Revolution' (Cooper, 1987). In one sense this constitutes yet another serious drain on military resources, at a time when they are clearly slotted for some financial sacrifice. On the other hand it can also be seen as a compensatory indirect extension of military influence; the manifestation of military interest and investment in developing a stronger civilian base, and partner; or, more properly, as a function of all of the above – another reflection of the symbiotic relationship between military and society.

Chinese developmental priorities underwent similar change: the particulars were different, but the essence was analogous. Again, there was a convergence of more sanguine threat perceptions, acceptance of current strength as minimally satisfactory, resignation to the fact that technological and other constraints precluded qualitative change within the foreseeable future, and a consequent shift in military attention from short-term to longer-term needs and requirements, together with consensus acceptance of the need for socio-economic restructuring. The functionally military sphere in society shrank. Military requirements were ranked fourth of the Four Modernizations now designated to define developmental priorities. Manpower was cut; non-essential and auxiliary military industry and other facilities were sold or transferred to civilian organizations. The military was directed to seek supplementary funding through pursuit of a non-restrictive policy of foreign arms sales. Yet, though military priorities may have faded, there is no question that the military in China also remains an integral part of the national leadership. In one sense, in fact, its role in society goes beyond the norm of symbiosis and cross-representation; in today's China the military retains a peculiar role as the consensual 'guardian of the Revolution' – as it once protected Deng Xiaoping from the extremes of Maoist persecution, so it now appears to be protecting the Maoist heritage from final dismemberment.[6]

4 Expansionist Ideology?

The nature, essence, and impact of expansionist ideology in the Soviet and Chinese contexts is impossible to define, for it has been both mirage and chameleon. The ideology of Trotsky and Lenin posed a mortal threat to 'capitalist' elites and norms, yet the beneficiary of expansionism was a transnational 'proletariat', not Muscovy – indeed: it postulated Germany and England as primary beneficiaries. Under Stalin, however, the internationalist credo became a fig-leaf for chauvinist nationalism. Expansionism was also restrained, and returned to its Tsarist mould: it sought dominance over Eastern Europe (it was Catherine who first drew the line on the map that was to become the Iron Curtain, as the line east of which Moscow could afford no leeway to an opponent), the borderlands to the south, and buffers against Chinese and Japanese power; but gains further afield (Tsarist troops had also seen African soil; Tsarist vessels had also been active in US waters – Kipp, 1977) were strictly dispensable – pawns on the chessboard of Great Power rivalry. There is something to be said for the old Cold Warrior's musing that revolution and ideology in fact constricted expansionism – the former by denying Russia the prize of Constantinople which would otherwise have been gained at the end of World War I, the latter by imposing the need at least to appear to conform to the anti-nationalist ethos.

But the immensely complicated task of dissecting the question of 'expansionist ideology' is perhaps not germane. Even if it could be argued that their ideology had expansionist content and that it defined or shaped State policy, neither the USSR nor China has had the relative power necessary to realize it – except in constricted circumstances. There can be little question that the primary propellant driving their arms procurement policies has, to the contrary, been the perception of threat from apparently superior enemies and hostile coalitions. That their military allocations have decreased when threat perceptions have faded undermines the case for expansionist ideology as either an independent or a dominant variable. The legal verdict of 'not proven' is apposite.

5 The 'Competition' Factor

The thesis that lack of 'democratic' control and absence of (price) competition gives undue licence to arms build-ups is peculiarly irrelevant to either Soviet or Chinese realities. Western-type checks and balances may not apply, but as the above survey makes clear, that has not diminished either societal control or restraint.[7] And competition has never been absent from Soviet or Chinese military procurement practices: there have always been competing design bureaux, and competing prototypes. The profit motive (both pecuniary and in the form of special privileges and status) has in fact been a permanent fixture. But the competition is still sharper than that suggested by elements of personal advantage: the real driving competition has been provided by the existence of more advanced and (potentially) more potent enemies, and the stakes – national survival.

The thesis concerning the impact of a competitive environment may in fact entail Soviet and Chinese advantage, not disadvantage. In the United States a degree of chauvinist arrogance and complacency (nurtured by decades of technological advantage), and perhaps corruption, has spawned a procurement system steeped in non-competitive bidding practices, 'gold-plating', and other forms of waste. US military industry, with its contractors and subcontractors, has in effect come to acquire many of the characteristics of the Soviet civilian economy: monopolistic practices, lack of competition, and resultant sloth – and of the two, today the Soviet civilian economy appears under the greater pressure to change, though the question of success remains open to some doubt. Soviet and Chinese military industries, on the other hand, constitute the one segment of their economies that truly do operate under 'capitalist'-type pressures.

6 Conclusion

Many of the dynamics identified by Western arms theory clearly do apply to 'socialist' societies – one can certainly identify cases of technology pull, and of developmental and bureaucratic momentum as independent variables and considerations.[8] Yet apparently obvious extrapolations from Western theory often prove hazardous, if indeed not wrong.

One problem concerns the fact that we are dealing with different politico-military cultures. Theorems that appear to apply in one context cannot be transposed indiscriminately to another.

Indeed, the distinction between 'Western' and 'socialist' realities may be misleading. The 'socialist' realities described in the text reflect, and may also be argued to have been moulded by, older cultural roots – roots that represent distinctly Asian cultural traditions. This may in fact be more important than the professed 'Marxist' superstructure!

But whereas this analysis may have dissected differences between European and Asian cultural traditions, rather than any that distinguish Adam Smith from Karl Marx, it is necessary also to inject a note of caution about future extrapolations. The 'Asian' aspect of Soviet and modern Chinese military-political culture may not be immutable. The ultimate aim and logic of Gorbachev's and Deng's reforms, which may yet succeed, are to divorce Party purpose from the tasks of day-to-day management and supervision. Gorbachevian reform contains the germ of separation of powers. Dengist reform contains elements of China's 'other' tradition, Confucianism. Thus the integrative nature of the respective establishment-composites may in the future become more diffuse.

Finally, we must acknowledge the problem of inadequacy of data. Quite often we simply do not know enough to offer judgement. And we must also caution ourselves that theory is just that – it is composed of postulates and hypotheses suggested by available evidence, but available evidence is far from exhaustive, and needs to be continuously tested against newer data. Theory is a working tool, not science in itself.

The study of politics, the interrelationships between functionally diverse societal organisms, sociology, and economics is the search for knowledge and insights about how society functions and evolves. Such a search can never be totally value-free. Sufficiency of data can never be assumed. 'Political science' is a misnomer of the first order. It is self-delusion: at best it is quasi-science; at worst (and most often) it is but pseudo-science. We can aspire to scholarship, not to science. There is no data that can prove us right; there is much data that can prove us wrong. Judgement is rarely final.

Notes

1. The text focuses on Soviet/Russian reality, and on the analogue that can be claimed for post-1949 Chinese reality and that is inherent in the older Chinese Sun Tsuian roots of Maoist

and CPC thought and approach. The reader should be aware that there is also a contrary Chinese tradition: that of Confucianism, which disparages military purpose and worth. The Chinese heritage in terms of 'military culture' is thus more ambivalent than Muscovy's. Current reality, however, clearly conforms to the pre-Confucian model, and that is the reality that must be addressed.

2. Nor did it change Moscow's underlying Clausewitzian view of war as a continuation of politics – though one must note that this constitutes an explanation of war, *not* a prescription!

3. For in-depth discussion, see Jacobsen (1987b).

4. The short answer to the problem of identifying and dissecting the 'military-industrial complex' of the USSR may indeed be that 'the USSR is a military-industrial complex' (Agursky & Adomeit, 1979, pp. 107–108).

5. The described 'open scissor' divergence concerns declaratory policy. Acquisition and implementing policies were less divergent. One might note that Eisenhower did contemplate nuclear warfighting during the early years of his Presidency, while Khrushchev may have seen his nuclear warfighting licence as a means to forcing US acceptance of MAD; President Kennedy's Secretary of Defense, Robert McNamara, did embrace MAD as a reflection of reality shortly thereafter – though other Establishment figures remained unconvinced. Declaratory doctrine is not always the sole determinant, but it usually serves the role of final arbiter; it does constitute the official consensual guideline for weapons usage.

Finally: 'acceptance of MAD', whether in Moscow or Washington, does of course not (and never did) entail necessary enthusiasm for the theory, or embrace of it: rather, it constitutes recognition of the reality and of the short- and medium-term technological imperviousness of the condition of MAD.

6. Cf. Jacobsen (1981), and the Far East reviews in Jones (annual).

7. The Bolsheviki were always acutely conscious of the danger of Bonapartism, and the need for civilian strategic control. The military-civilian symbiosis, and the privilege that this accords the military, does not in any way translate into military primacy or undue influence; it reflects the 'strategic culture' of its context – it reflects the fact of a leadership into whom an exceptionally high degree of security consciousness has been bred by historical experience, and by national and ideological expectations and convictions about the nature of international politics.

8. The history of the SS-20 is illustrative. There was no hint of hesitation when developing technology allowed replacement of older, inaccurate, stationary, and vulnerable Euromissiles with more accurate, smaller-warhead, mobile, and thus more survivable SS-20s. There was no thought of negative repercussions in the West. The SS-20 was in fact thought to be 'stability enhancing'; its survivability put it in a different category from the 'use or lose' missiles it was scheduled to replace. This strategic mindset clearly biased Moscow against appreciation of NATO's contrary military-political calculations. But it was Soviet bureaucratic momentum (or inertia) that prolonged the contradiction and, in the end, legitimized or enabled NATO counter-deployments that increased the jeopardy to Soviet security.

CARL GUSTAV JACOBSEN, b. 1944, Ph.D. in Political Science: Director of Soviet Studies at the Stockholm International Peace Research Institute (1985–87); now Director of East–West Studies at the Canadian Institute for International Peace and Security Studies and Professor of International Relations at Carleton University, Ottawa. His latest books are *The Soviet Defence Enigma: Estimating Costs and Burden* and *The Uncertain Course: New Weapons, Systems and Mindsets* (both Oxford University Press, 1987).

Chapter 16

Why the Soviets Buy the Weapons They Do*

MATTHEW A. EVANGELISTA

Department of Political Science, University of Michigan

1 Introduction

The increase in public concern about nuclear weapons in the early 1980s coincided with a resurgence of scholarly interest in determining the causes of the US–Soviet arms race. This chapter discusses three books which attempt to account for Soviet military developments; they employ a spectrum of possible explanations ranging from an analysis emphasizing bureaucratic politics and a 'Soviet military-industrial complex' to an approach stressing strategic 'requirements'. Antecedents of these types of analysis are found in the work of US social scientists and European peace researchers writing during the 1960s and early 1970s, mainly on US weapons policy.

I will begin by placing three books in the context of the earlier literature on arms control and military policy. Next, I will outline each author's approach through a discussion of how each relates Soviet weapons procurement to military doctrine. The authors' arguments will then be analyzed and assessed in relation to a particularly topical issue – Soviet regional nuclear force posture in Europe and the deployment of the SS-20 missile. Finally, I will put forward some tentative conclusions and recommendations for future research, again using Soviet regional forces as examples.

Scholarly attempts to explain the US–Soviet arms race in the wake of the 'missile gap' and the ABM debates of the 1960s resulted, by the end of that decade, in what James Kurth (1971) has called a 'thicket of theories'. Rational-actor models, favored in particular by economists and strategic analysts associated with the RAND Corporation,[1] came under fire from political scientists, mainly at Harvard University's Kennedy School of

---

* This chapter was originally published in *World Politics* (Evangelista, 1984) as a review of Berman & Baker (1982), Cockburn (1983), and Holloway (1983). It appears here in slightly edited form. I am grateful to Judith Reppy, Peter Katzenstein, and Myron Rush for helpful comments and criticism on earlier drafts of the essay. Reprinted with the permission of Princeton University Press. Copyright © 1984 by PUP.

Government, who focused on the role played by bureaucratic politics in determining US military developments (Allison, 1971; Halperin, 1974). Other observers thought US policy could be explained better with reference to a military-industrial complex (Barnet, 1972; Bottome, 1971; Melman, 1970). Related theories, set forth especially by European researchers, stressed the 'autistic' nature of military decision-making and, rejecting interpretations of rational actors responding to external threats, proposed instead models of an 'internal dynamic' (*Eigendynamik*) (Senghaas, 1972a). Kurth described the dilemma of choosing between such competing theories of weapons procurement as 'the problem of alternative causes or the problem of *a posteriori* overdetermination', and related it to the issue of level of analysis:

> In brief, *a posteriori*, the military policy is overdetermined by several alternative and analytically coequal explanations. The logical dynamic of the process of discovering or inventing alternative causes is to equalize explanations, to destroy degrees of validity among them, while not destroying the explanations themselves. We are left entangled within a thicket of theories. (Kurth, 1971, pp. 377–378)

As recent explanations of Soviet military policy resemble in many ways the analysis of US policy that preceded them, so too do they suffer from many of the same problems – not the least of which is overdetermination. One goal of this essay is to propose a possible means of coping with the problem of overdetermination in explanations of Soviet weapons procurement, by adopting an approach developed by Kurth. First, however, it is necessary to discuss the three books and how they relate to the earlier traditions.

Berman & Baker (1982) attempt what has become known in the literature as a 'requirements' of 'mission analysis' approach to explaining Soviet military policy.[2] This approach is generally considered apart from a rational-actor analysis, which posits cost-effective responses to objective threats. In a requirements approach, perceptions of threats are shaped by a country's specific history, geography, military traditions, and organizational structures. These factors in turn influence the nature of the response to external threats. Berman & Baker claim to have adopted this method of analysis (pp. 1–5); but, as I will attempt to demonstrate, their explanations more often resemble those of a rational-actor approach. In this regard, their analysis harks back to the early RAND studies of the vulnerability of the US Strategic Air Command (SAC) that spawned the bomber and missile gaps. The authors describe Soviet responses to existing US threats much as Albert Wohlstetter and others prescribed US responses to projected Soviet threats in the 1950s – as sensible, cost-effective, 'rational' responses based on objective 'threat assessment' (Wohlstetter et al., 1954). Furthermore, in discussing Soviet nuclear weapons doctrine, Berman & Baker often employ concepts that are not found in Soviet military writing on nuclear weapons (for example, the notions of 'strategic reserve' or 'theater reserve' forces, on pp. 19–21, 62–65, 130–132), but that are quite commonplace in the terminology developed at RAND for thinking about the unthinkable (Kaplan, 1983). Consideration of the factors that constitute a true requirements approach receives comparatively little attention.

Cockburn (1983) relies alternately on two competing types of explanation: a bureaucratic politics approach (emphasizing competition among military services and military-industrial interests), and a military-industrial complex approach (focusing on cooperation and collusion between military, political, and industrial interests). His work falls in the tradition of Graham Allison and Morton Halperin on the one hand, and of European peace researchers such as Dieter Senghaas and Johan Galtung on the other.

Holloway (1983) proposes a more complex explanation for Soviet military policy – one that incorporates aspects of the requirements and bureaucratic politics models but adds a historical dimension and an analysis based on study of the Soviet military 'research-production cycle'. The closest parallel among the earlier studies of US weapons policy is probably the work of Herbert York (1970, 1976), although in certain respects, Holloway's case studies of Soviet weapons decisions resemble studies of US weapons conducted by Allison, Frederic Morris (1975), Michael Armacost (1969), and others.

It should be noted that of the three works under consideration, only the Berman & Baker volume sets out directly to explain the Soviet Union's strategic posture.[3] Both Cockburn's book[4] and Holloway's[5] take broader approaches and cover a number of diverse issues. In focusing on the question of what drives the Soviet side of the arms race, I attempt to extract from the Cockburn and Holloway volumes explanatory approaches that the authors do not always make explicit.

2 Military Doctrine and Weapons Procurement

The distinction between military and political roles lies at the heart of the debate over the determinants of Soviet military policy. Strategic theories hold that the military is subordinate to the political leadership and does not exert autonomous influence on weapons procurement. Theories emphasizing bureaucratic politics or a military-industrial complex posit that weak political control over the military allows weapons to be produced that have no genuine strategic rationale. The requirements approach often neglects the broader political goals that influence military policies.

In principle, military doctrine defines the relationship between military and political leaders in the Soviet Union. Therefore, as a starting point for comparing the explanations for Soviet military policy offered by the three books, it is worth considering how each of them treats the relationship of Soviet military doctrine to weapons procurement.

According to Berman & Baker,

> In Soviet military writing the terms *military doctrine* and *military strategy* are used more precisely than in the West. Military doctrine, the highest level of military thinking, is dictated by the Communist party leadership as a set of official views about the types of warfare for which the Soviet military establishment must be prepared. Subordinate to Soviet doctrine are various levels of military thought, including military strategy, which develops the detailed organization, methods, and preparations for waging war. (1982, p. 24; emphasis in original)

The authors briefly mention 'broader purposes' for which Soviet doctrine and strategy may be intended, including their use

> in shaping public beliefs to conform with official thinking, [. . .] to influence the adversary's perceptions, [and] to rationalize away intractable problems and to promote various institutional interests. [. . .] Moreover, changes in Soviet statements on military doctrine and strategy may reveal the ideological, institutional, and technological influences that have shaped the Soviet Union's strategic posture. (p. 24)

Unfortunately, none of these broader purposes is explored throughout the rest of the book. Instead, the authors relate Soviet strategic posture to doctrine according to the formal definition: the political leaders determine the requirements of Soviet military forces on the basis of their perception of the foreign threat, and the military leaders carry out the political directives to meet that threat. The best summary of the explanation Berman & Baker provide for Soviet military developments is found in the subtitle of their book: Soviet military doctrine sets *requirements* for force posture, which are best explained as *responses* to foreign threats.

The requirements approach taken by Berman & Baker is in principle distinct from a rational-actor approach. Although not explicitly defined, it seems intended to take into consideration the role of military tradition and organization, geopolitical and historical factors, and perception of threat, whereas the rational-actor approach concerns itself only with threats and 'rational' responses to them.

Thus, Berman & Baker state at the start of their work that 'Soviet strategic forces are as much a product of military traditions as of changing circumstances' (p. 1). The argument here would seem to be that because the Soviet Union never had a tradition of strategic air power as did the United States, it never developed a strong strategic air command with a large fleet of intercontinental bombers. By contrast, the Soviet strategic posture derives from the fact that, as a land power, Russia had long emphasized artillery in its military policy; early Soviet interest in missiles, as opposed to bombers, should be understood in relation to the Russian artillery tradition. Indeed, the first Commander in Chief of the Strategic Rocket Forces, Marshal Nedelin, was a former artillery commander, and artillery officers have played a major role in shaping the missile forces.[6]

Berman & Baker mention, but do not fully develop, this notion (pp. 26, 47–48, 110). The concept seems particularly important for distinguishing a true-requirements approach (which explains an early emphasis on regional missiles) from a rational-actor approach (which does not explain why a regional posture should take preference over one that emphasizes intercontinental missiles, or even bombers, from the start).

Consistent with the military-requirements approach is a historical rationale for Soviet emphasis on regional systems. Berman & Baker argue that, 'historically, the most vital interests of and greatest threats to the USSR have been in neighboring areas. Hence the Soviet tendency – not fully appreciated in the United States – to attribute a strategic importance to its regional nuclear forces' (p. 2). The authors have in mind Russia's long history of invasions of its territory from both east and west; they mention in particular the impact that the German invasion of June 1941 had on Soviet military thinking (p. 22).

One wonders to what extent historical and military-traditional factors would have produced a similar Soviet regional nuclear policy in the absence of concrete threats – the formation of NATO and the deployment of US atomic bombers on bases surrounding the Soviet Union in the late 1940s, and the introduction of tactical nuclear weapons into Europe in the early 1950s. According to the requirements approach, such threats must be taken into consideration. In fact, however, by devoting relatively little attention to the organizational, military-traditional, and historical aspects of a requirements approach, Berman & Baker are left mainly with foreign threats as the basis for explaining Soviet military policy:

> In the past, Western actions have created or affected many basic requirements that have determined how the Soviet strategic forces would develop. [...] Clearly, [however,] the Soviet strategic force posture has developed not only in response to strategic developments in the United States and the countries adjoining the USSR. As part of a complex and interactive process, the USSR has sought to take account of external developments and develop a capability to counter them while attempting to fulfill its long-standing security requirements. (p. 72)

By providing only a superficial account of the 'complex and interactive process' by which threats are translated into security requirements, Berman & Baker make it difficult to distinguish 'long-standing security requirements' from rational-actor responses to external threats. It is not clear from their explanation, for example, that even if Russia throughout its history had never been invaded from the west, Soviet leaders would have responded any differently when faced in the 1950s with the threat of nuclear-armed aircraft on bases that encircled the USSR.

The authors try to explain the peculiarly Soviet nature of the response to external threat by attempting to understand Soviet targeting requirements. Once the targeting requirements are known (to the extent that is possible), the requirements approach differs little from the rational-actor approach.

An external threat causes a change in targeting requirement; the best means of fulfilling that requirement constitutes a 'rational' response.

The main problem in this exercise is arriving at an accurate understanding of Soviet targeting requirements. Berman & Baker infer Soviet targeting priorities from selected translations of Soviet military writings, from missile deployment locations, and from 'the presumed Soviet TVD [*teatry voennykh deistvii*, or theaters of military operations] planning framework' (p. 19, fn. 28). They come up with a list that, by including virtually everything, seems to provide little guidance:

> The broad list of requirements compiled by Soviet planners is likely to be composed of strategic nuclear targets, including missiles, submarines, strategic aircraft bases, naval bases, nuclear storehouses, and command-and-control centers; operational and tactical nuclear targets, including aircraft carriers, aircraft, cruise missiles and tactical missile deployments, tactical airfields, nuclear storage sites, and formations and reserves, logistical and fuel centers, naval bases and air defense bases and facilities; and administrative and economic targets, including critical industrial facilities, national administrative and political centers, transportation centers and ports, and centers of state administration. (p. 19)

In order to explain the appearance of a new Soviet weapon (or an apparent change in Soviet force structure), the authors speculate how their presumed list of Soviet targets may have changed as a result of foreign developments, and call the new Soviet weapon a response to those developments.

In contrast to Berman & Baker, Andrew Cockburn believes that foreign threats have rarely created requirements or generated responses that are helpful in explaining either Soviet or US military policies. With the exception of the development of Soviet interceptor aircraft as a counter to US strategic bombers, Cockburn finds 'very little evidence that either the Americans or the Russians have actually initiated research and development of a particular system in response to a move by the opposition'. On the contrary, 'the record indicates that the desire for the new weapon or a longer production line comes first; only afterward is the threat discovered that the weapon is supposed to meet' (1983, pp. 13–14). Thus,

> It may be that the military on either side is engaged not so much in an arms race as in simply doing what it wants to do for its own institutional reasons. The other side is relevant only in that it serves as a convenient excuse for these unilateral activities. (p. 12)

It should therefore come as no surprise that Cockburn's views of military doctrine are quite different from Berman & Baker's: 'Military doctrine tends to evolve in response to demands from generals for an excuse to justify whatever they happen to be interested in spending money on, and the Soviet marshals and generals are no exception' (p. 238).

Cockburn's approach here seems consistent with theories of the military-industrial complex (Aspaturian, 1973; McDonnell, 1975), and he specifically uses the US model as his point of comparison:

> Just as names like General Dynamics, Lockheed, and McDonnell Douglas are synonymous with American warplanes and missiles, so too the Russians have big-name defense contractors. They are called design bureaus and are named after the designers who originally set them up. [. . .] The relationship of these 'contractors' to their military customers and the manner in which the bureaus execute their contracts have many similarities with how American defense contractors conduct their business. (p. 79)

At times, Cockburn focuses more on bureaucratic competition between military services and between design bureaus than on cooperation within a complex. In any case, he argues that Soviet military policy can be explained better on the basis of these internal factors than as responses to external stimuli.

David Holloway's discussion of Soviet military doctrine indicates that he, too, believes that internal factors must be taken into account in order to understand Soviet military developments. He presents definitions of military doctrine (both its political and military-technical aspects), military science, and military art, as found in the official *Soviet Military Encyclopedia*, arguing that the formal definitions themselves 'are relevant to an understanding of Soviet policy making, for they express a definite conception of the proper relationship between political authority and professional military expertise' (1983, p. 30). In the 'proper relationship', the Party dominates the formulation of military doctrine. Holloway (1970, 1971) has found, however, that in the post-Khrushchev period the Soviet military has attempted to exert more influence on doctrine. Thus, 'these abstract definitions reflect a certain tension between Party and military prerogatives in Soviet military thought' (p. 31). Contrary to the emphasis in the Berman & Baker approach, Holloway maintains that

> Policy cannot be derived directly from military doctrine because doctrine is too general to do more than provide broad guidelines. Policy must be understood as the product of a political process, in which both low politics (bureaucratic infighting and struggles for power) and high politics (disagreement over the direction of policy or over its implementation) play their part. (p. 163)

Although Holloway's explanations resemble those of Cockburn in their emphasis on politics, his more detailed case studies of specific weapons developments also stress factors that are integral to a genuine requirements approach – organization of the research-production cycle, and the influence of military traditions and history.

3 Soviet Regional Forces and the Case of the SS-20

The emphasis that Berman & Baker place on Soviet regional requirements constitutes one of the most valuable contributions of their work, and holds considerable relevance for the current debate over nuclear weapons in Europe. In essence, the story they present is one of Soviet capabilities constantly lagging behind requirements and threats.

In response to the postwar atomic monopoly of the United States, the Soviets built up a system of air defenses (Berman, 1978; Evangelista, 1983) and accelerated programs for developing their own atomic weapons and delivery vehicles for carrying them. (See Holloway, 1983, ch. 2.) However, partly because of Stalin's unwillingness to allow even discussion of the role of nuclear weapons in modern warfare (perhaps because he thought it might discredit the 'permanently operating factors' he claimed to be responsible for the Soviet victory in World War II), Soviet troops received no nuclear weapons until after his death in 1953. The Soviets initially countered US air bases and military facilities in Europe with a fleet of Tu-4 bombers (copies of the US B-29) armed with conventional weapons. The first nuclear-capable bomber, the Tu-16, appeared in 1954. In 1959 the Soviets began deploying the SS-4 medium-range ballistic missile (MRBM), and two years later an intermediate-range system (IRBM), the SS-5. They deployed no new MRBMs or IRBMs until the SS-20 appeared in 1977. Berman & Baker argue that, throughout the postwar period, Soviet regional nuclear forces never successfully met the threat posed by US and NATO aircraft, cruise and ballistic missiles, and nuclear artillery.

The SS-4 and SS-5 missiles were particularly unreliable, requiring unstable liquid-fuel propellants; they were deployed at vulnerable, 'soft' sites rather than in hardened underground silos, and needed 8 to 24 hours to prepare for firing. Their vulnerability was increased dramatically, according to Berman & Baker, when the United States began deploying 'quick-reacting and highly survivable Polaris missiles [that] could effectively strike both Soviet regional nuclear missiles and strategic bomber bases' (1982, p. 59).

In the mid-1960s, the Soviets attempted to remedy these problems by developing the medium-range SS-14 and intermediate-range SS-15 missiles: both employed mobile launch systems (to decrease vulnerability), and solid-fuel propellants (to improve 'reaction time'). However, the Nadiradze design bureau that was charged with developing the missiles had considerable difficulty producing a satisfactory solid-fuel system (pp. 90–91), and neither missile was ever put into series production. Berman & Baker argue that because of this major technical failure, coupled with an increasing threat, the Soviets were forced in the late 1960s to adopt a 'quick-fix' solution to their regional security requirements. Their answer was to divert the variable-range SS-11 missile, apparently designed originally for maritime use (against US carriers with nuclear-armed aircraft), for employment as part of the regional force. By the early 1970s, some 120 SS-11 missiles were deployed in SS-4 and SS-5 missile fields in the western USSR, and another 200 or so along the Sino-Soviet border (pp. 60, 111, 122).

Berman & Baker believe that the SS-11 solution might have gone far toward fulfilling Soviet regional requirements but for the fact that deployment of the missiles was constrained by the SALT treaties. Although the Soviet Union had pressed from the beginning for inclusion of regional nuclear forces in the strategic arms talks, the United States was unwilling to discuss its forward-based systems in Europe, or the British and French nuclear forces (Sharp, 1982). Thus, Berman & Baker maintain, the Soviets were forced to develop a system specifically intended to fulfill the regional role that the SS-11s had satisfied. That system – the SS-20 IRBM – is the Soviets' first successful solid-fuel missile. It has been deployed with three independently targetable warheads (MIRVs), and is considered mobile (although it must be launched from pre-surveyed sites). Berman & Baker termed the SS-20 'a long overdue follow-on to the vulnerable SS-4 and SS-5 missiles', one that has gone a long way toward meeting Soviet regional requirements (p. 67). Nevertheless, the authors foresaw increases in Soviet requirements generated by NATO's deployment of Pershing II and ground-launched cruise missiles (p. 71).

By contrast, Cockburn does not interpret the emergence of the SS-20 as a rational response to US and NATO nuclear threats, although he, too, presents the technical failures of the SS-14 and SS-15 as part of his explanation. He accounts for the SS-20 in a manner consistent with a military-industrial complex approach. In essence, he argues that the SS-20 should be understood primarily as a means of keeping the Nadiradze design bureau in business, pointing out that the bureau 'has been trying and failing to build a solid-fueled ICBM for twenty years' (1983, p. 87). Its first attempt was the SS-13, which was considered a counterpart to the US Minuteman missile; only 60 were produced because of serious technical problems. Next came the mobile SS-14 and SS-15 missiles, derived from the SS-13, which were also unsuccessful. The SS-16 was the Nadiradze bureau's most recent try at developing a solid-fueled mobile ICBM. It has been flight-tested only once since 1975, and unsuccessfully at that (p. 200). This missile was such a failure that the Soviets were willing to bargain it away as part of the SALT II treaty.[7] Cockburn describes the sequence leading to the SS-20:

> Nadiradize [sic] and the strategic rocket forces did manage to salvage something of their reputation from the SS-16 debacle. By removing the third stage of the SS-16, they had a missile that could manage a flight of 3000 miles – not enough for the serious business of intercontinental warfare but sufficient for use against targets in Western Europe and China. There was a market for such a missile because the medium-range SS-4s and SS-5s, which had first been installed in their silos in the late 1950s, were, in the words of one report, 'crumbling in their silos'. (p. 201)

Thus, Cockburn's explanation for the SS-20 is the Soviet version of the 'bail-out imperative' that James Kurth (1973) has identified as a factor influencing the procurement of US aerospace weapons. According to

Cockburn, the SS-20 was needed to satisfy the parochial interests of the Nadiradze design bureau and its military backers in the Strategic Rocket Forces – to find a 'market' for their 'product'.

Holloway's explanation for the deployment of Soviet regional nuclear forces follows that of Berman & Baker fairly closely. Regarding the SS-20, for example, he discusses the problems inherent in the Soviet regional nuclear force, the exclusion of regional systems from SALT negotiations, and the advantages presented by the modern SS-20; he suggests that 'the case for deployment must have seemed overwhelming' (1983, p. 70). He also makes an important point about Western interpretations of Soviet policy and the extent to which they determined the reaction to the SS-20:

> Western governments appear to have regarded the Soviet SS-4s and SS-5s as no more than a stopgap, intended to hold Western Europe hostage until an effective intercontinental force was deployed. Because of this misunderstanding, they did not anticipate the deployment of new systems, now that the Soviet Union possessed powerful strategic forces capable of striking the United States. The new systems, therefore, have been interpreted not as a follow-on to the older ones, but as part of a Soviet attempt to tilt the balance of power in its favor by making NATO strategy unworkable. (p. 71)

The notion of 'competition in strategies' that Holloway introduces is a particularly important one. Whereas Berman & Baker stress only the new NATO weapons that threatened the force of SS-4s and SS-5s during the mid-1960s, Holloway emphasizes the impact of the new NATO strategy of 'flexible response' as well. He recounts how

> Soviet ideas about a war in Europe began to change in the late 1960s as a result of NATO's shift towards a strategy of flexible response, which envisages the possibility that war in Europe may begin with a conventional phase. The Soviet Union did not wish to be tied into an inflexible one-variant strategy of its own, and accordingly adjusted its policy to prepare for non-nuclear as well as nuclear operations in Europe. Since a European conflict might go nuclear at any time, flexible weapons, which could be fired quickly, were required. The SS-4s and SS-5s did not meet this requirement. (p. 69)

Holloway suggests that Soviet leaders view the planned deployment of new Pershing II and cruise missiles in combination with strategies for 'limited nuclear options' (the Schlesinger Doctrine and Presidential Directive 59) with the same (or greater) concern they evinced in response to changes in NATO weapons and strategies in the 1960s. He concludes that 'what has been taking place between NATO and the Warsaw Pact is not only a competition in arms, but also – and perhaps more importantly – a competition in strategies' (p. 72).

In discussing Soviet regional nuclear policies, Holloway touches on an important point that he develops more thoroughly in his chapter on Soviet thinking about nuclear war: the distinction between military responsibility for preparing for wars, and political responsibility for deterring them. The point is brought out in the author's discussion of Nikita Khrushchev's views on Soviet regional nuclear forces. Evidently the Soviet leader saw his medium-range missiles not only as military weapons, but as a deterrent broadly conceived. He maintained, for example, that the threat of nuclear destruction by Soviet missiles would keep France and Britain from joining the United States in a war over Berlin (p. 67). Moreover, Khrushchev's use of 'missile diplomacy' to support broad foreign policy goals is well documented (Horelick & Rush, 1966).

Holloway's analysis of Soviet regional forces suggests that it is important to consider the role of the top political leadership in certain types of decisions regarding Soviet force posture – particularly decisions related to broader foreign policy goals or requiring major changes in strategy. At the same time, he has identified other important factors – organizational, bureaucratic, historical – that are also emphasized by the other authors. It may therefore be argued that the level of analysis at which one studies Soviet military policy affects the nature of the explanations one derives. If all the relevant levels of analysis are considered, the result – as Kurth suggests – is overdetermination. It does seem possible, however, to study Soviet policy in such a way as to mitigate the level-of-analysis problem and to arrive at general conditions under which one type of explanation would be more appropriate than another. The issue of overdetermination would thereby be rendered less problematic.

4 Levels of Analysis and Types of Explanation

Not all phenomena are best explained with reference to a single level of analysis. Even explanations for a particular category of phenomena, such as decisions regarding Soviet weapons procurement, would seem to benefit from a more eclectic approach. The problem lies in deciding at which point a given level of analysis provides a more explanatory power than another. Students of international political economy have found it useful to consider the relationship between – and the relative strengths of – state and society as one way of helping to determine the appropriate level of analysis, and thus the most important explanatory factors for a given phenomenon.[8] In this section, I will first describe the level-of-analysis problem as it appears in the books under review. I will then consider the applicability of a state-society approach to the level-of-analysis problem in explanations of Soviet weapons decision-making. Finally, I will address the related problem of overdetermination by employing the taxonomy developed by Kurth for analyzing US weapons procurement.

Berman & Baker, after collapsing historical, military-traditional, and organizational factors into a Soviet target list, explain Soviet weapons decisions at the international level by assessing threats. This method has certain shortcomings when the authors are trying to explain weapons that seem redundant in terms of their missions. For example, even with their long Soviet target list, they can explain the fact that the SS-18 and SS-19 missiles seem to offer redundant capabilities only by arguing that the latter missile constitutes 'an additional hedge' (1982, p. 125). In this case, it might make more sense to focus on the level of the Soviet leadership, and observe, as Holloway does, the extent to which Soviet leaders are committed to numerical parity with the United States in nuclear forces. (See his ch. 3.) Such a policy, in the context of an ongoing arms race, would by definition eventually lead to redundancies. In order to maintain 'parity', the Soviets may feel obliged to match quantitative changes in US force posture, such as increases in warheads, even if these do not necessarily represent developments of great strategic significance. For example, an increase in the number of warheads on existing US missiles (through MIRVing) that does not add anything to the Soviet target list or render Soviet forces appreciably more vulnerable might engender a Soviet response for which a requirements explanation could not fully account.

Likewise, by relying only on the requirements approach, Berman & Baker would have trouble explaining the Soviet Union's current interest in developing modern ground-launched cruise missiles. Recent Soviet tests of such missiles indicate a 'requirement' that the authors do not recognize in their book.[9] That requirement, as Cockburn suggests, could be a political one – the perceived need to match the latest products of US technology, regardless of their utility in the Soviet context or of whether the technology in itself is effective. (See esp. pp. 134–137, 148–149, 154–155.)

In his explanations, David Holloway discusses a number of levels of analysis: the international system for evidence of threats; the overall Soviet economic system for allocation of resources; the research-production cycle for processes of weapons innovation and procurement; factors at the organizational level; and the influence of technology and history. He maintains that 'one reason why a historical perspective is important is that Soviet policy is not easily explained by the theoretical models of the arms race to be found in the social science literature' (1983, p. 178). Since Holloway has considered such models as 'action-reaction' and the 'autistic' or *Eigendynamik* (internal dynamic) approach in the current work and in earlier articles (Holloway, 1974, 1980), his contention seems well supported. It still, however, begs the question which factors are more important under which conditions.

Since Cockburn, in his 'theoretical model', borrows from the bureaucratic-politics and military-industrial-complex approaches, he looks mainly at the level of the military service and the design bureau for his explanations; he therefore finds the determinants of Soviet weapons decisions to lie in the competition between or cooperation among them. At times, he considers the higher level of the political leadership in order to explain the broad contours of Soviet military policy, but only by relating them to personal power struggles – for example, Brezhnev favored heavy industry and military production in order to gain military allies and win out over Kosygin, who supported consumer industries and cuts in the military budget.

For particular military procurement decisions and even major changes in force structure, Cockburn relies on an analysis at the level of bureaucratic politics. This type of explanation does not always work. In order to challenge the image of a monolithic Soviet military carrying out the dictates of the Party, Cockburn discusses the extent to which the Air Defense branch of the Soviet armed forces opposed the 1972 US–Soviet treaty limiting antiballistic missile systems – which was the responsibility of the Air Defense Command (p. 223). The fact that the ABM treaty was signed anyway, and the Air Defense budget was reduced, suggests, however, that in this case Cockburn's bureaucratic explanation is insufficient. The Air Defense forces are considered a separate branch of the Soviet armed forces, ranked third in the hierarchy (ahead of the Navy and Air Force); according to a bureaucratic-politics or military-industrial-complex argument, they should have won the ABM debate (Jones, 1981). The fact that the Soviet ABM was unsuccessful should not have mattered – as Cockburn argues, Soviet military bureaucracies are particularly adept at obtaining their desired weapons, whether or not they work. By the same token, Cockburn's assertion that the expansion of the Soviet fleet during the past decade or so can be attributed to the bureaucratic machinations of its commander, Admiral Gorshkov, is unconvincing when one considers the weak bureaucratic position of the Navy within the military and the government. Explanations based on the expanding requirements of the Soviet Navy (put forth by Western analysts) or the utility of a blue-water navy in supporting broader foreign policy goals would seem more accurate.[10]

Although the comparative perspective Cockburn has adopted – studying the Soviet military-industrial-complex with reference to the United States – can engender useful insights, it can be taken too far. There is no reason to believe, for example, that the situation that obtains in the USA – a weak state penetrated by a strong society – is duplicated in the Soviet Union. In fact, the United States appears to occupy an extreme position in its relationship of weak state to strong society, and it seems likely that the Soviet Union represents the other extreme (Brzezinski & Huntington, 1963; Katzenstein, 1978). Such a generalization should not be used to solve all problems associated with explaining Soviet weapons procurement. Nevertheless, it seems helpful in dealing with the problem of overdetermination, especially when considered in tandem with an approach Kurth (1971) developed for overcoming the analogous US problem.

Kurth attempted to cut through the 'thicket of theories' used to explain US military procurement, and to resolve the problem of overdetermination. His approach was to posit 'modes of change' and relate them to 'modes of causation' for application to types of weapons decisions and stages in the processes of research, development, and procurement. Specifically, Kurth found that four modes of change – quantitative, innovative, renovative, and redistributive – fit four modes of causation – bureaucratic politics, bureaucratic process, bureaucratic-corporate alliances, and the economic system. It is not surprising, in light of the state-society approach discussed above, that Kurth should find bureaucratic forces most important for determining decisions on weapons procurement in the United States – a country with a relatively weak state apparatus and strong interest groups.

Only detailed research will reveal how useful Kurth's taxonomy is for understanding Soviet developments (more research is necessary to assess its validity for US developments as well). At this time, it is worth attempting a tentative application in the context of Soviet regional forces.[11] Although Kurth's categories of change seem relevant to the Soviet case, his modes of causation do not always apply; indeed, those for the Soviet weapons procurement process are often the opposite of those for the US. Again, this conclusion is what a state-society analysis would predict.

For example, in Kurth's category 'innovative change' he argues that 'because an innovative change is unfamiliar and sometimes inexpensive, it normally begins not in a decision at the higher levels of policymaking and budget-making but in technical and organizational procedures for research and development. At this initial point, some sort of technocratic explanation seems best' (1971, pp. 396–397).[12] To go from research and development to production and deployment, Kurth argues, probably requires bureaucratic momentum and 'strategic fears'. He therefore divides innovative change into two stages: the first relies on a technocratic explanation, while the second emphasizes bureaucratic forces. This distinction is perhaps not necessary. If weapons designers want to promote technical innovations, they must act much as any other bureaucrat and contribute to the process of generating strategic fears.[13]

In the Soviet system, the situation is quite different; in fact, it is almost the reverse, as Holloway indicates:

> Soviet military R & D in the post-war period can be seen as the effort of a basically non-innovative system to cope with revolutionary technological change, which has been generated primarily by the Soviet Union's potential enemies. [. . .] Major innovation decisions cannot easily be handled within the standard operating procedure of the military R & D system, and require intervention from the top to authorize new funding and new institutional arrangements. (1983, pp. 148–149).

Thus, political intervention (based on strategic fears or technological opportunities) is necessary to generate bureaucratic momentum and to stimulate innovation. It is true that Soviet weapons designers have proposed innovative developments on their own initiative – particularly in some areas of aircraft and radar technology – but the successful implementation of their proposals has usually required strong political (and not simply bureaucratic) backing.[14] In the context of the Soviet regional forces, an important stimulus for research and development of rocket technology came from Germany during World War II, and top political support was crucial for developing ballistic missiles during the early postwar period (Holloway, 1977, 1982).

The next stage in the development of Soviet regional forces in the postwar period could fall into Kurth's rubric of 'redistributive change', (Kurth, 1971, pp. 399–400). Although in the US context Kurth has in mind primarily redistribution of economic rewards among industrial sectors, his examples find a close Soviet analogue in Khrushchev's creation of the Strategic Rocket Forces in late 1959 and the large-scale change from production of aircraft at aviation industry plants to production of medium-range missiles.[15] Clearly, the impetus for this type of change in the Soviet military posture meets Kurth's requirements of being 'both unusual in kind and general in scope'. As Berman & Baker recount, the major deployment of US nuclear weapons systems around the periphery of the Soviet Union during the early postwar years fits this description.

Kurth terms another type of change 'renovative'. In its 'pure form', it is defined as 'the production and deployment of a weapons system whose technical characteristics are generally familiar, whose strategic implications are generally minor, whose production renovates an established aerospace organization' (Kurth, 1971, p. 397). In the Soviet case, the deployment of the SS-20 seems to conform to this definition quite well. Its MIRV technology was certainly familiar, as was its solid-fuel propulsion system (albeit due to years of unsuccessful development). As Cockburn reminds us, the SS-20 served to renovate the flagging Nadiradze 'corporation' as well as the regional component of the Strategic Rocket Forces. And, although the strategic implications for the SS-20 were deemed anything but minor by NATO officials, there is reason to believe that when the Soviets first made the decision to deploy the SS-20, they perceived the system mainly as a follow-on and did not expect that type of response (Garthoff, 1980–81, 1983).

Kurth argues that for renovative change to occur in the absence of a major strategic threat, the proponent of the new weapons system must mobilize many allies in industry, government, and so forth. In the presence of a threat, 'bureaucratic–corporate alliances can be rendered unnecessary by bureaucratic–strategic anxieties. Whether this happens seems to be a function of the relative bureaucratic power of the nurturing military organization' (Kurth, 1971, p. 398). The Strategic Rocket Forces represent one of the strongest bureaucratic powers in the Soviet military. Furthermore, as Berman & Baker point out, the threat or requirement that the SS-20s were expected to meet was a longstanding one. Finally, it was not necessary to rally great support among the design bureaus or military industries because the Strategic Rocket Forces already had the candidate weapon – the two-stage version of the SS-16, which became the SS-20.

The case of the SS-20 also serves to illustrate Kurth's remaining category, that of 'quantitative change'. In the United States, Kurth (1971, pp. 400–401) argues, such change depends mainly on bureaucratic–corporate alliances. During an era of negotiated arms control agreements, this explanation does not adequately account for Soviet developments, however. One US participant in the SALT negotiations argues, for example, that at certain times the levels of Soviet missile deployments seemed quite sensitive to the political requirements of the arms control negotiators and were used as 'signals' of Soviet intentions.[16]

Do Soviet arms control proposals regarding the SS-20 reflect a similar process at work? Holloway suggests that the various proposals put forward by Brezhnev between October 1979 and March 1982 to limit Soviet regional nuclear forces in return for cancellation of the NATO decision to deploy Pershing II and cruise missiles were designed to maintain a large Soviet nuclear force targeted against Europe; they probably did not entail cutting back the amount of SS-20s deployed (pp. 76–78). At this stage one could argue, as Berman & Baker do, that military requirements demanded a large force regardless of NATO's decisions on further deployments, and that such deployments would call forth an even larger Soviet force as a response. Or one could imagine, as Cockburn does, that a bureaucratic–corporate alliance of the type described by Kurth was formed between the Strategic Rocket Forces and the Nadiradze bureau in order to press the political leadership not to limit the numbers of SS-20s deployed. At a later stage, however, if the Soviet leadership were more interested in obtaining an arms control agreement with the United States than in satisfying the desires of its military services and design bureaus, the 'bureaucratic–corporate alliance' explanation would no longer serve. Before breaking off negotiations in response to deployment of new US missiles in Europe, the Soviets indicated a willingness to negotiate a substantial reduction in the number of SS-20s deployed (in return for cancellation of the NATO deployment), although presumably neither the military 'requirement' nor the interest of the Nadiradze bureau in having its missile produced and deployed in great quantities had decreased.[17] Thus, when considering quantitative change, one must keep in mind the stage at which the quantitative decisions are being made, and whether the weapons under consideration are the subject of arms control negotiations.

5 Conclusion

In the above analysis, I have attempted to apply James Kurth's four 'modes of change' to Soviet weapons procurement in the context of the development of Soviet regional forces. Some tentative conclusions emerge: First, the 'modes of causation' for Soviet developments differ considerably from those Kurth identified in US weapons procurement, with a greater emphasis on political intervention and strategic threats and opportunities as the stimuli for Soviet decisions, and a lesser role for bureaucratic factors. Second, it is important to distinguish stages within each type of change; the sequence and characteristics of the stages may differ in the US and Soviet cases.

An analysis drawing on Kurth and informed by consideration of relative strengths of state and society would suggest that, for innovative change to occur in the United States, technocratic impulses must lead to bureaucratic momentum, which must be followed by the generation of strategic fears. In the Soviet case, strategic fears or technological opportunities lead to political intervention, which generates bureaucratic momentum and innovation. This interpretation seems consistent with the role that political leaders are supposed to play in the formation of Soviet military doctrine as formally defined. Although these conclusions are only tentative generalizations and can hardly serve to explain all US and Soviet weapons procurement decisions, they do seem to hold some value for comparative purposes. Further research is required to test and refine these general observations.

For conducting such research, the analysis presented here suggests the importance of applying a particular framework (such as that developed by Kurth) to the study of weapons procurement decisions, in order to begin to specify conditions under which certain factors are more likely than others to influence the decision-making process. Identification of these factors, and the conditions under which they are most relevant, will serve as a guide to the proper level of analysis on which to focus, and will help to mitigate the problem of overdetermination.

The three books discussed here provide important insights into the factors that influence Soviet decisions concerning weapons procurement. They demonstrate that much can be learned of specific cases of weapons development, production, and deployment by applying analyses based on military requirements, bureaucratic politics, organizational structures and processes, and historical factors. Two tasks of future research in this area might be the following: first, it would be useful to propose a framework for analyzing weapons decisions that will suggest generalized conditions under which particular factors come into play. A second step would be to undertake parallel studies of particular Soviet weapons decisions in order to make generalizations about sequences in decision-making and the relative weights of different types of determinants at different stages of the process. This kind of research can make an important contribution to understanding the main influences on Soviet military policy – influences that must be understood better if the dangers posed by the current arms race are to be addressed.

Notes

1. An excellent study of the RAND strategists – including, among others, Thomas Schelling, Herman Kahn, and Albert Wohlstetter – and the best work on the evolution of US nuclear policy is Kaplan (1983).

2. The best work using the requirements approach has been done by Michael MccGwire, particularly on Soviet naval policy. See his articles in Royal United Services Institution (1970); MccGwire (1973, 1980, 1981); MccGwire et al. (1975). Another good example is Garthoff (1983).

3. Although Berman & Baker do not fulfill their promise of providing a true requirements analysis, they display a number of compensating strengths. The authors deserve a good deal of credit for their attempt to present a relatively parsimonious explanation for Soviet strategic

posture, and also for the amount of detailed information they have compiled on characteristics of Soviet strategic weapons design and deployment. In addition, they provide useful material on US and NATO nuclear weapons deployments, which they see as having greatly influenced Soviet developments. The book – particularly the many informative tables and charts found in the appendices – constitutes a valuable source of reference for researchers in the field of US and Soviet military policy.

4. Cockburn's book is a highly readable and carefully researched work, written with one primary intention: to counteract the practice of 'threat inflation' by which some US military and government officials greatly exaggerate Soviet military strength in order to rationalize procurement of the new weapons they favor. Cockburn focuses on four aspects of the Soviet military: the 'hordes', or regular conscript army; the 'professional warriors', or officer corps; the 'weapons makers'; and the weapons themselves. For the purposes of this essay, the most relevant sections of Cockburn's book are those in which he discusses the politics of the Soviet High Command, the process by which new weapons are procured, and the characteristics of those weapons.

5. Holloway's book covers a number of topics, including the role of military power in the formation of the Soviet state; the early Soviet nuclear weapons program; Soviet thinking on nuclear war; the role of military power in Soviet foreign policy; Soviet arms control policies; the structure of military research and development; and the role of military production in the Soviet economy. This volume is especially valuable in that it brings together the results of Holloway's many years of research into Soviet military policy in a form more accessible – particularly to non-specialists – than his original articles and chapters in various books.

6. See the biography by Tolubko (1979). Holloway points out that the officers of the Strategic Rocket Forces 'have tended to see their missiles as extensions of artillery, not as pilotless bombers'. He suggest that the artillery concept of 'operation in depth' may account somewhat for early Soviet emphasis on regional missiles by encouraging 'Soviet designers to concentrate on extending the range of their rockets step by step, thus increasing gradually the Soviet capability to launch deep strikes against the enemy' (p. 153).

7. Cockburn has covered this issue in some detail in articles in the *Columbia Journalism Review*, 21 (July–August 1982), and the *New York Times*, 27 April 1982; see also Talbott (1980, pp. 133–135).

8. Most notably, Katzenstein (1978); see especially his introduction and conclusion.

9. See the Associated Press report on the SS-CX-4 in the *Washington Post*, 7 April 1983; see also Arkin (1983).

10. The expanding-requirements argument is MccGwire's (see references in note 2), while the foreign-policy rationale has been put forth by Gorshkov (1979).

11. For the purposes of this chapter, the order in which Kurth discussed his 'modes of change' will not be followed, so as to permit a chronological presentation of the Soviet cases.

12. Innovation is made even less expensive when weapons manufacturers are reimbursed by the government for unsolicited, 'independent' research and development costs (Reppy, 1976, 1977).

13. I am grateful to Judith Reppy for bringing this point to my attention. A good example of a weapon designer's engaging in bureaucratic politics in order to promote his product is provided by the inventor of the 'neutron bomb', Samuel Cohen (1983).

14. On radar developments, see the memoirs of a former Soviet radar designer Fedoseev (1976), and Erickson (1977). On aircraft, see the memoirs of Iakovlev (1966).

15. See Khrushchev's speech, *Pravda*, 15 January 1960, and his remarks in his memoirs (1974).

16. See Garthof (1975, esp. pp. 30–32). For a further discussion of the influence of arms control negotiations on military posture, see Sharp (1979).

17. For details of Soviet and US proposals, see the monthly *Arms Control Reporter* (Brookline, MA: Institute for Defense and Disarmament Studies).

MATTHEW EVANGELISTA, b. 1958, Ph.D. in Political Science (Cornell University); Assistant Professor of Political Science, University of Michigan; author of *Innovation and the Arms Race. How the United States and the Soviet Union Develop New Military Technologies* (Cornell University Press, 1988); current main research interests: sources of moderation in Soviet security policies and prospects for East–West cooperation.

Chapter 17

Economy, Power, and the Arms Race*

RAIMO VÄYRYNEN

Department of Political Science, University of Helsinki

1 Dimensions of Militarization

Arms races may be studied on subnational, national, or systemic levels. Research on subnational aspects of arms races usually focuses on development, production, and acquisition of weapons systems. The state-centred approach is geared to account for interactive dynamics in competitive weapons-acquisition decisions by major powers. Finally, the systemic approach is primarily interested in the military aspect of the world-system structure or in the historical fluctuations of military capabilities in that system.

The state-centred approach may rely on either domestic or external factors in explaining the arms race process, while the systemic approach largely neglects domestic factors. The present study focuses, in the first place, on the *systemic* and *historical* aspects of arms races. Analysing arms races only as a systemic phenomenon is misleading, however. That is why such an approach has to consider also linkages with the state level as well as its constraints on and opportunities for the arms races.

Arms races may be operationalized in two broad ways: either by considering major weapons systems as their building blocks, or by paying attention to the economic and human resources they absorb. A focus on weapons systems implies primary interest in specific military technologies, political decisions to acquire them, and strategic objectives guiding their employment. Such analysis treats weapons systems either as products of antecedent political, economic, and technological dynamics or as causes of a variety of domestic and international consequences.

A focus on specific weapons technologies often leads to emphasis on the subnational factors. In part, this is justified, as domestic factors provide a necessary explanation of the arms build-up. However, technology cannot be treated as a domestic factor: it transcends both national and cultural boundaries. In consequence, military technologies should not be assessed only by such narrow criteria as their costs and performance; instead, they

---

* I am grateful to Nils Petter Gleditsch and to Robert Schaeffer (Editor, *Nuclear Times*, Washington, DC) for detailed substantial and editorial comments on an earlier draft of this chapter.

should be understood as technical artefacts of a particular era as well. Military technologies reflect the social values and interests of the era as well as the level of scientific and technical development of societies which have produced them.

Major technological systems have a degree of autonomy that allows them to reshape social reality and create new 'forms of life'. Nuclear energy and major weapons are examples of technologies fostering particular types of social and political arrangements that are hierarchical and centralized rather than decentralized (Winner, 1986). Weapons systems express the technical constitution of societies in which they are developed, and transform national and international political arrangements.

Major weapons systems are introduced into operational use at irregular intervals, reflecting discontinuities in military-technological decisions. But the long lead-times needed in the development and procurement of weapons systems and the political-corporate follow-on imperative introduce an underlying logic of continuity in the arms races (see Kurth, 1973; Kaldor, 1986). Arms race continuities and discontinuities can be explored either by focusing on the introduction of major weapons systems to the arsenals, or by resorting to time-series information on national military capabilities. The latter approach provides a more systematic picture of historical fluctuations, while the development and deployment decisions of major weapons may reveal more about critical turning points in the technological aspects of arms races.

Measuring of national military effort is a complicated task. Military expenditures, and their share of the GNP or of government spending, are an appropriate measure of the opportunity costs of arms races. True, these indicators may not tell much of military innovations or the military capabilities and political intentions behind them. All the same, measuring military effort as a fraction of GNP appears the best single indicator of overall military allocation. One should bear in mind, however, that this method has shortcomings in historical and comparative cross-section analyses of militarization (Goertz & Diehl, 1986). I rely primarily on economic indicators of the arms race but, in the absence of reliable data, also use troop strengths, and weaponry may be used to describe the extent and dynamics of arms competition.

This chapter deals specifically with the *long waves of economic development* and *power transitions* as potential systemic explanations of arms races. The focus on economic cycles and power transitions links two different strands of research. Economic cycles reflect the development logic of the world economy and can only in part be reduced to the performance of individual national economies. Power transitions are based on a more state-centred model in which major powers have a prominent position. Economic cycles and power transitions provide potential explanations of arms races, but only in combination with national and subnational factors. In addition, cycles and transitions may be used to periodize history. Periodization suggests possible turning points in historical development and may help in the search for qualitative changes in international relations.

2 Long Waves and Arms Races

Historically, economic constraints have shaped the level and intensity of military efforts. Without a sufficient military-industrial base, the domestic development and procurement of arms are not possible. The international armaments industry has always been hierarchically organized, reflecting the asymmetries in the international economic division of labour. Advanced civilian and military technologies of each historical period are controlled by a few leading corporations of the core countries. The more advanced the technology, the fewer the number of states and corporations with access to it. From these centres, weapons systems and military technologies have radiated, either through arms transfers or various types of licence agreements, to semiperipheral and peripheral countries. (For a more extended analysis, see Neumann, 1984.)

The acquisition of national military power is thus constrained by that state's position in the global core–periphery structure. This is evidenced by the high correlations between the military expenditures and the GNP of individual countries; the greater the economic capability of a state, the more military power it acquires. Traditionally, the connection between economic and military power has often been interpreted as a deliberate policy pursued by economically powerful states to discipline weaker nations by the use or threat of military power (Baran & Sweezy, 1966). The heavy military burdens of major powers can also be explained by their political and economic rivalries pushing them to build up their military capabilities. Almost invariably, then, major powers are trapped in extensive military spending, while the resources of small countries are so scarce that they can never acquire a military potential to match the military capabilities of leading states.

The core–periphery structure of the world economy shapes the distribution of military capabilities between states and provides a static approximation of it. Any deviations of individual countries from the core–periphery pattern in the distribution of military capabilities can be observed and submitted to further theoretical and empirical scrutiny. The inclusion of economic cycles and power transitions lends a dynamic complement to static structural analysis. The static and dynamic structural parameters define the macrocontext in which states make their decisions on military allocations and the acquisition of weapons systems.

Long waves of capitalist development, or Kondratiev cycles, are directly related to economic opportunities to and constraints on the acquisition of military capabilities. During the boom phase of the long cycle, the overall prosperity of national economies increases, and more funds accumulate in state coffers. Such funds may be used to support economic and military expansion, characteristic of the upswing phases of long economic cycles. During these phases there are economic opportunities to accumulate more military capabilities, which in turn are further justified by the needs of external expansion.

An economic upswing directly releases resources for military uses, and affects military allocations. The long waves of capitalist development are often interpreted in the context of a capital investment theory which postulates that massive investments are made in capital goods during the boom phase, while capital is depreciated during the bust phase. Thus, 'the essence of every economic cycle, caused by fluctuations in investment, is the overshooting and undershooting of capital-goods production' (van Duijn, 1983, p. 144; see also Gordon, 1980, pp. 26–31). An attractive feature of this capital investment theory of long cycles is its endogenous character which distinguishes their economic dynamics from political and military consequences. Among its shortcomings is that it neglects the possibility of technological development spawning new civilian and military products and production techniques (van Duijn, 1983, pp. 122–124).

The capital or infrastructural investment theory of long economic cycles is relevant for analysing arms races. Industrial revolutions have made weapons systems bigger and more complex, requiring increased resources for their development and production. This development has been pronounced since the late 19th century. The increasing complexity and versatility of weapons systems has been inextricably linked with technological change. In fact, technology has gradually substituted complexity of weapons systems for their mere size. Complexity has been assumed to improve the technical performance of weapons and to help dominate the adversary. In reality, there has been a trade-off between quality and quantity and, perhaps more importantly, between reliability and complexity of weapons systems (see Fallows, 1982).

Joseph A. Schumpeter (1939, 1978) linked long waves of economic development to technological innovations. During the period of economic stagnation, old technological solutions and production structures lose their ability to generate new demand. New technological innovations are needed to overcome the crisis. For Schumpeter, innovations meant the 'setting up of a new production function'. Economic development is not a smooth process, but is a result of movements and countermovements within society. That is why 'new development proceeds from different conditions and in part from the actions of different people; many old hopes and values are buried forever, wholly new ones arise'. In the Schumpeterian perspective, the 'creative destruction' of old production structures is a precondition for the shift of an economy to a new upsurge (Schumpeter, 1939, pp. 84–86, and 1978, pp. 65–68, 216–219).

Technological innovations and reorganization of production appear 'discontinuously in groups or swarms' at the bottom of the economic upswing. Such swarms of innovations are generated by risk-taking entrepreneurs investing funds in capital-goods-producing industrial plants. In that way, new purchasing power and new markets are gradually created. In time, technological innovations begin to wear out: the market contracts, entrepreneurial profits decline, and unemployment increases (Schumpeter, 1939, pp. 102–109, and 1978, pp. 223–232). Empirical evidence supports the view that 'an upturn tends to dampen innovation, while a downturn in production stimulates innovation' (Goldstein, 1988, pp. 219–225). There is also contrary evidence to the statement that innovations cluster to the long-wave depression phases (Solomou, 1988, pp. 89–100).

The Schumpeterian approach contains two important observations. First, it pinpoints that economic cycles are not always reproductive (that the downturn is reversed endogenously), but may also be non-reproductive, requiring basic changes in the socio-political framework of the accumulation process. If the cycle is non-reproductive, society may have to undergo a political crisis before the economic downturn can be reversed (see Gordon et al., 1983). In such a crisis, the old and new social structures, and their agents, are pitted against each other. The dominant coalitions and their policies, inherited from the preceding period of prosperity, are challenged by new social forces which may form the next governing coalition. Economic crisis and the socio-political structure of accumulation have a two-way relationship (Gordon, 1980, pp. 19–20).

Another conclusion to be drawn from Schumpeter's analysis is that basic innovations and infrastructural investments made, whether by private entrepreneurs or the state, to overcome stagnation give rise to new leading industries. They are expected to lead the economy out of crisis and to dominate the subsequent long economic cycle (Schumpeter, 1939). This idea has been further specified by Rostow (1978), through a model in which successive leading industry complexes have a life cycle of their own. Such cycles of leading industries are closely associated with the rise and decay of the 'swarms' of technological innovations suggested by Schumpeter. A similar idea has been captured by the concept of 'natural trajectories', which postulates that the life cycles of technological innovations have properties of a logistic curve. The specific shape of such trajectories may vary, however, from one 'technological regime' to another. (See Nelson & Winter, 1977; Marchetti, 1980.)

Throughout history, the leading industries have succeeded each other in roughly the following order: textile industry, the railroad complex, steel, chemical and electrical industries, the vehicle industries, and the computer-telecommunications nexus. In speaking of 'succession', we must recall that in reality these industrial cycles, and the logistic curves describing their trajectories, have overlapped each other. Thus, the shifts from one industrial cycle to another have tended to be gradual rather than abrupt. We should also recall that the rise of each leading industry has, as a rule, started from the leading economic power which has managed to develop technologies at the cutting edge and to use them in mass production. Gradually, the technological innovation has spread, through transnational economic networks, to less advanced countries. By the time the innovation starts wearing off, the leading power (and potential catch-up powers as well) is already busy developing technological innovations intended to give rise to yet a new leading industrial sector.

Recently, the existence and timing of such Kondratiev cycles have been much debated, and today the lines of debate would seem to have converged. There is empirical support for the claim that there are long-term periodicities in the world economy, both in prices and in economic activity. The nature of such periodicities will vary from one national economy to another, nor are they necessarily as uniform as Kondratiev expected. Kondratiev cycles are too mechanical to provide a basis for the theory of international economic and political dynamics. Thus, the conception of uniform development patterns, embedded in Kondratiev cycles, needs to be modified (Beenstock, 1983, pp. 137–159; Menzel, 1985).

Long cycles may be used to periodize the world economic dynamics, without our putting too much theoretical premium on them. It will suffice to repeat the standard periodization of the downswing and the upswing phases of the cycle. 'Downswing' phases cover the periods of 1815–50, 1873–97, 1920–45, and from 1967 on. 'Upswing' phases cover, in turn, the remaining periods of 1850–73, 1897–1914, and 1945–67. World War I has at times been annexed to the preceding upswing, while the beginning of the most recent downswing has by some been dated to 1973 rather than 1967.

Such periodization should be considered a tool of analysis rather than the final word in economic time-series research. Empirical descriptions of economic cycles and transitions are useful, in fact indispensable. However, only theoretical explications of the causes and consequences of economic transitions can make analysis of their political and military correlates meaningful (see Kleinknecht, 1981). One theoretical perspective may be derived from research dealing with the phase periods of capitalist economic development and its crises.

The period from the Napoleonic Wars to about 1870 has been described as the era of irresistibly rising industrialism and deepening socio-political polarization. Another trend period extends from 1870 to 1914. During this 'new age of capitalism' industrialization continued, but was now accompanied with a new phase of imperialist expansion and exacerbation of domestic conflicts in major capitalist countries. During the third trend period, extending from 1914 to 1945 or 1950, new social contradictions appeared and the two world wars reorganized international relations. Thereafter, capitalism experienced a 'great leap forward': it was internationalized under the aegis of transnational corporations and banks. Maddison suggests that 1973 may have opened a new phase in the process of capitalist development (see Beaud, 1981; Maddison, 1982).

In Maddison's analysis the turning points in capitalist economic development occurred in 1913 and 1950. He is somewhat less certain whether similar turning points appeared in 1870 and 1973. In any case,

Maddison rejects the idea that long-term rhythms in economic development can be traced to recurrent cycles. Rather the transition from one phase to another is 'caused by system-shocks' which are 'specific disturbances of an ad hoc character' (Maddison, 1982, pp. 83–95). A major war may be a 'system-shock' rerouting the development of capitalist world economy, and such wars may be discerned in each of the phase transitions identified by Maddison. It is, however, difficult to observe any clear-cut association between these wars and the economic turning points. At any rate, they have to be scrutinized in the context of overall social and political contradictions (Väyrynen, 1987, p. 88).

Theoretically, Kondratiev cycles and Maddison's phase periods are at variance with each other. Empirically, however, this is not necessarily the case. This justifies an analytical focus on the long economic waves and associated cycles of technological innovations and leading industries, as set out in Table 17.1.

Table 17.1 *Economic and industrial cycles, 1815 to present*

Downswing	Upswing	Leading industrial complex
1815–49	1850–72	The railway complex (iron industry and steam engines)
1873–96	1897–1914	Steel, electrical, and chemical industries
1920–44	1945–67	The vehicle industry (cars and aircraft)
1968–		Telecommunications, computers, electronics, biotechnology

The outline in Table 17.1 is based on the Schumpeterian idea that each economic downswing generates a swarm of technological innovations, infrastructural investments, and new leading industries. They are carried over to the succeeding phase of economic upswing, when innovations and investments are consummated and pave the way for a new downswing and a subsequent wave of innovations. Politically, periods of stagnation tend to foster nationalism, conservatism, and parochialism, while the periods of growth are conducive to reformism and internationalism (Weber, 1981). This is supported by the observation that most socialist ideas have advanced during the upswing phases. However, economic growth itself may not produce reformism and radicalism: rather, it may be the transition from depression to prosperity – the recovery period in long-cycle terminology – that fosters 'new thinking' in society. Those people who have been 'heads down' during the depression are now alerted to new political opportunities opened to economic and political advance (Silverman, 1985).

The long cycles of economic development and industrial restructuring shape the political power structure of societies. During the upswing phase, new groups try to entrench their position in society. The rise of new groups is a result of the disintegration of policies and their support coalitions during the preceding economic crisis when 'patterns unravel, economic models come into conflict, and policy prescriptions diverge' (Gourevitch, 1986, p. 17). From the crisis, new policies and coalitions may emerge to manage the upswing phase of the economic cycle and to plunge into the ensuing period of decelerated growth and, ultimately, new crisis.

3 Power Transitions and International Conflicts

Kondratiev waves have been interpreted above as results of an endogenous economic logic. I have discarded, in other words, the exogenous interpretation which regards long cycles as products of external shocks and disturbances. In order to retain the possibility of an endogenous interpretation, political and military cycles (if any) in international history are better kept analytically separate from economic cycles. The relationships between different types of cycles should be ascertained by empirical research. This point of departure implies that the economic and politico-military subsystems of international relations are considered analytically distinct. Empirically, they are interrelated in a complex and dynamic fashion.

The dynamics of international relations cannot be understood without considering international power cycles composed of rising and declining states. Such cycles can be explored both nationally and internationally. The national perspective focuses on a nation's share of global economic and military power, its evolution over time, and its consequences for internal and external political relations. The turning points in the cycle of relative national power are particularly prone to abrupt changes in political orientation, and hence to warfare and arms races (Doran & Parsons, 1980; Doran, 1983).

The international perspective either compares several cycles of relative national power or develops a systemic model of polarity. The former approach yields a picture of power transitions in which rising and declining states confront each other in bilateral relationships. The latter approach creates a dynamic systemic model in which the historical transitions occur between unicentric and multicentric, i.e. bipolar and multipolar, international systems.

The model of power transition used here builds on the primacy of domestic economic, technological, and institutional factors in the generation of economic growth and expansion. International power transitions result from the internal dynamics of national economies and polities. The structure of the international system has an important and flexible role in enabling and constraining the growth of national economies within the hierarchy of the system. The variable impact of the international structure is reflected in the differential opportunities of peripheral and core nations for economic gain, and in the historical development of core powers.

The United States, for example, rose to the core of the world economy as a result of indigenous industrial dynamics, relatively free of any international constraints. Britain's economic and naval supremacy, on the other hand, was predicated on political and military equilibrium on the European continent. This does not mean that the international system does not impinge on domestic development, however. The issue is 'not whether the international system shapes domestic politics, but how and through what mechanisms' (Gourevitch, 1986, p. 65). In the US case, the South's dependence on the European market for cotton sales was an important factor in the national disintegration, and paved the way for the Civil War in the 1860s (Keohane, 1983).

Most power-transition models are based on the national cycles of power in which states traverse from potential to mature power and decline thereafter. The process of industrialization is pivotal to the accumulation of economic and military capabilities (Organski, 1964, pp. 300–306). Recently, the dynamics of ascending and declining hegemonies has provided a convenient framework for the analysis of international power cycles and power transitions. The concept of decline must be understood as a relative term – as a decline of national capabilities in relation to those of other, rising, powers. This observation has indeed been taken so far as to suggest that 'the major reason why power declines in the third stage has nothing to do with the mature nation itself. Its relative power declines because other nations are entering the second stage of transitional growth' (Organski, 1964, p. 305).

Organski's point contains an important observation, but it needs to be qualified. Decline can also be caused by internal and external developments in the leading power itself. Leading powers may suffer from economic and institutional 'slack', from the overextension of civilian and military bureaucracy, and, overall, from diminishing returns; the costs of their international primacy increase disproportionately in comparison to its benefits (Gilpin, 1981). Hegemonic decline is not solely due to better performance of rivals.

Differential growth rates and ensuing power transitions tend to create rivalries and even wars between major powers (Organski & Kugler, 1980; Houweling & Siccama, 1988). In addition to warfare, power transitions also foster arms races as mechanisms of competition between major powers. Power-transition conflicts contain both military and economic competition as a method of international change. In economic terms a main issue concerns the economic costs of military competition fostered by the power transition.

Historical record suggests that, in the long run, the military burden tends to become costly, draining the national resources and testing the economic endurance of nations. In effect, as Robinson (1900) put it, competition in economic endurance is 'one of the crucial tests in the struggle for existence'. It may develop into a substitute for war 'which ruins states and crushes nations' and is 'waged without firing a shot' (Robinson, 1900, pp. 619–622). In general terms, the economic rise of major powers seems to precede their military resurgence. Such a military preponderance does not necessarily produce security, however, and may, in fact, open the gates of economic decline (Kennedy, 1987).

The role of economic competition as a substitute for military war was also developed by Max Weber in his Freiburg address in 1895. There he elevated the economic and cultural struggle between nations into a dominant mode of international rivalry. In Weber's view, 'processes of economic development are in the final analysis also power struggles'. In this struggle 'the ultimate and decisive interests [. . .] are the interests of national power' (Weber, 1958, p. 14). Economic resources are a component of national power rather than a value to be shared by international trade.

Most recent theories see general wars as endogenous to the international power cycle. General wars are interpreted as means of solving the international political contradictions that have developed as a result of the redistribution of economic and military power. In the opinion of Modelski (1987), the general or global war 'is basic to thinking about long cycles, it is the trial-by-fire that decides the issue of leadership'. It is 'a system process that is persistent, pervasive and participated in by all the global powers; it is constitutive of new political arrangements and basic innovations' (Modelski, 1987, pp. 36–37). Such a theory-specific and functional interpretation of general wars is theoretically very neat. It also has obvious drawbacks, as it tends to overdetermine the causes of global wars, while neglecting a great deal of the collective violence embedded in other inter-state and civil wars (Väyrynen, 1987, pp. 83–84).

To avoid this pitfall, we must separate the power-transition process and international warfare from each other analytically and scrutinize their relationship empirically in appropriate theoretical contexts. This approach enables us to gauge the impact of intervening variables between the redistribution of economic power and technological initiative on the one hand, and the frequency and severity of warfare on the other. Such intervening exogenous variables mediate between shifts in economic capabilities and warfare and specify its intermediate causes.

Measures of military efforts are important intervening variables between economic power transitions and inter-state warfare. Intervening variables have varying degrees of independence from the distribution of material national power. For example, military expenditures and the nature of military technology are more closely connected with the underlying economic dynamics than political factors which include military alliances and international organizations. They may have the task of managing the political and military rivalries which power transitions foster.

For Modelski, World War I was a turning point in world leadership in which the United States replaced Great Britain. The principal challenger to Britain's leadership since 1792, and indeed since 1689, had been France, while Germany assumed this role in 1914. Until World War I world powers included, in addition to Great Britain and France, the United States, Russia, Germany, and Japan. Since 1914 the international system has been bicentric: the United States and the USSR have been the only truly global powers, challenged in the two world wars by Germany (Modelski, 1983, p. 119).

This suggestion is open to criticism. It is unfounded to regard France as the principal challenger to Great Britain, especially on the eve of World War I, as this ignores the Anglo-German military and political rivalry. It is also dubious to date the transition from a multicentric to a bicentric international system as early as 1914. If the dominant arms race is expected to take place between the main adversaries in the first place, then international relations before World War I should have witnessed a fierce military competition between Great Britain and France. After that war, the arms race should have poised the United States and Germany against each other. Yet this did not happen in reality.

Modelski himself has discerned some of these anomalies in his grand theory. He considers Germany the main challenger to Great Britain in 1874–1914, and expects the Soviet Union to pose in 2000–30 a major challenge to the United States as the world power (Modelski, 1987, p. 40). Such a formulation fails to account for the US–Soviet arms race after World War II and suggests that Modelski's long-cycle theory has only limited explanatory power as concerns arms races.

The world-system analysis argues that Great Britain, after its hegemonic ascent during the Napoleonic Wars, experienced hegemonic victory during the downswing of 1815–50 and then enjoyed hegemonic maturity during the upswing of 1850–73. After the decline of British hegemony in 1873–97, the United States embarked upon a similar cycle from the upswing of 1897–1914 on. US hegemonic victory occurred during the interwar period and culminated in its hegemonic maturity between 1945–67. Since then the United States has experienced a decline in its hegemony (Hopkins & Wallerstein, 1979; see also Väyrynen, 1983a, pp. 395–402).

The world-system tradition pairs the phases of Kondratiev cycles with those of the hegemonic transition. The transition towards unicentricity is assumed to occur during the upswing phases of the long economic cycles. The return towards multicentricity, characterized by intense political and economic conflicts, takes place during the economic downturns (Bousquet, 1980, pp. 48–50). For theoretical purposes, it may be justifiable to establish an analytical linkage between the long waves of economic development and the international power cycle. But for empirical purposes it is important to keep them analytically separate.

In the analysis of the international power cycles, the world-system approach is in better agreement with the historical record than is Modelski's long-cycle theory. Thus Kennedy (1981) dates the zenith of British power to the mid-1860s when Britain's relative industrial capacity started to decline quite rapidly and the centre of innovation began to switch to more promising sites, in particular to Germany and the United States (Kennedy, 1981, pp. 20–27). In a similar vein, Porter (1983, pp. 34–36) dates the beginning of the British economic decline to 1873.

4 Power Transitions in History

The process of economic power transition before World War I can be illustrated by the distribution of GNP among the major powers, as set out in Table 17.2.

Table 17.2 *Distribution of economic resources among major powers, GNP in 1870–1913 (%)*

	1870	1880	1890	1900	1913
Russia	19.8	19.1	17.7	17.1	16.9
USA	19.6	26.1	28.2	30.6	36.0
UK	19.3	17.5	19.3	17.8	14.3
France	17.8	15.6	14.1	12.8	10.3
Germany	16.8	16.3	15.7	16.4	17.0
Japan	6.7	5.4	5.0	5.3	5.5
Total	100.0	100.0	100.0	100.0	100.0

Source: Kugler & Organski, 1986, reprinted with permission.

The economic power transition before World War I saw, primarily, the rise of the United States and, secondarily, the decline of Great Britain, France, and Russia. However, Britain's decline was relatively slow during the last two decades of the 19th century, so Britain retained its leading economic and naval position (Kennedy, 1987, pp. 224–232). In fact, Britain's relative industrial decline reinforced its financial position (Hobsbawm, 1987, pp. 51–52). France experienced a far more rapid fall in its economic standing in relation to other major powers, most significantly with respect to Germany. In 1870, Russia and Germany were equal in economic power with the three other great powers. During the following decades they lost the race for economic predominance to the United States, but defeated France and Great Britain.

The same picture emerges with respect to the distribution of the production of manufactured goods and iron/steel. The only major deviation is the much more rapid rise of German heavy industry, which was to have significant consequences both for military competition and for international commerce (Kennedy, 1984, pp. 12–13, and 1987, pp. 198–202). Germany's industrial breakthrough occurred in two waves of technological innovations which coincided with two upswings of the long economic cycles (Trebilcock, 1981, pp. 48–50). Consistent with the Schumpeterian hypothesis, the recovery phase of the latter upswing in 1883–92 was characterized by a high rate of basic innovations, particularly in the United States and Germany (van Duijn, 1983, pp. 180–185).

Technological innovations and industrialization also shaped the European power structure. States failing to achieve broad-based industrialization, such as France and Russia, lost their chance to become dominant states. Industrial development 'made wealth and industrial capacity the decisive factor in international power' (Hobsbawm, 1979, pp. 84–86). The limited scope of US external expansion made the international political and military bearing of US economic potential smaller than it would have been otherwise. In Europe the situation was different because Germany did not hesitate to use its economic prowess to advance expansionist ends. That is why 'the industrialization of Germany was a major historical fact' (Hobsbawm, 1979, p. 40). The gathering economic competition between declining Britain and rising Germany, and their specific geopolitical relationship, pitted these powers in political and military competition against each other.

The full impact of Anglo-German military rivalry was not felt before the beginning of the 20th century. Until then, continental European powers did not challenge the colonial policy of Britain, except for some Russian involvement in the 'Great Game' as to control of Asia. In the absence of a serious challenge, Britain had an opportunity to deal with colonial rebellions one by one, without interference from other colonial powers (Porter, 1983, pp. 44–45). The Boer War of 1899–1902 demonstrated that Britain's ability to govern rebellious colonies by projecting force was beginning to fade.

Hegemonial decline may have also contributed to the British policy of concluding an alliance with Japan in 1902. This alliance was primarily intended to contain Russian expansion in the Far East, but it also recognized Japan's economic and political interests on the Asian mainland. The agreement was 'a stage in the working out of Japanese imperialism' (Beasley, 1987, pp. 76–77). After the Russo-Japanese War, Britain sought an understanding with Russia on spheres of influence in Asia. To this effect, a Russo-British convention was concluded in 1907 to complement a similar agreement between Russia and Japan.

David Gillard (1977) points out that these agreements marked in effect the end of the 'Great Game' because British perceptions of international rivalries had changed. From then on, the British perceived the 'growing power of Germany and the naval and imperial ambitions of its emperor as likely to constitute in future the central threat to British security. It was a threat which would have to be neutralized by the British throwing their weight against Germany in the European balance of power' (Gillard, 1977, pp. 170–177). Such an orientation had been brewing for years in the nationalist press; political opinion in Britain became, after 1902, increasingly hostile towards Germany (Kennedy, 1982, pp. 255–265).

The power-transition process pitted Great Britain and Germany against each other. Britain made efforts to strengthen its slipping position by aligning with Japan and France and regulating its competition with Russia. As the dominant European power, Britain tried to prevent Germany and Russia, as the leading Eurasian land powers, from joining forces. Britain was able to prevent a German–Russian alliance, but this did not suffice to maintain peace and stability on the Continent. The war was not waged between the declining hegemon, Great Britain, and the ascending hegemon, the United States, but between European powers. This fact, which undermines the credibility of hegemonic-war theories, may be explained in several different ways.

The geopolitical approach suggests that major arms races and general wars tend to take place between the leading sea and land powers. It has been suggested that general wars have been fought between a naval core alliance and a continental challenger. They have been triggered off when the core alliance denies the challenger access to the active economic zone of the world system. The defeat of the continental challenger has been a result of its half-hearted quest for sea power, due to its inability to extricate itself from continental conflicts and other commitments (Modelski, 1987, pp. 226–227; Modelski & Thompson, 1988, pp. 20–23).

The peaceful transition of power from Great Britain to the United States in the 20th century supports this general explanation. Both were sea powers and both belonged to the same core alliance against the continental challengers (Germany and Russia). As Great Britain became increasingly hard-pressed in its colonies, Britain conceded US predominance in particular in Central America and the Caribbean. The two powers also shared control of the sea lanes where the United States expanded its control under the influence of the Mahanian naval philosophy. The peaceful transition of hegemony from Great Britain to the United States was assisted by inflated fears of German expansion to the Western hemisphere and by traditional Anglo-Saxon affinities (Anderson, 1981).

The outbreak of World War I cannot be fully explained by the long economic cycles or by the process of power transition. True, the 'Great War' did start during an upturn in the cycle. In general, 'there is a one-to-one correspondence between the economic cycle and the war cycle until 1918. Each escalating war cycle ends near the end of an upswing phase period' (Goldstein, 1985, p. 247; cf. Goldstein, 1988, pp. 244–249). Before World War I, the economic upswing helped the emerging powers, especially the United States and Germany, to accumulate resources to underpin their revisionist policies. Their challenge to British predominance was more complex than a simple power-transition model would suggest (cf. Organski & Kugler, 1980, pp. 61–62). Instead of trying to beat Britain, the United States cooperated to wreck the challenge from the Wilhelminian Reich.

Before World War I, the United States was an economic giant but a military dwarf. This helps to explain why its contribution to the war effort was, in particular before 1917, primarily economic. In fact this economic contribution proved decisive to the outcome of war (Kennedy, 1984, pp. 23–26; Kugler & Domke, 1986, pp. 60–63). According to Modelski, the world leader is assumed to take systemic decisions on wartime coalitions and global war (Modelski, 1987, pp. 14–15). In that respect, the United States behaved in World War I only partially as world leader. But the United States made a decisive economic contribution to the war. Historically, such a contribution has entrenched the donor power in the postwar economic division of labour and opened new trade routes and markets for it (Pearson, 1987).

Finally, in the analysis of the German challenge standard theories of hegemonic war have to consider the social and political crisis that the country faced. The outbreak of World War I cannot be understood except in the context of the financial crunch and the domestic political polarization that preceded it in Germany (Väyrynen, 1988). The German economic crisis of 1911–13, which occurred at the end of a long-cycle upswing, created a political atmosphere conducive to the mobilization of opinion for war.

World War I transformed international relations at two different levels. It catalysed social and political revolutions in Russia and Germany, which temporarily removed them from a position of international power. By contributing to the dissolution of the Austro-Hungarian Empire and by weakening Germany, the war gave the United States a chance to return to a semi-isolationist policy. The United States profited enormously from the war by being able to produce for it, without having to experience its destructiveness at home, and gained access to new markets. After World War I, the United States became the most powerful country in the world, which enabled it to wield, even in its semi-isolation, a kind of veto power over the British in international relations.

The United States did not use this power effectively. Instead, it permitted Great Britain to reconquer much of its previous influence, which was possible because of the defeat of its prewar rivals. In such conditions 'Britain was given a further lease of life as world power', even though the resurrection was temporary and bound to last only so long as its rivals were recovering and the United States chose to return to its self-imposed isolation (Porter, 1983, pp. 84–86; Kennedy, 1984, pp. 32–37). The redistribution of economic resources among the major powers since World War I is illustrated in Table 17.3. During the interwar period, Great Britain and France were too weak to maintain the political order created for Europe at Versailles. France tried, however, a variety of approaches to safeguard stability in Europe and its own security (Mandelbaum, 1988, pp. 72–128).

Table 17.3 *Distribution of economic resources among the major powers, GNP in 1925–80 (%)*

	1925	1938	1950	1960	1970	1980
USA	42.5	36.3	50.0	42.5	40.7	36.6
USSR	15.1	20.8	20.1	24.8	21.5	21.8
UK	12.6	11.7	10.6	8.6	6.3	5.4
Germany	12.2	15.0	7.1	9.2	11.6	11.2
France	9.6	7.0	7.2	7.1	8.6	8.2
Japan	8.0	9.2	5.0	7.8	11.3	16.8
Total	100.0	100.0	100.0	100.0	100.0	

Source: Kugler & Organski, 1986, reprinted with permission.

Until the 1930s, all revisionist powers, in particular Germany and the Soviet Union, were weak. But this situation started to change from the late

1920s onwards. As a consequence of the Great Depression of 1929–33, the United States, Great Britain, and France suffered a decline in their relative economic standing. At the same time, forced industrialization in the Soviet Union, the alliance between state power and big companies in Nazi Germany, and the coalition between military bureaucrats and the *zaibatsu* in Japan captured a greater share of economic resources for challenging states. These powers based their economic expansion on autarky. This strategy assured economic growth and employment in the short run, but also created internal political impasses which increased, in turn, pressures for external expansion as a method of alleviating them.

Autarky and the international conflicts of the 1930s, initiated by the revisionist powers, destroyed the international division of labour. In Britain, the decline of its economic hegemony, a slow rate of innovation in basic industries, and the Great Depression contributed to the General Tariff of 1932 and the abandonment of free trade. The British iron and steel industry demanded more protection against external competition, primarily from the United States (Capie, 1983; pp. 63–75 and passim). Japan and Germany made rearmament a political priority. Economic policy was subordinated to rearmament once it became clear that resources and organization were inadequate to pursue both. In Germany, the crisis of governance towards the late 1930s resulted in the restoration of Nazi control over the economy and the military (Deist, 1981; Geyer, 1984, pp. 144–153).

In the mid-1930s, international relations were polarized between the revisionist and status-quo states, the preparation for war was well under way. In both groups, military spending helped overcome the economic depression. Eugen Varga (1935) perceptively predicted that both a general war and the economic crisis of the late 1930s were approaching. The economic crisis was due to the 'underproduction' of civilian and 'overproduction' of military goods by the revisionist countries. The German, Italian, and Japanese search for autarky, and the wars initiated by them, destroyed the international division of labour and overburdened their economies with huge investments in war preparations (Varga, 1935, pp. 122–138; Kerner, 1981, pp. 34–44).

The resulting domestic instabilities increased the need for external expansion already engraved in political action programmes. This development was facilitated in Germany by the military's professional confusion. Procurement decisions, deployment plans, and operational details became the main preoccupation of the military, which was unable to develop a coherent strategy to guide the acquisition and use of military hardware. The military's inability to develop a sound political framework for armaments policy had devastating international consequences. It gave Hitler a justification to take over the leadership of military affairs and handle them as ideological issues. Hitler's military policy precipitated an economic crisis in 1938–39 and accelerated the plunge into global war (Geyer, 1984, pp. 149–153, and 1985).

The system of collective security, inscribed in the Covenant of the

League of Nations, was ineffective in securing peace: it was neither collective nor secure. Its maintenance was primarily the responsibility of Great Britain and France. Britain, a declining power, preferred peace and practised appeasement, while France put more emphasis on military rearmament to counter Germany (Porter, 1983, pp. 96–98). With hindsight we may say that British policy was ineffective because it failed to deter German expansionism, and French policy because it lacked economic resources to back up its commitments. In capability terms, France was inferior to Germany, which made its army opt for a defensive strategy. Defence based on the preference for a continuous front and the expectation of slow-moving operations were to spell military disaster in 1940. France had prepared to fight the wrong kind of war (Mandelbaum, 1988, pp. 119–124).

The Axis Powers might have been deterred by the overwhelming capabilities of the Allied Powers acting in concert in the 1930s. Germany's expansionist policy worked only as long as it was able to attack its adversaries one by one (Kugler & Domke, 1986, pp. 63–65). The Ribbentrop–Molotov pact, instead of saving the Soviet Union, increased the ferocity of the German attack, as it permitted Germany to eliminate France. The Battle of Britain proved a turning point: Germany failed to defeat Britain and had to fight a two-front war from then on. The attack on the Soviet Union and the US decision to join the war made German defeat inevitable. The only real question was how long it would take the Allied Powers to achieve victory.

The United States was again able to benefit from the war by strengthening its productive capacity and by conquering new markets during and after. US hegemony was due both to its own strength and to the weakness of other major powers. In that regard, the US position did not differ appreciably from the experiences of previous hegemonic powers. The economic recovery of Japan and Germany increased their common share of the economic resources in the six-power system, from 12.1% in 1950 to 28.0% by 1980. The relative economic power of the United States, and of Great Britain for that matter, has declined consistently since the 1970s.

Post-WWII power competition differs from previous periods in that it has also had an antagonistic ideological character, in addition to the US–USSR power competition. In economic terms, the Soviet Union has been losing rather than winning this rivalry: increasingly it has become an 'incomplete superpower' whose comparative advantage has lain more in military capability (Dibb, 1986). The coming process of power transition appears more economic than military. The new complexity of international relations places a premium on economic and technological resources and reduces opportunities to wield military force effectively. This trend should indicate the need for caution in predictions that suggest the Soviet Union as the main challenger to US world leadership beyond 2000 (Modelski, 1987, p. 40).

5 National Military Efforts

The dynamics of militarization and its links with underlying structural factors can be explored by examining the historical growth of military capabilities. The point is to check whether long economic cycles or phase periods on the one hand and power transitions on the other have had any discernible influence on fluctuations in national military efforts. Standardized data have been used in the analysis here whenever available, in order to avoid the pitfalls of spurious growth figures. Because it is not feasible to examine all the major powers, this analysis will focus on critical cases illuminating the validity of my models of explanation. Such critical cases have been the United States and Germany as rising powers, while Britain and the United States qualify as declining powers. The Soviet Union will also be included in the analysis.

In gauging military expenditure, data provided by Banks (1982) are primarily used. He details the share of the total national budget devoted to military expenditures for the period 1850–1966. Flora (1983) has collected data on the proportion of military personnel among the male population aged 20–44 for the period 1850–1970. Data on the distribution of seapower with global reach over a 500-year period have been developed by Modelski & Thompson (1988). Kennedy (1987) has assembled relevant historical data to describe economic and military power transitions.

5.1 The United States

In the United States the heavy military burden during the upswing of 1850–72 was due to the Civil War (fought 1861–65). Some three-fourths of total national budget expenditures in 1862–63 went to the war. By the late 1860s, relative military expenditures had declined to their normal peacetime level – about 20% of the federal budget. They hovered around this figure until 1897, reaching their lowest relative level in 1886–88. The rapid though unstable and crises-ridden economic growth following the Civil War did not translate to any increase in relative military spending.

Relative decline in military expenditures does not necessarily preclude its absolute growth. A rapidly growing economy may permit the military to expand without adding to the relative military burden – as illustrated by post-World War II Japan and the post-Civil War United States. The emergence of US economic imperialism from the mid-1890s justified political and military demands to build up a battleship navy to protect US commerce and signal national greatness. Such a navy was politically conceived in 1893–94 and realized by the Cleveland Administration during the depression that followed (LaFeber, 1980, pp. 229–241). The share of the federal budget devoted to the military increased from 23.5% in 1897 to 47.4% in 1899.

The construction of new battleships was initiated during an economic depression, when the need to create employment could be used as justification. A truly significant increase in the relative military burden of the United States started after 1898 when the US economy underwent a very rapid horizontal and vertical expansion (Maddison, 1982, p. 173). In an upwardly mobile semi-peripheral country, such as the United States in the 1890s, military and economic growth are often linked. In the United States this dynamic phase of economic expansion was associated with external aggression and conflicts with a declining power, Spain, in Cuba and the Philippines. Military action in Cuba was fostered by both the fear of local revolution and the political self-confidence generated by the economic boom of 1898 (LaFeber, 1980, pp. 387–391). The growth in relative military expenditures levelled off after the turn of the century, while the US share of the naval power increased from 1897 to 1910 and then declined.

During the interwar period, US military expenditure in share of the federal budget reached its historical low: it never exceeded 20.7% and by 1935 had fallen to 8.6%. In this the United States differed from other major powers, which responded to the international economic and political crises of the 1930s by initiating rearmament programmes. This suggests that the international system explanation has only limited value in accounting for low US military expenditures in the interwar period (Gourevitch, 1986, pp. 63–66). The interwar experience also undermines the idea of a 'ratchet effect', as outlined by Russett (1970). By using military manpower data, he concludes that the US military establishment has failed to shrink back to prewar levels (Russett, 1970, pp. 2–5). Scrutiny of the US military's share of the federal budget reveals that the 'ratchet effect' failed to operate after World War I as well as the Vietnam War.

After World War II, the United States assumed a political and military role commensurate with its economic hegemony. Justification for this role was given by reference to alleged Soviet expansionism and the ideological divisions in Asia and Europe which opened Eurasian rimlands to US access. The new US image in the world was also reflected in its naval predominance. The US Navy outspent the British Navy as early as in 1919, but in the next decades the two agreed on rough parity and together controlled some two-thirds of the world's seapower. By the end of World War II, the United States controlled about one-half of global naval capabilities (Modelski & Thompson, 1988, p. 131).

Until 1949, US power relied on its vast economic resources and on the military deterrence provided by nuclear weapons. Economic power lent credibility to the policy of economic containment, which was a keystone in US policy towards Asia and Europe in the immediate postwar years. In 1949–50, US policy shifted its emphasis from economic containment to rearmament and military containment (Pollard, 1985, pp. 234–242). The US rearmament programme was justified by redefining the Soviet threat as a military challenge, both direct and indirect. Such a threat could be addressed only by building up more military power and creating, in the Achesonian style, situations of strength for containing the Soviet Union.

In Dean Acheson's metaphor, Soviet policy was like a river: 'One can dam it or deflect it, but not argue with it. Therefore, we had been at work to create strength where there had been weakness' (Acheson, 1969, p. 379). To create political strength, more military power was needed. To justify a military build-up, Achesonians resorted to hyperbole:

> At the end of the war we were the most powerful nation on earth, with the greatest army, navy, and air force, a monopoly of the most destructive weapon, and all supported by the most productive industry and army. But now our army had been demobilized, our navy put in mothballs, and our air force no longer had a monopoly of atomic weapons. In three or four years at most we could be threatened with devastating damage, against which no sure protection appeared. (Acheson, 1969, p. 376)

The twin policies of political strength and military rearmament tied Western Europe more closely to the United States and reduced the possibility of independent policy choices. Block has suggested that economic needs, in addition to the outbreak of the Korean War, encouraged the rearmament programme and the policy of containment spelt out in NSC-68. In economic terms, the existence of industrial surpluses and the fear of a depression remained basic problems in the United States. Previously, those problems had been handled by running permanent export surpluses in trade with Western Europe. A rearmament programme could also absorb such surpluses, as well as lowering unemployment (Block, 1977, pp. 102–108, and 1980). In this way, international and national economic instabilities contributed to a new wave of militarization. Since then, US military expenditures have remained at a high level, with dramatic increases during the Korean and Vietnam wars.

The relationship between the long economic cycle and fluctuations in US military spending is difficult to gauge. Relative military spending was low during the periods of slow economic growth 1873–97 and 1920–39, and higher during the periods of rapid growth in 1897–1914 and 1945–67. On the other hand, the Civil War and the Vietnam War confound the relationship between Kondratiev cycles and military spending. Involvement in external warfare and expansion have pushed military burdens upwards. This has served to foster inflation and other economic problems, in particular after the Vietnam War. Both world wars had, in turn, favourable impacts on US economic growth (Solomou, 1988, pp. 52–53; cf. Goldstein, 1988, pp. 265–266).

Some authors have rejected the Kondratiev cycle as incompatible with historical evidence and suggested that the 20–30-year Kuznets swings are more valid descriptions of economic growth paths (Solomou, 1987, and 1988, pp. 48–55). Kuznets did not attribute regular cyclicity to the variations he found in various time series; instead he spoke of 'secondary secular movements'. In the United States this approach seems to have but limited value in accounting for variations in military spending, except for the 1882–1913 period. The Kuznets swing defines 1899 as the turning point to high growth and 1906 to a low growth. This helps to account for the low level of military spending throughout most of the 1880s and the 1890s, its resurgence from 1898, and its decline again after 1909–10. The rearmament programme of the Kennedy Administration occurred during the Kuznets upswing of 1959–66.

Conclusions on the relationships of economic cycles and swings with fluctuations in military spending are confounded by patterns of power transition. In particular, after World War II the hegemonic position of the United States and its politico-military competition with the Soviet Union complicate the analysis. The coincidence of US hegemonic maturity with the long economic upswing made resources available for military programmes which were further justified by the confrontation with the Soviet Union. The military programme outlined in NSC-68 did not contain any cost estimate, as policymakers expected that the nation could afford it. According to Acheson (1969, p. 376), 'the added power and energy of America' was needed for 'the drama was now played on a world stage'.

5.2 The Soviet Union

In Russia the relative level of its military burden, measured by the military's share of GNP, remained rather stable until World War I, except for the peaks engendered by the Russo-Turkish War of 1877–78 and the Russo-Japanese War of 1904–05 (Köhler, 1980a). To be more precise: relative military spending tended to drop after the Crimean War, although its absolute value increased somewhat. This trend was partially reversed in 1863–66 when Russian military expenditure increased, while government spending remained stagnant (Banks, 1972, p. 131). Despite moderate growth in military spending after 1867, its share of government spending decreased. This was due to the vigorous expansion of the Russian economy from 1867–68 to the mid-1870s (Geyer, 1987, pp. 42–45).

The economic upswing permitted a simultaneous reform of the armed forces and the reduction of their economic burden for Russian society. Except for the Russo-Japanese War in 1904–05, the relative economic burden remained fairly constant until World War I (Jones, 1987, pp. 163–165). This tendency can be interpreted variously. In one respect it reflects the declining political status of Russia in the system of major powers. Russia's position as a latecomer in military competition and its defeats in the Russo-Japanese War and World War I suggest that Russia had lost its chances of prevailing in the transition of power.

On the other hand, Alexander II and his War Minister D.A. Milyutin were able to reform and streamline the Russian Army. The introduction of conscription in 1874 was part of the overall social emancipation promoted in Russia during the period of economic growth in the 1860s and the early 1870s. Until the reforms, the bulk of Russia's military spending had gone to provide subsistence for officers and recruits rather than to logistics and weapons. The nature of the Russian military was compatible with the agrarian economy from which it derived its means of subsistence (Pintner, 1984, pp. 237–241). It relied on masses instead of mobility and firepower.

The Milyutin reforms attempted to increase the efficiency of military administration, education, and procurement in order to make the army a more effective instrument in Russia's rivalries with other European powers. But the backward and dynastic character of Russian society blocked these reforms and led to incomplete results. 'The Russian army had modernized its structure but it still lagged behind the forces of potential European adversaries organizationally, technically, and psychologically. In an age of intensifying nationalism and imperialist rivalry these were serious shortcomings' (Keep, 1985, p. 378; see also Fuller, 1985, pp. 7–13). As an underdeveloped country, Russia faced a cruel dilemma, one to be experienced later by the Soviet Union: a strong fighting force had to be financed in an economy considerably weaker than that of its main adversaries.

In 1900, the absolute manpower figures of Russian Army matched those of the French and German armies combined, but its share of total population remained a low 0.8% (Pintner, 1984, p. 247). In practical terms this meant that Russian military power relied on demographic rather than on technological resources. In the 1890s and the early 1900s, deliberate efforts were made to increase military capabilities, resulting in higher growth rates in defence outlays than in any other European power.

Yet the military's share of total state expenditures declined, leading to an acrimonious debate between Kuropatkin and Witte after Russia's defeat by Japan. The relative decline in Russian military outlays compares with the constant share of state budget for the military in France and the decline in Germany (Fuller, 1985, pp. 47–52). This decline was reversed after 1909 when economic growth permitted the expansion of state expenditures and the allocation of a slightly greater share for modernizing the military. Increased allocation to the military, despite economic hardships, was motivated by the strong commitment of the Tsarist system to maintain Russia as a military great power, if necessary by borrowing money from abroad, especially from France. This policy meant heavy increases in the state debt and the burden on civilian society, and was to pave the way for the Revolution (Geyer, 1987, pp. 255–263; Jones, 1987, pp. 167–169).

The weakness of the Russian economy seriously limited the ability to sustain the heavy military burden which its (geo-)political position demanded. Starting in the 1890s, Russia underwent a surge of industrialization, which gave rise to modern heavy industry and domestic arms manufacturing. As a rule, state-directed industrialization in an underdeveloped economy results in polarized accumulation, i.e. in a major imbalance between the capital goods sector and the rest of the economy. This happened in Russia, and it all but blocked the development of an indigenous military industry. Innovation in military technology was sluggish: most military improvements were adopted from abroad (Trebilcock, 1981, pp. 236–238; Fuller, 1985, pp. 54–55, 73–74).

Russia's situation started to change after 1908, when a healthier balance was established between heavy and light industries and a more positive relationship emerged between the acquisition of top-notch foreign technology and domestic economic development. However, Western technology may have arrived 'too late to produce any enduring industrial effects [. . .] it operated for only a few years before being disrupted by the especially chaotic conditions of the imperial war economy' (Trebilcock, 1981, pp. 281–284). Russia remained dependent on advanced military technology acquired from leading arms manufacturers abroad (Geyer, 1987, pp. 267–271).

Before World War I, Russia made an effort – comparable in some ways with today's *perestroika* – to restore its economic and strategic parity with other major powers, in particular with Imperial Germany. But Russia was a backward empire trying to compete in a military power struggle with economically more advanced countries, and its socio-economic basis began to falter. The agrarian economy and class structure raised insurmountable obstacles to Witte's policy of transforming, by means of catch-up industrialization, the country into a more competitive power (Skocpol, 1979, pp. 93–94, 99).

This dilemma was further aggravated by Russia's involvement in the pre-World War I arms races and its overextension to the Far East. Both became serious liabilities to the Russian economy, draining its resources for suboptimal purposes (Fuller, 1985, pp. 56–57). The Russian case provides *prima facie* evidence for the territorial trap hypothesis: that expanding imperial powers become overcommitted to their territorial possessions; and, in consequence, their returns from economic and strategic expansion diminish, and their position in the systemic competition with other powers weakens (Thompson & Zuk, 1986).

After the Russian Revolution, the Soviet Union had to confront the same structural hurdles to military modernization that had faced the Tsarist government. The redefinition of the political situation in 1927, stressing the hostility and aggressiveness of capitalist powers, made the need to modernize the military imperative. The twin doctrines of capitalist encirclement and the inevitability of war were used to justify the policy of forced industrialization. In effect, the 'Stalinist regime viewed its race with the West as an all-out struggle in which industrial power, and especially military power, would be decisive' (Parrott, 1985, pp. 21–22). Stalinist technology policy permitted borrowing from abroad, but put even greater emphasis on expanding domestic research and development (R&D). This was manifested in the priority given to domestic military R&D and procurement, which helped to produce, by the late 1930s, massive amounts of modern weaponry (Parrott, 1985, pp. 47–48, 70–73).

During the first half of the 1920s, due to domestic turbulence, Soviet military spending as a percentage of the state budget remained at a level comparable with that of Tsarist Russia. It declined considerably towards the end of the 1920s and in the early 1930s, but experienced rapid growth from 1933 on. The swift transition of the Soviet military to the technological age can be explained by a combination of domestic push and intensifying rivalry with Germany. The net result was an increase in the share of Soviet military outlays of the national budget from 3.4% in 1933 to 25.6% by 1939 (Nove, 1978, pp. 227–228). The expansion of the Soviet military in the 1930s was facilitated by forced industrialization and the domestic development of technology. It was justified by the breakdown of the international system and the intensification of ideological and power rivalries.

After World War II, the Soviet Union's position as superpower encouraged the growth of military outlays. The growth of industrial capacity permitted investment in military technology and the substitution of technology for manpower. These emergency programmes were initiated by the US development of the atomic bomb in August 1945 and continued by the across-the-board development of military technology after 1949 (Holloway, 1983; Parrott, 1985, pp. 116–124). However, this substitution effect did not operate during Stalin's final years in the Cold War when both military manpower and financial outlays grew rapidly (Nove, 1978, pp. 319–320). Khrushchev attempted the substitution of technology for manpower in earnest, but by the early 1960s his policy faced stiff political and bureaucratic resistance.

Brezhnev did not try any novel solutions to reduce the military burden on the civilian economy. On the contrary, he made a bargain with the military and provided it, in exchange for political support, with greater internal autonomy and a greater number and variety of modern weapons. This deal precluded the possibility of the application of economic yardsticks in the decisions to develop and procure weapons systems. As a consequence, the privileged position of military spending and technology in the Soviet economy has contributed to its own stagnation. In a way, the military has become an enemy of its own development. Recent recognition of this fact has paved the way for civil–military consensus on the inextricable link between economic modernization and military strength.

Perestroika is motivated by Gorbachev's concern with the status of the Soviet Union as a 'complete' great power. However, the current civilian–military consensus on the priority given to Gorbachev's programme of economic reform is fragile. Military needs cannot be pushed aside in the daily management of the economy, because the long life-cycles of weapons systems require continuous military allocations. Their priority can be lowered only with the expectation that they can be increased in the future. A critical question, then, is how long the Soviet military's top brass is prepared to wait for *perestroika* to produce tangible results in the form of a broad range of technically advanced weapons (Rice, 1987).

The fluctuations of Russian and Soviet military expenditures can hardly be accounted for by Kondratiev cycles. This is largely due to the fact that the Russian/Soviet economy has been isolated from the world economy, which has transmitted cyclical dynamics only in an indirect way. However, it may also be that a closer integration of Russia to the world economy before World War I transmitted an economic upswing which reshaped its internal development and even gave a push to military preparations (Geyer, 1987, pp. 267, 270–271).

Even more clearly, Russian military preparations before World War I were reactions to external strategic pressures emanating from the escalating arms race between the major European powers. The power-transition model appears also to account for Soviet military spending after World War II, including the current phase of Soviet military-economic policy. The nature and magnitude of Soviet military arsenals closely reflect its great-power aspirations. A major motivation behind *perestroika* is to modernize the Soviet economy to assure its future status as a great power.

5.3 Great Britain

Measured in terms of its share of GNP, British military spending remained rather constant throughout the 19th century. In fact, a slight decline is evident during this period, except for the increase caused by British involvement in the Crimean War in the 1850s (Köhler, 1980b). Figures for military share of the national budget up to 1913 show a highly stable spending pattern, except for the Boer War: in 1899–1902 this share jumped from a standard 35% to 60% and more (Banks, 1982, p. 132). Long-term economic fluctuations had little effect on variations in British military spending before World War I. Indeed, the existence of any Kondratiev waves in the British economy has been disputed (Solomou, 1988, pp. 27–33).

An alternative explanation is that Britain's military policy and priorities were shaped by its hegemonic and colonial position in the world. Britain had both an economic and political aversion to a standing army, which it regarded as a drain on industrial development and a potential threat to the liberal political system. As a consequence, the British Army was kept rather small, although it expanded vigorously during the Boer War and again in 1912–13. In 1910 the share of military personnel of the male population aged 20–44 years was 4.5%, but it jumped to 6.4% in 1913 when it reached the same relative level as the German Army (Flora, 1983, pp. 249, 252).

The view that the British Army was insignificant appears to be somewhat of a myth in the years preceding World War I. Yet, Britain put its main emphasis on naval development, which was a necessary ingredient in the global economic and military power situation (Porter, 1983, pp. 18–20). The British share of global seapower was one-half, or slightly less, throughout the 19th century, but it started to decline from the late 1890s and onwards. Despite rapid growth of naval expenditures, Britain was not able to retain its quantitative and qualitative edge in comparison to the catch-up powers (Modelski & Thompson, 1988, pp. 121–123, 209–210).

Altogether, 'the maintenance of *Pax Britannica* [. . .] was a remarkably low-cost affair' (Chalmers, 1985, pp. 5–6). Great Britain was able to reap benefits from its dominant position in the world economy without investing any inordinate amounts of its own resources in the military protection of the empire. The Concert of Europe assured the balance on the Continent and permitted Britain to concentrate on commercial and colonial expansion: 'the managed balance of power can be seen as a kind of subsidy for British imperial expansion in the nineteenth century' (Mandelbaum, 1988, p. 36).

This situation started to change towards the end of the 19th century when Britain's industrial predominance gradually slipped and other powers began to challenge its position. To respond to these challenges, Britain had to devote a greater share of its economic resources to military purposes, but that could not ensure its continued supremacy. Instead, an industrial arms race with other European powers ensued. From the 1880s on, British military outlays started to increase, military production expanded, and military contracts were allocated more frequently than before to private manufacturers of weapons, including Vickers, Armstrong, and Yarrow (Kaldor, 1982, pp. 31–34).

The preference given to private companies was to create serious problems when Britain mobilized during the Boer War and, subsequently, during World War I. As the British Army was prepared for small colonial wars, the armaments industry was not strong enough for a lengthy war with other industrial powers (Kennedy, 1987, p. 229). In the absence of consistent governmental policy, the companies did not build up sufficient reserves of guns and shells.

This failure of public policy and armaments industry affected the Army more seriously than the Navy. Capital-intensive battleships had to be constructed before the war, while the Army needed to replenish constantly (Trebilcock, 1975). The problems of industrial mobilization in World War I were due, in part, to the British commitment to maintain naval superiority to counter the German challenge and to arrest the decline in its international position. The price of this commitment, reinforced by reliance on the market mechanism in arms production, was the arms industry's inadequate preparedness for general war.

Allocating military contracts to private companies was justified, in part, by the need to create employment in the conditions of depression which plagued the British economy in the mid-1880s. Arms contracts were intended to strengthen the economy and Britain's international position as well (McNeill, 1982, pp. 268–270). Military Keynesianism was used, much as it was later applied by the US Reagan Administration in the 1980s, to prop up the ailing economic position of the British hegemony. British naval programmes were predicated on the usefulness of battleships, which were considered 'symbols of the British victory at Trafalgar' (Kaldor, 1982, p. 34). The preference for battleships was typical of a dominant naval power, which liked to compare its fighting capacity directly with that of other powers. The dual-power standard adopted by the British is a good example of the tendency to confront, in peacetime comparisons, rival battlefleets head-on.

There are two types of challenges to this kind of naval thinking. Weaker powers may try to undermine a naval hegemony based on battleships by resorting to an indirect strategy such as commerce raiding. If the adversary is gaining sufficient economic resources, as Germany did, it may opt for head-on confrontation. Germany chose the latter strategy, and curiously neglected the development of weapons useful for indirect strategy, such as torpedoes and submarines. The dominant power, once it has attained a lead in critical military technologies, may try to freeze their development in order to perpetuate its advantage. This proved impossible, however, in the Anglo-German naval race at the turn of the century. Technological innovation, a critical ingredient in every new round of this arms spiral, became institutionalized in British and German industries (McNeill, 1982, pp. 277–281).

The battleship required constant technical improvements in its mobility, survivability, and firepower. Technological arms races are more expensive because improved quality usually costs more than increased quantity. This became visible before World War I when the technology intensiveness of the naval arms race drove up military outlays and reduced the number of ships that could be constructed. The cost escalation resulted in bottlenecks in construction programmes and exacerbated domestic conflicts between programme opponents and proponents. (See Berghahn, 1971; Lambi, 1984.)

The German determination to invest industrial and financial resources in constructing a battlefleet posed, in the eyes of naval strategists, a new and direct threat to the British Isles. This development called for the British to concentrate their battleships in the vicinity of the Isles, which created a painful trade-off between national security and imperial interests (Wainstein, 1971, pp. 162–165). A remedy to this dilemma was to switch, as Julian Corbett suggested, from an offensive to an active defensive naval strategy, to enable Britain to 'choose our own ground for the trial of strength', when the adversary's navy would be 'most dangerously exposed' (Corbett, 1911; see also Semmel, 1986). This suggests that British naval thinking changed as the idea of massive confrontation with the adversary was gradually replaced by the utilization of relative advantages.

Corbett's strategy also included the possibility that German power could be contained or even defeated outside the main European theatre of war by joint naval and army operations. In that way, a pitched battle in Europe with the German Army could be avoided. But World War I showed that Britain had faced a dilemma in which neither the new naval strategy nor the continental commitment had been any genuine alternatives at all. Britain had been 'a victim both of geography and of changing technology' (Kennedy, 1981, pp. 181–186).

In the interwar years, Britain's military burden declined in relative terms. The share of military manpower of the male population aged 20–44 declined in 1923–38 to the range of 3.7–4.3%, among the lowest figures in British history. Until 1936, the military's share of the national budget hovered around 13% – also very low by historical standards. The slump in defence spending and military personnel reflects both the scarcity of economic resources, due to the hegemonic decline and economic recession, and the political mood which favoured the preservation of peace and the status quo. Low military spending in the 1920s and the 1930s is clearly consistent with the low growth phase of the British economy during the same period, even if no Kondratiev cycles may have existed (Solomou, 1987, pp. 33–36).

Britain's defence policy was reassessed in 1931–32 as international tensions intensified. It was recognized, though not without hesitation, that all three services needed restocking and technical modernization (Kennedy, 1981, pp. 272–282). Britain launched its rearmament policy in earnest in 1935, more than doubling military expenditures by 1939. The Air Force was the main beneficiary of this programme, which consumed in 1939 as much as 38% of the national budget.

The economic consequences of the rearmament programme are a matter of controversy. Trebilcock has argued the case for the benefits that rearmament has historically produced. Before World War I the armament industry had, according to this argument, advanced the British economy as much as the railways had done a few decades earlier (Trebilcock, 1973). In a similar fashion Thomas and Meyers have suggested that the rearmament of the 1930s, as a public-works programme, contributed to economic growth and staved off a recession that was expected in 1937–38. On the other hand, scepticism has also been voiced on the economic benefits of rearmament (Thomas, 1983; Meyers, 1981).

But military-economic medicament could not arrest the spread of the malaise of British economic and political decline. In the aftermath of World War II, Great Britain had to face the unpleasant truth: no longer was it a world power. The British decided, however, to maintain a level of military spending higher, in relative terms, than during the interwar period. In the 1950s and the 1960s, the military's share of the state budget was about 20%, except for 1953–56 when it approached and even exceeded 30%. This high level of military spending can be explained largely by the international context. In addition to the remnants of the imperial burden, the political division of the world and its special relationship with the United States encouraged Britain to invest in military power. The special relationship is an example of a historical tendency: 'a former dominant power tends to sink into dependence upon its supplanter, when you might have expected an undying hatred' (Wight, 1978, p. 127).

In fact, this relationship committed Britain to a high level of military spending, to a nuclear role, and to sharing the imperial burden with the United States. In the beginning, nuclear weapons were regarded as a source of national power and as a reassurance against a US return to isolation. But they also created the illusion that Britain was still a world power capable of maintaining imperial commitments as well. In that way the nuclear force 'reinforced support for a world role and delayed a reappraisal' (Chalmers, 1985, pp. 19–23; see also Porter, 1983, pp. 121–123). The British economy was not strong enough to sustain such a heavy military burden, and has obviously suffered from the allocation of resources to the extensive domestic development and procurement of weapons.

Britain may be considered a prototype of an economy in which the use of scarce resources for military spending has crowded out funds and talents from productive civilian investments and technology programmes. This occurred despite the vigorous expansion of the world economy, under US leadership, in the 1950s and the 1960s. This growth effect was transmitted to the British economy as well, but was offset by Britain's inability to stimulate indigenous productivity and economic activity, particularly in the manufacturing sector. This state of affairs may be explained by the early start of Britain, by its premature maturity, to use Nicholas Kaldor's (1966) expression, which made it incapable of absorbing the full benefits of the postwar growth cycle.

6 Military Spending and Economic Development

A high level of military burden may be sustained so long as the economy as a whole is growing and moving upwards in the world economic hierarchy. In an upwardly mobile semi-peripheral country, the military and civilian aspects of economic modernization may reinforce each other. This positive association is forged by state intervention that provides both the political motivation and the institutional framework for a national programme of industrialization. Japan in the Meiji period (1868–1912) is a relevant example of how, in the quest for modernization, the state extends its control over heavy industry, typically including the armaments industry (Halliday, 1975, pp. 46–61).

The military element in the national growth project has coercive implications and contributes to imbalanced economic development. Structural distortions and repressive state policies foster both domestic turbulence and external aggression. That is why semi-peripheral countries tend to belong to the zone of political instability in the world economy (Wallerstein, 1979; Väyrynen, 1983b). Relatively high military spending, for industrialization and warfare, is often an integral part of the national growth trajectory (Sen, 1984).

Having attained a core position in the world economy, the state will usually have the resources to maintain a military capability commensurate with its political commitments. When the relative strength of a country's economy starts declining, military spending increasingly becomes a liability. The adverse impact of military expenditures is further increased if the world economy moves to a long period of slow growth. In such a situation, policymakers seldom have the wisdom to scale back military spending and invest the resources so released in economically more productive purposes. The inability to readjust national resources and strategies to each other is due to fear of losing international influence. Such decisions are rendered even more difficult by the adversarial nature of international relations, with two or more major powers locked in military competition.

The net result is that such powers are able to spare a smaller relative share than their less militarized economic competitors for investments to increase productivity and marketable civilian products. Thus military spending tends to slow down economic growth and erode a country's international position, instead of propping it up. This tendency has a multitude of social and political consequences. These include the exacerbation of tensions in the labour market and the decline of the welfare state, of which Britain provides tangible evidence. Naturally, also factors other than military spending have contributed to the domestic economic and political crisis of Britain, but this cannot be disentangled from the totality (Gourevitch, 1986, pp. 192–199). In Britain, the gap between economic and military resources on the one hand and strategic commitments on the other is probably greater than in any other major country (Kennedy, 1987, pp. 481–483). Remedies to eliminate Britain's economic ills are constrained by its position in the international political system which imposes the need to participate in military burden-sharing.

In the United States, the detrimental economic effects of high military spending were generally recognized during the Vietnam War. The discussion focused primarily on the inflationary impact of the war, even though inflation was caused by other factors as well (Calleo, 1982). Early on, military expenditures and production were observed to have also structural effects, steering resources away from civilian investment and R&D and contributing to a lopsided pattern of industrial development. More recently, this aspect of weapons development and production has been illustrated in detail by several studies (Dumas, 1982; DeGrasse, 1983; DiFilippo, 1986).

In a more immediate way, the deficit economy in the United States is due to the effort, initiated in 1978, to arrest the decline of US global influence by building up its military capabilities. US economic resources and Reagan's economic policy have not sufficed, however, to attain this objective. On the contrary, economic realities have forced US policymakers to recognize that military spending has to be scaled back and a more selective strategy advanced to preserve global influence. This is further necessitated by the present incompatibility between ambitious US political objectives and the meagre means available for pursuing them.

7 Conclusions

The empirical evidence presented here suggests that Kondratiev cycles cannot provide an adequate explanation for the fluctuations in relative military efforts. The conclusion appears to be the same if other cyclical patterns of economic development, such as Kuznets swings, are considered. Understandably, there is no simple diachronic correlation between economic fluctuations and the dynamics of military spending. Both are steered by so many factors that their co-variation over time can hardly be expected.

This does not preclude a more limited conclusion, however. Often the scarcity or abundance of economic resources associated with respective phases of economic cycles will constrain or facilitate policymaking. Economic resources available affect the political and military options open to policymakers. Constraints and opportunities associated with the economic cycles are, however, context-dependent and vary from one cycle to another. That is why it is difficult to discover any generalized pattern, although the impact of relative economic resources on military allocations can be discerned in individual periods.

The power-transition hypothesis provides a more potent explanation of military allocations. Upwardly mobile states have economic resources to accumulate military power to prop up their industrial and political prowess. Downwardly mobile states have difficulties in maintaining their previous levels of military spending. Even such levels may prove inadequate to underpin political and strategic commitments made at the pinnacle of relative power. The power competition between leading state(s) and their challengers fosters arms races, exacerbating political tensions and economic burdens.

Major arms build-ups in the 19th and 20th centuries have been carried out either by rising powers, such as Germany and the Soviet Union, or by dominant powers, particularly the United States after World War II. There is quite a difference between Great Britain and the United States in this respect. The military component of British hegemony, save in wartime, was relatively modest, while for the United States it has been more dominant. This can be explained in the 19th century by the balance of power in Europe, which released Britain from its continental commitment, and in the 20th century by its policy of appeasement vis-à-vis Germany. Instead, the United States chose to confront the Soviet Union on the European continent, which considerably increased its military burden.

Before declaring the long-cycle perspective unsuited to explain arms races, we must consider the possibility that arms races are more closely related to cyclical breakthroughs in military technology than to fluctuations in military expenditures. The starting point of this argument is that the development of military technology is associated with capitalist and socialist industrialization. By shaping industrial innovations and production, long-cycle dynamics have indirect influence also on military technology. The concept of 'leading industries' has particular relevance in this context, as it suggests that each long economic wave creates its own industrial sectors. Military technology and production cannot but be affected by the rise and decline of leading industrial sectors.

The indirect association between long waves and military technologies is not only based on a theoretical argument: it has been also substantiated by empirical research. Väyrynen (1983c) has explored how the development and production of weapons systems have been historically shaped by the emergence of new industrial sectors and the Kondratiev cycles behind them (see also Kaldor, 1987). Neither such cycles nor power transitions are fully able to account for all fluctuations in military capabilities and allocations; the answers will, in fact, depend on the kind of military indicators used. All the same, we may conclude that economic cycles and power transitions provide a material background which policymakers cannot neglect in deciding on the acquisition of military weapons and technologies.

RAIMO VÄYRYNEN, b. 1947, Director, Tampere Peace Research Institute (1972–78); Secretary-General, International Peace Research Association (1975–79); Professor of International Relations, University of Helsinki (1978–); Chairman, Disarmament Advisory Board, Finnish Foreign Ministry (1988–); Chairman, Finnish Social Science Research Council (1989–); Visiting Professor of War and Peace Studies, Princeton University (1986–87); current main research interests: macrohistorical change in international relations, international conflict.

PART IV:
THE RESEARCH AGENDA

Chapter 18
Systemic Confrontation, Armament Competition, and Armament Dynamics*

DIETER SENGHAAS
Department of Social Science, University of Bremen

1 Looking Back

Twenty years ago, 'armament dynamics' was a central theme in peace research. The concept of *armament dynamics* referred to the factors that determine the growth of military potential. Are these factors created primarily by constellations in the international or domestic realm? This question led on to a discussion over the priority of internal or external factors in armament competition that lasted several years.[1] Rivaling ideal models played a fruitful heuristic role in the discussion. Over time, mediating points of view developed, combining internal and external explanations of the growth of military potential. From empirical observations, the strength of different factors was assessed, and old findings sometimes revised. Thus, thematically limited, specific case studies were made, for instance of individual weapon biographies. However, comprehensive explanations of the armament problematique are lacking, especially as there are great methodological problems in adding individual findings to an explanation of the totality of the situation. New theoretical endeavors in a discussion of the armament problematique are long overdue. It is against this background that the following conceptual considerations are presented.

2 Three Levels of Analysis

An appropriate analysis of the armament problematique must take into account at least three levels of the problem: systemic confrontation (or power rivalry), armament competition, and armament dynamics.

---
* This chapter originated in a comment on an essay by Håkan Wiberg (Chapter 3 in this volume). An earlier German version has been published as Senghaas (1988a).

Systemic confrontation (or power rivalry) refers to the political framework within which armament competition is observed. This is an objective situation which is not a result of misperception, although misperception often plays an important role also on this level. Systemic confrontation comes about for several reasons, but primarily through struggle for dominance in conflicts over hegemony. Systemic confrontation is usually nourished by mutually incompatible socio-political and ideological motives. In the case of the East–West conflict, the systemic confrontation is a result of a primary conflict, as it would exist even without armament competition and armament dynamics. It is worth noting that such systemic conflict will be characterized at different times by different expressions of the conflict, which at times may rise to the antagonism of a cold war, with the constant danger of military confrontation, and at times may cool to a detente. It can be observed that the East–West conflict has passed through recurrent phases of cooperation and dissociation or confrontation. However, there has been a constant undercurrent of armament throughout.

A second level of analysis concerns *armament competition*: the competitive relation of potential opponents, and their search for advantageous military options and counteroptions. Military strategy and armament procurement programs are the manifestations of armament competition. There may be total convergence between these manifestations, although that will not always be the case. The goal in armament competition is to constrain the military options of the potential opponent. Actions and reactions can be both closely and loosely related to each other. Closely, when specific reactions are countermeasures to specific actions. Loosely, when the military programs of both sides confront each other, without being directly interrelated like cogs in a cogwheel. A mixed form exists when two military postures that have been founded on different assumptions face each other, such that there is an asymmetry, and when specific armament policies nevertheless forestall or somehow invalidate those of the adversary. Armament competition in Central Europe seems to correspond to this mixed form. Nuclear-strategic armament competition between the USA and the Soviet Union can be described as being loosely structured. Armament competition in the sense of tightly structured action-reaction processes can most likely be observed in conventional arms races outside the East–West context.

Armament competition is the military result of systemic confrontation and power rivalry. As the conflict lasts, the process on the level of armament competition gains its own momentum, becoming a strong independent force. The factor of systemic confrontation does create the political frame within which armament competition occurs, but it does not determine the specific process and characteristics of armament competition. Its specific characteristics are determined by an important group of armament factors.

The third analytical level concerns *armament dynamics*. This relates to multiple factors that characterize armament politics: the interests of the military apparatus, the interests of the armament industry, the technological momentum, the drive which state bureaucracy and political institutions create, i.e. interests of institutions which make armaments policy and doctrines of security. These factors mesh: technological developments influence the military apparatus and the armament industry, and they contribute to the reformulation of existing security doctrines. The military apparatus articulates its strategic preferences to the political elite, expects the armament laboratories to present new innovations in weapon technology, and requires the most modern equipment from the armament industry. Reformulations of strategic doctrines by civilian and military institutions can change military postures, so long as they are accepted by the political elite. In turn, the political elite can give impulses for new armament programs, accept to produce weapons that the weapon laboratories develop, etc.

The greater the armament efforts, the more these factors gain a momentum of their own, such that security policy ceases to give primary attention to the international environment, and becomes rather the object of a complex network of domestic decision-making processes. At times, the development of security policy may even be more contingent on domestic changes than on trends in the international situation.

3 Configurative Causality

The interaction between systemic confrontation (or power rivalry), armament competition, and armament dynamics cannot be grasped by a simple causal model. Though it is possible to find some causal links from the study of individual weapon biographies ('what was the cause of what, and with what effect?'), a comparison of several weapon biographies soon shows the futility of attempting to achieve an analytic grasp of the total situation. The situation is complicated, because armament programs are developed in the context of armament competition and systemic confrontation. This makes it imperative to think in terms of *configurative* causality. It is then important to consider the total context, created by structural factors, and feedback processes between some of the factors. In analyzing an individual case, one must consider its relation to the whole. An analysis is required which places the individual case in a greater context, attempting to differentiate its conclusions through comparison with other detailed analyses (the progressive-regressive method). In such a way, conclusions about the totality can be extracted from an empirical basis, while further case studies are set in a new light. Thinking in terms of configurative causality is a dialectic process.

4 The Armament Problematique: Eight Cases

Over time, systemic confrontation, armament competition, and the armament dynamics vacillate between coloring reality strongly and weakly: the systemic confrontation can become tense as in a cold war, or it may cool to a detente. The armament competition can escalate to an 'armament race', or continue at a lower level when there is no tension. Armament dynamic factors can be accentuated to a greater or lesser degree. Distinguishing between high and low value for the three dimensions, their combination gives eight cases, as shown in Table 18.1.

Table 18.1 *The armament problematique*

		Armament competition			
		+		−	
		Armament dynamics		Armament dynamics	
		+	−	+	−
Systemic confrontation (or power rivalry)	+	1	2	3	4
	−	5	6	7	8

Case 1. Here is an example of strong systemic confrontation, resulting in strong armament competition, further strengthened by strong impulses from armament dynamics. This is a broad-based cold war situation.

Case 2. Here is a combination of strong systemic confrontation, strong armament competition, and weak armament dynamics. This combination may appear when an armament race is building up. This is also the background for analyses in line with the Richardson model.

Case 3. Here is a combination of strong systemic confrontation, lack of armament competition, and strong input of armament dynamics. This is an autistic structure,[2] nevertheless within a frame of systemic confrontation. At the same time, armament dynamics factors have a momentum of their own.

Case 4. Strong systemic confrontation, with a low degree of armament competition and low degree of armament dynamics, is found in a sustained but demilitarized conflict. Within a strategy of conflict transformation, it is often a goal to establish this context. In this situation, it is possible to reduce armament competition and impair the armament dynamics factors. This can make it simpler to identify the primary conflict, which is the political and ideological systemic confrontation; and that will enhance chances for political conflict management.

Case 5. Here, strong armament competition and strong armament dynamics combine with weak systemic confrontation. Systemic confrontation has lost its importance for armament, which is driven by its own self-sustained momentum.

Case 6. Here is a very improbable case – strong armament competition driven neither by specific internal nor by specific external factors. This case is largely hypothetical.

Case 7. Here is a completely autistic case: strong armament dynamics, weak systemic confrontation, and weak armament competition. Armament is driven exclusively by internal factors.

Case 8. Here is a de-ideologized and demilitarized conflict. There is no ideological controversy, nor any notable condition of armament.

We should expect to find frequent instances of cases 1 and 3, i.e. combinations of strong systemic confrontation and strong armament dynamics, in situations with strong or weak armament competition. However, we could also expect to find developments toward cases 5 and 7, especially during periods of detente. These cases are characterized by strong armament dynamics, strong or weak armament competition, and weak systemic confrontation. A development through case 4 to case 8 should be the goal of a strategy of conflict transformation. What this means is a demilitarization of the conflict, over time leading to de-ideologization. In reality, all rigid cases (1, 3, 5, 7) are characterized by strong armament driving factors. Each has certain autistic tendencies.

5 Final Remarks

Numerous studies of the armament behavior of the two superpowers and their military allies concentrate on its variability over time: the rise and decline in expenditures; old procurement programs are completed, new ones commenced; old strategic doctrines are accentuated or appear in new guise. Peace researchers are often elated when they are able to document, for instance, that the US armament budget has a lower rate of growth than the economy, or has been cut by a few billion dollars. No heed is paid to the actual size or importance of armament expenditures, e.g. the order of magnitude. The focus is on mere ripples on a sea of spending. In fact, it is impossible to grasp the relation between systemic confrontation/power rivalry, armament competition, and armament dynamics, without applying an analysis of long-term perspectives to the total size and purpose of armament expenditures. The immensity of this size is no less important to explain than marginal changes. Primacy must be given to establishing a foundation for relevant theoretical statements about the orders of magnitude involved here.

The comparative analysis of cases with different degrees of systemic confrontation, armament competition, and armament dynamics is a task that peace research has yet to complete in a satisfactory manner. It is important to ensure that the dozens of case studies completed over the past twenty years have not been conducted in vain. Some of these studies will have to be 'contextuated', e.g. reinterpreted within the total context of which only specific aspects were analyzed originally. But many new studies will have to be initiated in a coordinated manner to yield comparable results. Due attention will have to be paid to factors of system antagonism/power rivalry, armament competition, and armament dynamics. So new research will have to be threefold and heuristically balanced. Such a basis can make possible a substantive theory of 'armamentism', covering international relations, politics, socio-economic structure, and technology as crucial dimensions.

Notes

1. For my own contributions to this debate, see Senghaas (1969, 1972a, 1972b, 1974a). An extensive English summary of my position is Senghaas (1974b). See also Chapter 2 of this volume.
2. The notion of 'autistic structure' is developed further in Senghaas (1974b).

Biographical details about DIETER SENGHAAS are found at the end of Chapter 2.

Chapter 19
Arms Races – Why Worry?

HÅKAN WIBERG
Lund University Peace Research Institute, and Centre of Peace and Conflict Research at Copenhagen University

1 What Kind of Problem?

In what ways does the arms race constitute a *problem*? The answer depends on what is understood by the very term 'problem'. To a politician or an entrepreneur, the primary connotation is something that for some reason is seen as threatening, so that *something must be done*. To the typical scholar, a 'problem' is primarily something *that is insufficiently known*, where a better description, explanation, or prediction is needed. Obviously, there are linkages between 'problems' in the first and in the second senses, but frequent mutual frustrations in the cooperation between practitioners and scholars testify that such linkages are far from simple. The scholar may tend to see the politician as 'formulating the problem the wrong way', when handing it over to the former in expectation of a solution; and when the scholar has reformulated it and treated it to the best of his/her ability, feeling that great progress has been made, the politician will often see the result as largely irrelevant, since it deals with 'why' rather than with 'how'.

What constitutes a *social problem* is defined from a perceived reality, including perceptions of social consequences, and a set of standards, values, and norms as to how things ought to be. What is seen as a *scientific* problem is defined by a perceived reality (but often not the same one) and a theoretical body, a 'paradigm'.

How does this apply to the arms race? Let us start by looking at how it can appear as a *social* problem when discussed by politicians, the peace movement, and others concerned. Stated concerns about armaments are usually based on one or more of the following assumptions, here listed in simplified forms:

- *War*: armaments increase the risks of war, whether by making their possessors more belligerent, more reckless, or more likely to become the targets of pre-emptive wars, or by making 'war by accident' more probable.

- *Waste*: military expenditures constitute waste by detracting from the societal or global resources available for constructive purposes. Armaments are therefore inimical to welfare and development.
- *Threat*: highly armed states can use their military power as leverage in forcing other states to make concessions that are detrimental to their sovereignty, security, and welfare.
- *Militarization*: heavily armed states also tend to get militarized in various other ways, from economy and political system to national culture.

These assumptions differ as to who is primarily harmed. In the case of the 'militarization' argument, it is primarily the state itself, in the case of the 'threat argument' primarily others, and in the case of the 'war' argument – and often the 'waste' argument – everybody is presumed to be harmed.

All these assumptions are controversial, empirically, theoretically, or normatively. Whether militarization is good or bad depends on ethical and political standpoints. Conservatives tend to embrace more of the traditional military values than do liberals and socialists (Eckhardt, 1969, 1980; Skjelsbæk, 1979) – but it is also possible to find 'red militarism' (Albrecht, 1980; Holloway, 1980). States or alliances that see themselves as 'peace-loving', 'status quo', etc. tend to argue that the 'threat' and 'war' arguments do not apply to them.

The 'waste' argument has also been the subject of much controversy. Against the armchair argument outlined above there is also an armchair argument with the opposite conclusion: that armaments contribute positively to the national economy – by technological spin-off, and by demand stimulation and thus the creation of jobs.

Empirical investigations abound – of the economic effects of armaments on national economies, the effects of hypothetical partial disarmament, the effects of alternative uses of resources now consumed for military purposes (the disarmament-development theme), etc. (for bibliography, see Wängborg, 1981); but the issue can hardly be regarded as conclusively resolved. The predominant result is that armaments tend to be negative to national economies by draining capital, manpower, and brainpower from the civilian sector – and giving much less back to it. Despite all these results, however, there are several grounds for caution. Some findings (Benoit, 1973, 1978) indicate a positive effect in at least some developing countries; many findings in either direction show rather weak correlations; and it has been argued (Kaldor, 1982) that the issue is too crudely defined, since military technology may be either 'progressive' or 'decadent' from the viewpoint of technological/economic growth, depending on whether military demands contribute to the development of new technologies (combustion engines, aircraft, etc.) or to society being stuck with old ones (the same examples in the late 20th century). Nevertheless, the predominant result in more recent studies (e.g. Nincic, 1982; Deger & Smith, 1983;

Cappelen et al., 1984; Rasler & Thompson, 1988) is that military expenditures tend to harm countries' economies.

How much more do they harm? The United Nations has sponsored an array of studies on the relations between disarmament and development (summarized in Hovstadius & Wängborg, 1981), as well as studies of alternative uses of resources (Thorsson, 1984a is a national follow-up), and here too the results tend to favour disarmament. However, we should not expect any straightforward *causal* mechanisms, since assumptions will usually have to be made about what *would be* alternative uses, depending on e.g. the economic system, the political traditions, and more ephemeral factors in the country under study. Assets removed from the military sector may be consumed, invested, or simply lie idle; and the decision-makers may be individuals, corporations, or state machineries. Net consequences are likely to vary with all this.

For all these reasons, a detailed examination of the 'waste' argument would require a monograph of its own. We have already mentioned what appear to be the best generalizations of a sweeping kind – and that there are a number of possible exceptions, as well as various complications of the issues. Let us therefore move to the main theme of this chapter: the 'war' argument.

2 Do Armaments Promote or Prevent Wars?

Let us begin by reformulating the question: Is there any causal relationship between arms races and the occurrence of wars? If so, what does it look like? We will first look at the theoretical arguments that have been adduced to answer these questions, and then try to discern to what extent existing empirical studies can shed any light on these controversies.

The typical answer to the first question is 'Yes', although authors then differ widely as to what direction the relationship has. Let us, however, also point out that the answer might be 'No' (Saaty, 1968; Lambelet, 1971; Chatterjee, 1974). If we portray military expenditures as being essentially governed by internal or domestic processes, and the dynamics of escalation into war as essentially depending on features of international interaction, then it is not obvious that these two processes need be much related to each other. It might also be that both armament dynamics and escalation processes are manifestations of more profound characteristics of the international system, that they therefore may be parallel without affecting each other very much. If 'No' is the 'correct' answer, then empirical studies should reveal this, either by finding zero correlations between indicators of armament and indicators of war, or by finding initial correlations between them to be spurious: that they vanish, when other factors are kept constant.

Among those that hold 'Yes' to be the answer there is a centuries-old controversy as to the direction. Let us glance at the arguments of each position before proceeding to a more detailed theoretical analysis.

First, we find an array of arguments to the effect that armaments *beget* war. The trivial one is that you cannot have wars without arms – from which it is then often extrapolated that the more arms you have, the greater is the risk that they will get used. Various assumptions may then be made to underpin this conclusion. The more armed a state is, the more militarized it becomes; and military influence tends to be more warlike than civilian. The more a state has invested in military might, the greater become the pressures to have something to show for it, and the greater the likelihood of aggressive policies. The more military capability a state has, the less cautious will it be in its foreign policies, and therefore the more likely will it be to get involved in processes leading to 'unintentional' war. The more armaments there are in an international system, the more will there be of mutual fear and/or competition, the more will competitive elements of interaction prevail over cooperative ones, and the greater becomes the likelihood of war. The more a state arms, the more likely is it that this will be seen as a threat by its neighbours, and thus become the target of pre-emptive attack. The more armed the states in an international system are, the greater is the likelihood of a premium on striking first in a crisis and therefore that international crises will escalate into war. Heavy armaments tend to increase the total 'conflict budget' between states by becoming a conflict element in themselves, thereby increasing the risk of war. The more rapid the process of armament, the more tension will there be in the system; and therefore the occurrence of crises will increase, whereas the prudence and rationality of the decision-makers in crises tend to decrease.

We also find an impressive array of arguments in the opposite direction, however. Many of them are variations of the *si vis pacem, para bellum* argument which is the normal justification used by states for their own armaments; and many of them flatly contradict the assumptions contained in the first set. The more militarily prepared I am, the more likely are you to be deterred from attacking me, or indeed from taking the risk of getting involved in a war with me. The more armaments there are in a system, the more destructive is a war likely to be, and the less willing will either side be to take risks of getting involved in one. They will therefore be more likely to avoid crises, as well as more likely to behave prudently and cautiously in case of crisis. The risk that someone will 'get ahead' by a sudden arms spurt is greater in a system with low levels of armament than in one with higher, so the system is more stable in the latter case. Arms races may serve as a substitute for military confrontations, making them less likely. As is often the case in social science, the conclusion from one set of premises that appear 'reasonable' is flatly contradicted by the conclusion from another set of premises that appear equally 'reasonable', and there are scant prospects of resolving the contradiction from the armchair. We must therefore consider how to make the different assumptions testable, and decide what is to count as admissible evidence. One obvious question will be what the relevant variables are.

At first glance, the dependent variable seems obvious: *war*. It appears to be easily observable and to be quantifiable in a number of ways: duration, casualties, amount of military forces engaged, number of participating states, etc. Yet this simplicity is partly spurious, as witnessed by the fact that different lists of wars for a given time period may vary by a factor of 10 – different authors having different criteria in terms of actors (states only, or other combinations as well), duration, continuity (whether to count a series of battles as one or more wars), and the numbers of combatants and casualties. There is quite a high degree of agreement at the upper end, but rather less at the lower (Richardson, 1960b). Nor is this only a matter of more or less arbitrary empirical delimitations, where some authors treat war as a 'yes/no' variable, whereas others count with it (or more than one category of armed confrontation) as the extreme value of some kind of scale. (For the state of this art, see e.g. Leng & Singer, 1988.)

Behind these considerations lie theoretical issues: Should we expect the same causal mechanisms and dynamics in smaller confrontations as in major wars? Should we expect 'war' to be just more of something than 'military confrontation', or should we assume the two to be importantly different? More sophisticated types of investigation (reviewed in Eberwein, 1981) have split the problem of establishing what factors are associated with war into two components: finding the correlates of the emergence of military confrontations, and finding the factors behind military confrontations escalating into war. (The latter has been one main preoccupation of the Correlates of War Project and studies emerging from it; for an overview, see Singer, 1981.)

In some cases, however, the variable under discussion is 'probability of war', rather than war itself, and the problem is then how to measure that variable independently of measurements of war. Quincy Wright (1971 [1942]) attempted to do so by means of informed judges, but found out that only very close to World War II were they able to assess who would get into war with whom considerably better than a random guess would have done. Goldmann (1974) has tried another way, by operationalizing 'tension' in terms of content analysis of official statements concerning the risk of war, relating that variable to, *inter alia*, nuclear strategic balance and different kinds of polarity.

With these – and a few more – exceptions, however, the occurrence of war has been the predominant variable (whether alone or in terms of escalation of a military confrontation) in attempts to test propositions about relationships between military preparedness and belligerence.

The *independent variable* is far more problematic, for several reasons. Statements like 'The more armaments, the more . . .' may refer to different *levels*: the individual state, the dyad, or the entire system under consideration. In many cases, especially in 'deterrence' arguments, what counts is not so much the levels of armaments in individual states as some comparison between them ('balance of power' in some sense of that notoriously ambiguous term). The magnitudes that are relevant to measure may also vary from one analysis to the other. Sometimes the argument is about the assumed effects of the armaments themselves; often it is about the perceptions of these magnitudes, or about the comparisons made in somebody's perceptions. In the latter cases, measures of armaments will only serve as proxies for measures of perceptions, being easier to measure and justified by (often questionable – Morgan, 1983, pp. 188f.) assumptions to the effect that the perceptions are approximately correct.

Nor is it self-evident *what* quantities to attempt to measure. Some arguments essentially revolve around *input*: how much of its assets a nation spends on military preparations, whether in absolute terms or in relation to its GNP, state budget, etc. (and even there it is controversial what divisor to use – cf. Leitenberg & Ball, 1977). In other cases *output* is assumed to count: the amount of military capability that a state gets out of its investment. We refer this discussion to Chapter 3, however, since with few exceptions (e.g. Naroll, 1969) those who have tried to correlate armaments and war have generally used input variables – whether because these have been seen as the directly relevant ones, or because they have been used as proxies for output on the basis of arguments of optimal allocation, etc. (Abolfathi, 1978, contradicted by Rattinger, 1975a).

There is another theoretically important problem concerning what to measure. In some arguments, it is the quantities of armaments, or the relations between these quantities in different states, that are assumed to count: whereas in other arguments (of the 'arms race' type), it is rather the first-order derivatives, indicating the pace of the arms race, that are seen as crucial. This involves no new problem of validity (if we have a valid measure of armaments, that obviously also entails having a valid measure of their pace), but it may greatly compound the problem of reliability: the relative uncertainty of a difference is greater, or far greater, than the relative uncertainty of the terms of the difference (Wiberg, 1983).

3 The Burden of Proof and the Logic of Worrying

What, then, is to count as evidence? The problem is, of course, not special to issues concerning arms races, but may have a particularly high relevance here. Let us start by looking at the problem in a more abstract way: with an activity widely regarded as having beneficial consequences (which are often given as the arguments for engaging in the activity), at the same time as there is some suspicion that it also has potentially harmful consequences, where does the burden of proof lie, and what is adequate proof?

This problem is obviously in itself an ethical one, the answer to which must depend, *inter alia*, on the ethical standards of the analyst. It may, however, give rise to at least two lines of inquiry. One of them is descriptive, and concerns what risks are accepted and who is regarded as having the burden of proof, in what cultures, at what time periods. The other line is conditionally prescriptive: *given* that an actor (legislative body, entrepreneur, etc.) has a certain preference order or utility function, and given that this actor has a certain degree of risk aversion, what procedures of assessing evidence is it *rational* for him to have? A tentative answer to the descriptive question seems to be that it is difficult to discern any coherent doctrine about risks, e.g. in modern Western societies. In the same state at the same time, the law of a country may require providers of medicines or foodstuffs to satisfy fairly rigorous criteria of evidence to the effect that their products do not have noxious side effects – and require trade unions or environmentalists to give strong positive (rather than just *prima-facie*) evidence of the harmfulness of a chemical substance that they want prohibited in industrial production.

The simplest answers to the simplest versions of the prescriptive question take as their point of departure that the rules of assessment must depend on the relative strength of the beneficial and the harmful effects. For example, many legal systems regard it as a far worse mistake to sentence and punish an innocent person than to acquit a guilty one. In that case, it becomes rational to put the burden of proof on the prosecution, and to make it fairly strong ('beyond reasonable doubt'). In societies where acquitting a guilty person is seen as the worse mistake, it instead becomes rational to require that the accused prove their innocence.

In science, it is generally regarded as a worse mistake to admit a false proposition to the body of established knowledge than to refuse admission to a true proposition. (We need not go into the underlying rationality of that preference here.) For that reason, scientific criteria of evidence tend to be fairly strong, as expressed e.g. in terms of levels of significance.

Now, what about armaments and their effects? What kinds of evidence is it rational to demand, and on the basis of what arguments?

The combination of beliefs and preferences in most states implies that armaments have beneficial effects for the state in question, e.g. in terms of capabilities for defence and deterrence or dissuasion. We shall take this for granted without discussing how well-founded that belief may be and must move on to the next question: What about the marginal utility of armaments? Military authorities (like other bureaucracies) try to argue that it is very high just around the present level of expenditure: even a slight reduction would lead to a dramatic loss of national security, and a very modest increase would solve major problems. Among others, however, the belief is widespread that the marginal utility is decreasing even at the present level: you get less additional security out of each new defence dollar, or each extra unit of equipment. Several of the arguments we have reviewed go even further, arguing that the marginal effect may well be negative, with unintended side effects outweighing any increases in defence and/or deterrence capability.

Where, then, is it rational to allocate the burden of proof? Should the military have to prove that the proposed increase would have positive net effects, or should those who worry be required to prove the opposite?

It is far beyond the scope of the present chapter to attempt to *answer* that question – and by implication whether the now predominant distribution of burdens of proof is a rational one or not. One observation should be made, however, in regard to the evidence we are about to survey. By observing normal scientific standards, writers have usually regarded hypotheses about the effect of armaments on wars as supported, only if there was fairly strong evidence for them (whether in terms of significance tests, or some other criteria): and otherwise they have been regarded as not supported. It lies implicit in this – even if not necessarily intended by the authors – that the burden of proof rests with those who worry. This may or may not be rational, depending on how we answer the question above, in attempting a political balance sheet. In any case, whatever standard of evidence we use for assessing whether a worry is justified or not, the criteria must be less stringent when it comes to whether to *start* worrying. Here, 'beyond reasonable doubt' cannot be the criterion: 'more likely than not' may be amply sufficient, or even 'there is some risk that . . .'. From this perspective, the evidence we will go through is highly cautious, in that it systematically underestimates the reasons for worrying, or at least for starting to worry.

4 Quantitative Evidence

We emphasize that we are restricting our survey to one type of evidence: that put forward in quantitative terms, by statistically testing hypotheses concerning the effects of war of armaments. Some hypotheses deal with the national level, others concern dyads of competing nations, and others still make statements about regions or entire international systems. Nor is there any a priori convincing reason why the relations between armaments and war should be the same on all levels.

We also find considerable variation in the complexity of the hypotheses. The simplest ones have dimensions of armaments only as independent variables, whereas others have other independent variables as well, such as the economic size of nations, or the number of boundaries that they have. In the simplest case, where all effects are assumed to be direct and no interaction is assumed between the independent variables, disentangling the effects of armaments as such becomes simple, and the other independent variables are primarily interesting for making comparisons between the effects of armaments and those of the other variables. In more complex models, effects may be assumed to be both direct and indirect, which calls for more statistical work in assessing them; or the effects may be assumed to be multiplicative, rather than additive. It may be that two phenomena have relatively few effects by themselves, but much more when combined, as seems to be the case with arms races and crises.

Let us start by looking at the very simple hypothesis: that armaments beget war. If this is true, then we should find that the greater the absolute level of armaments in a nation, the more wars will that nation get involved in. Even a casual inspection of data will reveal a strong tendency in this direction – but then, several reservations have to be made. First, this may have to do with the classical finding (Richardson, 1960b; Wright, 1971), replicated by several others, that great powers do get much more involved in wars than others. That still leaves open what aspect of great power status it is that counts most, since this finding recurs even when 'great power' is defined solely in terms of trade patterns (Wallensteen, 1973). Since economy and military size are closely related (Köhler, 1977), an observed correlation between military size and engagement in wars *may* signify armaments-induced belligerence: but it *may* also be spurious, with the belligerence and the amount of armaments stemming separately from the economic size of the state. This can be checked – as it has – to which we return shortly. Another simple objection to drawing too quick conclusions from correlations between armaments and wars can be phrased in chicken-or-egg terms. Even if the bivariate correlation between military expenditures and war participation is not exposed as spurious when we control for economic size (e.g. by correlating belligerence with GNP/cap rather than with GNP), the direction of causality still constitutes a problem. The correlation *might* be due to high military expenditures engendering a martial spirit, a reckless foreign policy or pre-emptive attacks from others, but it *might* also mean that a (correctly, as it turns out) predicted war has motivated the high and/or rapidly increasing armament level; and it *might* mean that some underlying factor causes *both* increased armaments *and* a stronger tendency to get involved in war.

Let us give one example of each type of further analysis. Newcombe & Wert (1973, continuing Newcombe, 1969) tried to control for economic size by first regressing military expenditures (milex) on GNP, then dividing actual milex with the thus theoretically expected milex to define a 'tension ratio', and then relating this ratio to participation in war in a longitudinal study. They found that nations with a tension ratio over about 150 (i.e. nations that spend in excess of 50% more on armaments than expected from their size) are several times more likely to get into war than those not overarmed in this sense. They also found that *moving* into being overarmed was strongly associated with participation in war (cf. Sylvan, 1976 on effects of getting military aid). Their study thus takes care of the first kind of objection, since they have controlled for economic size. It does, however, not conclusively take care of the second objection, since alternative explanations of the correlation can still be imagined – e.g. what Lebow (1981, p. 315) calls 'post-crisis military preparation': some underlying factor makes crises more frequent, one of the first in the series triggers off a rapid rearmament, and a later one escalates into war.

An example of trying to cope with the second objection can be found in Naroll (1969) in his very longitudinal study. Apart from trying to control for cultural factors and possible diffusion, he discusses his central finding that armament tends to make war more likely, irrespective of whether the state in question has a defensive or aggressive stance. Naroll's argument against the correlation being spurious is that he has four different indicators of military preparedness. If war frequency were the cause and armaments the effect, then we should expect these four indicators to correlate with each other, whereas in fact they have little or no interrelationship. On the other hand, since Naroll looks only at a fairly limited category of nations (approximately: regional or systemic major powers), the first objection cannot readily be taken care of.

Moving from examples to the whole universe of quantitative analyses of correlates of international violence – especially those relating it to armaments – we find a fairly vague picture. Vasquez (1976), in his encompassing survey of statistical findings in international politics, notes that most hypotheses have low success and low predictive power; and that when international violence is the dependent variable, both are lower than average. Among what, on the basis of his criteria, are characterized as 'null findings' we find: 'There appears to be no strong relationship between the military power or status of a nation. [. . .] and negative interactions between nations' (p. 200). The only type of hypothesis relevant to our inquiry that fares slightly better is that 'There appears to be no strong relationship between violence among nations and the military power or status of nations'. This, however, seems a borderline case, since it is cited both under 'null findings' (p. 202) and as a 'promising finding' (p. 203).

The picture found in other early surveys of quantitative studies is rather much the same. Rummel (1972), in addition to citing early – and methodologically rather unsatisfactory – attempts by Cattell (1949), Cattell & Gorsuch (1965), and Richardson (1960b), goes through the results from his own Dimensionality of Nations project (e.g. Rummel, 1968) as to how 'foreign conflict behaviour' is related to indicators of military effort (absolute and relative milex and military personnel). The correlations he finds by using varying measures and techniques range between 0.30 and 0.55, relative figures yielding somewhat higher correlations than absolute ones. His conclusion, nevertheless, is that there is little relationship between armaments and foreign conflict behaviour, or specifically war; and in his later major work (1979), armaments and increases in them play a very modest role in the theory construction: for example, they are not even included in the theory about action/reaction processes. Rummel obviously uses very strict criteria, e.g. in terms of amount of variance explained. With moderately strict criteria, the conclusion would rather have been that here *is* a relationship. (See also Weede, 1973 for a discussion of why he and Rummel arrived at different conclusions.)

Rummel is by no means alone, however. In such later surveys as those of van der Dennen (1981) and Zinnes (1980), the net verdict is also quite modest when it comes to how military efforts affect war. One reason may be that these authors have looked more generally at 'power' and at direct effects shown in bivariate correlations with indicators or factors.

In the 1970s we find a new generation of research, as represented by Haas (1974), Wallace (1972, 1973), and Choucri & North (1975). All of these work with more complex causal models, where military indicators appear 'in the middle' of the model; and all of them find various kinds of effects, only some of which are direct, however. Haas, in addition to finding a slight correlation between relative milex and his conflict index, tries different causal models in terms of how well they fit his totality of data. In all of them, arms build-up contributes to warfare, but in different ways for developing and for developed countries: other variables are seen as having a substantial part of their effects via arms build-up, which in addition has some direct and indirect effects of its own.

Much the same is true for Wallace: in his case, rank disequilibrium has much of its effects via milex indicators, which, however, also have some effects of their own. Likewise, in the model used by Choucri & North, military indicators mainly appear as intervening variables, e.g. as intermediary between 'lateral pressure' and war – but again having some effects of their own. This set of studies does not directly contradict those cited above: the *direct* contribution of milex indicators to war is modest. But they put the issue in context, underlining the role of milex as an early warning indicator as much as, or more than, being a causal factor on its own. Finally, let us return to the issue of what aspects of being a 'great power' primarily contribute to belligerence. Here, the work from the Correlates of War project provides some clues, especially Bremer (1980). (What appears to have been an earlier version, Stuckey & Singer, 1973, is discussed in Zinnes, 1980.)

On the basis of the finding that great powers are far more warlike than others (Small & Singer, 1982), different indices were constructed and correlated with warlikeness. The purely economic indicator (degree of industrialization) turned out to be the poorest predictor of war, whereas the combination of industrial development and military preparedness was far better, producing a very strong correlation with the tendency to go to war. One tentative conclusion here might be that the military aspect of being a great power counts more than the economic one – which then gives added strength to reasons for worrying about armaments on the basis of the repeated finding that great powers are warlike.

Let us now attempt a partial summation of findings on how military preparedness as a national attribute is related to warlikeness. At best, we may say that the picture is a mixed one. Some studies report a clear relationship, but then usually a rather modest one: others draw the conclusion that, with their criteria, the relationship is nil. Among the positive studies, several add – or should have added – reservations concerning the interpretation as a *causal* relation, and where causality is more closely examined, military preparedness tends to be a 'funnel' for other causal effects at least as much as being a causal agent on its own.

The net verdict, then, will depend on how strong the criteria we use. With fairly strong ones, there is not much reason to depart from the early verdict by Rummel (1968). With less strict criteria, we may rather say that the picture is mixed. We then have to add two things.

First, we should note *how* the picture is mixed, consisting of some results that seem to indicate a clear relationship between armament and warlikeness – or, to express it more cautiously, getting involved in war – and those that indicate a weak or nil relationship. There are no studies indicating a relationship in the opposite direction: that armaments make for peace. The debate on choice of criteria therefore essentially concerns whether to regard it as *proved* that military preparations (belong to the set of several factors that) beget war, or only to regard it as more likely than not on the basis of the available evidence.

Second, one reason for the relatively weak results may be that we have been looking in the wrong place – which brings us to the next section.

5 The Dyadic Level

With hindsight, we may say that the relatively meagre results from the nation level might have been expected on the grounds that war is essentially a relation between nations, rather than a behaviour of individual nations, for which reason we ought to look primarily at properties of dyads when searching for causes of war. In our particular case, the important questions will then concern how war in a dyad is related to armament characteristics of that dyad: the pair of armament levels of the members, as well as the sum of these levels and the relation between the levels.

The simplest hypothesis here would be that the more arms that can be brought to bear in a conflict, the more likely is it that they will actually be used. Some versions of balance-of-power or deterrence theorizing, however, contradict that hypothesis.

A first crude indicator can be found in the dyadic version of the 'great power finding': dyads of two great powers are far more likely than others to get into war, followed by dyads with one great and one other power (Wallensteen, 1973; Weede, 1975). The problems of spuriousness remain here, too. One way of coping with them is by limiting ourselves to dyads of major powers and looking at how the likelihood of war is related to armament levels in the dyad. First, however, we should reformulate the question (Eberwein, 1981; Singer, 1981; Waymen et al., 1983) to distinguish the issue of under what circumstances a dispute is likely to lead to a military confrontation, from that of when a military confrontation is likely to escalate into war.

In analysing the latter question, Singer (1979) finds that the risk of escalation increases with the level of military preparedness in a dyad: it increases from low–low dyads to low–high dyads, and further increases from low–high to high–high dyads, when such dyads consist of two major powers.

Those results seem to lend some credibility to the notion that armaments are dangerous – but dangerous as compared to what? Maoz (1983), in his study of the outcome of disputes, concludes that *resolve* (as operationalized by him) plays a greater role for the outcome of disputes than capability: initiators of disputes, as well as initiators of war, tend to win more often than the others. For our purpose, the important result in his study is that when both parties in a dispute pursue reckless policies, the risk of war becomes particularly high (40%, as against the average of 12%). This means that the policies of the parties make more of a difference for the risk of war than do variations in their capabilities.

The more general question concerns how the risk of war is related to the relations between the capabilities of the parties. Several versions of balance-of-power thinking hold this to be the crucial variable – and more important than the individual levels or their sum. In the very simplest version, the hypothesis is that the risk of war in a dyad is less when there is equality of capability. Several studies, however, disconfirm this simple hypothesis. Singer (1979), studying major powers since 1816, finds that the risk of escalation of a military confrontation into war is higher (20%) when both sides have a high level of military preparedness than when only one of them has (13%). Studying different regions in a shorter time perspective, Weede (1976) finds that peace is most likely in a dyad when one of the parties has overwhelming preponderance; concurrently, Garnham (1976) finds that there is most violence in a dyad in a dispute when the parties are approximately equal in military power. This is also implied by the results of Houweling & Siccama (1988), who find that *overtaking* is most strongly related to war: overtaking presupposes approximate equality, so this result, too, contradicts (the equality version of) the balance-of-power hypothesis of peace.

Other studies have tried to investigate versions of balance-of-power or deterrence hypotheses more systematically, by comparing several different measures of relations of capability with several different versions of such hypotheses. The study most relevant for our question, using quantitative measures of capabilities, is that of Smith (1982), who does not find much support for deterrence theory, either.

One obvious possible objection here is that present, post-1945, history is not really comparable with past, due to the combination of nuclear weapons and fairly rigid pact systems. Weede (1981, 1983, 1985) attempts to study the effects of extended deterrence by comparing (overall, or within a subset of prima-facie conflict-prone dyads) the dyads whose members belong to opposite military blocs with the other dyads. He concludes that the former dyads have a lower (in fact, nil) frequency of wars, so that extended deterrence seems to work. If Modelski & Morgan (1985) are right in arguing that there has been little risk of a global war anyhow in the post-1945 period, then that circumstance, rather than extended deterrence, accounts for this absence of war in inter-bloc relations.

So far we have only looked at static aspects of the relationship between armaments and war. It remains to look at the dynamic aspect, at the relationship between *arms races* and war. The very term 'arms race' is controversial (Buzan, 1987, ch. 5). Those authors who have attempted more systematic quantitative studies have taken pains to make their terms more clear by characterizing arms dynamics in dyads in terms of how quick, how long, and how linked (or some combination of these) a dyadic process of rearming is.

6 Arms Races and War

The first scholar to combine theory building and rigorous empirical research was Lewis Fry Richardson (1960a), whose analysis of arms races is discussed in Chapters 3–5 in the present volume. For our present analysis, only his hypotheses about the relationship between arms races and war are of interest. Richardson's central hypothesis was that what he called *unstable* arms races would terminate in war, whereas stable ones would not necessarily do so. It should be noted here that his use of the terms 'stable' and 'unstable' is completely different from that found in strategic studies or international politics. A 'stable arms race' is Richardson's shorthand for 'an arms race in a stable regime', which in turn means an arms race where – in the model – one can predict that it will eventually lead to the armaments of the two sides stabilizing at a combination (X, Y), calculable from the model and the data. By contrast (the interesting version of) an 'unstable' arms race is one where it can be predicted that arms expenditures will spiral upwards endlessly. The conditions for stability and the absence of stability were studied by Richardson; later authors, like Zinnes (1976), have made further refinements.

What is relevant for us here is Richardson's way of linking armaments and war. Unlike his very careful work with the models, there is no theoretical derivation of his hypothesis about a linkage: it is just stated, seemingly as more or less self-evident, and later authors have questioned it on various grounds. To Huntington (1958), the interesting distinction is that between quantitative arms races, which he assumes to be destabilizing (in the strategic studies sense), and qualitative arms races, which may be stabilizing. Lambelet (1971) has argued that arms races and war are largely independent, and holds (1975b) that Richardson's distinction between stable and unstable arms races may not be so relevant in some cases: it depends on where the calculated point of stability lies in relation to the budget lines of the opposing parties (which are not necessarily constant over time). To see this, compare Figures 19.1 to 19.4, which illustrate where the armaments equilibrium $(\bar{X}, \bar{Y})$ may lie in relation to the budgetary limitations (B_X, B_Y) for military expenditures of the parties. We get the following four combinations, depending on whether the equilibrium is stable (indicated by arrows towards it) or unstable (arrows pointing from it), and on whether it is affordable (lying inside the 'budget box') or not (outside it).

	Stable	Unstable
Affordable	Figure 19.1	Figure 19.2
Non-affordable	Figure 19.3	Figure 19.4

Figure 19.1 *A stable, affordable arms race*

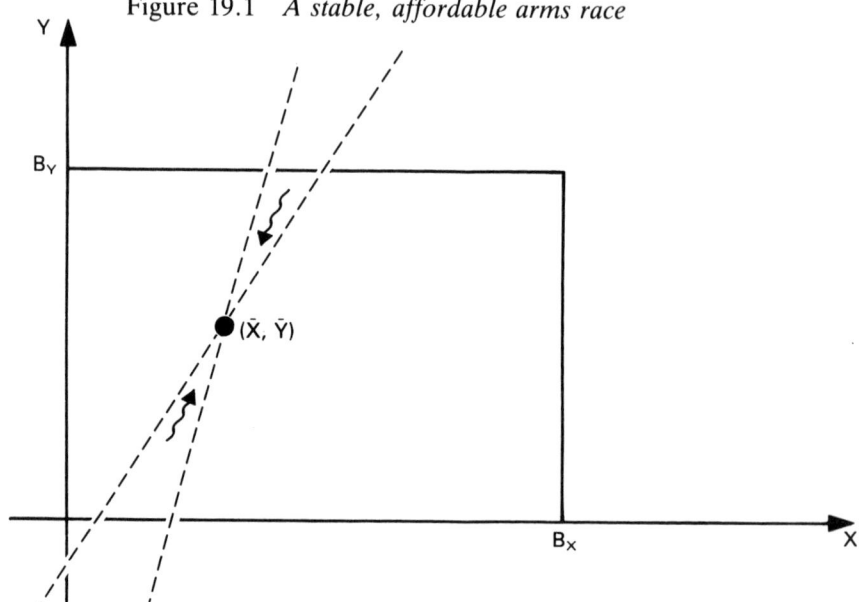

Figure 19.2 *An unstable, affordable arms race*

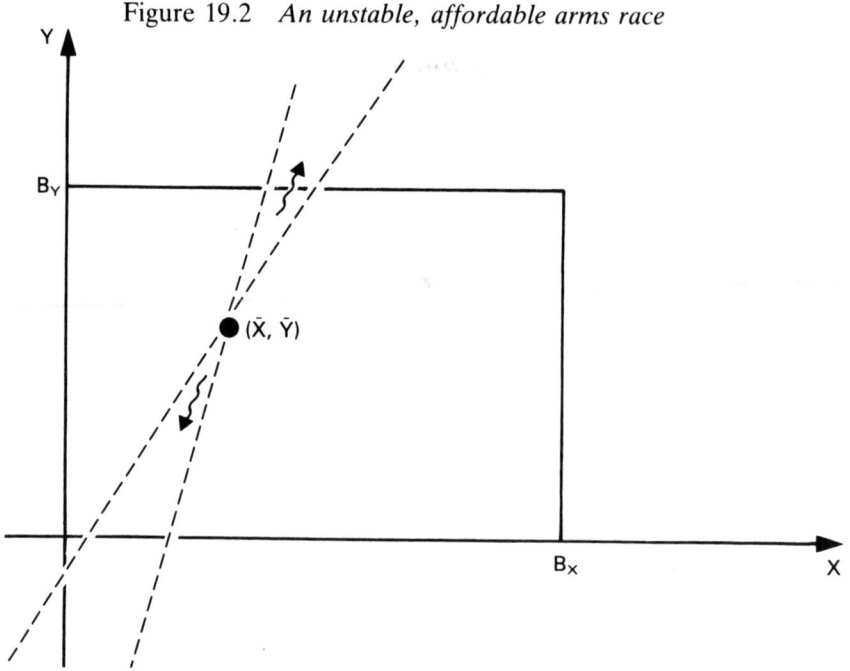

Figure 19.3 *A stable, non-affordable arms race*

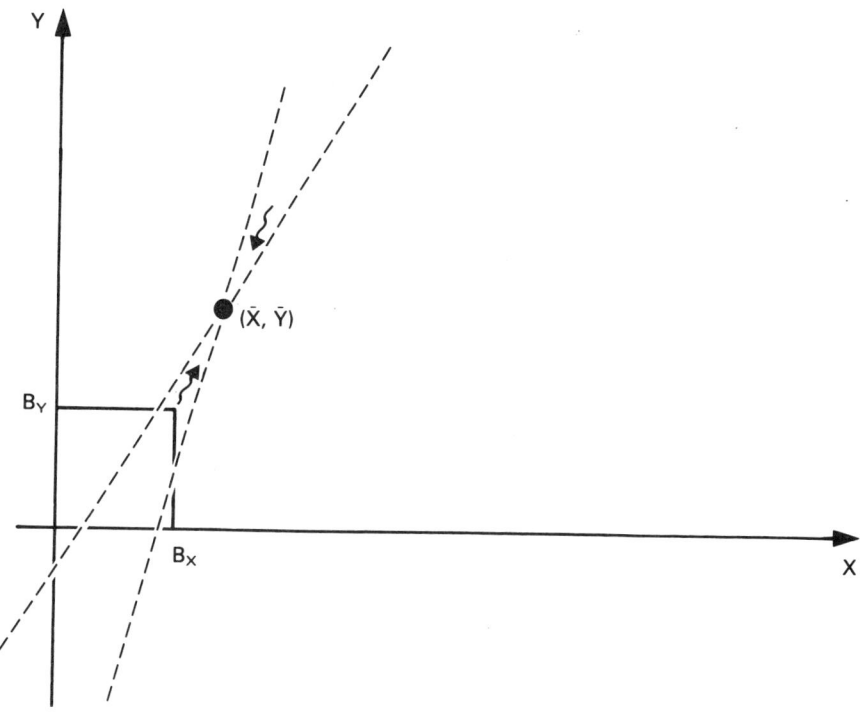

Figure 19.4 *An unstable, non-affordable arms race*

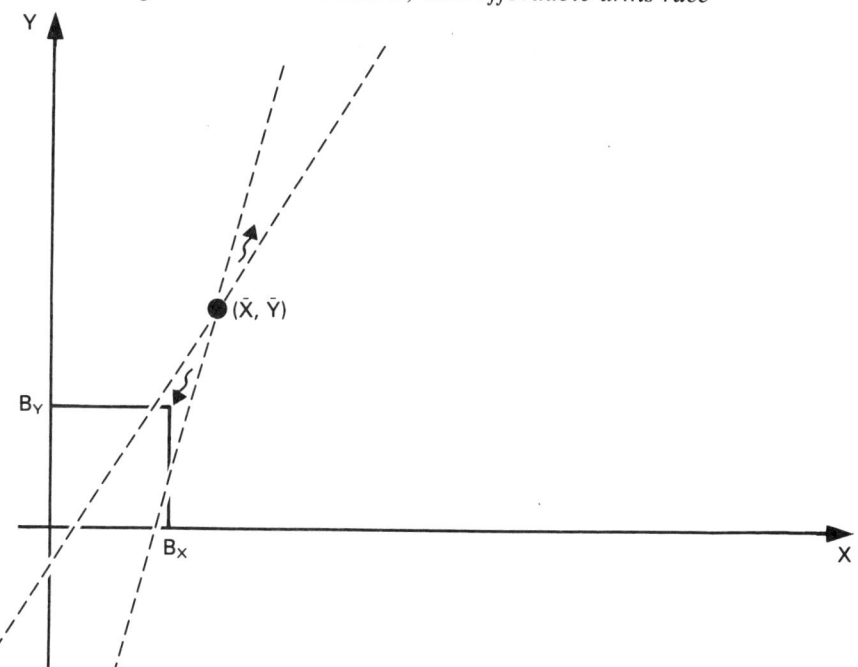

From Richardson's theoretical point of view, the crucial distinction is that between stable and unstable: and he assumes that unstable arms races will lead to war. To this, Lambelet has two objections: (1) they might just as well end in bankruptcy as in war; and (2) from that view point, the situation depicted in Figure 19.3 is not interestingly different from those depicted in Figures 19.2 and 19.4. All three describe arms races where the momentum tends to drive the race outside the economically possible, and additional hypotheses are required for the model to predict what will happen then. Will the budget box define an imposed stability (in which case *all* arms races end in the 'stable' category, which according to Richardson may or may not end in war)? Or should we hypothesize that lying close to the budget line creates a danger of war in itself (in which case the stable race in Figure 19.3 is just as dangerous as the unstable ones)?

Richardson also assumes, although without formally deriving it from his model, that disarmament moves by one or both sides will increase the probability of peace. This has been challenged by several authors: Lambelet (1975b) again, as well as several works by Dagobert Brito and Michael Intriligator (see e.g. Intriligator & Brito, 1984, or Chapter 4 in the present volume). In essence, their arguments are based on assumptions about the effects of force ratios in terms of deterrence, temptation to attack, and temptation to pre-empt, and their conclusions are that, given suitable assumptions, *any* relationship between armament/disarmament and war/peace may obtain. (Cf. the critique by Mayer, 1986; and the reply by Intriligator & Brito, 1986b.)

In very broad terms, this agrees with the conclusions that may be drawn from some versions of classical balance-of-power thinking, which is also Lambelet's point of departure. Intriligator & Brito's model, although phrased in more abstract terms, is primarily about nuclear war: or, to be more specific, about under what circumstances an intentional nuclear war would appear rational or irrational to hypothetical decision-makers with certain beliefs and preferences. Their conclusion is that an area around (0, 0) is dangerous, due to considerations of temptation and pre-emption, whereas there is a 'cone of deterrence' surrounding the upper parts of the line $X = Y$, so that under certain circumstances even mutual rearmament into that cone may increase the prospects for peace: essentially the MAD situation.

If we want an assessment of the more general links between armaments and war, however, we have to expand such a model of intentional nuclear war in two respects. What about nuclear war by accident? And how is the risk of non-nuclear war affected by the nuclear balance?

In the first respect, we find a hiatus between the vast literature modelling nuclear war decisions, and the growing literature on the risks of nuclear war by accident (Bracken, 1983; Frei & Catrina, 1983; Hellmann & Bjørnsson, 1985; Wallace et al., 1986; Smoker & Bradley, 1988). With very few exceptions (like Dumas, 1979), the risk of unintentional war has not been incorporated into rational-actor models: and analysts of accidental nuclear war have not attempted that integration either.

Nevertheless, the conclusion to be drawn in the most abstract terms appears obvious: even if, by the logic of Mutually Assured Destruction, mutual nuclear rearmament may make for (nuclear) peace by getting deeper into the 'cone of deterrence', such expansion of nuclear arsenals at the same time increases the risk of accidental nuclear war. Exactly where the latter effect outweighs the former (given these premises) nobody seems to have tried to calculate, but that boundary was probably passed a long time ago. The already existing vast overkill capability must mean that the marginal stabilizing effects of further rearmament are very small, at the same time as it seems reasonable to assume that the risks for accidental war grow at least proportionally to the number of missiles, perhaps even faster.

Nor is it self-evident how the nuclear balance should be assumed to affect the risk of non-nuclear war, or of military confrontations that might escalate into war. Here are found a number of sometimes contradicting hypotheses, all of which have at least some plausibility (Goldmann, 1974, ch. 5.4). We have already referred to the analyses by Weede, (1981, 1983, 1985) where he concludes that extended deterrence has worked, in the sense that members of the alliance systems of the two nuclear powers have not gone to war with each other. It should then be pointed out that this does not mean that nuclear powers do not go to war – on the contrary, they tend to get into considerably more war than others – only that they do not get into war *with each other*.

This is not the place for a general discussion of theories of deterrence (see e.g. Morgan, 1983; Buzan, 1987). From the perspective of our problem, however, one problem appears crucial, and that is conceded even by conditional protagonists of deterrence like Weede: the risk of accidental war is cumulative, whereas – in that sense – deterrence is not. In other words, even if the risk of accidental war in a given year is quite small, the chances of surviving many years without such a war get smaller and smaller with the number of years, so that in the long run a war is virtually certain (unless we make the very strong assumption that the annual risk decreases at least exponentially).

7 Some Empirical Evidence

Let us now move from the discussion of various hypotheses about the relationship between arms races and war to inspecting the empirical evidence produced so far. First, we shall have to consider how to delimit the universe and how to operationalize the terms – neither of which is unproblematic. Depending on the operationalization, we find between a few dozen and several hundred wars since 1816; and the number of arms races also varies, between a handful and about three dozen.

Richardson himself (1960a, ch. 6) notes that 'Historians mention arms races only for 10 out of 84 wars between 1820 and 1929', making it plain that most wars have *not* been preceded by arms races. In addition, most of the arms races he looked at were classified by him as stable ones. His study cannot be considered a systematic one, since he makes virtually no attempt at identifying the entire set of arms races in the period, so as to find out whether wars were more frequent in that set than in the complementary set. In his opinion, the modern type of unstable arms races came into being between the 1870s, when the Franco-German and Russo-Turkish wars were not preceded by unstable arms races, and the Russo-Japanese War in 1904, which was. Thus his only cases of unstable arms races are this one and the two periods preceding the world wars.

Huntington's (1958) list of arms races is also rather short, and to some extent controversial. It was only in the 1970s that the systematic quantitative study of the relationship between arms races and wars was taken up, foremost by Smith (1980, 1982), and by Wallace (1979).

Smith (1980) systematically goes through data on military expenditures – where available – for the period between 1860 and 1977. She sets up clear criteria for distinguishing 'arms races' from other kinds of rearmament, the essential ones being (1) that there are expressions of hostile intentions in the dyad under consideration, (2) that both members of it do increase their military expenditures, and (3) that this goes on for at least four years. On this basis, Smith identifies 32 arms races. These are then divided into 'Richardsonian' and 'non-Richardsonian' on the basis of whether the arms expenditures of *both* nations could be at least moderately well fitted to a simple Richardson model. Among the 14 Richardsonian arms races, 3 were still going on at the end of the period (USA/USSR, North/South Korea, and USSR/Albania). Among those that have ended, only two were unstable in Richardson's sense (Chile–Peru in 1869–79, and India–Pakistan in 1957–64), both of which ended in war. So, however, did 6 out of the 9 stable arms races, and the attempt to predict war or peace on the basis of that distinction only yielded an unimpressive score of 5/11.

Therefore Smith took a closer look at the stable races, expecting (like Ward, 1984b) that it would make a difference whether the Richardson analysis of them indicates that they would approach their equilibrium point and slow down considerably rather soon ('interestingly stable races'), or whether this could be expected to take a long time ('uninterestingly stable ones'). It was then assumed that, from the point of view of war-proneness, the latter category ought to be put together with the unstable ones. In fact, all four of the 'uninterestingly stable' arms races ended in war (USSR–Japan 1921–38, France–Germany 1936–39, Israel–Arab states 1949–55, and again 1968–73), whereas among the five 'interestingly stable' arms races, two ended in war and three did not. By this re-categorization, then, predictive success improved to 9/11; and the author might have claimed even a bit more than that, since the basis for that score is the version of the hypothesis that stable arms races will *not* end in war, which is stronger than Richardson's own.

Since Smith's period largely overlaps with that studied by Wallace (1979) – 1816–1965 – and since they use rather different operationalizations, it is interesting to see to what extent their conclusions agree. In this 1979 work,

Wallace moves from his earlier (1972, 1973) analyses of nations to the dyadic case, although limited to dyads of major powers. From the Correlates of War list of military confrontations, he finds 99 such dyads in the entire period. He then constructs a fairly complex 'arms race index' as – essentially – a product of the extrapolated rates of increase in the armaments of the two parties, aimed at ensuring that 'only long-term, intense, bilateral growth in arms expenditures will score high' (Wallace, 1979, p. 13). With this index, 28 out of the 99 disputes were preceded by an arms race, and 23 of them ended in war, whereas only 3 out of the 71 disputes not preceded by arms races ended in war. We thus note a very strong and by any criterion statistically significant relationship between arms races and (escalation of military confrontations into) war. While Wallace appropriately warns that this statistical association does not *necessarily* indicate a causal relationship (both phenomena *might* be caused by a third one) he insists that, at the very least, it makes the arms race index an early warning indicator – especially since three of the five cases with arms races without war were situations that historians tend to regard as having been at the brink of war: the remilitarization of the Rhineland, the Munich crisis, and the Cuban missile crisis.

Given the difference in time periods, operationalizations, and cases, it is difficult to say much more about the relationship between Smith's and Wallace's studies than that both point in the same direction. Later critiques do shed some more light over the robustness of the results.

Weede's (1980) main objections to Wallace's methodology are (1) that there have been long time periods without any case of escalation; (2) that 19 out of the 23 escalating arms races belong to the two complexes involving World War I and World War II, respectively; and (3) that Wallace does not distinguish between status-quo powers and revisionist powers, so as to be able to assess better the *para bellum* hypothesis. In his reply, Wallace (1980) points out (1) that the relationship between arms races and escalation holds for each time period; (2) that even when the data are rearranged in the ways suggested by Weede to get more statistical independence between the cases, we get strongly significant statistical relationships between arms races and wars; and (3) that the status-quo/revisionist variable does indeed have an effect of its own, but at the same time, there remains a strong relationship between arms races and wars, even when we control for this variable – and in addition, the arms race index turns out to be a better predictor of escalation than the ratio of military expenditures between the status-quo nation and the revisionist nation.

In a later article, Wallace (1981) makes a more thorough attempt at comparing the explanative power of two versions (superior power or quicker armament rate) of the *para bellum* hypothesis with that of the arms race index. His conclusion is that the two former variables explain very little by themselves ($R^2 = 0.074$) in comparison with the arms race index ($R^2 = 0.759$), and also that they add very little explanative power (from

0.759 to 0.799), when combined with the arms race index in the same causal model: for which reason 'it is those who would seek "peace through preparedness", who have misread the historical record and, as a consequence, are advocating a dangerously unrealistic course' (p. 95).

Another replication was made by Houweling & Siccama (1981), who questioned Wallace's methodology and definitions on several counts, e.g. that he could not distinguish the effects of arms races from those of serious disputes, having looked only at *when* serious disputes escalated into wars. The essential result of their replication is that the occurrence of serious disputes is statistically associated with the occurrence of a (direct or indirect) arms race, that both serious disputes, arms races, and the combination of the two are associated with outbreak of war in a way statistically significant, but that the *direct* effects of disputes are much stronger than the *direct* effects of arms races. Houweling & Siccama also checked Wallace's own conclusion by seeing what happened when one used Smith's, rather than Wallace's own, operationalization of 'arms race'. They found that, in this case, the statistical association was still in the direction of arms races engendering war, but now quite weak and not statistically significant.

Another test of the robustness of Wallace's results is found in Diehl (1983), who also revised some of the definitions and measures on the basis of a methodological critique. He still found the same relationship as Wallace, even if considerably weaker: arms races do increase the risk of confrontations escalating into war. (Further light is shed on the underlying mechanisms by Diehl 1985, studying how the outcomes of such confrontations that did *not* escalate into war were affected by the presence or absence of arms races.) Finally, in addition to finding that rough parity between the parties increases the risk of a confrontation escalating into war from 13% to 20%, Singer (1979) found that the risk increased further to 75% when this parity was combined with a rapid military build-up in the three years prior to the dispute.

Thus all studies have found that arms races are positively associated with war; in nearly all it is statistically significant, and in a couple of them strong. There is absolutely no support for the direct version of the *para bellum* hypothesis. Empirical results do not logically exclude that in some sub-universe of the cases, there might be a negative relation between arms races and wars; however, such a sub-universe has not been empirically identified.

8 Higher Levels of Aggregation

So far, we have reviewed the results of studies using nations, or dyads of nations, as statistical individuals. In some of these, the level of aggregation is actually slightly higher: note Israel vs. the Arab states. When we move to still higher levels of aggregation, we can find a number of studies that relate belligerence to e.g. degree of polarity, degree of alliance formation, measures of balance of power – and the first-order derivatives of such measures. (See the review by Zinnes, 1980 for the rather confusing results.) There seems to be no study, however, that tries to relate the armament levels of regions to the incidence of wars in regions. In all likelihood, the result would be rather puzzling, at least for the post-1945 period, when we have had unusually little war both in regions with very high armaments density (Europe) and in regions with low density (South America), at the same time as the regions with high armaments density include both Europe and the Middle East.

For methodological reasons, it is even more difficult to assess the effects of variations in global military efforts on global peace. For a long time, we have had only one international system, and when we go further back in time, reliable data can hardly be found. The only way of identifying such effects must therefore be by means of time-series analysis, where the chicken-and-egg problem is likely to loom large, if the period investigated includes the two tremendous peaks of the world wars. Alcock (1972) seems to have made the most ambitious attempt, looking at the post-1945 period only. His theory implies that we should find disproportionately much war in periods when the rate of increase in arms expenditures has just shifted from acceleration to deceleration: when arms expenditures are still going up, but more slowly than before.

Alcock also claims to have found support – in effect very strong support – for his theory in the data he presents. Thompson et al. (1979) criticized Alcock's study on a number of counts, from the periodization to his using ad hoc interpretation rather than systematic testing. Their attempts at replication, having rectified these things, is not quite comparable to Alcock's, however, since Thompson et al. studied a different subject: the set of great powers in 1900–65. In any case, they found no systematic support for the hypothesis, which they ought to have done, had it had generalizable validity.

9 Summing Up

What conclusions can we draw from these overviews of empirical studies of relationships between armaments and wars? That depends on two things: the findings themselves, and the criteria we use in assessing the findings. If we use very strong criteria for awarding the epithet 'beyond reasonable doubt', then it is difficult to find anything that is really *proved*. Even those results that are quite respectable, or even impressive, by the standards used in social science for sampling, measurement, systematic comparisons, and assessment of statistical significance are unable to produce *the cause* of wars. They can do no more than identify causal components and show tendencies. Having proved that major powers, on average, are far more likely to enter wars than other states does not mean we have demonstrated that there is *no* relatively peaceful great power. Having demonstrated that a category of arms races is dangerous, in the sense that members of this category are far more likely to escalate into a war than other dyads of nations, we still have not shown that any arms race in this category *must* end in war. There are no natural laws in social science – whether we relish or deplore that fact. If the burdens of proof are made that strong, those who worry about increasing armaments have no solid evidence to produce – but the advocates of increases have even less.

If we limit the burden of proof to what professional social scientists would normally accept as evidence, we have more to offer. Several studies of the effects of – absolute or relative – armament levels associate them with getting into disproportionally much war. This may then be tentatively accepted as a fact, even if some reservations have to be made: some studies do not find a systematic relationship (but *no* study associates high armament levels with peacefulness); the relationship is usually a rather weak one (weaker than some other variables); and in several cases it may be doubted whether, or to what extent, the statistical relationship reveals a causal one, alternative explanations not having been systematically excluded.

If it is a weakness in the nation case that some studies find a nil relation, the dyadic case stands stronger. Here all studies point in the same direction, even if they result in ascribing differing strength to the relationship and if they differ in the extent to which the statistical relationship has been demonstrated to reflect a causal one. This is particularly true for the dynamic case of dyadic studies: that of 'arms races', however we define them. Studies on higher levels of aggregation, however, are too few, and too weak and/or methodologically questionable for us to base any firm conclusions on.

It should be noted that on this level of rigour, too, there is still very little support for those who worry about their own nation or alliance having *too few* arms, at least if that worry is phrased in terms of risks of war. (For a more general discussion of 'security', see Wiberg, 1986.) What comes closest to such a support is the fact that the superpowers are less likely than other dyads to go to war *with each other* – but then, that was taken to demonstrate that 'extended deterrence works' – and if this is the case, it must also be true for the first post-1945 decades, when nuclear arsenals were very much smaller than today's.

If we lower the criteria even more, to 'more likely than not', even quite small differences will count, and many more studies become relevant. This is where very many studies of correlates of wars belong. Even in those cases where the results are – barely – statistically significant, they are normally so weak that they account for only a few per cent of the total variation found in military conflicts among states. By selectively picking among such studies, one might construct a case for not worrying about too many arms, just as for worrying about them; and I would not a priori exclude that on this level of evidence a case might even be made for worrying about too few arms even from the 'war' viewpoint.

If we attempt an overall conclusion, however, not repeating all the reservations once more, it must be that the reasons for worrying about arms races are clearly stronger than the reasons for not worrying, at least as long as we go by empirical research rather than untested hypotheses. The essential remaining question is to what extent it can be said that a causal relationship between high armament levels (or rapid increases in armament) and high risks for war has been *conclusively proved* or not – but that is neither here nor there when it comes to whether the reasons for worrying are stronger than those for not worrying.

Whatever the political conclusions to be drawn from that, it definitely provides a valid argument for trying to find more solid knowledge than we have today about how arms races actually work – and that is what this book is about.

Biographical details about HÅKAN WIBERG are found at the end of Chapter 3.

Chapter 20
A Possible Future for the Arms Race*

MICHAEL D. INTRILIGATOR
& DAGOBERT L. BRITO

Center for International and Strategic Affairs, University of California, Los Angeles; Department of Economics, Rice University, Houston, Texas

1 A Potential Shift in the Character of the Arms Race

What is the arms race of the future? Our conjecture is that the future of the arms race could be radically different from its past, with the late 1980s forming a break with the past. The 'new' arms race, of the end of this century and the beginning of the next century, will, we believe, differ in three fundamental ways from the 'old' arms race of the past 40 years.

In the past the arms race was primarily the competition between the two superpowers, the United States and the Soviet Union; it was characterized by the use of high technology; and it resulted, according to our analysis, in a stabilizing regime of mutual deterrence.[1]

By contrast, the future arms race could be radically different, with multiple races among the medium and smaller powers; with these races characterized by the use of medium and low technology; and potentially resulting in instabilities and regional conflicts or wars.

2 The Superpower Arms Race

The arms race of the last 40 years has been primarily one between the two superpowers and their allies in NATO and the Warsaw Treaty Organization.

The US and Western arms buildup was stimulated in part by the Soviet takeover of Czechoslovakia in 1948 and its invasions of Hungary in 1956, of Czechoslovakia in 1968, and of Afghanistan in 1979. Of key importance were the 1949 Soviet first atomic bomb explosion, demonstrating its nuclear weapons capabilities; the 1953 Moscow flyby of Soviet long-range bombers, showing its delivery capabilities; and the 1957 Sputnik launch, showing its ICBM capabilities. Of all these perhaps most important were

---

* This chapter is based on remarks presented by the first author at the concluding session, on the future of arms races, of the symposium which forms the basis for the present volume.

the Soviet bomber and Sputnik shocks, which demonstrated US vulnerabilities and which led to the mobilization of the US political, scientific, and military communities.

The Soviet and Eastern arms buildup was stimulated in part by the Truman Doctrine in the Balkans in 1947, the formation of NATO in 1949, and the outbreak of the Korean War in 1950. Of key importance were the 1950s buildup of US bomber capabilities, the 1953 US first hydrogen bomb explosion, the 1962 Cuban missile crisis, and in 1964, China's first atomic bomb explosion. Of all these, perhaps the most important were the Cuban missile crisis shock and the Chinese acquisition of nuclear weapons capabilities, which led to the mobilization of the Soviet political, scientific, and military communities.

The result of these events was a change on the part of both superpowers in their perception of the capabilities and the intentions of the potential enemy, leading to an enormous acquisition of arms by the US following 1955–57 and by the Soviet Union following 1963–64. Capabilities built up vastly, resulting by the 1970s in huge and unprecedented arsenals on both sides, of not only strategic long-range nuclear capabilities (a frequent measure of armament) but also other military capabilities – tactical, conventional, etc.

This arms race has been characterized by both a quantitative and a qualititative dimension, as both sides not only add numbers of missiles, warheads, etc. to their arsenals but also use newer technologies for weapons, their means of delivery, and their control.

At the same time as arms buildups were occurring on both sides, steps were taken in the area of arms control. These include the Austrian State Treaty in 1955 and the Antarctica Treaty in 1959 to keep nuclear weapons out of Austria and Antarctica, respectively, and later agreements to keep nuclear weapons out of the seabeds and space; the Limited Test Ban Treaty in 1963 to stop atmospheric testing of nuclear weapons and later agreements to limit yields on such tests; the NPT Treaty in 1968 to prevent nuclear proliferation, with later measures to strengthen the non-proliferation regime; the SALT Treaties in 1972 and 1979 to limit strategic weapons; the ABM Treaty in 1972 to limit anti-ballistic missile deployments; and the INF Treaty in 1987 to eliminate intermediate and shorter range missiles.

The result of both these arms deployments and these arms control measures was that, probably by 1970 and certainly by 1980, there existed a regime of mutual deterrence, with each side restrained not only from attacking the other but even from seriously provoking the other for fear of the consequences. In that sense, the superpower arms race and arms control agreements resulted in a more stable world than that of the earlier period, by creating a regime of mutual deterrence. It is not by accident that the recent period has not seen crises comparable to those of the late 1950s and early 1960s, especially the 1958 Quemoy–Matsu crisis and the 1962 Cuban missile crisis. By establishing a mutual deterrence regime, the arms race and arms control contributed to strategic stability.

The future will probably see a continuation of the superpower arms race, with further weapons deployments and innovations; but with a leveling off of the arms race, both quantitatively and qualitatively, due to mutual recognition of the existence of the deterrence regime, further arms control agreements, and budgetary limitations imposing constraints on both sides. All three factors exist today, but they will probably play an even more significant role in the future. The result will be a tapering off of the superpower arms race – not its end and certainly not its reversal (which could threaten the mutual deterrence regime and thus overall strategic stability) but its gradual reduction in size, scope, and significance.

3 A New Set of Arms Races?

As the superpowers' arms race gradually tapers off, there is a substantial likelihood that other nations will simultaneously accelerate their arms acquisitions. The result could be a new set of arms races: new in terms of the actors involved, the nature of the arms acquired, and the implications for conflict and war.

The first set of actors is comprised of the *smaller nuclear powers* of the United Kingdom, France, and China, which are planning major deployments and will be upgrading their weapons, both nuclear and conventional. Past acquisitions by these three nuclear powers have generally been ignored, as analysts and policy-makers have concentrated on the superpower arms race. Past arguments have been that Britain was so closely tied to the USA that it could be treated as a minor addition to US capabilities. Past arguments have also been that French and Chinese capabilities were negligible. Now, however, all three smaller nuclear powers have a complete triad of bomber-, missile-, and submarine-based nuclear weapons, and are both improving them and building them to substantial levels. The result of this arms race will be a shift from a bipolar world to a multipolar world. This will involve additional potential initiators of a conflict or a war, shifting coalitions of major actors, an increase in global uncertainty, and thus a more dangerous world than the bipolar one.[2]

The second set of actors is comprised of the *potential proliferators* – nations with the potential of building nuclear weapons. Apart from the five great power nuclear weapons states, only India has detonated a single nuclear device, but it is widely suspected that certain nations have a covert stockpile of untested nuclear weapons. These nations with 'bombs in the basement' have followed the alleged Israeli pattern of covert nuclear weapons development, no weapons tests, secret weapons production and stockpiling, and a stated policy of denial or ambiguity. There may, in fact, be as many covert nuclear weapons nations today as there are overt nuclear weapons nations, including possibly Israel, India, Pakistan, South Africa, Taiwan, South Korea, Argentina, and Brazil. In the future these states may possibly be engaged in a covert nuclear arms race, adding to and modernizing their secret stockpiles. Other nations may also follow this route. Meanwhile the other highly industrialized European nations have the technology and infrastructure to acquire or develop nuclear weapons whenever they want, in a very short period of time, but have chosen not to do so up to now. The presence of these nations – the Federal Republic of Germany, Switzerland, Sweden, Italy, Spain, and others – has created the potential for a cascading instability if there were any indication that any one of these was, in fact, acquiring or developing nuclear weapons. Another important actor, Japan, has recently surpassed the political and psychological barrier of limiting defense spending to no more than one percent of GNP; it could have a substantial increase in its conventional forces, and it has the technology to develop nuclear weapons in the future if it can overcome its 'nuclear allergy'. Yet another factor affecting nuclear proliferation is the advent of second-tier nuclear supplier states.[3] These nations were believed to be nuclear importing states at the time, over twenty years ago, of the signing of the Nuclear Nonproliferation Treaty; over time, they have become current or potential future nuclear exporting states. Included are Brazil, Argentina, India, Pakistan, and South Africa, none of which are parties to the Nuclear Nonproliferation Treaty.

The third set of actors is comprised of the *newly industrialized countries*. These include South Korea, Taiwan, and such growing countries as Brazil and India which, in addition to having a nuclear weapons potential, could be building conventional capabilities due to the combination of a perceived security threat, greater recent economic capabilities to acquire weapons, the perceived status conveyed by weapons, and the desire to keep the existing political and military leaders in power. Brazil is an important case because of its recent establishment of a huge arms industry aimed at exporting conventional weapons, which has played an important role in helping to pay its foreign debt. Other countries with large foreign debts, including not only Latin America's major debtors, Argentina and Mexico, but also others, including countries in Eastern Europe, may follow Brazil's example of expanding their arms export industries as a way of earning foreign exchange. Already Czechoslovakia and North Korea are major arms exporters.

The fourth set of actors is comprised of *Third World nations*. Civil wars and international wars are being fought in Africa, Asia, the Middle East, and Central America, and additional such wars are likely to occur in the future. Such wars and the potential for additional wars provide a strong incentive for Third World countries to acquire weapons, whether for defensive or offensive purposes. The Iran–Iraq war, a major war which continued over a long period without superpower intervention, has provided an important recent lesson for Third World countries. In fact, the Iran–Iraq war may be seen in the future as playing the role of a stimulus to the Third World in the same way that Sputnik was a stimulus to the USA and the Cuban missile crisis to the USSR. This war, which has involved the third largest number of casualties of any war in this century and which has involved the use of chemical weapons and human wave tactics, has shown that major wars can occur in such regions. It has demonstrated that Third World countries will have to rely on their own arms capabilities or imported weapons for defense. The likely result will be an acceleration of the arms race in Third World countries, leading to instabilities in these regions.

Finally, the fifth set of actors is comprised of *non-nation-state actors*, including various subnational groups of liberation fronts, terrorist organizations, and private armies and various supranational groups of international drug organizations and crime syndicates. These actors will probably play an increasingly important role in seeking and obtaining arms and even manufacturing their own arms to advance their own causes or interests.

Thus the scene of action for the arms race will probably move away from the bipolarity of the superpowers to the multipolarity of the rest of the world, with a new set of actors in the arms race. At the same time there is likely to be a shift from an emphasis on high-technology weapons and a qualitative arms race, as in the superpower arms race, to an emphasis on low- or medium-technology weapons and a quantitative arms race. High-technology arms races of the sort characterizing the superpower arms race are beyond the capabilities of other nations, with the exceptions of the smaller nuclear powers and the highly industrialized nations of West Europe and Japan. The race will therefore change its character from nuclear to non-nuclear, involving low or medium technology – such as small arms, artillery, armored personnel carriers, small planes, coastal ships, and possibly chemical and biological/bacterial weapons. The race will be more of a quantitative than a qualitative one, given both the lack of access to sophisticated technology and the relatively low starting levels of weapons inventories in most of the countries involved. Furthermore, there will be multiple arms races in different regions.

4 Implications of the New Arms Races

Such new arms races, involving newer nations acquiring low- or medium-technology conventional weapons, chemical weapons, biological/bacteriological weapons, and covert nuclear weapons, have ominous implications. The 'old' arms race, of the superpowers, while perhaps a waste of resources, had at least the advantage of contributing to stability through the establishment of a mutual deterrence regime. By contrast, the 'new' arms races will probably not have this redeeming feature. The acquisition of weapons, particularly by nations in the Third World, is likely to contribute to the outbreak of war, with Third World nations acquiring enough weapons to strike their regional rivals but not enough to deter these rivals.[4] Thus the new arms races could be qualitatively of a different and much more dangerous type than the superpower arms race.

Nuclear proliferation, whether overt or covert, could be particularly destabilizing. Nations with nuclear weapons could use nuclear threats or even nuclear strikes in extreme situations, e.g. where their survival is at stake. Subnational groups or even terrorist organizations could also acquire nuclear weapons, e.g. by theft, and use nuclear threats or nuclear strikes to promote their goals. The circumstance when nuclear weapons are probably most likely to be used is when one nation in a conflict or war has a nuclear weapons monopoly.[5] Such a situation could occur today in several regions as a result of the new arms races. Furthermore, with more overt or covert nuclear weapons states, there is a growing probability of inadvertent or accidental nuclear war, due to human error, technical failure, or terrorist action. (See Intriligator & Brito, 1988d.)

In addition to adverse consequences for strategic stability, increasing the chance of conflict or war, the new arms races have adverse consequences for arms race stability. If one nation were to begin to acquire weapons, that could incite similar acquisitions by other nations in that region or elsewhere, triggering an arms race. The large number of nations with a nuclear weapons potential suggests that the acquisition of such weapons by one country or by a non-nation actor could trigger their acquisition by others, continuing the chain of proliferation from the USA to the USSR to the UK, France, and China, to India to Pakistan to . . .

Another factor in the instability of the new arms races is the presence of newer arms-exporting nations and their dependence on such exports, given their lack of other export potential and their foreign debt. Competition can be intense among arms-supplying states, due both to the expansion of arms industries in current arms-producing states and to the buildup of such industries in newer arms-producing states. Such states will require customers, and it is not out of the question for them to incite or to fuel conflicts or wars in various regions in order to stimulate sales. In the new arms races there could be commercial reasons for promoting instability or even the outbreak of war.

Thus the new arms races, unlike the old superpower arms race, could be characterized by substantial instabilities, including both arms race instability and strategic instability, with the arms races potentially leading to the outbreak of war. Also, they will result in fundamental challenges to the hegemony of the United States and the Soviet Union. A military as well as a political and an economic challenge to the supremacy of the superpowers is that they will not be able to intervene successfully in regional conflicts and wars in order to promote stability. This decline in hegemony will be a further factor in the increase in global instability, which will act as both a cause and a consequence of the new arms race.

5 Policy Questions

The instabilities inherent in the new arms races thus lead to the possibility of conflict or the outbreak of war, particularly among Third World nations.

Two important policy questions are whether the arms race can be prevented and whether such potential conflicts or wars can be avoided.

The new arms race probably cannot be avoided, although attempts can be made through the actions of the superpowers, through international organizations, and through collective action of the countries involved. The superpowers are not in a good position to stop the new arms races, as they have set an example in their own arms race which other countries may try to follow. Nevertheless, they could work both individually and cooperatively to exert pressure against arms buildups in the Third World, individually through pressure on their client states and cooperatively through the establishment of a new international regime to limit arms transfers. International organizations can play a role if there could be coordination of economic and security policy, such as United Nations–World Bank–International Monetary Fund economic pressures to prevent or limit arms buildups. Finally there could be collective action of the countries involved, possibly assisted by the superpowers and international organizations, to prevent or limit arms buildups.

If, nevertheless, these new arms races do take place, conflicts and wars will probably occur. However, attempts could be made to stop these wars, again through the actions of the superpowers, through international organizations, and through collective action. While the superpowers could attempt to intervene to prevent or to stop a war, given the precedent set by the Iran–Iraq war, it is likely that, at least in some situations, they would not succeed. International organizations could play a role, although once again the precedents set by either powerlessness or lack of involvement in recent wars suggest that they would fail to prevent the outbreak of wars. Collective action also is largely a record of failure.

Given the past record, then, it is probably more feasible to prevent the new arms races than to prevent the outbreak of war if such arms races do occur. The prevention of the new arms races, however, will require an unprecedented degree of cooperation between the superpowers, coordination among international organizations, and collective action among the countries involved. If the new arms races are to be prevented, major initiatives must be taken – and taken soon – to ensure the cooperation, coordination, and collective action needed to achieve this goal.[6]

Notes

1. For a formal development of the potential for certain arms races to reduce the chance of war and thus contribute to strategic stability via mutual deterrence, see Intriligator & Brito (1984). Our paper identified certain arms races likely to lead to war and, conversely, certain arms races likely to reduce the chance of war. It concluded that the USA–USSR arms race since the 1960s has, in all likelihood, reduced rather than increased the chance of war. See also Intriligator & Brito (1985a, 1986a, 1986b, 1987a), Mayer (1986), and Wolfson (1987). Note that stability against the outbreak of war is not the same as arms race stability. The superpower arms race has involved arms race instability as weapons are built to higher levels or improved, but it has involved strategic stability via deterrence (see Intriligator & Brito,

1986a). The superpower arms race has led to a 'regime' by providing a cooperative solution among nation states to a type of Prisoner's Dilemma problem, here the problem of war pre-emption (see Intriligator & Ramberg, 1983).

2. In Intriligator & Brito (1988c) it was noted that the global geostrategic conflict could, in the future, resemble that of the Middle East, with many interacting actors, shifting coalitions, etc., but without the potentially restraining influence of the superpowers.

3. See Jones et al. (1985), and Potter (1987).

4. As analyzed in Intriligator & Brito (1984), an arms race starting at low levels could result in war initiation or even forced pre-emption, with each side able to attack the other and neither side able to deter.

5. See Intriligator & Brito (1981), and Brito & Intriligator (1978, 1985, 1987a), for an analysis of nuclear proliferation.

6. This analysis and its policy implications suggest that new priorities need to be established in research on the arms race, so as to shift the emphasis from the old superpower race to the potential new arms races involving smaller and developing nations and their implications for the outbreak of war.

Biographical details about MICHAEL D. INTRILIGATOR and DAGOBERT L. BRITO are found at the end of Chapter 4.

Bibliography

The following list includes all the references contained in the individual chapters. We hope that this list can serve a useful function of its own, as a comprehensive bibliography on the subject. A few non-cited items are listed to make the bibliography more complete in its core area. Another good bibliography on arms dynamics and military technology, focusing in particular on strategic weapons and ballistic missile defense, is found in Brauch (1989d).

The German letters ä, ö, and ü appear in their usual position in the alphabet, as if they were written ae, oe, and ue. The Scandinavian letters æ (ä), ø (ö), and å appear at the end of the alphabet.

Abolfathi, Farid, 1978. 'Defense Expenditures in the Persian Gulf: Internal, Interstate, and International Factors in the Iraqi–Iranian Arms Race, 1950 to 1969', pp. 99–129 in W. Ladd Hollist, ed. *Exploring Competitive Arms Processes: Applications of Mathematical Modeling and Computer Simulation in Arms Policy Analysis*. New York: Dekker.

Acheson, Dean, 1969. *Present at the Creation. My Years in the State Department*. New York: Norton.

Acland-Hood, Mary, 1985. 'Military Research and Development Expenditure', pp. 287–293 in *World Armaments and Disarmament. SIPRI Yearbook 1985*.

Acland-Hood, Mary, 1986. 'Military Research and Development', pp. 235–241 in Thee, 1986b.

Acland-Hood, Mary, 1987. 'Military Research and Development', pp. 153–158 in *World Armaments and Disarmament. SIPRI Yearbook 1987*.

Adams, Gordon, 1982. *The Politics of Defense Contracting. The Iron Triangle*. New Brunswick, NJ: Transaction.

Aglietta, Michel & Anton Brender, 1984. *Les Métamorphoses de la société salariale*. Paris: Calmann-Lévy.

Agrell, Wilhelm, 1981. *Rustningens drivkrafter*. Lund: Studentlitteratur.

Agrell, Wilhelm, 1985. *Alliansfrihet och atombomber – kontinuitet och förändring i den svenska försvarsdoktrinen 1945–82*. Stockholm: Liber.

Agrell, Wilhelm, 1989. *Vetenskapen i försvarets tjänst – de nya stridsmedlen, försvarsforskningen och kampen om det svenska försvarets struktur*. Lund: Lund University Press.

Agursky, Mikhail & Hannes Adomeit, 1979. 'The Soviet Military–Industrial Complex', *Survey*, vol. 24, no. 2, Spring, pp. 106–124.

Ahlmark, Per, 1965. *Den svenska atomvapendebatten*. Stockholm: Prisma.

Albrecht, Ulrich, 1980. 'Red Militarism', *Journal of Peace Research*, vol. 17, no. 2, pp. 135–149.

Albrecht, Ulrich, 1986a. 'Der militärische Gebrauch von Forschung und Entwicklung', pp. 449–462 in Beate Kohler-Koch, ed. *Technik und internationale Politik*. Baden-Baden: Nomos.

Albrecht, Ulrich, 1986b. 'Rüstungstechnologien und internationale Sicherheit', pp. 199–214 in Hans-Hermann Hartwich, ed. *Politik und die Macht der Technik*. Opladen: Westdeutscher Verlag.

Albrecht, Ulrich, 1987. 'Militarismus und Rüstung', pp. 404–411 in Jörg Calliess & Reinhold E. Lob, eds. *Praxis der Umwelt- und Friedenserziehung*, vol. 1, *Grundlagen*. Düsseldorf: Schwann.

Albrecht, Ulrich, 1988. 'Die Bomber sollen gleichsam auf leisen Sohlen daherkommen', *Frankfurter Rundschau*, no. 262, 9 November, p. 14.
Albrecht, Ulrich & Randolph Nikutta, 1989. *Die sowjetische Rüstungsindustrie*. Wiesbaden: Westdeutscher Verlag.
Alcock, Norman Z., 1972. *The War Disease*. Oaksville, Ontario: Canadian Peace Research Institute Press.
Alker, Hayward & Cheryl Christensen, 1972. 'From Causal Modeling to Artificial Intelligence: The Evolving of a UN Peace Making Simulation', pp. 177–224 in J.A. Laponce & Paul Smoker, eds. *Experimentation and Simulation in Political Science*. Toronto: University of Toronto Press.
Alker, Hayward R. & John Mallery, 1988. 'From Events Data to Computational Histories: A Relatus-Based Research Program on the Collective Management of International Conflict'. Paper prepared for the 29th Convention of the International Studies Association, St. Louis, 29 March–2 April.
Allison, Graham T., 1971. *Essence of Decision*. Boston, MA: Little, Brown.
Allison, Graham T. & Morton H. Halperin, 1972. 'Bureaucratic Politics: A Paradigm and Some Policy Implications', pp. 40–79 in Richard H. Ullman & Raymond Tanter, eds. *Theory and Policy in International Relations*. Princeton, NJ: Princeton University Press.
Allison, Graham T. & Frederic A. Morris, 1976. 'Armaments and Arms Control: Exploring the Determinants of Military Weapons', pp. 99–129 in Franklin A. Long & George W. Rathjens, eds. *Arms, Defense Policy, and Arms Control*. New York: Norton.
Anderson, Stuart, 1981. *Race and Rapprochement. Anglo-Saxonism and Anglo-American Relations, 1895–1914*. Rutherford, NJ: Fairleigh Dickinson University Press.
Anderton, Charles H., 1985a. 'A Selected Bibliography of Arms Race Models and Related Subjects', *Conflict Management and Peace Science*, vol. 8, no. 2, pp. 99–122.
Anderton, Charles H., 1985b. *Arms Race Modeling: Systematic Analysis and Synthesis*. Ithaca, NY: Cornell University. [Ph.D. Dissertation.]
Andrén, Nils, 1971. *Försvar utan kärnvapen*. Stockholm: Folk och Försvar.
Angell, Norman, 1935. *The Great Illusion*. London: Heinemann. [First published in 1910.]
Arkin, William M., 1983. 'Soviet Cruise Missile Programs', *Arms Control Today*. vol. 13, no. 4, May, pp. 3–4.
Armacost, Michael H., 1969. *The Politics of Weapons Innovation: The Thor-Jupiter Controversy*. New York: Columbia University Press.
Art, Robert J., 1968. *The TFX Decision: McNamara and the Military*. Boston, MA: Little, Brown.
Art, Robert J., 1973. 'Bureaucratic Politics and American Foreign Policy: A Critique', *Policy Sciences*, vol. 4, no. 4, December, pp. 467–490. Reprinted in shortened form in Art & Jervis, 1985, pp. 467–490.
Art, Robert J. & Robert Jervis, eds., 1985. *International Politics. Anarchy, Force, Political Economy, and Decision Making*. 2nd ed. Boston, MA: Little Brown.
Aspaturian, Vernon, 1973. 'The Soviet Military-Industrial Complex: Does it Exist?', pp. 103–134 in Rosen, 1973.
Atomenergiutredningen 1955 års, 1956. *Atomenergien*. Stockholm: SOU 1956: 11.
Atomkommittén, 1946. *Betänkande rörande preliminära organisatoriska åtgärder för atomenergiforskningens främjande*. Stockholm: Riksdagen.
Atomkommittén, 1947. *Betänkande med förslag till organisation av och ekonomiskt stöd åt atomenergiforskningen*. Stockholm: Riksdagen.
Aviation Week and Space Technology, 1962a. 'Washington Roundup', vol. 76, no. 20, 14 May, p. 25.
Aviation Week and Space Technology, 1962b. 'Live Polaris Launch', vol. 76, no. 20, 14 May, p. 35.
Aviation Week and Space Technology, 1987. 'GE Will Compete for Guidance System', vol. 127, no. 25, 21 December, p. 31.
Balassa, Bela, 1969. 'Industrial Development in an Open Economy: The Case of Norway', *Oxford Economic Papers*, new series, vol. 21, no. 3, pp. 344–359. Reprinted in *Articles*

from the Central Bureau of Statistics, no. 30, 1969, pp. 5–23. Oslo: Central Bureau of Statistics.
Ball, Desmond, 1980. *Politics and Force Levels. The Strategic Missile Program of the Kennedy Administration*. Berkeley, CA & London: University of California Press.
Ball, Nicole & Milton Leitenberg, 1983. *The Structure of the Defense Industry*. London & Canberra: Croom Helm.
Banks, Arthur, 1982. *Cross-Polity Time-Series Data*. Cambridge, MA: MIT Press.
Baran, Paul & Paul Sweezy, 1966. *Monopoly Capital*. New York: Monthly Review Press.
Barnaby, Frank, 1980. 'The Military Tail Wagging the Political Dog', *The Guardian*, 23 October.
Barnes, Barry, 1982. *T.S. Kuhn and Social Science*. London: Macmillan.
Barnet, Richard J., 1972. *Roots of War*. New York: Atheneum.
Bataille, Georges, 1949. *La Part maudite. Essai d'économie générale*, vol. 1, *La Consumation*. Paris: Minuit.
Baudrillard, Jean, 1966. *Le Système des objets*. Paris: Gallimard.
Baugh, William H., 1984. *The Politics of Nuclear Balance. Ambiguity and Continuity in Strategic Policies*. New York & London: Longman.
Beard, Charles A., 1956. 'Historical Relativism', pp. 314–328 in Fritz Stern, ed. *The Varieties of History*. New York: Meridian.
Beard, Edmund, 1976. *Developing the ICBM: A Study in Bureaucratic Politics*. New York: Columbia University Press.
Beasley, W.G., 1987. *Japanese Imperialism 1894–1945*. Oxford: Clarendon.
Beaud, Michael, 1981. *Histoire du capitalisme 1500–1980*. Paris: du Seuil.
Beenstock, Michael, 1983. *The World Economy in Transition*. London: Allen & Unwin.
Beglov, Spartak, 1988. 'Security – Ours and Theirs', *International Affairs* [Moscow], no. 5, May, pp. 34–42.
Benoit, Emile, 1973. *Defense and Economic Growth in Developing Countries*. Lexington, MA: Heath.
Benoit, Emile, 1978. 'Growth and Defense in Developing Countries', *Economic Development and Cultural Change*, vol. 26, no. 2, January, pp. 271–280.
Bergh, Trond & Tore J. Hanisch, 1984. *Vitenskap og politikk*. Oslo: Aschehoug.
Berghahn, Volker R., 1971. *Der Tirpitz-Plan. Genesis und Verfall einer innenpolitische Krisenstrategie unter Wilhelm II*. Düsseldorf: Droste.
Berghahn, Volker R., 1981. *Militarism. The History of an International Debate, 1861–1979*. Leamington Spa: Berg.
Berman, Robert P., 1978. *Soviet Air Power in Transition*. Washington, DC: Brookings.
Berman, Robert P. & John C. Baker, 1982. *Soviet Strategic Forces: Requirements and Responses*. Washington, DC: Brookings.
Betts, Richard K., ed., 1981. *Cruise Missiles: Technology, Strategy, Politics*. Washington, DC: Brookings.
Bielfeldt, Carola, 1977. *Rüstungsausgaben und Staatsinterventionismus*. Frankfurt a.M.: Campus.
Bielfeldt, Carola & Peter Schlotter, 1980. *Die militärische Sicherheitspolitik der Bundesrepublik Deutschland. Einführung und Kritik*. Frankfurt a.M.: Campus.
Bijker, Wiebe E.; Thomas P. Hughes & Trevor J. Pinch, eds., 1987. *The Social Construction of Technological Systems: New Directions in the Sociology and History of Technology*. Cambridge, MA: MIT Press.
Blackaby, Frank, 1986. 'The Strategic Defense Initiative and its Implications', pp. 123–125 in Thee, 1986b.
Blechman, Barry M. & Stephen S. Kaplan, 1978. *Force Without War, US Armed Forces as a Political Instrument*. Washington, DC: Brookings.
Block, Fred L., 1977. *The Origins of International Economic Disorder*. Berkeley: University of California Press.
Block, Fred L., 1980. 'Economic Instability and Military Strength: The Paradoxes of the 1950 Rearmament Decision', *Politics & Society*, vol. 10, no. 1, pp. 1–34.

Bloor, David, 1976. *Knowledge and Social Imagery*. London: Routledge & Kegan Paul.
Bloor, David, 1982. 'Durkheim and Mauss Revisited: Classification and the Sociology of Knowledge', *Studies in the History and Philosophy of Science*, vol. 13, no. 4, December, pp. 267–297.
Bobrow, Davis B. & Stephen R. Hill, 1985. 'The Determinants of Military Budgets. The Japanese Case', *Conflict Management and Peace Science*, vol. 9, no. 1, Spring, pp. 1–18.
Böhme, Gernot; Wolfgang van der Daele & Wolfgang Krohn, 1973. 'Die Finalisierung der Wissenschaft', *Zeitschrift für Soziologie*, vol. 13, no. 2, pp. 183–227.
Bottome, Edgar M., 1971. *The Balance of Terror: A Guide to the Arms Race*. Boston, MA: Beacon.
Boulding, Kenneth, 1962. *Conflict and Defense: A General Theory*. New York: Harper.
Boulding, Kenneth, 1985. *The World as a Total System*. Beverly Hills, CA: Sage.
Bousquet, Nicole, 1980. 'From Hegemony to Competition: Cycles of the Core', pp. 46–83 in Terence K. Hopkins & Immanuel Wallerstein, eds. *Processes of the World System*. Beverly Hills, CA: Sage.
Boyer, Robert, 1986. *La Théorie de la regulation. Une analyse critique*. Paris: La Découverte.
Bracken, Paul, 1983. *The Command and Control of Nuclear Forces*. London: Yale University Press.
Brauch, Hans Günter, 1976. *Struktureller Wandel und Rüstungspolitik der USA (1940–1950), Zur Weltführungsrolle und ihren innenpolitischen Bedingungen*. Ann Arbor, MI & London: University Microfilms.
Brauch, Hans Günter, 1979a. *Entwicklungen und Ergebnisse der Friedensforschung (1940–1950)*. Frankfurt a.M.: Haag & Herchen.
Brauch, Hans Günter, 1979b. 'Ein neues Feindbild gegen die Entspannung in den USA?', *Vorgänge*, no. 39, pp. 117–122; no. 40/41, pp. 147–156.
Brauch, Hans Günter, 1980. 'Armaments Dynamics and Presidential Elections in the United States (1948–1976)', *Korean Journal of International Studies*, vol. 11, no. 4, pp. 273–318.
Brauch, Hans Günter, 1981. 'Rüstungsabhängigkeit und amerikanische Präsidentschaftswahlen: Eine Fallstudie zum Verhältnis von Rüstungsabhängigkeit und Wahlverhalten', pp. 167–205 in Gert Krell, ed. *Die Rüstung der USA – Gesellschaftliche Interessen und politische Entscheidungen*. Baden-Baden: Nomos.
Brauch, Hans Günter, 1984. *Angriff aus dem All. Der Rüstungswettlauf in Weltraum*. Berlin & Bonn: Dietz.
Brauch, Hans Günter, 1986. 'Rüstungsdynamik und Waffentechnik: Ein Versuch zur Interpretation der amerikanischen strategischen Raketenabwehrsysteme mit Hilfe von Theoremen aus dem Bereich der Rüstungsdynamik', pp. 411–448 in Beate Kohler-Koch, ed. *Technik und internationale Politik*. Baden-Baden: Nomos.
Brauch, Hans Günter, ed., 1987. *Star Wars and European Defence. Implications for Europe: Perceptions and Assessments*. London: Macmillan/New York: St. Martin's.
Brauch, Hans Günter, 1989a. 'Military Technology – Armaments Dynamics – Strategic Stability: Implications for Arms Control', pp. 3–38 in Brauch, 1989d.
Brauch, Hans Günter, 1989b. 'Strategic Defence Initiative or Strategic Defence Response? An Attempt to Interpret the Emergence of the SDI Programme in Terms of Theorems of Armaments Dynamics', pp. 352–445 in Brauch, 1989d.
Brauch, Hans Günter, 1989c. 'Military Technology, Armaments Dynamics and Disarmament: A Select Bibliography', pp. 505–538 in Brauch, 1989d.
Brauch, Hans Günter, ed., 1989d. *Military Technology, Armaments Dynamics and Disarmament – ABC Weapons, Military Use of Nuclear Energy and of Outer Space and Implications for International Law*. London: Macmillan/New York: St. Martin's.
Bredow, Wilfried von, 1983. *Moderner Militarismus. Analyse und Kritik*. Stuttgart: Kohlhammer.
Bremer, Stuart A., 1980. 'National Capabilities and War Proneness', pp. 57–82 in J. David Singer, ed. *Correlates of War II: Testing Some Realpolitik Models*. New York: Free Press.
Brewer, Anthony, 1979. *Marxist Theories of Imperialism*. London: Routledge & Kegan Paul.

Brito, Dagobert L., 1972. 'A Dynamic Model of an Armaments Race', *International Economic Review*, vol. 13, no. 2, pp. 359–375.

Brito, Dagobert L. & Michael D. Intriligator, 1972. 'A General Equilibrium Model of the Stability of an Armaments Race', in *Proceedings of the Sixth Asilomar Conference on Circuits and Systems*. New York: Institute of Electrical and Electronic Engineers.

Brito, Dagobert L. & Michael D. Intriligator, 1973. 'Some Applications of the Maximum Principle to the Problem of an Armaments Race', *Modeling and Simulation*, vol. 4, pp. 140–144.

Brito, Dagobert L. & Michael D. Intriligator, 1974. 'Uncertainty and the Stability of the Armaments Race', *Annals of Economic and Social Measurement*, vol. 3, no. 1, January, pp. 279–292.

Brito, Dagobert L. & Michael D. Intriligator, 1977. 'Nuclear Proliferation and the Armaments Race', *Journal of Peace Science*, vol. 2, no. 2, Spring, pp. 231–238.

Brito, Dagobert L. & Michael D. Intriligator, 1978. 'Nuclear Proliferation and Stability', *Journal of Peace Science*, vol. 3, no. 2, Winter, pp. 173–183.

Brito, Dagobert L. & Michael D. Intriligator, 1980. 'A Game–Theoretic Approach to Bureaucratic Behavior', pp. 223–236 in Pan-Tai Liu, ed. *Dynamic Optimization and Mathematical Economics*. New York & London: Plenum.

Brito, Dagobert L. & Michael D. Intriligator, 1981. 'Strategic Arms Limitation Treaties and Innovations in Weapons Technology', *Public Choice*, vol. 37, no. 1, pp. 41–59.

Brito, Dagobert L. & Michael D. Intriligator, 1985. 'Conflict, War, and Redistribution', *American Political Science Review*, vol. 79, no. 4, December, pp. 943–957.

Brito, Dagobert L. & Michael D. Intriligator, 1987a. 'Deterrence May Require Mixed Strategies', pp. 54–62 in Stephen J. Cimbala, ed. *Challenges to Deterrence in the 1990s*. New York: Praeger.

Brito, Dagobert L. & Michael D. Intriligator, 1987b. 'Arms Races and the Outbreak of War: Application of Principal-Agent Relationships and Asymmetric Information', pp. 104–120 in Christian Schmidt & Frank Blackaby, eds. *Peace, Defence and Economic Analysis*. London: Macmillan.

Brodie, Bernard, 1946. *The Absolute Weapon*. New York: Harcourt Brace.

Brokaw, Tom, 1988. Interview with Secretary-General Gorbachev, *Europa Archiv*, vol. 43, no. 1, pp. D3–D10.

Brzezinski, Zbigniew & Samuel P. Huntington, 1963. *Political Power: US/USSR*. New York: Viking.

Brzoska, Michael & Thomas Ohlson, 1987. 'The Flow of Arms: Main Trends', pp. 1–14 in Michael Brzoska & Thomas Ohlson, eds. *Arms Transfers to the Third World, 1971–1985*. Oxford & New York: Oxford University Press.

Bülow, Andreas von, 1985. *Die eingebildete Unterlegenheit*. Munich: Beck.

Bulletin of Peace Proposals, 1988. Military Use of Research and Development: The Arms Race and Development, vol. 19, no. 3–4. (Special issue)

Bunn, Matthew & Kosta Tsipis, 1983. *Ballistic Missile Guidance and Technical Uncertainties of Countersilo Attacks*. Cambridge, MA: MIT Program in Science and Technology for International Security, report no. 9.

Burns, Arthur, 1959. 'A Graphical Approach to Some Problems of the Arms Race', *Journal of Conflict Resolution*, vol. 3, no. 4, December, pp. 326–342.

Busch, Peter A., 1970. 'Appendix: Mathematical Models of Arms Races', pp. 193–233 in Russett, 1970.

Buzan, Barry, 1987. *An Introduction to Strategic Studies*. London: Macmillan.

Caldwell, Dan, 1977. 'Bureaucratic Foreign Policy-Making', *American Behavioral Scientist*, vol. 21, September/October, pp. 87–110.

Calleo, David, 1982. *The Imperious Economy*. Cambridge, MA: Harvard University Press.

Capie, Forrest, 1983. *Depression and Protectionism: Britain between the Wars*. London: Allen & Unwin.

Cappelen, Ådne; Nils Petter Gleditsch & Olav Bjerkholt, 1984. 'Military Spending and Economic Growth in the OECD Countries', *Journal of Peace Research*, vol. 21, no. 4, November, pp. 361–373.

Carlgren, Wilhelm, 1985. *Svensk underrättelsetjänst 1939–45*. Stockholm: Liber.
Carr, Edward H., 1945. *The Twenty Years' Crisis 1919–1939*. 2nd ed. London: Macmillan. [First published in 1939.]
Carter, Ashton B., 1987. 'Assessing Command System Vulnerability', pp. 555–610 in Ashton B. Carter, John D. Steinbrunner & Charles A. Zraket, eds. *Managing Nuclear Operations*. Washingt,on, DC: Brookings.
Caspary, William R., 1967. 'Richardson's Model of Arms Description, Critique, and an Alternative Model', *International Studies Quarterly*, vol. 11, no. 1, March, pp. 63–88.
Cattell, Raymond B., 1949. 'The Dimensions of Culture Patterns Discoverable in the Syntal Dimensions of Existing Nations', *Journal of Social Psychology*, vol. 44, no. 2, pp. 215–253.
Cattell, Raymond B. & Richard L. Gorsuch, 1965. 'The Definition and Measurement of National Morale and Morality', *Journal of Social Psychology*, vol. 67, no. 1, pp. 77–96.
Central Bureau of Statistics, 1978. *Historical Statistics 1978*. Oslo: Central Bureau of Statistics.
Chalmers, Malcolm, 1985. *Paying for Defence. Military Spending and British Decline*. London: Pluto.
Chatterjee, Partha, 1974. 'The Equilibrium Theory of Arms Races: Some Extensions', *Journal of Peace Research*, vol. 11, no. 3, pp. 203–211.
Choucri, Nazli & Robert C. North, 1975. *Nations in Conflict: Population, Expansion and War*. San Francisco, CA: Freeman.
Cimbala, Stephen, 1987. *Artificial Intelligence and National Security*. Lexington, MA: Heath.
Civilförsvarsstyrelsen, 1955. *Civilförsvaret inför atomåldern. Kontakt med Krigsmakten*, no. 4. Stockholm.
Cochran, Thomas B.; William M. Arkin & Milton M. Hoenig, 1984. *Nuclear Weapons Databook*, vol. I, *US Nuclear Forces and Capabilities*. Cambridge, MA: Ballinger.
Cochran, Thomas B., William M. Arkin, Robert S. Norris & Milton M. Hoenig, 1987. *Nuclear Weapons Databook*, vol. II, *US Nuclear Warhead Production*. Cambridge, MA: Ballinger.
Cockburn, Andrew, 1983. *The Threat: Inside the Soviet Military Machine*. New York: Random House.
Cohen, Samuel, 1983. *The Truth about the Neutron Bomb*. New York: William Morrow.
Committee of Soviet Scientists for Peace, Against the Nuclear Threat, 1985. *Space Strike Arms and International Security*. Moscow: Novosti.
Committee of Soviet Scientists for Peace, Against the Nuclear Threat, 1987. *Strategic Stability under the Conditions of Radical Nuclear Arms Reductions*. Moscow: Novosti.
Common Security: A Programme for Disarmament. The Report of the Independent Commission on Disarmament and Security Issues under the Chairmanship of Olof Palme, 1983. London: Pan.
Cooper, Julian, 1987. 'Technology Transfer between Military and Civilian Ministries', pp. 388–404 in Joint Economic Committee, Congress of the United States, *Gorbachev's Economic ʹPlans*, vol. 1. Washington, DC: Government Printing Office.
Corbett, Juliet S., 1911. *Some Principles of Maritime Strategy*. London: Longmans & Green.
Coser, Lewis, 1956. *The Social Functions of Conflict*. Glencoe, IL: Free Press.
Coulam, Robert F., 1977. *Illusions of Choice: The F-111 and the Problem of Weapons Acquisition Reform*. Princeton, NJ: Princeton University Press.
Cowen, Regina, 1986. *Defense Procurement in the FRG: Politics and Organization*. Boulder, CO: Westview.
Crabb, Cecil V. & Kevin V. Mulchany, 1986. *Presidents & Foreign Policy Making*. Baton Rouge, LA: Louisiana State University Press.
Curti, Merle, 1929. *The American Peace Crusade, 1815–1860*. Durham, NC: Duke University Press. [Facsimile reprint, 1973: New York: Octagon.]
Cusack, Thomas R. & Michael D. Ward, 1981. 'Military Spending in the United States, the Soviet Union, and the People's Republic of China', *Journal of Conflict Resolution*, vol. 25, no. 3, September, pp. 429–469.
Czempiel, Ernst-Otto, 1966. *Das amerikanische Sicherheitssystem, 1945–1949. Studie zur Aussenpolitik der bürgerlichen Gesellschaft*. Berlin: de Gruyter.

Dalgleish, D. Douglas & Larry Schweikart, 1984. *Trident*. Carbondale, IL & Edwardsville, IL: Southern Illinois University Press.
David, Donald E. & Walter S.G. Kohn, 1977. 'Lenin's "Notebook on Clausewitz" ', pp. 188–222 in Jones, 1977.
Davidson, Donald, 1975. 'Thought and Talk', pp. 7–24 in Guttenplan, 1975.
Davis, Otto A.; M.A.H. Dempster & Aaron Wildavsky, 1966. 'A Theory of the Budgetary Process', *American Political Science Review*, vol. 60, no. 3, September, pp. 529–547.
Deger, Saadet & Ron Smith, 1983. 'Military Expenditure and Growth in Less Developed Countries', *Journal of Conflict Resolution*, vol. 27, no. 2, June, pp. 335–353.
DeGrasse, Robert W., Jr., 1983. *Military Expansion, Economic Decline*. New York: Council of Economic Priorities.
Deist, Wilhelm, 1981. *The Wehrmacht and the German Rearmament*. Toronto: University of Toronto Press.
DeWitt, Hugh E., 1984. 'Labs Drive the Arms Race', *Bulletin of the Atomic Scientists*, vol. 40, no. 9, November, pp. 40–42.
Dibb, Paul, 1986. *The Soviet Union: The Incomplete Superpower*. London: Macmillan/Chicago, IL: University of Illinois Press.
Diehl, Paul F., 1983. 'Arms Races and Escalation: A Closer Look', *Journal of Peace Research*, vol. 20, no. 3, September, pp. 205–212.
Diehl, Paul F., 1985. 'Armaments without War: An Analysis of Some Underlying Effects', *Journal of Peace Research*, vol. 22, no. 3, September, pp. 249–260.
DiFilippo, Anthony, 1986. *Military Spending and Industrial Decline. A Study of the American Machine Tool Industry*. Westport, CT: Greenwood.
Discriminate Deterrence, 1988. *Report of the Commission on Integrated Long-Term Strategy*. Washington, DC: US Government Printing Office.
Donovan, Robert J., 1982. *Tumultuous Years. The Presidency of Harry S Truman, 1949–1953*. New York & London: Norton.
Doran, Charles F., 1983. 'Power Cycle Theory and the Contemporary State System', pp. 162–182 in William Thompson, ed. *Contending Approaches to World System Analysis*. Beverly Hills, CA: Sage.
Doran, Charles F. & Wes Parsons, 1980. 'War and Cycle of Relative Power', *American Political Science Review*, vol. 74, no. 4, December, pp. 947–965.
Draper, Charles S., 1959. 'Submarine Inertial Navigation – A Review and Some Predictions'. Paper presented to Polaris Steering Task Group, 22 October. [Copy in Charles Stark Draper Laboratory, Inc., Library, Cambridge, MA, CSD-107.]
Duffy, Gavan, 1988a. 'Time Space: Representing the Temporal Domain of SherFACS International Conflict Events'. Paper prepared for the 29th Convention of the International Studies Association, St. Louis, 29 March–2 April.
Duffy, Gavan, 1988b. 'Theory and Text: How Textual Analysis can Help Build International Relations Theory.' Paper prepared for the 29th Convention of the International Studies Association, St. Louis, 29 March–2 April.
Duhem, Pierre, 1954. *The Aim and Structure of Physical Theory*. Princeton, NJ: Princeton University Press. [First published in 1906.]
Dumas, Lloyd J., 1979. 'Armament, Disarmament, and National Security: A Theoretical Duopoly Model of the Arms Race', *Journal of Economic Studies*, new series, vol. 6, no. 1, May, pp. 1–38.
Dumas, Lloyd J., 1982. 'Military Spending and Economic Decay', pp. 1–26 in Lloyd J. Dumas, ed. *The Political Economy of Arms Reduction*. Boulder, CO: Westview.
Dupuy, Trevor N., 1964. 'Quantification of Factors Related to Weapon Lethality', Annex III-H, in R. Sunderland et al., *Historical Trends Related to Weapons Lethality*. Report prepared under contract for the Advanced Tactics Project of the Combat Developments Command, HQ US Army, Washington, DC.
Dupuy, Trevor N., 1980. *The Evolution of Weapons and Warfare*. London, New York & Sydney: Jane's.
Dörfer, Ingemar, 1973. *System 37 Viggen - Arms Technology and the Domestication of Glory*. Oslo: Norwegian University Press.

Eberwein, Wolf-Dieter, 1981. 'The Quantitative Study of International Conflict: Quantity and Quality', *Journal of Peace Research*, vol. 18. no. 1, pp. 19–38.

Eckhardt, William, 1969. 'The Factor of Militarism', *Journal of Peace Research*, vol. 6, no. 2, pp. 123–132.

Eckhardt, William, 1980. 'The Causes and Correlates of Western Militarism', pp. 323–353 in Asbjørn Eide & Marek Thee, eds. *Problems of Contemporary Militarism*. London: Croom Helm.

Edgerton, David, 1988. 'The Relationship between Military and Civil Technology: A Historical Perspective', pp. 106–114 in Gummet & Reppy, 1988.

Egerton, George, 1983. 'Great Britain and the League of Nations. Collective Security as Myth and History', pp. 95–117 in *The League of Nations in Retrospect*. Berlin, New York: Walter de Gruyter.

Eisenhower, Dwight D., 1961. 'Farewell Radio and Television Address to the American People, January 17, 1961', pp. 1035–1040 in *Public Papers of the President of the United States, Dwight D. Eisenhower 1960–61*. Washington, DC: United States Government Printing Office.

Ekman, Stig, ed., 1986. *Stormaktstryck och småstatspolitik - aspekter på svensk politik under andra världskriget*. Stockholm: Liber.

Engelhardt, Klaus & Karl-Heinz Heise, 1974. *Militär-Industrie-Komplex und staatsmonopolistischen Herrschaftssystem*. Berlin: Staatsverlag der DDR.

Engels, Friedrich, 1877. *Anti-Dühring*. Also, vol. 20 in Karl Marx & Friedrich Engels, *Werke*. Berlin: Dietz.

Enloe, Cynthia, 1983. *Does Khaki Become You?* London: Pluto.

Erickson, John, 1972. 'Radio Location and the Air Defense Problem: The Design and Development of Soviet Radar, 1934–40', *Science Studies*, vol. 2, no. 3, July, pp. 241–268.

Ericsson, Stig H:son, 1968. *Kuling längs kusten*. Stockholm: Bonniers.

Erlander, Tage, 1976. *1955–60*. Stockholm: Tiden.

Evangelista, Matthew A., 1983. 'The Evolution of Soviet Tactical Air Forces', pp. 451–479 in Jones, 1983.

Evangelista, Matthew, 1984. 'Why the Soviets Buy the Weapons They Do', *World Politics*, vol. 36, no. 4, July, pp. 597–618. [Slightly revised version as ch. 16 of this book.]

Evangelista, Matthew, 1986a. 'Case Studies and Theories of the Arms Race', *Bulletin of Peace Proposals*, vol. 17, no. 2, May, pp. 197–206.

Evangelista, Matthew, 1986b. *Technological Innovation and the Arms Race: A Comparative Study of Soviet and American Decisions on Tactical Nuclear Weapons*. Ithaca, NY: Cornell University. [PhD dissertation.]

Evangelista, Matthew, 1986c. 'Explaining NATO's Nuclear Weapons', *Occasional Papers*, Peace Studies Program, Cornell University & Peace Research Institute, Frankfurt a.M.

Evangelista, Matthew, 1988. *Innovation and the Arms Race: How the United States and the Soviet Union Develop New Military Technologies*. Ithaca, NY: Cornell University Press.

Fairbanks, Charles H., Jr., 1985. 'Arms Races: The Metaphor and the Facts', *The National Interest*, vol. 1, no. 1, Fall, pp. 75–90.

Fallows, James, 1982. *National Defense*. New York: Vintage.

Falsche Gewichte, 1983. Militärpolitik Dokumentation, no. 30/31. Frankfurt a.M.: Haag & Herchen.

Faramazyan, Rajik Artasjesovitsj, 1974. *USA: Militarism and the Economy*. Moscow: Progress.

Fedoseev, A., 1976. *Zapadnia: Chelovek i Sotsializm*. Frankfurt a.M.: Possev-Verlag.

Ferejohn, John, 1976. 'On the Effects of Aid to Nations in Arms Races', pp. 228–251 in Zinnes & Gillespie,1976.

Fieldhouse, Richard W., 1986. 'Chinese Nuclear Weapons: An Overview', pp. 97–113 in *World Armaments and Disarmament: SIPRI Yearbook 1986*.

Fitchett, Joseph, 1988. 'New Missile Strategy Urged', *International Herald Tribune*, 11 January, pp. 1, 5.

Fitzgerald, Mary, 1985. *Marshal Ogarkov on Modern War: 1971–1985*. Alexandria, VA: Center for Naval Analysis.

Flora, Peter, 1983. *State, Economy and Society in Western Europe 1815–1975*, vol. I. *The Growth of Mass Democracies and Welfare States*. Frankfurt a.M.: Campus.

Fontanel, Jacques & J.F. Guilhaudis, eds., 1986. *Arés. La course aux armament et le désarmament*. Grenoble: Université de Grenoble II, Centre d'Etudes de Défense et de Sécurité Internationale.

Forland, Astrid, 1987. 'På leiting etter uran. Institutt for Atomenergi og internasjonalt samarbeid 1945–51', *Forsvarsstudier*, no. 3. Oslo: Research Centre for Defence History.

Forland, Astrid, 1988. 'Atomer for fred eller krig? Etableringa av Institutt for Atomenergi 1945–48', *Forsvarsstudier*, no. 2. Oslo: Norwegian Institute for Defence Studies.

Forsvarskommisjonen, 1978. *Forsvarskommisjonen av 1974, NOU* 1978: 9. Oslo: Norwegian University Press.

Foucault, Michel, 1969. *L'Archéologie du savoir*. Paris: Gallimard.

Freedman, Lawrence, 1978. *Arms Production in the United Kingdom*. London: Royal Institute of International Affairs.

Frei, Daniel & Christian Catrina, 1983. *Risks of Unintentional Nuclear War*. London: Croom Helm.

Freud, Sigmund, 1930. *Civilization and its Discontents*. London: Hogart Press and Institute of Psycho-Analysis/New York: Cape & Smith.

Fritiofsson, Karl, 1966. 'Säkerhetspolitiska perspektiv på frågan om svenska kärnvapen', *Kungliga Krigsvetenskapsakademiens tidskrift*, vol. 170, no. 9, pp. 303–315.

FRUS, 1950. *Foreign Relations of the United States*, vol. 1, *National Security*. Washington, DC: US Government Printing Office, 1977.

Fuller, William, 1985. *Civil-Military Conflict in Imperial Russia, 1881–1914*. Princeton, NJ: Princeton University Press.

Føllesdal, Dagfinn, 1975. 'Meaning and Experience', pp. 25–44 in Guttenplan, 1975.

Galbraith, John, 1969. *How to Control the Military*. New York: New American Library.

Galbraith, John, 1972. *The New Industrial State*. Harmondsworth: Penguin. [First published in 1967.]

Galtung, Johan, 1980. *The True Worlds. A Transnational Perspective*. New York: Free Press.

Galtung, Johan, 1988. 'The Cold War as an Exercise in Autism. The US Government, the Governments of Western Europe and the People', ch. 5, pp. 81–108 in *Transarmament and the Cold War*, vol. 6 of *Essays in Peace Research*. Copenhagen: Ejlers. Also in: *Alternatives*, vol. 14, no. 2, April 1989, pp. 169–193.

Gansler, Jacques S., 1980. *The Defense Industry*. Cambridge, MA: MIT Press.

Gantzel, Klaus Jürgen, 1973. 'Armaments Dynamics in the East–West Conflict: An Arms Race?', *Peace Science Society (International) Papers*, vol. 20, pp. 1–24.

Gantzel, Klaus Jürgen, 1974. 'Zur Analyse internationaler Rüstungsdynamik', *Mannheimer Berichte aus Forschung und Lehre an der Universität Mannheim*, no. 8, February, pp. 227–233.

Gantzel, Klaus Jürgen & Jörg Mayer-Stamer, eds., 1986. *Die Kriege Nach dem Zweiten Weltkrieg bis 1984. Daten und erste Analyzen*. Munich: Weltforum.

Gantzel, Klaus Jürgen; Volker Rittberger & Burkhard Luber, 1972. 'Internationale Faktoren der Rüstungsdynamik im Ost–West-Konflikt', *Mitteilungen der Hessischen Stiftung Friedensund Konfliktforschung*, no. 4.

Garnham, David, 1976. 'Power Parity and Lethal International Violence, 1969–73', *Journal of Conflict Resolution*, vol. 20, no. 3, pp. 379–394.

Garthoff, Raymond L., 1975, 'SALT and the Soviet Military', *Problems of Communism*, vol. 24, no. 1, January-February, pp. 21–37.

Garthoff, Raymond L., 1980–81. 'Brezhnev's Opening: The INF Tangle', *Foreign Policy*, no. 41, Winter, pp. 82–94.

Garthoff, Raymond L., 1983. 'The Soviet SS-20 Decision', *Survival*, vol. 25, no. 3, May-June, pp. 110–119.

Garthoff, Raymond L., 1985. *Detente and Confrontation: American–Soviet Relations from Nixon to Reagan*. Washington, DC: Brookings.

George, Alexander L., 1979. 'Case Studies and Theory Development: The Method of

Structured, Focused Comparision', pp. 43–68 in Paul G. Lauren, ed. *Diplomacy: New Approaches in History, Theory, and Policy.* New York: Free Press.

George, Alexander L.; Philip J. Farley & Alexander Dallin, eds., 1988. *US–Soviet Security Cooperation – Achievements, Failures, Lessons.* New York & Oxford: Oxford University Press.

Geyer, Dietrich, 1987. *Russian Imperialism. The Interaction of Domestic and Foreign Policy, 1860–1914.* New Haven, CT: Yale University Press.

Geyer, Michael, 1984. *Deutsche Rüstungspolitik 1890–1980.* Frankfurt a.M.: Suhrkamp.

Geyer, Michael, 1985. 'The Dynamics of Military Revisionism in the Interwar Years. Military Politics between Rearmament and Diplomacy', pp. 100–151 in Wilhelm Deist, ed. *The German Military in the Age of Total War.* Leamington Spa: Berg.

Giddens, Anthony, 1986. *The Nation-State and Violence.* Cambridge: Polity.

Gillard, David, 1977. *The Struggle for Asia 1828–1914. A Study of British and Russian Imperialism.* London: Methuen.

Gillespie, John V. & Dina A. Zinnes, eds., 1976. *Mathematical Systems in International Relations Research.* New York: Praeger.

Gillespie, John V.; Dina A. Zinnes & G. S. Tahim, 1976. 'Deterrence as Second Strike Capability: An Optimal Control Model and Differential Game', pp. 367–385 in Gillespie & Zinnes, 1976.

Gillespie, John V.; Dina A. Zinnes, G. S. Tahim, Martin W. Sampson, Philip A. Schrodt & R. Michael Rubison, 1979. 'Deterrence and Arms Races: An Optimal Control Systems Model', *Behavioral Science*, vol. 24, no. 4, July, pp. 250–262.

Gilpin, Robert, 1981. *War and Change in International Relations.* Cambridge & New York: Cambridge University Press.

Gleditsch, Nils Petter, 1987. 'The Local Impact of Reduced Military Spending. A Case Study of Norway', pp. 213–235 in Jürgen Kuhlmann, ed. Edited papers from Research Committee 01 'Armed Forces and Conflict Resolution', XI World Congress of Sociology, New Delhi, August 1986, in *Forum International*, vol. 7. Munich: Sozialwissenschaftliches Institut der Bundeswehr.

Gleditsch, Nils Petter; Olav Bjerkholt & Ådne Cappelen, 1988. 'Military R&D and Economic Growth in Industrialized Market Economies', pp. 198–215 in Peter Wallensteen, ed. *Peace Research: Achievements and Challenges.* Boulder, CO & London: Westview.

Goertz, Gary & Paul F. Diehl, 1986. 'Measuring Military Allocations. A Comparison of Different Approaches', *Journal of Conflict Resolution*, vol. 30, no. 3, September, pp. 553–581.

Goldblat, Jozef, ed., 1985. *Non-Proliferation: The Why and Wherefore.* London: Taylor & Francis.

Goldblat, Jozef & David Cox, 1988. *Nuclear Weapon Tests: Prohibition or Limitation?* Oxford & New York: Oxford University Press.

Goldmann, Kjell, 1974. *Tension and Detente in Bipolar Europe.* Stockholm: Esselte Studium.

Goldstein, Joshua S., 1985. 'Kondratieff Waves as War Cycles', *International Studies Quarterly*, vol. 29, no. 4, December, pp. 411–444.

Goldstein, Joshua S., 1988. *Long Cycles. Prosperity and War in the Modern Age.* New Haven, CT: Yale University Press.

Gordon, David M., 1980. 'Stages of Accumulation and Long Economic Cycles', pp. 9–15 in Terence K. Hopkins & Immanuel Wallerstein, eds. *Processes of the World-System.* Beverly Hills, CA: Sage.

Gordon, David M.; Thomas E. Weisskopf & Samuel Bowles, 1983. 'Long Swing and the Nonreproductive Cycle', *American Economic Review*, vol. 73, no. 2, pp. 152–157.

Gorshkov, Sergei G., 1979. *Morskaia Moshch' Gosudarstva.* Moscow: Voenizdat. [English version, 1980. *The Sea Power of the State.* Oxford: Pergamon.]

Gourevitch, Peter, 1986. *Politics in Hard Times. Comparative Responses to International Economic Crises.* Ithaca, NY: Cornell University Press.

Gowing, Margaret, 1965. *Britain and Atomic Energy, 1939–1945.* London: Macmillan.

Gray, Colin S., 1971. 'The Arms Race Phenomenon', *World Politics*, vol. 24, no. 1, October, pp. 39–79.
Gray, Colin S., 1974. 'The Urge to Compete: Rationales for Arms Racing', *World Politics*, vol. 26, no. 2, January, pp. 207–233.
Gray, Colin S., 1976. *The Soviet-American Arms Race*. Westmead: Saxon House & Lexington, MA: Heath.
Gray, Robert C., 1979. 'Learning from History: Case Studies of the Weapons Acquisition Process', *World Politics*, vol. 31, no. 3, April, pp. 457–470.
Greenwood, Ted, 1975. *Making the MIRV: A Study of Defense Decision-Making*. Cambridge, MA: Ballinger.
Gummett, Philip & Judith Reppy, eds., 1988. *The Relations between Defence and Civil Technologies*. Dordrecht: Kluwer.
Guttenplan, Samuel, ed., 1975. *Mind and Language*. Oxford: Oxford University Press.
Gøthe, Odd, 1988. *Ærlig talt!* Oslo: Tiden.
Haas, Michael, 1974. *International Conflict*. New York: Bobbs-Merrill.
Habermas, Jürgen, 1962. *Strukturwandel der Öffentlichkeit*. Neuwied: Luchterhand.
Habermas, Jürgen, 1968. *Technik und Wissenschaft als 'Ideologie'*. Frankfurt a.M.: Suhrkamp.
Habermas, Jürgen, 1973. *Legitimationsprobleme im Spätkapitalismus*. Frankfurt a.M.: Suhrkamp.
Habermas, Jürgen, 1981. *Theorie des kommunikativen Handelns*. Frankfurt a.M.: Suhrkamp.
Habermas, Jürgen, 1985. *Der philosophische Diskurs der Moderne*. Frankfurt a.M.: Suhrkamp.
Halliday, Jon, 1975. *A Political History of Japanese Capitalism*. New York: Pantheon.
Halperin, Morton H., 1974. *Bureaucratic Politics and Foreign Policy*. Washington, DC: Brookings.
Halperin, Morton H., 1975. *National Security Policy-Making. Analyses, Cases, and Proposals*. Lexington, MA: Heath.
Halperin, Morton H., 1987. *Nuclear Fallacy: Dispelling the Myth of Nuclear Strategy*. Cambridge, MA: Ballinger.
Halperin, Morton H. & Arnold Kanter, 1973a. 'The Bureaucratic Perspective', pp. 3–40 in Halperin & Kanter, 1973b. Reprinted in shortened form in Art & Jervis, 1985, pp. 439–466.
Halperin, Morton H. & Arnold Kanter, 1973b. *Readings in American Foreign Policy: A Bureaucratic Perspective*. Boston, MA: Little, Brown.
Hanisch, Tore J. & Even Lange, 1986. *Veien til velstand*. Oslo: Norwegian University Press.
Hanning, Hugh, ed., 1970. *The Soviet Union in Europe and the Near East*. London: Royal United Services Institution.
Hansen, Chuck, 1988. *US Nuclear Weapons: The Second History*. Arlington, TX: Aerofox.
Harberger, Arnold C., ed., 1960. *The Demand for Durable Goods*. Chicago, IL: University of Chicago Press.
Harris, Geoffrey, 1986. 'The Determinants of Defence Expenditures in the ASEAN Region', *Journal of Peace Research*, vol. 23, no. 1, March, pp. 41–49.
Haug, Wolfgang Fritz, 1987, *Commodity Aesthetics. Ideology and Culture*. New York: International General.
Hellmann, Sven & Britta Bjørnsson, 1985. *Nuclear War by Mistake – Inevitable or Preventable?* Report from an International Conference in Stockholm, 15–16 February 1985. Stockholm: Swedish Physicians Against Nuclear Arms.
Hempel, Carl G., 1966. *Philosophy of Natural Science*. New York: Prentice-Hall.
Herken, Gregg, 1987. 'The Earthly Origins of Star Wars', *Bulletin of the Atomic Scientists*, vol. 43, no. 8, October, pp. 20–28.
Herrmann, Richard, 1988. 'The Empirical Challenge of the Cognitive Revolution: A Strategy for Drawing Inferences about Perceptions', *International Studies Quarterly*, vol. 32, no. 2, June, pp. 175–203.
Hesse, May, 1974. *The Structure of Scientific Inference*. London: Macmillan.
Hintze, Otto, 1906. 'Staatsverfassung und Heeresverfassung', pp. 61–85 in Volker R. Berghahn, ed., 1975. *Militarismus*. Cologne: Kiepenheuer & Witsch.

Hoag, David G., 1971. 'Ballistic-Missile Guidance', pp. 19–106 in Bernard T. Feld et al., eds. *Impact of New Technologies on the Arms Race*. Cambridge, MA: MIT Press.
Hobsbawm, Eric, 1979. *The Age of Capital 1848–1875*. New York: Mentor.
Hobsbawm, Eric, 1987. *The Age of Empire 1875–1914*. New York: Pantheon.
Hobson, John A., 1988. *Imperialism. A Study*, 3rd ed. London: Unwin Hyman. [First published in 1902.]
Holland, Lauren H. & Robert A. Hoover, 1985. *The MX Decision: A New Direction in US Weapons Procurement Policy?* Boulder, CO: Westview.
Hollist, W. Ladd, 1977a. 'Alternative Explanations of Competitive Arms Processes: Tests on Four Pairs of Nations', *American Journal of Political Science*, vol. 21, no. 2, May, pp. 313–340.
Hollist, W. Ladd, 1977b. 'An Analysis of Arms Processes in the United States and the Soviet Union', *International Studies Quarterly*, vol. 21, no. 3, September, pp. 503–528.
Holloway, David, 1970a. 'The Role of the Military in Soviet Politics', pp. 7–15 in *The Soviet Union in Europe and the Near East: Her Capabilities and Intentions*. London: Royal United Services Institution.
Holloway, David, 1970b. 'New Ideas in Soviet Decision-Making', pp. 68–73 in *The Soviet Union in Europe and the Near East: Her Capabilities and Intentions*. London: Royal United Services Institution.
Holloway, David, 1971. *Technology Management and the Soviet Military Establishment*. Adelphi Paper no. 76. London: International Institute for Strategic Studies.
Holloway, David, 1974. 'Technology and Political Decision in Soviet Armaments Policy', *Journal of Peace Research*, vol. 11, no. 4, pp. 257–279.
Holloway, David, 1977. 'Military Technology', pp. 407–489 in Ronald Amann; Julian Cooper & R. W. Davies, eds. *The Technological Level of Soviet Industry*. New Haven, CT: Yale University Press.
Holloway, David, 1980. 'War, Militarism and the Soviet State', *Alternatives*, vol. 6, no. 1, March, pp. 59–92. [Shortened version with the same title, pp. 129–169 in Edward P. Thompson & Dan Smith, eds. *Protest and Survive*. Harmondsworth: Penguin.]
Holloway, David, 1982. 'Innovation in the Defence Sector: Battle Tanks and ICBMs', pp. 368–414 in Ronald Amann & Julian Cooper, eds. *Industrial Innovation in the Soviet Union*. New Haven, CT: Yale University Press.
Holloway, David, 1983. *The Soviet Union and the Arms Race*. New Haven, CT: Yale University Press.
Holst, Johan Jørgen, 1973. ' "Comparative" US and Soviet Deployments, Doctrines, and Arms Limitation', pp. 53–95 in Morton A. Kaplan, ed. *SALT: Problems and Prospects*. Morristown, NJ: General Learning Press.
Hopkins, Terence K. & Immanuel Wallerstein, 1979. 'Cyclical Rhythms and Secular Trends of the Capitalist World-Economy: Some Premises, Hypotheses and Questions', *Review*, vol. 2, no. 4, Spring, pp. 483–500.
Horelick, Arnold L. & Myron Rush, 1966. *Strategic Power and Soviet Foreign Policy*. Chicago, IL: University of Chicago Press.
Hounshell, David A., 1983. *From the American System to Mass Production 1800–1932. The Development of Manufacturing Technology in the United States*. Baltimore, MD: Johns Hopkins University Press.
Houweling, Henk & Jan G. Siccama, 1981. 'The Arms Race-War Relationship: Why Serious Disputes Matter', *Arms Control*, vol. 2, no. 2, September, pp. 157–197.
Houweling, Henk & Jan G. Siccama, 1988. 'Power Transitions as a Cause of War', *Journal of Conflict Resolution*, vol. 32, no. 1, March, pp. 87–102.
Hovstadius, Bo & Manne Wängborg, 1981. 'The United Nations Study of Disarmament and Development: An Overview', *Journal of Peace Research*, vol. 18, no. 2, pp. 209–217.
Howard, Michael, 1976. *War in European History*. Oxford: Oxford University Press.
Hughes, Thomas P., 1983. *Networks of Power*. Baltimore, MD: Johns Hopkins University Press.
Hughes, Thomas P., 1986. 'The Seamless Web: Technology, Science, Etcetera, Etcetera', *Social Studies of Science*, vol. 16, no. 2, May, pp. 281–292.

Huisken, Ron, 1974. 'The Dynamics of World Military Expenditure', pp. 123–139 in *World Armaments and Disarmament. SIPRI Yearbook 1974*.
Huisken, Ron, 1981. *The Origin of the Strategic Cruise Missile*. New York: Praeger.
Huntington, Samuel P., 1958. 'Arms Races: Prerequisites and Results', *Public Policy. A Yearbook of the Graduate School of Public Administration, Harvard University*, vol. 8, part 1, ch. 2, pp. 41–86.
Huntington, Samuel, 1961. *The Common Defense*. New York: Columbia University Press.
Hurlen, Bjarne, 1966. 'Statens anskaffelsespolitikk og den industrielle utvikling', *Norsk Militært Tidsskrift*, vol. 136, no. 8, pp. 445–450.
Hussain, Farooq, 1981. *The Future of Arms Control: Part IV. The Impact of Weapons Test Restrictions, Adelphi Papers*, no. 165. London: International Institute for Strategic Studies.
Hägglöf, Gunnar, 1958. *Svensk krigshandelspolitik under andra världskriget*. Stockholm: Norstedt.
Iakovlev, A.S., 1966. *Tsel' Zhizn'*. Moscow: Politizdat.
Intelligence Community Report, 1982. 'Intelligence Community Report on Soviet Acquisition of Western Technology', *US Export Weekly*, 13 April, pp. 58–70.
Intriligator, Michael D., 1964. 'Some Simple Models of Arms Races', *General Systems*, vol. 9, pp. 143–164.
Intriligator, Michael D., 1967. *Strategy in a Missile War: Targets and Rates of Fire*. Security Studies Paper no. 10. Los Angeles, CA: Security Studies Project, University of California, Los Angeles.
Intriligator, Michael D., 1968. 'The Debate over Missile Strategy: Targets and Rates of Fire', *Orbis*, vol. 11, no. 4, Winter, pp. 1138–1159.
Intriligator, Michael D., 1971. *Mathematical Optimization and Economic Theory*. Englewood Cliffs, NJ: Prentice-Hall.
Intriligator, Michael D., 1975. 'Strategic Considerations in the Richardson Model of Arms Races', *Journal of Political Economy*, vol. 83, no. 2, April, pp. 339–353.
Intriligator, Michael D., 1982. 'Research on Conflict Theory: Analytic Approaches and Areas of Application', *Journal of Conflict Resolution*, vol. 26, no. 2, June, pp. 307–327.
Intriligator, Michael D., 1988. 'Calculating the Benefits and Costs', in Sanford A. Lakoff, ed. *Beyond Start?* IGCC Policy Paper no. 7. La Jolla, CA: Institute on Global Conflict and Cooperation, University of California, San Diego.
Intriligator, Michael D. & Dagobert L. Brito, 1976a. 'Strategy, Arms Races, and Arms Control', pp. 173–189 in Gillespie & Zinnes, 1976.
Intriligator, Michael D. & Dagobert L. Brito, 1976b. 'Formal Models of Arms Races', *Journal of Peace Science*, vol. 2, no. 1, Spring, pp. 77–88. Also published as ACIS Working Paper no. 2, Los Angeles, CA: Program in Arms Control and International Security, University of California, Los Angeles.
Intriligator, Michael D. & Dagobert L. Brito, 1981. 'Nuclear Proliferation and the Probability of Nuclear War', *Public Choice*, vol. 37, no. 2, pp. 247–260.
Intriligator, Michael D. & Dagobert L. Brito, 1984. 'Can Arms Races Lead to the Outbreak of War?', *Journal of Conflict Resolution*, vol. 28, no. 1, March, pp. 63–84.
Intriligator, Michael D. & Dagobert L. Brito, 1985a. 'Heuristic Decision Rules, The Dynamics of an Arms Race, and War Initiation', pp. 133–160 in Luterbacher & Ward, 1985.
Intriligator, Michael D. & Dagobert L. Brito, 1985b. 'Non-Armageddon Solutions to the Arms Race', *Arms Control*, vol. 6, no. 1, May, pp. 41–57.
Intriligator, Michael D. & Dagobert L. Brito, 1986a. 'Arms Races and Instability', *Journal of Strategic Studies*, vol. 9, no. 4, December, pp. 113–131.
Intriligator, Michael D. & Dagobert L. Brito, 1986b. 'Mayer's Alternative to the I-B Model', *Journal of Conflict Resolution*, vol. 30, no. 1, March, pp. 29–31.
Intriligator, Michael D. & Dagobert L. Brito, 1987a. *Arms Control: Problems and Prospects*. IGCC Research Paper no. 2. La Jolla, CA: Institute on Global Conflict and Cooperation, University of California, San Diego.
Intriligator, Michael D. & Dagobert L. Brito, 1987b. 'The Stability of Mutual Deterrence',

pp. 13–19 in Jacek Kugler & Frank C. Zagare, eds. *Exploring the Stability of Deterrence*. GSIS Monograph Series in World Affairs. Boulder, CO: Lynne Rienner.

Intriligator, Michael D. & Dagobert L. Brito, 1988a. 'The Richardsonian Arms Race Model', pp. 219–236 in Manus I. Midlarsky, ed. *Handbook of War Studies*. Boston, MA: Unwin Hyman.

Intriligator, Michael D. & Dagobert L. Brito, 1988b. 'Arms Control', pp. 213–232 in Edward A. Kolodziej & Patrick Morgan, eds. *National Security and Arms Control*. Westport, CT: Greenwood.

Intriligator, Michael D. & Dagobert L. Brito, 1988c. 'Arms Races and Arms Control in the Middle East', in Gideon Fishelson, ed. *Economic Cooperation in the Middle East*. Boulder, CO: Westview.

Intriligator, Michael D. & Dagobert L. Brito, 1988d. 'Accidental Nuclear War: A Significant Issue for Arms Control', *Current Research on Peace and Violence*, vol. 11, no. 1–2, June, pp. 14–23.

Intriligator, Michael D. & Dagobert L. Brito, 1988e. 'The Potential Contribution of Psychology to Nuclear War Issues', *American Psychologist*, vol. 43, April, pp. 318–321.

Intriligator, Michael D. & Bennett Ramberg, 1983. ' "International Regimes": Would You Know One If You Saw One?', *CISA Research Note*, no. 13, Los Angeles, CA: Center for International and Strategic Affairs, University of California, Los Angeles.

Isard, Walter & Charles H. Anderton, 1985. 'Arms Race Models: A Survey and Synthesis', *Conflict Management and Peace Science*, vol. 8, no. 2, Spring, pp. 27–98.

Jacobsen, Carl G., 1975. 'Soviet Civilian Fleets', in *Soviet Oceans Development*. Washington, DC: Government Printing Office.

Jacobsen, Carl G., 1981. *Sino-Soviet Relations since Mao: the Chairman's Legacy*. New York: Praeger.

Jacobsen, Carl G., 1982. *The Nuclear Era: Its History; its Implication*. Cambridge, MA: Oelgeschlager, Gunn & Hain/Nottingham: Spokesman.

Jacobsen, Carl G., ed., 1987a. *The Uncertain Course: New Arms, Strategies, and Mindsets*. Oxford: Oxford University Press.

Jacobsen, Carl G., ed., 1987b. *The Soviet Defence Enigma: Calculating Costs and Burden*. Oxford: Oxford University Press.

Jahn, Egbert, 1975. 'The Role of the Armaments Complex in Soviet Society. (Is There a Soviet Military-Industrial Complex?)', *Journal of Peace Research*, vol. 12, no. 3, pp. 179–194.

Jasani, Bhupendra, 1986. 'The Military Use of Outer Space', pp. 137–143 in *World Armaments and Disarmament. SIPRI Yearbook 1986*.

Jaurès, Jean, 1911. *L'Armée nouvelle*. Paris: J. Rouff.

Jervas, Gunnar, 1983. 'Sverige, Norden och kärnvapen', pp. 58–90 in Bertil Heurlin, ed. *Kernevåbenpolitik i Norden*. Copenhagen: Det sikkerheds- og nedrustningspolitiske udvalg.

Johnsen, Katherine, 1961. 'Senate Vote Emphasizes Proven Weapons', *Aviation Week and Space Technology*, vol. 74, no. 21, 22 May, pp. 22–23.

Jones, David R., ed., annual 1977–. *Soviet Armed Forces Review Annual*, Gulf Breeze, FL: Academic International Press.

Jones, David R., 1987. 'The Soviet Defence Burden through the Prism of History', pp. 151–174 in Jacobson, 1987b.

Jones, Rodney W.; Cesare Merlini, Joseph F. Pilat & William C. Potter, eds., 1985. *The Emerging Nuclear Supplier States and Nuclear Nonproliferation*. Lexington, MA: Heath.

Jünger, Ernst, 1932. *Der Arbeiter. Herrschaft und Gestalt*. Hamburg: Hanseatische Verlagsanstalt.

Kaldor, Mary, 1982a. *The Baroque Arsenal*. London: Deutsch/New York: Hill & Wang.

Kaldor, Mary, 1982b. 'Warfare and Capitalism', pp. 261–287 in New Left Review, eds. *Exterminism and Cold War*. London: Verso.

Kaldor, Mary, 1986. 'The Weapons Succession Process', *World Politics*, vol. 38, no. 4, July, pp. 577–595.

Kaldor, Mary, 1987. 'The Atlantic Technology Culture', ch. 10, pp. 143–162 in Mary Kaldor & Richard Falk, eds. *Dealignment. A New Foreign Policy Perspective*. Oxford: Blackwell.

Kaldor, Mary & Julian Perry Robinson, 1978. 'War', pp. 343–379 in Christopher Freeman & Marie Jahoda, eds. *World Futures. The Great Debate*. London: Robertson.

Kaldor, Nicholas, 1966. *Causes of the Slow Rate of Economic Growth of the United Kingdom*. Cambridge: Cambridge University Press.

Kapitza, Sergej, 1988. 'Is There a Soviet Military-Industrial Complex?' Moscow. [Unpublished paper.]

Kaplan, Fred, 1983. *The Wizards of Armageddon*. New York: Simon & Schuster.

Kaplan, Lawrence S., 1980. *A Community of Interests: NATO and the Military Assistance Program, 1948–51*. Washington, DC: Office of the Secretary of Defense Historical Office.

Kaplan, Stephen S., 1981. *Diplomacy of Power. Soviet Armed Forces as a Political Instrument*. Washington, DC: Brookings.

Kappus, Wolfgang, 1985. *Abrüstung und Wirtschaftswachstum. Die Erfahrungen der USA mit der Rekonversion 1968–1976*. Frankfurt a.M.: Campus.

Karp, Aaron, 1984/85. 'Ballistic Missiles in the Third World', *International Security*, vol. 9, no. 3, Winter, pp. 166–195.

Katzenstein, Peter J., ed., 1978. *Between Power and Plenty: Foreign Economic Policies of Advanced Industrial States*. Madison: University of Wisconsin Press.

Keeny, Spurgeon M., Jr. & Wolfgang K.H. Panofsky, 1981/82. 'MAD versus NUTS', *Foreign Affairs*, vol. 60, no. 2, Winter, pp. 287–304.

Keep, John L. H., 1985. *Soldiers of the Tsar. Army and Society in Russia 1462–1874*. Oxford: Clarendon.

Kende, Istvan, 1971. 'Twenty-five Years of Local Wars', *Journal of Peace Research*, vol. 8, no. 1, pp. 5–23.

Kende, Istvan, 1978. 'Wars of Ten Years (1967–76)', *Journal of Peace Research*, vol. 15, no. 3, pp. 227–241.

Kennedy, Paul, 1981. *Realities behind Diplomacy. Background Influences on British External Policy 1865–1980*. Glasgow: Fontana.

Kennedy, Paul, 1982. *The Rise of the Anglo–German Antagonism, 1860–1914*. London: Allen & Unwin.

Kennedy, Paul, 1984. 'The First World War and the International Power System', *International Security*, vol. 9, no. 1, Summer, pp. 7–40.

Kennedy, Paul, 1987. *The Rise and Fall of the Great Powers. Economic Change and Military Conflict from 1500 to 2000*. New York: Random House.

Kent, Glenn A., 1963. *On the Interaction of Opposing Forces under Possible Arms Agreements*, Cambridge, MA: Center for International Affairs, Harvard University.

Keohane, Robert O., 1983. 'Associative American Development, 1776–1860: Economic Growth and Political Disintegration', pp. 43–90 in John Gerard Ruggie, ed. *The Antinomies of Interdependence. National Welfare and the International Division of Labor*. New York: Columbia University Press.

Kerner, Manfred, 1981. *Staat, Krieg und Krise*. Cologne: Pahl-Rugenstein.

Khrushchev, Nikita S., ed. by Strobe Talbott, trans., 1974. *Khrushchev Remembers: The Last Testament*. Boston, MA: Little, Brown.

Killian, James R., Jr., 1982. *Sputnik, Scientists, and Eisenhower*. London & Cambridge, MA: MIT Press. [First published in 1977.]

Kipp, Jacob W., 1977. 'Russian Naval Reformers and Imperial Expansion', pp. 118–148 in Jones, 1977.

Kissinger, Henry A., 1979. 'The Future of NATO', *Washington Quarterly*, vol. 2, no. 4, Autumn, pp. 3–17.

Kleinknecht, Alfred, 1981. 'Lange Welle oder Wechsellagen? Einige Methodenkritische Anmerkungen zur Diskussion', pp. 107–112 in Dietmar Petzina & Ger van Roon, eds. *Konjunktur, Krise, Gesellschaft*. Stuttgart: Klett-Cotta.

Köhler, Gernot, 1977. 'Structural-Dynamic Arms Control', *Journal of Peace Research*, vol. 14, no. 4, pp. 315–326.

Köhler, Gernot, 1980a. 'The Soviet/Russian Defense Burden, 1862–1965', *Bulletin of Peace Proposals*, vol. 11, no. 2, pp. 131–140.

Köhler, Gernot, 1980b. 'Determinants of the British Defense Burden 1689–1977', *Bulletin of Peace Proposals*, vol. 11, no. 1, pp. 79–85.

Koistinen, Paul A. C., 1980. *The Military-Industrial Complex. A Historical Perspective.* New York: Praeger.

Kolko, Joyce & Gabriel Kolko, 1972. *The Limits of Power: The World and United States Foreign Policy, 1945–1954.* New York: Harper & Row.

Kossiakoff, Alexander, 1980. 'Conceptions of New Defense Systems and the Role of Government R&D Centers', pp. 61–88 in Long & Reppy, 1980.

Krass, Allan, 1981. 'The Evolution of Military Technology and Deterrence Strategy', pp. 19–67 in *World Armaments and Disarmament: SIPRI Yearbook 1981*.

Krell, Gert, 1976. *Rüstungsdynamik und Rüstungskontrolle: Die gesellschaftlichen Auseinandersetzungen um SALT in den USA 1969–1975.* Frankfurt a.M.: Haag & Herchen.

Krell, Gert, ed., 1981. *Die Rüstung der USA. Gesellschaftliche Interessen und politische Entscheidungen.* Baden-Baden: Nomos.

Krippendorff, Ekkehart, 1985. *Staat und Krieg. Die historische Logik politischer Unvernunft.* Frankfurt a.M.: Suhrkamp.

Kubbig, Bernd, 1984. *Gleichgewicht oder Überlegenheit. Amerikanische Rüstungskontrollpolitik und das Scheitern von SALT II.* Frankfurt a.M.: Campus.

Kubbig, Bernd, 1988. *Amerikanische Rüstungskontrollpolitik. Die innergesellschaftlichen Kräfteverhältnisse in der ersten Amtszeit Reagans (1981–1985).* Frankfurt a.M.: Campus.

Kugler, Jacek & William Domke, 1986. 'Comparing the Strength of Nations', *Comparative Political Studies*, vol. 19, no. 1, pp. 39–69.

Kugler, Jacek & A.F.K. Organski, 1986. 'Hegemony and War'. Paper presented at the International Studies Association meeting, Anaheim, CA, 25–29 March.

Kuhn, Thomas S., 1970. *The Structure of Scientific Revolutions.* 2nd ed. Chicago, IL: University of Chicago Press. [First published in 1962.]

Kungliga Majestät, 1956. *Angående riktlinjer för utvecklingsarbetet på atomenergiområdet*, Proposition no. 176. Stockholm: Riksdagen.

Kupperman, Robert H. & Harvey A. Smith, 1972. 'Strategies of Mutual Deterrence', *Science*, vol. 176, no. 4030, pp. 18–23.

Kupperman, Robert H. & Harvey A. Smith, 1976. 'Deterrent Stability and Strategic Warfare', pp. 139–166 in Gillespie & Zinnes, 1976.

Kurth, James, 1971. 'A Widening Gyre: The Logic of American Weapons Procurement', *Public Policy*, vol. 19, no. 3, Summer, pp. 373–404.

Kurth, James, 1973. 'Why We Buy the Weapons We Do', *Foreign Policy*, no. 11, Summer, pp. 33–56.

Kuznets, Simon S., 1930. *Secular Movements in Production and Prices.* Boston, MA: Houghton Mifflin.

LaFeber, Walter, 1980. *The New Empire. An Interpretation of American Expansion 1860–1898.* Ithaca, NY: Cornell University Press.

Lakatos, Imre, 1970. 'Falsification and the Methodology of Scientific Research Programmes', pp. 91–196 in Imre Lakatos & Alan Musgrave, eds. *Criticism and the Growth of Knowledge.* Cambridge: Cambridge University Press.

Lambelet, John C., 1971. 'A Dynamic Model of the Arms Race in the Middle East, 1953–1965', *General Systems*, vol. 16, pp. 145–167.

Lambelet, John C., 1973. 'Towards a Dynamic Two-Theater Model of the East-West Arms Race', *Journal of Peace Science*, vol. 1, no. 1, Autumn, pp. 1–38.

Lambelet, John C., 1974. 'The Anglo-German Dreadnought Race, 1905–1914', *Papers of the Peace Science Society (International)*, vol. 22, pp. 1–45.

Lambelet, John C., 1975a. 'A Numerical Model of the Anglo–German Dreadnought Race', *Papers of the Peace Science Society (International)*, vol. 24, pp. 29–48.

Lambelet, John C., 1975b. 'Do Arms Races Lead to War? Some Preliminary Thoughts', *Journal of Peace Research*, vol. 12, no. 2, pp. 123–128.

Lambelet, John C., 1976. 'A Complementary Analysis of the Anglo–German Dreadnought Race, 1905-1916', *Papers of the Peace Science Society (International)*, vol. 26, pp. 49–66.
Lambelet, [John C.] Jean-Christian, 1985. 'Arms Races as Good Things?', pp. 161–174 in Luterbacher & Ward, 1985.
Lambelet, John C.; Urs Luterbacher & Pierre Allan, 1979. 'Dynamics of Arms Races: Mutual Stimulation vs. Self-Stimulation', *Journal of Peace Science*, vol. 4, no. 1, Fall, pp. 49–66.
Lambi, Ivo Nikolai, 1984. *The Navy and the German Power Politics, 1862–1914*. London & Boston, MA: Allen & Unwin.
Lapp, Ralph, 1970. *Arms Beyond Doubt. The Tyranny of Weapons Technology*. New York: Cowles.
Larson, Deborah W., 1988. 'Problems of Content Analysis in Foreign-Policy Research: Notes From the Study of the Origins of Cold War Belief Systems', *International Studies Quarterly*, vol. 32, no. 2, June, pp. 241–255.
Larsson, Christer, 1985. 'Historien om en svensk atombomb 1945–1972', *Ny Teknik*, no. 17, 25 April, pp. 54–83.
Lebow, Richard Ned, 1981. *Between Peace and War*. London & Baltimore, MD: Johns Hopkins University Press.
Leebaert, Derek, ed., 1979. *European Security: Prospects for the 1980s*. Lexington, MA: Heath.
Leebaert, Derek, ed., 1981. *Soviet Military Thinking*. London: Allen & Unwin.
Leidy, Michael P. & Robert W. Staiger, 1985. 'Economic Issues and Methodology in Arms Race Analysis', *Journal of Conflict Resolution*, vol. 29, no. 3, September, pp. 503–530.
Leine, Johs., 1968. 'Forsvarsmidlene og det private næringsliv', *Norsk Militært Tidsskrift*, vol. 138, no. 8, pp. 419–422.
Leitenberg, Milton, 1978. 'Base Closing in the United States: A Note on the Office of Economic Adjustment', pp. 135–139 in Wallensteen, 1978.
Leitenberg, Milton, 1979. 'The Counterpart of Defense Industry Conversion in the United States: The USSR Economy, Defense Industry, and Military Expenditure', *Journal of Peace Research*, vol. 16, no. 3, pp. 263–277.
Leitenberg, Milton & Nicole Ball, 1977. 'The Military Expenditures of Less Developed Nations as a Proportion of their State Budgets. A Research Note', *Bulletin of Peace Proposals*, vol. 8, no. 4, pp. 310–315.
Leng, Russell J. & J. David Singer, 1988. 'Militarized Interstate Crises: The BCOW Typology and Its Applications', *International Studies Quarterly*, vol. 32, no. 2, June, pp. 155–173.
Lens, Sidney, 1970. *The Military-Industrial Complex*. Philadelphia, PA: Pilgrim.
Levy, Jack S., 1985. 'Theories of General War', *World Politics*, vol. 37, no. 3, April, pp. 344–374.
Liebknecht, Karl, 1958: 'Militarismus und Antimilitarismus', pp. 247–456 in *Gesammelte Reden und Schriften*, vol. 1. Berlin: Institut für Marxismus-Leninismus beim ZK der SED. [First published in 1907.]
Lilienthal, David, 1964. *Journals*, vol. 2, *The Atomic Energy Years, 1945–50*. New York: Harper & Row.
Liossatos, Panagis, 1980a. 'Socio-Economic Dimension of the Arms Race', *Conflict Management and Peace Science*, vol. 5, no. 1, Fall, pp. 55–68.
Liossatos, Panagis, 1980b. 'Modeling the Nuclear Arms Race: A Search for Stability', *Journal of Peace Science*, vol. 4, no. 2, pp. 169–185.
Ljungdahl, Axel, 1972. *En flygofficers minnen*. Stockholm: Norstedt.
Lockheed Missiles and Space Company, Inc., n.d. *The Fleet Ballistic Missile System*. Sunnyvale, CA: Lockheed.
Lomas, Peter, 1988. 'Attitudes of the Nuclear Threshold Countries', pp. 311–318 in Goldblat & Cox, 1988.
Long, Franklin A. & Judith Reppy, eds., 1980. *The Genesis of New Weapons. Decision Making for Military R&D*. New York: Pergamon.
Lucier, Charles E., 1979. 'Changes in the Values of Arms Race Parameters', *Journal of Conflict Resolution*, vol. 23, no. 1, March, pp. 17–39.

Luterbacher, Urs, 1975. 'Arms Race Models: Where Do We Stand?', *European Journal of Political Research*, vol. 3, no. 2, June, pp. 199–217.

Luterbacher, Urs, 1976. 'Towards a Convergence of Behavioral and Strategic Conceptions: The Case of American and Soviet ICBM Build-Up', *Peace Research Society (International-Papers*, vol. 26, pp. 1–21.

Luterbacher, Urs & Michael Ward, 1985. *Dynamic Models of International Conflict*. Boulder, CO: Lynne Rienner.

Lutz, Dieter S., ed., 1979. *Die Rüstung der Sowjetunion. Rüstungsdynamik und bürokratische Strukturen*. Baden-Baden: Nomos.

Lutz, Dieter S., 1986. *Towards a Methodology of Military Force Comparison*. Baden-Baden: Nomos.

Luxemburg, Rosa, 1923. *Die Akkumulation des Kapitals*. Berlin: Vereinigung Internationaler Verlags-Anstalten. [Originally published in 1913.]

McDonnell, John, 1975. 'The Soviet Defense Industry as a Pressure Group', pp. 87–122 in MccGwire et al., 1975.

McGuire, Martin C., 1977. 'A Quantitative Study of the Strategic Arms Race in the Missile Age', *Review of Economics and Statistics*, vol. 59, no. 3, August, pp. 328–339.

MccGwire, Michael, ed., 1973. *Soviet Naval Developments: Capability and Context*. New York: Praeger.

MccGwire, Michael, 1980. 'The Rationale for the Development of Soviet Sea Power', *United States Naval Institute Proceedings*, vol. 106, no. 5, May, pp. 155–183.

MccGwire, Michael, 1981. 'Soviet Naval Doctrine and Strategy', pp. 125–181 in Leebaert, 1981. [Revised ed. of 'Naval Power and Global Strategy', *International Security*, vol. 3, no. 4, Spring 1979, pp. 134–189. Also in Steven E. Miller & Stephen Van Evera, eds., 1988. *Naval Strategy and National Security. An International Security Reader*, pp. 115–170. Princeton, NJ: Princeton University Press.]

MccGwire, Michael; Ken Booth & John McDonnell, eds., 1975. *Soviet Naval Policy: Objectives and Constraints*. New York: Praeger.

MacKenzie, Donald, 1986. 'Missile Accuracy - An Arms Control Opportunity', *Bulletin of the Atomic Scientists*, vol. 42, no.6, June/July, pp. 11–16.

MacKenzie, Donald, 1987. 'Missile Acccuracy: A Case Study in the Social Processes of Technological Change', pp. 195–222 in Bijker et al., 1987.

MacKenzie, Donald, 1988a. 'The Soviet Union and Strategic Missile Guidance', *International Security*, vol. 13, no. 2, Fall, pp. 5–54.

MacKenzie, Donald, 1988b. 'Stellar-Inertial Guidance: A Study in the Sociology of Military Technology', pp. 187–241 in Everett Mendelsohn, Merrit Roe Smith & Peter Weingart, eds. *Science, Technology and the Military: Sociology of the Sciences Yearbook*, vol. 14. Dordrecht: Reidel.

MacKenzie, Donald & Judy Wajcman, eds., 1985. *The Social Shaping of Technology*. Milton Keynes: Open University Press.

McNamara, Robert, 1967. 'Address by Secretary of Defense McNamara to United Press International Editors and Publishers, September 18, 1967', pp. 382–394 in US Arms Control and Disarmament Agency, ed. *Documents on Disarmament 1967*. Washington, DC: US Government Printing Office.

McNamara, Robert & Hans A. Bethe, 1986. 'Reducing the Risk of Nuclear War', *Bulletin of Peace Proposals*, vol. 17, no. 2, June, pp. 121–130.

McNeill, William H., 1982. *The Pursuit of Power: Technology, Armed Force and Society since AD 1000*. Oxford: Blackwell/Chicago, IL: University of Chicago Press.

Maddison, Angus, 1982. *Phases of Capitalist Development*. Oxford: Oxford University Press 1982.

Majeski, Stephen J., 1983a. 'Dynamic Properties of the US Military Expenditure Decision-Making Process', *Conflict Management and Peace Science*, vol. 7, no. 1, Fall, pp. 65–86.

Majeski, Stephen J., 1983b. 'Mathematical Models of the United States Military Expenditure Decision-Making Process', *American Journal of Political Science*, vol. 27, no. 3, August, pp. 485–514.

Majeski, Stephen J., 1985. 'Expectations and Arms Races', *American Journal of Political Science*, vol. 29, no. 2, May, pp. 217–245.
Majeski, Stephen J. & David L. Jones, 1981. 'Arms Race Modeling: Causality Analysis and Model Specification', *Journal of Conflict Resolution*, vol. 25, no. 2, June, pp. 259–288.
Maktutredningen, 1982. *Maktutredningen. Sluttrapport. NOU 1982: 3.* Oslo: Norwegian University Press.
Mandelbaum, Michael, 1981. *The Nuclear Revolution. International Politics Before and After Hiroshima.* Cambridge: Cambridge University Press.
Mandelbaum, Michael, 1988. *The Fate of Nations. The Search for Security in the Nineteenth and Twentieth Centuries.* Cambridge: Cambridge University Press.
Mann, Michael, 1986. *The Sources of Social Power*, vol. 1, *A History of Power from the Beginning to AD 1760.* Cambridge: Cambridge University Press.
Maoz, Zeev, 1983. 'Resolve, Capabilities, and the Outcomes of Interstate Disputes, 1816–1976', *Journal of Conflict Resolution*, vol. 27, no. 2, June, pp. 195–230.
Marchetti, Cesar, 1980. 'Society as a Learning System: Discovery, Invention and Innovation Cycles Revisited', *Technological Forecasting and Social Change*, vol. 18, no. 2, pp. 267–282.
Mayer, Arno, 1982. *The Persistence of the Old Regime.* New York: Pantheon.
Mayer, Thomas, 1985. 'Transform Methods and Dynamic Models', pp. 175–219 in Luterbacher & Ward, 1985.
Mayer, Thomas F., 1986. 'Arms Races and War Initiation: Some Alternatives to the Intriligator-Brito Model', *Journal of Conflict Resolution*, vol. 30, no. 1, March, pp. 3–28.
Mechtersheimer, Alfred, 1977. *Rüstung und Politik in der Bundesrepublik. MRCA Tornado, Geschichte und Funktion des grössten westeuropäischen Rüstungsprogramms.* Bad Honnef: Osang.
Medick, Monika, 1977. *Waffenexporte und auswärtige Politik. Gesellschaftliche Interessen und politische Entscheidungen.* Meisenheim am Glan: Hain.
Melman, Seymour, 1970. *Pentagon Capitalism.* New York: McGraw-Hill.
Menzel, Ulrich, 1985. *Lange Wellen und Hegemonie. Eine Literaturbericht.* Bremen: Projekt Hegemoniekrise und Kriegswahrscheinlichkeit.
Meyer, Stephen M., 1984. 'Soviet National Security Decisionmaking: What Do We Know and What Do We Understand?', pp. 255–29,7 in Jiri Valenta & William C. Potter, eds. *Soviet Decisionmaking for National Security.* London: Allen & Unwin. [Earlier version with the same title published as *ACIS Working Paper* no. 33. Los Angeles, CA: Center for International and Strategic Affairs, University of California.]
Meyers, Reinhard, 1981. 'Die vierte Teilstreitkraft. Industrie, Handel und Finanz in der britischen Aufrüstung der dreissiger Jahre', *Neue Politische Literatur*, vol. 26, no. 2, pp. 191–212.
Michels, Robert, 1958. *Political Parties. A Sociological Study of the Oligarchical Tendencies of Modern Democracy.* Glencoe, IL: Free Press. [First published in German in 1911.]
Mills, C. Wright, 1956. *The Power Elite.* New York: Oxford University Press.
Mink, Louis O., 1966. 'The Autonomy of Historical Understanding', pp. 160–192 in William H. Dray, ed. *Philosophical Analysis and History.* New York & London: Harper & Row.
Misgeld, Klaus, 1984. *Sozialdemokratie und Aussenpolitik in Schweden - Sozialistische Internationale, Europapolitik und die Deutschlandfrage 1945–1955.* Frankfurt a.M.: Campus.
Modelski, George, 1983. 'Long Cycles and World Leadership', pp. 115–140 in William R. Thompson, ed. *Contending Approaches to World System Analysis.* Beverly Hills, CA: Sage.
Modelski, George, 1987. *Long Cycles in World Politics.* London: Macmillan.
Modelski, George & Patrick M. Morgan, 1985. 'Understanding Global War', *Journal of Conflict Resolution*, vol. 29, no. 3, September, pp. 391–418.
Modelski, George & William R. Thompson, 1988. *Seapower in Global Politics, 1494–1993.* London: Macmillan.
Moll, Kendall D. & Gregory M. Luebbert, 1980. 'Arms Race and Military Expenditure Models: A Review', *Journal of Conflict Resolution*, vol. 24, no. 1, March, pp. 153–185.

Morgan, Patrick M., 1983. *Deterrence: A Conceptual Analysis*. London: Sage. [First published in 1977.]
Morgenthau, Hans, 1946. *Scientific Man vs. Power Politics*. Chicago, IL: University of Chicago Press.
Morris, Fredric A., ed., 1975. 'Acquiring Weapons', Part II, pp. 111–215 in *Commission on the Organization of the Government for the Conduct of Foreign Policy*. Washington, DC: US Government Printing Office, June, Vol. IV, Appendix K, 'Adequacy of Current Organization: Defense and Arms Control'.
Moss, Norman, 1987. *Klaus Fuchs*. London: Grafton.
Moto-oka, T., ed., 1982. *Fifth Generation Computer Systems*. Amsterdam: North Holland.
Mulhern, John J., 1987. 'Market Research Can Boost Competition for DoD Dollars', *Defense Management Journal*, vol. 21, no. 2/3, pp. 13–17.
Müller, Erwin, 1985. *Rüstungspolitik und Rüstungsdynamik: Fall USA. Zur Analyse der Rüstungsmotive einer Weltmacht und zur Theorie moderner Rüstungsdynamik*. Baden-Baden: Nomos.
Müller, Erwin, 1987. 'Rüstungsdynamik', pp. 262–267 in Dieter S. Lutz, ed. *Lexikon Rüstung, Frieden, Sicherheit*. Munich: Beck.
Myrdal, Alva, 1976. *The Game of Disarmament. How the United States and Russia Run the Arms Race*. New York: Pantheon.
Naroll, Roul, 1969. 'Deterrence in History', pp. 150–164 in Dean G. Pruitt & Richard C. Snyder, eds. *Theory & Research on the Causes of War*. Englewood Cliffs, NJ: Prentice-Hall.
Nelson, Richard R. & Sidney G. Winter, 1977. 'In Search for a Useful Theory of Innovation', *Research Policy*, vol. 6, no. 1, January, pp. 36–77.
Nelson, Richard R. & Sidney G. Winter, 1982. *An Evolutionary Theory of Economic Change*. Cambridge, MA & London: Harvard University Press.
Neumann, Stephanie, 1984. 'International Stratification and the Third World Military Industries', *International Organization*, vol. 38, no. 1, Winter, pp. 167–198.
Newcombe, Alan G., 1969. 'Toward the Development of an Inter-Nation Tensiometer', *Peace Science Society (International Papers)*, vol. 13, pp. 11–27.
Newcombe, Alan & James Wert, 1973. 'The Use of an Inter-Nation Tensiometer for the Prediction of War', *Peace Research Society (International) Papers*, vol. 21, pp. 73–83.
Nieburg, Harold L., 1966. *In the Name of Science*. Chicago, IL: Quadrangle.
Nikutta, Randolph, ed., 1986. 'Rüstungswirtschaft in der Sowjetunion', *Militärpolitik Dokumentation*, nos. 47–49, Frankfurt a.M.: Haag & Herchen.
Nincic, Miroslav, 1982. *The Arms Race. The Political Economy of US Military Spending*. New York: Praeger.
Norman, Colin, 1981. *The God That Limps: Science and Technology in the Eighties*. New York & London: Norton.
North, David M., 1987. 'Seven Nations Curb Nuclear Weapon Launch System Exports', *Aviation Week and Space Technology*, vol. 126, no. 16, 20 April, pp. 28–29.
Nove, Alec, 1978. *An Economic History of Russia*. Harmondsworth: Penguin.
Oakeshott, Michael, 1966. 'Historical Continuity and Causal Analysis', pp. 193–212 in William Dray, ed. *Philosophical Analysis and History*. New York: Harper & Row.
Oakeshott, Michael, 1983. *On History and Other Essays*. Oxford: Blackwell.
OECD, 1969. *The Technological Gap. Analytical Report*. Paris: Organization of Economic Cooperation and Development.
Olson, Mancur, Jr., 1965. *The Logic of Collective Action*. Cambridge, MA: Harvard University Press.
Olson, Mancur, Jr. & R. Zeckhauser, 1966. 'An Economic Theory of Alliances', *Review of Economics and Statistics*, vol. 48, no. 3, August, pp. 266–279.
Olsson, Ulf, 1977. *The Creation of a Modern Arms Industry. Sweden 1939–1974*. Gothenburg: Department of Economic History, University of Gothenburg.
Organski, A.F.K., 1964. *World Politics*. New York: Knopf.
Organski, A.F.K. & Jacek Kugler, 1980. *The War Ledger*. Chicago, IL: University of Chicago Press.

Ostrom, Charles W., Jr., 1978. 'A Reactive Linkage Model of the US Defense Expenditure Policymaking Process', *American Political Science Review*, vol. 72, no. 3, September, pp. 941–957.
Paine, Christopher & Gordon Adams, 1980. 'The R&D Slush Fund', *The Nation*, vol. 230, no. 3, 26 January, pp. 72–75.
Panofsky, Wolfgang K.H., 1981. 'Science, Technology and the Arms Build-Up'. Paper presented at Colloque Science and Disarmament, Paris: Institute Français des Relations Internationales, 15–17 January.
Panofsky, K.H., 1987. 'A Physicist Looks at SDI', *Arms Control Today*, vol. 17, no. 5, June, pp. 26–29. [Interview.]
Pareto, Vilfredo, 1968. *The Rise and Fall of the Elites. An Application of Theoretical Sociology*. Totowa: Bedminster Press. [First published in Italian in 1901.]
Parrot, Bruce, 1985. *Politics and Technology in the Soviet Union*. Cambridge, MA: MIT Press.
Patel, Kumar N. & Nicolaas Bloembergen, 1987. 'Strategic Defense and Directed Energy Weapons', *Scientific American*, vol. 257, no. 3, September, pp. 31–37.
Pearson, Stanley, 1987. 'Financing Global Wars. The Political Economy of Global War Coalition Leadership'. Paper prepared for the Annual Convention of the International Studies Association, Washington, DC, 14–18 April.
Perlo, Victor, 1973. *The Unstable Economy: Booms and Recessions in the US Since 1945*. New York: International Publishers.
Perry, Robert, 1980. 'American Styles of Military R&D', pp. 89–112 in Long & Reppy, 1980.
Pickering, Andrew, 1981. 'The Hunting of the Quark', *Isis*, vol. 72, no. 262, June, pp. 216–236.
Pintner, Walter, 1984. 'The Burden of Defense in Imperial Russia 1725–1914', *The Russian Review*, vol. 43, no. 3, pp. 231–259.
Pitman, George R., Jr., 1969. *Arms Races and Stable Deterrence*. Security Studies Paper no. 18. Los Angeles, CA: Security Studies Project, University of California, Los Angeles.
Polanyi, Karl, 1944. *The Great Transformation*. Boston, MA: Beacon.
Pollard, Robert, 1985. *Economic Security and the Origins of the Cold War, 1945–1950*. New York: Columbia University Press.
Ponomarjev, Alexandr N., 1984. *Aviatsija Nastoiashtshevo i Buduishtshevo*. Moscow: Aviamotornaya.
Popper, Karl R., 1966. *The Open Society and its Enemies, Vol. 2, Hegel and Marx*, 5th ed. London and Henley: Routledge & Kegan Paul. [First published in 1945.]
Porter, Bernard, 1983. *Britain, Europe and the World 1850–1982: Delusions of Grandeur*. London: Allen & Unwin.
Posen, Barry, 1984. *The Sources of Military Doctrine: France, Britain, and Germany between the World Wars*. Ithaca, NY: Cornell University Press.
Potter, William C., 1987. 'Creating a Database on International Nuclear Commerce', *CISA Working Paper*, no. 59. Los Angeles, CA: Center for International and Strategic Affairs, University of California, LA.
Prawitz, Jan, 1967. 'Ny atomdoktrin', pp. 196–219 in Lennart Grape & Bengt Ysander, eds. *Säkerhetspolitik och försvarsplanering*. Stockholm: Folk och Försvar.
Pruitt, Dean G. & Richard C. Snyder, eds., 1969. *Theory & Research on the Causes of War*. Englewood Cliffs, NJ: Prentice-Hall.
Pursell, Carroll W., Jr., 1972. *Military-Industrial Complex*. New York: Harper & Row.
Quester, George H., 1970. 'Sweden and the Nuclear Non-Proliferation Treaty', *Cooperation and Conflict*, vol. 5, no. 1, pp. 55–64.
Quine, Willard van Orman, 1964. *From a Logical Point of View*. 2nd ed. Cambridge, MA: Harvard University Press. [First published in 1953.]
Quine, Willard van Orman, 1975a. 'The Nature of Natural Knowledge', pp. 67–81 in Guttenplan, 1975.
Quine, Willard van Orman, 1975b. 'Mind and Verbal Dispositions', pp. 83–96 in Guttenplan, 1975.

Radzicki, Michael, 1987. 'Institutional Dynamics: An Extension of the Institutionalist Approach to Socioeconomic Analysis'. Notre Dame, IN: Institute for International Peace Studies, University of Notre Dame. [Unpublished paper.]

Rajewsky, Christiane & Dieter Riesenberger, 1987. *Wider den Krieg. Grosse Pazifisten von Kant bis Böll.* Munich: Beck.

Rapoport, Anatol, 1957. 'Lewis F. Richardson's Mathematical Theory of War', *Journal of Conflict Resolution*, vol. 1, no. 3, September, pp. 249–304.

Rapoport, Anatol, 1960. *Fights, Games, and Debates.* Ann Arbor: University of Michigan Press.

Rapoport, Anatol, 1966. 'Models of Conflict: Cataclysmic and Strategic', pp. 259–287 in Anthony V.S. de Reuck et al., eds. *Conflict in Society.* London: Churchill.

Rapoport, Anatol, 1967. 'Games Which Simulate Deterrence and Disarmament', *Peace Research Reviews*, vol 1, no 1 (whole issue).

Rapoport, Anatol, 1987. 'Conflict Escalation and Conflict Dynamics', pp. 163–178 in Väyrynen et al., 1987.

Rasler, Karen & William R. Thompson, 1988. 'Defense Burdens, Capital Formation and Economic Growth', *Journal of Conflict Resolution*, vol. 32, no. 1, March, pp. 61–86.

Rathjens, George, 1969. 'The Dynamics of the Arms Race', *Scientific American*, vol. 220, no. 4, April, pp. 15–25; also pp. 177–187 in York, 1974.

Rattinger, [Hans] Johannes, 1975a. *Rüstungsdynamik im internationalen System. Mathematische Reaktionsmodelle für Rüstungswettläufe.* Munich: Oldenbourg.

Rattinger, Hans, 1975b. 'Armaments, Detente, and Bureaucracy: The Case of the Arms Race in Europe', *Journal of Conflict Resolution*, vol. 19, no. 4, December, pp. 571–595.

Rattinger, Hans, 1976a. 'From War to War to War: Arms Races in the Middle East', *International Studies Quarterly*, vol. 20, no. 4, December, pp. 501–531.

Rattinger, Hans, 1976b. 'Econometrics and Arms Races: A Critical Review and Some Extensions', *European Journal of Political Research*, vol. 4, no. 4, December, pp. 421–439.

Reinhardt, George C. & William R. Kintner, 1953. *Atomic Weapons in Land Combat.* Harrisburg, PA: Military Services Publishing Company.

Reppy, Judith, 1976. 'The IR&D Program of the Department of Defense', *Cornell University Peace Studies Program Occasional Papers*, no. 6., March.

Reppy, Judith, 1977. 'Defense Department Payments for "Company-Financed" R&D', *Research Policy*, vol. 6, no. 4, October, pp. 396–410.

Reppy, Judith, 1985. 'Military R&D and the Civilian Economy', *Bulletin of the Atomic Scientists*, vol. 41, no. 9, October, pp. 10–14.

Reppy, Judith, 1987. 'Military Research and Development and International Trade Performance'. Paper prepared for the Annual Meeting of the International Studies Association, Washington, DC, 14–18 April.

Rice, Condoleezza, 1987. 'Defence and Security', pp. 192–209 in Martin McCauley, ed. *The Soviet Union under Gorbachev.* London: Macmillan.

Richardson, Lewis Fry, 1939. 'Generalized Foreign Politics', *British Journal of Psychology*, Monographs Supplement, no. 23, pp. vi–91.

Richardson, Lewis Fry, 1951. 'Could an Arms Race End without Fighting?', *Nature*, vol. 168, September 29, p. 567.

Richardson, Lewis Fry, 1960a. *Arms and Insecurity: A Mathematical Study of the Causes and Origins of War.* Pittsburgh, PA: Boxwood/Chicago, IL: Quadrangle.

Richardson, Lewis Fry, 1960b. *Statistics of Deadly Quarrels.* Pittsburgh, PA: Boxwood/Chicago, IL: Quadrangle.

Richmond, B., 1985. *A User's Guide to STELLA.* Lyme, NH: High Performance Systems.

Riesman, David; Nathan Glazer & Reuel Denny, 1950. *The Lonely Crowd.* New Haven, CT: Yale University Press.

Risse-Kappen, Thomas, 1986. 'Applying Arms Race Theory to NATO's Nuclear Weapons Deployments. A Reply to Matthew Evangelista', *Bulletin of Peace Proposals*, vol. 17, no. 2, June, pp. 207–213.

Roberts, Alan, 1985. 'Preparing to Fight a Nuclear War', pp. 279–294 in MacKenzie & Wajcman, 1985.

Robinson, Edward van Dyke, 1900. 'War and Economics in History and Theory', *Political Science Quarterly*, vol. 15, no. 4, pp. 581–628.
Rokkan, Stein, 1970. 'Numerical Democracy and Corporate Pluralism', pp. 70–115 in Robert A. Dahl, ed. *Political Oppositions in Western Democracies*. New Haven, CT & London: Yale University Press. [First published in 1966.]
Rosecrance, Richard, 1982. 'Reply to Waltz', *International Organization*, vol. 36, no. 3, Summer, pp. 682–685.
Rosen, Steven, ed., 1973. *Testing the Theory of the Military Industrial Complex*. Lexington, MA: Heath.
Rosenberg, David A., 1979. 'American Atomic Strategy and the Hydrogen Bomb Decision', *Journal of American History*, vol. 66, no. 1, June, pp. 62–87.
Rosh, Robert M., 1987. 'Ethnic Cleavage as a Component of Global Military Expenditures', *Journal of Peace Research*, vol. 24, no. 1, March, pp. 21–30.
Rostow, Walt W., 1978. *The World Economy. History and Prospect*. Austin: Texas University Press.
Royal United Services Institution, 1970. *The Soviet Union in Europe and the Near East: Her Capabilities and Intentions*. London: RUSI.
Rummel, Rudolph J., 1968. 'The Relationships between National Attributes and Foreign Conflict Behavior', pp. 187–214 in J. David Singer, ed. *Quantitative International Politics*. New York: Free Press.
Rummel, Rudolph J., 1972. *Dimensions of Nations*. London: Sage.
Rummel, Rudolph J., 1979. *Understanding Conflict and War*, vol. 4, *War, Power, Peace*. Beverly Hills, CA: Sage.
Russett, Bruce M., 1970. *What Price Vigilance? The Burdens of National Defense*. New Haven, CT: Yale University Press.
Rørholt, Bjørn, 1966. 'Forsvarsbevilgningene og den norske industri', *Norsk Militært Tidsskrift*, vol. 136, no. 1, pp. 17–22.
Saaty, Thomas L., 1968. *Mathematical Models of Arms Control and Disarmament*. New York: Wiley.
Sandberg, Irwin, 1974. 'On the Mathematical Theory of Interactions in Social Groups', *IEEE Transactions*, vol. SMC-4, pp. 432–445.
Sapolsky, Harvey M., 1972. *The Polaris System Development: Bureaucratic and Programmatic Success in Government*. Cambridge, MA: Harvard University Press.
Sarkesian, Sam C., ed., 1972. *The Military-Industrial Complex. A Reassessment*. Beverly Hills, CA: Sage.
Scheiderbauer, Sven, 1981. 'Uppbyggnaden av flygvapnets första radarsystem 1949–53', *Militärhistorisk Tidskrift*, pp. 85–120.
Schelling, Thomas C., 1966. *Arms and Influence*. New Haven, CT: Yale University Press.
Schiller, Herbert I. & Joseph D. Phillips, eds., 1972. *Super-State: Readings in the Military-Industrial Complex*. Urbana: University of Illinois Press.
Schilling, Warner A., 1961. 'The H-Bomb Decision: How to Decide Without Actually Choosing', *Political Science Quarterly*, vol. 76, no. 1, March, pp. 24–46.
Schlotter, Peter, 1975. *Rüstungspolitik in der Bundesrepublik. Die Beispiele Starfighter und Phantom*. Frankfurt a.M.: Campus.
Schmidt, Manfred G., 1975. *Staatsapparat und Rüstungspolitik in der Bundesrepublik Deutschland (1966–1973). Schranken und Folgeprobleme des Staatsinterventionismus im Militär- und Rüstungssektor*. Giessen & Lollar: Achenbach.
Schrodt, Philip, 1987. *Artificial Intelligence and International Relations: A Guide to the Perplexed*. Paper prepared for the Convention of the Midwest International Studies Association, Lawrence, Kansas, 6–7 November.
Schroeer, Dietrich, 1984. *Science, Technology and the Nuclear Arms Race*. New York: Wiley.
Schroeer, Dietrich, 1985. 'Quantifying Technological Imperatives in the Arms Race', pp. 60–71 in David Carlton & Carlo Schaerf, eds. *Reassessing Arms Control*. London: Macmillan.
Schumpeter, Joseph A., 1919. 'Zur Soziologie der Imperialismen', in *Archiv für Sozialwissenschaft und Sozialpolitik*, vol. 46, no. 1, pp. 1–39 & no. 2, pp. 275–310. Tübingen: J.C.B.

Mohr. [English translation, 1951. *Imperialism and Social Classes.* New York: Augustus Kelley.]
Schumpeter, Joseph A., 1939. *Business Cycles. A Theoretical, Historical and Statistical Analysis of the Capitalist Processes*, vol. 1. New York: McGraw-Hill.
Schumpeter, Joseph A., 1978. *The Theory of Economic Development.*₁ New York: Oxford University Press. [First published in 1911.]
Scott, Harriet F. & William F. Scott, 1984. *The Armed Forces of the USSR.* Boulder, CO: Westview.
Sejersted, Francis, 1984. *Høyres historie*, vol. 3. *Opposisjon og posisjon.* Oslo: Cappelen.
Semmel, Bernard, 1981. *Marxism and the Science of War.* Oxford: Oxford University Press.
Semmel, Bernard, 1986. *Liberalism and Naval Strategy. Ideology, Interest and Sea Power during the Pax Britannica.* Boston, MA & London: Allen & Unwin.
Sen, Gautam, 1984. *The Military Origins of Industrialisation and International Trade Rivalry.* London: Pinter.
Senghaas, Dieter, 1969. *Abschreckung und Frieden. Studien zur Kritik organisierter Friedlosigkeit.* Frankfurt a.M.: Europäischer Verlagsanstalt.
Senghaas, Dieter, ed., 1971. *Kritische Friedensforschung.* Frankfurt a.M.: Suhrkamp.
Senghaas, Dieter, 1972a. *Rüstung und Militarismus.* Frankfurt a.M.: Suhrkamp.
Senghaas, Dieter, 1972b. *Aufrüstung durch Rüstungskontrolle: Über den symbolischen Gebrauch der Politik.* Stuttgart: Kohlhammer.
Senghaas, Dieter, 1972c. 'Arms Race Dynamics as Restrictive Conditions to Detente', pp. 187–196 in Ulrich Albrecht, Johan Galtung, Pertti Joenniemi, Dieter Senghaas & Sergiu Verona, *Is Europe to Demilitarize?*, special issue of *Instant Research on Peace and Violence*, no. 4.
Senghaas, Dieter, 1973. 'Arms Race by Arms Control', *Bulletin of Peace Proposals*, vol. 4, no. 4, pp. 359–374.
Senghaas, Dieter, 1974a. *Gewalt – Konflikt – Frieden. Essays zur Friedensforschung.* Hamburg: Hoffmann & Campe.
Senghaas, Dieter, 1974b. 'Towards an Analysis of Threat Policy in International Relations', pp. 59–103 in Klaus von Beyme, ed. *German Political Studies*, vol. 1. London & Beverly Hills, CA: Sage.
Senghaas, Dieter, 1979. 'Arms Race Dynamics and Arms Control in Europe', *Bulletin of Peace Proposals*, vol. 10, no. 1, February, pp. 8–19. [Revised version as ch. 2 of this book.]
Senghaas, Dieter, 1986. *Die Zukunft Europas.* Frankfurt a.M.: Suhrkamp.
Senghaas, Dieter, 1988a. 'Systemantagonismus, Rüstungskonkurrenz und Rüstungsdynamik. Konzeptuelle Überlegungen zu einem alten Thema der Friedensforschung', pp. 209–216 in Bernhard Moltmann, ed. *Perspektiven der Friedensforschung.* Baden-Baden: Nomos.
Senghaas, Dieter, 1988b. *Konfliktformationen im internationalen System.* Frankfurt a.M.: Suhrkamp.
Shapin, Steven, 1982. 'History of Science and its Sociological Reconstructions', *History of Science*, vol. 20, part 3, no. 49, September, pp. 157–211.
Shapley, Deborah, 1978. 'Technology Creep and the Arms Race: ICBM Problem a Sleeper', *Science*, 22 September, pp. 1102–1105.
Sharp, Jane M., 1979. 'Is European Security Negotiable?', pp. 261–296 in Leebaert, 1979.
Sharp, Jane M., 1982. 'Four Approaches to an INF Agreement', *Arms Control Today*, vol. 12, no. 3, March, pp. 1–3; 6–8.
Silverman, Lawrence, 1985. 'Long Waves of Ideology'. Paper prepared for the European Consortium for Political Research Joint Sessions, Barcelona, 26–30 March.
Simaan, Marvin & Jose B. Cruz, Jr., 1975. 'Formulation of Richardson's Model of Arms Race from a Differential Game Viewpoint', *Review of Economic Studies*, vol. 42, no. 1, pp. 67–77.
Simaan, Marvin & Jose B. Cruz, Jr., 1976. 'Equilibrium Concepts for Arms Race Problems', pp. 342–356 in Gillespie & Zinnes, 1976.
Simmel, Georg, 1955. *Conflict.* New York: Free Press. [First published in German 1908.]

Singer, J. David, 1979. 'The Management of Serious International Disputes'. Ann Arbor, MI: University of Michigan, Department of Political Science. [Unpublished paper.]

Singer, J. David, 1981. 'Accounting for International War: The State of the Discipline', *Journal of Peace Research*, vol. 18, no. 1, pp. 1–18.

SIPRI, 1972. *The Near-Nuclear Countries and the NTP*. Cambridge, MA: MIT Press.

SIPRI, 1974. *Nuclear Proliferation Problems*. Cambridge, MA: MIT Press.

SIPRI Yearbook, see *World Armaments and Disarmament*.

Sirjacques, Françoise, 1977. *Determinanten der französischen Rüstungspolitik*. Frankfurt a.M.: Campus.

Sirjacques, Françoise, 1979. *Frankreich und die NATO*. Frankfurt a.M.: Campus.

Sivard, Ruth L., annual. *World Military and Social Expenditures*. Washington, DC: World Priorities.

Skjelsbæk, Kjell, 1979. 'Militarism, its Dimension and Corollaries: An Attempt at Conceptual Clarification', *Journal of Peace Research*, vol. 16, no. 3, pp. 213–229.

Skocpol, Theda, 1979. *States and Social Revolutions. A Comparative Analysis of France, Russia and China*. Cambridge: Cambridge University Press.

Skolnikoff, Eugene, 1987. 'The Technological Factor Shaping East–West Relations'. Paper presented at the Sixth Annual Conference of the Institute for East–West Security Studies, Espoo (Finland), 11–13 June.

Small, Melvin & J. David Singer, 1982. *Resort to Arms. International and Civil Wars. 1816–1980*. Beverly Hills, CA: Sage.

Smith, Gaddis, 1972. *Dean Acheson*, vol. 14 in Robert H. Ferrell, ed. *The American Secretaries of State and their Diplomacy*. New York: Cooper Square.

Smith, Merritt Roe, 1985. *Military Enterprise and Technological Change: Perspectives on the American Experience*. Cambridge, MA: MIT Press.

Smith, Theresa Clair, 1980. 'Arms Race Instability and War', *Journal of Conflict Resolution*, vol. 24, no. 2, June, pp. 253–284.

Smith, Theresa Clair, 1982. *Trojan Peace: Some Deterrence Propositions Tested. Monograph Series in World Affairs*, vol. 19, book 2. Denver, CO: University of Denver.

Smoker, Paul, 1987. 'Simulation of International Conflict', pp. 149–176 in P.G. Bennett, ed. *Analysing Conflict and its Resolution*. Oxford: Clarendon.

Smoker, Paul & Morris Bradley, eds, 1988. *Accidental Nuclear War*, special issue of *Current Research on Peace and Violence*, vol. 11, no. 1–2.

Socialdemokratiska partistyrelsen, 1960. *Neutralitet, försvar, atomvapen*. Stockholm: Tiden.

Solomou, Solomos, 1987. 'Kondratieff Long Waves in Economic Growth 1850–1913', *Review*, vol. 10, no. 3, pp. 507–534.

Solomou, Solomos, 1988. *Phases of Economic Growth, 1850–1973. Kondratieff Waves and Kuznets Swings*. Cambridge: Cambridge University Press.

Sorel, Georges, 1925. *Reflexions sur la violence*, 6th ed. Paris: Riviere. [First published in 1908.]

Spector, Leonard S., 1984. *Nuclear Proliferation Today*. New York: Vintage.

Spencer, Herbert, 1876–1896. *Principles of Sociology*. Published in *A System of Synthetic Philosophy*, vols. 6–8. London: Williams & Norgate/New York: Appleton. [First published in 1897.]

Spitzer, Hartwig, 1987. 'Lässt sich die Rüstungsdynamik Steuern?', *Sicherheit und Frieden*, vol. 5, no. 4, December, pp. 247–253.

Stein, Harold, 1963. *American Civilian–Military Decisions. A Book of Case Studies*. Birmingham: University of Alabama Press.

Stein, Jonathan B., 1984. *From H-Bomb to Star Wars: The Politics of Strategic Decision Making*. Lexington, MA: Heath.

Stein, Jonathan B., 1985. 'Political Pull, Technological Push', *Bulletin of the Atomic Scientists*, vol. 41, no. 6, June/July, pp. 40–41.

Stein, Josephine Anne & Frank von Hippel, 1986. 'Laboratories Versus a Nuclear Ban', *The New York Times*, 28 March.

Steinberg, Gerald M., 1983. 'Two Missiles in Every Garage', *Bulletin of the Atomic Scientists*, vol. 39, no. 9, October, pp. 43–48.

Steinberg, Gerald M.; Anselm Yaron; Jack Ruina & Mark Balaschak, 1981. *Assessing the Comparability of Dual-Use Technologies for Ballistic Missile Development*. Cambridge, MA: MIT Center for International Studies. [Report for Arms Control and Disarmament Agency.]
Stokke, Ivar, 1968. 'Norsk industri og forsvarsanskaffelser', *Norsk Militært Tidsskrift*, vol. 138, no. 1, pp. 37–40.
Strauss, Robert P., 1972. 'An Adaptive Expectations Model of the East-West Arms Race', *Peace Research Society (International) Papers*, vol. 19, pp. 29–34.
Strauss, Robert P., 1978. 'Interdependent National Budgets: A Model of US-USSR Defense Expenditures', pp. 89–97 in W. Ladd Hollist, ed. *Exploring Competitive Arms Processes*. New York: Dekker.
Strum, S.C. & Bruno Latour, 1984. 'Redefining the Social Link: From Baboons to Humans'. Paper presented at International Primatological Society meeting, Nairobi, July.
Stuckey, John & J. David Singer, 1973. 'The Powerful and the War-Prone: Ranking the Nations by Relative Capability and War Experience, 1820–1964'. Paper presented at the conference on Poder Social: America Latina en El Mundo, Mexico City.
Svensk kärnvapenforskning 1945–1972, 1987. Stockholm: Försvarsdepartementet.
Sylvan, Donald A., 1976. 'Consequences of Sharp Military Assistance Increases for International Conflict and Cooperation', *Journal of Conflict Resolution*, vol. 20, no. 4, December, pp. 609–636.
Taagepera, Rein, 1979/80. 'Stockpile-Budget and Ratio Interaction Models for Arms Races', *Peace Science Society (International) Papers*, vol. 29, pp. 67–78.
Taagepera, Rein; G.M. Scheffler, Ronald T. Perkins & David L. Wagner, 1975. 'Soviet–American and Israeli–Arab Arms Races and the Richardson Model', *General Systems*, vol. 20, pp. 151–158.
Talbott, Strobe, 1980. *Endgame: The Inside Story of SALT II*. New York: Harper Colophon.
Tammen, Ronald L., 1973. *MIRV and the Arms Race: An Interpretation of Defense Policy*. New York: Praeger.
Tamnes, Rolf, 1986. 'Ettpartistat, småstat og særinteresser', *Nytt Norsk Tidsskrift*, vol. 3, no. 3, pp. 42–64.
Thee, Marek, 1978. 'The Dynamics of the Arms Race, Military R&D, and Disarmament', *International Social Science Journal*, vol. 30, no. 4, pp. 904–925.
Thee, Marek, 1986a. *Military Technology, Military Strategy and the Arms Race*. London: Croom Helm/New York: St. Martin's.
Thee, Marek, ed., 1986b. *Arms and Disarmament: SIPRI Findings*. Oxford & New York: Oxford University Press.
Thee, Marek, 1987. 'Military Technology, Arms Control and Human Development', *Bulletin of Peace Proposals*, vol. 18, no. 1, March, pp. 1–11. [Reprinted in *Physics and Development*, International Centre for Theoretical Physics, Trieste, no. 8, 1987, pp. 40–64.]
Thee, Marek, 1988. 'Science and Technology for War and Peace: The Quest for Disarmament and Development', *Bulletin of Peace Proposals*, vol. 19, no. 3–4, September, pp. 261–292. [Reprinted under the title 'Recovering Research and Science', pp. 67–109 in Ken Coates, ed., 1988. *Perestroika: The Global Challenge: Our Common Future*. Nottingham: Spokesman. A shorter version of this article appears as ch. 7 of this book.]
Thee, Marek, 1989. 'Military Technology – A Driving Force Behind the Arms Race and an Impediment for Arms Control and Disarmament', pp. 39–64 in Brauch, 1989d.
Thomas, Mark, 1983. 'Rearmament and Economic Recovery in the late 1930s', *Economic History Review*, vol. 36, no. 4, November, pp. 552–579.
Thompson, Edward P., 1980. 'Notes on Exterminism, the Last Stage of Civilization', *New Left Review*, no. 121, May/June, pp. 3–31.
Thompson, William R., ed., 1986. *Contending Approaches to World System Analysis*. Beverly Hills, CA: Sage.
Thompson, William R.; Robert D. Duval & Ahmed Dia, 1979. 'Wars, Alliances and Military Expenditures', *Journal of Conflict Resolution*, vol. 23, no. 4, December, pp. 629–654.

Thompson, William R. & Gary Zuk, 1986. 'World Power and the Strategic Trap of Territorial Commitments', *International Studies Quarterly*, vol. 30, no. 3, September, pp. 249–268.
Thorson, Stuart J. & Donald A. Sylvan, 1982. 'Counterfactuals and the Cuban Missile Crisis', *International Studies Quarterly*, vol. 26, no. 4, December, pp. 539–571.
Thorsson, Inga, ed., 1984a. *Med sikte på nedrustning. Omställning från militär till civil produktion i Sverige*, vol. 1, *Huvudbetänkande*; SOU 1984: 62; vol. 2, *Särskilda rapporter*, SOU 1985: 43. Stockholm: Liber.
Thorsson, Inga, ed., 1984b. *In Pursuit of Disarmament. Conversion from Military to Civil Production in Sweden*, vol. 1A, *Background, Facts and Analyses*; vol. 1B, *Summary, Appraisals and Recommendations*; vol. 2, *Special Reports*. Stockholm: Liber. [Translation of Thorsson, 1984a.]
Tiedtke, Stephan, 1978. *Die Warschauer Vertragsorganisation. Zum Verhältnis von Militär- und Entspannungspolitik in Osteuropa*. Munich: Oldenbourg.
Tolubko, V., 1979. *Nedelin*. Moscow: Molodaya Gvardiya.
Trebilcock, Clive, 1973. 'British Armaments and European Industrialization, 1890–1914', *Economic History Review*, vol. 26, no. 2, pp. 254–272.
Trebilcock, Clive, 1975. 'War and the Failure of Industrial Mobilization: 1899 and 1914', pp. 139–164 in J.M. Winter, ed. *War and Economic Development*. Cambridge & New York: Cambridge University Press, 1975.
Trebilcock, Clive, 1981. *The Industrialization of Continental Powers 1780–1914*. London: Longman.
Triska, Jan & David Finley, 1965. 'Soviet–American Relations: A Multiple Symmetry Model', *Journal of Conflict Resolution*, vol. 9, no. 1, March, pp. 37–53.
Tuchman, Barbara W., 1966. *The Proud Tower*. New York: Macmillan.
Tullberg, Rita, 1986. 'World Military Expenditures', pp. 17–22 in Thee, 1986b.
Turner, John, 1985. *Arms in the '80s: New Developments in the Global Arms Race*. London: Taylor & Francis.
United Nations, 1971. *Economic and Social Consequences of the Arms Race and Its Extremely Harmful Effects on World Peace and Security*. New York: UN, Office of the Secretary-General.
United Nations, 1982. *The Relationship between Disarmament and Development*. UN Study Series, no. 5. New York: UN.
United Nations, 1987. *The Military Use of R&D, A Report Pursuant to General Assembly Resolution 37/99J*. New York: UN, Department of Disarmament Affairs.
US Bureau of the Census, 1985. *Statistical Abstract of the United States 1986*, 106th ed. Washington, DC: US Government Printing Office.
US News & World Report, 1987. 'A Frightening New Number Game', 28 September.
Utrikespolitiska institutet, 1965. *Svenska kärnvapenproblem*. Stockholm: Prisma.
Vagts, Alfred, 1960. *A History of Militarism, Civilian and Military*, revised ed. London: Hollis & Carter. [First published in 1938.]
van den Dungen, Peter, 1977. 'Varieties of Peace Science: An Historical Note', *Journal of Peace Science*, vol. 2, no. 2, Spring, pp. 239–257.
van der Dennen, Hans, 1981. 'On War: Concepts, Definitions, Research Data: A Short Literature Survey and Bibliography', section 3.2, pp. 128–189 in *Unesco Yearbook on Peace and Conflict Studies 1980*. Westport, CT: Greenwood.
van Duijn, Jacob J., 1983. *The Long Wave of Economic Life*. London: Allen & Unwin.
Varga, Eugen, 1935. *The Great Crisis and its Political Consequences. Economics and Politics 1928–1934*. London: Modern Books.
Vasquez, John A., 1976. 'Statistical Findings in International Politics: A Data-Based Assessment', *International Studies Quarterly*, vol. 20, no. 2, June, pp. 171–218.
Veblen, Thorstein, 1964. *Imperial Germany and the Industrial Revolution*. New York: Kelly. [First published in 1915.]
Volger, Helmut, 1987. *Der Wandel der Perzeption von Abrüstung, Entwicklung und Konversion in der UNO*. Frankfurt a.M.: Haag & Herchen.
von Sydow, Björn, 1978. *Kan vi lita på politikerna? Offentlig och intern politik i socialdemokratins ledning*. Stockholm: Tiden.

Väyrynen, Raimo, 1983a. 'Economic Cycles, Power Transitions, Political Management and Wars between Major Powers', *International Studies Quarterly*, vol. 27, no.4, December, pp. 389–418.
Väyrynen, Raimo, 1983b. 'Semiperipheral Countries in the Global Economic and Military Order', pp. 163–192 in Helena Tuomi & Raimo Väyrynen, eds. *Militarization and Arms Production*. London: Croom Helm.
Väyrynen, Raimo, 1983c. 'Economic Fluctuations, Technological Innovations and the Arms Race in a Historical Perspective', *Cooperation and Conflict*, vol. 18, no. 3, September, pp. 135–160.
Väyrynen, Raimo, 1987. 'Global Power Dynamics and Collective Violence', pp. 80–96 in Väyrynen et al., 1987.
Väyrynen, Raimo, 1988. 'Domestic Crises and International Wars', pp. 70–102 in Peter Wallensteen, ed. *Peace Research: Achievements and Challenges*. Boulder, CO: Westview.
Väyrynen, Raimo; Dieter Senghaas & Christian Schmidt, eds., 1987. *The Quest for Peace*. London: Sage.
Vårt framtida försvar, 1947. Stockholm: Centralförbundet Folk och Försvar.
Wagner, David L.; Ronald T. Perkins & Rein Taagepera, 1975. 'Complete Solution to Richardson's Arms Race Equations', *Journal of Peace Science*, vol. 1, no. 2, Spring, pp. 159–172.
Wainstein, Leonard, 1971. 'The Dreadnought Gap', pp. 153–169 in Robert J. Art & Kenneth N. Waltz, eds. *The Use of Force. International Politics and Foreign Policy*. Boston, MA: Little, Brown. Originally published in *US Naval Institute Proceedings*, vol. 92, no. 9, September, 1966, pp. 78–91.
Wallace, Michael D., 1972. 'Status, Formal Organization and Arms Levels as Factors Leading to the Onset of War', pp. 49–70 in Bruce M. Russett, ed. *Peace, War and Numbers*. Beverly Hills, CA: Sage.
Wallace, Michael D., 1973. *War and Rank among Nations*. Lexington, MA: Heath.
Wallace, Michael D., 1979. 'Arms Races and Escalation', *Journal of Conflict Resolution*, vol. 23, no. 1, March, pp. 3–16.
Wallace, Michael D., 1980. 'Some Persisting Findings: A Reply to Professor Weede', *Journal of Conflict Resolution*, vol. 24, no. 2, June, pp. 289–292.
Wallace, Michael D., 1981. 'Old Nails in New Coffins: The Para Bellum Hypothesis Revisited', *Journal of Peace Research*, vol. 18, no. 1, pp. 91–95.
Wallace, Michael D. & Judy M. Wilson, 1978. 'Non-linear Arms Race Models', *Journal of Peace Research*, vol. 15, no. 2, pp. 175–192.
Wallace, Michael D.; Brian L. Crissey & Linn I. Sennott, 1986. 'Accidental Nuclear War: A Risk Assessment', *Journal of Peace Research*, vol. 23, no. 1, March, pp. 9–28.
Wallensteen, Peter, 1973. *Structure and War*. Stockholm: Rabén & Sjögren.
Wallensteen, Peter, ed., 1978. *Experiences in Disarmament: On Conversion of Military Industry and Closing of Military Bases*. Report no. 19. Uppsala: Department of Peace and Conflict Research, Uppsala University.
Waller, Douglas C. & James T. Bruce, 1987. 'SDI's Covert Reorientation', *Arms Control Today*, vol. 17, no. 5, June, pp. 2–8.
Wallerstein, Immanuel, 1979. *The Capitalist World-Economy*. Cambridge: Cambridge University Press.
Waltz, Kenneth N., 1959. *Man, the State, and War: A Theoretical Analysis*. New York: Columbia University Press.
Waltz, Kenneth N., 1979. *Theory of International Politics*. Reading, MA: Addison-Wesley.
Ward, Michael D., 1984a. 'Differential Paths to Parity. A Study of the Contemporary Arms Race', *American Political Science Review*, vol. 78, no. 2, June, pp. 297–315.
Ward, Michael D., 1984b. 'The Political Economy of Arms Races and International Tension', *Conflict Management and Peace Science*, vol. 7, no. 2, Spring, pp. 1–23.
Ward, Michael D. & A.K. Mahajan, 1984. 'Defense Expenditures, Security Threats and Government Deficits: A Case Study of India, 1952-1979', *Journal of Conflict Resolution*, vol. 28, no. 3, September, pp. 382–419.

Wayman, Frank W.; J. David Singer & Gary Goertz, 1983. 'Capabilities, Allocations, and Success in Militarized Disputes and War, 1816–1976', *International Studies Quarterly*, vol. 27, no. 4, pp. 497–515.
Weber, Max, 1921. *Wirtschaft und Gesellschaft*. Tübingen: Mohr.
Weber, Max, 1958. 'Der Nationalstaat und die Volkwirtschaftpolitik', pp. 1–25 in Johannes Winckelmann, ed. *Gesammelte Politische Schrifte*. Tübingen: Mohr. [First published in 1921.]
Weber, Robert Philip, 1981. 'Society and Economy in the Western World System', *Social Forces*, vol. 59, no. 4, June, pp. 1130–1147.
Weede, Erich, 1973. 'Nation-Environment Relations as Determinants of Hostilities among Nations', *Peace Research Society (International) Papers*, vol. 20, pp. 67–90.
Weede, Erich, 1975. 'World Order in the Fifties and Sixties: Dependence, Deterrence and Limited Peace', *Peace Research Society (International) Papers*, vol. 24, pp. 49–80.
Weede, Erich, 1976. 'Overwhelming Preponderance as a Pacifying Condition among Contiguous Asian Dyads', *Journal of Conflict Resolution*, vol. 20, no. 3, September, pp. 395–412.
Weede, Erich, 1980. 'Arms Races and Escalation: Some Persisting Doubts' [Response to Wallace, 1979], *Journal of Conflict Resolution*, vol. 24, no. 2, June, pp. 285–287.
Weede, Erich, 1981. 'Preventing War By Nuclear Deterrence or by Detente', *Conflict Management and Peace Science*, vol. 6, no. 1, Fall, pp. 1–18.
Weede, Erich, 1983. 'Extended Deterrence by Superpower Alliance', *Journal of Conflict Resolution*, vol. 27, no. 2, June, pp. 231–254.
Weede, Erich, 1985. 'Some (Western) Dilemmas in Managing Extended Deterrence', *Journal of Peace Research*, vol. 22, no. 3, September, pp. 223–238.
White, Morton G., 1965. *The Foundations of Historical Knowledge*. New York: Harper & Row.
Wiberg, Håkan, 1983. 'Measuring Military Expenditures: Purposes, Methods, Sources', *Cooperation and Conflict*, vol. 18, no. 3, pp. 161–177.
Wiberg, Håkan, 1986. 'The Security of Small Nations: Challenges and Defences', *Journal of Peace Research*, vol. 24, no. 4, December, pp. 339–364.
Wicken, Olav, 1984. 'Vekst og våpen', pp. 156–184 in Rolf Tamnes, ed. *Forsvarsstudier*, vol. 3. Oslo: Tanum-Norli.
Wicken, Olav, 1987a. 'Norske våpen til NATOs forsvar', *Forsvarsstudier*, no. 1. Oslo: Norwegian Institute for Defence Studies.
Wicken, Olav, 1987b. 'Militære anskaffelser: Forsvars- eller industripolitikk?', pp. 54–72 in Klaus-Richard Böhme, ed. *Krigsmaterialanskafning 1987*. Stockholm: Militära Högskolan.
Wicken, Olav, 1988. 'Stille propell i storpolitisk storm', *Forsvarsstudier*, no. 1. Oslo: Norwegian Institute for Defence Studies.
Wiesner, Jerome, 1960. 'Foreword to the issue "Arms Control"', *Daedalus*, vol. 89, no. 34, Fall, pp. 677–680.
Wight, Martin, 1978. *Power Politics*. [Edited by Hedley Bull & Carsten Holbraad.] Harmondsworth: Penguin.
Wilkes, Owen & Nils Petter Gleditsch, 1987. *Loran-C and Omega: A Study of the Military Importance of Radio Navigation Aids*. Oslo: Norwegian University Press/Oxford: Oxford University Press.
Wilson, George C., 1964. 'GOP to Capitalize on LeMay's Charges', *Aviation Week and Space Technology*, vol. 80, no. 16, 20 April, pp. 26–27.
Winner, Langdon, 1986. *The Whale and the Reactor. A Search for Limits in the Age of High Technology*. Chicago, IL: University of Chicago Press.
Wittrock, Björn & Stefan Lindström, 1984. *De stora programmens tid – forskning och energi i svensk politik*. Stockholm: Akademilitteratur.
Witzel, Rudolf, 1988. *Rüstungskontrollpolitik und Machtverständnis in den USA: die inneramerikanische Kontroverse um die äussere Sicherheit 1968–1976*. Frankfurt a.M.: Campus.
Wohlstetter, Albert, 1974a. 'Is There a Strategic Arms Race?', *Foreign Policy*, no. 15, Summer, pp. 3–20.

Wohlstetter, Albert, 1974b. 'Rivals, but No Race', *Foreign Policy*, no. 16, Fall, pp. 48–81.
Wohlstetter, Albert, 1975. 'How To Confuse Ourselves', *Foreign Policy*, no. 20, Fall, pp. 170–198.
Wohlstetter Albert, 1984. 'Staatsmänner, Bischöfe und sonstige Strategen über Bombenangriffe auf Unschuldige', *Pro Pace*. Bonn: Deutsches Strategie-Forum.
Wohlstetter, Albert; T.S. Hoffman; R.J. Lutz & H.S. Rowen, 1954. *Selection and Use of Strategic Air Bases*. Report R–266. Santa Monica, CA.: RAND. [Declassified 1962.]
Wolfson, Murray, 1987. 'A Theorem on the Existence of Zones of Initiation and Deterrence in Intriligator-Brito Arms Race Models', *Public Choice*, vol. 54, no. 3, pp. 291–297.
World Armaments and Disarmament: SIPRI Yearbook, annually. Stockholm: Almquist & Wiksell (1970–77). London: Taylor & Francis (1978–85). Oxford: Oxford University Press (1986)).
Wright, Quincy, 1965. *A Study of War*. 2nd ed. Chicago: University of Chicago Press. [First published in 1942. Abridged version published 1964.]
Wängborg, Manne, 1981. 'Disarmament and Development – A Bibliographical Introduction to the United Nations Study', pp. 193–241 in *UNESCO Yearbook on Peace and Conflict Studies 1980*. Westport, CT: Greenwood.
Yanarella, Ernest J., 1977. *The Missile Defense Controversy: Strategy, Technology, and Politics, 1955–1972*. Lexington, KY: University of Kentucky Press.
Yergin, Daniel H., 1977. *Shattered Peace – The Origins of the Cold War and the National Security State*. New York: Houghton Mifflin.
York, Herbert F., 1970. *Race to Oblivion. A Participant's View of the Arms Race*. New York: Simon & Schuster.
York, Herbert F., 1973. *The Origins of MIRV*. Report no. 9. Stockholm International Peace Research Institute.
York, Herbert F., ed., 1974. *Arms Control. Readings from* Scientific American. San Francisco, CA: Freeman.
York, Herbert F., 1975. 'The Origins of MIRV', pp. 23–35 in David Carlton & Carlo Schaerf, eds. *The Dynamics of the Arms Race*. London: Croom Helm.
York, Herbert F., 1976. *The Advisors: Oppenheimer, Teller, and the Superbomb*. San Francisco, CA: Freeman.
York, Herbert F., 1988. *Making Weapons – Talking Peace: A Physicist's Odyssey from Hiroshima to Geneva*. New York: Basic Books.
Zinnes, Dina A., 1976. *Contemporary Research in International Relations*. New York: Free Press.
Zinnes, Dina A., 1980. 'Why War? Evidence on the Outbreak of International Conflict', pp. 331–360 in Ted Robert Gurr, ed. *Handbook of Political Conflict*. New York: Free Press.
Zinnes, Dina A. & John V. Gillespie, eds., 1976. *Mathematical Models in International Relations*. New York: Praeger.
Zuckerman, Solly, 1980. 'Science Advisers and Scientific Advisers', *Proceedings of the American Philosophical Society*, vol. 124, no. 4, August, pp. 241–255.
ÖfiaB–54, 1954. *Alltjämt ett starkt försvar*. ÖfiaB-förslaget 1954. *Kontakt med krigsmakten*, no. 9–10. Stockholm: Försvarsstaben.
ÖfiaB–57, 1957. *ÖfiaB-utredningarna 1957. Kontakt med krigsmakten*, no. 10–12. Stockholm: Försvarsstaben.
ÖfiaB–62, 1962. *Riktlinjer för krigsmaktens fortsatta utveckling*. Stockholm: Försvarsstaben.
ÖfiaB–65, 1965. *Utredning om det militära försvarets fortsatta utveckling*. Stockholm: Försvarsstaben.

Subject Index

accelerometer 128–129
action-reaction model 1–3, 6, 9, 10–11, 33, 48–49, 79–80, 85, 112, 114–116, 171, 220, 347
  critique 2, 12, 15–16, 19, 26, 40–57, 87–88, 95–96, 215, 239
  internal 9–10, 22–23, 52, 188
  and US 5, 92, 178, 186, 188, 190, 193–194, 197, 207–208, 226–228
  and USSR 5, 296–299, 306
Afghanistan, Soviet invasion 194–195, 376
alliances, and decision-making 8, 9, 33, 41–42
Antarctica Treaty 377
anti-ballistic missile (ABM) systems 92, 176, 177, 184, 188, 190, 192, 198–199, 200–202, 207–208
Anti-Ballistic Missile (ABM) Treaty 1972 73, 111, 212, 307, 377
anti-submarine weapons 197
Apollo project 205
Argentina, weapons technology 378, 379
armament dynamics 346, 347–350, 349, 354
Armed Services Committee (US) 133–134
arms, types and levels 12
arms control 24–30, 68, 74–76, 91, 114, 169, 309–310, 377–378
arms race,
  bipolar 59
  cataclysmic models 32, 78–79, 82, 84, 86
  causal models 33, 49–57, 78
  consequences 352, 354–363, 365–373
  covert 378–379, 381
  definitions 10–12, 59, 89–90, 91
  dynamics 1–13, 15–30, 29, 31–32
    essential features 22–24, 91
  future possibilities 17, 376–382
  mathematical models 31–48, 58–60, 78, 81
  multipolar 74–75, 76, 108, 378–380
  new 11, 13, 378–381
  parameters 39–40, 42–46, 50, 55–56, 81
  as problem 31, 352–354
  qualitative 3, 11, 15–17, 21, 25, 74, 90–91, 100, 108, 365, 377, 380
  quantitative 365, 380
  stable/unstable 35–37, 61–62, 64, 71–74, 76, 191–192, 365–370, 366–367, 381, 382
  stage-centred approach 314, 315

  strategic 16–17, 53, 65–69
  strategic models 32–33, 34, 78–79, 82, 84, 86
  systemic approach 8, 9, 10, 314
  testing models 40–41, 47, 49, 56
  and war 365–373
  see also action-reaction models; artificial intelligence models; asymmetric models; internal factors model; US–USSR arms race
artificial intelligence models 3, 81–86
asymmetric models 1–3, 61, 72, 116
ASW Terne missiles 146
Atlas missile 134, 190
Austrian State Treaty 377
autistic model 1–2, 50, 79–80, 92, 124–125, 178, 194, 221, 296, 306, 349–350

B-1 bomber 94, 118
B-29 bomber 302
B-36 bomber 235
balance of power 21, 70, 85, 111, 178, 188, 217, 234, 356, 363–364, 368
bargaining chips 5, 9, 170
Basic Principles Agreement 289
behaviourism 82
bilateralism 68, 69
BMD system, *see* defence, ballistic missile
bombers,
  strategic 165, 176–177, 193, 196, 207, 235
  US 377
  USSR 376–377
Brazil, weapons technology 378, 379
Britain,
  decision-making 71
  power 322, 323–324, 325–330, 338–342, 343–344
  weapons 378
  see also expenditure, military
Brito model 58, 63–64, 80
Bullpup missile 146
bureaucratic politics 5, 6, 12, 72, 116, 117, 220
  and foreign policy 2
  USA 54, 178, 184, 186–189, 192–208, 210–212, 214, 227–228, 296, 309–310
  and USSR 4, 295, 297, 306–311

416 ARMS RACES

capabilities 38, 46, 53, 60, 72, 201, 364, 377–379
capitalism,
   and arms race 2, 22, 94, 97, 178, 189, 316–320
   and militarism 247–275, 251–267, 277–280, 281, 282–284
   case studies 225–244 *passim*
'catch-up' theorem 8, 9, 100, 336, 338
causality, configurative 23–24, 91, 348
causation, redundant 7, 23–24, 91, 209
China,
   weapons technology 124, 285–293, 378
   see also military-industrial complex
Circular Error Probable 123
civil society, and militarism 248, 250–264, 270, 272–274, 276–279, 280
command, control, communication and intelligence (C^3I) technologies 110–111, 114
Committee on the Present Danger (US) 195
comparison, structured focused 217, 221, 225–226, 229–230, 238–245
competition,
   armament 347, 348–350, 381
   inter-service 8, 220, 297, 301, 306
     USA 175, 179, 185, 187, 189, 190, 192, 200–201, 204
   international 189, 260–261, 265–266, 285, 292, 316, 322–323, 325–330
   technological 94, 118, 171–172
computers 123, 129–130
confrontation, systemic 347, 348–350
consensus building, USA 227–228
containment 232
core-periphery system 316, 321, 327, 342
Correlates of War Project 356, 362, 371
counterforce capability 12, 92, 129, 136, 184
cruise missiles 4–5, 73, 94–95, 109, 119, 239
   ground-launched 12, 303–304, 306, 310
Cuban missile crisis 70, 371, 377
culture, military 285–288, 293

decision rules 59, 71–73, 76
decision-making 41–42, 54–55, 56–57, 78–79, 83, 95–96, 117, 145, 348
   historical studies 220–245
   USA 178–179, 183–187, 189, 192–193, 195–212
   USSR 5, 212
defence,
   ballistic missile (BDM) 176, 177, 193, 207, 289
   research and development initiatives 111–114

'total' 157
Defense Advanced Research Projects Agency (DARPA) 97
détente policies 15
determinism, technological 3, 5, 88, 123, 236–237
deterrence,
   and arms build-up 116, 168, 232, 288, 332, 355
   extended 364, 368–369, 374
   mutual 11, 17, 18, 66–69, 70–75, 197, 376–378, 380
differential game model 58, 64–65
diplomacy, and arms control 24–25, 27, 28, 116, 238
Directed Energy Weapons (DEWs) 112
disarmament, *see* arms control; bilateralism; unilateralism
Draper Laboratory, and weapons technology 128–129, 136
Duhem-Quine thesis 130–131, 134–135

economy,
   and arms race,
     long waves 9, 10, 316–321, 324, 327, 331, 333, 337–338, 343–344
     and militarization 331–342
     and military expenditure 315, 316, 342–343
     and power transitions 321–330
   effect on politics 96, 97, 99, 150, 189, 195, 213, 216
   expansion 8, 98, 143, 161, 332
Egypt, *see* expenditure, military
Eigendynamik, *see* autistic model
expansionism 8
   German 330
   Russian 285, 291–292, 332
expenditure, military 31, 35, 38, 42–43, 47, 315, 316, 323, 329
   Britain 51–52, 91, 107–108, 338–342
   China 105, 107
   curtailment 27–28, 234–235, 350
   determinants 32–33, 260–261, 331
   and economic development 315, 316, 342–343
   Egypt 55
   France 91, 107–108
   Germany 51–52, 94, 107
   Israel 55
   Japan 107
   Sweden 165
   Switzerland 94
   USA 11, 48, 53–54, 91, 94–95, 105–108,

INDEX

113–114, 179–180, 194–196, 234–235, 331–334
USSR 11, 53–54, 91, 105–108, 289, 334–338
and war 360–362, 370
as waste 353–354

F–16 aircraft 95
F–111 aircraft 176, 177, 188, 190, 193, 203, 213
F–111B aircraft 193
fatigue effect 42, 43–44, 60–62, 79
fleet ballistic missile (FBMs) 205
Flexible Response 304
'follow-on theorem' 8, 9, 13, 20, 88, 92, 118, 189, 315
force reduction 25–26, 110
France,
    power 323–324, 325, 326, 328–330
    weapons technology 124, 378
    see also expenditure, military

Gaither Report (US) 194–195
Germany,
    power 323–324, 325–330, 328, 339–340, 344
    weapons technology 379
    see also expenditure, military
graduated reciprocation in tension reduction (GRIT) 85
grievance factor 2, 35, 60–62, 79
guidance technologies 3, 94, 124–130, 135–137, 184

historical studies 93, 220–245, 306
    methodology 221–225, 226, 229–230, 233, 244–245
hydrogen bomb, case studies 226–241

ICBMs see missiles, intercontinental ballistic
identification problem 9–10
India, weapons technology 378, 379
industrialism,
    and arms race 93, 97, 100–103, 141–143, 155, 171, 318–319, 322, 325–326, 329, 335–339, 344–345, 362
    and militarism 88, 96, 100–102, 155, 171, 251, 263–264, 268, 270, 279, 282
input-output model 215–218
Integrated Long-Term Strategy report (US) 110–113
intelligence, and weapons procurement policies 193–195, 198, 207–208, 217, 242

interests,
    industrial 23, 189
    national 78–80, 96
    socio-political 5, 8, 17–19, 20, 29, 43, 183, 192
Intermediate Nuclear Forces (INF) Treaty 13, 74, 110, 290, 377
internal factors model 2, 6, 7–10, 12, 16, 22–24, 26, 33, 48–52, 56, 79–81, 94, 140, 171, 178
    limitations 87–88, 124–125, 215, 314
    and USA 184, 186, 209, 210–211, 296
    and USSR 306
internationalism 269–272, 283
interwar period, models 52
investment, military 25–26, 27, 90–91, 94–95, 150
Iran-Iraq war 59, 379–380, 382
IRBMs, see missiles, intermediate range ballistic
Israel,
    weapons technology 125, 378
    see also expenditure, military
Italy, weapons technology 379

Japan 325, 326, 328, 329–330, 342
    weapons technology 379
Jupiter IRBM 190, 238–239

Kinetic Energy Weapons (KEWs) 112
Kongsberg model 145–147, 149–150

laser technology 16, 94, 103, 112, 126
launchers 176, 190, 197, 302
Limited Test Ban Treaty 377

macro-response model 194
Manhattan Project 158, 179, 205, 242
Marxism 96–97, 178
Massachusetts Peace Society 31
Massive Retaliation 288–289
mathematical models, limitations 81–82
Max Planck Institute 98
militarism,
    and anti-militarism 258–259, 266–275, 278, 279–280
    archives 247–249, 276–284
    and civil society 248, 250–264, 270, 272–274, 276–279, 280
    as consumption 101, 260–262, 267–269, 280–282, 284
    definitions 247–250
    industrial 88, 96, 100–102, 155, 171, 251, 263–264, 268

militarism *cont.*
  Lebenswelt and *Systemwelt* 249–250, 262–275, 278, 279–282, 284
  and post-industrialism 101–102
militarization 18, 89, 331–342, 353, 355
military fix model 9, 239
military mission model 5, 8, 13, 18, 109, 213, 296–297
military-industrial complex 1, 4–5, 8, 18, 54, 79, 88, 92, 101, 116, 140, 215, 261, 316
  China 4, 285, 291, 292
  Eisenhower warning 2, 150–152, 190–191, 286, 288
  Germany 102
  Japan 102
  Norway 2, 140–152
  Sweden 144, 157
  USA 96, 140, 150, 152, 178, 186, 209, 213, 292, 296
  USSR 2, 4, 96, 102, 285, 287–288, 290–291, 292, 294, 295, 297, 300–301, 303, 306–307
Minuteman missile 129, 188, 190, 198, 204–205, 206–207, 303
missiles,
  accuracy 100, 109, 113, 122, 123, 125–130, 136
  air-launched 95
  intercontinental ballistic 54, 95, 100, 109, 123, 133–135, 176, 188, 190–192, 196, 203–204
  intermediate-range ballistic 99, 128, 187, 190, 196, 238–239, 302–303
  medium-range ballistic 302, 305, 309
  sea-launched ballistic 176
  small intercontinental ballistic 126, 128
  submarine launched 125, 128, 129–130, 137, 190
  see also guidance systems; launchers; weapons
models, descriptive/normative 58–64
Multilateral Force (MLF) 238–239
multiple independently targetable re-entry vehicles (MIRVs) 73, 92, 109, 119, 122, 129
  USA 176, 188, 190–192, 197–198, 201–202, 205–208, 216, 218, 306
  USSR 216, 303, 309
Mutual Assured Destruction (MAD) 289–290, 368–369
MX missile 118, 125, 126, 128, 183–184, 187, 189, 192, 197, 199–200, 204–205, 213

'National Security State' 175
National Socialism 265–269, 274, 280

NATO 142, 197, 299
  deployment decisions 5, 14, 110, 303–304, 310
navigators, inertial 125–127, 136–137
neutron bomb 239–240
Nike Zeus ABM system 190, 207
Norway,
  Defence Research Establishment 145–148, 150
  Institute for Atomic Energy 146
  modernization 141–145, 151
  Royal Norwegian Council for Science and Technology 147
  see also military-industrial complex
nuclear energy 158–159, 161–162, 169, 171, 235
Nuclear Nonproliferation Treaty 377, 379
nuclear weapons, *see* missiles; weapons

Off-Shore Procurement Program 143
organizational imperative 19–20
overdetermination 6–7, 9, 91, 220, 226, 238–241, 296, 305, 307, 311
overkill capabilities 21, 110, 369

pacifism 267
Pakistan, weapons technology 378, 379
Palme Commission 89
paramilitarism 266–267
parity, doctrine of 21, 85, 306, 372
Partial Test-Ban Treaty 134, 169
peace policies 25, 26–27, 29
Peace Science Society 3
perestroika 337–338
Pershing II missile 12, 239, 290, 303–304, 310
Pershing III missile 100
PIGA (pendulous integrating gyro accelerometer) 128–129
PIPA (pulsed integrating pendulous accelerometer) 128–129
Polaris missiles 12, 134, 135, 190, 196, 205, 302
politics, and technology 3, 88, 122–123, 124, 135–137
Poseidon missile 129, 137, 188, 206–207
postwar period, models 52–56
power, military,
  and economy 316
  historical studies 325–330
  transitions 9, 321–324, 331, 334, 338, 344–345
Prisoners' Dilemma 78–79, 80, 85, 382
proliferation, nuclear 108, 156, 377, 378–381

Quemoy-Matsu crisis 377

radio-frequency weapons 112
RAND Corporation 295, 296–297
rational actor approach 2, 3, 9–10, 33, 53, 95–96, 295–296, 298–299, 368
Reaction-Linkage model 42, 55
reactors, heavy-water 154, 159, 161–162, 167, 168
requirements model 295, 297–303, 306, 310–311
research and development (R&D),
  and armaments dynamics 10, 114–119
  conversion 103
  future-oriented 111–114, 119
  magnitude 105–108, 179–184
  militarization 105–108, 143–144
  privately funded 94–95, 102
  restriction 26, 91, 190
  role in arms build-ups 3, 87–103, 105–119, 308
  secrecy 105, 118, 179, 184, 193
  strategic nuclear weapons 176, 192
  styles 182–183
revisionist approach 2, 178, 215, *see also* internal factors model

SALT agreements 5, 28, 176, 190, 202, 204, 216, 289, 303–304, 377
saturation, nuclear weapons 99–100, 108
security,
  collective 258, 329–330
  dilemma 80
  policy oligarchies 18–19
self-interest, *see* interests, national
Sentinel system 190
Sidewinder missile 146
simulations 65–67
SIPRI, on global R&D 106–108
social inertia model 10, 22, 116
socialism,
  and armaments 4, 22, 285–293
  and militarism 259–260, 262–265, 272, 274, 353
South Africa, weapons technology 378, 379
South Korea, weapons technology 378, 379
space, militarization 74, 94, 109, 111–113
Spain, weapons technology 379
Spartan missiles 177
Sprint missiles 177
Sputnik 74, 148, 190–191, 194, 205, 376–377
SS–4, SS–5 missiles 302–304
SS–11, SS–13, SS–14, SS–15 missiles 302–303
SS–18 missile 99, 305–306
SS–19 missile 305–306
SS–20 missile 294, 295, 302–305, 309–310

SSM Penguin weapons system 146
stability,
  doctrine of 21
  strategic 70–71, 72–73, 85, 191–192, 197, 213, 214–218, 377–378, 380–381
Star Wars *see* Strategic Defense Initiative
state,
  and military-industrial complex 141, 148–152, 261, 283, 285–388, 353
  and society 305–308, 310–311
  and technological change 121
  and war 93, 286
  see also arms race, state-centred approach
stealth technology 73, 92, 94–95, 113
stock adjustment model 58, 62–63, 72
stock, weapons 39, 99–100, 108, 110, 157, 228, 377
Strategic Arms Reduction Talks (START) agreement 11, 74
Strategic Defense Initiative (SDI) 111–113, 117–118, 135, 176, 177, 180, 193, 288–290
strategies, psychostrategies 20–21, 122
submarine systems 12
submissiveness factor 52
sufficiency, doctrine of 21, 289
superiority 5, 21, 90, 108, 208, 228, 289
Sweden,
  AB Atomenergi 158–159, 161–162, 169
  Defence Research Agency (FOA) 154, 158–164, 167–170
  nuclear weapons programme 3, 154–172
  weapons technology 379
Switzerland, weapons technology 379

Taiwan, weapons technology 378, 379
technology,
  development 121–127, 138, 337, 340
  and economic cycles 317–320, 323, 325, 335–336, 344–345
  entrepreneurship 5, 8, 228, 239
  historical study 124, 127–130, 155–156
  momentum of 3, 19–20, 74, 76, 97, 102–103, 105–119, 189, 202, 220, 231, 236, 243, 344
  out of control 8, 89, 121–123, 124–125, 137, 151
  and qualitative arms race 16–17, 108–111, 144, 348
  sociological study 130–137, 155
  technological imperative 6, 9, 10, 119, 130, 185, 188, 200–202, 206–207, 209, 308, 314–315
  see also determinism, technological; research and development

terrorism, and nuclear weapons 380, 381
TFX fighter bomber 176, 177, 187, 190, 193, 213
Third World, militarization 89, 93, 108–109, 112–113, 379–380, 381–382
Thor missile 128, 190, 238–239
'threshold countries' 108–109, 156
Titan II 128, 190
translation, indeterminacy of 223–225, 240–241
Trident 12, 187, 189, 197
　C4 129, 137
　D5 128–130
Tu–4 bomber 302
Tu–16 bomber 302

unilateralism 26–27, 28, 68, 69
United Nations, reports 19, 106, 119
US Mutual Defense Assistance Program 141, 143, 147
US–USSR arms race 70, 73–76, 94–96, 155, 171, 176, 295, 376–378
USA,
　deployment decisions 12, 54–55, 71–72, 296, 307–308
　and military R&D 88, 94–95, 100, 102–103, 105–108, 111–114, 179–185, 192–209, 212
　power 321–322, 323–324, 325–330, 331–334, 343–344
　studies 4, 8
　weapons stockpile 11, 70, 99–100, 110, 228, 292
　weapons technology 124–130, 133–134, 155–156, 175–218
USSR,
　decision-making 5–6, 8, 12, 192
　and militarism 264–266
　and military R&D 88, 97, 102–103, 105–108, 112, 183–184, 193, 202, 212, 336
　military doctrine and arms procurement 297–301, 311

　power 323–324, 325–326, 330, 334–338, 344
　targeting requirements 299–300, 305–306
　weaponry 70, 124–125, 285–293, 295–311
　　regional 299, 301–305, 308–309, 310
　see also expenditure, military; military-industrial complex

verification 75, 85, 114
Vladivostock Accord 95

war,
　accidental 73, 75–76, 352, 355, 368–369, 381
　and arms race 37, 70–71, 352, 354–357, 365–369, 376, 380–382
　　evidence 357–363, 369–373, 374
　discriminate 113
　dyadic level 363–365, 374
　and economic competition 322–323
　global 323, 327
　limited 168
　nuclear 122, 289, 368–369
　see also stability, strategic
weapons,
　acquisition cycles 180–183
　conventional 100, 168, 380
　lethality 98–99
　quantity 90, 105–108, 110–111
　reduction 110–111, 113–114, 177
　redundancy 110, 119, 306
　research projects 186–215
　role in peace/war 65–66
　strategic 155, 175–218
　　cancelled 177, 188
　　input/output factors 191–202, 204–209, 213, 216–217
　testing 133–135, 377
　see also missiles; proliferation; specific weapon systems; technology, military
worst-case doctrine 17, 118

Name Index

Acheson, Dean 227, 231–234, 236–237, 243, 332–334
Acland-Hood, Mary 106, 108
Agrell, Wilhelm 3
Ahlmark, Per 174
Albrecht, Ulrich 3, 155, 171, 178
Alcock, Norman Z. 373
Alexander II, Tsar 334
Alker, Hayward R. 83, 84
Allison, Graham T. 187, 218, 296–297
Almgren, Carl-Eric 166, 174
Andersson, Sven 164, 166
Andropov, Yuri 290
Angell, Norman 258
Arendt, Hannah 268
Armacost, Michael H. 4, 176, 187, 189, 195–196, 198, 203, 297
Art, Robert J. 176, 187, 189, 195, 198, 203, 213

Baker, John C. 296–303, 304, 305–306, 309–310
Balassa, Bela 142
Ball, Desmond 4
Ball, Nicole 357
Banks, Arthur 331
Barnaby, Frank 122
Bataille, Georges 268
Baudrillard, Jean 268, 281
Baugh, William H. 183, 186
Beard, Edmund 176–177, 187–189, 196, 198–199, 203, 246
Beasley, W.G. 326
Beglov, Spartak 110
Benoit, Emile 353
Berghahn, Volker 101
Berman, Robert P. 296–303, 304, 305–306, 309–310
Block, Fred L. 333
Bloor, David 133
Bobrow, Davis B. 45
Boulding, Kenneth 82
Brauch, Hans Günter 4, 12, 155, 226, 244
Bredow, Wilfried von 101
Bremer, Stuart A. 362
Brezhnev, Leonid 289, 306, 310, 337
Brito, Dagobert L. 3, 11, 13, 80–81, 368
Brzezinski, Zbigniew 110

Busch, Peter A. 46
Buzan, Barry 6, 10

Carlgren, Wilhelm 172
Carr, Edward H. 272–274
Carter, Jimmy 199, 205, 288
Caspary, William R. 43
Catherine the Great 291
Cattell, Raymond B. 361
Chalmers, Malcolm 338, 341–342
Choucri, Nazli 40, 51–52, 361–362
Christensen, Cheryl 83, 84
Clark, William A. 110
Clausewitz, Carl von 286
Cochran, Thomas B. 99–100, 110
Cockburn, Andrew 297, 300–301, 303–304, 306–307, 309–310
Cohen, Samuel 312
Cooper, Julian 290–291
Corbett, Juliet 340
Coser, Lewis 14
Coulam, Robert E. 176, 187–189, 195, 198, 203, 213
Crabb, Cecil V. 231
Croce, Benedetto 226
Curti, Merle 31
Czempiel, Ernst-Otto 192–193

Dalgleish, D. Douglas 177, 189, 197
Davidson, Donald 223–224, 240
Davis, Otto A. 14
Deng Xiaoping 291, 293
Diehl, Paul F. 372
Draper, Charles Stark 136–137, 139
Duffy, Gavan 84
Duhem, Pierre 130, 134–135
Duprés, Eugène 13

Egerton, George 269–270
Eisenhower, Dwight 2, 150–152, 190–191, 286, 288
Eklund, Sigvard 162
Engels, Friedrich 93, 96, 259–260, 267
Enloe, Cynthia 121
Erasmus Roterdamus 87
Erlander, Tage 162–167
Evangelista, Matthew 4–6, 8, 12, 152, 178–179, 183–186, 193–194, 212, 220, 238–240, 244

Fairbank, William 132
Fairbanks, Charles H. 11
Fellows, James 317
Finlay, David 13
Fitchett, Joseph 113
Flora, Peter 331
Forland, Astrid 158
Foucault, Michel 247, 279, 280, 282, 284
Freud, Sigmund 255–256, 282
Fritiofsson, Karl 168
Fuchs, Klaus 241–243

Galbraith, J.K. 43
Galtung, Johan 2, 297
Gansler, Jacques S. 180, 183, 189
Gantzel, Klaus Jürgen 1, 13, 178
Garnham, David 364
Garthoff, Raymond 218
George Alexander L. 4, 214, 217, 225–226
Geyer, Michael E. 2, 276–284
Giddens, Anthony 259, 283
Gillard, David 326
Gleditsch, Nils Petter 94, 138
Goldmann, Kjell 356, 369
Goldstein, Joshua S. 318, 327
Goldwater, Barry 134
Gorbachev, Mikhail 120, 290, 293, 337
Gorshkov, Sergei G. 307
Gorsuch, Richard L. 361
Gourevitch, Peter 322
Gowing, Margaret 172
Graham, Daniel 193
Gray, Colin S. 11, 14, 70, 194, 246
Greenwood, Ted 4, 177, 187–189, 192, 198, 201–202, 206–208, 209–210, 213, 246
Gøthe, Odd 150

Haas, Michael 361–362
Habermas, Jürgen 278–279, 282–283, 284
Halperin, Morton H. 187, 296–297
Hansen, Chuck 138
Harris, Geoffrey 47
Haug, Wolfgang Fritz 247
Hauge, Jens Christian 145–146, 150, 151, 152
Herrmann, Richard 231
Hesse, May 131
Hill, Stephen R. 45
Hintze, Otto 93, 253–254
Hobsbawm, Eric 325–326
Hobson, John A. 256
Holland, Lauren H. 177, 183–184, 187–189, 192, 197, 199–200, 204–205, 210–211
Hollist, W. Ladd 54, 55
Holloway, David 213, 297, 301, 304–306, 308, 310, 312
Holst, Johan Jørgen 11
Hoover, Robert A. 177, 183–184, 187–189, 192, 197, 199–200, 204–205, 210–211
Houweling, Henk 364, 372
Hughes, Thomas P. 137, 152
Huisken, Ron 4–6, 94, 108
Huntington, Samuel P. 365, 370
Hurlen, Bjarne 144

Intriligator, Michael D. 3, 11, 13, 80–81, 368

Jacobsen, Carl G. 4
Jaseni, Bhupendra 112
Jaurès, Jean 260
Jervas, Gunnar 169–170
Johnsen, Katherine 133
Johnson, Louis 227, 233, 234, 236, 242
Johnson, Lyndon Baines 190, 195, 202
Jünger, Ernst 267–269, 281

Kaldor, Mary 13, 99–100, 253
Kaldor, Nicholas 342, 399
Keep, John L.H. 335
Kende, Istvan 13
Kennan, George F. 224–225, 232
Kennedy, John F. 134, 190, 195, 334
Kennedy, Paul 324, 331, 340
Keynes, John Maynard 268–269
Khrushchev, Nikita 288–289, 304–305, 309, 337
Killian, James R. 148
Kipp, Jacob W. 291
Kissinger, Henry 14, 110
Köhler, Gernot 360
Kossiakoff, Alexander 180–182, 183
Krass, Allan 122
Krell, Gert 1
Krippendorff, Ekkehart 93
Kuhn, Thomas S. 138
Kurth, James 6–7, 13, 88, 184–185, 201, 208, 295–296, 303, 305, 307–311
Kuznets, Simon S. 333
Lakatos, Imre 138
Lambelet, John C. 38–39, 51, 53, 55–56, 365–368
Larson, Deborah 224
Larsson, Christer 159–160, 169
Lasswell, Harold 274
Lebow, Richard Ned 360

Leitenberg, Milton 357
LeMay, Curtis 134
Lenin, V.I. 286, 291
Lie, Trygve 143
Liebknecht, Karl 259–260, 283
Lied, Finn 147–148, 151, 152
Lilienthal, David E. 227, 233, 236
Liossatos, Panagis 43
Long, Franklin A. 179
Lucier, Charles E. 52
Ludendorff, Erich 268
Luebbert, Gregory E. 51
Luterbacher, Urs 41, 53–54, 84
Luxemburg, Rosa 260, 261–262, 283–284

McGwire, Michael 311, 312
MacKenzie, Donald 3, 121–139
McNamara, Robert 187, 190, 193–196, 198, 202–203, 206–207, 209, 213
McNeill, William 121
Maddison, Angus 319–320
Majeski, Stephen J. 42
Mallberg, John 83
Mandelbaum, Michael 339
Mann, Michael 121
Maoz, Zeev 363–364
Mark, Carson 230
Marx, Karl 87, 259, 293
Mayer, Arno 282
Mayer, Thomas F. 368
Meyer, Stephen M. 3, 5, 13, 214, 341
Meyer-Stamer, Jörg 13
Michels, Robert 256, 280
Millikan, Robert Andrews 131–132
Mills, C. Wright 150
Milyutin, D.A. 334–335
Mjøset, Lars 2
Modelski, George 323–324, 327, 331, 364
Moll, Kendall D. 51
Mondale, Walter 14
Morgan, Patrick M. 364
Morgenthau, Hans 273, 274
Morris, Frederic 297
Moto-oka, T. 86
Müller, Erwin 103
Mulchany, Kevin V. 231
Myrdal, Alva 89, 170

Naroll, Roul 357, 360–361
Nedelin, Marshall 298
Nelson, Richard R. 125
Neumann, John von 230
Newcombe, Alan 360
Nieburg, Harold 95

Nitze, Paul 233
Nixon, Richard M. 190, 289
Njølstad, Olaf 4
Nordenskøld, Bengt 174
Norman, Colin 105–106
North, Robert C. 40, 51–52, 361–362

Oakeshott, Michael 223
Ogarkov, Marshall 289–290
Olson, Mancur 42
Olsson, Ulf 156
Oppenheimer, J. Robert 227
Organski, A.F.K. 322
Ostrom, Charles W. 42, 54–55

Paine, Christopher 94
Palme, Olof 164–167
Panofsky, Wolfgang 119
Pareto, Vilfredo 256, 280
Parrott, Bruce 336
Perry, Robert 182–183, 212
Pickering, Andrew 132
Polanyi, Karl 280
Popper, Karl 241
Porter, Bernard 324

Quester, George C. 169–170
Quine, Willard van Orman 130, 134–135, 223, 240

Radzicki, Michael 82
Rapoport, Anatol 32, 40, 60, 76, 78, 80, 119
Rapp, Torsten 166
Rathjens, George 92
Rattinger, Hans 38–42, 55
Reagan, Ronald 11, 14, 110–114, 177, 179–180, 193, 198–200, 288–290, 339, 343
Reinhardt, George C. & Kintner, William R. 173
Reppy, Judith 94, 179–180, 312
Richardson, Lewis F. 1–3, 10–12, 31–57, 36, 37, 58–76, 78–85, 221, 349, 356, 361, 365–370
Rickover, Hyman 137
Riesman, David 87–88
Risse-Kappen, Thomas 5, 12, 240
Roberts, Alan 122
Robinson, Edward van Dyke 322
Rokkan, Stein 150
Rosenberg, David 220, 228–230, 234–237, 242
Rosh, Robert M. 14, 47
Rostow, Walt W. 318
Rummel, Rudolph J. 361–362

Rumsfeld, Donald 199
Russett, Bruce M. 332

Sapolsky, Harvey M. 177, 187–189, 200, 205, 246
Sappuppo, Mike 128
Scheiderbauer, Sven 172
Schilling, Warner A. 137, 220, 227–228, 230, 232–233
Schlesinger, James 199, 288, 304
Schrodt, Philip 81–84
Schroeer, Dietrich 122, 123–124, 125, 129, 138
Schumpeter, Joseph A. 255, 282, 317–318, 320, 325
Schweihart, Larry 177, 189, 197
Sejersted, Francis 151
Senghaas, Dieter 1–2, 4, 7, 12, 13, 43, 91–92, 102, 178, 188, 194, 209, 221, 296–297
Shapin, Steven 132
Shapley, Deborah 122, 125
Siccama, Jan G. 364, 372
Simmel, Georg 14
Singer, J. David 6, 356, 362–364, 372
Skolnikoff, Eugene 107
Small, Melvin 6, 362
Smith, Adam 293
Smith, Theresa Clair 364, 370–372
Smoker, Paul 3
Sorel, Georges 256, 280
Souers, Sidney 237
Spencer, Herbert 255–256, 282
Spitzer, Hartwig 91
Stalin, Joseph 291, 337
Stein, Jonathan B. 3, 122, 220, 228, 230–234, 236–237, 242
Stratmann, Franziskus Maria 101
Strauss, Lewis 230
Strauss, Robert P. 53
Strum, S.C. 121
Swedlund, Nils 164, 166, 174
Sweezy, Paul 269
Sylvan, Donald A. 83

Taagepera, Rein 42, 50, 52–53, 55
Tammen, Ronald L. 177, 187–189, 191, 197–198, 200–201, 205–206, 208, 213
Tamnes, Rolf 152
Teller, Edward 137, 193, 230–231
Thee, Marek 3, 43, 89, 91, 105–120, 122
Thomas, Mark 341
Thompson, Edward P. 122
Thompson, William R. 331, 373
Thorson, Stuart J. 83
Thorsson, Inga 89
Tidemand, Otto Grieg 147, 151

Tolubko, V. 312
Trebilcock, Clive 336, 341
Triska, Jan 132
Trotsky, Lev 291
Truman, Harry S. 226–231, 233, 234–238, 242–243
Tuchman, Barbara W. 52
Tullberg, Rita 108
Turner, John 122

Ulam, Adam 230
Undén, Östen 162, 173

Vagts, Alfred 273–274
Van der Dennen, Hans 361
Van Duijn, Jacob J. 317
Varga, Eugen 329
Vasquez, John A. 361
Väyrynen, Raimo 8, 10, 14, 314–345
Veblen, Thorstein 257
Vegetius, Flavius V. Renatus 87
von Sydow, Bjorn 164–165, 173

Wagner, David L. 41, 53
Wallace, Michael D. 361–362, 370–372
Wallensteen, Peter 360–363
Ward, Michael 84
Weber, Max 254, 272, 280, 323
Weede, Erich 363–364, 369, 371
Wert, James 360
White, Morton G. 223
Wiberg, Håkan 3, 7, 58, 78, 81–82
Wicken, Olav 2, 140–153
Wiesner, Jerome 14
Wight, Martin 341
Wilkes, Owen 138
Wilson, Judy M. 51
Winner, Langdon 315
Wohlstetter, Albert 296
Wooldridge, Dr 95
Wright, Quincy 275, 356

Yanarella, Ernest 177, 187–189, 192, 198, 202, 208–209, 212, 213
Yergin, Daniel H. 175
York, Herbert F. 92, 117, 120, 122, 139, 208, 218, 220, 228, 230–233, 236–237, 297

Zinnes, Dina A. 361, 365, 373
Zuckerman, Solly 122, 137

Øen, Bjarne 152

Index compiled by Meg Davies (Society of Indexers)